SOUTH-WESTERN
™
THOMSON LEARNING

Business to Business Marketing:
Analysis & Practice in a Dynamic Environment
By Robert P. Vitale and Joseph J. Giglierano

Vice President/Editor-in-Chief:
Jack W. Calhoun

Vice President/Team Director:
Melissa S. Acuña

Acquisitions Editors:
Pamela M. Person
Steven W. Hazelwood

Developmental Editor:
Mardell Toomey

Marketing Manager:
Marc Callahan

Production Editor:
Salvatore N. Versetto

Manufacturing Coordinator:
Diane Lohman

Compositor:
Shepherd, Inc.

Printer:
Quebecor World Taunton

Design Project Manager:
Michelle Kunkler

Internal Designer:
Imbue Design/Kim Torbeck, Cincinnati

Cover Designer:
Imbue Design/Kim Torbeck, Cincinnati

Cover Images:
© PhotoDisc, Inc.

Photography Manager:
Deanna Ettinger

Photo Researcher:
Feldman & Associates, Inc.

Media Developmental Editor:
Christine A. Wittmer

Media Production Editor:
Robin K. Browning

Library of Congress Cataloging-in-Publication Data
Vitale, Robert P.
    Business to business marketing: analysis and practice in a dynamic environment/
Robert P. Vitale, Joseph J. Giglierano.
        p. cm
    Includes bibliographical references and index.
    ISBN 0-324-07296-1
    1. Industrial marketing. I. Giglierano, Joseph J. II. Title.
HF5415.1263.V58 2001
658.8'4—dc21   2001049193

Business to Business

Marketing

Analysis & Practice in a Dynamic Environment

Robert P. Vitale

Joseph J. Giglierano

San Jose State University

SOUTH-WESTERN

★

THOMSON LEARNING

Australia · Canada · Mexico · Singapore · Spain · United Kingdom · United States

To our wives and children—

Susan and Sam, and Allison and Vincent.

For your patience, tolerance, support, and occasional reality check.

Please welcome us back.

ABOUT THE AUTHORS

Rob Vitale is an experienced marketing consultant with clients in the automotive, electronics, materials, and transportation industries. His corporate experience includes engineering positions with Boston Edison and Ford Motor Company, marketing and marketing management positions with General Electric, and division management with Fiberchem. He has been published in a variety of outlets in the transportation, marketing and education fields.

Joe Giglierano has consulted with companies of all stripes, focusing mainly on startup technology companies. He has taught San Jose State University's (SJSU) corporate MBA program at Advanced Micro Devices, Inc., Apple Computer, Inc., Hewlett-Packard Co., and National Semiconductor, Inc. Widely published, his principle areas of research are marketing and entrepreneurship, new product strategies, online marketing and electronic commerce.

Both have taught marketing at SJSU since the late 1980s, and serve on numerous industry boards, panels and councils.

Preface xix

1   Introduction to Business-to-Business Marketing 2

2   Classifying Customers, Organizations, and Markets 30

3   Organizational Buying and Buyer Behavior 58

4   The Legal and Political Environment 88

5   Concepts and Context of Business Strategy 110

6   Assessing and Forecasting Markets 144

7   Segmenting , Targeting, and Positioning. 188

8   Planning and Positioning the Value Offering 220

9   Innovation, Branding, and Competitiveness 256

10   Pricing in Business-to-Business Marketing 290

11   Business-to-Business Selling: Developing
and Managing the Customer Relationship 336

12   Channel Relationships 372

13   Communicating with the Market 416

14   Business Ethics and Crisis Management 456

Case Study 1: LastMile Corporation: Choosing
a Development Partner 486

Case Study 2: Automotive Headlamps 498

Case Study 3: Marketing Plastic Resins: GE and BW 506

Glossary 510

Subject Index 520

Name Index 531

Company and Product Index 533

CONTENTS

Preface .... **xix**

1   **Introduction to Business-to-Business Markets** **2**

Marketing Fundamentals in Business-to-Business Markets 4

  Business Markets and Business Marketing Defined 5

  The Marketing Mix 5

  Marketing Philosophy and Culture 9

Further Differences between Business Marketing and Consumer Marketing 9

  Derived Demand 10

  Complexity—A Rationale for Relationship Marketing 14

  Market Structure 16

  Some International Considerations 16

An Examination of Value 17

The Value Chain 18

  Direct versus Support Activities 19

Misunderstanding of the Value and Value Chain Concepts 21

Trends and Changes in Business Marketing 23

  Hypercompetition 23

  Formation of Partner Networks 24

  Adoption of Information Technology and the Internet 24

  Supply Chain Management 25

  Time Compression 26

2   **Classifying Customers, Organizations, and Markets** **30**

Practical Application of Market Generalizations 34

Types of Organizational Customers 35

  Commercial Enterprises 35

  Government Units 36

  Nonprofit and Not-for-Profit Organizations 37

  Producer Types 37

  Customer Needs Influenced by Classification of Markets 39

Classifying the Business-to-Business Market Environment 40

  Publics 40

  The Macroenvironment 42

  Usefulness of Classification 47

The Concept of a Value Network 47
  Using the Value Network Concept 48
Changes in Markets over Time 50
  The Product Life Cycle 51
  The Technology Adoption Life Cycle 53

3   Organizational Buying and Buyer Behavior **58**

The Nature of Buying 60
  The Consumer Buying Decision Process 60
  Organizational Buying 61
  The Buying Center 62
Organizational Buyers' Decision Process: A Stepwise Model 63
  Intricacies of the Buying Decision Process 64
Organizational Buyers' Decision Process: A Process Flow Model 65
  Stage 1: Definition 66
  Stage 2: Selection 68
  Stage 3: Solution Delivery 71
  Stage 4: End Game 71
Two Examples of Buying Decision Processes 72
  Straight Rebuy Example: Buying Office Supplies 72
  New Task Example: Acquiring Automated Sales and Customer Management System 74
Transition of Buying Decision Process: New Task Becomes Rebuy 77
Influences that Shape the Buying Decision Process 78
  Other Organizational Influences 79
  Other Interpersonal and Individual Influences 79
Implications for Business Marketing 79
The Variability of Rational Buying Decisions 80
  Human Factors in Business Decisions 80
  Mutual Dependence and Customer Loyalty 81
  A Brief Psychology of This Process 82

4   The Legal and Political Environment **88**

Business Regulation in a Free Market 90
Enforcement Responsibilities 91
Legislation Affecting Marketing 92
  Sherman Antitrust Act (1890) 92
  Clayton Act (1914) 92
  Federal Trade Commission Act (1914) 93
  Robinson-Patman Act (1936) 94
  Celler-Kefauver Act (1950) 95
  Consumer Goods Pricing Act (1975) 95
  Securities Laws 96
  The Uniform Commercial Code 96

Business Legislation Issues 96
 Intercorporate Stockholding. 96
 Interlocking Directorates 97
 Price Maintenance 97
 Refusal to Deal. 98
 Resale Restrictions 98
 Price Discrimination 99
 Quantity Discounts 102
Substantiality Test 102
Company Size. 104
Intellectual Property 104
 Antitrust Implications of Intellectual Property 106
Political Framework of Enforcement 106
Pacific Drives Revisited 107

5   Concepts and Context of Business Strategy **110**

What Is Strategy? 113
 Key Strategy Concepts 113
 Recent Trends. 114
The Hierarchy of Business Strategy. 115
 Strategic Resource Allocation 115
 Strategic Business Units 116
Tools for Designing Strategy. 117
 The Growth-Share Matrix 117
 An Illustration of Matrix Analysis. 120
 Multifactor Portfolio Matrix. 122
Corporate Strategy: Creating a Portfolio of Businesses 125
 Incompatibility of Cultures within Organizations 125
 Portfolios and Value 126
The Spirit and Dream of the Entrepreneur 126
 The Organization Mission 127
 Changing the Rules 128
Strategy-Making and Strategy Management Processes 129
 Reconciling Theory with Practice 130
Performing Strategic Management in the Business-to-Business Company. 131
 Step 1. Develop Goals and Objectives 131
 Step 2. Environmental Analysis 132
 Step 3. Strategy Design. 132
 Step 4. Implementation Plan Design. 133
 Step 5. Strategy Implementation 133
 Step 6. Monitoring of Environment and Performance Results 133
 Step 7. Analysis of Performance 134
 Step 8. Adjustments 134

A Critique of the Model 134

The Balanced Scorecard 135

Special Issues in Business Strategy 136

Strategy Development and the Internet 136

Volatility and Uncertainty Require Flexibility 137

Strategy Implications of Value Networks 137

Strategic Implications of Market Ownership 138

Strategy Development in New Businesses 138

6   Assessing and Forecasting Markets **144**

Market Research 146

Market Research Fundamentals 148

Implications of Types of Decision Support 150

Designing the Research—Differences from Market Research in Consumer Markets 154

Designing the Research Approach—Other Special Circumstances
in Business-to-Business Market Research 155

Practical Advice for Performing Market Research in Business-to-Business Markets 157

Summary of Market Research 162

Competitive Analysis 162

The Six Sources of Competition 163

Information to Collect on Individual Competitors 164

Sources of Competitive Information 167

Summary of Competitive Analysis 169

Forecasting Markets 169

Forecast Types and Techniques 172

Marketing Operations Forecasts in Depth 174

Summary of Forecasting 178

Appendix 6–1: Typical Research Problems to Be Overcome by Attention
to Good Research Methodology 182

Appendix 6–2: Useful Sources of Customer Information 182

Appendix 6–3: Working with Market Research Vendors 186

7   Segmenting, Targeting, and Positioning **188**

The Relationship between Segmenting, Targeting, and Positioning 191

Market Segmentation 193

Basic Ideas of Segmentation 193

Value-Based Segmentation 195

The Process of Determining Segmentation 197

Summary of Segmentation 203

Choosing Target Segments 203

Attractiveness of Segments 203

Choosing Targets 206

Positioning 210
Further Issues in Segmentation, Targeting, and Positioning. 211
   Segmentation and Positioning Based on the Technology Adoption Life Cycle 212
   Positioning a Product Line 213

8   Planning and Positioning the Value Offering **220**

The Product Life Cycle. 223
The Product Life Cycle and Life Stages of Offerings 225
   Offering Development Stage. 225
   Offering Introduction Stage 226
   Offering Growth Stage. 227
   Offering Maturity Stage. 230
   Offering Decline Stage 231
   Knowing Where a Product Is in Its Product Life Cycle. 231
The Product Life Cycle from the Viewpoint of an Established Offering 233
   Product Elimination Decisions 234
Basic New Product Development Process 235
   Customer/Market Orientation 238
   Team Approach 239
   Invest in the Early Stages 240
   Stage Gates 240
   Concurrent Development 241
   No Shortcuts 242
The Role of Marketing in the Product Development Process 242
   Marketing Defines the Outcomes 242
Reducing the Risk of New Product Failures 244
   Why Do New Products Fail? 244
   Contrary Perceptions of Innovation 246
Collaborators 246
Make-or-Buy Decisions. 248
   Factors in the Decision 249
   Supplier Role in the Decision 251

9   Innovation, Branding, and Competitiveness **256**

Marketing Entrepreneurially. 260
   Changing the Rules 263
   Practical Aspects of Creating an Entrepreneurial Orientation 263
Competing through Innovation 265
   Innovation across the Offering 266
   Pursuit of Disruptive Technologies 270
   Pursuit of Sustaining Innovation 272
   Practical Aspects of Accomplishing Innovation 273

Competing by Building a Brand. 277
 Importance of Brand in Business-to-Business Buyer Behavior 278
 Branding as a Standard 280
 Defending the Brand 282
 Building a Strong Brand 283

10 Pricing in Business-to-Business Marketing 290

Pricing Basics 295
 Pricing to Reflect Customer Value 297
 Relevant Costs 303
 Demand Functions and Pricing 305
Managing Price as Part of Marketing Strategy 308
 Strategic Context of Pricing 309
 Pricing throughout the Product Life Cycle and the Technology Adoption Life Cycle 310
 Penetration Pricing and Price Skimming 313
 Pricing in Discovery Mode 315
 Pricing for International Marketing Efforts 316
Managing Pricing Tactics 317
 Summary of Managing Price 322
Pricing Implementation: The Case of Negotiated Pricing 322
 Two Types of Situations 323
 Preparation for Negotiation 325
 Last Thoughts on Negotiation 327
Pricing and the Changing Business Environment 328
 Pricing, Time Compression, Hypercompetition, and the Internet 328
 Appendix 10–1: Contribution Analysis 334

11 Business-to-Business Selling: Developing and Managing
the Customer Relationship 336

The Nature of Sales and Sellers 338
Characteristics of Business-to-Business Selling 339
 Repeated, Ongoing Relationship 340
 Solution-Oriented, Total System Effort 340
 Long Time Period before Selling Effort Pays Off 340
 Continuous Adjustment of Needs 341
 Creativity Demanded of Seller by Buyer 341
The Role of Sales in a Modern Organization 341
 Relationship Sales and Marketing 342
 Four Forms of Seller Roles 345
 Other Types of Selling Roles 350
 Post-Sale Customer Service 352
 Management Perspective 354

The Mutual Needs of Buyer and Seller. 355
   The Needs of the Job Function. 355
   The Needs of the Organization 356
   The Individual Needs of the Buyer and Seller 358
Selling—The Structure. 358
   Sales Force Organization 359
Direct Sales Force 359
   Sales Force Deployment 360
   Sales Force Compensation 361
Manufacturers' Representatives. 364
   Market Conditions That Favor Either Manufacturers' Representatives
   or a Direct Sales Force 366
   Combinations of Representation. 368

12 Channel Relationships **372**

The Rationale for Marketing Channels. 375
Marketing Channels Deliver Value 376
   Economic Utility. 377
   Channel Flows and Activities That Create Value. 378
   Marketing Channels Meet Customer Needs and Expectations 381
   Industrial Distributors Serve Industrial End Users. 382
   Industrial Distributors Serve Industrial Suppliers. 384
   Value Networks Are Marketing Channels 385
Business Logistics Management. 387
   The Physical Distribution Concept—A Cost-Service Relationship 388
   Economic Utility of Business-to-Business Markets 390
Channel Design 391
   Dual Distribution and Multidistribution 392
   Reduce Discrepancy of Assortment 392
   When Use of Distributor Channels Is a Good Channel Design. 393
Distribution and the Product Life Cycle. 397
   Introduction 397
   Growth. 398
   Maturity/Decline 398
Managing Channels of Distribution. 399
   Selecting and Caring for Distributors. 399
   Power and Conflict in Marketing Channels. 400
   Channel Patterns and Control 401
Channels and the Internet 404
   The Internet's Potential Role in Business-to-Business Marketing. 405
   Development of New Types of Channels 407
   What Went Wrong 409
   Future Adoption of Internet Technology for Channel Management. 410

13   Communicating with the Market **416**

A Communications Model 420
    Losing Meaning in the Translation 420
    Media Can Impact the Message 421
    Feedback 422
    Noise 423
    Capabilities of Promotion 424
The Elements of the Promotion Mix 424
    Personal Selling 424
    Advertising 425
    Sales Promotion 425
    Public Relations 427
Promotional Methods in Business-to-Business Marketing 429
    Convergence of the Promotion Mix 432
    Print Promotion 432
    Corporate Advertising 435
    Direct Mail 436
    Sales and Support Literature 436
    Channel Promotions 438
    Promotional Merchandise 439
Public Relations, Trade Shows, Conferences, and Corporate Positioning 439
    Trade Shows and Conferences 439
    Public Relations and Positioning 442
    Sensacon Applications of Public Relations, Trade Shows, and Positioning 444
Internet and Web Communications in Business-to-Business Marketing 445
    Web Site 446
    Attracting Visitors to a Web Site 449
    Opt-In E-Mail 450
    Newsletters 450
    Newsletter Advertising 450
    On-Line Seminars 451
    Effective Internet Communications 451
Promotion and the Impact of Trends in Business-to-Business Markets 452
    Promotion and Time Compression 452
    Promotion and Hypercompetition 453

14   Business Ethics and Crisis Management **456**

Ethical Issues and the Marketing Concept 461
The Societal Marketing Concept 461
    Societal Marketing as an Ethical Base 463
A Clash of Ethical Standards 463
    Ethical Standards among Different Stakeholders 464

Ethical Standards at Different Levels in the Organization 465
Ethical Standards of the Individual and Performance Standards of the Organization 466
Individual Ethical Behavior. 470
Win-Win, Win-Lose, and Zero-Sum 470
Ethical Behavior and Value Networks 473
Crisis Management 473
Crisis Preparation. 475
Media Relations during a Crisis 478
Minor Crises: Preparation for and Handling of Incidents 479

Case Study 1: LastMile Corporation: Choosing a Development Partner **486**

Case Study 2: Automotive Headlamps **498**

Case Study 3: Marketing Plastic Resins: GE and BW **506**

For additional case studies, visit our Web site at **http://vitale.swcollege.com**

Glossary **510**

Subject Index **520**

Name Index **531**

Company and Product Index **533**

Business to Business Marketing: Analysis and Practice in a Dynamic Environment is intended to capture the dynamic realities of the marketplace while emphasizing the most important principles that students need to learn to be effective, competent professionals in the real world. After almost twenty-five years of industry experience, Rob Vitale began preparing to teach Business-to-Business Marketing to juniors and seniors in the College of Business at San Jose State University. He was frustrated by his preliminary review of available textbooks, finding that none reflected his experiences as a practitioner or would be understandable to students with only an introductory course in marketing. Joe Giglierano, Rob's colleague at San Jose State, suggested *Rethinking Business to Business Marketing* by the late Paul Sherlock. Eureka! Here was a book that captured the excitement of the subject without abandoning its complexity. Even though *Rethinking* was not a textbook, we felt that we could present students with enough transitional material to bridge to an understanding of the book. Rob and Joe subsequently wrote a "minimalist" student guide, including lecture notes, cases, and readings. Over a five-year period, that student package grew into an almost five hundred page manuscript. Thus the foundations of *Business to Business Marketing* have been classroom-tested in graduate and undergraduate courses in Business-to-Business Marketing and Marketing Management.

Several principles guided the book's development. First, several key ideas form the conceptual grounding. Porter's *value chain* provides the underpinning for the *marketing concept,* its application, and implementation. The *product life cycle* and Moore's *technology adoption life cycle* form the basis for considering the dynamics of market evolution. Hamel and Prahalad's ideas on business strategy and Dickson's thoughts on competitive market behavior form the basis for the discussion of marketing strategy formulation. The *societal marketing concept* is a key element of ethical marketing behavior. In each of the individual topic areas addressed, we build on the concepts that we believe are most central and useful.

The material in each chapter also builds on our own experiences performing business-to-business marketing. Between the two of us, we have about fifty-five years' experience in working for and consulting with organizations that perform business-to-business marketing (curiously, we both began our careers doing electric utility emergency planning). Each chapter benefits from observations made in real-world situations. Our academic and consulting research also has contributed ideas and examples. Further, we have discussed our observations and concepts with an extensive network of industry contacts. Thus each chapter benefits from the multiple dialogues conducted with executives and managers over the past decades, and particularly over the past five years since we began work on this project.

We depart a bit from traditional approaches to textbooks. Our experience has shown us that students' assumptions about business-to-business marketing are often based on their familiarity with consumer marketing. For that reason, we have created many comparisons and contrasts between the two fields throughout the text to clarify the most important differences and to give weight to the distinguishing characteristics of business-to-business principles and practices.

Planning, strategy design, and decision-making are important skills that are common to all current areas of business; we offer opportunities to hone these skills through applications-driven cases, examples, and Internet experiences. Whenever possible, we attempt to strengthen students' critical thinking skills. The examples we use include familiar companies, people, and events in the business world. A practical and real-world approach is enlivened through interesting scenarios and sidebars, and emphasizes changes brought about by technology, entrepreneurship, relationships, and globalization.

FEATURES

The pedagogical style includes consistently previewing and reviewing concepts and approaches. Highlighted text in the margins clarifies terms or concepts that may be unfamiliar to students. Special care has been given to assure that material is presented clearly and coverage is thorough.

- Each chapter begins with an informal overview that prepares students for what they will learn in the chapter, including the opening vignette and other chapter features.

- The overview is followed by a vignette. These vignettes, read after the overview, should deepen students' understanding of new material and prepare them for the main chapter content.

- Learning objectives follow the overview and opening vignette. These are more easily understood and appreciated at this point in the chapter since students already have a sense of the topical coverage from the overview and opening vignette.

- eB2B features provide opportunities to explore Web sites related to topics in each chapter.

- Each chapter ends with "Thoughts to Take with you into the Next Chapter," designed to build on students' learning and help them integrate their knowledge and understanding to prepare them for the next chapter.

- Key terms and questions for review and discussion also reinforce learning.

- Finally, Internet exercises provide a variety of learning experiences through Internet use and exploration. This feature is designed to provide students with a more in-depth experience than the eB2B boxes.

- Case studies, both in the book and on the Web site, reinforce text materials with practical experience, based on real-world situations.

SUPPLEMENTS

The product family that accompanies this text is of equally high quality, as follows.

Instructor's Manual with Test Bank (ISBN 0-324-12150-4)

The Instructor's Manual includes an outline of chapter content interspersed with teaching suggestions, answers to end-of-chapter questions, and case analysis. The Test Bank includes fifteen multiple-choice questions, ten true/false questions, and two essay questions. Answers are included.

Instructor's Resource CD (ISBN 0-324-15657-X)

The Instructor's Resource CD (IRCD) includes the Instructor's Manual, Exam View Electronic Test Bank, and PowerPoint slides.

The Electronic Test Bank consists of fifteen multiple-choice questions, ten true/false questions, and two essay questions. The advantage of using the Electronic Test Bank is the instructor's ability to easily manipulate content to create new tests.

There are over thirty PowerPoint slides per chapter, which include coverage of the most salient chapter material, compelling art, and questions to incorporate into the slide presentation. These slides are designed to hold student interest and prompt questions that will help students learn.

Video (ISBN 0-324-13456-8)

Video scenarios cover topics that relate to various chapter content.

Web Site

Instructors and students alike will find useful and exciting resources on our Web site. The Web site, like the main text, is designed to bring the practices of business-to-business marketing to life. Visit us at **http://vitale.swcollege.com**

ACKNOWLEDGMENTS

We wish to thank numerous people for their contributions, without whom this text would not exist.

We first acknowledge our various mentors. Rob extends his heartfelt appreciation to Joe Byrne, Claude Martin, Conrad Zumhagen, and Jim Hartley, as each has contributed style and substance when appropriate. Joe wishes to thank Peter Dickson for the conceptual grounding and perspective he provided as Joe's advisor at Ohio State and for his help, advice, and collaboration over the years since. Many thanks are owed to Anne Perlman, who guided Joe's efforts at Tandem when the Internet was first presenting its commercial potential.

Together we'd like to thank our colleagues who contributed their time and talents: Dan Evans of San Jose State for his review and suggestions about the legal environment, Gene Robillard for material on sales management, and Jeff Kallis for information on marketing to government agencies that will appear on our Web site. Thank you also to Roger Grace, of Roger Grace Associates, for his review and suggestions on promotion and corporate positioning; to Conrad Zumhagen for his review and suggestions regarding innovation and entrepreneurship, as well as his contribution of Case Study 2, "Automotive Headlamps"; to Herb Rammrath, for his permission and review of case material; and to Jim Shaw, of Shaw Resources, who provided his company as a case study.

Several other individuals have given us much to think about, as we have discussed ideas and observations with them over the years. Especially generous and helpful, among others too numerous to name, were Mike Adams, Michael Cruz, Chuck Erickson, Joe Giglierano Sr., Ravi Kaiwar, Cathy Kitcho, Luanne Meyer, Dave Riker, Jim Robbins, Dave Rosenberg, Eric Schmidt, Jim Shaw, Lindsay Snyder, Orton Snyder, and Tim Wild. Extra special thanks go to Susan Bayerd and Allison Baker, who made important contributions with legal insights and perspectives on marketing in the telecommunications industry.

Our friend and compatriot Julia Rosenberg kept us going in the early years, for which we are eternally grateful. Our students contributed their thoughts, questions, and insights, and words cannot come close to expressing our thanks to them. In particular, we would like to express our gratitude to three students—Paul Haayer, Jaya Konduri, and Diane Vo—who helped greatly in preparing case material.

We express our deepest gratitude to our friends at South-Western College Publishing. They believed in this project and have guided its transformation from a class reader with high aspirations into tangible reality. Our developmental editor, Mardell Toomey, holds a cherished place in our hearts. She has shown extraordinary skill in managing this project through to fruition while maintaining a sense of purpose and a sense of humor. Out of deference to her, we abandoned our surprise ending. We also thank Pamela Person and Steve Hazlewood, acquisitions editors; Marc Callahan, marketing manager; and Sam Versetto, production editor. Michelle Kunkler, design project manager, should also be thanked for her help in developing a functional and eye-catching text design. Everyone worked very hard, and it is much appreciated.

We would also like to extend our deepest thanks to our colleagues who reviewed this text. We extend a special thanks to Jonathan Hibbard of Boston University, who carefully dissected each chapter, always had so many reliable suggestions, and was flexible enough to even work with us from Singapore! The reviewers include Mark L. Bennion, Bowling Green State University; Robert D. Green, Indiana State University; Jonathan Hibbard, Boston University; Daniel E. Innis, Ohio University; Susan K. Jones, Ferris State University; Ajay Menon, Colorado State University; Dr. Carolyn Nicholson, Stetson University; Richard E. Plank, Haworth College of Business; Henry H. Rodkin, DePaul University; Sanjit Sengupta, San Francisco State University; and Dr. Michael Weber, Barry University.

There are undoubtedly persons we should have thanked, but have not. To those folks, we assure you this was not intentional, but merely a memory lapse. We are most grateful for your contributions as well.

And of course, there are no words for the gratitude and love we feel for our families, who, after all is said and done, are apparently taking us back after this effort (we hope).

Robert P. Vitale
Joseph J. Giglierano

1

Introduction to Business-to-Business Marketing

overview... In this first chapter, we introduce you to business-to-business marketing, provide you with an overview of the differences and similarities between business-to-business and consumer marketing, and, finally, provide you with an approach for studying this field that is built around the concept of value for customers. Value includes both customer benefits and customer costs incurred in realizing these benefits. We close the chapter by introducing several trends currently changing the face of business-to-business marketing. These trends, which are important for you to keep in mind as you progress throughout the book, raise the question of whether we need to change our ideas about what works in business-to-business marketing.

In our opening example, two "new economy" companies—Yahoo! and Tibco—form a partnership to address a new, business-to-business market need that they believe exists. Later in the chapter, you will have an opportunity to visit areas of the companies' Web sites.

© JOSE LUIS PELAEZ INC./STOCK MARKET

YAHOO MOVES INTO BUSINESS MARKETING

Web **portal** and Internet directory Yahoo, Inc., has recently launched a new product/service named Corporate My Yahoo! It is teaming with Tibco Software, Inc., which offers software for connecting applications to a network to offer **Intranet portals** for businesses. This move reflects many of the dynamics occurring in business marketing today. Yahoo/Tibco will go up against some hefty competitors, including Sun Microsystems and Microsoft. The market is small, but growing rapidly, and will probably attract more competitors.

The first step toward success of this business combination is for Yahoo and Tibco to create a working **partnership** that will offer customers a complete solution. As offerings have become complex and single companies have been unable to complete the offerings alone, partnerships have become quite common. Successful partnerships require a clear, agreed-upon vision that capitalizes on the strengths of the combination.

Second, the Yahoo/Tibco partnership represents competition from an unusual source, perhaps a somewhat unexpected source, from the viewpoint of Sun or Microsoft. Yahoo has been principally a consumer marketer, and this competitive move places them firmly in the business marketing camp as well. Such moves to new markets can create entire categories of new competitors.

Third, Yahoo's opportunity is currently nebulous. Uncertainty pervades this market. It is unclear how fast this market will grow, whether the real opportunity is in larger or smaller firms, or whether the market will ever evolve at all. However, the more experience Yahoo gets in providing service to businesses, the stronger its position if this market develops.

Finally, the product provided is a combination of tangible product, intangible service, and virtual entity. The Internet and the Web have permeated business markets and changed the way many things are done.

A **portal** is a Web site that serves as a launch site for other sites or programs. An **Intranet portal,** then, is a site that operates on a company's internal Web network. It provides the employees with a personalized Web site from which they can access internal or external Web-based resources, such as news, employee benefits, and programs.

Yahoo/Tibco must now complete a solid product/service offering and present it to the market. It is not clear yet how the partnership will segment the market, what segments will be targeted, and how the two companies will combine to sell the product/service. Given the nature of this business, they will have to get into the market rapidly and adapt as they go.

- ◆ Reinforce the basics of marketing from your marketing principles course.
- ◆ Gain an appreciation for the main differences between consumer marketing and business-to-business marketing.
- ◆ Understand the marketing concept and its implications for business-to-business marketing.
- ◆ Understand the meaning of value.
- ◆ Gain a sense of how the value chain is structured.
- ◆ Gain an understanding of the implications of the value chain for business-to-business marketing.
- ◆ Obtain a sense of the changing nature of the business environment.

introduction. . .

Business markets present different types of challenges and opportunities than those presented by consumer markets. The concepts of *relationships, value,* and *buyer decision making* function in very different ways than would be expected in consumer markets. As you may conclude from what you have just read, Yahoo's performance could go in several directions—winning combination, abject failure, or somewhere in between. What should Yahoo do to deal with the situation and create a high chance of turning it into a profitable enterprise? As an organization, how should it modify its behavior to suit a completely different market? This chapter sets the stage for answering these questions.

To fully appreciate the differences and similarities between business-to-business and consumer marketing, we need an understanding of marketing basics and how these basics apply in business-to-business marketing. For those of you who have already taken a marketing principles course, this will be a review of what you have already learned. These basic marketing concepts, presented in a business-to-business context, will ensure that everyone reading this book starts with approximately the same background—a level playing field.

MARKETING FUNDAMENTALS IN BUSINESS-TO-BUSINESS MARKETS

Many students face difficulties in the study of business-to-business marketing because they come into it from their existing viewpoint as consumers. Students as consumers often feel inundated by promotional messages from what seems to be an unlimited number of sources, and they may begin to believe that these messages are all there is to the entire marketing effort. Here, as in any introductory marketing courses, students can begin the process of separating their marketing analysis from their perspectives as consumers. We are not suggesting, however, that students abandon their understanding of consumer behavior. Quite the contrary—decision makers in business-to-business marketing situations often behave similarly to consumers in buying situations, albeit with different and often more complex motivations.

Business Markets and Business Marketing Defined

To see how marketing principles apply in business-to-business markets, you first need an understanding of what business-to-business markets and marketing are. So, as you read this chapter, please keep these definitions in mind:

- ◆ **Business markets** consist of all organizations that purchase goods and services to use in the creation of their own goods and services. These are then offered to their customers. Generally, business markets consist of fewer but larger customers than consumer markets and are involved in purchases of significantly large value having complex economic, technical, and financial considerations.

- ◆ **Business marketing** is the process of matching and combining the capabilities of the supplier with the desired outcomes of the customer to create value for the "customer's customer" and, hence, for both organizations. The many facets of the business buying decision process and the needs of many stakeholders in the buying organization create a behavioral situation usually far more complex than in the consumer market.

The Marketing Mix

You may recall from your marketing principles course the concepts of the **four Ps:** product, price, place, and promotion. These are still the four Ps of marketing whether operating in a consumer or a business market. There are, however, some differences that require explanation.

Product   In general marketing theory, the term *product* refers to a core product (or service) that can be augmented by additional features and options that will appeal to different buyers. In a consumer product such as a new car, buyers can add many options to the core vehicle, such as a premium sound system or a sports suspension package. Beyond those options made available by the vehicle manufacturer, the dealer may provide options to assist in the ownership process, such as financing, acceptance of a trade-in, or insurance. Taken together, these options, those that modify the performance of the vehicle and those that facilitate purchase and ownership, create the augmented product. Buyers have the choice to customize—to design—their vehicle to their own tastes and needs.

In contrast, consider the product when an automobile company markets a fleet of new cars to a car rental company. The core product is still the cars, but now the quantity and assortment of models become important as well and can be considered part of the core product. In addition, the car company arranges an availability and delivery schedule. A contract for spare parts delivery becomes part of the deal. The arrangement would also include training of service personnel. Depending on the capabilities of the rental company, the car company may provide some or all maintenance and service.

In this text, we define the augmented business-to-business product as the **total offering** that will provide a complete solution to the buyer's needs. This may encompass features such as financing terms and delivery options or, based on the buyer's preference, simply be the core product. The desirability of the augmented portions of the offering will vary among different business-to-business buying organizations, requiring flexibility of the marketer and the marketing organization.

A note about terminology is important here. In the previous paragraph, we introduced the term **total offering** to describe the augmented product. This is an intentional avoidance of the word *product*, as we want to reinforce throughout the text that the value provided to customers often goes far beyond "just the product."

There are often fundamental differences between core product characteristics in business-to-business and consumer markets. Because business-to-business products are often incorporated into the buyer's offering to their own customers, they are often defined and created by a partnership between the buying organization and the marketing organization. This process produces a product that is specific to the buying unit's needs while maximizing the value creation capabilities of the marketer. Because the specifically tailored product is often more technical in nature, it is often defined by a written specification whose purpose is to maintain a given level of performance.

> **Total offering** is the offering that provides a complete solution to the buyer's needs. This may include financing, delivery, service, or, based on the buyer's preference, only the core product.

Price

As in any transaction, price is the mutually agreed-upon amount (of money or something else of worth) that satisfies both sides in the exchange. Both the buyer and the seller realize an increase in the value they hold as a result of the transaction. Price, the measure of value exchanged, is determined by the market—not by the costs associated with the creation of the offering. In business-to-business markets, price determination can be the final step in a complex design, development, and negotiation, particularly when the product is the result of a collaborative effort. For less-complex or standardized products, price may be the result of a competitive bidding process. Only for the most generic of products will price in business-to-business markets be based on a "list" price as in consumer markets.

Continuing with the automotive example, the price for the new car is a fixed price based on the manufacturer's suggested retail price (MSRP). Each of the options has a list price as well, and several options may be bundled together and priced as a single package. Automobiles are relatively unique as consumer products in that price negotiation is acceptable and expected. Most consumers—in the United States, at least—do not expect to negotiate on price for most products that they buy.

Consider again the fleet offering from the car company aimed at the rental company. The price undoubtedly is a negotiated price for the whole fleet rather than individual prices for individual cars. In addition, the automaker probably offers financing that is more complicated than financing offered to a consumer. The package may include special incentive discounts or allowances for performance of various activities. Suppose the car company wants to have the rental company promote the fact that the rental company has chosen this brand of cars for much of its fleet. The car company offers an allowance—a price reduction—off the total price to compensate the rental company for its promotional efforts. Just as in the product portion of the four Ps, the price component differs between consumer marketing and business-to-business marketing. Prices for consumers are often fixed and discounted, with some financing provided for high-cost purchases. Pricing for business customers often varies from fixed price, includes far more special discounts and allowances, and involves complex financing. Business-to-business pricing may also involve forms other than a one-time price payment or fee, such as commissions or profit sharing. In many deals involving small growing companies, services may even be done in exchange for stock options. Pricing internationally may also be more complex, particularly if the customer company is multinational. Prices may have to be adjusted for different currencies and may have to change dynamically as exchange rates shift.

Place   In consumer markets, **place** is about getting the product to the customer in the right **form** (size package, quantity, etc.); at a useful **time** (availability of extended retail hours, short waiting periods for special orders, etc.); with minimum inconvenience associated with the place of purchase; and with **possession** ease (transfer of ownership, such as cash, credit, acceptance of personal checks). Form, time, place, and possession comprise the four types of economic utility and are a critical part of the value delivered to the customer. In consumer markets, **economic utility** often refers to consumer preferences in locational convenience, required purchase quantities/sizes, temporal convenience, and acquisition convenience. In the automobile example, the car company provides economic utility to consumers by locating dealerships near population centers or heavily trafficked shopping routes. The dealerships are set up to foster single car purchases in which the car is available immediately or can be quickly ordered. All the activities that facilitate purchasing the car (credit check, financing, registration, etc.) make it possible for the buyer to start the transaction and drive off with the car in less than a couple hours.

Economic utility is a necessary (though not sufficient), pivotal part of the concept of value in business-to-business markets, which often takes on the form of supply chain management, inventory services, and material resource planning. In the example of the auto manufacturer marketing to the rental car company to add to its fleet, the car manufacturer offers cars in appropriate quantities in the appropriate time interval. The right cars are shipped to the right locations. Spare parts are made available in appropriate quantities as well. They also are shipped to the right locations at the right times. This is no easy accomplishment when car companies have production schedules to match with delivery schedules and the assembly plants are not all located near the myriad of rental company outlets.

Businesses design their marketing channels to provide maximum value to their customers while minimizing costs associated with the creation of economic utility. This is true for both consumer and business-to-business channels. The major differences lie in the length and concentration of the channel. The quantities purchased in business-to-business marketing are substantially larger than consumer purchases with timing of delivery a critical factor, leading to direct relationships between manufacturer and customer and eliminating channel intermediaries.

Promotion   Business-to-business marketing places different emphasis on the parts of the promotion mix (advertising, sales promotion, personal selling, and public relations) than is commonly found in consumer marketing. Consumers are inundated with advertising as manufacturers attempt to create awareness of and interest in their products. In consumer markets, advertising plays the largest role in the promotion mix.

In business-to-business markets, the capabilities of advertising can seldom be leveraged. Generally, we know advertising as a monologue—a one-way communication.[1] Feedback from the customer is not always encouraged and is not automatic. Advertisers must make a separate and purposeful effort to know how their customers have responded to promotion campaigns (or wait for sales results). In the new car example, the carmaker advertises heavily in television, radio, print, and the Internet to build brand awareness and beliefs. Dealers also advertise in television, radio, and newspapers to provide information and incentives to buy (sales promotion). Dealerships have salespeople who work with consumers to help them through the buying process. The relationship formed is usually a temporary one, focused on completing the transaction and getting the consumer happily through the first few weeks after acquiring the new car.

In business-to-business markets, personal selling is the most used and effective type of promotion. Personal selling, as a dialogue, allows rapid and accurate feedback to the marketer. As noted earlier, products in business-to-business marketing are often the result of collaboration between the supplier and the customer. This collaboration requires the building of relationships between individuals in their respective organizations, necessitating a strong personal selling (dialogue) effort. The carmaker in our example may have a sales team that manages the account with the car rental company. The efforts of the sales team focus on providing information and personal service to the executives and employees of the car rental company involved in purchasing, managing, and maintaining the rental car fleet.

Two of the major differences, then, between consumer and business-to-business promotion are the closeness and the duration of the relationship. In business-to-business marketing, the relationship is often closer and longer lasting than in consumer marketing, with the individuals having developed personal ties. For many consumer products, contact between the consumer and the marketer is confined to

[1]Regis McKenna, "Marketing Is Everything," *Harvard Business Review* (January–February 1991).

advertising, the relatively short-lived transaction period, and maybe a consumer response to a follow-up survey.

Marketing Philosophy and Culture

The preceding section has discussed the traditional four Ps of the marketing mix, highlighting the differences between the four Ps in consumer marketing and the four Ps in business-to-business marketing. Configuration of the four Ps, whether in consumer marketing or business-to-business marketing, should be driven by the **marketing concept**.

The marketing concept has been the philosophy at the forefront in the field of marketing over the last fifty years. It says that, to be successful, a company should understand customers' needs, meet those needs with a coordinated set of activities, and do so in a way that meets organizational goals.[2] A firm that operates under the culture of the marketing concept focuses all of its efforts and resources toward satisfying the needs of its customers. This is distinctly different from organizations that operate in a production, sales, or marketing department culture.[3] In each of these cultures, marketing is a distinct yet dependent part of the organization, often viewed as an expense rather than as a generator of margin. The marketing concept implies that marketing is the driving force in the organization, defining the roles of other functions in meeting the needs of customers.[4]

FURTHER DIFFERENCES BETWEEN BUSINESS MARKETING AND CONSUMER MARKETING

Exhibit 1–1 summarizes several potential differences between business marketing and consumer marketing. Depending on specific circumstances, all these factors may or may not be present in any given business situation. While all of these differences are discussed in the following chapters, a few are crucial for understanding the context of business-to-business marketing and are highlighted in the immediate discussion. The first is the nature of demand; of particular note is the difference between **consumer demand** and **derived demand**.

> The **marketing concept** states that, to be successful, the firm should be contextually market sensitive, understand customer needs, meet those needs in a coordinated way that provides value to the customer, and do so in a way that meets organizational goals. A firm that is (or claims to be) a market-driven/customer-driven firm is applying the marketing concept, recognizing that every employee of the firm contributes to the marketing effort.

> **Consumer demand** is the quantity of goods or services desired to be bought, given market conditions (usually expressed as a function of market price). **Derived demand** is the demand experienced by the chain of suppliers and producers that contribute to the creation of a total offering. Without initial consumer demand, there is no demand on the chain of suppliers.

[2]Kotler has introduced a societal element to the marketing concept. This is discussed in Chapter 14. See Philip Kotler, *Marketing Management: The Millennium Edition*, 10th ed. (Upper Saddle River, N.J.: Prentice-Hall, 2000), 25.

[3]William D. Perreault Jr. and E. Jerome McCarthy, *Basic Marketing*, 13th ed. (New York: McGraw Hill), 1999), 33–35.

[4]For a complete treatment of the concept of marketing as the defining parameter in the organization, readers are directed to Regis McKenna, "Marketing Is Everything," *Harvard Business Review* (January–February 1991).

EXHIBIT 1–1   Business-to-Business versus Consumer Marketing—Summarizing the Differences

Business-to-Business	Consumer
Market Structure	
♦ Geographically concentrated ♦ Relatively fewer buyers ♦ Oligopolistic competition	♦ Geographically dispersed ♦ Mass markets, many buyers ♦ Monopolistic competition
Products	
♦ Can be technically complex ♦ Customized to user preference ♦ Service, delivery, and availability very important ♦ Purchased for other than personal use	♦ Standardized ♦ Service, delivery, and availability only somewhat important ♦ Purchased for personal use
Buyer Behavior	
♦ Professionally trained purchasing personnel ♦ Functional involvement at many levels ♦ Task motives predominate	♦ Individual purchasing ♦ Family involvement, influence ♦ Social/psychological motives predominate
Buyer-Seller Relationships	
♦ Technical expertise an asset ♦ Interpersonal relationships between buyers and sellers ♦ Significant info exchanged between participants on a personal level ♦ Stable, long-term relationships encourage loyalty	♦ Less technical expertise ♦ Nonpersonal relationships ♦ Little information exchanged between participants on a personal level ♦ Changing, short-term relationships ♦ Short-term relationships encourage switching
Channels	
♦ Shorter, more direct	♦ Indirect, multiple relationships
Promotion	
♦ Emphasis on personal selling	♦ Emphasis on advertising
Price	
♦ Either competitive bidding or the result of a complex purchase process	♦ Usually list or predetermined prices
Demand	
♦ Derived ♦ Inelastic (short run) ♦ Volatile (leveraged) ♦ Discontinuous	♦ Direct ♦ Elastic ♦ Less volatile

Derived Demand

The demand for nylon fibers by consumers does not exist. Nylon is, however, demanded to spin yarn because yarn is demanded to weave fabric because fabric is demanded to make clothes; all of these demands are **derived demands**—a result of the ultimate **consumer demand** for nylon clothing items. Demand in business markets is derived from consumer demand. Because of the derived nature, demand in business markets is leveraged—greater swings occur than in consumer markets— thus the term *volatile* in Exhibit 1–1. A small percentage change in consumer markets leads to much greater changes in business markets.

The Bullwhip Effect

The volatility of derived demand is partially explained by the **bullwhip effect**.[5] As consumer demand varies, either as a result of seasonality or other market factors, "upstream" suppliers of services and components that contributed to the total offering experience a leveraged impact. This leveraging can cause wide swings in demand. Suppliers in the chain forecast production and inventory levels based on existing order rates. When consumer demand drops, the order rate drops and supply chain members compensate with lower production and inventory levels. The initial correction is often greater than the difference between the old forecast and the actual demand. This can happen for several reasons. First, because the preexisting inventory level is excessive when related to the new (lower) order rate, management attempts to adjust levels to be more in line with the new rate. Second, customers with closely monitored inventory control systems adjust orders often—in some instances, daily. Suppliers receiving such daily adjustments may elect to utilize longer order cycles, accumulating these daily changes over time.[6] This delay is possible if there are high costs associated with processing frequent orders. Another contributor to the delay could be the materials requirements planning system in use. It may have minimum order quantities related to economies of scale.[7] Additional variability results when trade promotions exist that are intended to influence buying patterns in the channel.[8] Thus, small frequent adjustments can accumulate into large inventory problems. Multiply these effects throughout the supply chain, and the volatility of derived demand becomes easily evident.

A good example of the bullwhip effect can be seen in Exhibit 1–2, a story about Ford and Firestone. Because of the recall of tires, Ford stopped production in

---

[5]Philippe-Pierre Dornier, Ricardo Ernst, Michel Fender, and Panos Kouvelis, *Global Operations and Logistics* (New York: John Wiley & Sons, 1998). Chapter 7 provides a complete discussion of the bullwhip effect and its relationship to supply chain management.

[6]Hau L. Lee, V. Padmanabhan, and Seungjin Whang, "The Bullwhip Effect in Supply Chains," *Sloan Management Review* (spring 1997): 96.

[7]Ibid.

[8]Ibid., 97. This subject is also dealt with again in this text in Chapter 12.

EXHIBIT 1–2   Assembly Lines (and Tires) Stop Rolling

In response to the tremendous need to find replacements for 6.5 million tires recalled by Firestone, Ford Motor Company halted production of its popular Explorer sport utility vehicles (SUVs) and Ranger pickup trucks at three facilities in August 2000. The tires, originally intended for use in approximately 3 percent of annual production of these vehicles, were redirected to the replacement market. Most of the recalled tires were used as original equipment on Ford SUVs and were the primary tire installed on current production models. The production shutdown was estimated to cost Ford $100 million in profits for the quarter. Overall, the Firestone tire recall is expected to reduce Ford 2000 profits by $500 million.

Ford and Firestone are not the only companies whose profits will suffer from the production shutdown. Ford builds the largest-selling SUVs in their market. Each vehicle is comprised of many components and systems provided by several major automotive suppliers. Though not common household names as they are not major participants in consumer markets, companies such as Dana, Eaton, ArvinMeritor, TRW, Lear, and Visteon are major suppliers to Ford SUVs, many of the items specifically designed and built for these vehicles and not used by other manufacturers. In a dramatic example of the volatility of demand in business-to-business markets, all of these suppliers have announced reduced earnings, either partly or substantially a result of the Ford production halt.

Eaton Corporation reported a 49 percent drop in third-quarter net, partly because of the Ford production cuts (previous reports set the reduction attributable to Ford at 10 percent of quarterly results), and Dana Corporation said its third-quarter results were 82 percent below the prior year's results. While not entirely attributable to the Ford production halt (Dana is a supplier to the heavy truck market, also in a slump), Dana announced it would cut 2,000 jobs from its workforce of 80,000 in an effort to boost fourth-quarter earnings.

The impact of the production shutdown does not end with components and systems. The International Natural Rubber Organization (INRO) has reported that rubber producers who sold rubber to INRO as buffer stock are now enthusiastic bidders to put the inventory back on the market. The now defunct INRO has been seeking bidders for its 138,000 metric tons of buffer stock. Heavy rains in Indonesia have cut raw materials supplies at the same time there is increased demand from tire makers to replace the recalled tires. Of course, there are additional complications. While rubber producers are interested in buying back the stock they sold to INRO, they are concerned about possible product degradation due to less than ideal storage conditions. The Firestone tire recall has generated concern about using old rubber to manufacture tires. Anyone purchasing the material will be told that it was INRO buffer stock. One rubber trader related the feeling that INRO rubber may be old but it could still be used in low-demand applications, such as bicycle tires, canvas shoes, tires for vehicles used in China (low-speed applications), or on agricultural vehicles.

Sources: The Wall Street Journal, various articles (September 6–October 19, 2000); *Business Week* (September 18, 2000).

---

its assembly plants. This had a ripple effect back through the supply system feeding the assembly plants. Ford "sneezed," and the industry "caught a cold."

Another factor in the leveraged, **discontinuous demand** of business markets is the issue of capacity throughout the supply chain resulting from the desire of manufacturers to closely monitor capacity utilization. A supplier tailors its capacity based on forecasts of demand. When a consumer goods manufacturer experiences an increase in demand, additional raw materials and supplies are consumed. Suppliers of these items experience greater demand and are required to increase production capacity, thus increasing their demand for raw materials and supplies. When the demand on suppliers reaches a level that requires capitalization of new production capability, a discontinuity in supply capability results. If the supplier elects to invest in additional capacity, this increase provides capacity to the marketplace and demand for production and infrastructure-related products. The entire supply chain is impacted by increased demand for equipment and facilities. Multiply this scenario by all the consumer goods manufacturers who are experiencing a business increase and all their suppli-

Discontinuous demand is the condition in which quantity demanded in the market makes large changes up or down in response to changes in market conditions. The transition from one market state to another occurs in large increments rather than small incremental changes in demand.

ers, and the leveraged impact of consumer demand is obvious. This volatility can be considered a cause and an effect, as in the adage, "a rising tide raises all ships."[9]

While demand fluctuates more in business markets, it is also **inelastic** in the short term. Your customer, a manufacturer who has incorporated your product into the design of its own offering to customers, may not be able to substitute another component for that item, particularly if, as a business marketer, you have managed to maintain a significant differentiation from your competitors. If the item's cost is driven up by unforeseen factors, the manufacturer has the choice of continuing production by paying the higher price or ceasing the manufacturing process, alienating its own customers who may be expecting delivery. Your customer's reluctance to alienate its customers is a major source of *inelasticity*. If the change in the supply situation that caused the price increase is expected to continue, the manufacturer eliminates use of the component *by design* in the next generation of its product offering.

> **Price elasticity** of demand refers to the percentage change in quantity demanded relative to the percentage change in price. If a price change produces a change in demand that is less in percentage than the percentage price change, then demand is said to be **inelastic**.

Volatility　The bullwhip effect, or leveraging, described here can help us understand logistics-oriented supply chain effects on business-to-business demand. The bullwhip effect, however, is only part of the cause of volatility in business-to-business markets. Because of the volatility of business-to-business demand, small changes in consumer buying attitudes are closely watched as potential indicators of changes in our economy. The inelastic nature of derived demand may lead the uninitiated business marketer to a false sense of security, believing that the short-term persistence of demand translates into long-term stability.

We have seen many examples in history in which sudden environmental changes have destabilized entire markets. Rapid changes in the economy can have medium-term—or faster—impacts on derived demand. The almost 30 percent plunge in consumer purchases of certain model automobiles in 1974 and again in 1979, coincident with each oil crisis, is an example of a fast-acting economic event. Many suppliers to the automotive industry found orders stopping immediately, not to return until it was financially too late for the supplier to recover. Again, in the Ford and Firestone example discussed in Exhibit 1–2, the situation in which Ford ceased production of a very profitable, high-volume vehicle was caused by a combination of events. The resulting lower earnings reported by suppliers of components for the Ford Explorer could not have been anticipated.

---

[9]Some large business customers often provide suppliers with several forecast levels. Worst-, likely-, and best-case forecasts are often part of business-to-business arrangements. These forecasts are only as good as the business-to-business customer's forecast of its market and is subject to the same frailties of all forecasts. It is in the best interest of the business-to-business supplier to "know its customers' customers" and develop its own forecast of the market. (See Chapter 6 and Chapter 7 regarding forecasts and understanding markets.) When it is not customary for a business-to-business customer to provide best-/likely/worst-case forecasts, it is critical for the business-to-business supplier to obtain, either internally or through outside assistance, good market forecasts.

An example of a slower-acting event was the downturn in the Asian economy in 1997 and 1998. The effects in the United States were not felt immediately in most sectors because the Asian crisis took several months to fully develop. Inventory took awhile to clear through the distribution channels. Eventually, effects were felt in the United States and Europe, but these were partially attenuated by increases in demand in other parts of the world. Both of these examples, the oil crises of the 1970s and the Asian economic difficulties of the 1990s demonstrate that, more than we may want to acknowledge, modern business-to-business marketing operates in a global environment.

Complexity–A Rationale for Relationship Marketing

One of the major implications of derived demand is that business marketers must understand their customers' customers. Only if marketers are customer focused are they able to fully understand their customers' network of derived demand. The business marketer can design products and services to fully benefit customers and, hopefully, anticipate changes in levels of demand instigated by the customers' market. The impact of the discontinuous nature of demand can be mitigated by business marketers' participation in the relationship with the customer on a continuing, ongoing basis. If, as a result of its complacency, a business marketer allows a competitor to take advantage of its inattention by offering a lower price or better product, the loss of short-term business could translate into lost opportunities to be the supplier of the customer's next generation needs. Consequently, business marketers must be diligent in their efforts to continually reinforce buying decisions and create more value for their existing customers.

Another factor that separates business-to-business markets from consumer markets is the complexity created by the various attributes that make up the total business offering. Partly in response to this complexity is the "other side of the coin," the complex nature of the buying decision process. Complexity on both sides is obvious when one studies the **outsourcing** of product research and development, the acquisition of such things as computer information systems, manufacturing facilities or equipment, or a new power plant. However, on the other end of the spectrum lie products that are not very complex, such as office supplies. While the products themselves are not particularly complex, very often features such as quantity discounts, complementary products, and delivery schedules create complexity. All in all, this pervasive complexity reinforces the differences between business-to-business and consumer marketing. The differences that we have discussed do not stand alone but combine to create unique difficulties and opportunities.

Outsourcing is the purchasing of part of the company's continuing operations, such as recruiting or manufacturing, rather than investing in the infrastructure to accomplish the task internally.

Opportunities through Relationships

In business-to-business markets, additional product design effort is often needed to ensure that a product's complexity will enhance customer value rather than detract from it. The dialogue between customer and marketer must quickly and dramatically convey complex concepts that are generally more difficult to understand than those required in consumer marketing. As already noted, communications in business marketing must often focus more on personal selling than in consumer marketing. The sales force becomes the focal point for developing the relationships that will enhance the position of the selling organization in its attempt to address the complex and diffused buyers' decision processes. Marketing based on building close relationships with customers becomes the glue that holds all the other pieces together to create value by ensuring that the customers' uniqueness is accommodated. In contrast, relationships in consumer marketing are often part of "Customer Service" and are often treated as sources of costs rather than enhancement to interaction with customers.

For example, EMC, a company that markets high-end data storage systems, employed a strategy during the 1990s of building direct relationships with customers to become the leader in corporate-wide information storage. While IBM was reducing its efforts to maintain relationships with customers, EMC was focusing on working with customers to understand their problems. With this acquired understanding, EMC launched products that made data storage and management faster, easier, and more effective. In 1993, EMC passed IBM in the number of storage systems used with IBM mainframe computers.[10]

One effect of the necessity for close relationships is that switching costs—the costs of switching suppliers—become very high for both the customer and the supplier. In consumer markets, switching costs usually are not nearly so constraining. High switching costs in business-to-business markets can result from the investment that the partners make in matching buying, ordering, inbound logistics, and delivery systems to each other. High switching costs can also come from the working relationships established on a personal level, which may be less tangible than the logistical linkages. However, such personal linkages can be just as close and binding and just as difficult to break. Because buyers realize that commitment to a vendor creates such high switching costs, they become very careful about whom they choose as suppliers and often establish backup, second source relationships with other suppliers. Meanwhile, suppliers seek out other buyers so that they are not so reliant on a single large customer. Once all these primary and secondary relationships are established, the high switching costs make the supplier-customer relationships difficult to split, making it difficult for new partners to enter the picture. Partners need to realize, though, that they cannot abuse these locked-in relationships with poor quality or service or untenable

---

[10]Hassan Fattah, "It's Not Easy Being King," *Marketing Computers* 20, no. 5 (May 2000): 74.

demands. Though durable, partnerships break at times and the aggrieved partner makes it difficult for the penitent party to reestablish the relationship.

Market Structure

Another highlighted difference between business-to-business and consumer markets is that, usually, business marketers face markets with a much smaller number of customers than consumer marketers face. The reasons for this are quite simple. First, there are simply fewer organizations in existence than there are consumers. Second, organizations differ greatly in what they do and how they do it. Hence, their needs for products and services differ greatly. This means that many market segments (a topic discussed in Chapter 7) have relatively few organizations populating them.

Having many market segments with differing needs implies that mass marketing approaches will not be particularly useful. Our natural instincts as consumers are often contrary to effective business-to-business marketing logic. As an example, mass communications are not particularly efficient or effective. Access to mass media is expensive. In consumer markets, cost in mass media is spread out over a large audience such that cost per contact is low. If mass media do not or cannot reach enough numbers of prospects, due to small numbers in target segments as occurs in many business markets, then cost per contact remains high and other, more efficient means of communications must be sought. This high-cost business model analogy extends to other aspects of marketing as well. Since business segments often have small numbers of buyers (see the discussion of oligopolistic markets in Chapter 2) and it is likely that each buyer has a different idea of what product provides the best value, marketers are likely to tailor offerings to specific value definitions. As a result, product costs will tend to be high, since economies of scale are more difficult to come by. Either the product has to have a great deal of value built in, so that high prices are tolerated by customers, or the marketer has to target numerous similar segments whose needs allow a basic product design with minor customized modifications.

Some International Considerations

As we examine the differences between business-to-business and consumer markets, it is appropriate to note a few international implications. In part because of international standards-setting organizations, the complexity of doing business beyond our own borders is less for business-to-business markets than for consumer markets. International consumer markets are subject to many more cultural, language, regulatory, and individual value differences than business-to-business markets. An exporter of a packaged food product must be concerned not only with packaging, promotion, and language differences but also with cultural beliefs and values about ingredients, colors, and style as well as buying habits. Additionally, international standards in foods and packaging of consumer products vary greatly. Conversely, business-to-business products have fewer hurdles to clear.

While business-to-business products are subject to the same politics of tariffs and other trade barriers, many materials and supplies meet standards that are con-

> ### Participation Exercise
>
> Examine a recent product purchase you made as a consumer. Did the brand of this product play an important role in your selection process? Note the different components and elements that make up the product. Did the producer of the consumer product manufacture all of the components, or do you think some parts may have been purchased from other producers? What considerations do you think the producer of the consumer product had when selecting the manufacturer of the various components and parts that make up the final product? What values did the producer look for (cost, reliability, durability, power consumption, etc.)? As you make your examination, you may be surprised by the number of different manufacturers who contributed to the final product. [Careful! Don't create any hazards or damage your recent purchase during this examination!]

sistent across borders. Plastic materials have been nearly standardized through the voluntary effort of the Society of Plastic Engineers (SPE); and the transportation industry, through the Society of Automotive Engineers (SAE), has created performance standards for vehicle systems. These are but two examples. Steel, plastic, pulp and paper products, chemicals, and electronics industries have technical standards that are applied worldwide. Organizations such as the International Standards Organization (ISO) have created a common language to define and specify the technical performance of manufacturing and quality systems. Compliance with many of these standards has become mandatory at many global firms.

Another area of commonality across international borders is the importance of the dimensions of functionality, performance, and productivity. The diversity of product needs in business-to-business markets across borders is somewhat reduced when compared to consumer markets in which dimensions such as style, fashion, and cultural tastes take precedence.

AN EXAMINATION OF VALUE

Throughout this chapter, as well as the rest of this text, a recurring theme is the customer's perception of value and that perception's impact on buying decisions. The notions of value, the value chain, the networks that build value, and the nature of competition are very powerful in giving depth to business marketers' decisions. For example, the role and management of marketing channels and business logistics become much more clear when value for the final customer is understood as the necessary outcome of an extended value chain. Value and the value chain deserve a close look, then, in some detail. In this chapter, we elaborate on the value chain as described by Porter[11]; in Chapter 2, we expand the discussion to better reflect changes implied by new and emerging business styles and formats.

This brings us to the point where we must make explicit the concept of value. The adage, consumers who purchase a quarter-inch drill bit do not want a quarter-inch

---

[11]Michael E. Porter, *Competitive Advantage: Creating and Sustaining Superior Performance* (New York: Free Press, 1985).

drill bit—they want a quarter-inch hole, is quite appropriate. As consumers, we do not purchase music CDs because we like the shiny plastic discs; we buy them because we are interested in the entertainment value of the music. The disc is merely a container for the value. Customers do not purchase products; they purchase offerings that create solutions and satisfaction. Consumer and business markets are alike in the exchange process. All parties who are part of an exchange must leave the transaction believing they acquired more than they gave up. The value of an offering is determined not by the cost to create it but, rather, by the net value of satisfaction delivered to the customer.

So what is value? Treacy and Wiersema[12] define **value** as the sum of all of the benefits that the customer receives in the process of buying and using a product or service less the costs involved.[13]

The concept is quite simple. The tricky part of value is that lots of things contribute to benefits and lots of things contribute to costs. When you sum all the customer's benefits from buying and using a product or service, you are trying to add terms with different units. The same goes for costs incurred by the customer. There are certainly costs involved in purchasing and costs of maintenance and upgrades, but there are time costs and aggravation costs in the purchasing process, as well. Purchasers also encounter hidden costs associated with usage, such as learning time and the cost of mistakes made while learning how to use the product. We refer to the sum of these costs as the **evaluated price.** Additionally, purchasers' definitions of what is the best value changes with time, experience, technology, and competitive positioning. Accordingly, the concept of value is often hard to quantify. However, this does not mean that the concept is not a useful one. In fact, if we explore the idea of value in a theoretical sense, we can learn a great deal about how business marketing works.

> **Evaluated price** is the total cost of owning and using the product. This may include transportation, inventory carrying costs, financing costs, potential obsolescence, installation, flexibility to upgrade, cost of failure, and obsolescence of existing products or equipment, plus the price paid to the vendor.

THE VALUE CHAIN

In the mid-1980s, Harvard business professor Michael Porter put forth the idea of a value chain.[14] When the value chain is understood and applied wisely, it is a powerful concept that can help a company create competitive advantages that competitors often do not even know exist. As with any management tool, however, if misunderstood and misapplied, the results can sometimes be disastrous. Let us examine the fundamentals and propose an adaptation.

---

[12]Michael Treacy and Frederick Wiersema, *The Discipline of Market Leaders* (Reading, Mass.: Addison-Wesley, 1995).

[13]We prefer the expression of value as a remainder of benefits minus costs rather than as a ratio of benefits to costs, as presented by Kotler and others. Something with relatively low benefits can have a high ratio value if the costs are low. In most cases, a minimum benefit level must be reached before an offering is attractive. Consequently, we feel it better to represent value as an amount subject to a maximum budget constraint. For the ratio expression, see Philip Kotler, *Marketing Management: The Millennium Edition,* 10th ed. (Upper Saddle River, N.J.: Prentice-Hall, 2000), 11.

[14]Porter, op. cit.

Yahoo/Tibco Partnership

Go to the Web site for Tibco (http://www.tibco.com). Click through on "Customers" and then click through on "Yahoo!" You should see a description of how Yahoo is contributing the Corporate Intranet portal to the offering of Tibco. You might also browse through Tibco's presentation of products and services. Now, can you describe the kinds of benefits the Yahoo/Tibco partnership is attempting to provide? What do you think are the components of evaluated price? What kinds of conditions do you think a customer would be facing to find a high level of value in the Yahoo/Tibco offering?

Porter's basic idea is that companies compete to be chosen by buyers. Buyers choose from among competitors' offerings based on the buyers' perceptions of where they will receive the most value (subject to the realities of budgets). Each vendor who is competing, then, tries to do so by offering more value, *as perceived by the customer,* than is offered by the other vendors. The **value chain,** then, is the chain of activities that creates something of value for the targeted customers. The "something of value" is an offering (which was implied by Porter but not made explicit). The offering is everything that the customer or prospect perceives as contributing to benefits and costs. This includes the product and the service but goes much further. The offering also includes brand image, the economic utility provided by distribution such as availability and appropriate quantity, and, as noted earlier, evaluated price. Evaluated price includes all the costs that are subtracted from benefits to produce value—the "cost of doing business" with a supplier. The left-hand portion of Exhibit 1–3, The Value Chain and Offering, represents the value chain.

Exhibit 1–3 also shows the created offering as a combination of product, service, image, availability, and quantity—all part of the factors that make up the evaluated price. Note that these factors are created by the supplier's direct and support activities; yet, their value is as perceived by the target customer. This is an important distinction as we move on. The decision to select a particular supplier is based on the customer's perception of the created value, not the creator's perception.

Direct versus Support Activities

Porter's conceptualization of the specifics of a value chain, internal to an organization, includes both direct and support activities. The direct activities contribute directly to the offering. The support activities make it possible to perform the direct activities. For instance, marketing creates brand image, which is valuable to customers because it provides assurances of quality, upgradability, and the like. Marketing is

EXHIBIT 1–3   The Value Chain and Offering

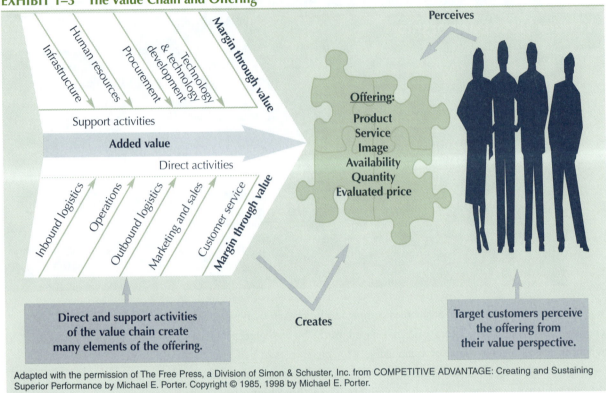

Adapted with the permission of The Free Press, a Division of Simon & Schuster, Inc. from COMPETITIVE ADVANTAGE: Creating and Sustaining Superior Performance by Michael E. Porter. Copyright © 1985, 1998 by Michael E. Porter.

then a direct activity. Human resources management defines positions and recruits, hires, trains, and motivates the people who are necessary to do the marketing and other activities. Therefore, human resources management is a support activity.

The specifics of direct and support activities are shown in Exhibit 1–4. The implications of all this are fairly simple and familiar, but they are also quite powerful. The first implication is that the organization should start by really understanding its prospective customers. The organization should fully understand what prospects would perceive as valuable. Further, the organization should understand how prospects might be persuaded to change their minds about what is valuable. This is not manipulation but customer education. It is focused on getting the customer to better appreciate the value that it is possible to obtain from the offering. The market-driven organization is able to demonstrate superior value in its offering, enabling improved margin through customer recognition of that value. The organization is focused on providing more value, not on giving less value and then convincing customers it is the best that they can expect. The organization must itself recognize all of the factors that provide value to its offering.

The second implication is that not all prospects are alike. Segments exist, based on what value the prospective customers seek and what they can afford. Once this is understood, it becomes apparent that our traditional means of determining segments—demographically or by industry—are perhaps misguided. (This is discussed more in Chapter 7.)

The third implication is that direct and support activities are equally important. Without critical links, the whole chain falls apart and the customer's value is

EXHIBIT 1–4 Direct and Support Activities of a Value Chain

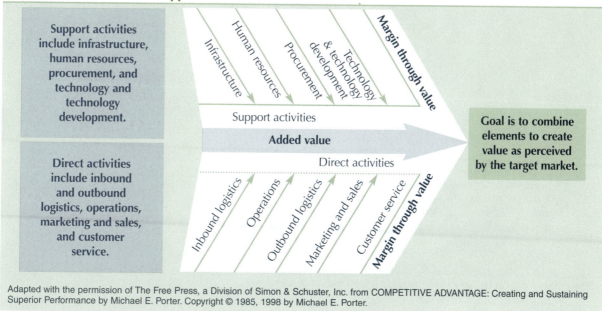

Adapted with the permission of The Free Press, a Division of Simon & Schuster, Inc. from COMPETITIVE ADVANTAGE: Creating and Sustaining Superior Performance by Michael E. Porter. Copyright © 1985, 1998 by Michael E. Porter.

degraded. One of the misuses of the value chain concept during the recession in the early 1990s was to see value creation only in activities that produced or sold products. Significant cuts were made in "non–value producing" activities without realizing the impact these cuts would have on value perceived by customers.

The fourth implication is that the value chain truly extends from the customer back through distribution channels, through manufacturers, through component suppliers, finally to raw material providers (Exhibit 1–5). This representation is not unlike the more logistics-oriented notion of a **supply chain,** which is discussed in Chapter 12. Because of the nature of derived demand, business buyers define what is valuable to them in terms of what value they are providing to their own customers. Each purchase by a business contributes to the value it provides to its customers.

The idea of value and its competitive implications is quite straightforward. The value chain concept gives a powerful argument for following the marketing concept. As previously noted, the marketing concept says that, to do well, the organization should know its customers, meet their needs, and do so in a way that meets organization goals. The value chain concept goes further to provide a framework for pursuing the marketing concept.

> A **supply chain** is the chain of entities and activities that results in products provided to end users. It starts with raw materials and traces the flow of materials and subassemblies through suppliers, manufacturers, and channel intermediaries to the final customer.

MISUNDERSTANDING OF THE VALUE AND VALUE CHAIN CONCEPTS

The concepts of value and the value chain are very basic, so much so that marketers sometimes lose sight of their implications. It appears that this happens in three principal ways.

EXHIBIT 1–5   The Extended Value Chain

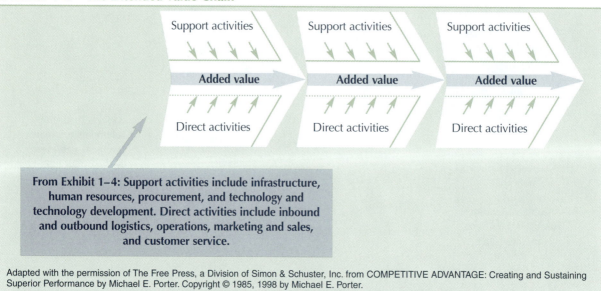

From Exhibit 1–4: Support activities include infrastructure, human resources, procurement, and technology and technology development. Direct activities include inbound and outbound logistics, operations, marketing and sales, and customer service.

Adapted with the permission of The Free Press, a Division of Simon & Schuster, Inc. from COMPETITIVE ADVANTAGE: Creating and Sustaining Superior Performance by Michael E. Porter. Copyright © 1985, 1998 by Michael E. Porter.

First, marketing managers often get so caught up in trying to create profits for their companies that they lose sight of what customer value really means. They forget that customers will not choose to buy a product unless it provides superior value to the customers. To create profits, managers sometimes think that they can forgo some customer value to reduce costs by taking shortcuts on quality, service, or availability; or, they lose sight of customer value altogether and wind up creating me-too or inferior products or offerings whose value is easily copied and soon surpassed. Marketers need to be reminded that perceived value must be better than value from competitors' offerings. Without this fundamental driver, profits do not happen.

Second, managers often lose sight of what creates value for the customer. As already noted, customers get value from more than just the core product or service. Some products provide prestige, some provide upgradability, some have the support of a stellar service organization, and others never need service. Too often, managers get bogged down getting the product (or service) features right and they forget that communications, positioning, distribution, and pricing also create value.

Third, there are often so many different kinds of businesses that want a product or service and derive value from it in so many different ways that it is difficult to pin down exactly what combination of features in an offering is truly valued by the most important customers. When this occurs, it indicates that a poor job has been done in defining segments and/or choosing target markets. If segments have been defined well, they are practically homogeneous when it comes to benefits sought. If there is a great deal of heterogeneity within the target segments, then the segmentation needs to be rethought (see Chapter 7).

In all of the preceding situations, marketers lose sight of the fact that they need to be truly customer value driven. This means that they have to maintain the discipline of focusing on customers and finding a way to provide superior value for them. Time and again, when companies lose sight of this, they get into trouble.

TRENDS AND CHANGES IN BUSINESS MARKETING

To this point, we have suggested that it is important to study business-to-business marketing separately from consumer marketing. We have also discussed the concepts of value and the value chain as the bases for thinking about business marketing. The business-to-business marketing environment is changing rapidly, and adaptation to this change may require some new ways of thinking and acting. Things are changing so rapidly that it is tempting to say that all the "rules" no longer apply and it is time to write the new rules of business.[15]

Many concepts in business marketing are just as germane as they were in the past: understanding customers and building relationships with them, understanding segmentation, applying branding concepts, and careful management of the marketing channels and business logistics, just to name a few. However, there are some trends appearing, not just in technology industries but also across many other industries. These trends may require some new business and marketing approaches—approaches that may be extensions of existing business marketing concepts but that may not always be easily recognized.

Throughout this book, we elaborate on trends that, at this time, appear to require attention from business-to-business marketers. While these changes are mostly obvious, how to address them may not be so obvious.

Several of these trends are interrelated: they cause each other. Together they produce second- and third-level effects that become trends in and of themselves.

Hypercompetition

Several factors have combined, seemingly in the short term, to create many smart, fast competitors across many industries. New companies that emerge quickly or create new markets and industries almost overnight challenge established companies. In the face of this new, rapidly appearing **hypercompetition,** existing companies are rapidly embracing new, unproven methods and techniques. Every time organizations lay off employees, they tend to create more competitors for themselves. This trend continues with the continued desire to cut costs. As companies learn to do more with fewer people, at least some of these companies downsize. This leaves many skilled people who are looking for work; some start companies, and more go to work for new companies, often with a well-established network of relationships in place. The venture capital market of the 1990s fueled much of this activity, creating instant competitors. In the past, a company could see who its future competitors were going to be as they started and slowly entered the market. Recently, venture capital and **initial public offerings (IPOs)—** first offerings of a company's stock on a public exchange—provide sufficient resources to turn start-ups into full-fledged competitors much more quickly than would have

---

[15]Karen Southwick, *Silicon Gold Rush* (New York: Wiley, 1999).

happened in the past. Even though the hot venture capital and IPO markets have cooled and many new competitors have gone out of business, the events of the late 1990s showed that, when capital is available, quick creation of viable competitors can occur.

The rapidly changing competitive landscape means that business marketers must anticipate a hypercompetitive environment even though they are unable to anticipate who tomorrow's competitors will be. This, in turn, means that competitive analysis techniques and competitive actions, which once focused on addressing competition from specific competitors, must be adapted to accommodate this heightened uncertainty. Techniques that can be used in such an environment are discussed in Chapter 6.

Formation of Partner Networks

Products, projects, and systems have become so complex and interrelated that no company can provide a "whole product" by itself. For instance, software providers need to partner with hardware vendors, other software vendors, and systems integrators to provide enterprise-level software systems (such as enterprise resource planning—ERP—systems). What was once a sales channel—the software company to the systems integrators—has become a sales, service, and distribution cluster. Similar partnering occurs for new product development and filling product lines. Larger companies are recognizing that, often, other companies have crucial pieces of technology or complementary products. These trends are not just occurring in the computer industry and related industries. The same kinds of partner networks are occurring in industries as diverse as construction, energy production and distribution, consulting, and employment services.

This seems straightforward, and the solutions for addressing this trend seem to look a lot like extensions of channel management. However, the business marketer realizes that things are different when the marketer is approached by an arch rival competitor with the offer of partnering on a new venture or in a new market. This is not collusion, because the competitor remains a competitor in other markets; and the competitor may break the partnership—probably will break the partnership—in the future and compete in this market that the two partners have pioneered together. The implications of this trend in partnering are examined more closely in Chapters 8 through 12.

Channel facilitators are those service providers to the channel that are not necessarily part of channel design but who make possible the efficient operation of the channel. Channel facilitators are financial institutions, transportation and logistics companies, third-party service providers, and so on. These organizations provide outsourced services to facilitate the effective operation of the channel.

Adoption of Information Technology and the Internet

Another trend changing the face of business marketing is the increased pace of adoption of information technology. Internet technology, of which the Web is a subset, offers enhanced communication, enhanced customer service, and reduced costs. The concepts of total offering and evaluated price combine to demonstrate that these benefits accrue to buyers as well as sellers. Channel members and other intermediaries obtain all these benefits as well, as they act as buyers, sellers, and **facilitators.**

Supply Chain Management

Supply chains extend from raw material and component suppliers, through the manufacturer, and through the distribution channel to the final buyer. We have had **electronic data interchange (EDI)** in use for a couple decades to manage supply chains. While it is used and useful, as a facilitator of supplier/buyer relationships, EDI has never lived up to its full promise. It is expensive to install and maintain. It requires that everyone involved be using compatible systems. This has caused real problems for any supply chain member who wanted to be involved in several supply chains, thus requiring investment in multiple systems. Only those supply chains in which there were clear channel leaders and enough resources could arrange such an integrated system.

> **Electronic data interchange (EDI)** is a technology for exchanging information concerning ordering of goods. The information exchanged consists of order and fulfillment information as well as payments through electronic funds transfer. EDI is facilitated through value-added networks—these are private, secure networks, inaccessible to non-members of the network.

The Web has and will continue to impact the dynamics of supply chain management. Now the participants do not have to have compatible equipment, just Internet access and an up-to-date browser (it is actually more complicated, but the compatibility issue is much more tractable using the Internet). A single supplier or distributor can participate in multiple channels, even though the channel leaders use different platforms. The supplier or distributor must still reconcile different tracking and accounting systems, but such efforts still cost less than maintaining several different information technology (IT) systems.

On-line ordering, inventory and delivery tracking, coordination of marketing programs, and automated sharing of market information have the potential to squeeze a great deal of the costs out of the supply chain, while making the supply chain faster and more effective. Market-driven pricing methods are challenged as well. Auctioning software allows excess inventory to be sold over the Web, allocating the inventory to the channel outlets where it will be valued the most. Using the auctioning concept from the other direction, manufacturers or distributors can run on-line bidding for supply contracts. In a very short time frame, they can get better prices and more effective delivery contracts. Auctioning can make existing suppliers, whose offerings do not provide good value, subject to quick termination of their contracts for nonperformance, because the transaction costs of switching have been minimized (other switching costs still exist, of course, and may give the incumbent supplier some breathing room).

The Web has begun to change the nature of the relationship between the business marketer and his customer, as well. The Web can streamline communications and make it possible to have closer ties with more customers. Today, the buying decision process (discussed at length in Chapter 3) almost always includes at least some information search on the Web. If a marketer is to be seriously considered, he must have a Web site with relevant information readily available. The Web site must also be easy to find and navigate. Once contact and a relationship are established with a prospective or current customer, the Web can be used to quickly share new information, obtain feedback, place orders, and track order progress. Thus, the Web is integral to customer service, too.

The Web is also the conveyor of a product or a service. Many products now are digital, including, of course, software; but a product such as an insurance policy or a consulting report can be a document, which can be transmitted in digital form. Drawings, photographs, videos, or combinations of these may constitute part or even all of a product. These, of course, can be delivered via the Internet or Web. Many software products that were once sold as "shrink-wrapped" products, or as major installations, now are sold as Web-enabled services. Customers do not have to install the application on their own systems. All they have to do is access the software on a central site and input their own data by completing forms on a Web site, and the central site runs the application. The output is returned to the customer through a custom-generated Web page. Selling such services via the Web provides a great deal of value to business buyers in that installation time is small and the overhead costs of installation and maintenance are shared with other users of the centralized service. The implication is that many more business customers now have access to the software, presumably making their business operations more efficient and effective. At the same time, the business model of the software company has changed from a software product manufacturer to that of a service provider. Many software companies, such as Oracle and IBM, are developing this model for addressing smaller company markets. All this changes the business environment for the companies that used to provide installation, training, and maintenance services for customers installing new software and hardware. A great deal of the business that used to be generated is now potentially going away. On the other side of the coin, the installation, training, and maintenance business that is left tends to be high value and high margin.

Even as this book was in production, new business forms and profit models were created that we could not have imagined at the outset. The Web enables efficiency and productivity in new schemes of partner networks and value collaborations. Chapter 2 introduces the logical outcome of these circumstances when combined with the philosophy of customer value—value networks. The rest of the book highlights the directions information technology is taking business marketing and the accommodations that business marketers are making.

Time Compression

Several factors combine to create **time compression**—an increase in the "speed" of doing business. How organizations react to this acceleration has both short-term and long-term effects on their survivability and performance. With hypercompetition, competitive pressures cause companies to try to get new products out faster and to replace these products with succeeding generations of products even more rapidly. Having offerings in the market with more value than competitors' offerings wins customers; but, then, competitors are trying to do the same thing, so the pace quickens.

Over the last twelve to eighteen months, our discussions with executives and managers have yielded disquieting results. Responses to the question, "How are you dealing with time compression?" range from well thought out, seemingly effective methods to some version of "work harder and faster." There seem to be too many of the latter.

With all the change occurring in the business marketer's world, we believe that some ideas, such as the value chain and its implications, continue to have validity and can provide guidance. We contend that the best way to be successful and profitable is to focus on creating superior value for prospective customers. Do this first, and prospective customers will be willing to pay, commensurate with perceived value. Then the focus can turn to managing costs in such a way that value is not diminished. With proper management, companies will be creating enough cash flow to pay for the value that is provided to them by their own upstream suppliers.

In the Yahoo/Tibco partnership, the key to its success is how much value can be created for large company users. The first step taken by the partnership is promising; they have created an Intranet portal, run as an internal test for Yahoo employees. As this book was being written, they were also creating test portals for several initial customers. If the marketers in the partnership pay close attention to users' reactions, the partnership may be able to get insight into what is valuable and how to communicate this. The question then becomes whether the partnership can deploy a targeted offering more effectively than do its competitors.

Chapter 2 concerns other key ideas that describe how business-to-business markets operate and how marketing implications are drawn from these concepts. Keep in mind, though, that providing value is still at the foundation of these concepts. Customers' perceptions of value change over time, and the ways that value is created through organizations changes as well. Throughout this book, and indeed throughout your career as a marketer, the search for creative ways to provide new value to your current and future customers must continue.

Key Terms

bullwhip effect
business marketing
business markets
channel facilitators
consumer demand
derived demand
discontinuous demand
economic utility
electronic data interchange
  (EDI)
evaluated price

form
four Ps
hypercompetition
inelastic demand
initial public offerings
  (IPOs)
Intranet portals
marketing concept
outsourcing
partnership
place

portal
possession
price elasticity
supply chain
time
time compression
total offering
value
value chain

Questions for Review and Discussion

1. Describe the differences between business-to-business and consumer marketing for the following market elements:

   Products   Buyer behavior   Decision making

2. What is meant when we say that decision making in business-to-business markets moves through observable stages?

3. Describe the difference between derived demand and consumer demand. How does the leveraging phenomenon occur?

4. What is the difference between value as perceived by the customer and value as perceived by the supplier?

5. We learned in economics the difference between elasticity and inelasticity. What is meant when we say that business-to-business demand is inelastic in the short term and discontinuous in the long term?

6. Ultimately, who is the long-term benefactor of application of the value chain?

7. Considering all of the elements of evaluated price, would value to the customer's customer be a major consideration? Why, or why not?

8. How is value created in the transaction process?

9. As consumers, how do our "shopping instincts" make it difficult to understand business-to-business marketing philosophy?

10. What factors can contribute to a customer remaining with a particular supplier even though lower-cost substitutes may be available?

Internet Exercises

Using a search engine such as Yahoo! or Google, find an example of an industry outside of high technology for which a Web-based market or exchange has been created for buying and selling products, services, supplies, parts, or feedstock. Trace the links back through to the member companies. By searching through their Web sites and following links to articles about the industry, determine how the companies and the industry have changed over the past three years from the introduction of the Web-based market or exchange.

Go to the Web site for Yahoo!: **http://www.yahoo.com** Click on "My Yahoo." Investigate what features My Yahoo offers. You can even configure your own My Yahoo page, if you like (or, if you already have one, try reconfiguring it). How does Yahoo pursue the marketing concept by offering My Yahoo? What will Yahoo have to do to pursue the marketing concept to adapt My Yahoo to a corporate Intranet portal, as described in the opening story? As you think about your answer, try to address the three elements of the marketing concept: understanding customers, meeting their needs, and meeting Yahoo's company goals. You will probably find that it is more difficult than you might think to accomplish the first and third elements!

Go to Tibco's web site: **http://www.tibco.com** Look up five of their strategic partners, as identified in the Press Releases section or in the Customers section of the Web site. Can you determine how each partnership contributes to Tibco's offering?

2

Classifying Customers, Organizations, and Markets

overview. . . In this chapter, several key ideas are introduced that are used throughout this book. Categorization of businesses as customers helps the marketer begin to understand the business environment in which she operates. Categorization of businesses as suppliers helps the marketer to begin to understand the competitive environment. Looking inward, the marketer can also begin to understand the constraints faced by her own company as a member of a supplier category. Building on the value chain idea introduced in Chapter 1, the concept of value networks aids in the marketer's understanding of relationships that currently exist and that need to be built to create superior value for customers. To give a framework for understanding how business environments change, two useful models of business evolution are provided: the product life cycle concept and the technology adoption life cycle. All in all, these concepts provide frameworks for understanding the business-to-business marketer's environment from a large-scale viewpoint. Of course, the "devil is in the details," but these ideas help the marketer frame the problems and opportunities that need to be addressed.

© EYEWIRE COLLECTION

The opening example shows how TRW operates in multiple categories, how its customers operate in multiple categories, and how TRW's business and marketing strategies are affected. The example also points out how operating in multiple modes creates management problems.

Though the brands are not well known to consumers, TRW products contribute value to practically every car and truck produced. In 1999, TRW sales to the automotive segment totaled over $11 billion. Does your car or truck have antilock brakes? TRW, including the Kelsey Hayes brand, has provided a greater number of antilock brake systems to the automobile manufacturers market than any other company, beginning in 1969 with the first electronically controlled automatic brake system (ABS) launched on the Lincoln Mark IV. Does your car or truck have an air bag? You have an even chance that TRW manufactured the sensors that detect the severity of an accident and trigger the air bag—also provided by TRW. It does not stop with these products. Lucas electrical components, sodium-cooled engine valves, vehicle suspension systems, and engine management systems are all part of the TRW basket of offerings. Of course, should you require service or replacement of any of these components, the repair technician can pinpoint the problem with TRW diagnostic service equipment and install TRW after-market parts. Not bad for a company that started in 1901 as a fastener manufacturer in Cleveland, Ohio.

Did we mention aerospace and information systems? In 1999, TRW revenues from these markets exceeded $5.5 billion. In 1958, NASA launched Pioneer 1, built by TRW, into space. Since that time, TRW has built approximately 200 spacecraft, including the Chandra X-ray Observatory, recently launched from the space shuttle Columbia.

How does an organization continuously provide value to such diverse markets over a long period? By understanding the market, anticipating future value, and partnering with other market participants to create that value. TRW is organized to mirror the needs of the markets in which it participates. The market for TRW products and services is divided into two large segments: Automotive and Aerospace & Information Systems. This initial segmentation might imply that customers within each segment have similar buying habits. This is, however, not likely. Volkswagen purchase habits for braking systems are quite different from an individual's purchase habits for the same products as repair or maintenance items. While providing the same core product (e.g., brakes) to both customers, TRW recognizes that the value sought is a well-designed braking system that will safely stop the vehicle.

The Volkswagen perception of this value includes engineering design and development assistance, durable

TRW OPERATES IN MULTIPLE CATEGORIES (CONT'D)

components and reliable supply, and interaction with production planning to ensure effective supply logistics (the right quantity at the right time and place for this customer)—all at a competitive price. In this instance, the brakes are components specified and purchased by Volkswagen for incorporation into a Volkswagen product; Volkswagen becomes the end user of the components. There is little if any recognition of TRW parts by the purchaser of a new Volkswagen.

In the aftermarket, TRW recognizes that the customer wants quick diagnosis of the vehicle problem and immediate availability of replacement components. In this case, the end user is the repair technician or the vehicle owner whose primary interest is getting the vehicle roadworthy. While the core product is the same, the offerings are not alike. Volkswagon purchases millions of identical brake components directly from TRW. The repair technician buys brake components individually, as needed, and of many different designs and variations to match the different vehicles being serviced. TRW recognizes these fundamental differences in value sought and treats these markets as completely different segments.

TRW marketing is organized not along product lines but along customer value and buying habits. The aftermarket organization at TRW represents all TRW products in the automotive sector. Aftermarket headquarters is located in the United Kingdom, with a global service network covering more than 120 countries. **Original equipment manufacturer (OEM)** markets are managed from a headquarters operation in Livonia, Michigan, with support centers for vehicle manufacturers in seventeen countries. While this may appear as logistics management, it is much more than that.

TRW partners with its customers and its suppliers. As a supplier, TRW must know the methods and culture of customers as well as the immediate supply needs. TRW must examine customers not just as buyers of components but also as participants in demanding markets. TRW's awareness of these demands, the needs of its customers' customers, helps TRW anticipate customer needs. With this additional market sensitivity, TRW can work with its suppliers to enhance the value of the offering throughout the entire value chain. TRW's Value

TRW: Web Site Layout and Presentation

Go to the Web site for TRW (http://www.trw.com). Examine the layout of the Web site and the way that offerings are presented. To what extent are customers accommodated by the organization of the Web site?

Look at the different markets that TRW participates in. Note that OEM and aftermarket, while often involved with identical core products, have completely different branches in the Web site. Each is addressed by the needs of the market segment. Compare milestones for OEM and aftermarket. You should be able to notice that milestones and significant events are related to markets being served, not to products being "served up."

Chain Management Center (VCMC) manages efforts in this area to understand and apply successful "best practices" while improving communications and alignment with TRW customer goals. In 1999, TRW partnered with Magna International, Incorporated, to open Advanced Car Technology Systems (ACTS), the most advanced independent automotive development and testing center in the world for modular, functional, and safety systems. This joint venture of two major automotive suppliers is intended to continue to push the envelope of value-related offerings for both partners and customers.

Complete braking and traction control systems or complete suspension systems (or satellite systems, for that matter) are designed and developed in conjunction with major customers. The performance of the system impacts the reputation of the customer. The customer seeks suppliers who demonstrate not just product or technology competence but an understanding of their markets and how the supplier can contribute value to the customer's offering. How does an organization continuously provide value to markets over a long period? It is by knowing its customers and their organizations and the markets in which they make decisions.

- ◆ Understand the different kinds of business customers.
- ◆ Understand the different categories of business marketers.
- ◆ Gain an appreciation of the different kinds of competitive market structures and their effects on buying behavior.
- ◆ Understand how the value chain concept is extended by the value network concept. Think through the implications for marketing.
- ◆ Reinforce and extend your understanding of the product life cycle and its impacts on business-to-business markets.
- ◆ Gain an initial introduction to the technology adoption life cycle and its implications for targeting and positioning.

introduction. . .

Customer organizations and markets evolve over time just as products and technologies do. At the start of Chapter 1, we saw an example of Yahoo!, a consumer-oriented Internet organization, collaborating with Tibco, a software developer, to offer Intranet portals for businesses. What may seem like a natural combination of two organizations in today's fast-changing Internet arena actually redefines Yahoo! and Tibco and their competitive positioning. However, changes in competitive form and business environment are not a creation of the Internet. Markets and organizations have life cycles not unlike products.

In this chapter, we examine traditional business patterns and see how organizations and markets have evolved as the value needs of customers react to an ever-changing environment. The concept of evolving business patterns and value as seen by the customer is not a new notion to industry; rather, it is just one that seems to have a large number of convenient exceptions. Firms engaged in fast-paced markets often claim that they usually do not have time to "study" their customers. Smart competition uses this as an opportunity to move ahead with new offerings better geared to meet customer desires. Toward the end of this chapter, we discuss what we believe to be a common misunderstanding about value and the marketing concept.

PRACTICAL APPLICATION OF MARKET GENERALIZATIONS

The following discussion may sound a bit esoteric, and the student may wonder how these concepts are applied. In and of themselves, the concepts discussed in this chapter hold no prescriptions for specific actions that a business-to-business marketing manager can take. However, these concepts can be used to begin the manager's thinking process. The practical aspect of categorizing products, analyzing the nature of competition in the market, tracking product life cycles, and understanding the technology adoption life cycle is the framework provided for perceiving the business environment. All of these concepts provide insight into how the other actors in the marketer's environment will generally act and react. They also give some clues as to how the environment is likely to change in time—though not specific changes and when they will occur.

There are several standard forms of product, competition, and market combinations that make up the business environment. Common configurations often have sets of marketing activities that tend to be associated with them. An understanding of these generalizations can assist the marketer to better understand how customers in certain environments will behave, how they will perceive value, and how competitors will try to create superior value.

TYPES OF ORGANIZATIONAL CUSTOMERS

Many business-to-business marketers have their own systems for classifying customers. What these systems are and how they are applied depend on the marketer's company's particular situation. Understanding different customer groups and why they are clustered together can provide insight into how and why customers view value. In this section, we present a standard way of thinking about categories of businesses. These categories represent a beginning for the marketer in trying to understand segmentation in her market and give a first clue concerning what strategies the customers will pursue and how they will be constrained. The categories are presented in no particular order.

Commercial Enterprises

The classification of *commercial enterprises* reflects a segmentation of for-profit organizations based on how the products or services in question are going to be used. This group includes industrial distributors and dealers, resellers, original equipment manufacturers (OEMs), and users or end users (E/U).

Industrial Distributors   Also known as industrial wholesalers, these organizations act as middlemen providing the economic utilities of form, time, place, and possession to manufacturers and segments of customers of those manufacturers. The creation of assortments of products from many manufacturers to closely match the needs of customer segments is a major added value of middlemen. Business marketers often elect to use middlemen to reach customers whose purchase volumes do not justify direct sales efforts. Chapter 12 contains a complete discussion of marketing channels, including appropriate products for this type of representation and the value provided by these middlemen. For now, note that these intermediaries take ownership of goods from manufacturers and provide their customers timely access to these goods.

Value-Added Resellers   The addition of **value-added resellers (VARs)** to the marketplace has broadened traditional intermediary concepts. More than distributors or wholesalers, VARs provide unique offering enhancements to manufacturers' products. Typically, a VAR provides systems to its customers (computer software and hardware integration, communications systems, etc.) tailored to a particular customer's needs. The VAR draws on goods and services from many manufacturers to create these custom systems, often developing unique expertise in the integration of many different products. The combined offering may include portions of products and services from different organizations who, without the VAR, would normally be competitors. Thus, the VAR's integration of offerings from many sources is, in effect, the creation of a **value network** at the user level. Later in this chapter, we look at value networks, coalitions to satisfy specific segment needs, as the next logical competitive form.

Original Equipment Manufacturers
Original equipment manufacturers (OEMs) purchase goods to incorporate them into goods they produce and sell to their customers. Business-to-business marketers spend the major part of their resources approaching, learning about, developing, and satisfying these customers. OEMs are usually the largest-volume users of goods and services, particularly in oligopolistic markets, as we discuss later in this chapter.

For example, General Motors (GM) purchases tires from Goodyear; Compaq purchases processors from Intel. General Motors and Compaq use tires and processors, respectively, as an original part of the products they offer to their customers. Note that Goodyear and Intel, both OEM suppliers in this scenario, offer their products to customers in the replacement market through industrial distributors as well. While the total offer is significantly different (tires through distribution are aimed at local dealers with lower volumes and greater geographic diversity than vehicle manufacturers), the core products, tires and processors, remain unchanged.

Users or End Users
Manufacturers that purchase goods and services for consumption, either as supplies, capital goods, or materials for incorporation into their products such that the identity of the purchased product is lost, are known as **users** or **end users (E/Us).** When providing tires to GM, Goodyear is an OEM in the preceding example. When purchasing steel for fabrication into steel tire belts, Goodyear is an E/U. The supplier of steel views Goodyear as its end user. Business marketers find that this traditional relationship is changing as OEMs attempt to place some responsibility for their products with their suppliers and suppliers begin to recognize the importance of branding in the business-to-business market.[1]

When users purchase goods and services in support of their operations, the buying pattern is significantly different. When Goodyear purchases fuel for its trucks, it is a routine rebuy usually involving one purchasing individual. If Goodyear were purchasing a new robotic tire manufacturing facility, a very large number of individuals would participate in this one-time, but very unique, purchase. In either situation, Goodyear is the E/U in the transaction. (We discuss the buying decision process for different levels of buying complexity in Chapter 3.)

Government Units

In 1998, purchases by more than 85,000 local, state, and federal government units made up approximately 35 percent of our gross national product (GNP). Govern-

---

[1] Gerry Kobe, "The Demise of Brand X," *Automotive Industries* (May 1999): 53.

ment is the largest consuming group in the United States. Widely dispersed with large numbers of players, government markets are influenced by specifying agencies, legislators, and evaluators, as well as, hopefully, the eventual users. What business marketers have come to appreciate as value in the private sector takes on a completely different meaning in the public sector.

Complicated procurement laws and regulations often have social goals and policies as the driving force. Preference to certain types of suppliers, socially motivated general contract provisions, and the potential impact of quotas and other regulations that seemingly have nothing to do with the product can be frustrating to business marketers. In theory, however, this is little different from the private sector, provided the marketer is focused on customer needs rather than the product. It is necessary to examine what value is expected by the government customer and who/what the influencing factors will be.

The specialized role that government functions play in our society (national defense, disaster relief, education, social and political agenda, etc.) leads to nonstandard products. This complexity and the lack of standardization are often the result of significant negotiation by a diverse group of stakeholders. While competitive bidding is often required to avoid demonstrating any favoritism or undue influence, negotiated contracts are also possible, particularly where research and development is necessary or there is no competition to the value provider in question. The value chain approach combined with recognition of buying center influences (Chapter 3) is particularly suited to doing business with government or, for that matter, any complex organization.

Nonprofit and Not-for-Profit Organizations

Institutional customers such as hospitals, churches, colleges, nursing homes, and so on are part of this customer category. At first glance, it may appear that the major part of the marketing mix used to appeal to this customer base is price. As with any customer group, however, the best value recognized in the exchange is important. Many of these organizations are subject to significant public scrutiny. As a result, their buying habits may become similar to those of government units, particularly if there is a strong social agenda associated with the organization.

Producer Types

Business-to-business organizations may also be classified by the goods they produce. As previously stated, these classifications may all be related to potential segmentation variables.

Raw Materials Producers   Depending on the goods or materials position in its life cycle (its degree of uniqueness or distinction from competition), producers of materials may find markets more sensitive to price. Raw materials suppliers, particularly those that have significant competition from generic types, seek added-value positions unrelated to the core product. A supplier of sugar to a large bakery may find that the texture or granule size of its product or how well it dissolves may be a distinctive advantage. Raw materials (such as steel, plastics, and glass) are usually supplied by a few very large producers who sell their products directly to large end users, relying on industrial distributors to serve smaller customers.

Often, raw materials lose their "identity" when combined into a customer's product. The fabricator's customers know the sheet steel purchased by a metal fabricator as a sturdy frame for a computer housing, not as a branded material supplied by a particular steel company. The commodity nature of the steel has been replaced by the added value of the form and function of the frame.

Component Parts and Manufactured Materials Producers

Components and manufactured materials (e.g., upholstery fabric for furniture) usually retain their identity even when fully incorporated into the customer's product. These goods are more easily differentiated from their direct competition by the value added to the core product. Component parts such as the small motors used in computer disk drives are incorporated by disk drive manufacturers in essentially the same form as provided by the motor manufacturer. The component producer's core product contribution is still recognizable after its inclusion in the customer's offering.

Capital Goods Manufacturers

Capital goods—those goods used to produce output—are usually purchased with input from many parts of the organization. These are "big ticket" purchases with considerable risk involved for the customer. The process is lengthy and usually includes the development of a rather sophisticated specification to ensure that the needs of the organization are met and that it gets what it has been promised. When customers invest in a capital item, they must place a tremendous amount of trust in the supplier—and write a good specification.

Suppliers should realize that, from the customer's viewpoint, the specification is a device to level the playing field. By demanding strict adherence by all potential suppliers to the terms of a specification, the customer reduces opportunities for differentiation between competing suppliers. Obviously, this is exactly the opposite of what the supplier wants. The supplier searches for any possible way to make its offering distinctive—better and different—from the competition. This buying behavior is discussed in Chapter 3.

Customers of capital goods expect an offering that includes installation, equipment, and accessories. Often, trials or evaluation installations are required. As a substitute, suppliers may provide testimonials of successful installation and application for other customers, provided confidentiality concerns of both the current and previous customers can be accommodated.

Accessory Equipment Suppliers

Companies that make equipment that works with some other offering are known as **accessory equipment** suppliers. The accessories may be added to a bundled offering by a systems integrator or other channel intermediary of some kind; they may be added to a bundle offered by

an OEM; or the business customer may purchase them separately. Some examples of accessory equipment include clean room supplies for semiconductor manufacturing, floppy disks for computers, and telephone headsets for businesses' telecommunications systems. In most cases, the vendor of the primary product or service does not make the accessory equipment because an independent supplier can make it more quickly with higher quality or for less cost—if the accessory equipment line of business has been well established (i.e., it is in the late growth stage or maturity stage of the product life cycle; see the section in this chapter on the product life cycle). Accessory equipment suppliers have generally gained enough expertise and volume of production to be able to have all three advantages—faster, better, and cheaper—than providers of the primary offering.

If a company is providing accessory equipment—or providing an accessory service, such as cleaning uniforms or moving trade show equipment—the key to providing value is to be compatible with the industry standards for the primary offering. For instance, keyboard manufacturers for computers must conform to standards for data input and connection to the computer. Makers of add-on gadgets for personal digital assistants (PDAs), such as the Palm Pilot, must conform to the physical connection requirements of the devices and to the PalmOS software operating system. To ensure high financial performance, the accessory equipment supplier must pick the right standard. If no standard has emerged as the winner, the marketer for the accessory supplier must either gamble or adapt the product to all the major standards competing for ascendancy. Once a standard has been set, the surviving accessory suppliers need to focus on driving their costs down and, if possible, branding. Since the value provided by the accessory is usually secondary to the value provided by the primary offering, there are limits to the price the accessory provider can charge. Good branding strategy and execution earn a price premium (see Chapter 9), but this, too, is limited by the relative value and price of the primary offering.

Customer Needs Influenced by Classification of Markets

By now, you may be asking yourself why these classifications are important. As they stand alone, they are of little value other than for creating data. No one classification method serves all marketing needs. In fact, rigid organizational classification systems can get in the way of effective benefit-based segmentation; but they can also be a significant factor in development of strategies.

Each of these different types of products and organizations, however, has different levels of involvement by people involved in the customer's purchase decision. Capital items used to produce output are often the end game of a major investment decision by the organization, involving many people within the customer organization who play varying roles in the purchase (see the discussion concerning the buying center in Chapter 3). A routine purchase of materials and parts has a smaller group of interested parties; the supplier who recognizes and assists these participants to maximize the value of the offering for the particular situation can have a substantial advantage.

CLASSIFYING THE BUSINESS-TO-BUSINESS MARKET ENVIRONMENT

Our discussion so far has dealt with classifying individual companies based on the kind of offering they provide. The marketer can use these classifications to get a sense of what kinds of needs the customer organization has, what sorts of motives and constraints drive the competitors, and what constraints the marketer faces in designing marketing strategy.

We now shift our viewpoint to classifying the market environments in which business-to-business marketers must operate. We classify the elements of the environment that can affect the marketer's strategy. As part of this, we briefly examine the effects of different economic market structures. In examining the effects of these environmental structures, we focus on how the relationships between market participants are affected.

Publics

Recall from your marketing principles course the factors that make up the market environment. These generally apply as well to business markets as to consumer markets. They include the various **publics,** or communities of interested parties who are not direct participants in a market as customers, channel members, suppliers, or competitors. These publics have interests because of economic or societal effects of activity in the market or because they provide financing to the direct participants.

Financial Publics   Financial publics include banks and other lending institutions, investors, investment banks, venture capital firms and investors, stock exchanges, brokerage houses and financial analysts, and investment institutions such as retirement funds and mutual funds investment houses. The members of this community seek to maximize the financial performance of the companies they invest in. They develop and share a great deal of information on companies and industries. Very often, they attempt to impact corporate action with their ability to influence the perception of the company in the financial community. Financial publics can be large employee retirement plans responsible for investing their funds for specific growth goals. (For example, the California State Employees Retirement System, CalPERS, has significant funds to invest and can influence the companies in which they choose to invest.) Or they can be fund managers at major investment banks and firms (e.g., Fidelity Investments). Many independent (as well as institutional) investors are sensitive to the views and directions taken by the financial publics.

© EYEWIRE COLLECTION

Business-to-business marketers need to understand the role played by these entities in making resources available. Accordingly, much marketing effort is spent in communicating with the members of the financial public and in working to meet their particular needs. Most medium- to large-sized companies now have specialists in investor relations devoted to maintaining relationships with the financial community. These specialists usually are part of corporate marketing or corporate finance within the organization. While these specialists handle most of the communication with the financial community, higher-level marketing managers are sometimes called upon to make presentations to venture capitalists, bankers, or brokerage house analysts to explain the company's marketing vision and strategy.

As is shown in Chapter 13, one of the most difficult tasks for corporate marketing communications specialists is to ensure that all outgoing communications have compatible and cross-reinforcing messages. The financial public must be considered another audience that perceives communications. They are not isolated from communications intended for customer groups, and vice versa. Accordingly, marketers must be careful to consider the financial public in efforts to keep consistency in all marketing messages.

Independent Press   The media can publish news that can enhance or destroy a market position. On the positive side, it is important for companies to maintain good relationships with the news media in their industry so that good news about a company can receive the most notice. When negative things concerning the company arise, media attention can be devastating. We have sometimes referred to this as "the 60-Minutes syndrome," named after the CBS long-running news magazine program. As is discussed in Chapter 13 and Chapter 14, the best defense for a company in this type of situation is a proactive public relations effort that "inoculates" against a single incident causing serious damage.

Public Interest Groups   Many public interest groups, though comprising a minority in the population, are often able to get the attention of the media or opinion leaders and thus focus "popular" attention on their issues. In some instances, this effort can succeed in attracting the attention of the financial publics, leading to an impact on investors. Again, a good public relations effort combined with an effective inoculation strategy can minimize the negative impact of these groups. A market-driven organization, however, should recognize its societal role and that public interest groups may be an early indication of shifts in the mainstream market.

As an example of a firm's societal role and the attention interest groups can bring to bear, consider how the soaring gasoline prices during the first six months of 2000 invigorated environmentalists' efforts regarding fuel consumption. These efforts were focused particularly on large sport utility vehicles (SUVs), also a target of vehicle safety groups. The largest and most profitable producer of these vehicles, Ford Motor Company, reacted by adding safety features to its larger SUVs and making a commitment to improve the fuel economy of its entire line of SUVs by 25 percent within three years. Were these actions recognition of societal responsibility, good marketing, or a clever public relations position? Whatever the answer, the result is the same.

Internal Publics   Every employee is a representative of the organization to the general public, and every employee is a representative of her part of the organization to the other components of the organization. The reputation and the image of a firm or its parts are greatly impacted by the attitude of its employees. Firms are known as "good to work for" primarily based on the word of mouth from current and past employees, just as different parts of a firm are impacted by conversation among employees. A major aim of internal marketing programs is to promote belonging and ownership among employees that is reflected in their attitudes when away from the job.

The Macroenvironment

Also included in the market environment are existing trends and other macroenvironment factors. The seven macroenvironment factors generally addressed in marketing texts are the demographic, economic, sociocultural, natural, technological, competitive, and legal and political environments. In this chapter, we focus on the first six factors in this list, with emphasis on how they influence value creation. The legal and political environment is fully discussed in Chapter 4.

The Demographic Environment   **Demographics** are the vital statistics that describe a population. The demographic environment includes the characteristics of the population in the geographic regions in which the company does business. Demographic variables include the distribution of ages, incomes, wealth, mobility, education, family composition, religion, ethnic background, and living conditions. All of these variables have an influence on consumer consumption, which translates into business consumption in the effort to meet consumer needs.

Businesses themselves have demographic characteristics, including the type and size of industries that exist, the size and location of companies, the ages of the businesses, and the size of the functional areas within the companies. Demographic characteristics may be associated with particular needs and buying behaviors. Marketers should thus be aware of the relevant demographics of the populations and businesses that comprise their environments.

The Economic Environment   The macroeconomies of regions in which the company does business also influence how business-to-business customers buy and consume. The **macroeconomy** of a region or jurisdiction is the sum total of all economic activity in the area and certain economic characteristics of note. These characteristics include how fast the economy is growing (or declining) in size, the level of employment, the rate of unemployment, interest rates, and exchange rates of currency between different economies.

The state of the economy affects customers' willingness and ability to buy, principally by affecting personal income (which influences derived demand in business-to-business markets), interest rates, and company profits. The economy influences channel members similarly. Competitors may have lowered ability to respond to perceived threats and undertake new initiatives in an unfavorable economy. On the other side of the coin, competitors may be more desperate and willing to attack when the economy has hurt them. Public policy may also be influenced by the state of the economy. Finally, the internal environment of a company will probably be affected by the economy: individual employees may be more cautious when the economy is not favorable, and it is likely that fewer resources will be available for new initiatives. A grasp of the trends in the economy will help a marketer to anticipate how all of the participants within the marketer's environment will tend to behave.

The Sociocultural Environment   Just as in consumer marketing, the culture of the society in which the business operates has an impact on what people buy, why they buy it and use it, how they buy, and how they react to marketing stimuli. A **culture** is all the symbols and themes that reflect a society's norms and values. In any large society, multiple cultures and subcultures may be relevant. Social trends within a culture define the topics of interest to people in a society and further define what is acceptable and unacceptable in products, services, communications, and even prices. The business marketer must be aware of the cultural norms and social trends affecting customers, competitors, partners, and employees. This becomes a larger challenge as the business operates in more cultures.

The Natural Environment   The natural environment includes natural resources, raw materials, the ecology, the weather, and, on occasion, geologic activity. Much of the effect of the natural environment comes from raw materials, water, and energy resources, which of course are needed in some degree by almost every company. Marketers perceive the impacts of the natural environment principally as constraints on the products that they can offer. The constraints are imposed by the availability and quality of raw materials for products and water and energy for operations. For most marketers, the impacts of availability and quality are an interaction between the natural resources themselves and the companies involved in the supply chain. Accordingly, marketers must understand both the physical and supply chain aspects to fully understand the constraints imposed by the natural environment.

In the last several decades, the environment has taken on another set of influences as societal preferences and public interest groups have taken to the cause of environmental protection and conservation of natural resources. The effects of this movement are influenced as much by consumer perceptions as by reality in the natural environment. The leveraging of public attitudes through the filter of the actions taken by business-to-business customers can have a dramatic impact on a business.

A good example is the McDonald's switch from plastic foam packaging to wax-coated paper packaging for most of its menu items.[2] Consumers perceived foam packaging as unfriendly to the environment and paper as biodegradable and a good environmental choice. (In fact, foam packaging techniques no longer use chlorofluorocarbons—CFCs—in the manufacturing process and polystyrene foam is generally recyclable.) The wax-coated paper would not biodegrade. McDonald's made the change because of consumer perceptions, not reality. Consider the loss to their foam packaging supplier.

The lesson for business-to-business marketers is to pay attention to trends in the perceptions of consumers and try to anticipate how this will affect the behavior of businesses attempting to provide value to consumers.

The Technological Environment

The Technological Environment   Advanced technology is developed and housed in companies; universities; research institutes; government agencies and laboratories; and, sometimes, in industry consortiums, such as the semiconductor industry's Sematech. Business-to-business marketers need to be scanning the technological environment for developments that can change their markets. This may include changes in a competitor's product or process technology, competition arising from outside the industry because a new technology meets customers' needs, changes in channel members' technology that alter their competitive position, or changes in customers' technology that change their needs or buying behavior. News of technology developments can surface in several forums. Trade journals, trade conferences, and trade shows often feature technology trends. Research symposia feature new developments; the hallway chatter may be even more helpful. Research journals and academic conferences in science and engineering disciplines can provide new technology ideas and hints of developments in the works. Finally, patent filings can often provide useful information. Much of this information seeking falls within the realm of competitive intelligence gathering (see Chapter 6); but, certainly, only a part does. It may be more important for a marketer to gain an understanding of customers' technology development and acquisition efforts.

---

[2]Robert Grace, "McD's & Politics of Perception," *Plastics News,* 12 November 1990, 6.

The technological environment has been both a blessing and a curse for business-to-business marketers. Through technology, customer service can be improved and more information is readily available to marketers. Technology, however, is changing at an everincreasing pace. Still, this is no excuse for not being prepared. Technology was ultimately a major contributor to the demise of vacuum tube electronics powerhouses such as Sylvania, TungSol, GE, and RCA; and the railroads were victims of changing technology in business logistics and passenger travel. More recently, an unwillingness and an inability to adapt to technology trends spelled the fall of Digital Equipment Corporation (DEC). When these changes were happening, technology, compared to today, was changing at a snail's pace, emphasizing the need for marketers to be even more vigilant in today's environment.

The warning that rapid technological change brings to business-to-business marketers is really very simple: *Product technology should not play a major role in your customer's decision to buy your product.* Technological advantage is fleeting. If you do not replace your technology with the next generation, your competitor will—and it is likely to be a competitor that you did not even know you had! On the other hand, the marketer still needs to pay attention to customers' technology, whether it is in their products or in their processes. Not anticipating a technological change that affects their buying behavior offers another way for competitors to gain an advantage against you.

The Competitive Environment

From Levitt's "Marketing Myopia"[3] to McKenna's "Marketing Is Everything"[4] significant effort has been made to get business marketers to recognize their competitors. The IBM Selectric typewriter was not replaced in the market by another typewriter (not even the next-generation IBM replacement); it was replaced by a new technology. Dedicated word processor manufacturers (e.g., Lanier, NBI) should have seen that electronics technology and third-party software would lead to full-function desktop computers.

Exhibit 2–1 describes four common types of competitive markets (you may recognize these from your economics principles course). Although all of these forms can be found in business-to-business markets, as indicated in the examples for each of the four types, **oligopolies** have traditionally dominated the industrial competitive arena. For example, the small number of major automobile producers in the United States (GM, Ford, Daimler-Chrysler, Toyota, Honda, etc.) purchase the large majority of all synthetic rubber, lead, and glass produced in the United States. A similar situation exists in the grain markets, with companies like Kellogg's, General Mills, and a few others purchasing most grains produced. Even when there are smaller players in the market, evolutionary trends are often established by the competitive positioning of the major players. Three major competitors and a host of

---

[3]Theodore Levitt, "Marketing Myopia," *Harvard Business Review* (July–August 1960).

[4]Regis McKenna, "Marketing Is Everything," *Harvard Business Review* (January–February 1991).

EXHIBIT 2–1   Competitive Forms in Business-to-Business Markets

Pure Competition

- Many buyers and sellers exist with no single entity having much effect on the price—no leverage positions. The market is significantly larger than any one entity (buyer or seller).
- Generally exists in commodities, such as raw materials and agricultural products.
- Price is a major component of the marketing mix, and products are not differentiable; thus, sellers seldom deviate from the price.

Monopolistic Competition

- Many buyers and sellers, but product is differentiable such that a range of prices is possible.
- Products can vary in terms of quality, features, style, and so on, such as in specialty steel fabrication or in advertising services
- Branding, advertising, personal selling, and so on, important to differentiate branding.

Oligopolistic Competition

- Market consists of a few sellers who are highly sensitive to each others' strategies.
- Products can be uniform or nonuniform. Typical examples include autos, airlines, steel industries.
- Few sellers exist because of barriers to entry.
- Price has often been aimed at maintaining stability (note chaos in airline industry).

Pure Monopoly

- Consists of one seller.
- Examples are Postal Service; utilities; and, before government action, Standard Oil.
- "New" competitors to the products and services provided by this group (Federal Express, Windmill power companies, etc.) are generally small, niche players indistinguishable (or barely visible) in the market.

smaller niche players seem a natural state of competition in an oligopoly. Fewer than three major players tends to drive a market to collusion.[5]

Accordingly, if a marketer competes in an oligopolistic market, strategy depends on the marketer's current position within the oligopoly. Strategy is discussed more thoroughly later in the book, but, for now, a quick summary will suffice. If the company is one of the leaders in the market, strategies should be pursued to differentiate from the other leaders while building volume. If the company is a smaller player, then its marketers should be looking for smaller, defensible niches in which the company can dominate.

From the viewpoint of a company that is marketing to customers who are in an oligopoly, the key is building relationships. As you would expect, oligopolies are natural examples of the *80/20 rule*—80 percent of a vendor's sales volume is likely to come from 20 percent of its customers. It is imperative to build strong, collaborative relationships with those large-volume customers.

In many other business-to-business markets, monopolistic competition or pure competition exists. As already noted, strategy is discussed in more detail later in the text. For now, though, the key in either market is to look for ways to differentiate the offering, creating superior value compared to competitors' offerings. Even after differentiation has been established, the offering must be constantly updated to create more value.

---

[5]Jagdish N. Sheth and Rajendra Sisodia, "Only the Big Three Will Thrive," *The Wall Street Journal*," May 1998.

Commodity markets might seem resistant to differentiation, but it can be done with some creativity. Consider a sugar processor who differentiated its offering to a cereal manufacturer. The company worked with the manufacturer to alter the formula for the sugar so that the sugar would adhere to the cereal better when doused in milk. The change in the composition of the sugar was only part of the differentiation, however. The value to the cereal company also resided to a great deal in the supplier's willingness to collaborate in the relationship built between the two companies.

Usefulness of Classification

Marketers should *not* believe that the act of classifying the market and its actors will provide *all* of the information necessary for choosing target segments and designing strategy. The insights gained are not fine-grained enough.

However, classification can help marketers begin to frame the issues, threats, and opportunities they face. Classification provides a good starting place for understanding the business environment. Obviously, it may be difficult to obtain a thorough understanding of the environment and its implications all in one analytic effort. Marketers should make this an ongoing effort, adding to the information base as new pieces of information surface, as new trends emerge, and as new interpretations are developed.

THE CONCEPT OF A VALUE NETWORK

The next two sections of this chapter concern ideas that further help to frame an understanding of the business environment. The classifications that have been described help the marketer see patterns in the business environment. However, the classifications are static and do not reflect the complexity or dynamics of the market. The concepts in this section and the next will help the marketer appreciate such an environment and the implications that emerge.

The first idea extends the concept of the value chain introduced in the previous chapter. The concept of the value chain (Exhibit 2–2) has more than a coincidental similarity to supply chain analysis, notwithstanding the implied value added by support functions. The ebb and flow of market relationships that exist in today's complex markets, however, do not perfectly fit the flows of the supply chain. From a marketing perspective, the implications of partnerships and alliances can create a multidimensional network of relationships that change frequently.

In fast-paced markets, organizations are finding that the most productive way to create an offering with maximum value for a particular market or customer contains elements of offerings from several parties. These parties, or collaborators, can either be companies that the organization has previously allied with or may be a competitor in another market. The chain expands into a multidimensional network. This network of collaborators includes nontraditional partners in a way that all partners in the network "win" as part of the team that provides the offering of greatest value. For

EXHIBIT 2–2   An Adaptation of the Value Chain

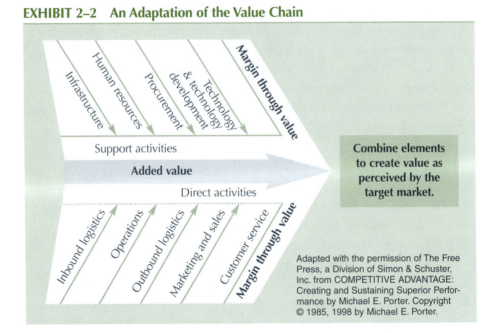

Combine elements to create value as perceived by the target market.

Adapted with the permission of The Free Press, a Division of Simon & Schuster, Inc. from COMPETITIVE ADVANTAGE: Creating and Sustaining Superior Performance by Michael E. Porter. Copyright © 1985, 1998 by Michael E. Porter.

another customer or in another market, the network of partners may be completely different. When a marketer looks to enter a new market, a new network may be formed. This new network may include some or all of the members of the previous network. A firm's value network may be different for every major customer. Exhibit 2–3 represents the complexity of the network when multiple value chains are combined. Imagine how this network would look if more partners were added.

Companies that elect to operate through value networks must be well aware of the markets of their customers and their network partners. The network alliance will create opportunities to disclose, willingly or inadvertently, many facets of each partner's operations. Proper barriers are needed to prevent undesired information exchange and can be developed to encourage the alliance while protecting other business interests.

Using the Value Network Concept

What does this mean for the business marketer? Three sets of implications are examined more closely in later chapters, because they concern specific analyses that must be done and specific actions to be taken:

1. In analyzing competition, the marketer needs to look at competitive clusters of partnered companies rather than stand-alone, single-company competitors (see Chapter 6).
2. In designing offerings, the marketer must decide on what pieces to outsource to partners, which to provide from the company's internal resources, and which to develop jointly with customer or supplier partners (see Chapter 8).
3. In building relationships, partners have to be sought, screened, contracted with, managed, and—in many cases—severed (see Chapter 12).

EXHIBIT 2–3   The Multidimensional Value Network

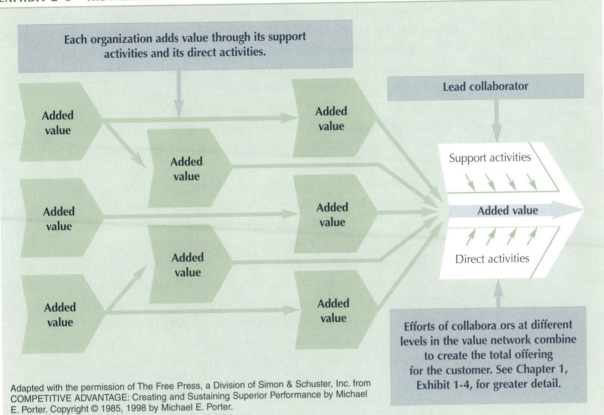

Adapted with the permission of The Free Press, a Division of Simon & Schuster, Inc. from COMPETITIVE ADVANTAGE: Creating and Sustaining Superior Performance by Michael E. Porter. Copyright © 1985, 1998 by Michael E. Porter.

The value network is introduced here to broaden your perspective as you continue through these first several chapters concerning understanding the environment. While it is difficult enough to try to anticipate the effects of the business environment on several customers, competitors, and on one's own company, the marketer facing real-world situations must deal with an added layer of complexity in trying to understand the effects on a network of partners. In the context of this chapter, though, the question becomes "How is a marketer's analysis of the marketer's own industry affected by consideration of partnership relationships?"

One principal concern arises when a marketer considers the nature of competition in the market or industry. Monopolies, monopsonies (a **monopsony** is a market with one dominant buyer, much as a **monopoly** has a dominant vendor), and oligopolies tend to have some staying power, since the actors in such markets and the market forces themselves (such as high entry barriers) can prevent substantial competition from arising. This is why we have antimonopoly laws (see Chapter 4). However, when a market is dominated by a partnership instead of a single-company powerhouse, the partnership's dominance would seem to be more precarious. Partnerships can break apart or run into internal decision-making problems more easily than can a self-contained company. Thus, the competitive forms in which some players clearly dominate are in danger of transitioning rapidly into monopolistic competition due to shifting competitive forces. Also, partnerships can quickly produce sizable new competition that quickly changes the competitive landscape. For example, Microsoft, in its recent antitrust case, made the argument that the partnerships between Netscape, Sun Microsystems, America Online, and others rapidly changed the nature of competition in many of the markets that were under scrutiny in the case.

Another concern arises in the technological environment. One of the key kinds of partnerships that has evolved over the last ten to fifteen years is the joint development partnership. Very few companies have the resources to pursue basic research or comprehensive technical development of new products in complex technical areas. Joint ventures for such research and development can overcome many of the resource limitations problems. When examining the technical environment, then, a business marketer should look closely at the partnerships that exist to address new technology. The strengths and weaknesses of these alliances need to be examined to fully understand what technical progress is likely to occur—or not occur—in the foreseeable future.

The impact on the assessment of the macroenvironment, of the trend toward value networks, then, is a need to examine the partnership relationships that exist and can exist within the elements of the business environment. These networks may be synergistic, producing more value than the partners could produce independently; or, they may actually produce less value than is possible. Business marketers need to look at value networks as presenting opportunities as well as threats.

CHANGES IN MARKETS OVER TIME

It is not enough to understand the nature of competition in a market and what benefits are perceived as having value at a given point in time. Markets evolve as competitors, channels, customers, and technologies change. In this section, two ideas are introduced that help the marketer think about how her situation will change and how these changes might be successfully addressed.

It is important to have a sense of how a market has developed and how it is likely to change in the future. For instance, oligopolistic markets are generally not oligopolies from the very beginning. Usually they start out as a temporary monopoly when a company introduces a product with a radically new technology. As this product is improved and as prospective customers learn more about the product and its technology, the market becomes more competitive as it draws more entrants. If the product easily becomes a commodity and there are minimal barriers to entry, the market often moves toward pure competition with many players and slim margins. Over time, a few competitors may emerge that create brand identity and operating efficiency. As competitors who cannot match costs or differentiation drop out, the market evolves to an oligopoly.

An oligopoly may also emerge after the market has gone through a period of monopolistic competition. After the introductory period, new entrants enter the market and are able to differentiate their offerings along several dimensions. They continue to develop the product technology but also make improvements on costs, business configurations, and the other three Ps of marketing. The market undergoes rapid or hyper growth until the rate of new adoptions falls off. With the reduction in the growth rate, the inefficient competitors drop out and a slower-growing oligopolistic market emerges. A few companies dominate the mainstream market, and smaller companies serve relatively small market niches.

Over the years, marketers, strategists, and academics have noticed patterns in how markets change over time. The following two ideas, the product life cycle (PLC) and the technology adoption life cycle (TALC), provide some generalizations about these patterns and what they mean. Of these two, the product life cycle is more generally usable. The technology adoption life cycle has particular applicability in the case of breakthrough innovations.

The Product Life Cycle

Marketing students will recognize characteristics of the product life cycle from prior discussion. The concept of the **product life cycle (PLC)** is that product categories go through several "life" stages, as shown in Exhibit 2–4.

Over the years, the PLC has drawn criticism on several fronts. Note that not all products follow the PLC as it is shown in the exhibit. Divergence from the classic bell-shaped PLC is partly dependent on the level of abstraction. The PLC for a single incarnation of a given technology (e.g., Version 2 or Release 3a) may deviate substantially from the shape of the PLC and is really only a contributing element to the total sales curve for the product category as a whole.

The level at which the PLC has the most relevance is at the "category" level. Product category is still a nebulous concept and can create some ambiguity. For instance, one might ask whether Pentium-type microprocessors are a relevant category. The question arises when the marketer is trying to understand competitive

EXHIBIT 2–4   The Product Life Cycle

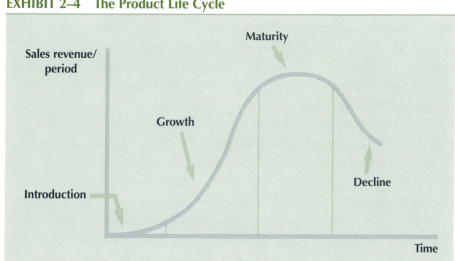

dynamics for, say, Pentium III processors from Intel and competitive offerings from Advanced Micro Devices (AMD). Should the marketer consider the Pentium III to be part of the Pentium life cycle, or does it deserve to have its own life cycle analyzed?

The answer lies in the purpose for trying to understand a product life cycle. The principal reasons that marketers want to understand the PLC for their offering or market is *to anticipate the general behavior of customers and the general nature of competition* that will be faced in the near future. Accordingly, the most useful level of abstraction for the Pentium/Pentium III example is probably at the level of the Pentium, overall. The nature of competition reflects a mature industry more so than it does an introductory market. Customers, such as Dell Computers, Compaq, and IBM, know their needs and how to meet them. Competition exists and is well entrenched. The market is oligopolistic, with Intel the dominant player and AMD a smaller but viable second company. In the next round of microprocessor innovations, though, the new technology may be so advanced that the product market behaves in a way that is consistent with the introductory stage of the PLC, in which the innovator has a temporary monopoly.

The usefulness of the PLC has two limitations. The PLC gives only general guidance on what to expect. It *does not provide a means for predicting changes* from one stage of the PLC to the next. Similarly, it *does not provide prescriptions for strategies or actions* that a firm should take during the current PLC stage or some future stage.

Concerning the first limitation, the inability to predict when the shape of the sales curve will change, realize that markets change as the various factors driving their nature change. Predicting when changes will occur is like predicting when the weather will change. Oftentimes a forecaster will get close, particularly when the prediction is for the very near future. However, inflection points in the PLC sales curve occur because several factors interact concurrently that lead to these changes in trends in total sales. Predicting the effects of these interactions is difficult if not impossible. For instance, in the latter half of the 1980s, pundits predicted at the beginning of each year that that year would be the "Year of the LAN" (local area network). Finally, at the end of the decade, when Novell had a stable operating system available and the principal software vendors had stable network-enabled versions of their software available, and when customers were ready to buy new equipment and software, LAN system sales rocketed. Several pundits were correct in predicting this growth period. However, they had been inaccurate in the prior two or three years for having predicted the same thing.

Concerning the second limitation, the inability to derive specific strategies from the PLC, the same difficulties arise. Any individual company faces a unique combination of multifaceted factors. The PLC provides a framework for organizing these in the marketer's mind. However, the PLC model is too simplistic to help much beyond this. The marketer must assess the opportunities and threats that are posed at any given time and construct strategy based on matching the firm's strengths and weaknesses to these opportunities and threats. The PLC, then, can suggest some general directions in which to go, but the marketer's job is to find a unique strategy that provides superior value to targeted customers. Marketers must take care to not create a self-fulfilling prophecy. Changing the marketing mix for an offering based solely on a cursory analysis of the PLC can create unwanted conditions in an otherwise healthy market.

The Technology Adoption Life Cycle

While the PLC has limitations on its usefulness, it still provides a reminder to the marketer that things will change and the marketer must adapt. In the case of breakthrough innovation, additional insight may be gained by examining another life cycle that can be superimposed on the PLC, the **technology adoption life cycle (TALC).** The TALC focuses more on the kinds of customers and how they come to adopt the new technology.

Bridging a Chasm

The TALC describes how a breakthrough innovation becomes adopted in a market. Geoffrey Moore[6] has taken the innovation diffusion model described by Everett Rogers[7] and extended it. Rogers divided adopters of a new innovation into groupings he called *innovators, early adopters, early majority, late majority,* and *laggards.* Moore updated these groupings based on his own research on high-tech, business-to-business products. He called the groupings *technophiles, visionaries, pragmatists, conservatives,* and *laggards.*

Moore did not just change the names of the groups, though. He uses the TALC as a framework for explaining two principal observations about how technology markets evolve. The first observation is the existence of a **chasm,** a break in the sales growth curve for a new technology. The second observation is the chaos that occurs in a period of rapid growth, which Moore calls the **tornado.** The tornado eventually produces the emergence of a dominant supplier. These two observations and the implications of the TALC have potential for providing useful guidance to the business marketer.

Moore suggested that there were natural breaks in the TALC curve that occurred between each group or segment. Note on Exhibit 2–5 that a relatively large break—the chasm—occurs in the TALC curve between visionaries and pragmatists.[8] Moore claims this occurs because pragmatists will not treat visionaries as credible references when it comes to adoption. Pragmatists want proven solutions, with little trauma in their adoption. Pragmatists will not buy until other pragmatists buy and provide references. It is difficult, though, to find the pragmatists who buy first and then provide references for other pragmatists. Visionaries, on the other hand, try to make quantum jumps in the way they compete. Hence, they adopt an innovation before all the pieces are in place to make the product work well, that is, before a "whole product" exists. The visionary buyers then create or

---

[6]Geoffrey A. Moore, *Crossing the Chasm: Marketing and Selling Technology Products to Mainstream Customers* (New York: Harper Business, 1991).

[7]Everett M. Rogers, *Diffusion of Innovations,* 4th ed. (New York: Free Press, 1995).

[8]A similar approach to customer adoption and market development can be found in Roger J. Best, *Market-Based Management,* 2d ed. (Upper Saddle River, N.J.: Prentice-Hall, 2000), Ch. 3.

EXHIBIT 2–5   The Technology Adoption Life Cycle

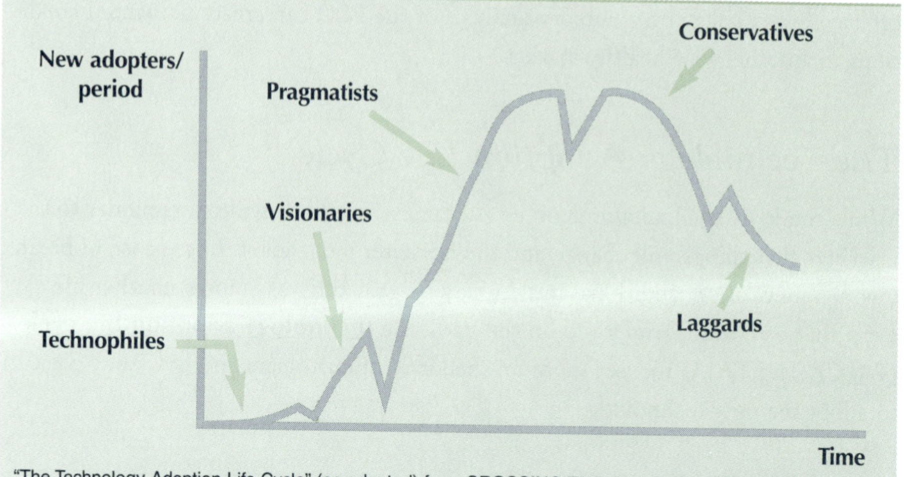

"The Technology Adoption Life Cycle" (as adapted) from CROSSING THE CHASM by GEOFFREY A. MOORE. Copyright © 1991 by Geoffrey A. Moore. Reprinted by permission of HarperCollins Publishers, Inc.

buy customized pieces of the system to make the whole thing work. The trial-and-error process of sculpting such a customized solution can create a state of chaos within the adopting organization. Thus, visionaries tend to obtain a reputation for wreaking havoc within their organizations.

To cross this chasm, Moore claims that the vendor of an innovation must pass through the first two segments—the technophiles and the visionaries. These are necessary because the whole product cannot be defined and then developed until enough experience has been gained. Then the vendor must find a "beachhead," or foothold, niche among pragmatists on the other side of the chasm. This niche must have need for the product that is so compelling that pragmatist buyers will take the risk of buying without the assurance of references from other pragmatists who have already adopted. The vendor must find such a niche, create a whole product to meet the compelling need of these buyers, and offer the whole product to these buyers through proper positioning. The proper positioning means that the one or two most compelling benefits of the whole product are clearly communicated and delivered.

The chasm, or **market development gap**,[9] marks a major change in the way an organization does business. Externally, the entire marketing mix—the type customer as well as what the customer will perceive as of value—changes. Internally, the company's production capability; size; and, with dramatic growth, culture changes. None of this change is automatic.

Across the Chasm and into the Tornado

Once this first beachhead is addressed, pragmatist buyers talk to other pragmatists and a chain reaction spreads across many niches within the market. Naturally, if an organization successfully capitalizes on a new technology, either its own or that of a supplier, competitors for that market segment with similar value offerings will gravitate to the

[9]Ibid., 64.

new technology. Instead of customer acceptance of the technology, the *market* begins to accept the technology. Eventually, this acceptance can lead to standardization within a segment or an industry.

If the market is large enough, a groundswell of demand can develop. The market goes into a period of rapid sales growth, the tornado.[10] This portion of the TALC superimposes directly onto the growth period of the PLC. Moore claims that, in a tornado, the market wants to support the market leader. This occurs because the buyers, pragmatists that they are, face the least internal chaos if the systems they are buying are the recognized standard. There will be plenty of peripherals and software that will work easily with the leader's product. There will be plenty of consultant expertise available to help them through problem periods. As upgrades become available, adoption of these upgrades causes the least internal upheaval if they are backward compatible with the leader's product that was purchased earlier in the tornado.

The market-chosen leader, then, has the opportunity to become the "gorilla," as Moore dubs it. The gorilla can do what it wants as long as it does not deviate too far too often from what the pragmatist buyers desire. In return, the gorilla receives the "gorilla's share" of the sales and obtains a healthy margin on these sales. This, of course, allows the gorilla to invest in new technology to reinforce its leadership position in the market.

Moore suggests that the way to become the gorilla in a tornado involves a certain amount of luck combined with smart coordination of several factors. The gorilla must have assembled the "whole product," and this product must be standardized so that the members of the mainstream market can all obtain roughly the same product (with minor customized features).

Moore goes into other aspects and implications of the TALC. Moore's ideas give business marketers a framework for interpreting the dynamics of their markets. Though many of these ideas remain untested by scholarly research, they provide food for thought that may give marketers considerable insight.

Readers should compare Moore's viewpoint, at least through this portion of the TALC, with the concept of market ownership expressed by Regis McKenna.[11] A major difference is that market ownership implies an organization that continues to "push the envelope" within its market niche to maintain a growth market. The ownership focus is on innovating the value presented to the market rather than on technology itself.

---

[10]Geoffrey A. Moore, *Inside the Tornado* (New York: Harper Business, 1995).

[11]McKenna, *Marketing Is Everything,* op. cit.

The concepts described in this chapter—classifying products, defining different types of competition, emerging value networks, the product life cycle, and the technology adoption life cycle—help marketers to begin to think about their business environments. Differences in products help marketers understand how differing kinds of value may be desired by differing kinds of customers. The product life cycle and the technology adoption life cycle help marketers think about how value desired by customers and competition will change over time. The nature of competition helps marketers think about how to develop and maintain competitive advantage.

These "mental models" are not enough upon which to base marketing strategy. Now the marketers must delve deeper into the specifics of their markets. In Chapter 3, you will get more of a sense of how individual business customers attempt to obtain value from their suppliers. If you keep in mind the concepts we have discussed in this chapter, you can then begin to understand how value is pursued differently under differing market conditions, by different types of organizations, and even by different types of individuals within those organizations. Beyond Chapter 3, subsequent chapters help build an understanding of legal constraints (Chapter 4) and the context of company strategy (Chapter 5). Chapter 6 and Chapter 7 provide guidance on obtaining and utilizing information about the market. Together, these chapters provide the detail necessary to create strategy and tactics that provide superior value to target customers, thus making it possible to beat the competition.

Key Terms

accessory equipment

capital goods

chasm

culture

demographics

end user (E/U)

macroeconomy

market development gap

monopoly

monopsony

oligopoly

original equipment
   manufacturer (OEM)

product life cycle (PLC)

publics

technology adoption life
   cycle (TALC)

tornado

user

value-added reseller
   (VAR)

value network

Questions for Review and Discussion

1. What are some of the differences between marketing to typical commercial enterprises and marketing to government agencies?
2. Classify the following businesses as VARs, users, component producers, or raw material producers.

   a. A supplier of copper to a wire manufacturer
   b. A supplier of rear axle assemblies to a heavy truck manufacturer
   c. A distributor of private telephone exchange equipment (PBX) and installation services

d. A supplier of pigments to a paint manufacturer

e. A maker of automated assembly equipment

f. A supplier of small motors to disk drive manufacturers

3. How can the agenda and focus of financial publics and public interest groups create seemingly opposite goals for business-to-business marketing managers?

4. Defend the validity and importance of internal publics.

5. How can market-sensitive internal publics improve a firm's competitiveness?

6. If technology is so important to business-to-business marketers, should it also play a major role in your approach to your customers? Why, or why not?

7. How do oligopolies support the 80/20 rule?

8. Describe the areas of validity and fallacy associated with the study of the PLC.

9. What market characteristics make it unlikely that pragmatists will easily follow the role model of visionaries?

10. Relate the PLC and the chasm, with particular emphasis on the market factors that undergo change from introduction to rapid growth of an offering.

Internet Exercises

Go to the Web site for Grainger.com, the on-line catalog of W. W. Grainger, Inc.: **http://www.grainger.com** Note how the site is organized. Grainger is a supplier to the maintenance, repair, and operations (MRO) market. What competitive form do you think best characterizes the competitive environment of most of Grainger's customers in this market? How does this affect the way that Grainger addresses this market? Contrast this with the competitive form that TRW's customers face in their automotive market. Describe how the differences you have observed in customers' competitive environments lead to different kinds of marketing approaches.

Go to the Web site for GotMarketing: **http://www.gotmarketing.com** Look at the portion that describes its e-mail campaign management service. Look at some other sites for e-mail campaign services, for example: **http://www.epiphany.com**, **http://www.marketfirst.com**, and **http://www.annuncio.com** Based on what you have seen, in what stage of the product life cycle do you think e-mail marketing services are? Why? What are the implications for marketing of such services to GotMarketing's target customers—small- and medium-sized businesses? What do you think GotMarketing should do next to market e-mail marketing services to these target customers?

Go to the TRW Web site: **http://www.trw.com** Read the section on the history of the company. In recent years, TRW has begun a program they call a "technology bank." Explain what this program is about. Why do you think TRW has chosen to invest in start-up companies rather than undertake the development and launch of these ventures on its own?

3

Organizational Buying and Buyer Behavior

overview. . . Chapter 1 introduced business-to-business marketing, and Chapter 2 established the nature of the many types of participants in business-to-business markets. Successful business-to-business marketing involves understanding how organizations buy and how individuals are likely to behave in the roles of decision makers within the organization. This chapter examines the nature of buying and individual behaviors associated with the buyer's decision process.

Organizations "buy" to satisfy rational needs that result from their desire to be successful in their markets; however, it is individuals within organizations who make the buying decisions. Those individuals have a stake in the outcome of the purchase decisions and desire to influence the decision process. In this chapter, we demonstrate that the need of the organization may be quantifiable but that behavior in organizations has many qualitative elements that influence the buying decision. It is in the qualitative elements of decision making that the importance of the vendor/supplier relationship becomes a critical factor in the success of the marketing effort.

The complexity of the business buying process varies with the complexity of the purchase. Routine purchases are automatic, repeated with an almost mechanical approach. More complex needs require greater involvement by a larger number of stakeholders in the organization. We examine the levels of buying complexity and how the marketer's relationship and approach are impacted by this complexity.

© TERRY VINE/STONE

THE AGE OF RELATIONSHIPS ON THE INTERNET*

A big screen at the front of the room shows industrial items grouped into "lots" that United Technologies Corporation wants to purchase for its Carrier and Otis divisions. Sixty-four prescreened suppliers will enter their bids from their home operations via the secure network. The auction will last most of the day. "Where else can you get this many players in this short a time?" says the senior engineer for Carrier who is coordinating this bidding effort companywide. A commodity purchasing manager observing the auction says he sensed that his current supplier would be aggressive in its bidding. Sure enough, ten minutes into the event, the price for his items has dropped steadily to 14 percent less than what he has paid in the past. Any savings to United Technologies of course must be significant enough to warrant a change from their existing supplier, and complex or technology-oriented items do not lend themselves to this type of bidding. FreeMarkets Inc., the auction company that has coordinated this effort for United Technologies, screens potential new supplies based on United Technologies' technical specifications quality requirements and supplier standards.

It soon becomes clear that pricing in the event is being driven by a foreign supplier who has never done business with the company before. "We're going to India," says the commodity purchasing manager, as he sees a sharply lower bid pop onto the screen from a company with operations in India.

The on-line bids are only a small part of the buying process. The buyer, United Technologies, still has to check out the capabilities of any new supplier and make sure that switching makes sense. While United Technologies is hoping to narrow its supplier base to a smaller group of the most competent players, price is only one factor in evaluating the value of the supplier relationship. The low bidder does not necessarily win.

*"Bidding for E-Nuts and E-Bolts on the Net," The Wall Street Journal, 12 March 1999.

- Develop an understanding of the difference between quantifiable organizational needs and the often qualitative process used to fulfill those needs.

- Understand how organizations develop and satisfy the requirements for selecting and maintaining relationships with suppliers.

- Understand how individuals within organizations develop and satisfy the requirements of their professional responsibilities as dictated by their organizations and, within that framework, their own individual needs.

- Discuss the vendor/customer relationship as the principal defining factor in the success of business-to-business marketing efforts.

- Examine the different levels of complexity of decisions made in the buying process and how the business-to-business marketer can influence the process.

introduction. . .

The scenario in the opening example took place during the first quarter of 1999, effectively demonstrating the way a major corporation can select suppliers for generic or commodity items. Technology made possible the broad dissemination of United Technologies' component requirements, and rapid communications provided an almost instantaneous bidding frenzy. Obviously, organizations are buying differently than they did just a few years ago and buyers are making decisions in a different manner than before.

Or are they? The Internet is a great tool in the process, but what happens to the relationships between supplier and customer that have in the past been considered so important? This chapter examines the often-taught classical buying process and its value, as well the interpersonal dynamics and relationship aspects of how organizations and individuals make buying decisions—whether at the pace of the Internet or more conventional means.

THE NATURE OF BUYING

Many consumer purchases (i.e., buying decisions) are spur of the moment, often associated with the availability of funds to make the purchase. While consumers seldom conduct a conscious value evaluation, by making the purchase they have decided that the value they are about to receive is greater than the value they are giving up (i.e., their costs). If this were not the case, the exchange would not take place. The value assigned by the customer is influenced by many factors beyond the serviceability of the core product or service. The nature of the buyer decision process in a business-to-business environment is not unlike the consumer process, though the steps are often thought to be more visible and theoretically more quantifiable. Let us further compare the processes.

The Consumer Buying Decision Process

Our purchases as consumers are influenced by the roles we play in our daily lives. As parents, teachers, students, children, managers, and individuals, we are influenced to "do what's right" within the framework of the role we are playing. Sometimes that is a responsible decision with a broad range of beneficiaries; at other times, what is right is an impulsive, self-satisfying choice (e.g., "I bought it because I liked the color"). In any event, though we are influenced by many factors, we make the buying decision as individuals and are usually accountable to only ourselves for the outcome. What we have just described is part of the need-recognition stage in the classical five-stage consumer buyer decision process:

1. Need recognition
2. Information search
3. Evaluation of alternatives
4. Purchase decision
5. Postpurchase behavior

This process, or a similar representation, is familiar to every student who has completed a marketing principles course. As presented, these five stages imply that the process consists of five discrete, sequential events. Depending on whether the purchase is a repeat of an earlier purchase or an entirely new task (or is low involvement or high involvement), some parts of the process may be de-emphasized or extended. As consumers, we know that this process is more of a simultaneous than a sequential process. Consumer beliefs about legitimacy of information sources, brand reputations, and the influences of others coalesce into a final purchase decision by the individual consumer or family group. Afterward, the consumer evaluates the purchase relative to either individual or family expectations.

Organizational Buying

How do organizations "buy" compared to how we, as consumers, "buy" in the retail market? The initial response from an inexperienced observer might be that organizations purchase whatever is cheapest, that is, that organizations must make the most rational, lowest-cost, most-profitable decision. While the ultimate profitability of the buying organization (or minimized cost for the nonprofit organization) plays a major role, price is only a part of the delivered value.

Organizational purchases involve inputs from many of the professional specialties in the organization. The organization relies on decision makers and influencers at many levels and from different disciplines to contribute their expertise to satisfy a diverse set of needs. The inputs from these **stakeholders** aim to ensure that the best possible buying decisions are made for the organization. Individual stakeholders may contribute their expertise to the decision process without full knowledge or appreciation for the requirements of other stakeholders. Seldom is any one individual entirely responsible for the purchase decision.

The process requires communication among stakeholders within the buying organization. It is necessary for the supplying organization to *simultaneously* approach all influencers in the decision process with a message tailored to the needs of each individual influencer. It is not unusual for the supplying firm's communications with different stakeholders to substitute for, or instigate, greater communication among stakeholders.

> **Stakeholders** are the individuals and organizations that have an interest—a "stake"—in the company, its operation, and its performance. The interest may or may not be financial.

The Buying Center

The **buying center** is a collection of individuals with a stake in the buying decision, individuals who contribute to the final purchase decision. Members of the buying center determine, within their own specialties, the organization's needs and the methods the organization uses to satisfy them. Buying center complexity changes depending on the complexity of the need. Contrary to what the term implies, a buying center is not one central location where buying decisions are made. The term is simply marketing jargon for the representatives of the various independently operating portions of an organization (finance, production, purchasing, engineering, etc.) that influence the selection of the best solution for the organization's needs. Depending on the size and complexity of the organization, influencers (stakeholders) in the decision may be physically located a great distance (across the hall, locally, nationally, internationally, etc.) from each other. One of the major tasks of the business marketer is to simultaneously but individually influence all stakeholders by satisfying their individual professional *and* personal needs.

The needs of the organization are determined by customer needs, internal goals and objectives, and by external environmental factors. Stakeholders are accountable for the development of buying requirements that satisfy all of these influences. Depending on the intended market and customers of the organization, influences may include government agencies and independent standards-setting organizations and publics, as well as the quantifiable and relationship needs of the vendor and the customer. Exhibit 3–1 shows the various professional disciplines and organizations that may contribute to or influence the buying center.

The professional needs of engineering or technical specialists in the buying center are related to the physical performance of the product that is being supplied. Their concerns center on how well the component will meet design requirements and reliably perform in their application. Production or manufacturing specialists in the buying center are concerned with how well the component will

---

EXHIBIT 3–1   Many Disciplines Can Contribute to the Buying Center

Internal Factors

- Technology
- Management
- Legal
- Finance
- Accounting
- Production/Manufacturing
- Marketing
- Service

External Factors

- Customer needs and buying behavior
- Government agencies
- Independent standards-setting organizations
- Various publics

Stakeholders in each discipline within the organization contribute their expertise to the decision such that both internal and external factors are accommodated.

integrate into their manufacturing process. Service professionals are interested in how and what service the component will require when the product is in the field. If the purchase is a significantly large investment, the customer's finance organization is concerned with alternatives to fund the purchase. Each member of the buying center has a concern unique to his responsibilities and presents an opportunity for the business marketer to demonstrate a unique value of the offering his company seeks to provide.

For instance, in the United Technologies example that opened this chapter, consider the differences between the senior engineer for Carrier who is coordinating the reverse auction and the commodity purchasing manager. Based on the brief remarks reported in the example, we could well imagine that the most important dimension of value for the senior engineer would be a smooth process with no problems. He wants to prove that the system works so that it can be used more widely in the future. On the other hand, we could imagine that the purchasing manager is most concerned with getting good prices from qualified vendors. If problems occur, he is not too concerned unless they cannot be fixed. FreeMarkets, then, would focus different aspects of its service offering on these two members of the buying center. For the senior engineer, the FreeMarkets account team would work to make sure that the system works with no technical flaws. Meanwhile, to address the concerns of the purchasing manager, FreeMarkets will give special effort to finding and qualifying enough suppliers that they can be assured that pricing will be very competitive. If FreeMarkets had only focused on the needs of the senior engineer, they might not have gotten enough good qualified suppliers, instead focusing on proving the technology. The result could easily have been that a dissatisfied purchasing manager would now be reluctant to support wider use of the auctioning technique.

Summarizing the differences discussed so far,

- Organizational buying involves more buyers—more decision makers or contributors to portions of the decisions.

- Committees (the buying center) are involved, with professionals in each discipline (stakeholders) making decisions that are driven by their particular needs.

- Different types of decisions are often occurring simultaneously in the process, spread throughout the buying organization.

ORGANIZATIONAL BUYERS' DECISION PROCESS: A STEPWISE MODEL

Exhibit 3–2 shows the business buyers' decision process as it is usually presented. We believe this model is a little misleading. Before noting problems with the model, let us discuss what is important to understand about the buying decision process.

EXHIBIT 3–2   Steps in the Buying Decision Process

1. Problem recognition	5. Proposal solicitation
2. General need description	6. Selection
3. Product specification	7. Make the transaction routine
4. Supplier/Source search	8. Evaluate performance

Intricacies of the Buying Decision Process

Successful business marketers understand the buying processes of their customers and work with these processes to provide value to customers and win their business. Several key concepts lead to successful interaction with customers' decision processes.

Individual Roles and Personal Needs   Several people in the buying center are involved in any stage or step of the process. Each of them has individual needs related to his role in the buying center. Each of them has personal needs as well.

Interaction Creates Fluidity   The people within the buying center interact, for better or worse. At times, interaction is necessary to move the process ahead. At other times, interaction slows the process or stops it completely. Interaction can change the buying center members' perceptions of the organization's needs and of their own needs, as well, creating a fluid situation that the marketer must continuously reevaluate.

The Buying Process Is Simultaneous, Not Sequential   The buying decision process progresses only loosely as a stepwise process. Particularly in new task situations (which is explained later in the chapter), a grouping of the steps into stages better represents the process. The steps within each stage may overlap, occur simultaneously, recycle, or change their character in midstream.

Relationships and Loyalty   The quality of the relationships between organizations and individuals of the organizations are a key influence. If the buying center members trust a supplier and the supplier's representatives—and if the supplier has an ongoing consultative relationship with the buying center's members—the buying center tends to use the supplier's information, take advice from the supplier, and buy its products. A key factor in the degree of influence that the relationship has is the track record of previous successes and the loyalty those successes have created between the participants.

Three Kinds of Needs   The members of the buying center try to meet three kinds of needs through the buying decision process. The first type of need is the organization's need for benefits from the product or service once it is finally purchased and used. The second type of need is the buying center individual's need stemming from his role in the buying center. The third type of need is the buying

---

Participation Exercise

Think about the personal needs of the senior engineer and the commodity purchasing manager in the United Technologies example. List two or three personal needs that you might imagine these individuals have related to the acquisition and use of the auctioning service bought from FreeMarkets. If you were the marketing manager or the account manager for FreeMarkets, how might you address these personal needs?

---

center member's personal need. The second and third types of needs may be particular to a step or stage in the decision process.

Cluster of Stakeholders' Values

All of this adds up to the fact that a supplier's successful offering is really a cluster of values, each aimed at individuals in the buying center at given points in the process. The core product or service is only part of this cluster and really does not directly meet the organization's needs until after the product has been purchased and put into use. Needless to say, this makes business-to-business offerings very complex.

ORGANIZATIONAL BUYERS' DECISION PROCESS: A PROCESS FLOW MODEL

Based on the previous discussion, the stepwise model presents some problems. Recognizing the value of relationships in the decision process and that the value offering is a cluster of values, we prefer a stage model. The "formal," step-by-step process implies a beginning and an end to each step, as well as the notion that each step must be completed before starting the next. For simple, familiar, or low-involvement decisions, this may be the case. Our experience of how buying decisions are really made, particularly for new task purchases, strongly suggests a process flow with significant overlap and feedback loops and without borders between steps. We have presented the flow as a series of stages because, even in the most free-form decision process situations, there generally are milestones, transitions, or break points that occur between the stages. Within the stages, actions generally include the previously discussed steps, but they flow in a loose sequence from start to transition point and then on to the next stage. Exhibit 3–3 shows the buying decision process as a **process flow model** rather than as a step model, as was shown in Exhibit 3–2. It also shows the correlation between the two models.

Notice that in Exhibit 3–3 we show almost all the classical decision steps in the definition and selection stages. We then expand the steps "Make the transaction routine" and "Resell the job." We do this because there is so much activity—especially marketing activity—that occurs in these last steps, particularly when the purchase is complex. These two stages become an integral part of the relationship

EXHIBIT 3–3   Stages in the Process Flow Model of the Buying Decision Process

Process Flow Stages	Buying Decision Process Steps
Definition Stage	
◆ Problem definition ◆ Solution definition ◆ Product specification	◆ Problem recognition ◆ General need description ◆ Product specification
Selection Stage	
◆ Solution provider search ◆ Acquire solution provider(s)	◆ Supplier/Source search ◆ Proposal solicitation ◆ Contract for supplier(s)
Deliver Solution Stage	
◆ Customize as needed ◆ Install/Test/Train	◆ Make the transaction routine
End Game Stage	
◆ Operate solution ◆ Reach end result ◆ Evaluate outcomes ◆ Determine next set of needs	◆ Evaluate performance ◆ Resell the job

that forms between buyer and supplier organizations. Hence, these two stages become the precursor activities for the next buying decision process undertaken by the buying organization.

To understand how business marketers can address buying center needs, let us examine each stage in greater detail.

Stage 1: Definition

In this first stage of the process, the buying center attempts to learn more about what its organization needs and about what options are available to address those needs. In Exhibit 3–3, this stage is shown as having the following kinds of activities: recognizing and defining the organization's problem, defining the broad outlines of a solution, and specifying the product or service features sought. The stage ends with a first determination of what is specifically sought by the organization. This specification may be revised later, but it sets the organization's buying center on a path with a specific direction.

A key thing to understand about the definition stage is that it includes "problem recognition," which determines how the buying center carries out the rest of the decision process. Problem recognition is analogous to organizational need awareness. The way that the buying center defines the problem and the general nature of the solution determines whether they approach the buying decision as a familiar or an unfamiliar task. At one extreme, the problem and its likely solution may be defined as a completely **new task.** The rest of the buying deci-

A **new task** is a need that has not been faced by the organization previously. An entirely new offering, the incorporation of a new technology, or a combination of factors can create this level of task. The organization has a significantly steep learning curve in a new task buying situation and will initially seek many sources of information and assistance, utilizing the complete buying process to investigate alternatives.

sion process then tends to be more thoughtful, rigorous, and time-consuming as a result. At the other extreme is determination that the organization simply needs the same thing it obtained last time it had this particular problem. This results in a **straight rebuy** situation. A straight rebuy involves abbreviated steps in the process, fewer people in the buying center, and less time to completion. In the middle lie **modified rebuy** situations in which the buying center determines that the problem or solution is somewhat similar to past problems or solutions. Such a determination results in a buying decision process that examines alternatives but within a limited scope. As one would expect, it involves fewer people than the new task situation and more than the straight rebuy. It takes less time than a new task and more time than a straight rebuy.

> A **straight rebuy** is a buying situation that is routine and has established solutions. Straight rebuys are "more of the same" and often involve simply the reorder of a previous product. A marketer should strive to derive straight or **modified rebuy** situations from new task situations to limit established business to exposure from competitive forces.

It is important to note that the astute supplier benefits greatly from involvement with its customer in this early process stage. An understanding of the buying center's needs, both organizational and individual, during this stage allows the supplier to create value for the buying center by helping the buying center through the process. The supplier also has the opportunity to adapt its product or service through the process of helping the buying center define its problems and solution set.

As the decision moves through the stages, a general need and solution is defined. The buying organization's technical team fully details the need and solution through the development of a product specification. It is at this point that the technical team members of the buying center determine the extent of the product's intricacy. Prototypes are built and reviewed for how well the original need is satisfied. Component technology and appropriate alternatives from a cost and performance viewpoint are examined. The technical value assessment is made, and the product specification is created. The development of the specification should be the result of extensive collaboration between supplier and customer. It is in this process that technology alternatives are narrowed and designs begin to rely on the specific nature of the remaining alternatives.

This description can lead one to believe that this is the end of the defining process, that after this point the product design is frozen. In reality, this is too narrow a view. As was noted in the *value chain* discussion, concluding that all possible customer value can be quantitatively specified is a major misstep in the application of the value chain concept.

The Meaning of a Specification

What purpose does the product specification serve? The obvious answer is that the specification is what you give to the potential supplier that completely describes what the product must be and how it must perform. It is then the responsibility of the supplier, if it wants the business, to quote the lowest possible per unit price on the product. Perhaps this is an accurate analysis in a straight rebuy situation and is true for Web-based transactions. Not only does the specification give the customer a method to say what the product must be should there be any future disagreement, it also provides the supplier with a very clear indication of what the product does not need to be—also useful in future disagreements.

The functions performed by the specification, however, are not limited to resolving conflicts between the buyer and the seller. Specifications are an attempt by the buyer to generalize the need description, regardless of its complexity. The specification seeks to reduce differences between different potential suppliers of the product, making it easier to choose from among competing proposals. Internally, the specification serves as an assurance to the buying center that, when a supplied component meets the specification, all of the requirements of the organization have been met. In this regard, the specification serves as an **internal brand** much the same way a national consumer brand reassures buyers about quality, function, and value in the consumer market. Thus, a well-written specification that virtually eliminates differences between competing suppliers is an enabling factor in successful transactions.

The development of a product specification is a step where the business marketer can have significant input, particularly if the value provided by the seller goes beyond easily quantifiable needs. Successful suppliers will have worked with the buying organization such that the specification describes attributes of their total offering while minimizing the impact of differentiating attributes of competitors' offerings. The development of early prototypes, as noted earlier, the selection of component technology, and appropriate alternatives from a cost and performance viewpoint are all areas where suppliers can meet the buying organization's needs that exist during this phase of the process. Concurrently, such assistance provides assurance to the buying center that the supplier can provide superior value when the final solution is delivered at the end of the decision process.

Beyond this point in the process, it is much more difficult for a potential supplier who has not yet been involved in the definition stage to be truly competitive. The new supplier finds the buying center already predisposed to a particular form of solution.

RFQ/RFP are acronyms for the common business practices of asking a supplier to quote a piece of business. RFQ is a request for quotation, usually associated with an offering that can be thoroughly and quantitatively defined. An RFP is a request for proposal, usually defined by a set of needs, specifications or outcomes that have greater leeway with regard to the final form or technology of the offering.

Stage 2: Selection

Once the buying center knows what it wants to acquire, it seeks a vendor to provide it in the selection stage. The choice of vendor may be a foregone conclusion, particularly if, as noted earlier, the vendor has collaborated throughout the specification process. The buying center may go through the steps of the selection stage, though, just the same. As shown in Exhibit 3–3, the activities performed in this stage include development and issuance of a **request for quotation (RFQ)** or **request for proposal (RFP)** evaluation of offers, initial selection of a supplier, negotiation of terms, and specification of an order or contract. While the steps can occur simultaneously and in varying order, the stage ends and transitions to the next stage with the contract or order.

This stage usually begins with specification of a request for proposal or quote. In most large and mid-sized organizations, this is a formal procedural step that has been well defined by the finance or purchasing function of the buying center's firm. It usually has a close relationship to the product or service specification established earlier. As already discussed, if the supplier organization can help the buying center through the process, the supplier stands a greater chance of becoming the supplier chosen. At this step, if a supplier is in a position to help write the RFP, then the RFP can be biased to ask for proposals to do exactly what the supplier intends to do. Obviously, the proposal then will match very well with the buyer's requirements and will at least stand a good chance of being picked for a final round of proposal presentations.

After the RFP or the RFQ is issued, proposals or quotes are received and evaluated by members of the buying center. Depending on the complexity of the need, the competing suppliers' marketers are called on to marshal their writing and presentation skills as well as their knowledge of their own and their customers' markets. Straight rebuys of somewhat generic items, such as the scenario described in the United Technologies opening vignette, may require only a brief (perhaps only on-line, if suppliers are adequately prequalified) response to an RFQ that stresses price as the dominant part of the marketing mix. For new tasks and, to a certain degree, modified rebuy situations, however, successful and profitable responses to RFQs require a combination of elements well beyond price.

Distinction from Public Sector Purchasing

This process of issuing an RFP or an RFQ often runs a little differently in the case of government purchasing. Fairness is often a legislatively mandated goal in structuring the proposal/quote and selection process. The request for proposal or quote often has to be published in specified newspapers or other outlets. Prospective suppliers have to meet a set of rigid criteria that are often much less flexible than criteria in private sector purchasing. This does not mean that suppliers' marketers are ignored in the design process for the RFP or the RFQ. Marketers addressing governmental markets can still establish relationships with government buying centers and assist in designing and specifying the solution. They may face more competition, though, in the selection process. Indeed, they may also face fewer straight rebuy situations due to legislatively mandated rebidding on purchase contracts over time.

Buyers Seek Sellers with Best Total Offering and Capabilities

In evaluating proposals, buying organizations seek to protect themselves from single-source and inflexible price situations by seeking additional or alternate suppliers. The search for qualified, acceptable suppliers leads to a list of those suppliers who, *in the view of the buying organization,* can meet the needs of the buying center. Depending on the stature of the buying organization, their reputation as a customer, and the nature of the supply opportunity, they may attract proposals from all or a few of the available qualified suppliers. If the buying organization is hindered by previous difficulties with suppliers or is experiencing other environmental situations (e.g., severe financial difficulties, etc.) the RFQ or proposal solicitation may require a marketing effort to appear attractive to potential suppliers.

As was discussed in Chapter 2, business markets are often oligopolies, with only a few companies having capabilities in any particular area. Many organizations may be capable of making exceptional one-of-a-kind items (that special cake that resulted from customization of the general recipe), but this capability does not automatically transfer to an ability to supply several thousand items each month (how big is that kitchen?). Organizations have many concerns in acquiring a product or service and seldom have the luxury of many choices. Yet the supplier is an integral part of the success or failure of the efforts of the buying organization. So, business buyers must screen supplier organizations with regard to their capabilities beyond the creation of one component. Years in business, size and reputation, manufacturing capacity, and customer service commitment are among the screening factors, in addition to the supplier's product quality and ability to meet the technical specification. These screening factors can be the most difficult for a supplier to satisfy, especially for the small, technology-oriented young company without a track record of large volume production.

When it comes to selection, the classical process implies that the buying center weighs all factors as defined by the specification and selects the supplier that best meets those specified needs. If there is an outstanding provider, the selection among potential suppliers can be obvious. However, all facets of the offer come into play, those quantifiable as well as those value chain features that are not as easily measured.

Assuming that all potential suppliers are qualified and that all have met the minimum performance requirements specified, the buying center selects from a group of providers who have worked very hard to meet the specification. The problem with this, from the suppliers' viewpoint, is that in all their hard work they have probably accomplished exactly the worst outcome—to be just like each other. Under such circumstances, the customer selects the supplier with the lowest price. From this result comes the entrenched myth that the successful supplier is the one that offers the lowest price. This does not follow good marketing logic.

Why would suppliers want to work to be just like each other? Smart suppliers work very hard to distinguish their offerings from each other. Market-driven suppliers do not use price as a marketing tool but will look to the buying center's broad and diverse needs to assemble an added-value approach that demonstrates qualitatively the advantages of their offer. This does not mean to imply that price is not important; it is, but competitive offerings need to be distinguished in other ways as well.

The buying center eventually arrives at a decision on which supplier it chooses. The final selection may be contingent on negotiations on some of the solution's features, on terms of the contract, or even on the final price. The selection stage reaches completion when the contract is signed.

Stage 3: Solution Delivery

Once the supplier is chosen, the supplier begins the process of delivering on its promises. This portion of the overall process may take a longer period of time than the first two stages combined. When the product is complex and involves a high degree of customization and even technical development, this stage is an extended set of activities. The solution delivery stage ends when the "delivery" is complete and approved by the buying organization. An astute supplier already involved in the definition and selection stages has, in many cases, had its offering approved or is proceeding through the approval process. Early approval can then speed up the supplier's cash flow.

Activities that can be included in this stage include all solution development that remains to be done, customization of the product or service based on a diagnosis process, testing of early versions of the solution, delivery of prototypes and incorporation into manufacturing trials, installation and testing of the full-scale solution, training of the buyer's employees who will operate the solution or interact with the service provider, resolution of any supply chain or logistics management issues, and perhaps other readiness activities.

The process of merging the supplying logistics of the supplier with the consumption logistics of the customer occurs during this stage. It is incumbent on the supplier to match the operational buying needs of the customer. Suppliers must recognize "how their customers buy" and meet that pattern. The transaction process should be routinized in a way that it is invisible to the buying organization. The supplier will want to match such things as materials planning, shipping quantities, inventory location, delivery times, and invoice routines (i.e., the utilities of business logistics—form, time, place, and possession) to the buyer's methods.

How the supplier delivers on its promises up to this point is watched closely by the buying organization. All through this delivery stage, the buying organization evaluates how good the supplier is and what the likelihood is of a good working relationship in the future. If the supplier can provide this value during the delivery stage, it stands a good chance of making a successful transition into future buying decisions.

Stage 4: End Game

All of the prior activity has a purpose—to provide the buying organization with the products, materials, or capabilities necessary for the buying organization to reach its goals. These goals might be stated in terms of market share, position, market ownership, or, ultimately, profitability. Often, buying organizations formally evaluate purchase outcomes and these are the criteria by which the outcomes are judged. Individual members of the buying center also evaluate the purchase, the process, and the supplier after the purchase is in use. The needs at this point are the benefits that were anticipated to begin with. Along with this is a need for reasonable (and usually predictable) costs.

The supplier should use every opportunity to reinforce the validity of the buying center decision. Suppliers that continue to show an interest in the changing needs of a buying center after the supplier has been selected are preparing for the next RFQ from the customer as well as making it far more difficult for a competitor to encroach on the business. The quality with which the supplier meets the logistics needs described in the discussion of the delivery stage should be a positive influence in the business relationship, and suppliers should solicit feedback regarding these processes. The manner in which the supplier "resells the job" can be tangible evidence of otherwise nonquantifiable factors that can make price less of an issue.

The end game of a specific supply situation should also be the definition stage of the next—a natural flow in the involvement of the customer and supplier organizations. The degree to which this happens automatically is an indicator of the degree of success of the relationship viewed from either organization.

TWO EXAMPLES OF BUYING DECISION PROCESSES

Let us look at two hypothetical examples (based on real situations) to illustrate what happens in the buying process. The two examples represent the two ends of the spectrum: a straight rebuy on the one hand and a new task on the other.

Straight Rebuy Example: Buying Office Supplies

For the straight rebuy, let us examine a small advertising agency buying office supplies. Their need for the supplies is triggered when the office manager notices that some inventory levels are low. Maybe, though, they are a little more organized and the office manager places a monthly order. In either case, a *problem is recognized* (office supplies need to be replenished) and the process starts (see Exhibit 3–4). The next step involves checking the inventory to see if some items have sufficient inventory or need an extra large order. The office manager may also ask someone in each department (e.g., from the creative, media, traffic, account management, and administration departments) whether they have any special supply needs coming up soon. The office manager then makes out his list of things to order. This represents the *definition of need* and *definition of solution* steps, and this stage is complete (refer to Exhibit 3–3). The *definition* stage took all of maybe an hour to complete, most of which was spent waiting for the administrative

EXHIBIT 3–4   Summary of the Straight Rebuy Example

Stage	Result
Definition	Monthly rebuy of office supplies; office manager fills in the order form.
Selection	Minimal consideration; decided to use their regular supplier; order faxed to supplier.
Deliver solution	Supplier delivers order.
End game	Supplies used; invoice arrives and is paid; supplier calls to check on satisfaction.

FreeMarkets: Buying Decisions

assistant in the creative department to return the office manager's voice mail message. Notice that the ad agency did not actually need the supplies at this time. Their need was for information on what supplies they were going to need in the coming month.

The next step is for the office manager's assistant to place the order. The assistant prepares a purchase order that is faxed to the agency's regular office supply dealer. The assistant follows up with a phone call to the dealer's customer service rep that handles the ad agency account. The phone call verifies some unusual quantities that are being ordered. That's the extent of the *selection* stage. Notice that a selection of supplier was made very quickly: the office manager determined, almost unconsciously, that the agency would use its regular dealer. Again, the agency does not actually need the supplies at this time; it needs only to have a reliable supplier chosen and an order easily placed by the end of this stage. In a straight rebuy, this part of the process is almost trivial, unless something has happened to cause the office manager to re-evaluate whether the choice of supplier should be reopened.

The *solution delivery* begins with delivery of the order. Let us say that the dealer makes its own deliveries. Three days after the order was placed, the delivery van shows up and drops off the supplies. The driver, along with the office manager's assistant, checks the packing list against the purchase order. The assistant signs off the delivery, and this stage is complete. The agency's needs in this stage are on-time delivery, the right products received, and the convenience of the transaction.

In the *end game,* the invoice from the dealer is received and the agency's accountant pays the bill. Perhaps the dealer's customer service rep calls the office manager's assistant and checks to see whether the order was received with no problems. Perhaps the service rep also checks quickly to verify that no changes in procedure are expected for the next month's order. All these steps reinforce the *routinization of the transaction* and even quickly *resell the job.* The needs of the organization during this stage are the availability and usefulness of the office supplies, as well as reassurance that the same thing will happen in the future. Note that it is during this stage that the actual need for the products is realized. It is at this stage, too, that the price of the order is actually realized.

The office manager may make a cursory evaluation of the process to verify that the value received was satisfactory. If a problem has occurred during this process, the office manager will pay more attention to the evaluation. Some problems that

might occur include an increase in prices, a slow delivery, the delivery of the wrong
items, the back ordering of some crucial items on the order, or a churlish attitude
from the service people. Any one of these may cause the office manager to try to
rectify the situation or to re-open the search for a new supplier. A significant advantage exists for the current supplier (the "defending source"). Keeping existing customers is far more productive than finding new ones. Any incident that detracts
from the routine experience of the customer can create an opportunity for the supplier waiting in the wings to move to center stage.

New Task Example: Acquiring Automated Sales and Customer Management System

Let us contrast the preceding process with another example that illustrates a new
task buying situation. For this second example, we quickly describe the whole
process and then go back to identify stages, steps, and needs. This avoids a lengthy
discussion of highly involved activity and illustrates the main points without delay.

Consider a value-added reseller (VAR) of computer systems. They come to the
realization that they want to improve their own sales and pre-sale service operations. They find that they are losing some existing customers to competitors
because the competitors provide better pre-sale service. To complicate this problem, the competitors seem to have controlled their costs to the point that they can
offer superior service while charging lower prices. Also, the VAR believes that it
is losing sales opportunities by not being able to identify prospects quickly enough.
Competitors are finding them, qualifying them, and "getting in the door" before the
VAR even knows that an opportunity exists. At this point in time, the VAR has
not determined what sort of solution to seek.

The next step for the VAR involves undertaking an analysis of its current
sales and customer service processes. With the help of a consultant, the VAR and
the consultant arrive at the conclusion that several processes would be improved
with the installation of an automated sales and customer management system. The
consultant has brought in a business development person from a reputable vendor
of software for automated sales and customer management. A discussion with the
business development person from the software vendor launches the VAR into a
new task buying process to acquire such a system.

They begin this process by writing general specifications of the kind of system
they are looking for. The consultant and a missionary salesperson from the software vendor help them write this specification. The consultant suggests several
other suppliers who would probably be good alternatives as vendors. These suppli-

ers are contacted and asked to make proposals based on the specifications that have been written. The suppliers ask detailed questions concerning the VAR's situation. Three of the vendors prepare detailed proposals and make presentations to the VAR's executives and several other managers within the organization.

The executives and the VAR's IT manager confer to select a vendor. In their discussions, they discover that new selection criteria have arisen from some of the vendor presentations. They revise their criteria and determine that they need more information from a couple of the vendors. After additional discussions with the vendors, they finally select one vendor. It happens to be the first vendor, who helped them write the specifications and request for proposal. Discussions with the vendor's sales team shift into negotiation mode, specifying the contract for the project. After negotiating the work and the terms, a deal is signed by executives for both the vendor and the VAR. The technical team for the vendor begins talking at length with the future users of the system and begins designing the system. Early versions of the system are tested with users and demonstrated for the VAR's executives. Modifications are made; some renegotiation of features and price results. First modules of the new system are installed, and the first batch of users is trained. They begin using the system, with mixed results. The vendor fixes some bugs and provides some additional training. Meanwhile, the users are becoming more proficient—some of the problems take care of themselves.

Over the next six months, the process to design, test, build, train, launch, and fix is repeated for the remaining modules of the system. The VAR's IT manager and the sales vice president begin to discuss how well the system is working. A sales assistant collects some evaluative information on system performance. The vice president and the IT manager generally conclude that they like the system, that they would have done a few things differently, and that they need more modules. Meanwhile, the system vendor's sales team has been helping the VAR evaluate the system. They suggest some improvements and introduce the vice president and the IT manager to new modules that have been developed in the time during which the system was installed. It is some of these new modules that the vice president and the IT manager suggest to the VAR's CEO for improving the automated system.

This example shows how the process might flow in a new task buying situation. The buying center took more time and effort throughout the whole process than was taken for the straight rebuy. In fact, the buying center itself was larger and involved people higher in the organization than were involved in the straight rebuy. The individual stages and steps did not occur in a stepwise fashion. While there was a general flow, the steps tended to recycle and repeat to a certain extent. For instance, the analysis of sales and service processes that occurred in the *solution definition* step probably further refined the definition of the organization's problem. When the selection team entered its initial deliberations on the selection of the vendor, they discovered new criteria to consider, which sent them back to the solution definition step and took them through more information search on the vendors.

One feature of this process that stands out is the amount of time and effort that transpire between the time a contract is signed and the delivery of the "final"

EXHIBIT 3–5   Summary of the New Task Example

Stage	Result
Definition	Recognized problem; analyzed with help of consultant; supplier helps write specifications and RFP; suppliers submit proposals
Selection	Discussions and negotiations with suppliers; supplier selected (the one who helped initially); contract negotiated and signed
Deliver Solution	System delivered in modules; tested; users trained; system modified as needed
End Game	System operated; results observed and analyzed; discussions begin with supplier for acquisition of new modules and upgrades

product (see Exhibit 3–5). In fact, it might be argued that there is no final delivery as such; the end game stage of this process overlaps and flows into the early process stage of the next buying process. Another feature that stands out is the amount of uncertainty at each step. The recycling that occurs does so in part because so much uncertainty remains when the organization progresses from step to step. The organization uses much more information in the whole process to try to combat the uncertainty. The organization also makes use of the consultant in an attempt to help handle the complexity, newness, and uncertainty.

As was pointed out for the straight rebuy process, the VAR's needs differ from step to step. The organization does not need an actual product until it is well into the solution delivery activities. In the problem definition step, the VAR needs a good definition of the problem it is trying to solve. In the next step, it needs a good description of the parameters of a solution to its problem. It needs assistance in defining those parameters. It needs further help in designating prospective vendors. In the selection process itself, it needs good information, not only of the vendors' capabilities but also of other characteristics such as their flexibility, their reliability, and the ease of working with them. The underlying need is the need for assurance that the vendor chosen will be able to deliver the value desired.

In the step in which the solution is defined, the needs include a need for increasing detail on how the new system will work and how it will help the VAR provide new value. This helps the VAR start to redesign its processes to take advantage of the system and to begin to plan to adapt and adopt. The VAR also needs further reassurance that it will get the desired value boost. As the system gets closer to implementation, the VAR needs the system to perform to specifications. Further, the VAR needs ease of use, ease of adoption, training of its employees, and merging with processes in place.

Exhibit 3–6 shows how needs progress through the stages of the buying decision process. Notice that we have distinguished between the buying organization's needs and the individual needs of the members of the buying center. Notice, as well, that individual needs can be classified as personal needs or needs related to the individual's role within the organization. In general, the needs of the organization tend to be addressed by the product and service portions of the supplier's offering. The

EXHIBIT 3–6   Examples of Organizational and Individual Needs in the Buying Decision Process

Steps in Flow	Organizational Needs	Individual Needs
Define problem	Clear, concise, tractable	Information and time
Define solution	Appropriate, affordable	Design assistance
Acquire provider	Choice, speed	Information, assurance
Develop solution	Speed, easy use	Execution help
Install, test, train	Ease of integration, speed	Knowledge, comfort
Operate solution	User friendly	Easy to maintain
End result	Effective, low cost	Recognition
Evaluation outcomes	Information	Communication, reward

individual needs, both personal and role-related, of the buying center members are addressed mostly by the supplier's efforts to build a relationship with the customer.

TRANSITION OF BUYING DECISION PROCESS: NEW TASK BECOMES REBUY

If the supplier's marketing efforts are done well and have the desired effect, the new task buying situation for a particular customer will transition into some form of rebuy situation in the next round, as illustrated in Exhibit 3–7. If the marketing effort fails for some reason—a mistake is made, a competitor performs better, or the customer's situation changes drastically, for instance—the decision process may revert to an earlier stage or the customer may decide to choose an alternative supplier. Exhibit 3–8 shows such contingencies as having a recycling effect in the process. The supplier then has to change its approach, determining what stage the decision process is now in and looking for ways to provide value to the customer at that stage.

EXHIBIT 3–7   Buying Decision Evolution

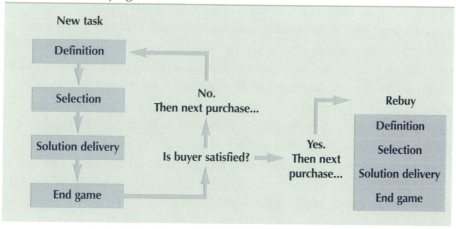

EXHIBIT 3–8   More Buying Decision Evolution

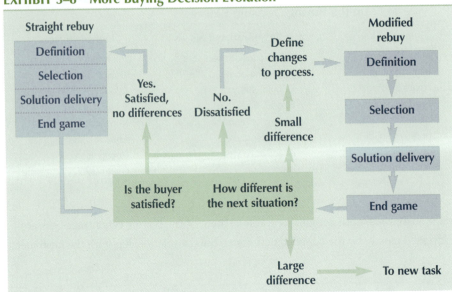

INFLUENCES THAT SHAPE THE BUYING DECISION PROCESS

The preceding discussion described the effect of familiarity on the nature of the process. Also emphasized was the effect of the supplier's marketing efforts, particularly in the early stages of the buying process. Other factors that similarly affect the nature and flow of the decision process are the complexity of the problem and solution, the risk aversion of the decision makers and influencers, the importance of the decision (related to the importance of the problem), and the speed with which the solution needs to be in place. Complexity tends to make the process more complex and lengthen it. Importance and risk aversion tend to make the process proceed with more rigor or care and tend to involve people higher in the organizational hierarchy. A requirement for speed, of course, tends to work against rigor and care and tends to reduce the scope of investigation.

As has been noted, the business marketer must fully recognize the impact of joint decision making in the buying center. The ability of the supplier to influence each of these decision makers requires recognition not only of the rational facets of the process but also of the complexity of center members' simultaneous but individual influence in the process. Just as different ingredients in a recipe interact with each other throughout the baking process, the interaction among members of the buying center is a continuous process.

As individual members of the buying center influence the decision, they are guided not by the classical decision process but by conventions related to the organization. These may include

◆   The characteristics/corporate culture of the firm

◆   The degree of risk aversion present in the culture

◆ The reward system in place at the time of the decision

◆ The amount of vertical and horizontal management involvement

In addition to these organizational conventions, the social dynamics of the situation play a large role in the decision process. Missionary sellers can find themselves in the center of a conflict internal to the customer. This can be a disaster or an opportunity for the seller. The missionary seller can play roles as a communicator, a boundary person, a diplomat, and a liaison between different customer interests. Treating these roles with respect can gain the trust and confidence of the various customer stakeholders. All require a marketer who understands the interpersonal dynamics of the situation and what each participant defines as a win. Individuals within the buying center may be politicking as they plan for their own advancement and/or operating in a framework neither entirely rational nor beneficial to the organization as a whole. Individuals in these roles are influenced by several factors.

Other Organizational Influences

The mission, goals, and objectives of an organization determine its attitude toward many projects. Policies and procedures are created to reinforce those goals and objectives and impact the organizational structure. The degree to which an organization is innovative or bureaucratic, dynamic or static, impacts business decisions. If the marketer's goal is to enlist a customer as partner in a new development, the customer organization should be one that rewards innovation and leadership. Certainly this should be one of the considerations in selecting which customer in an oligopolistic market would be the best candidate to approach with new ways of doing things.

Other Interpersonal and Individual Influences

Individuals in organizations react to situations with the same belief systems as in their private lives. Though in different roles, personality types and individual preferences influence decision making. Customer reactions to authority and status, though not "rational," may be perfectly human. Understanding aspects of social styles and human relationships can significantly contribute to the persuasiveness of a marketer's position.

An individual's age, income, education, and job position all contribute to attitude. Personal assessments regarding risk and beliefs about how things are supposed to be done can overshadow the most logical and rational decision process. The personal assessment of the participants in the decision process, both the buyers and the sellers, have a greater influence on the decision than product and price.

IMPLICATIONS FOR BUSINESS MARKETING

Recognizing the concurrent nature of the decision process, the business marketer can influence each step to enhance the supplier's position relative to the competition. The continuous relationship between the supplier and the customer should contribute to the supplier's knowledge of where the customer's market is going and, within that market, where the customer sees its role. This provides insight into possible new product development by the customer. This "need recognition" by the customer is an opportunity for the supplier to place information about its new products and technologies into the decision mix. As buying center individuals develop the initial general need description, they usually are not aligned with one type of solution or technology. The business marketer should participate with the buying center to influence the process. The added-value features and attributes of the marketer's offering and its suitability for the buyer's needs should be presented to individuals in the buying center in a way tailored to their individual focus. If customers are considering a major investment in a new facility, they may have concerns about financing the project and, as with any major facilities investment, be concerned about obsolescence. The finance professionals in the buying center should be approached with offering attributes that appeal to their needs, while manufacturing management should be counseled about the long-term flexibility of the facilities.

The business marketer must simultaneously appeal to all levels and disciplines in the buying center. If the marketer's offering has real added value to the customer, the supplying organization is able to assist in the customer's decision process. It is not unusual for suppliers to jointly develop product specifications with customers. This is advantageous to both the customer and the supplier. The customer gets a component or service that is specifically tailored to its needs, often unique in the market and quite possibly a competitive advantage. The supplier gains from the development of the tailored product, both technically and through the enhanced relationship with the customer. The enhanced relationship can demonstrate not only a financial investment by the supplier in the business of the customer but also an emotional one. Competition is locked out, at least initially, of the business opportunity. If the supplier has a distinctive competence that is prominent in the offering, the competition may decide to not even pursue the business.

THE VARIABILITY OF RATIONAL BUYING DECISIONS

Many texts and training sources have proposed that business selling is primarily technical selling. A business presents logical benefits of its product relative to the competition's; and, provided its product is better, its product is selected. This is simplistic—nice in theory. In reality, as can be seen from this discussion so far, the business buying decision process has many elements of consumer decision making in it. Humans still make the decisions, so the decisions are still subject to many of the factors that are involved in consumer buying decisions.

Human Factors in Business Decisions

When human factors are involved, an entirely objective decision may not be possible. With this in mind, what can be said about the traditional stepwise process?

- Objective means are used to narrow choices. In many instances, several suppliers will be completely capable of providing the basic need of the organization. There will be a select group of suppliers, however, that match the cultural, interpersonal, value, and relationship needs of the organization.

- Suppliers that recognize the cultural, interpersonal, value, and relationship needs of the organization are more likely to be the "in" supplier, favored by more members of the buying center, than those who rely merely on the capabilities and features of their core product. Members of the buying center will be more comfortable and receptive to a supplying organization they believe has their best interests (their organization's and their own) in mind, as well as selling a product.

- A review of the facts is often done because the cultural process says it is supposed to be done. There is safety in having made a decision in a conventional way. You can always say, "But I did it the way I was supposed to."

- Facts are arranged to justify the decision that individuals in the buying center want to make. As decision makers, they are influenced by many intangible factors. Why do we think they can make a decision without regard to those influences? Why should they?

- People seek reinforcement for their beliefs in every factor that is presented to them. It is human nature to want to be right. Individuals want what they already believe to be true. In consumer buying, this is acceptable. In business buying, there is a need for rational justification to narrow choices and serve as a backup to decisions.

Mutual Dependence and Customer Loyalty

While not completely irrational—the needs of the organization must be satisfied—business buying decisions also must satisfy the members of the buying center. Marketers can work hand in hand with a customer. Ideally, the goal is to create a mutually rewarding relationship in which the customer becomes dependent on the solution/system rather than on just the core product. The focus is to create customer loyalty. This can make it expensive for the customer to change to another supplier. This investment is mutual and visible in a number of ways:

- *Long-term contracts.* As in any relationship, long-term commitments increase both the risk and the reward for the parties involved. The reduced uncertainty of long-term commitments makes it possible to better utilize resources for both organizations.

- *Financial and emotional investment by both the selling organization and the buying organization in the success of the effort.* When the vendor and the customer have mutual financial interests that favor the success of their cooperation (not to be confused with any arrangements that may be termed illegal—see Chapter 4), there is more motivation to continue the relationship through the difficult times. In addition, the relationships among individuals in each organization develop an emotional investment in the success of "members of the team."

A Brief Psychology of This Process

Like any managerial decision, decisions made in the supplier selection process are made with a degree of uncertainty. They must be. For a decision to be made with absolute certainty, all rational details and rational outcomes must be known. If these factors are known, the decision can be made by a series of binomial choices—a computer program—thus not requiring attention of management judgment or intuition.[1] Simon made the observation that decisions are made by "bounded rationality."[2] This model states that decision makers do not know all possible outcomes or payoffs and have limited motivation to search for additional alternatives, opting for the first alternative that meets the minimum standard of performance. This can lead to satisfactory, but not necessarily optimum decisions. Simon called this *satisficing* behavior.

In the buying center, behavior that reflects this thinking would lead the marketer to believe that being the first supplier with a plausible offering may be sufficient to win the business. Satisficing can be seen as the first step beyond core product offerings, but experienced marketers know this often is not enough to capture business, let alone create a lasting relationship. While being first to market is often cited as a good positioning strategy, marketers interested in maximizing the value offering should look for optimal rather than sufficient positioning.

> **Value image,** the total of all impressions that a customer has of the firm, is a very powerful motivator—perhaps because so much of an individual's beliefs about a firm, situation, or occurrence are based on forgotten experiences. While the concept of value image is more obvious in consumer markets, it has application in business-to-business markets as well.

Sherlock states that customers form a **value image** associated with supplier alternatives.[3] This image is the sum total of all impressions and experiences that the buyer has of the supplier, whether or not pertinent to the current buying situation. These impressions act at the individual, organizational, and personal levels. This value imaging is not unlike conscious product/market positioning in that it is entirely in the customer's mind. The value image is formed by the customer and may have little to do with the actual product or service. Marketers should actively seek to maximize (not satisfice!) value image in the "mind" of the customer.

Application in Business Relationships

So how do we apply this in business marketing? Individuals have attitudes and beliefs about a number of things. Images and symbols are associated

---

[1] R. Richard Ritte and G. Ray Funkhouser, *The Ropes to Skip and the Ropes to Know,* 3d ed. (New York: John Wiley & Sons, 1987), 66.

[2] Herbert A. Simon, "Rational Decision Making in Business Organizations," *American Economic Review* (September 1979): 493–512.

[3] Paul Sherlock, *Rethinking Business-to-Business Marketing* (New York: The Free Press, 1991), 24.

in memories with values and experiences: a pink bunny beating a drum—batteries;[4] a red circle with white script writing—a soft drink; two lizards arguing at the edge of a pond—a popular brand of beer. These symbols represent whatever value, positive or negative, customers associate with those images and the type of outcomes they expect from those values. People relate to the roles that others play in the same way. If a fellow student says he wants a career in politics, we associate a particular image with that student. Customers, the members of the buying center, have associations with the company, products, and marketing and sales professionals—all aspects the supplier brings to the table in the process of marketing. These associations create powerful expectations of behavior. In some instances, these are positive associations that aid the marketing effort; in others, they may unknowingly work against the marketer. Unfortunately, they are difficult to generalize. We cannot make a table of five things to do, in typical business book style, to be successful; this cake has no recipe.[5]

As an example of rationalized decision making that seeks to satisfy more than core needs, say that you are a junior in college about to purchase your first new car. You have saved a long time, working two part-time jobs to get through school and still be able to afford this new car. You can purchase a small, economical (boring) car that, financially, is the logical choice for a student with at least one year of college remaining; or you can purchase that GT Convertible (exciting) that you would, "logically," keep beyond your graduation, eliminating the need to sell the economical car and buy another as a step up when you graduate. Which choice will you make? Either can be made to sound logical and rational.

This same type of rationalized decision making occurs in business buying decisions. In a business context, suppose you are the information systems manager for a start-up company. You must decide between Hewlett-Packard (HP) desktop computers for your employees or lower-cost clones assembled by a local reseller.

---

[4]The "Eveready Energizer Bunny" advertising campaign was named as one of the top ten commercials in 1990 by Video Storyboard Tests, Inc. Ironically, a full 40 percent of those who selected the ad as an outstanding commercial thought it was for Duracell—Eveready's strongest competitor. Duracell's previous positioning (value image?) was able to negate the commercial's popularity! (As cited by Regis McKenna, "Marketing Is Everything," *Harvard Business Review,* January–February 1991.)

[5]In *Rethinking Business-to-Business Marketing,* Sherlock applies the principles of Carl Jung to the decision process. Sherlock observes that the conscious mind (the area where we think we function) with its rational analysis; combined with the personal unconscious (forgotten personal experience); and the collective unconscious (where our inherent nature combines with archetypical roles—mother, child, hero, seller, etc.) with its power and drive are the three regions of the mind responsible for decision making. Sherlock emphasizes that this unconscious-driven decision process is justified by an after-the-fact rationalization through the use of the classical decision model.

For example, our conscious mind is where we think we make willful decisions, where we have willpower in decisions such as dieting, studying rather than partying, saving rather than spending. With willpower, we are not utilizing all of our capabilities and resources, which is why we are often unsuccessful in these pursuits. Our belief systems, created by our experiences and stored in less-than-conscious parts of our minds, exert tremendous influence on our decision process. To deny this would be to deny many of the motivational aspects of buyer behavior.

© JOHN TODD/AP/WIDE WORLD PHOTOS

Depending on your attitude toward risk and your need for quality assurance, after-purchase support, and ability to upgrade, you could, logically, select either supplier:

HP rationale. HP has been in business for a long time and will continue to be able to support us. Their product may not be the latest, hottest computer for the best price, but their quality and reliability make them the right choice. They better fit the image of the type of company we want to do business with, and we cannot get hurt choosing HP. Besides, upgrading is not important since technology changes so fast we will not want to bother to upgrade old computers but will purchase new ones when necessary.

Local reseller rationale. Fast Freddie Computers (FFC) is a local business on the cutting edge of new systems integration. FFC can pick the best components from many suppliers to assemble computers tailored to our individual needs. They are local, in our community, and more able to understand the needs of a small start-up company. Reliability and service will not be an issue because they are nearby and will be onsite immediately if there are any problems. We will be a big customer to them, while HP will not know we exist. Besides, they will be able to upgrade our computers with the latest technology at a lower cost than purchasing new units.

How do marketers reconcile this theory of decision making with what is supposed to be a logical business approach? First, recognize that a good marketing plan and a good business marketer assist the buying center through the decision process. The marketer should recognize the steps previously discussed as components of the decision that can be influenced. The marketer that fully understands the nature of the customer's business, his own organization's supply capabilities, and the role he can play will seek opportunities to enhance his image with respect to the needs of the customer at every possible opportunity. All of these factors combine to create the "way the customer buys." It is impossible to standardize these factors into an eight-step routine decision process.

Think back to the United Technologies example at the beginning of this chapter. UTC has instituted a process that unilaterally changes its relationships with suppliers. If you were the marketing manager for one of these suppliers, what would UTC's actions tell you about the nature of your prior relationship with UTC? With their buyer behavior in mind, what would you do now?

The process by which organizations select suppliers is difficult to generalize. Learning the way a particular customer buys is critical to the business marketer. The differences in consumer and business buying models have been discussed, with emphasis on the broad array of different types of decisions occurring simultaneously in the buying center. The marketer should address the different aspects of value sought by the different members of the buying center. Only in this way can the marketer provide superior value to the customer's entire organization.

Perhaps the most important observation to come out of this chapter is the importance for the business marketer's organization to be involved in the early portion of the customer's buying decision process. As the customer develops the general statement of need, the business marketer should be of assistance in offering alternatives and pointing out the supplier's unique values. The development of a specification should be a joint effort of the supplier and the buying center. When complete, the supplier's offering should be a natural fit with the specification and the organization's needs.

The development of a specification by the customer is often a method used by the customer to reduce differences between potential suppliers. The ability of the supplier to influence the specification is attributable in many ways to the expected value that the customer believes will be provided by the supplying firm. These expectations are the result of images and beliefs formed about potential suppliers long before this actual business episode.

Customers rely on suppliers for assistance throughout their design, development, and specification process. Particularly with new technologies, customers need coaching as to how to get maximum value from the supplier's products. A strong alliance with major suppliers to ensure that their best interests are protected is of value to customers. Suppliers do not become significant to the customer without forging these alliances. As we hope to demonstrate throughout this book, mutual trust, respect, and professionalism are essential to the business-to-business relationship.

Building relationships with customers, then, is key to succeeding in business-to-business marketing. This chapter has shown that understanding the buying center and the buying decision process is key to building such relationships. In the chapters that follow, we discuss how to learn about customers and the business environment and how to turn this knowledge into executable strategy. A key component of this strategy focuses on meeting customer needs through the development of relationships with customers.

Key Terms

buying center

internal brand

modified rebuy

new task

process flow model

request for proposal (RFP)

request for quotation (RFQ)

stakeholders

straight rebuy

value image

Questions for Review and Discussion

1. Contrast the consumer buying decision process with the organizational buying process.

2. What is a buying center?

3. What organizations or departments are usually considered to be in a buying center?

4. How does the buying center change for different types of purchases (straight rebuy, modified rebuy, new task)?

5. Relate the value network discussed in Chapter 2 with the buying center. How can they be intertwined to provide value for the customer?

6. Discuss how a "cultural code" works against rational, quantifiable decision making but results in satisfying decision outcomes.

7. Compare cultural codes and their impact in consumer decision making and business decision making.

8. Why is it difficult to generalize the process of business buying behavior?

9. Relate the buying process model to organizational and individual needs. How do they change through the process?

10. What types of purchases are likely to experience extensive activity occurring in the following portions of the buying decision process model?
    a. Definition stage
    b. Selection stage
    c. Solution delivery stage
    d. End game stage

11. What types of purchases and purchase decisions lend themselves to the Internet or other Web-based decision strategies?

12. An influential member of the buying center has confided to a supplier's representative that she wants help to "be a hero" in her organization. Into what part of the individual needs description does the "request" seem to fit? When is such a request likely to occur?

13. Your company has been a reliable and trusted supplier of somewhat generic, frequently purchased hardware items. One of your largest regular customers has announced that all purchases of hardware and supplies will be subject to an on-line bidding service. Your company has a choice of either submitting to the bidding system or lowering your current prices by 5 percent (thus avoiding exposure to the on-line process). How would you respond?

Internet Exercises

Suppose you are the office manager for the small advertising agency discussed in the chapter. Go to the Web sites for iPrint and OfficeMax: **http://www.iprint.com** and **http://www.officemax.com** Explore the custom printing options available at each. Which supplier do you think better accommodates customers' decision processes? Why?

Suppose you are still with the small advertising agency discussed in the chapter. You want to do business with the federal government. Go to the Web site for FirstGov: **http://www.firstgov.gov** Follow the link for "Doing Business with the Federal Government." Explore this site and determine what decision process federal agencies would go through to hire the services of a small agency. What might you do to work with this system?

Go to the Web site for United Technologies: **http://www.utc.com** Find the part of the site for the Hamilton Sundstrand Corporation. Go to the part of the Hamilton Sundstrand site for e-business and look at the resources for prospective suppliers, including small businesses. Does the process described on the site offer opportunities for prospective suppliers, especially small businesses, to build relationships with UTC or Hamilton Sundstrand? Why, or why not?

4

The Legal and Political Environment

overview. . . The impact of law and politics on business is usually greater than imagined by students and consumers. In this chapter, we examine the logic of legal restraints applied to business-to-business activities in a market-driven economic system and introduce the primary legislative controls on business-to-business markets. Many of these regulations overlap, support, or clarify prior regulations. To assist you in understanding the regulatory environment, we discuss the combined focus of these regulations with a review of the activities they regulate.

© PHOTOLINK/PHOTODISC

One of the most complicated and easily misunderstood issues in marketing is the legal environment. Contributing to this confusion is that, like many pieces of legislation, the laws and acts are subject to interpretation. The discussion that follows does not attempt to legally interpret legislation beyond that which has already been done in marketing and legal literature. The focus of this chapter is to define the parameters of the legal environment that business-to-business marketers face each day. We believe that it is more important to understand when a business practice can be considered illegal rather than to be able to state specifically which act(s) the practice is governed by. Within this context, we demonstrate the legal issues and offer some insight into antitrust and price discrimination law enforcement.

A central part of business legislation concerning the marketing mix is price. This chapter presents an in-depth, albeit hypothetical, example of the limitations placed on a business-to-business marketer's price-setting freedom to ensure a level playing field in the ultimate consumer market. The price scenario is followed by a discussion of intellectual property and antitrust legislation.

YOUR PLIGHT AS OWNER OF PACIFIC DRIVES

Suppose that you are the owner of Pacific Drives, a small computer hard drive company in a Northwestern state. Your potential customers are major producers of laptop computers. Your two largest competitors, DynaDrive Peripherals and Spin Technologies, are large companies with extensive product lines, established customers, and market access.

When you attempt to contract the shipping of your products to your customers, you find that the major logistics provider in your area with the best service will not ship your products because their nationwide contract with DynaDrive Peripherals gives them 100 percent of the DynaDrive business but only if they do not ship any competitors' products. As a result, you are forced to use a regional shipper with neither the reputation nor the market reach to completely satisfy your needs. Your customers complain about slow and costly delivery service, putting you at a competitive disadvantage in the market place.

As e-commerce grows, however, you find an alternative to your present way of doing business. You begin to offer your products directly to customers over the Internet. You make arrangements with a worldwide parcel service to handle all of your deliveries.

It looks like your problems are solved, until your Internet service provider (ISP) refuses to provide secure transmission capabilities for your ordering system. It seems that your ISP is a division of a conglomerate that is also the parent company of Spin Technologies. The parent company thinks the Internet operations are a good idea and wants to use it, so they are going to use their leverage to keep you out of the market.

LEARNING OBJECTIVES

- ◆ Understand the primary goals and objectives of business legislation and its implications in a market economy.

- ◆ Understand the basic U.S. antitrust and business regulatory legislative acts.

- ◆ Gain a sense of the interaction of legislation and the activities it restricts or prohibits.

- ◆ Recognize the business-to-business marketing implications and nuances of those restrictions.

- ◆ Understand the methods and variability in enforcement of the acts.

- ◆ Understand the substantiality test in enforcement decisions.

- ◆ Understand specific market issues related to price discrimination.

- ◆ Be introduced to intellectual property protection, licensing, and the relationship to antitrust laws.

introduction. . .

Does the treatment of Pacific Drives in this opening case sound like a fair scenario? No? Why not? The logistics provider is just giving a quantity discount to its larger customers, and the Internet service provider cannot be expected to provide service features to a customer that competes with its parent company. In fact, the fictitious example contains two restraints of trade that are violations of antitrust law. First, while the logistics provider can give quantity discounts to large customers, the discounts must be justified by the cost savings associated with the economies of scale and the contract cannot shut out competitors from using the same logistics provider. The second violation is exclusive dealing, committed by the Internet service provider. Companies cannot selectively restrict access to products and services in a way that lessens competition in the market.

In most situations, it is not likely that violations of business legislation are created by management with intentional harm or malice as a goal. Good marketers want to make the best deals for their organizations. Marketing managers, who daily make decisions regarding price and components of total offerings to customers, must have a working knowledge of the potential pitfalls, traps, and nuances of antitrust and price discrimination laws. Application of this working knowledge not only avoids embarrassing situations with customers but, through the use of a proactive approach to avoid legal entanglements, can enhance the customer relationship.

BUSINESS REGULATION IN A FREE MARKET

Though the United States has what can be called a "free market" economy, there are some necessary restrictions that must be placed on business to assure equal access to the market by all competitors and protect consumers in the market. As a result, business-related legislation has been focused in three areas:

1. *Protect companies from each other.* While competition is one of the fundamental strengths of a free market system, some organizations are much more able to compete than others. Smaller companies are often at risk of being overpowered by large companies attempting to dominate markets. Laws that prevent unfair pricing or restricted access to markets are often aimed at such situations.

2. *Protect consumers.* Without business legislation, some firms would misrepresent their products, lie or bait in their advertising, deceive in their packaging, or provide unsafe products. Unfair consumer practices have been a major area of enforcement. Generally, business laws attempt to maximize choice to the consumer while providing maximum access to markets by business.

3. *Protect the interests of society.* Most new legislation has focused on holding businesses responsible for the social and environmental cost associated with their processes or products. Thus, environmental legislation has significant impact on the conduct of business.

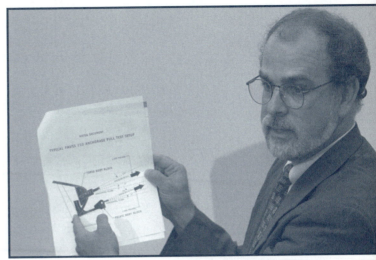

© RICHARD SHEINWALD/AP/WIDE WORLD PHOTOS

ENFORCEMENT RESPONSIBILITIES

At the federal level, enforcement of business law is usually the responsibility of a federal administrative agency or of the Justice Department in the executive branch of the U.S. government. Though many state-level agencies exist, their diversity puts them beyond the scope of this book. Administrative agencies are neither legislative nor judicial bodies.[1] While some agencies reside in the executive office of the President of the United States (for example, the Department of Health and Human Services and the Department of Agriculture), most are independent agencies like the Consumer Product Safety Commission (CPSC) and the Federal Trade Commission (FTC). The President can exercise a degree of control through his authority to appoint agency administrators, though a major difference between executive agencies and independent agencies is the term of administrators. Independent agency administrators serve for a fixed term whose period is staggered with the President's term, slightly reducing executive branch influence.[2]

It is very difficult to generalize about enforcement of business legislation because enforcement is often the *choice* of an agency or the Justice Department. Though traditional patterns have blurred in recent years, enforcement priorities can change with the change of a presidential administration or political party in power in Congress. Thus, the successful and astute marketer has an up-to-date working knowledge of the legal aspects of marketing and the current attitude of enforcement agencies.

---

[1]Marianne Jennings, *Business: Its Legal, Ethical, and Global Environment* (Cincinnati: South-Western College, 2000), 172.

[2]Richard A. Mann and Barry S. Roberts, *Smith and Roberson's Business Law,* 11th ed. (Cincinnati: South-Western College, 2000), 83–89.

LEGISLATION AFFECTING MARKETING

This section summarizes major legislation in the United States related to business-to-business marketing situations. The acts themselves and their primary focus are summarized in Exhibit 4–1. Because of the interrelationship of these laws, this summary is followed by an explanation of a number of issues that may not clearly lie within any one act.

Sherman Antitrust Act (1890)

The Sherman Antitrust Act was the first to prohibit "monopolies or attempts to monopolize" and "contracts, combinations, or conspiracies in restraint of trade" in interstate or foreign commerce. The Sherman Act provides for injunctions to restrain activities found to be in violation and allows anyone injured to recover, in a civil action, **treble damages.** Sherman Act jurisdiction is not strictly limited to interstate commerce but includes intrastate activities that have a substantial impact on interstate commerce.

> **Treble damages** are three times the actual loss incurred by the injured party as a result of a violation of antitrust law. The injured party must prevail in a civil court.

The Sherman Act provides for criminal felony penalties for both individuals and corporations. Corporations are subject to substantial fines, and individuals may be fined and imprisoned for up to three years.[3]

Clayton Act (1914)

The Clayton Act supplemented the Sherman Act by prohibiting certain specific practices before they advance to the definition of a restraint of trade as held by the

---

[3]Jennings, op. cit., 524.

EXHIBIT 4–1 Summary of Antitrust Acts and Their Focus

Statute	Focus
Sherman Antitrust Act (1890)	Monopolies, attempts to monopolize. Provided for both civil and criminal penalties. Broad coverage was base for later legislation.
Clayton Act (1914)	Tying agreements, interlocking directorates, intercorporate stockholding. Provides for civil penalties only.
Federal Trade Commission Act (1914)	Broadly defined unfair competition or competitive situations.
Robinson-Patman Act (1936)	Often known as "the price discrimination act", provided penalties for both buyers as well as sellers. Requires proportionally equal terms to buyers in common markets.
Celler-Kefauver Act (1950)	The "Antimerger Act." Broadened power to prevent acquisitions where they may substantially impact competition.
Consumer Goods Pricing Act (1975)	Repealed Miller-Tydings Act (1937), which had allowed "fair trade," a form of price maintenance.

Sherman Act. Clayton includes limitations on **tying contracts, exclusive dealing, intercorporate stockholding, interlocking directorates,** and mergers in which competition may be substantially reduced. The Clayton Act also provides that corporate officers and officials may be held individually responsible for violations. The Clayton Act, however, can be applied only to transactions and persons *engaged in* interstate commerce, rather than the more broadly defined jurisdiction of *affecting* interstate commerce under the Sherman Act.[4]

While the Clayton Act added teeth to Sherman, it specifically exempted labor and agricultural organizations from antitrust legislation.[5] Though the Clayton Act has no criminal penalties specified, intentional price discrimination carries criminal penalties under other acts.

Federal Trade Commission Act (1914)

The Federal Trade Commission (FTC) was initially established by this act to prevent unfair methods of competition and deceptive practices. The FTC has powers to investigate and enforce the federal legislation already mentioned. Its powers were broadened by the Wheeler-Lea Act (1938), which granted the FTC the power to regulate unfair or deceptive practices whenever the public is being deceived, regardless of the competitive environment. Thus, the commission is charged with the duty of preventing "unfair methods of competition in commerce and unfair or deceptive acts or practices in commerce." The broad power of the commission was described (and strengthened) by the U.S. Supreme Court in 1953 (*FTC v. Motion Picture Advertising Service Co.*) as follows:

> The unfair methods of competition which are condemned by . . . the Act *are not confined* to those that were illegal at common law or that were condemned by the Sherman Act. . . . It is also clear that the FTC Act was designed to supplement and bolster the Sherman Act and the Clayton Act to stop *in their incipiency acts and practices which, when full blown, would violate those Acts.* [Italics added for emphasis.][6]

A common pattern of enforcement by the FTC is to enter into consent orders with potential violators to minimize the possibility of future violations. Exhibit 4–2 provides an example of how consent orders are used to limit the anticompetitive nature of mergers and acquisitions.

Tying contracts are requirements to purchase ancillary goods or services "in a bundle" to get the offering really desired. Example: A manufacturer of hammers will only sell you a hammer if you agree to also buy all of the nails you need from it.

Exclusive dealing occurs when a seller sells to only one buyer in a region such that competition is lessened. Example: A manufacturer restricts access to its products via only one distributor and prevents the distributor from carrying competitive offerings. Both exclusive dealing and tying contracts are attempts to restrict buyers' access to competitive products. In specific circumstances, judgments about the legality of these situations often depend on the size and market power of the firm attempting to limit choice in the market.

Intercorporate stockholding occurs when one company controls the stock of another company and exercises control such that trade is restrained.

Interlocking directorates are firms that are in competition with each other but have common members on their boards of directors.

---

[4]Ibid.

[5]Mann and Roberts, op. cit., 876.

[6]Ibid., 880.

EXHIBIT 4–2   Companies and Regulators Agree to Agree

Companies faced with legal challenges from the FTC have an alternative to a court battle not unlike a plea bargain between a prosecuting attorney and a defendant. This alternative, called a **consent decree,** is a written agreement between the agency and the company. When this type of negotiated settlement is possible, significant time and expense can be saved in the resolution of specific issues. These agreements are often used to alleviate agency concerns that arise when mergers and acquisitions might limit access to markets. By reaching an agreement, the company involved can proceed with the intended acquisition in a timely manner. Consider the following examples.

Silicon Graphics and the FTC

Silicon Graphics, Inc. (SGI), provides 90 percent of the software used to produce three-dimensional high-resolution graphics. This software has made possible the images for movies such as *Jurassic Park, Terminator 2,* and similar high-image–oriented movies. SGI acquired two of the three leading entertainment graphics software firms. The FTC became concerned that, as a result of the acquisitions, SGI would no longer support independent graphics software producers and might deny competitors access to the software of the firms it was acquiring. Such actions by SGI could limit choices in the graphics software market as well as make it more difficult for hardware suppliers to provide compatible equipment for the software market. Without resolution of these concerns, the acquisition would likely have been challenged by the FTC.

Under the consent order, SGI agreed to maintain an open architecture for independent software developers and publish an application interface to give other graphics software producers the capability to write software for SGI workstations. SGI also agreed to assure that the acquired software could be run on hardware other than that provided by SGI.

Boston Scientific and the FTC

Boston Scientific Corporation (BSC), a principal player in the market for intravascular ultrasound imaging catheters (IVUS), intended to acquire its main competitor. The combination would give BSC 90 percent of the IVUS catheter market. In addition to this acquisition, BSC was acquiring another firm that was considered to be the only new competition in that market. To assuage FTC concerns, BSC proposed the licensing of a package of its patents and technologies and those of the acquired firms to Hewlett-Packard (now known as Agilent Technologies) or another FTC-designated firm to help launch a strong competitor. The FTC added two requirements: (1) BSC must provide the licensee, for three years, with IVUS catheters and technical assistance to obtain Food and Drug Administration approval of their own catheters; and (2) BSC cannot enter into any exclusive contracts with manufacturers of IVUS imaging consoles (consoles necessary to use the catheters). In other words, BSC was prevented from excluding any competitors from the market for other necessary equipment and was required to help their licensee successfully enter the market.

As you can see, the FTC has the authority to act *before* a violation of law or restraint of trade actually occurs. This power acts as an incentive to bring firms desiring mergers or acquisitions to communicate with the FTC prior to actual acquisition or merger. The agency and the firm(s) agree to create a mutually acceptable set of circumstances that will maintain a competitive market place.

Source: "Antitrust Policy, an On-Line Resource Linking Economic Research, Policy and Cases," Owen Graduate School of Management, Vanderbilt University, http://www.antitrust.org

Robinson-Patman Act (1936)

The Robinson-Patman Act amended and strengthened portions of the Clayton Act and made it unlawful for a buyer to knowingly "induce or receive" a discriminatory price.[7] Buyers as well as sellers could now be held liable for actions that violate antitrust laws. Particularly for large firms engaged in interstate commerce, Robinson-Patman has been known as "the" price discrimination act. It specifically defines price discrimination as unlawful, subject to certain specific exceptions. Robinson-Patman

---

[7]Ibid., 878.

also provides enforcing agencies with the right to limit quantity discounts, prohibit brokerage allowances except to independent brokers, and prohibit promotional allowances or furnished services/facilities except when made available equally to all participants. This **equality** can be defined as **proportionately equal terms** and can be based on several factors.

> **Equality/proportionately equal terms** means that a seller must provide to buyers in horizontal competition with each other substantially equal offers. The offers may differ in specific attributes but must be relatively equal in value. The offers may be proportioned by the volume of business received from each buyer.

Celler-Kefauver Act (1950)

Often referred to as the *Antimerger Act* the Celler-Kefauver Act amended the Clayton Act and broadened the power to prevent acquisitions where they may substantially impact competition.[8] Even with this legislation, many business combinations have occurred in recent years, such as BP-Amoco and Worldcom-MCI. In each of these mergers, enforcement agencies ordered that certain portions of one or both parties' holdings in specific markets be divested to avoid any opportunity to monopolize the market.

Consumer Goods Pricing Act (1975)

The Consumer Goods Pricing Act (CGPA) repealed the Miller-Tydings Act, which had allowed *fair trade* pricing of consumer goods. Fair trade was intended to protect small retailers from the buying power of large chains. Independent retailers could feel confident that they would not face price competition from the larger retailers while manufacturers were able to control retail prices. This control assisted in positioning products as well as managing marketing channel margins. Fair trade evolved into a form of resale price maintenance, which is further described later. The CGPA prohibits price maintenance agreements among manufacturers and resellers.

---

[8]Philip Kotler and Gary Armstrong, *Principles of Marketing*, 6th ed. (Upper Saddle River, N.J.: Prentice-Hall, 1994), 83.

Securities Laws

Complicated federal and state securities laws, beyond the scope of this book, are designed to protect the investing public, not business competitors and customers. Nevertheless, the effect of securities laws on the way we conduct business is enormous. In brief, business people in companies that have issued stock to outsiders cannot defraud the investing public and must "disclose" important information about the company and its business. If you are involved with your company in an initial public offering or an issue of stock to "the public," you absolutely need the guidance of securities law professionals.

The Uniform Commercial Code

Most business transactions are defined by some form of written document. These may be as simple as the terms of sale of an individual purchase or may comprise many pages of conditions of the sale and rights and remedies of the parties involved. The law that governs these contracts is either **common law** or the Uniform Commercial Code (UCC). The UCC is a standard set of laws that govern the contracts and associated case law. For clarity and uniformity, most portions of the UCC have been adopted by all states except Louisiana. Business contracts, particularly those concerning the sale of goods (UCC Article 2) across state lines are assisted by the consistent provisions of the UCC.

> **Common law** really is a method of interpreting law. Judges interpret any law based upon all case decisions already made about the same issue. This accumulation of decisions, called precedence, was developed in England.

It has been our experience that most students will have only limited need for extensive knowledge of contract law and, when necessary, will consult with legal professionals. Further coverage of the UCC and contract law, beyond topical discussions in other portions of this text (for example, pricing and sales, Chapter 10 and Chapter 11), is left to business law courses.

BUSINESS LEGISLATION ISSUES

Marketers should have a working knowledge of the combined nature and effect of these regulations. Since the regulatory powers of the acts overlap and amend each other, the best way for business marketers to approach this is with a discussion of the issues rather than the individual acts.

Intercorporate Stockholding

As already noted, intercorporate stockholding occurs when a company owns another company in the same market or own shares of another company in the same market in an attempt to control that company such that competition in the marketplace is reduced. It is important to emphasize that ownership of more than one company that participates in a marketplace by a parent firm is not, in and of itself, illegal. However, manipulating that ownership in a manner that reduces choice and competition in the marketplace is considered a violation. Consider a manufacturer of chemicals and plastics that has significantly large stock holdings in an automotive manufacturer such that the purchases of chemicals and plastics by the automotive manufacturer can be influenced. Applying this influence so that it is very difficult for any other chemical and plastics company to be considered as a supplier would be a restraint of trade.

Interlocking Directorates

A company may attempt control of another firm by having members of its board of directors serve as directors of the other company, a practice referred to as interlocking directorates. Companies that participate (ostensibly, compete) in the same market cannot have common directors such that actions could be influenced that would lessen competition between the companies or in the markets in which they participate, either as buyer or seller. Important to the particular situation is how "the market" is defined by enforcers. "Market" may be region, market segment, product line, or any factor in the competitive arena. Exhibit 4–3 provides an enforcement example.

Price Maintenance

A manufacturer's attempt to dictate the resale price of an item is called **price maintenance,** and it is specifically illegal. The problem usually arises in marketing channels, either at the wholesale or at the retail level. Once an intermediary (wholesaler, retailer, etc.) purchases a product, it can sell it at any price it wishes. Obviously, price is a part of the marketing mix and manufacturers would like to control it. Oddly enough, this practice was legal at the retail level under the Miller-Tydings Act (1937) until 1975 and was actually called *fair trade!* Suppliers may suggest or recommend pricing, but this must not be interpreted as having coerced the reseller into price maintenance. While manufacturers' suggested retail prices (MSRPs) are often used as tools to position the offering in the market and a retailer may elect to follow the suggested price as part of a promotional plan, the retailer cannot be coerced to sell at that price. If a retailer elects to discount the items below the MSRP, the manufacturer cannot use other means (e.g., refusal to deal, which follows) to force the seller to maintain a specified price.

There are circumstances in which a manufacturer is allowed to exert some control over the resale price of an offering. When suppliers are contributing to the value of the offering (e.g., providing financing for inventory, selling through a consignment agreement, providing support services, etc.), they are allowed more influence on the final price. This, ostensibly, is allowed to reduce the impact of **free riders**—retailers who provide a reduced-service package to customers, enabling profitability at a lower sales price than full-service retailers. Full-service retailers who provide a full package that may include such items as product demonstrations, installation advice, and local parts availability incur costs associated with these services. Manufacturers can protect full-service retailers by limiting the discounts that limited-service retailers can provide. Without such an accommodation, customers would seek information from the full-service retailer and make purchases at the lower-cost alternative.

> **Free riders** are those retailers who, either through mail order, e-commerce, or other means, provide a reduced-service package to customers, enabling a lower sales price. Often this service package takes the form of purchase assistance, product information, and customer education.

EXHIBIT 4–3   Legally Defined Markets

In the view of the Justice Department, whether mergers and acquisitions create a restraint of trade often depends on the definition of the impacted market. Here are two examples in which the market definition has significant impact on the proposed acquisitions.

Kraft General Foods, Inc. v. The State of New York

Kraft General Foods, Inc. (KGF), acquired the breakfast cereal business of Nabisco (Shredded Wheat, etc.). At the time of the acquisition, KGF's breakfast cereal line included *Post*-brand cereals. The state contended that the acquisition would have adverse effects in the ready-to-eat (RTE) adult breakfast cereal market. By defining the market as *adult RTE,* the state hoped to show that the two popular cereals, Post Grape-Nuts and Nabisco Shredded Wheat would dominate the "market."

The court found evidence of both supply-side and demand-side substitutability. The "kid" and "adult" RTE cereal markets overlapped, with the dominant selection characteristic being variety. Thus, the "market" was expanded to include more than 200 RTE cereals. From a supply-side perspective, the court determined that the RTE cereal industry manufacturing processes were flexible enough that if, as a result of the Post-Nabisco combination, adult cereals experienced a significant increase in market price, additional competitive substitutes would become available.

Community Publishers, Inc. v. Donrey Corporation

In this example, we can see the potential restraint of trade implied by interlocking directorates as well as the impact of market definitions. Community Publishers, Inc. (CPI), publisher of the *Daily Record,* a newspaper in northwest Arkansas, challenged the acquisition of the *Times,* a competing local newspaper, by an organization indirectly controlled by the same family that owned another Arkansas newspaper, the *Morning News.* In defense of the acquisition, the defendant argued that the market for news was served by a broad array of providers, including radio, television, and national- and state-level newspapers. Additionally, the defendant claimed that the market of each newspaper was different because the papers did not compete directly for advertisers nor was there significant switching of subscriptions between the papers. The court, however, defined the market narrowly as local daily newspapers in the northwest Arkansas geographic area. Under this definition, the combined newspapers had an 84 percent market share; the geographic area was integrated "socially, politically, and economically"; and everyone involved with each of the newspapers considered the other to be a competitor. The need of advertisers to promote in a "dominant newspaper" could, through an increase in advertising rates, "soak up" advertising revenue from other newspapers. The court found that the combined newspapers could, through regional expansion, create an entity that would have little competition for subscribers or advertisers.

As corrective action, the court rejected the idea of divestiture by the defendant, as this would allow the defendant to still have significant say as to the fate of the divested newspaper. The court therefore ordered rescission of the acquisition, restoring the market to its condition prior to the acquisition.

Source: The Merger Guidelines and Statutory Law, Chapter III, http://www.antitrust.org/law/us

Refusal to Deal

When used as a method to enforce or encourage one of the preceding issues, such as price maintenance, **refusal to deal** is illegal. This may take the form of not restocking or not providing associated services to dealers that have not followed suggested pricing. The courts have, however, recognized the right of a seller to sell (or not sell) to whomever it wants, provided the motivation is not to restrain trade or fix prices.

Resale Restrictions

The courts have not come down firmly on either side of the issue of **resale restrictions,** which usually refers to suppliers maintaining house accounts (customers that, while they are located within a reseller's market area, remain a direct customer of the manufacturer) or limiting resellers to certain territories. The manage-ment of exclusive territories and house accounts is further discussed in Chapter 12.

Price Discrimination

Price discrimination is one of the most difficult areas about which to generalize because court interpretations have been somewhat inconsistent. Essentially, price discrimination occurs when a supplier sells the same product to the "same class" of buyers at different prices such that the price differentials lessen competition. Prices for products that would be considered discriminatory but are sold to customers who are not in competition with each other is not illegal. Confused? Let us con-sider a sample scenario:

> Your company, Pacific Drives (Pacific), manufactures hard drives for personal computers. Among Pacific customers are two large computer manufacturers, NBM and PaloAlto Computers (PaloAlto). NBM and PaloAlto are rivals, each competing for the desktop computer market. Both companies purchase Pacific Model 1000 hard drives in large quan-tities, 5,000 units per month, for their products. Since Pacific is selling the same product, in similar quantities, within the same time frame (so that obsolescence or seasonal pricing is not a factor) to customers who compete with each other, Pacific is required to sell at the same price, $38, to both. In this scenario, illustrated in Exhibit 4–4, Pacific provides quantity discounts based on the size of the purchases.

This is a simple example that assumes comparable logistical considerations. Basically, neither PaloAlto nor NBM has an advantage in the marketplace as a result of any pricing irregularities on the part of Pacific Drives; but, wouldn't each customer strive for an advantage? Wouldn't Pacific be seeking opportunities to

EXHIBIT 4–4   Pacific Drives Supplies the Same Product to Two Customers Who Compete in the Same Market

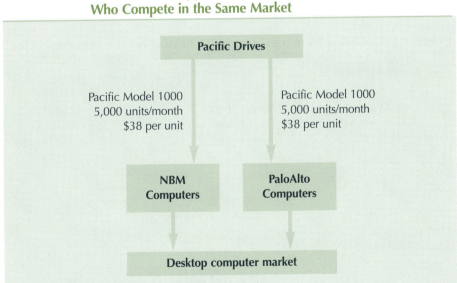

adjust pricing, up or down, as part of its value offering to its customers? The answer to both questions is yes. Let us add another factor to this scenario:

One of Pacific's competitors, United Memories (UniMem), has become very aggressive. It is attempting to increase its market share by targeted price reductions at major customers in Pacific's market. UniMem approaches NBM with a special price on its Model UniMem300 drive, which is comparable to Pacific Model 1000. The Pacific selling price to NBM has been $38 per unit in quantities of 5,000 drives per month. UniMem offers the UniMem300, at the same quantities and service logistics as Pacific, for $32 per unit. This is a significant enough savings for NBM that it decides to take advantage of the offer and informs Pacific of its decision to change suppliers.[9] Of course you (Pacific) are interested in retaining the business and offer to meet the UniMem price of $32 per unit. (See Exhibit 4–5.)

Wait a minute. Is this fair (or legal)? What about the Pacific price of $38 to PaloAlto? Doesn't this lower price to NBM give it an advantage over PaloAlto in their competitive battles?

In fact, pricing regulations allow a defending supplier (the one with the business—in this case, Pacific) to match the price of a competitor attempting to take away the business. Pacific Drives is not *required* to lower its price to any other customers. (In fact, an across-the-board price reduction on the part of Pacific could be interpreted as a **predatory pricing** move.)[10]

---

[9] The method and timing of notification to change suppliers can be indicative of the quality of the relationship between the supplier and the customer. Many businesses will not easily change suppliers unless there is a substantial incentive, particularly when everything is going well.

[10] The most serious marketing considerations here are not price. While pricing to different customers is considered confidential and customers theoretically do not tell each other what they are paying for components, Pacific Drives should be concerned about PaloAlto finding out that NBM is getting a better deal. Aside from the embarrassment at NBM (it could look like Pacific is overcharging them), it is likely that UniMem will approach PaloAlto with its Model UniMem300, using the business at NBM as supporting evidence of the quality and value of their offering.

Marketing professionals at Pacific should be asking themselves how UniMem could surprise them in the marketplace like this. Pacific's knowledge of its competitors and the dynamics of the market seem to be wanting. As we discuss in Chapter 10, price is a very dynamic part of the marketing mix. Pacific needs to be aware of product life cycles and the leading edge of technologies that could impact demand and price for their product.

EXHIBIT 4–5   United Memories' Aggressive Price at NBM Computers

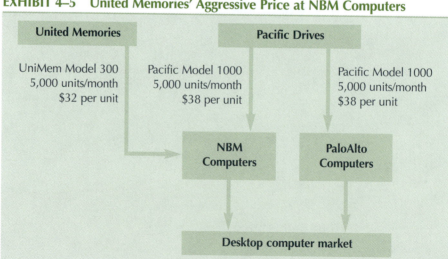

So far, our discussion has been relatively easy to follow within the guidelines of the Robinson-Patman Act. We now consider a situation in which price discrimination can occur notwithstanding adherence to the guidelines:

> **Predatory pricing** occurs when a firm with a dominant position in a market, threatened by a new or smaller firm, changes its pricing structure such that the new firm cannot operate profitably.

The desktop computer market is attractive to the entrepreneurial spirit and is a relatively easy market to enter. A small start-up company, Spartan Computers, contacts Pacific about supplying its hard drive needs. Spartan will manufacture desktop computers locally. Among its competitors will be PaloAlto and NBM. Spartan anticipates its volume will be approximately 500 units per month, but it will experience "significant growth" and would like Pacific to consider this in its offer. Of course, Spartan has also asked UniMem to quote the business. The Pacific response to the Spartan request for quote is $55 per unit, the standard "list" price for the anticipated volume of 500 units per month. Competitive information and the historic reaction patterns of UniMem convince Pacific marketers that this is what UniMem is likely to quote. Since discounts for large-quantity purchases are legal, Pacific does not anticipate any conflicts with its lower unit prices for higher volumes at NBM and PaloAlto. The addition of Spartan as a potential customer is shown in Exhibit 4–6.

It is not unusual for start-up companies to attract the employees of their larger competitors, and this has happened at Spartan. It does not take long for Spartan to realize that the Pacific offer of $55 per unit is significantly higher than the price to its larger competitors. Spartan's concern, beyond its cost of the hard drive, is that higher component prices in general will make it difficult, if not impossible, to compete in the market with NBM and PaloAlto. Spartan asks Pacific to reconsider the offer, notwithstanding the established list prices.

Pacific's initial reaction to Spartan is to stand by the standard prices. However, Spartan has pointed out that these prices will make it difficult for its products to compete in the market and that could be interpreted as a restraint of trade. It may be time for Pacific to re-examine discount policies for quantity purchases.

EXHIBIT 4–6 Spartan Computers Enters the Markets

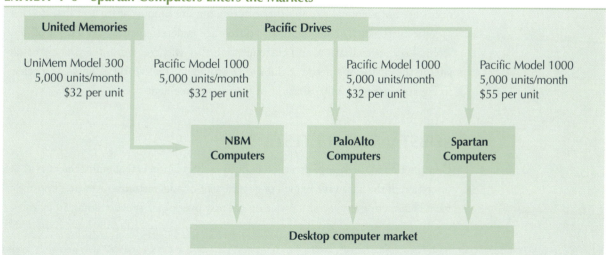

United Memories	Pacific Drives		
UniMem Model 300 5,000 units/month $32 per unit	Pacific Model 1000 5,000 units/month $32 per unit	Pacific Model 1000 5,000 units/month $32 per unit	Pacific Model 1000 5,000 units/month $55 per unit
	NBM Computers	PaloAlto Computers	Spartan Computers

Desktop computer market

Quantity Discounts

Quantity discounts for volume purchases are normal business practice and entirely legal, provided the discounts are cost justified. In other words, lower costs to serve high-volume customers may be passed on to the customer.[11] However, artificially low volume discounts can be (they are not always but can be) interpreted as discriminatory if they substantially impact the ability to compete in the customer's marketplace. Thus, Spartan is justified in asking for a lower price *if* Pacific quantity-scaled discounts cannot be justified by its cost to serve at those volumes.

In the foregoing examples, what happens if a purchasing agent from NBM told Pacific that NBM had an offer of a lower price than Pacific's current price and asked Pacific to match the competitive offer but the competitive offer does not really exist? Well, the Robinson-Patman Act also makes it illegal for the purchasing organization to knowingly create a discriminatory pricing situation. Generally, any action that will create an imbalance in the marketplace or restrict competitors from equal access to the market can invite regulatory oversight.

Let's summarize the major tenets of price discrimination regulation:

Offerings sold

for different uses,

to separate markets,

at different times,

that are not identical,

to government agencies, or

at prices to meet a competitive threat,

are generally not a violation of price regulations.

While this scenario is simplified and exaggerated, it nonetheless depicts real possibilities. Good marketing programs avoid possible regulatory problems. This summary provides some insight into how this is done. Most notably, offerings that are the result of a collaboration between customer and supplier, created through the process of partnering, or the result of customization for a particular customer's needs are not identical to any other offering but are unique, at least at first, to that specific customer. The degree of this difference is determined by the extent of new technology, specialization, and customization that was created in the process of satisfying the customer's needs. Exhibit 4-7 provides a real-world example of a price-fixing conspiracy and Department of Justice enforcement.

SUBSTANTIALITY TEST

Contributing to the lack of precision in business regulation is that enforcement is at the discretion of the executive branch of government or administrative agencies. Enforcement is discretionary, just as a police officer may overlook a speeder doing 50 in a

---

[11]Chapter 10 discusses the importance of different costing methods. A thorough understanding of costs related to different channels, volumes, and customers is essential as a good justification for pricing decisions.

EXHIBIT 4–7 The International Graphite Electrode Price-Fixing Conspiracy

On January 19, 2000, Mitsubishi Corporation, a distributor of graphite electrodes, and a former executive of UCAR International (a 50 percent owned joint venture of Mitsubishi during the period 1991 to 1995 and the world's largest manufacturer of graphite electrodes) were indicted in an international graphite electrode price-fixing conspiracy. Shortly thereafter, on March 13, 2000, the President and Chief Executive Officer of Carbone of America Industries Corporation and the corporation pleaded guilty and agreed to pay more than $7 million in fines for participating in an international cartel to fix the price of isostatic graphite.

Graphite electrodes, made of fine grain carbon with great strength and chemical resistance, are largely known as isostatic graphite and are used in, among other things, electric arc furnaces in steel-making mini mills, the fastest growing method of making steel in the United States. The electrodes generate the heat necessary to melt and refine steel. The total sales of graphite electrodes during a four-year period in the early 1990s were more than $1.7 billion. Steel makers, as a result of the conspiracy, paid higher noncompetitive prices for the electrodes used in steel manufacturing.

As of March 2000, several corporations *and individuals* had been charged and criminal fines assessed as a result of the Justice Department's Investigation. In the two years leading up to these actions, the following companies and individuals pled guilty to participating in the conspiracy:

- UCAR sentenced to pay a $110 million fine;
- UCAR's former CEO sentenced to serve seventeen months in jail and assessed a $1.25 million fine;
- UCAR's former COO, through a plea agreement, agreed to serve nine months in jail and pay a $1 million fine;
- SGL Carbon AG (a German corporation) sentenced to pay a $135 million fine;
- SGL's CEO sentenced to pay a $10 million fine (to this date, the largest ever antitrust fine imposed on an individual);
- Showa Denko Carbon, Inc., (U.S. subsidiary of a Japanese firm) sentenced to pay a $32.5 million fine;
- Tokai Carbon Co., Ltd., (a Japanese corporation) sentenced to pay a $6 million fine;
- SEC Corporation (a Japanese corporation) sentenced to pay a $4.8 million fine;
- Nippon Carbon Co., Ltd., (a Japanese corporation) sentenced to pay a $2.5 million fine.

Other participants in the conspiracy were accepted into the Justice Department's Corporate Leniency Program.

In the matter of Carbone of America Industries Corporation, the guilty pleas were to charges that the company and its executive participated in meetings and conversations with cartel members to discuss prices, agreed to certain price scenarios, agreed to market share maintenance, and participated in several other anticompetitive actions.

At first, antitrust enforcement against makers of carbon electrodes used in steel manufacture may seem far removed from the consumer markets where business regulation aims to maximize choice and keep a level playing field. Steel, however, is an essential material in many consumer goods, medical devices, appliances, transportation, and construction, impacting practically every element of business and consumer consumption. As you read the list of enforcement actions, note the penalties levied against individuals who took part in the conspiracies. Review also the "Substantiality Test" as described in this chapter.

Source: U.S. Department of Justice, press releases for January 19, 2000, "Mitsubishi Corporation and Former UCAR Executive Indicted in International Graphite Electrode Price-Fixing Conspiracy", and March 13, 2000, "New Jersey Company and Chief Executive Officer Agree to Plead Guilty to International Price-Fixing Conspiracy", available from http://www.usdoj.gov/atr

45 mph zone but will ticket a vehicle traveling at 60 mph in the same zone. Agencies responsible for enforcing business legislation prefer to prosecute infractions with a high likelihood of successful prosecution and conviction. With limited resources available for investigation and prosecution, violations are often subject to a *substantiality test* to determine the extent of the discriminatory practice. The substantiality test, arising out of a court decision regarding exclusive dealing, serves as an excellent tool for the marketer to judge the intensity of a situation. Three considerations make up this test:

1. *The size of the organizations involved ("size" may be sales volume, financial resources, market power, etc.).* Is a large company attempting to coerce the behavior or business practices of a smaller company?

2. *The volume of business involved.* Is the dollar amount large relative to the size of the market? Does the offending company have a significant share of the market?
3. *Market preemption.* Does the questionable business practice or arrangement prevent competitive products from access to a substantial portion of the market?

COMPANY SIZE

Business practices that are overlooked by regulators as not substantial when the company is small may receive much greater attention as the company grows and develops leverage in the marketplace. As this text was written, a federal appeals court upheld Judge Thomas Penfield Jackson's ruling that Microsoft violated U.S. antitrust laws but sent back to the district court the proposed remedy to split up Microsoft, directing the lower court to develop an alternative. Whether Microsoft and the Justice Department will reach a settlement or continue in court is not yet known, though Microsoft has not demonstrated any changes in marketing strategy as a result of the ruling. It is unlikely that Microsoft started out to violate any antitrust legislation. Microsoft business practices that may have been acceptable or at least overlooked when they were small became questionable as the company and its market strength grew. (Review the three considerations of the substantiality test. Do you think Microsoft substantially violated any part of antitrust or pricing regulations?) Market domination attracts scrutiny. Organizations must recognize the risks associated with business practices that will attract attention, be regarded as predatory, or construed as limiting competition or choice in the marketplace. Marketers can avoid confrontations by providing fair customer value and developing offerings and strategies that avoid scrutiny.

INTELLECTUAL PROPERTY

Intellectual property law provides creators/owners of intellectual property the right to benefit from its creation, use, and dissemination. Intellectual property is

Participation Exercise

By the time this book reaches your classroom, there may be significant progress toward resolution of the Microsoft antitrust case. Because of the many issues involved in the case and the number of stakeholders that may have "spun" the outcome, you may need several sources of information to make an informed judgment. Select at least three information sources that will likely report on this case from different viewpoints, such as *The New York Times, The Wall Street Journal,* and a trade publication in the software industry. Do the different information sources cast the outcome differently? It is likely that you will see a different emphasis from each source. After assimilating the information, with your understanding of antitrust legislation and its intent, how do you view the outcome?

regarded, for legal purposes, as essentially comparable to any other form of property. We focus on issues related to intellectual property in technology transfer and innovation, such as **patents, copyrights,** and **trade secrets.** This distinction removes trademarks, usually considered as symbols of identity and goodwill, from consideration. From an antitrust enforcement view, trademarks are considered product or organization differentiating devices and are treated differently, though many of the same legal principles apply.[11,12]

Patents are protection or ownership rights granted by the U.S. government to inventors for their original products, processes, or composition of matter. The patent owner may exclude the use, sales, or manufacture of the invention for a period that depends on the type of patent. Functional patents that cover machines, processes, and devices have a protection period of twenty years. This time period was lengthened from seventeen years in 1995 in an effort to harmonize U.S. patent law with other nations. Design patents, applying to the features of a product, are granted protection periods of fourteen years. Patent owners may sell, license, or trade patents just as they would any tangible property.[13]

Copyrights apply to original works of, among others, authors, musicians, and photographers. Copyrights protect the expression of ideas, not the underlying ideas themselves. Copyrights are granted to individuals for their lifetime plus fifty years and apply to work automatically since 1989. Signing nations of the Berne Convention also recognize international status for U.S. copyrights.[14] While registration of original works is not necessary, it is always recommended, particularly if ownership is intended to produce income. Like patent owners, copyright owners may sell, license, or grant permission for use of the copyrighted material.

Trade secrets are unusual in that their value is dependent on their secrecy. A trade secret is a process, technique, or competitive advantage whose owner has chosen not to seek additional legal protection, either in an effort to maintain the secret by avoiding disclosure or because the secret does not meet legal tests for originality. Protection has no definite term and is conditioned on efforts to keep the secret a secret. Trade secrets are an unusual category. By their very nature, owners are not able to license, sell, or trade them with the same degree of protection as patents and copyrights. Notwithstanding this, however, trade secrets can be the subject of use agreements between organizations.

---

[11]Readers interested in a broader discussion of trademark law, particularly as it relates to the Internet, are encouraged to reference Gerald Ferrera et al., *CyberLaw, Text and Cases* (Cincinnati: West/Thompson Learning, 2001).

[12]U.S. Department of Justice and the Federal Trade Commission, Antitrust Guidelines for the Licensing of Intellectual Property, issued April 6, 1995.

[13]Jennings, op. cit., 489.

[14]Ibid., 490.

Antitrust Implications of Intellectual Property

At first glance, intellectual property laws, which grant rights of exclusive use, and antitrust laws, which are aimed at maintaining an open market, may seem to be in total opposition to each other. This is, however, not the case. Intellectual property protection aims to protect creators and inventors of novel and useful inventions from copying, bootlegging, plagiarism, and other forms of theft. Without such protection, there would be significantly less incentive to innovate as the market value of intellectual property would be significantly reduced. Innovation is a primary motivator in competition and market growth. Businesses spend millions of dollars on research and development programs to create a competitive advantage.

Intellectual property is but one tool in the creation of an offering for the customer. Just as the use of other tools (e.g., production, distribution, market dominance) may or may not be in compliance with business legislation, intellectual property can be used or abused in the marketplace. In business-to-business markets, competitors often **license** or **cross license** each other's intellectual property. Businesses do this because they recognize that the target market(s) for a particular offering will adopt a new product, feature, or technology faster if both organizations are participating in its market development. (The relationship between innovation and competition is discussed in Chapter 9.)

Just as would occur with any restraint of trade, antitrust concerns arise when the leverage provided by the intellectual properties is used to limit access to or competition in the market. For example, firms may not use cross licensing to prevent new competitors from entering a market, to divide the existing market between themselves, or to create tying agreements to move unwanted merchandise.

A **license** is permission to use an asset as one's own without any right of ownership, granted by the owner of the asset. Licenses can be for specific time periods, regions, or countries. All forms of intellectual property may be licensed.

Cross licensing occurs when two businesses each have patents or other intellectual property that is of value to the other. The cross license may be structured to allow both firms a greater advantage in the same market, or the agreement may be related to separate markets. At times, firms will establish a jointly owned third firm to operate in a particular market with licenses of both firms' properties.

POLITICAL FRAMEWORK OF ENFORCEMENT

Marketing professionals cannot ignore the politics of business regulation. Different viewpoints and philosophies are represented by different administrations in our government. Though some recent examples have blurred the generalization, historically, the political affiliation of an administration in power has been an indicator of the aggressiveness of regulatory enforcement. Regardless of political affiliation or beliefs about regulation versus the free market, there have been times when government intervention was appropriate as well as times when intervention was either insufficient or overzealous. Even within an administration, legal opinions vary as to the nature and extent of particular violations and even as to whether the government should play a role in controlling the marketplace. The marketer should recognize that different views of the markets as well as historical precedent can impact the marketing environment.

U.S. Department of Justice

This thorough but legalistic Web site (http://www.usdoj.gov) contains many reviews of the intricacies of U.S. Code and case examples.

PACIFIC DRIVES REVISITED

Recall the opening of this chapter and the difficulties Pacific Drives was having getting its offering to its customers. With consideration for the legal factors we have discussed, what do you now think of this situation? Should the obstacles faced by Pacific Drives be considered aggressive competition or illegal activities? Would your opinion change if you were the marketing manager for Pacific Drives? In the opening situation, what recourse does Pacific Drives have?

Well, if you were the marketing manager for Pacific Drives, you might first discuss the situation with your firm's attorneys. Your next step might be to contact the organizations (possibly with your attorney—avoid the appearance of collusion!) that you believe are engaged in illegal activities impacting Pacific Drives and see if a negotiated resolution is possible. Certainly all parties will have an incentive to avoid litigation. If that strategy is not successful, you have the option of civil litigation. Who knows? You may not be the only victim of DynaDrive and Spin Technologies. You might even find that the Justice Department or the FTC takes up your cause.

As with most any illegal activity, ignorance of the law is not an adequate defense. Marketing managers cannot successfully plead a lack of understanding should their organization become the target of an antitrust or price discrimination investigation. Unfortunately, without a sufficient understanding of the "ins and outs" of business laws, managers may, when operating in a small organization or market that is not likely to draw attention, establish practices that become habit or increase in intensity as the organization or market grows. Certain business practices may seem like "just aggressive competition" or "finding an edge." If they infringe on any of the three areas described in the beginning of this chapter—protecting companies from each other, protecting consumers, and protecting the interests of society—*and* meet the substantiality test, they are likely to draw enforcement attention.

Successful market-driven strategy can help avoid many legal entanglements. As you progress to Chapter 5 and your understanding of business-to-business marketing continues to grow, we hope you will see that one of the best ways to avoid difficult legal situations is an ethical, market-driven approach from the start. In later chapters, pricing, channels, and personal selling are discussed. These activities are particularly vulnerable to the imprecise nature of the legal environment. Understanding the legal issues discussed in this chapter will greatly assist in the development and practice of market programs that provide long-term value to your customers.

Key Terms

common law	free rider	price discrimination
consent decree	intercorporate	price maintenance
copyrights	stockholding	refusal to deal
cross license	interlocking directorates	resale restrictions
equality/proportionately	license	trade secrets
equal terms	patents	treble damages
exclusive dealing	predatory pricing	tying contracts

Questions for Review and Discussion

1. How can intercorporate stockholding exist without raising FTC or Justice Department concerns?

2. What market factors must be present under Robinson-Patman to require a supplier to offer the same product to two (or more) different customers?

3. What market factors must be present for a manufacturer to legally refuse to continue to offer its products through a particular channel (what are the circumstances when a "free rider" condition can exist)?

4. Describe the practical importance of good market intelligence in addressing potential competitive pricing situations under the Robinson-Patman Act.

5. When a marketing manager questions whether an action may or may not be interpreted as a violation of a competitive legislative act, what consumer-level factors can ultimately be used as guidelines?

6. What extenuating circumstances must usually be present for a business practice to be scrutinized by the Justice Department? What limits the Justice Department from investigating all potential violations?

7. When there is significant disparity in size of competitors seeking the same customers, how do Clayton and Robinson-Patman fail to maintain the fabled "level playing field"?

8. How can continuous innovation and close partnerships with customers reduce the likelihood that market managers will be concerned with price discrimination issues?

9. Rather than the "letter" of the law as related to specific acts and legislation, understanding business regulation has often been described as understanding the intent of the law and the temperament of the enforcers. Explain.

10. How are the myriad of state and federal legislative acts and commissions consistent with a free market philosophy?

Internet Exercises

Go to R. M. Steuer's summaries of antitrust law: **http://profs.lp.findlaw.com/antitrust/index.html** Also see a review of Antitrust Policy: **http://www.antitrust.org** Review interpretations of the Robinson-Patman Act found at these sites. How often do you find what seem to be inconsistencies? What factors change to make what appears inconsistent fit with the intent of the law?

Go to the Covisint Web site: **http://www.covisint.com** Review the site to obtain a basic understanding of the partnership structure. Find articles on the antitrust concerns associated with Covisint using a search engine of your choice. What are the key problems that founders of electronic marketplaces have to solve to avoid antitrust concerns?

Using a search engine of your choosing, look for articles on the merger between AOL and Time Warner. A principal reason for the merger was the synergies that can be gained in marketing their services to businesses. Given your introduction to the legal limits on mergers and collusion, what do you think are reasons for a merger rather than a co-marketing partnership?

5

Concepts and Context of Business Strategy

overview. . . This chapter presents introductory material on the nature of strategy and strategic planning. While corporate executives are usually responsible for creating corporate and business unit strategies, marketers at many levels are called upon to contribute to the planning process. Accord-

© KEITH BROFSKY/PHOTODISC

ingly, this chapter presents material to help the marketing student think strategically and make a substantial contribution to the process.

The opening example is a presentation of strategy management concepts and processes at work in an organization. Corporate strategy chooses the businesses to be in and the performance levels that will be achieved. Analytic tools are presented in the chapter to aid in determining which businesses should be pursued. Business unit strategy concerns a translation of corporate goals into business unit goals and objectives. It also includes the configuration of the functions of the business to achieve the business unit's goals and objectives.

This chapter concludes with a discussion of the strategy management process. This process can be used, with minor modifications, at any level of the organization. Understanding the basic process, as well as its limitations, will help the student who enters a career in business-to-business marketing take an effective approach whenever the need arises.

The opening example shows how Siemens ties together internal operations and choice of external markets to boost its performance.

SIEMENS CHANGES ITS STRATEGY*

In 1998, Siemens of Germany faced a growing crisis. The company was making progress in making productivity improvements in most of its lines of business. However, it seemed that all its efforts were working well but were simply five years too late. The problems Siemens addressed—those of quality and costs—were the problems of the late 1980s and early 1990s. Meanwhile, its competitors, such as GE, Cisco, and Nokia, were adapting products and marketing efforts to adjust to new and changing markets. Net income at Siemens was slim and falling. Not surprisingly, Siemens' stock price was headed in the same direction.

CEO Heinrich von Pierer created a ten-point plan to revamp Siemens. The plan placed emphasis on growing areas of business, such as telecommunications and automotive electronics. Acquisitions were made to bolster these areas. Existing businesses such as medical engineering and semiconductors received attention to increase innovation and customer focus while improving operating efficiency. Nonperforming business lines were sold off. Organizational structure and working relationships were reshaped. Management positions were trimmed, and top executive positions were filled by key hires.

CEO von Pierer produced encouraging results. Profits and share prices are up. Morale among employees has improved greatly. Technology development has taken on a customer focus as marketing people and engineers collaborate in the design of new products.

Because a principal thrust of the new strategy is a focus on telecommunications, Siemens still faces stiff challenges. Technology changes rapidly in this industry, and the competitors are among the toughest in the world. It remains to be seen whether Siemens can keep up.

*Based on Jack Ewing, "Siemens Climbs Back," Business Week, 5 June 2000, 79–82.

- ◆ Understand the value of strategy and its role in a complex organization.

- ◆ Understand the planning process for defining and executing business strategy.

- ◆ Relate mission, goals, and objectives of an organization to the process of developing strategy.

- ◆ Develop an understanding of how an entrepreneurial approach to marketing is not limited to small, start-up organizations.

- ◆ Be able to identify ways in which a marketing organization can be made more entrepreneurially oriented.

- ◆ Know how corporate strategy differs from business unit strategy and how, in turn, both differ from marketing strategy.

- ◆ Have a sense of how strategies using today's strategy concepts differ from strategies using the concepts of prior periods.

- ◆ Be able to demonstrate an understanding of different strategy tools (growth-share and business-attractiveness matrices and balanced scorecards).

- ◆ Recognize what it means to create a strategy that "changes the rules" for a market or for an industry.

Goals are usually the first quantification of a business mission statement. Goals are a general statement of desirable outcomes, directly supportive of and aligned with the mission.

introduction. . .

The Siemens example illustrates how a change in strategy, well executed, can change the fortunes of a company. As you read this chapter, ask yourself what Siemens is doing that is consistent with the strategy concepts described in the chapter. Also, ask yourself what they are doing that is not consistent with these concepts. When they are inconsistent with the concepts discussed, what special risks are created for Siemens?

Strategy is important for three reasons. First, business marketers must live with the company strategy that has been defined by executive management. This strategy generally defines the marketer's direction, that is, the parameters the marketer has to live within on a day-to-day basis. Daily efforts by all members of the organization must be consistent with the **mission**, **goals**, **objectives**, and **strategies** of the firm. Knowing what strategies do and how they work will make the business marketing manager's decision making more informed and more closely tied to the intent of the company's strategy.

Second, higher-level management is likely to ask the marketer to participate in the creation of corporate and business unit strategy. To be effective, the business marketer should have a sense of the nature of strategy and strategy making at the company level.

Third, the marketer has to create and implement his own marketing strategy to serve the company strategy. Strategy at the functional or program level is somewhat different than company-level strategy. The marketer must understand what is needed, in terms of both concepts and tools, to accomplish this. This chapter concerns the "what, why, and how" of corporate or business unit strategy. The three chapters that follow produce the "what and how" of marketing strategy.

In addition to the concepts of strategy, this chapter examines how strategies are created and managed. Too often, popularized strategy methods overlook useful ideas and tools because they are not "fashionable." In this chapter, some useful ideas and tools are provided that, while updated, have their roots in the past and, when fully understood, are as useful today as when they were the "in" tools.

WHAT IS STRATEGY?

Strategy is, literally, the "art of the general." Strategic thinking has been around in military matters for thousands of years. While business strategy has been around for centuries, at least, business people and academics have only recently focused on "strategy" as something a businessperson does or a scholar studies. At its most basic, strategy is the determination of goals or objectives and the general means for reaching them.

Business strategy usually is comprised of "targets" for business performance metrics, coupled with a set of actions chosen to achieve those objectives. The objectives generally include target levels for profitability, sales, growth, and perhaps other measures important to the firm. The firm's business strategy also includes a determination of what businesses or markets to address, what kinds of products or services to offer in these markets, what kinds of actions need to be performed to obtain paying customers, and what resources need to be deployed to accomplish these actions.

The **mission** of an organization is the contextual definition of who the organization is and what it expects to accomplish. Usually a qualitative description, it is further defined by goals and objectives. A good mission statement should be useful to all members of the organization as a guide to proper decision making and direction.

Objectives are specific, measurable expressions of the stated goals, with specific targets and time periods.

Key Strategy Concepts

Executives and scholars have developed philosophies of how strategy should be formulated. They have also paid close attention to the practical side of strategy, documenting what works and what does not. Philosophies and approaches have evolved over time, and a great deal of what has been developed in the past still has relevance for today's markets and industries. Key ideas that have survived the tests of time to form the basis for traditional strategic management are:

1. Business strategy designers should seek to establish a **fit** between the business environment and the strategy.
2. The key element of *fit* in business strategy revolves around providing superior value for customers.
3. Superior value means that the offering of a company must be differentiated from the offerings of competitors in the minds of the targeted customers.
4. Differentiation is produced by using core competencies to advantage; the more distinct a company's core competencies, the higher the customer value that can be achieved and the better the profit margins that can be produced.
5. Quality and process improvement are fundamental to providing superior value.
6. Measuring results and tracking results create learning and set the stage for later improvements.

Fit between the business strategy and the business environment means that the organization pursues purposes and takes actions that are consistent with the needs, perceptions, and behaviors of the other actors within the environment.

Recent Trends

New ideas arose in the 1990s as well.[1] Strategy itself became focused on driving change rather than on adapting to it. Hamel and Prahalad[2] espouse the idea of changing the rules, both internally within a company and externally within the industry. The company identifies its **core competencies** that give it **differentiation.** It builds a vision of how the industry will change over the next two to five years. Then it builds a vision of how the company can influence change to create a favorable situation for itself. Core competencies to drive that change and differentiate its offering in the future are identified, and methods for building those competencies are laid out. Learning objectives, opportunities, and methods are also spelled out and implemented. This proactive approach is somewhat different from the traditional model of adapting to change.

> **Core competencies** are a company's skills, capabilities, and knowledge assets that are necessary to compete in its markets. They may be competencies that the company currently has or ones that it will need to obtain.
>
> **Differentiation,** as discussed in Chapter 1, is something that a company does better than its competitors. To be differentiation, it must be something that provides superior value to customers.

More recently, the concurrent trends of rapid technological change and the growth of the Internet have spurred more rethinking of the nature of strategy and strategic planning. Quick communication, rapid creation of new ventures, and rapid technical and business model innovation produce a highly turbulent environment, even within once-mature industries such as chemicals and metals.

With the tools of competition under rapid revision, strategists have sought to find ways to shape the rules and to prepare for radically reconfigured futures. It is in this framework that we find the concept of **market ownership**, (see box on page 120), proactively changing the market landscape, coming to fruition.

Some new views of competitive dynamics have emerged that form the basis for a great deal of this thinking about strategy. The notion of "co-opetition"[3] says that companies operate in a business ecosystem, where their efforts involve cooperation as well as competition. Partnerships and alliances form to create combination offerings; the combinations may be driven by customers seeking to obtain whole products that no one company has produced or even coordinated. Value creation occurs through the kinds of value networks described in Chapter 2. These new observations on the nature of strategy can be summed up as follows:

♦   Change in customers, channels, and competitors interact to create discontinuities in the evolution of industries or markets; these are somewhat predictable, with a high level of imprecision.

♦   While companies can have an influence on *how* markets change, they can seldom appreciably impact the *pace* of change.

---

[1] John A. Byrne, "Strategic Planning," *Business Week,* 26 August 1996, 46–52.
[2] Gary Hamel and C. K. Prahalad, *Competing for the Future* (Boston: Harvard Business School Press, 1994).
[3] Adam M. Brandenburger and Barry J. Nalebuff, *Co-opetition* (New York: Currency Doubleday, 1996).

♦ Companies need to look for ways to "change the rules" of the markets they compete in; this means proactively creating conditions for success that favor their own **business model** instead of those of the competitors.

♦ Such changes in the rules are still subject to the constraints of the business environment; constraints may have some flexibility, and this flexibility must be recognized.

♦ Strategists need to identify the core competencies that will translate into advantages in the future when the rules have changed.

♦ Advantages are not sustainable for long, so the company must continue to innovate, changing the rules on an ongoing basis, to stay ahead of the competition.[4] (See box on page 120 for a definition of market ownership.)

> A **business model** is a configuration of the elements of a business, how they work together, and how they produce profits.

A combination of strategy principles, both the old and the new, provide guidance and context to today's marketing managers who must help create and manage company strategies. As is presented later in this chapter, much of the world is uncertain and much of strategy making is creative; hence, a company should create processes and structures that manage uncertainties and creativity.

THE HIERARCHY OF BUSINESS STRATEGY

To help understand the nature of strategy that a business-to-business marketing manager contributes to or works within, one must recognize that strategy is largely hierarchical. Exhibit 5–1 is a representation of this. We can think of strategy as the general means to achieve a general purpose. The ploy in defining strategy is to define what *general* means. In practice, we have found that you get into a great deal of semantic hopscotch if you do not think situationally.

The distinction between strategy and tactics depends upon one's perspective or point of view. If you are the CEO, corporate goals, corporate objectives, and the means to achieve them define strategy. Everything else is "just" tactics. If you are a customer service specialist providing assistance on a twenty-four-hour toll-free line, your strategy will be designed to support customer service metrics that have been defined by your business unit.

Strategic Resource Allocation

Yesterday's world of corporate strategy stopped with a determination of which businesses to pursue and how resources would be allocated across them. Today's conception of corporate business strategy goes beyond this, as we have already discussed. In

---

[4]Peter Dickson, "Toward a General Theory of Competitive Rationality," *Journal of Marketing* 56, no. 1 (January 1992): 69–83.

EXHIBIT 5–1   Hierarchy of Strategy

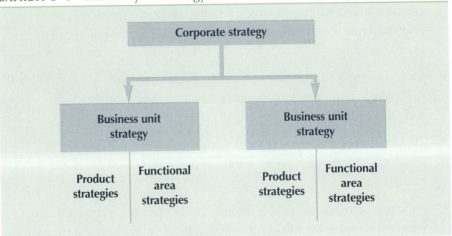

today's corporate strategy, the strategists still choose businesses or markets to pursue and allocate resources to them. However, strategists are also concerned with choosing a future vision to pursue (the question of which businesses to pursue is answered as part of this). This requires an anticipation of future core competencies, some of which the company must develop or acquire. So corporate strategy now includes a plan to develop a set of core competencies from where the competencies are today to the set needed in the period five to ten years hence. Development of these core competencies cannot happen overnight. Accordingly, a successful corporate strategy must include a development path to create these core competencies. Within this corporate strategy must be elements of organizational motivation. Resources need to be allocated to creation of the required personal skills and to rewarding their application in appropriate ways. All of this is structured to address the organization's "strategic intent."[5] This is the vision of the future, the goals to be reached to realize this future, and the measures to be met so that the organization can tell if that future is indeed at hand. All in all, this is a much more workable version of corporate strategy than was created under the "old" way of doing things.

Strategic Business Units

Determination of *corporate* strategy creates the "strategic architecture" that will guide the organization over the next five to ten years. Business unit strategy is strategy at the next level down in the hierarchy and is guided by the corporate strategic architecture. These **strategic business units** (SBUs) are the organizational entities within a corporation that address a single (usually) business. From

A **strategic business unit** (SBU) is a business, department, organization, or possibly even a product line within the larger organization that has separate goals and objectives. These business units must be capable of being planned and measured separately from the rest of the organization. Note that separate planning and measurement do not mean complete independence from the larger organization or other SBUs within the larger organization.

[5]Hamel and Prahalad, op. cit.

the point of view of the business unit—perhaps run by a general manager—strategy is the determination of what goals and objectives the SBU must meet, what markets to address, and generally how to address them.

Ideally, the SBU will have established an ongoing strategy management process that assures alignment with corporate mission, objectives, and budget. The business unit must trade off rigor for speed, especially if the corporate process has taken half a year or more. However, if organizations adapt the strategy creation viewpoint suggested by Hamel and Prahalad and others, business units will most likely go through some gut-wrenching trauma. If this is done well, though, then annual updates will not be so traumatic.

Usually within an SBU there is a marketing function. From the point of view of the marketing function, strategy is the choice of market segments to address and positioning of the SBU's offering (e.g., product lines) for these market segments (we discuss segments and positioning in Chapter 7). Marketing strategy must operate in concert with strategy at the product line or product level. The management of the SBU defines, in general, the kinds of customers that will be targeted and how the SBU will compete for their business. The product marketer (or service marketer) determines in more detail what different groups of customers exist and then chooses the specific target segments. The customers within a target segment exist at a pre-strategy state of mind (unaware, awareness, liking for the product, intention to buy). The strategy is the combination of a desired state of mind for the segment inhabitants and the design of the offering that will get them there. There are layers below this. Within the product strategy, there is also a product development strategy, a channel strategy, a partnership strategy, a communications and sales strategy, and a pricing strategy. All of these strategies must be made to be consistent—knitted together to form a cohesive plan that supports the SBU and, ultimately, the firm's mission, goals, and objectives.

TOOLS FOR DESIGNING STRATEGY

The prior discussion should give the future business marketing manager some idea of what will be asked of him concerning strategy and strategy development. The question then arises regarding what tools are available for strategy planners to use. In the next section, we discuss two tools that are fairly old but still have relevance for gaining insight to aid in the development of strategy. One, the growth-share matrix, may have its most relevance as a tool for students to understand some of what business strategists attempt to do with corporate strategy. The other, the multifactor matrix or attractiveness-strength matrix, has relevance when it is updated to reflect the strategy ideas of Hamel and Prahalad.

The Growth-Share Matrix

Exhibit 5–2 shows the **growth-share matrix,** which was developed by the Boston Consulting Group some thirty years ago. Students may recognize this

EXHIBIT 5–2   Growth-Share Matrix

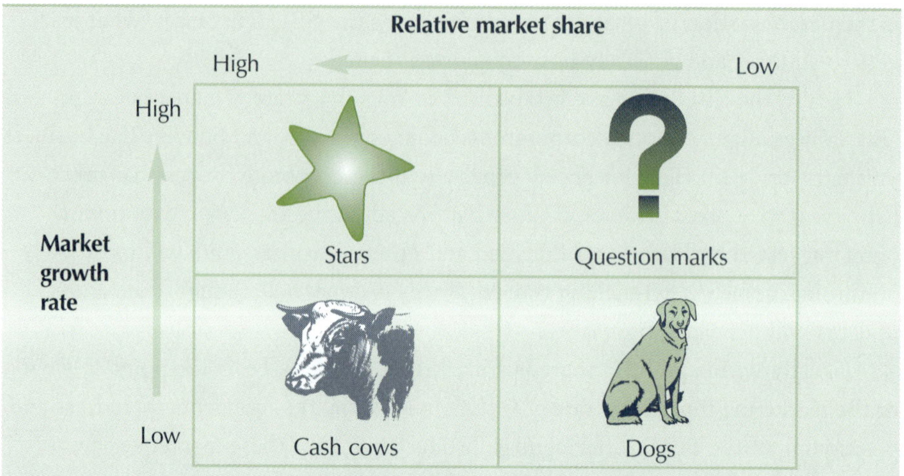

Reprinted from *Long Range Planning,* Volume 10, Barry D. Hedley, "Strategy and the 'Business Portfolio,'" 10, Copyright 1977, with permission from Elsevier Science.

A **business portfolio** is a collection of strategic business units that serve various needs in the corporate structure. An ongoing firm will need (1) sources of cash to fund investment in growing markets and (2) new possibilities emerging from research and development that may be valuable business opportunities in the future. This balance should be consistent with the culture of the organization. This is not unlike the combination of investments individuals have in their personal portfolios—resources that are consistent with the goals and culture of the individual.

resource allocation tool and its categorizations of SBUs as stars, cash cows, dogs, and question marks. This tool is probably best used to illustrate one of the purposes of corporate strategy, the construction of **business portfolios** to create a company that will evolve and remain profitable over time. The idea underlying the growth-share matrix is that organizations seek to develop and nourish those business opportunities with the greatest potential for growth; maintain those that are self-sustaining producers of resources; and "harvest"—exit, while reaping as much benefit as possible—those that are no longer able to function productively within the organization—not unlike an individual seeking the greatest return from his personal investment portfolio.

The basic idea is to identify those businesses (or products, if used at a lower level of abstraction) that generate resources for the parent organization (cash cows); those that need resources from the parent organization to keep pace with a fast-growing market—and because they can provide substantial returns in the future (stars); and those that may have reached the end of their run as significant contributors to the corporation (they may need cash, but that may never generate much in the future, i.e., they may experience substantial losses). Without a thorough understanding of the tool and its nuances, the complexities of today's business environment will not be well reflected in its use. However, we believe the matrix provides a useful starting point to discuss and illustrate corporate strategy issues. This discussion also sets up a nice transition to the attractiveness-strength matrix, which can be more useful in light of today's strategy concepts.

The definitions of the four elements of the matrix follow. Note the addition of the analogy to the product life cycle (PLC). Just as an offering can move through the stages of the PLC, a business unit will often evolve from question mark to star, star to cash cow, and cash cow perhaps to dog, counterclockwise around the grid:

- *Stars.* High growth markets and large market share. The organization must invest heavily to maintain position in the growing market. A star could likely be a business unit with a prominent position in a product/market that is in the growth stage of the product life cycle. Stars should be managed with market ownership as an objective.

- *Cash cows.* Relatively slower-growth markets where the business unit has prominent market share and may be the market owner, albeit in a slower market. As the name implies, these business units generate cash that fuels other parts of the organization. Business units identified as cash cows are often in the late growth, mature, or even decline stages of the product life cycle.

- *Dogs.* Slow or negative growth relative to the goals of the organization, with a less-than-prominent market share. Dogs can occur at any stage of the product life cycle except growth. Organizations must choose to either divest of the business or continue to harvest it for short-term cash. In some instances, a dominant market share is not sufficient to make these SBUs attractive.

- *Question marks.* Significantly attractive market potential, though the business unit does not have a significant share. Question marks are appropriately named. The business may require significant investment, may not be directly associated with the competencies of the firm, and may never grow to be a prosperous business. This situation could exist when an organization discovers a technology or business opportunity not aligned with corporate goals in a new and unfamiliar market or not consistent with the company's core lines of business. Question marks raise the question "Should the organization diversify (new product/new market) or divest?" Question marks can be viewed as in the introductory or early growth stages of the product life cycle.

Rethinking the Matrix

Several problems exist with the growth-share matrix that limit its usefulness in today's business environment. First, one of the key assumptions is questionable: the relationship between market share and profitability is suspect. This tends to undermine the validity of the analysis and its implications, depending on the organizational measurement of success. Second, the distinctions between the categories of star, cash cow, question mark, and dogs tend to be circumstantially defined. Organizations place business units in the matrix based on internal standards and perceptions of the relative market positions and growth opportunities of the business. Thus, there is an inherent subjectivity in the analysis that makes it less likely that a business will be viewed the same way by two different organizations (e.g., one organization's dog could be another organization's star; see the box on page 125, "General Electric Leaves the Small Appliance Business"). Since there are no universal rules, an SBU's position in the matrix is meaningful only when compared to SBUs within the same organization. Third,

Market Share Is Not Market Ownership

In "Marketing Is Everything,"* McKenna discusses owning a market. From his discussion, we can form three indicators of market ownership:

1. Market owners define a market niche as theirs and work toward dominating it. Their brand is immediately identified as the standard in that market. Examples are Hewlett-Packard Laser-Jet printers and GE Lexan Polycarbonate Resin. These products are defacto standards in their industries. Competitors to both products note their equivalence to those offerings.
2. Market owners continue to evolve their offerings with the next generation as defined by the value presented to the customer.
3. Market owners benefit from other organizations developing ancillary products and markets that serve the owners' customer base. Third parties define their products as compatible with market owners. In this ancillary product development process, the market owner may be consulted by the developer to ensure compatibility with future products. The owner thus gains insight to other points of view about his market.

Market share is not a defining parameter that leads to market ownership. Market share is a result of, not a cause of, ownership.

*Regis McKenna, "Marketing Is Everything," *Harvard Business Review* (January–February 1991).

because of the subjectivity of the measurements, the investment implications of the categories are not consistent. Stars may not provide the investment return suggested by the model when compared to opportunities not on the matrix but available if the organization were to look outside their own portfolio; cash cows may not throw off as much cash as would be expected; dogs and question marks may be very viable businesses when freed from the restraints placed on them through the relationship to the other SBUs in the portfolio.

The fourth problem is perhaps the most telling. The matrix is a snapshot in time. Current market growth may have little to do with future market growth, and, indeed, that future market growth may be very unpredictable. Such unpredictability is one of the key reasons that Hamel and Prahalad advocate trying to change the rules of the market or industry. Notwithstanding these considerations, growth-share analysis still illustrates for the student the ideas underlying consideration of the portfolio of businesses within a corporation.

An Illustration of Matrix Analysis

Consider the case of Siemens' Wireless Mobile line of business.[6] The following analysis uses both the growth-share matrix and the attractiveness-strength matrix. While, for ease of understanding, the analysis is somewhat abbreviated, it does

---

[6]Based on Siemens' Web site: http://www.ic.siemens.com/mobile/en/index.html Please note that the following discussion of Siemens' situation is a simplification. This example is included solely to illustrate the use of the tools presented here.

**EXHIBIT 5–3   Hypothetical Growth-Share Matrix for Siemens'
Business-to-Business Wireless Businesses**

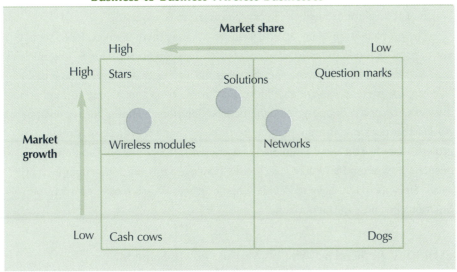

illustrate how the tools can be used to gain insight. However, it also shows that a
fair amount of creativity must be exercised in choosing what measures to use and
interpreting the current and foreseeable situations in light of the chosen metrics.

In 2001, Siemens' mobile line of business has five divisions, three of which are
business-to-business businesses. These three are:

◆ *Wireless modules.* These are miniature components, sold to OEM product producers, that make wireless communications possible.

◆ *Networks.* These are digital cellular networks systems offered to wireless network operators.

◆ *Solutions.* These are applications and solutions for various kinds of enterprises
to enable mobile business.

Let us look at how the growth-share matrix might look for Siemens' Wireless
Mobile businesses. Based on the limited information available, Exhibit 5–3 shows,
hypothetically, that two businesses are currently stars and one is a question mark.
This assumes a positive assessment of the outlook for the Solutions line of business,
which is not yet well defined in terms of size and growth rate. The implications of
this portfolio are very good in most respects. The prospects for the Wireless Modules business are very good, and this business should be supported. The Networks
line of business faces a stiff challenge from other competitors. Siemens may want to
look for a submarket within this business that it can dominate and, through redefinition of the market, turn this business into a star. The prospects for the Solutions
business are also good if the market develops. There is probably synergy between
the Solutions business and the Networks business that is not reflected in the model.
Since success in one area will probably help sell Siemens' offering in the other area,
Siemens should probably consider investments in these two lines of business as also

being linked. The definition of the Solutions market and Siemens' share of this business should probably also be tracked over time so that Siemens can re-evaluate the worth of the Solutions business as new information is acquired.

The problem with Siemens' situation here is that there is no cash cow apparent to provide funds to invest in the stars and question marks. This is a bit misleading since we have not shown other Siemens businesses that are generating cash. We can assume that there is enough cash available from somewhere to fund good business prospects. Suppose, though, that the Solutions business turns out to be a market that does not sustain a high growth rate. Then the Wireless Mobile growth-share matrix would look like that shown in Exhibit 5–4. The Solutions business now would look like a cash cow. However, this business might be quite small. Siemens would have to decide whether it was worth it to even keep the Solutions business in the portfolio.

EXHIBIT 5–4   Siemens' Wireless Mobile Growth-Share Matrix with New Data for Solutions

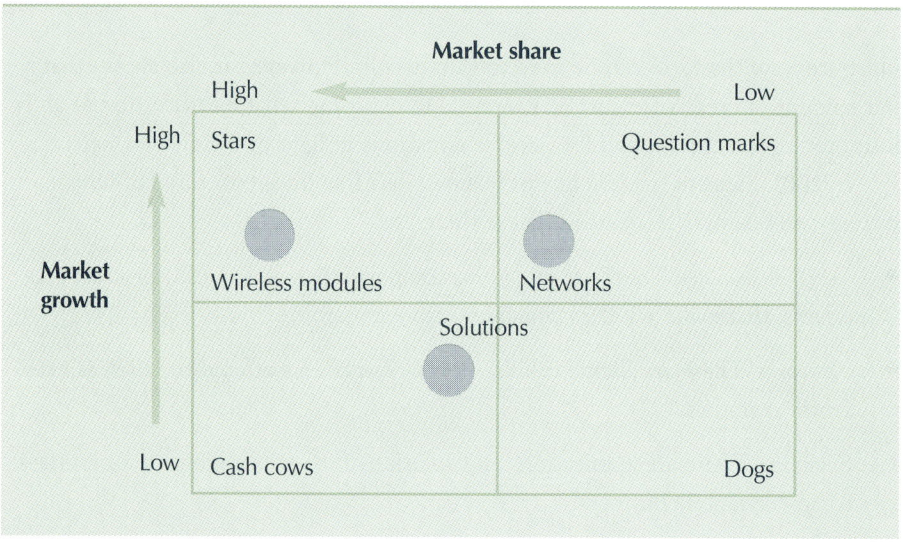

Multifactor Portfolio Matrix

Another tool often discussed in business portfolio analysis is the GE **market attractiveness–business strength matrix,** shown in Exhibit 5–5. This model assumes that, at lower levels of abstraction, no new competencies will be built and gives preference to those businesses or products in which the company already has competencies in place. So, if we redefine the horizontal axis as "capability to create business strength," we have a tool that is more in line with the new way of creating business strategy.

Again, the tool does not directly consider synergies between businesses or products. Unlike the growth-share matrix, though, future business strength can be defined in such a way to give a higher score to a business or product that makes better use of available resources.

Siemens: Cash Cows?

Go to the Web site for Siemens (http://www.siemens.com). Then go to the part of the site that discusses Siemens' divisions. Find the Wireless Mobile division; look at their lines of business. Are there any cash cows among these businesses? Are there any problems if the cash cows are consumer businesses and the stars and question marks are business-to-business businesses?

EXHIBIT 5–5   Attractiveness-Strength Matrix

Market attractiveness

	Strong	Medium	Weak
High	Protect position	Invest to build	Build selectively
Medium	Build selectively	Build selectively or manage for earnings	Limited expansion or harvest
Low	Protect and refocus	Manage for earnings	Divest

Invest/grow
Selectively earn
Harvest/divest

Business strength

From STRATEGIC MARKET PLANNING: THE PURSUIT OF COMPETITIVE ADVANTAGE by George S. Day. © 1984. Reprinted with permission of South-Western College Publishing, a division of Thomson Learning.

Even though the idea of building a business portfolio is not new, it still has relevance today. It makes sense to have businesses that create resources that can be used in other businesses that require investment. Then, augmenting the portfolio idea with today's strategy concepts, a company may stick to businesses in which it has special competencies. Augmenting further with today's concepts, the company may outsource (e.g., value networks as a replacement for vertical integration) several pieces of its operations in noncritical areas where it does not possess unique competencies. Thus, the company, which may be looking to build new competencies in other areas that executive management believes will be key in the future, is able to use its investment capabilities more wisely.

Return to the Siemens example. Exhibit 5–6, the attractiveness-strength matrix for Siemens' Wireless Mobile businesses (in business-to-business markets), shows a

EXHIBIT 5–6   Siemens' Wireless Mobile Attractiveness-Strength Matrix

Market attractiveness	Strong	Medium	Weak
High	Protect position **Wireless modules**	Invest to build	Build selectively
Medium	Build selectively	Build selectively or manage for earnings **Solutions**	Limited expansion or harvest **Networks**
Low	Protect and refocus	Manage for earnings	Divest

Invest/grow
Selectively earn
Harvest/divest

Business strength

story similar to that shown in the growth-share matrix, although with a slightly different twist. All the businesses exhibit high levels of business strengths. Wireless Modules also shows a high level of market attractiveness. The other two lines of business show less market attractiveness, for differing reasons. The Solutions business is less attractive because of the uncertainty around the definition of this market. The Networks business is less attractive because of the competition. We can imagine that the Solutions business would be even less attractive if the market grows more slowly than desired. The analysis shows that the problem is not in company strengths but in the markets being addressed. One approach to this might be to examine the markets and determine how to change the rules so that they become more attractive, then rethink the strengths needed to accomplish this. To make these businesses more attractive might require more in the way of missionary selling or industry education. Siemens would then have to evaluate the company's strengths in these areas as well.

The Siemens analysis using both the growth-share matrix and the attractiveness-strength matrix has necessarily been somewhat shallow. As noted though, it illustrates how the tools can be used to gain insight and that a fair amount of creativity must be exercised in choosing what measures to use and interpreting the current and foreseeable situations in light of the chosen metrics.

The attractiveness-strength matrix might be updated to better reflect the ideas of Hamel and Prahalad. In light of Hamel and Prahalad's ideas on proactively changing the dynamics of an industry or market, the matrix tool ought to be updated to reflect a desire to be in businesses in which such changes can lead to market dominance. The simple solution is to redefine the market attractiveness dimension. The traditional components of attractiveness still hold relevance: market size, competitive strength, growth rate, and addressability of market needs. We might add a component for the receptiveness of the market to be changed and to be owned or dominated. Markets that can be changed have a great deal of dissatisfaction among the customers or distribution channels concerning suppliers' methods of operation. A market will tend to move toward having a dominant supplier if economies of scale would give a supplier a large advantage or if there are other factors driving the market toward supplier concentration.

CORPORATE STRATEGY: CREATING A PORTFOLIO OF BUSINESSES

The preceding discussion describes ways that a corporation can address two important aspects of corporate strategy: choice of businesses to pursue and how to allocate resources. The idea of a portfolio of businesses has merit and can be made consistent with the current thinking on business strategy. The Siemens example introducing the chapter illustrates this point.

In the opening Siemens example, Siemens has business lines in computers, gas turbine engines, and cell phones, among many others. It does this to make use of its competencies and resources, to increase its revenue base, and to spread risk across several economic sectors. Siemens has focused on the areas where it has special competitive advantages in growth industries by selling off some of its businesses and operations. Siemens does not make its own screws for its mobile phones—it used to! However, it is building new competencies by focusing more on building its marketing and innovation capabilities.

Incompatibility of Cultures within Organizations

Companies whose culture feeds on rapid change and "pushing the envelope" of new markets and technologies find that they must quickly abandon established,

---

General Electric Leaves the Small Appliance Business

An example of "one organization's dog could be another organization's star," albeit a consumer example, is the departure of GE from the small appliance ("countertop") market.

Under CEO Jack Welch, GE established guidelines to create a more dynamic organization. These guidelines said essentially that a GE SBU must be #1 or #2 in its market, fit with the vision and goals of the "new" GE, and meet certain levels of profitability. The small appliance SBU, while the major market player, was faced with a changing yet slow-growing market, and poor (by GE standards) profitability. If placed on the growth-share matrix and compared to other SBUs, this business would likely be a "dog" by its internal measurements.

Black & Decker, the tool manufacturer, was interested in establishing a presence beyond the garage. The GE small appliance business was an ideal opportunity to obtain a major market presence. By Black & Decker measures, the return was more than acceptable and the technology fit very well into existing competencies. When Black & Decker acquired the SBU from GE, it is unlikely they considered it a dog.

older offerings—their dogs. Alternately, they may become multioffering companies with several businesses at different stages of the PLC.

This evolution to a large, multioffering (read "bureaucratic") company is not natural to many technology-oriented or entrepreneurially oriented companies—in fact, it may be considered an aberration! Thus, portfolio analysis creation may be naturally resisted. Older products are often discontinued rather than harvested. When two lines of business operate differently, such as cash cows versus stars, a rivalry for resources will likely arise. The corporation that does not handle this situation will see its cash cows stifle its future stars.

Portfolios and Value

Another factor that must be considered in this discussion of portfolio strategy is the relationship to customer value and the value network. As noted in Chapter 2, the most productive way to create an offering with maximum value for a particular market or customer is often to include several elements from other organizations. As designed, the matrix tools provide little assistance in partnership and network development. The internally defined rules do not provide effective evaluation of businesses across organization borders, and, as is often the case with internal metrics, a market perspective of what has value is ignored.

This oversight, not fully considering customer value, can be problematic whether the company is engaged in a value network or not. The organization engaged in a value network to create unified solutions for customers may lose the possible synergies between internally generated businesses. At the same time, the conglomerate that uses portfolio analysis without recognizing synergies across businesses may find that different business units are qualitatively supportive of each other in the marketplace. Consider the consumer example: "General Electric Leaves the Small Appliance Business." General Electric brand identification in the major appliance market was likely aided by the small appliance market presence. Satisfied users of GE small appliances (usually members of entry-level household units) would likely place GE in their evoked set of brands when making major appliance purchases (as they equip their first home). Will the sales of GE major appliances suffer without this positioning advantage?

In summary, then, portfolios are a useful way to think about corporate strategy, but corporate strategy requires consideration of other important factors.

THE SPIRIT AND DREAM OF THE ENTREPRENEUR

As seen in the opening Siemens example, business strategy often includes elements for shaping the internal workings of the company. It has become evident that building an entrepreneurial culture within a company helps the company adapt to environmental changes. In the last decade, entrepreneurial companies have also proven that they can create change as well.

As a first step in creating an entrepreneurial culture, companies begin by setting a mission for the company that sets the tone or context. In the new strategic-planning environment, company executives are likely to ask business marketers to participate in these efforts, either directly in a planning group or indirectly through a representative participating in such a planning group. To assist the business marketing manager to think in these terms, it is useful to discuss what goes into a good mission statement. Then we recast this with the spirit and dream of the entrepreneur, which enlivens an otherwise static mission.

© CAMAY SUNG/AP/WIDE WORLD

The Organization Mission

The mission for the organization must be an informed mission. In preparation for creating or reviewing/revising the mission, information should be developed on the future scenarios that the company is likely to face. This task should be done by whoever in the organization is responsible for tracking industry trends. If no one is responsible, then outside consultants can be utilized for this purpose. The information needs to be digested and disseminated to planning participants. Participants then work toward envisioning how the company will help create its future, as is discussed in the first section of this chapter. From this vision, the mission and broad goals are derived.

So how do you know that you have an enlivened mission and a good set of useful goals? The principal criterion is a sense of "ownership." If individuals at all levels of the organization have a sense that they are working toward something that they feel is significant to them—that the goal is their own—they will be motivated to pursue it. If they feel that this is the goal of the "company's executives," something separate from themselves, and they are pursuing it because they are being paid to do so, then the goal will take second position to the individuals' own agenda items. Similarly, if they feel the goal comes from the company's internal cultural code, they will have less sense of motivation. This will result from one or both of the following reasons.[7] Cultural codes generally do not produce a vision or goal that is particularly challenging. Culturally imposed goals generally reflect regression to the mean, where average performance and conservative action (or even inaction) are desirable. This is particularly true in large organizations. Second, as with the executive-imposed goals, culturally imposed goals are not owned by the individual and hence will be sublimated to the individual's own motivators.

Creation of an entrepreneurial culture and approach to strategy is presented here, as well as in Chapter 8, because the approach can be instituted at any level. If

---

[7]Paul Sherlock, *Rethinking Business-to-Business Marketing* (New York: The Free Press, 1991).

the business marketing manager is involved in setting strategy at the corporate or business unit level, he may want to address the reward system and organizational structure for creating a flourishing entrepreneurial orientation companywide. If the manager is working on strategy at the business unit or the functional level, an entrepreneurial orientation can also be created with rewards and structure. However, the constraints of the overall company organization must then be accommodated while doing so.

Fostering Ownership   How is ownership created? It is done best by involving individuals in determining vision and goals. A particularly entrepreneurial person may arrive at a unique vision for the organization. To get others on board, the executives need to provide support for such individuals and help them in persuading the other employees in taking ownership of the entrepreneur's vision and goals. Innovation should be rewarded with both monetary and organizational compensation. Innovators should be given freedom from traditional organizational constraints in the pursuit of their ideas. Management needs to be cognizant of the social effects of their reactions to the innovators. Management creates the context in which innovation can grow by its role model and attitudes toward innovation and should help create an environment in which the "whole is greater than the parts." Management can foster this by ensuring that all participants reap rewards from the new venture, commensurate with their contribution. Efforts to enhance the dream and the design of the product, project, or new venture should be encouraged and reinforced, as well.

Changing the Rules

The ultimate way for a company to act entrepreneurially is to change the rules of the market, as was discussed in the early part of this chapter. However risky it is to attempt to change the rules, if the new rules come to be adopted by the market, the action may have the effect of upsetting the current competitive balance and starting the process of establishing a new market owner.

Sun's Java language and the way it is marketed can be seen as an attempt to change the rules. Such a change would make Sun's version of the UNIX operating system, run on Sun workstations, a viable alternative to the Windows NT (Network version of Microsoft Windows) onslaught in the networking world. As Intel's microprocessor and Microsoft's Windows NT operating environment (the combination is often dubbed *Wintel*) advance to rival the capabilities of workstations, UNIX looks less viable as a long-term player in the market. UNIX's installed base is smaller than "Wintel's," so the growth vector points in "Wintel's" direction. However, if applications, written in Java, can run on any platform, then it does not matter what the customer's installed base is. Customers can upgrade with any platform and trust that their users will still be able to run old applications and new ones besides. Sun can compete on its technical capabilities and its marketing (specifically its distribution network and brand name) without "betting the farm" on UNIX.

STRATEGY-MAKING AND STRATEGY MANAGEMENT PROCESSES

Up to now, we have discussed the nature and the content of strategy. Strategy must come from somewhere, though. The complexity of the business environment, the complexity of potential interactions of the competitors' moves in the market, and the complexity of companies' internal organization structures make the process of developing and managing strategy necessarily complex itself.

Over the last half century, when strategic management has received direct attention from management and academics, different approaches have been tried and tested. We present here some of the key ideas that have emerged as useful in managing processes.

One idea that has survived over time is a stepwise progression of actions to conceive, implement, and adjust strategy. Stages in this **strategic management process** are shown in Exhibit 5–7.

Over the years, this process has been tried in both centralized and decentralized fashions. The centralized forms used groups of strategic planners at the corporate and business unit levels. They had the advantage of having a broad viewpoint that could understand the larger context within which the organization operated. The disadvantages of centralized planning were the planners' distance from the customers and from the company's operations. Often, centrally produced strategic plans were difficult to reconcile with reality, and so they had little impact on what the company actually did. Decentralized planning, planning done by line-level managers, had the advantage of having a good dose of reality. However, line-level managers were often too close to the action to understand broader strategic issues, interactions with other parts of the organization, and alternative target markets.

Strategy planning today still recognizes the value of decentralization. Involving the people closest to the customers and to the company's processes tends to produce strategies that are better informed. It also produces strategies that are "owned" by the people who have to implement them, thus increasing the likelihood that action will be taken and that the action will work toward common goals. Many of the corporate or companywide strategy-planning efforts undertaken by companies today involve relatively large groups of participants, numbering in the hundreds or even thousands. Direct participants obtain input and feedback from the rest of the workforce, so that virtually everyone in the organization takes part

EXHIBIT 5–7   Strategic Management Process

1. Setting goals and objectives
2. Analysis of the current situation
3. SWOT analysis: strengths, weaknesses, opportunities, and threats
4. Strategy design and choice of the best strategy
5. Implementation plan design
6. Strategy implementation
7. Monitoring of environment and performance
8. Analysis of variance from desired performance levels
9. Adjustments based on analysis of variance

in some way or another. Such a strategy development process can take a year or more to produce a company-wide strategy. The length of time is so long because so many people are involved and because it is often difficult to gain insight into complex industries.

Two implications arise from the amount of effort and time required to reach a company-wide strategy. First, if a marketing manager wants to create fast change, he should probably try to do so with a piece of the organization first, rather than trying to change the whole organization all at once. Second, when a marketing manager becomes involved in addressing corporate strategy, he must be prepared to handle the messiness and duration of this process. This requires emotional preparation as much as it requires having good data sources. The manager must realize that the seeming lack of progress is a part of the process and must learn to not get frustrated.

Reconciling Theory with Practice

Another view of strategy-making processes has developed from close observation of managers making strategic decisions. Mintzberg[8] and Quinn[9] have discussed the process of developing emerging strategies. Mintzberg has observed that **emergent strategy** is a combination of intended strategy and ad hoc, unintended strategy. In **logical incrementalism,** Quinn sees the organization taking small steps to create and change strategy. Due to the necessity of making short-term decisions with unknown long-term impacts, strategies evolve and migrate from their original intentions.

> **Logical incrementalism** refers to creating the direction of the organization through a series of decisions that produce small changes. These small changes can add up to a very large change overall.

These two attempts to reconcile the theory of strategy with the practice of actual strategic management have come to extend the original strategic management model. As it stands, the model suggests that strategy is purposeful and largely complete when it is initially developed. Mintzberg and Quinn have noted that when a company does environmental analysis (Step 2 in the strategic management model), very often it performs this stage of the process with outdated data and outmoded ways of looking at the market or industry. Hence, initial, "intended" strategies (Step 3 in the model) do not present a good fit with the environment. As the company implements such a strategy, the mismatch becomes evident and must be adjusted. Other factors also drive change in the strategy. Events occur that change the nature of the business environment. New opportunities may come along. Mistakes may be made that must be accommodated. Managers may become inspired and dramatically alter the strategy (for better or worse); so, a significant portion of the company's strategy is unintended. The result of intended strategy combining with unintended strategy is an **emergent strategy.** In terms of the strategic management model, the steps of the list that occur after the strategy is designed can seriously

---

[8]Henry Mintzberg and James A. Waters, "Of Strategies, Deliberate and Emergent," *Strategic Management Journal* 6 (1985): 257–72.

[9]James Brian Quinn, *Strategies for Change: Logical Incrementalism* (Homewood, Ill.: R. D. Irwin, 1980).

change the shape of the strategy that is actually applied. Whether this strategy performs well still depends on the fit with the actual environment.

The lessons from the emergent or incrementalist views of strategy serve as warnings to any strategist. One must allow for strategy to change and accept those changes. Things happen; new information emerges. At the extreme, managers must deal with crises (see Chapter 14). At a minimum, adjustments must be made. Strategy-making processes must include ways to obtain and react to new information, new insights, and unforeseen events.

PERFORMING STRATEGIC MANAGEMENT IN THE BUSINESS-TO-BUSINESS COMPANY

We have talked with executives, managers, employees, and consultants over the last several years asking whether the changing business environment has required the complete abandonment of the strategic management model presented in Exhibit 5–7. The answer we get is "not really," though some adaptation is necessary. So we present it here as a template for application, but we add some caveats and adaptations.

Step 1. Develop Goals and Objectives

First, we must distinguish between goals and objectives. Essentially, this is the distinction between the general and the specific. Some authors say goals are general; objectives are specific. Other authors reverse the definitions, saying goals are specific and objectives are general.

It does not really matter which is used, so long as consistency is maintained. For our purposes, we will say that goals are general, qualitative descriptions of some desired state of affairs. For a business, one might say, for example, that it is desirable for the firm to achieve superior profitability and leadership in its industry. Objectives, then, are specific expressions of these goals, with specific targets in specific time periods. For example, members of executive management might say they want to achieve a return on investment of 20 percent, after taxes, on a sustainable basis, by the end of fiscal year 2003. In that same time period, they might want to achieve at least 35 percent market share in their principal lines of business. Further, they might want to achieve recognition by at least 75 percent of purchasing managers in their markets in which their offerings set the standards for product and service quality. These targets are specific in ways that allow measurement of performance against them.

When goals and objectives are set at the corporate level, the relevant criteria are that performance must be in line with the expectations of the relevant stakeholders, such as investors, management, employees, and the community in which our firm is located. The objectives must be reachable, challenging, and internally consistent (not contradictory, so that reaching one objective makes it impossible to reach one of the others). At lower levels in the hierarchy, goals and objectives become expressions of the corporate goals and objectives. The strategy planners must decide what objectives will accurately measure the contributions of their business unit, product line, or program to the corporate objectives.

After strategy and implementation methods are set, the planners may decide that the objectives ought to be revised. They may believe that the strategy cannot achieve the objectives they originally set or that the strategy can surpass them.

Step 2. Environmental Analysis

In this step, the current situation and future possibilities are explored. At any level, the environment includes the following elements:

Markets, segments, and customers

Competition

Channels of distribution

Internal company environment

Effects of the economy

Effects of technology change

Public policy

At the corporate level, the environment also includes other stakeholders such as the financial and investment communities, as well as supplier markets.

The analysis is usually arranged in the form of an analysis of the current situation and a SWOT—strengths, weaknesses, opportunities, and threats—analysis that is more future oriented. The elements of the analysis from a business marketing manager's perspective are described in more detail in the next two chapters.

Step 3. Strategy Design

Strategy design is the step in which strategy planners decide how to meet or exceed the objectives they have set out, given the realities of the business environment. The tools discussed earlier can aid in the determination of what businesses to pursue and how to pursue them. In large measure, activity should be a creative effort.

The preferred method espoused by strategic management authors has been to create alternative strategies and choose the best from among the alternatives. In reality, strategy planners begin formulating strategies as they perform the SWOT analysis. Very often, a single best strategy is already in mind when they complete the analysis. When this occurs, little is gained from creating an alternative or two. These tend to be "strawman" strategies, purposely designed to be inferior to the original strategy. To recap, strategy at the corporate level includes:

♦   A vision of the business and its industry in the future

♦   The choice of goals and objectives (which may be revised or refinements of goals and objectives established in Step 1)

- The choice of which businesses to pursue

- The determination of allocation of resources across businesses

- Determination of which strategic competencies to emphasize and build in the future

- Allocation of resources to invest in building strategic competencies

Business unit strategy involves these same elements, scaled down to the business unit level and adapted to fit within the corporate strategy. The content of marketing or product strategy is addressed in Chapter 7 and Chapter 8.

Step 4. Implementation Plan Design

After the strategy is designed, the planners must decide what actions need to be done to accomplish this strategy. In this step, planners or managers decide who will do what, when, with whom, and at what cost.

It is at this stage that resources must be set aside to measure results, analyze the measures, and make adjustments. Too often, strategy plans—at any level—do not include a specific allotment to accomplish the post hoc data collection and analysis. As a result, the organization does not learn much about why it did poorly or did well.

Once the implementation plan is laid out, the costs, personnel resources, skills needed, and time required must be assessed. If the implementation plan requires more than the organization can afford, revisions in the strategy, or even in the objectives, need to be made.

Step 5. Strategy Implementation

Actions need to be taken and supervised, as required in the implementation plan. Systems should be in place for checking to see that actions are started and completed per plan. If actions are not being taken or accomplished as scheduled, remedies need to be sought.

Step 6. Monitoring of Environment and Performance Results

As noted in Step 4, part of the implementation activities should be designated for collecting and analyzing data. These data should track progress toward the objectives determined in Step 1. In the implementation plan, subobjectives may have been set to track progress toward meeting some higher-level performance target. Data and analysis need to be performed on these as well.

Meanwhile, data need to be collected about the business environment. If anything new or contradictory is reported, the organization must decide whether it is important to note. In some cases, the change in knowledge of the environment may lead to significant changes to strategy or implementation.

Step 7. Analysis of Performance

The idea is to track performance relative to objectives. Any significant variance from desired performance levels needs to be examined. Both under- and over-achievement need to be assessed. The purpose of the analysis is to determine why the variance occurred. This may require interviews with participants, collection and assessment of satisfaction surveys, or other market research.

Step 8. Adjustments

Based on the analysis of performance, adjustments may need to be made to strategy, implementation, environmental knowledge, or any other planning element. Small adjustments can probably wait until the next planning cycle. Big adjustments may require an entirely new plan to be produced. Most organizations close the strategic management loop by starting from scratch once a year; though in rapidly changing markets this timing may not be sufficient.

A Critique of the Model

The implementation of this strategic-planning model is a long, drawn out process, no matter at what level it is performed. It takes commitment to both undertake the planning process and to tolerate the "time to strategy." Our experience has been that the outcome is usually worth the wait. The process can be fast-tracked to a certain extent by running some activities in parallel and by making assumptions rather than collecting data. With the advent of collaborative software, either using the Web or running internally on a company's network, much work can be done "together." This also helps reduce time or makes the plan better.

To reduce the "time to strategy," planners may want to use software from reputable software vendors that helps the planner organize and analyze data about the business environment. The drawback to using template software is that the software does calculations that are invisible to the user and may imply a certain direction not entirely consistent with the unique situation at hand. The planner then does not get the feel for the operation of the market model or the company's profit model. Perhaps a better approach is the use of off-line templates[10] that take the user through analysis quickly but rely on the user to understand the data and to do the calculations.

In the end, we feel it is better to take the time to go through the analysis and planning steps rather than to give in to the temptation to not do the planning and rely on the company's ability to adjust "on the fly." The insight gained from taking at least some time to collect data, analyze it, and think about the meaning of the data seems to outweigh any advantage of "being first" but without a plan.

[10]Robert W. Bradford and J. Peter Duncan, *Simplified Strategic Planning* (Worcester, Mass.: Chandler House Press, 2000).

Another problem that this planning process will encounter is the tendency to drain the life out of a strategy. Related to this problem is the tendency to miss opportunities to innovate or change the rules of the market or industry, both potential outcomes from stifling the creative process. This problem stems from a tendency to get stuck in the analytic portion of the planning process. When it comes to designing strategy, time needs to be taken for a creative exercise. The difficulty here is to recognize that planners may have already created most of their preferred strategy while they were in the analysis phase, which may or may not have been done with a close understanding of the market and its participants. This suggests that a creative exercise may have to be done during the analysis phase rather than waiting for the strategy design phase to do it.

In summary, the process laid out here is based on the "old way" of designing strategy. We believe the drawbacks of doing this process, particularly in light of the time compression forced by the Internet, can be overcome. The benefits from taking a little time to do this will pay off in most cases. With adaptations, the process works at any level of strategy making. One tool that can have an impact on making the process work more effectively is the balanced scorecard.

The Balanced Scorecard

Another tool—one that can integrate the steps of the strategic management process—has received a great deal of attention over the last eight to ten years. The **balanced scorecard**[11] is as much a process itself as a tool for strategy content. It focuses on the goals of the organization and quantifies these into specific performance targets. The idea is to get away from sole reliance on measures that are rooted in the past—such as return on investment (ROI), sales growth, and market share—and concentrate also on measures that are forward looking, given the company's particular situation. Goals and measures are specified in four core areas: financial performance perspective, customer perspective, internal business perspective, and shareholder value perspective. Linkages between these perspectives are defined, and a limited number of measures are sought.

The process pursued in developing the scorecard starts with executive managers discussing their vision of the future and what will contribute to it. A facilitator draws a list of potential scorecard criteria from these discussions and presents it to the strategy-making participants. They discuss these and come to some agreement on strategy and a shorter list of measures. Further discussions set the vision, objectives, and measures. A set of activities to address the performance targets is designed and implementation plans instituted. Data are collected and compared to the targets. Performance is then the driver for strategy and strategy changes. Note that this approach is consistent with the strategic management model.

---

[11]Robert S. Kaplan and David P. Norton, "The Balanced Scorecard—Measures that Drive Performance," *Harvard Business Review* (January–February 1992), and "Putting the Balanced Scorecard to Work," *Harvard Business Review* (September–October 1993): 134–42.

> ### Participation Exercise
>
> Create a balanced scorecard for yourself or for your career over the next five years. Define your personal mission or a vision of your future that you would like to fulfill. Now develop goals and measures in each of the four core areas: financial performance, customer satisfaction, your own operations, and "stakeholder" value (include yourself, those closest to you, and any other interested parties as your stakeholders). Define these in ways that make sense to you. How will you track your performance over time?

SPECIAL ISSUES IN BUSINESS STRATEGY

This chapter provides an introduction to the nature of strategy and the process for developing and managing strategy. In this final section, we explore the implications of the principal issues and themes we have raised in this text.

Strategy Development and the Internet

A special consideration is what happens to strategy management with the increased use of the Internet. Not an end in itself, the Internet is an excellent communications channel. As with most dramatic improvements in communications ability, markets can change more rapidly and with potentially different patterns. The Internet is thus a tool that can improve value to both suppliers and customers. Even in the most staid of business markets, such as chemicals or assembled components for air-conditioning equipment, the nature of competition can change almost overnight. In many business markets, new intermediaries have created market exchanges of one sort or another. Competitive dynamics, customer requirements, and the nature of relationships have all changed as a result (see Chapter 12 for a discussion of the dynamics of the new on-line market exchanges).

Even in markets in which market exchanges have not yet materialized, the Internet has changed the ways that business is conducted. Suppliers have established networks to manage relationships with their customers. Large buyers have likewise set up networks to streamline their purchasing relationships. Much of this activity is experimental in nature. As technology changes, new experimentation will occur over the foreseeable future. As new methods evolve, the business environment is difficult to precisely predict.

The Internet can be used to do several things that ought to factor into the strategist's thinking:

♦ It can increase the speed with which the environment changes.

♦ It can reduce transaction costs, shipping costs, information costs, and inventory costs.

- It can increase the level of information available to customers and competitors.

- It can increase the capability to create an offering that is seamlessly pieced together from several partners' offerings, particularly when a Web site is a principal delivery mechanism for the offering.

Volatility and Uncertainty Require Flexibility

If we examine the strategy elements in light of these changes, some implications for strategy and strategy making emerge. First, in developing a vision of the future, the increased uncertainty and speed of change make visions even more inexact than before. These conditions also create what will seem to be an atmosphere of volatility. For instance, in 2000, industry-specific and cross-industry electronic marketplaces were seen to be the next greatest development in business-to-business marketing. The inability of most of the new marketplaces to establish ongoing operations completely changed the outlook for this kind of business model. Setting specific objectives becomes less meaningful under this kind of uncertainty. Any quantitative objectives set by marketers in this environment in 2000—for example, sales volume, number of customers, profits—were largely irrelevant to the realities of 2001.

Second, choice of the businesses to pursue becomes less enduring as the definition and boundaries of a business are blurred. The decision on the contents of the company's portfolio of businesses must retain a degree of flexibility.

Third, resource allocations across businesses become more critical. When it is difficult to know what kinds of investment will be needed to compete and grow, budgets are difficult to set. There may not be a second chance.

Fourth, core competencies take on increased importance in this new environment. Since an increased pace of change makes it more difficult to predict what competencies will have strategic merit, the company will be either drawn to invest in a broader spectrum of competencies than before or may be induced to cut investment in new competencies and resort to more outsourcing. The former would seem to be more attractive but will require increased resources invested with longer-term payouts than the company and investors will feel comfortable with.

Strategy Implications of Value Networks

In this volatile environment, we suspect the winning strategies will hinge on developing a portfolio of core competencies. One of these competencies must be flexibility to change strategies and operating models rapidly. The value network concept, discussed in Chapter 2, provides a model for businesses to rapidly forge new offerings through a combination of both internal and external resources. This process can be viewed as analogous to a "fast vertical integration." Business opportunities to pursue ought to include one or more SBUs that can generate cash flow immediately in order to fuel future growth and adaptation. However, the business portfolio should also include one or more SBUs in which the company's position in the market can play a dominant role in the future, based on its core competencies.

Strategic Implications of Market Ownership

The portfolio of strategic competencies—either internal, the result of diversification or integration, or external, the result of relationships developed through a network of value providers—is key to pursuing market ownership. If the company chooses competencies to develop that are important in multiple businesses, the company can hope to produce value for customers across a range of possible futures. By taking a proactive approach and "pushing the envelope" within a market, the company can shape that market and the nature of its participants. The process to produce this strategy does not have to differ much from the process described earlier. While traditional strategic-planning processes are not geared for the uncertainty or speed of change engendered by the Internet, the process can be adapted to focus on monitoring the environment and performance, updating knowledge of the environment, and adjusting strategy accordingly. A yearly planning cycle, in which major adaptations to change are done once in a year, is simply too slow. Adaptations need to be addressed perhaps quarterly or at least in a time frame that recognizes the rapid life cycle of many offerings. If the organization uses a balanced scorecard method to track performance and adapt, it should give careful thought to the appropriate performance metrics. A sizable portion of the internal metrics needs to be associated with learning and putting the knowledge gained to commercial use.

Strategy Development in New Businesses

Strategy development in new business-to-business organizations is a particularly relevant topic in light of the activity in business-to-business Internet start-ups over the past year or so. One advantage of starting a business-to-business operation is that often one customer can be the principal reason for going into business. That customer can provide all the financing, in whatever form, that the new business needs. The danger is that the new venture's business will become completely dependent on the one customer and will ignore any opportunities elsewhere. This may leave the new company in the unenviable position of having "all its eggs in the same basket"—being too dependent on the one customer. Accordingly, executives of new firms must actually have a strategy that at least avoids this pitfall. In new businesses, the strategy is often very fluid. In Mintzberg's terms, the strategy is mostly emergent.

The process of developing strategy for a new business poses some difficult problems. There is often a shortage of time to get a strategy in place. Availability of funds may make it difficult to create a good strategy quickly. Often there is neither time nor money available to do a good environmental analysis. There is always the possibility that the effort spent on learning about the environment may be wasted when the emergent strategy responds to a sudden new stimulus and the new venture makes a sharp change in strategic direction. The new direction may have little need for the information collected in the environmental analysis (while this perception may exist, usually effort spent to understand a market is not wasted).

Even though these problems persist, executives in new companies should not forgo the strategy-planning process. New ventures that plan tend to do better than new ventures that do not, even if their plans rapidly become works of fiction as the environment changes. This is why venture capitalists require a business plan before they will consider funding a new venture. The planning process for a start-up is not so onerous—other than the founders' loss of sleep—than the process in an established company. Fewer people are involved; hence, fewer arguments occur over interpretation of trends and courses of action. The business is usually not as complex as that of an established company. Also, the people involved are routinely energized and enthusiastic. The important factor, though, is that the founders know the market and the business better after having done the planning. The pieces of the business tend to fit together much better as a result.

Much of the last forty years' thinking on business strategy and strategy development processes still has relevance today. Businesses develop goals and objectives and then find ways to try to reach those goals. Businesses try to reach those goals by providing superior value to targeted customers. The strategy must fit the requirements of the business environment, including the requirements of all the relevant stakeholders. A portfolio of businesses is chosen that allows the business to grow and create profit into the future. The process for creating and managing strategy starts with developing goals, then using knowledge of the environment to create strategy that can be implemented and adjusted.

Newer thinking on strategy and processes changes the nature of strategy to include a vision of the future and core competencies required to create that future. The process today is often more encompassing, involving more people throughout the organization. Very often it is driven by close attention to performance measurement that is customized for the company's particular situation. Measures are set and performance tracked. Performance against the measures is the basis for making adjustments.

The business-to-business marketing manager has to live with the strategy that is developed at the corporate level and may have to participate in its development. Knowing what is being done and why helps the manager to be a full participant and guides the manager's attempts to implement the strategy.

The Siemens vignette introduced at the beginning of this chapter illustrates several of the points made in this chapter. It shows Siemens altering its portfolio to improve its performance. It shows Siemens changing its core competencies to improve its performance in current and future lines of business. It shows Siemens attempting to alter its internal environment, making the company more customer focused and entrepreneurially oriented. One thing it does not show is a company that has changed its strategy through a drawn out strategic-planning process. Rather, the CEO, Heinrich von Pierer, initiated the changeover. Think about the advantages and disadvantages of this approach. Would the outcome have been better or worse if von Pierer had involved hundreds of people within the organization to rethink Siemens' strategy?

Now that we have examined strategy at the corporate and business unit level, we can move on to the development of marketing strategy within this strategic context. Chapter 6 presents the specifics of gathering and analyzing data concerning the relevant business environment. Chapter 7 and Chapter 8 discuss using this data to develop the specifics of the marketing strategy.

Key Terms

balanced scorecard

business model

business portfolio

core competencies

differentiation

emergent strategy

fit

goals

growth-share matrix

logical incrementalism

market
  attractiveness–business
    strength matrix

market ownership

mission

objectives

strategic business unit

strategic management
  process

strategy

Questions for Review and Discussion

1. What is the difference between corporate strategy and marketing strategy? What are the similarities?

2. What are the differences in the ways that corporate strategy and marketing strategy ought to be formulated?

3. How can a company mission statement be made to provide motivation and guidance for a company rather than just giving lip service to a set of unrealistic values and goals?

4. Suppose you are working on constructing a portfolio of businesses for your company to pursue in the next three to five years. What makes for a good portfolio of businesses? What makes for a good portfolio of products?

5. Is the balanced scorecard consistent with the strategic management process outlined in Exhibit 5–7? Explain any inconsistencies.

6. Suppose you are involved in starting a new business in a fast-changing environment, such as e-services delivered to businesses. To what extent would the strategic management process be useful in planning strategy for such a new business?

7. Suppose a company follows the strategic management process with a degree of diligence. Yet, the company executives recognize that strategy is as much emergent as intentional. How might such a company use the strategic management process yet still accommodate emergent strategy development?

8. To what extent are entrepreneurial marketing and the strategic management process consistent? Inconsistent? Explain.

9. Discuss the relationship between market ownership (or, as noted by Moore, "the gorilla"), value networks, and the likelihood of vertical integration in today's market.

10. Discuss typical planning cycles other than the often-used annual cycle. How should rapid innovation and fast-paced change impact the frequency and duration of strategy planning?

Internet Exercises

Go to the Web site for Siemens: **http://www.siemens.com** Examine its business lines. What are Siemens' strategic business units? Why did you choose these as being SBUs? What do you think are the implications of defining SBUs the way you did instead of being more general or more fine-grained in your classification?

Go to the Monsanto Web site: **http://www.monsanto.com** Assess the lines of business in which Monsanto is currently engaged. Using a search engine, find what information you can on the Web that describes the markets for these businesses. How would you place these businesses on a growth-share matrix? What do you think are the implications for Monsanto? How would you place these businesses on a multifactor (strength-attractiveness) portfolio matrix? What do you think are the implications from this matrix?

Pick an industry in which you have a particular interest. Use a search engine to find articles and analyst reports on the industry. What are the key "rules" of the industry—the recognized factors that distinguish between success and failure? Explain why they are key. Find the most recent example of a company that changed the rules for this industry. How did the industry change?

6

Assessing and Forecasting Markets

overview. . . In this chapter, we examine the market climate created by two influences—customers and competitors. The first section concerns learning about customers. In Chapter 3, you learned about the nature of the buying center and the business buying decision process, thus gaining an understanding of buyers, their decisions, and the behaviors that impact them. This chapter demonstrates various methods to obtain that understanding. As has been stressed in prior chapters, business-to-business marketing is different from consumer marketing, necessitating somewhat different approaches for understanding buyers than are commonly used in consumer markets.

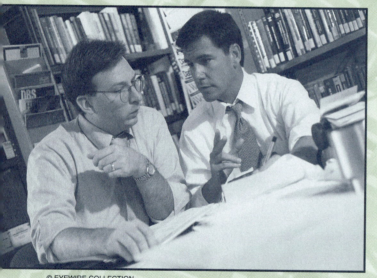

© EYEWIRE COLLECTION

The second part of this chapter examines methods for obtaining competitive intelligence. The key in gathering competitive data is to look for it in bits and pieces from multiple sources. You then put the pieces together like a mosaic to form a larger picture of the competitive landscape.

In the last part of this chapter, we discuss forecasting, particularly the kinds of forecasts that are used for planning marketing operations. The marketing operation forecast (MOF) is presented as a tool to gather timely data related to the logistics of current and future business and technology as well as the competitive environment. We show how these forecasts can provide useful information to many components of a market-driven organization.

Lou Gerstner Learns about the Customers First*

In 1993, Lou Gerstner took over the reigns at IBM. Previously, he had been at American Express. At the time, IBM was in a funk. Their stock price was slipping, and they had lost their industry position in personal computers. The old adage had been that "no one was ever fired for buying IBM"; but IT managers could not count on that any more!

Gerstner took IBM back to its roots to begin the turnaround. He began visiting major customers personally. He held customer meetings with twenty or more CEOs of other customers. He asked questions. He listened. For the better part of a decade, IBM had moved away from this model of customer learning. Increasingly, they had called on lower and lower levels in the customer organizations, down to the IT manager level. Their strategy was more push than pull. They lost touch with corporate customers' problems. Now Gerstner was setting the example of visiting and listening and prodding his marketers and salespeople to do the same. New products followed, as well as new software and service initiatives. By 1996, IBM was back to being a major force in the information industry.

The important part of the strategy for the purposes of this chapter is the way that Gerstner pursued his initiation into the computer industry. His approach to learning the markets was to go to customers and find out what their problems were. Then he sought solutions to their problems, and the customers responded. This is a very typical kind of market research in business-to-business markets. It works because the number of customer companies is relatively small. The more that you talk with and listen to customers, the greater your empathy for their situations and problems and the more likely that you will find something that can meet their needs. Notice that the focus was on customers, not on competitors. By understanding customers, a strong competitive positioning evolved.

Today, IBM continues to perform well and to lead or mingle with the leaders in most major parts of the industry. One of the strongest parts of its business remains in services and consulting. This gives IBM a natural way to continue to listen to its customers and learn where the new problems are cropping up.

*Based on Ira Sager, "How IBM Became a Growth Company Again," Business Week, 9 December 1996, 154–62.

LEARNING OBJECTIVES

- Gain an appreciation for market research in business-to-business markets.

- Understand the differences in market research between consumer and business-to-business marketing.

- Understand the kinds of market research methods employed in business-to-business marketing versus consumer marketing.

- Obtain a sense of how current trends are influencing how market research is done in business-to-business marketing.

- Obtain practice in designing interview questions appropriate for business-to-business market research.

- Understand the theoretical context guiding the collection of competitor data.

- Know what kinds of data need to be collected on competitors and likely sources for these data.

- Understand the effect of current trends on competitive information collection. Obtain practice in performing competitive analysis in a business-to-business setting.

- Understand the different types of forecasts and how they are used.

- Understand the construction and use of a marketing operations forecast.

introduction. . .

A marketing orientation necessitates that you know as much as you can about customers, competitors, and the business environment in which you compete. This implies that you will collect information about markets, your customers, your prospective customers, your customers' markets and customers, and your existing and potential competitors. All of this information collection and interpretation falls in the general domain of **market intelligence.** The portion of market intelligence that involves the design of a research approach and the systematic collection, analysis, and interpretation of data belongs to the subset of market intelligence known as either *market research* or *competitive research.* The boundaries between research and intelligence are somewhat fuzzy. Much of competitive and market research, especially in business-to-business marketing, can be called *informal* research, which is more fluid and less rigorous than *formal* research. The intent of all this type of effort, though, is to learn about the market, its players, and the directions the market is taking.

In this chapter, we specifically address market and competitive research in business-to-business marketing. We begin with a review of the fundamentals of the market research process and the role it plays in the organization.

MARKET RESEARCH

In a customer-oriented organization, the marketing process begins with knowing the organization's customers and prospective customers, just as Lou Gerstner sought to do when he went to IBM. To truly know customers, the business marketer needs to understand the following elements:

- *The customers' technologies.* Learn how your customers' technology and willingness to apply it will impact the application of your products.

- *The customers' products.* What is your customer going to use your product or service for? What will he expect of it? By understanding your customers' products and their fit in the market, you can better anticipate needs and head off problems—and competitors.

◆ *The customers' markets and customers.* Your distinctive competency may well provide an opportunity for your customers in their market; but first you have to know what they are attempting to achieve. Know where their next opportunity is and make it your next opportunity.

◆ *The customers' competitors.* This should not be a surprise, but your customers' competitors are your customers also—or should be—unless they are excluded from considering your organization as a supplier by other considerations.

◆ *The customers' channels.* How do your customers reach their customers? What levels of missionary sales effort, such as customer education and inventory assistance, do your customers use? Can you assist with channel logistics in any way? Are there buying habits in the end user market that dictate a particular channel behavior that is not ordinary (i.e., accompanying a companion product or offering, or a channel dictated by the way customers buy related products)?

◆ *The customers' buying center and buying patterns.* How do your customers make decisions? Do they have several levels of decision making, or are decisions made quickly with little oversight? Are there patterns to their buying that you can correlate to other events, such as climate, holiday seasons, and natural calamities?

◆ *The customers' culture.* Just as you may treat a market or technology differently from your competitors in an attempt to differentiate yourself from them, your customers are doing the same thing. "Certain companies buy from certain companies." Tradition, long-term relationships, logistical considerations, common enemies, and many other factors contribute to the cultural make up of your customers. There are some things some companies will be reluctant to do and some risks that they may not be willing to accept.

Take, for instance, the following example. Suppose you are the marketing manager for IBM's WebConnections service begun in 1999. This is a service that involves hardware, software, and a subscription service in which IBM provides smaller companies with the means to enhance their local area networks (LAN) with e-business capabilities. In this instance, **e-business** means the capability to run a commercial Web site. It might include performing transactions and customer service over the Web, as well.

The marketing manager must understand prospective customers' technologies. In this case, the LAN technologies that prospective customers have must be known so that the product can be made to work with them. To provide a Web management software package that creates and manages useful Web sites, the marketer must understand how smaller businesses want to run their businesses on-line. Similarly, an understanding of their customers' preferred ways of interacting with small business Web sites helps IBM create Web site interfaces that end-use customers will like to use. Understanding the different channel configurations that

> ### An Example of Different Cultures and the Effect on Choices of New Markets
>
> Two major competitors in the supply of silicone rubber are General Electric and Dow Corning. As the two major American companies with silicone rubber technology, they were very sensitive to each other's market actions. When the silicone breast implant market was flourishing, Dow Corning took a commanding lead, aggressively promoting its products, technologies, and services to the cosmetic surgery industry. GE, apparently expressing reservations about the potential sales in the market versus the associated risk, elected not to compete with Dow Corning for the business.
>
> Suppose your company is a supplier of silicone feedstock. The level of risk acceptance of your customers can play a significant role in your decision process. Where will your new technology be most readily accepted? How will you have to prove its viability?

small businesses might use allows IBM to design the Web site tools that will help small businesses support their channels; while understanding their customers' competitors will allow IBM to design all these elements of the offering so that their customers gain competitive advantages. Finally, understanding how small business prospective customers go through their buying decision processes allows IBM's marketing manager to design marketing and sales programs that will be successful.

There are many ways to obtain this understanding of customers. Very often, the marketing manager has experience in the customer's company, perhaps as an engineer or salesperson. In such a case, the marketer understands customers

Primary market research is the collection of data directly from respondents in the population in question. The marketer determines what data needs to be collected and sets out to obtain it.

because she *was* one! A marketer might also obtain this understanding by talking with salespeople and customer service people who deal directly with the customers. She might talk with channel partners who also deal directly with customers. The marketer might obtain research from a research firm that has studied the customers. Often, the marketer will decide that this information is not enough; she needs direct knowledge about specific customer needs, preferences, and behavior. In such a case, the marketer needs **primary market research**.

Market Research Fundamentals

Market research is a powerful tool, but it is only a tool. Like any tool, it can be used properly, it can be abused, or it can be used to complete a task without providing the required result. (Have you ever been in the kitchen and, needing a screwdriver, ruined a butter knife?)

The steps of the market research process are shown in Exhibit 6–1. This is a general depiction of the market research process, and is applicable in both consumer market research and business-to-business market research. The validity and usefulness of market research are strongly impacted by the quality and accuracy of

EXHIBIT 6–1 Steps in the Market Research Process

1. *Define the problem and research objectives.*

   What decisions will be supported?
   What information is needed to make these decisions?
   Should the type of research be exploratory or confirmatory?

2. *Design the research method.*

   What respondents will be sought?
   What sampling method will be used?
   Design the research instrument.

3. *Collect the data.*

   Control the quality of data collection.
   Enter the data in a database.

4. *Analyze the data and draw conclusions.*

   Apply appropriate analysis techniques.
   Control for nonrandom error.
   Draw appropriate conclusions, given the results and quality of data.

5. *Present the findings.*

   Apply information to decisions.

each step in the process. Marketers should be reminded that market research results are a snapshot in time and that markets will change.

The following discussion summarizes some of the more elementary but salient points of the steps in the process. The discussion is presented as if the process involves two principal participants, the marketing manager and a market researcher. In reality, the marketing manager may take both roles, or several people may be involved on the side of the manager and several more on the side of the researcher.

Define the Problem and Research Objectives

In this first phase of the market research process, the marketer and researcher must define the problem and research objectives. One of the most often cited reasons for poor market research is a failure to separate symptoms of problems from the actual problem. It is often said that poor sales are not really the problem but a symptom of other factors. The researcher must investigate the "problem" or purpose to know what answers are needed in the resolution of the problem or support of decisions. Without this guideline, the marketer and researcher can collect lots of information about markets without having much use for it.

Design the Research Method to Achieve the Research Objectives

Who or what part of the market has the information needed to support the decision process? The results of the research will be greatly impacted by the selection of respondents.

What is asked and how it is asked will also impact the results. **Sample** size, the size of the respondent group, will determine the accuracy of statistical analyses; but, more importantly, the method of sampling and the design of the research method (survey style; open-ended

A **sample** is the members of the population who are chosen to be respondents in a research study. If you want to obtain an accurate representation of the population, you will need to be careful about how a sample is selected. Ask your instructor to recommend a market research text to review sampling issues.

or closed-ended questions; delivery via mail, in person, or electronically; personal interview; etc.) must be tailored to the type of market segment under investigation. Oligopolistic business-to-business markets (only a few customers—see Chapter 2) will require an entirely different approach than market research in business-to-business markets with many buyers and sellers.

Collect the Data

In any primary market research effort, data collection has traditionally been the most expensive step because it is usually the most labor-intensive step. The quality of data collection is highly dependent on the knowledge, training, and attention to detail of the research personnel. In business-to-business market research where there is a need for in-depth personal interviewing, interviewers must have an adequate knowledge of the market, acquired through either personal experience or secondary research efforts prior to the interviewing process. The services of an outside market research firm may be appropriate, particularly when expertise in specific markets is desirable (see Appendix 6–3, Working with Market Research Vendors, at the end of this chapter). The specific costs associated with collecting data will vary depending on whether the organization elects to use outside vendors and the vendor size, reputation, and previous relationship with the organization.

Analyze the Data and Draw Conclusions

In doing good research, it is necessary to remember what to do with the information collected and knowledge gained. While the type of research instrument will determine the style and character of the generated information, the researcher must avoid drawing any conclusions not directly supported by the data or by the respondent group. As is true in any market research, marketers need to be wary of **evidence seeking**—interpreting the data optimistically in a way that supports the conclusions the marketer wants to reach.

Present the Findings

As simple as it may sound, applying the information to decisions can be difficult. One common failure, though occurring more often in consumer markets than in business-to-business markets, is failure to apply the findings or act on decisions in a timely manner.

Implications of Types of Decision Support

It is important to keep in mind that good market research supports better decision making. There are three basic decision types that research can be used to support. The first is a **targeting decision,** supported by an understanding of market segmentation. The second is a **design decision**, supported by an understanding of customer needs and customer reactions to design variables. The third kind of decision is a **go/no-go decision** made before launch of a new strategy, product or program.

Research to Support Targeting Decisions

In deciding on target segments, the researcher must either have information that is generalizable to the market as a whole or be confident that segments that are identified are large enough to deserve attention. To get generalizable information, the researcher must use sampling that is done well enough to represent the whole market. In addition, the research instrument must include questions that are sufficient to categorize respondents into groups representing market segments. It is very difficult to formulate segments effectively (see Chapter 7 for a discussion of useful and effective segmentation schemes) after the data have been collected. Accordingly, the researcher must have a good idea of how the market will be segmented prior to starting the research.

Unfortunately, it is often not possible to have a good idea about likely segments without doing some research. The implication of this is that good segmentation research is usually a two-stage research design. The first phase is **exploratory research** and produces the basis for effectively segmenting the market (usually based on differences in kinds of value sought—see Chapter 7). The second phase is **conclusive research.** It divides the sample into segments according to the segmentation basis found in the first phase. It also tests to see whether the segments are indeed distinct. If the sample is representative, then the research can produce estimates of relative and absolute segment sizes. See Exhibit 6–2 for a discussion of exploratory research compared to conclusive research.

EXHIBIT 6–2   Defining the Purpose of the Research: Exploratory or Conclusive

Before designing the project, the marketer and researcher need to decide whether the project is to be exploratory or conclusive. This decision depends on how much is already known about customers and prospects.

Exploratory research differs a great deal from conclusive research. Exploratory research is intended to get a sense of context and maybe some insight into possible relationships, trends, causes, and effects. Typical exploratory methods include analysis of secondary data, in-depth personal interviews, and focus groups. Conclusive research is theory-testing research. It answers questions such as "Will our new product be attractive in the market?" or "Which message gets the most interest from our target audience?" or "Do customers prefer on-line technical support or waiting to have a technical support person visit them?" A conclusive study might use laboratory experiments; large-scale sampling for mailed or interview surveys, with multivariate analysis of this primary data; or direct observation of customer behavior.

In determining whether to do exploratory or conclusive research, the business marketer must first understand what is known about the intended target markets. If the marketer knows largely how a particular market works and wants to make some important choices about some specific parts of the marketing plan, then conclusive research is called for. If the marketer knows only a little bit about how a market works and really is only guessing when making marketing decisions, then exploratory research is called for. Some other factors to consider are the cost, both in terms of money and time. Conclusive research is usually more costly in both money and time than exploratory research would be. However, exploratory research is not costless. Sometimes focus groups can be more costly and difficult to arrange than performing a series of phone interviews. Another strike against exploratory research is the difficulty in keeping bias out of the research. If a company decides to do a series of phone interviews instead of a carefully prepared mailed questionnaire, for instance, and uses one or two of its own marketers to do the interviews, the data can become very misleading. The interviewers may tend to hear only what they want to hear. Also, they may ask questions in such a way that they subtly lead the respondent to the answer most desired by the interviewer. If precision of the data and representativeness of the market are large issues, the marketer may want to "bite the bullet" and use more rigorous, conclusive research.

Other data about the segments are also collected in the same study to aid in choosing which segments to target. The additional data may include such things as strength of need, channels of distribution accessed, size of budget, and so on. All of these data help the decision maker envision the attractiveness of each segment.

Research to Support Design Decisions

Segmentation research is very different than the market research intended to provide insight for designing strategy, positioning, products, advertising, sales promotion, selling techniques, channel programs, or pricing. To design marketing strategy, or the offering, a company needs information for specific segments on benefits desired; the nature of the buying decision process; and reactions to product, service, or communications features. Notice that the segments have to be defined before this research can begin. Without the segments defined, design-related research produces information for offerings that tends to be unfocused or generic.

It has been our experience that collecting data for both segmentation and design at the same time is a bad idea. To design the offering, targeted to a group of customers, the marketer needs detailed, in-depth understanding of the customers' situation, needs and preferences, and buying behavior. Suppose many segments exist and the marketer is going to choose from among them. Usually the targeting decision is made based on no more than five or six dimensions. For example, in the IBM WebConnections example discussed earlier in the chapter, IBM uses only three dimensions to define the target segment, as shown in Exhibit 6–3: the size of the company's LAN, the intensity level of the internal information technology development, and the customer's strategic direction. If the researcher is collecting data for design decisions, as well, the dimensions studied will go far beyond the limited number needed for segment targeting. The design data will then be collected and analyzed for several segments that are not targeted. To do so is costly, time-consuming, and, on occasion, misleading. Consequently, we believe it is far better to address these two purposes in separate research efforts.

Research to Support Go/No-Go Decisions

The third type of research is for go/no-go decisions. In the process of launching new initiatives (e.g., new products, new channel programs, new sales programs), market-related go/no-go decisions occur at two or three steps, depending on how new the market is. (There are also go/no-go decisions concerning the technological aspects of the

EXHIBIT 6–3   IBM WebConnections Value Dimensions Defining Target Segment

Value Dimension	Indicator Variable for Value Dimension	Target Segment Characteristic
LAN enhancement desired	Size of LAN	10 to 100 users
Desire to outsource IT	Intensity of internal IT development	Low to moderate IT intensity
Desire to conduct e-business	Desire to conduct e-business	High level of desire to conduct e-business

product or the feasibility aspects of new programs. Please see Chapter 10 to see how these decisions are made.)

The first go/no-go decision (see Exhibit 6–4) concerns whether the market opportunity is worth considering. If the opportunity has many new elements to the organization and the market is not well understood, this go/no-go decision point is necessary. To determine whether the opportunity is a "go," a quick assessment of the size of the potential market and the rate of market growth needs to be made. This requires data similar to the exploratory assessment of market segments, plus **secondary data** sufficient to gauge the number of potential buyers of the product (or respondents to a new program).

The second go/no-go decision concerns whether the market is sufficiently interested in the offering concept. This decision occurs after the idea for the offering is well developed but prior to the execution of the offering. Product engineering, development of promotion, and definition of channel support programs have not begun in earnest. Very often, when a product is being designed for a particular customer with the participation of members of the customer's buying center, there is little need for a formal concept test. If the product or program is intended to be offered to a wider audience, the research will look more like a concept test for a consumer product.

The third go/no-go decision concerns whether the intended target market responds positively enough to the finished (or nearly finished) design of the offering or marketing program. This step occurs automatically in a collaboration with the customer. In other situations, it is necessary to determine whether the intended target market will respond as desired and, if not, whether simple changes be made to reach the desired effectiveness level. Many companies accomplish

Secondary data can be internal information compiled for other purposes, such as existing sales-tracking information, as well as research conducted by someone else, such as a market research company, usually for a purpose somewhat different than the marketer has in mind. For instance, companies such as IDC, Gartner Group, and Jupiter perform generalized market research related to computer and software markets. They then sell the research reports to interested companies. The marketers who buy the reports do not have control over the kinds of questions that were asked or issues addressed. Secondary data can also be the results of a research effort developed for another reason.

EXHIBIT 6–4   Major Go/No-Go Decision Points in the New Marketing Initiative Process

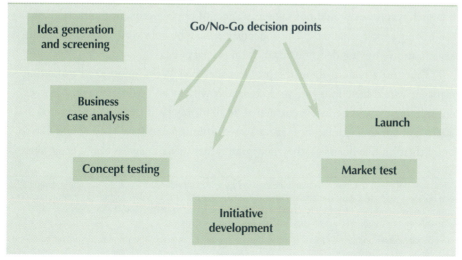

A **beta test** is a second test of a new product or technology, done at customer sites. An **alpha test** is a test done with a product or prototype internally within the company developing it. Alpha tests determine the viability of the product or technology.

this as part of **beta tests** performed for technical reasons, that is, the product or service is tested with a select group of real customers to see if the product works properly.

Designing the Research–Differences from Market Research in Consumer Markets

Market research in business markets has a different flavor than it does in consumer markets. In Chapter 1, we noted the differences between consumer markets and business-to-business markets. Given these peculiarities of business markets, marketers must address several problems that are specific to market research in business markets.

Concentrated Markets   When a business marketer addresses oligopolistic markets, the traditional tools of quantitative market research lose their relevance: *Too few buyers exist* for estimation of population characteristics from statistical inference.[1] Accordingly, data collection through large-sample surveys, such as are used in consumer research, cannot be performed. Data analysis techniques based on deriving unbiased estimation of population parameters and statistically testing their differences have little or no relevance. This means that business marketers need to use **personal interviews** for data collection in oligopolistic markets. Personal interviews are discussed later in the chapter.

Diversity of Interests in the Buying Center   The *number of people in the buying center* produces another major difference from consumer market situations. In households, one or two people usually make decisions. A consumer researcher can address questions to the member of the household most likely to make a decision in a product area, and the response will generally be valid. In a buying center for an organization, several people may strongly influence a decision, making it difficult for any one of them to predict the decision's outcome. Further, if you could question them all, they may be able to give their preferences *at the time,* but such responses would not take into account any subsequent interaction among the buying center members.[2] Consequently, it may be very difficult to predict an organization's buying decisions even from primary data.

Think for a minute about the problem the IBM WebConnections marketing manager would have in trying to do research with small business buying centers considering expanding into e-commerce. If all members of the buying center are queried about their preferences for a system solution and how they would like to build their on-line business, they may give rather naive answers about their likes

---

[1] This does not mean that business marketers can get by without understanding statistical analyses. Recall that business marketers must understand their customers' customers. So a thorough understanding of the customers' markets usually requires a basic statistical knowledge to understand the secondary research available on consumer markets or large-population business markets.

[2] The buying center and its members' relationship to different elements of the value chain are addressed in Chapter 3.

and dislikes. However, after they have had a chance to develop more understanding and knowledge about the value of the WebConnections system, they may have some very definite ideas about what they would really like to be able to do.

Addressing the problem of multiple actors within the buying center requires the business market researcher to pay close attention to the purpose of the research. If the research is intended to learn the roles of the buying center, the approach is simple: interview people in as many roles as possible. If the research is intended to estimate demand for a new product or response to a marketing program, the solution holds less-satisfying results. It still requires interviewing people in all the principal roles. If the research shows that buying center interaction is likely to be extensive, with little predictability in outcome, the solution is more managerial than research-based. The manager must create coordinated, well-designed efforts to influence the whole buying center, not just one or two roles. The accuracy of any predictions hinges on the level of understanding of the buying center members' roles, interests, and preferences.

Technical Expertise

Technical Expertise   A third difference arises from the *technical expertise that resides in the buying center.* For complex products, there is usually someone in the buying center who understands (or is considered to understand by other members of the buying center) the workings of the product or service technology. Accordingly, the language used in market research data collection instruments needs to reflect the technical nature of the product or service as understood by the target market. (As an example, consider the jargon applied to the device that, attached to an automobile engine, makes electric energy to charge the battery and provide power for electrical systems. Generally speaking, these devices are called *generators* in the motor/generator industry, whether producing alternating current or direct current. In the auto industry, the term *generator* means a direct current–producing device. The term *alternator* is applied to alternating current–generating devices.) This becomes particularly important when the technical expert in the buying center comes from a different field than the technical people on the vendor side. Market researchers then must translate the technical language of the vendor into the technical language of the buyer; similarly, they must translate the buyer's answer back into technical language the vendor can understand. At the same time, if the market research is also aimed at nontechnical people within the buying center, the technical language of the vendor needs to be framed in the language usage that is understood by the buyers.

Designing the Research Approach – Other Special Circumstances in Business-to-Business Market Research

Problems in performing market research in business markets worsen when the two overarching trends we have been discussing since the first chapter—time compression and heightened uncertainty—have an effect.

Time Compression

Time compression can have several impacts. The first problem is the time pressure applied to the market research process. Market researchers must obtain data, analyze it, and make recommendations in periods that are often measured in weeks, or even days, rather than months. While technology is making the data collection and analysis less time-consuming, analysis and interpretation of the data still require time for "human processing." Some things just take time.

Time compression can also reduce the respondents' ability and desire to respond to market research inquiries. Prospective respondents have diminishing amounts of time to participate in interviews, focus groups, or surveys. Hence, **response rates** to traditional market research methods (with standard incentives for respondents[3]) are decreasing. High response rates require increasingly valuable incentives to be offered to respondents.

> Research **response rates** are the number of responses to the research inquiry, stated as a percentage of the total number of potential respondents contacted.

Because most data collection methods obtain data for a "snapshot in time," time compression further reduces the duration for which research results are valid. Because the environment can change rapidly, much of this data has a short lifespan reflecting the state of the environment only so long as conditions are similar to the way they were at the time the data were collected.

---

[3]Standard incentives for business-to-business respondents in the past might have been entry of the respondent in a sweepstakes, giving the respondent a small gift, or payment of a small honorarium (maybe as high as $50 for higher-level managers). With increasing compensation and decreasing time available, these have become less effective. More recently, more meaningful incentives have shown to be effective, such as offering to donate $25 to charity in the respondent's name.

Rapid Changes in the IT Market

If asked in the summer of 1999 what Web-related technologies would be the highest priorities in the summer of 2000, IT managers might have said building transaction processing and tracking into their customer-facing and supplier-facing Web sites. In fact, while these are important, equally important or higher in importance are such things as integrating with application service providers (ASPs)* and deploying customer relationship management (CRM)† software. CRM software was just becoming Web-friendly in 1999, and the term ASP had not even come into common usage. If the researcher asked the question, the respondent would have answered; but the rapidly changing environment would have made the answer inaccurate.

*An application service provider (ASP) is a company that rents the use of commonly used computer programs to other companies. These programs, or applications, are stored on a centrally maintained server computer. The clients connect to the server through the Internet or through a private network.

†Customer relationship management (CRM) software helps a company's salesforce and customer service department track all of the interactions with individual customers. It is a database application that matches contact information with order history, order status, and other information useful in providing value to the customer.

Similarly, respondents' capabilities to project their future conditions are necessarily shortened. If an IT manager is asked what problems are going to be most pressing one year from now, the manager is unlikely to be able to give accurate answers. Even if the manager *thinks* she knows, the reality twelve months into the future may be very different.

<u>Uncertainty</u>   While time compression itself is one source of *uncertainty,* other factors such as unforeseen competition and changing customer preferences also heighten uncertainty. Additionally, globalization of markets increases both the chance that new competition will arise and also the chance that new customer segments will become evident. As competitors introduce new offerings at an increasing pace, reactions of buyers to these new choices become more and more unpredictable. Hence, new competition itself introduces new uncertainty in customers' preferences.

All of this uncertainty drives marketers away from the use of market research, especially for innovative, complex products or services. For such products, prospective customers have a hard time reacting to concept descriptions as they often cannot see the usefulness of a new product that is outside their experience. It would be easier if the marketer could offer respondents a working prototype to see, try, and think about. However, the complexity of many potential offerings makes it difficult for product developers to create representative prototypes to which respondents can react. Consequently, marketers and product developers often decide to spend their money where it will have the biggest bang for the buck—probably on product engineering—rather than on questionable research in which they will have little faith or trust. This problem is persistent but not insurmountable. And it is important to get as much information as possible about customer preferences and needs as early as possible To this end, the marketing operation forecast (MOF) and the role of missionary sales/field marketing personnel are discussed later in this chapter.

Practical Advice for Performing Market Research in Business-to-Business Markets

In the preceding sections, some of the problems of doing market research in business-to-business markets in today's turbulent environment have been highlighted. However, nothing has been said so far about how to address these problems. Let us start by summarizing the key problems that must be overcome:

◆   Small number of prospective customers within many business markets

◆   Size, complexity, and informality of the buying center

◆   Unpredictability of buying center interactions

◆   Technical or complex nature of products in many business markets

◆   Short time horizons for making decisions

◆ Lack of time for respondents to participate

◆ Heightened uncertainty about market dynamics

When a target market has a small number of buyers, the marketer must obtain data from enough of them to have data from an overwhelming majority of the market. In many cases, the largest three to five organizations will represent as much as 75 percent of the market or more. This means that the marketer or researcher must gain cooperation from potential respondents in these largest buying organizations and perhaps get a "representative" sample of the rest, making sure to cover any important market niches. Addressing the next issue, technical or complex nature of the product, will actually help in getting cooperation from the respondents. One of the principal ways to foster cooperation is to show an understanding of the customer's business and respect for their technical capabilities. The researcher (or marketer, acting as the researcher) wants to make it easy and comfortable for the respondent to provide information. When the researcher has done her homework, learning as much as possible before talking with prospective respondents, respondents generally appreciate the fact that they do not have to translate too much for the researcher. In areas where the respondent has special knowledge and skills, the researcher should acknowledge the respondent's expertise, know enough to be able to ask intelligent questions, and let the respondent educate her.

In markets in which the marketer has experience and contacts, the marketer generally takes this approach naturally. We have noticed, though, that marketers' everyday contacts may occur at lower levels in the buying organization, since these people, such as design engineers or plant supervisors, have direct knowledge of product and service features that are desired. These are good contacts, necessary for understanding the important dimensions of the value sought by customers. Marketers should make special efforts, though, to make contacts at higher levels in the organization and throughout the buying center. Part of the marketer's job is to have brief meetings with upper-level managers, purchasing managers, R&D researchers, and corporate vice presidents to update them on new products and marketing initiatives and to learn about the buying center, its processes, and things it finds valuable.

All of this contact activity has two market research effects. It helps the marketer know the customer and its buying center intimately. Long-term contact with exchanges of bits and pieces of information builds a rich knowledge of what is valued and how the buying center processes work. Second, when the marketer needs a lot of information in a hurry, she is likely to have access to the people with the right information. Also, a context has been established that will make data gathering and interpretation easier—the "translation" barriers to market research will have been already breached.

Doing Personal Interviews   One of the inescapable conclusions from the preceding discussion about performing market research in business markets is that personal interviews are appropriate in many circumstances. Sometimes, business marketers will need to hire a market research consultant or vendor to perform this research; often the marketer will decide to do the research with available resources in-house. If the marketer decides to do the interviews in-house, she should keep several guidelines in mind.

First, if the research is more exploratory than conclusive, the questions should tend to be open-ended. Such questions allow the respondent to give the questioner the benefit of her wisdom and insight. If the research is more toward the conclusive side, the questions should be designed more with multiple-choice answers. To get more insight, the researcher/marketer can then give the respondent a chance to explain her answer.

Second, questions for all respondents should be the same. In exploratory research, the researcher should use follow-on questions to get rich data. In conclusive research, it is even more important to get each respondent's choice or score for each question. The questioner will need to be diligent in getting respondents to answer appropriately—too often the respondent will want to expound. The researcher should tolerate a certain amount of this but in the end must induce the respondent to answer the question as it was asked.

Third, and perhaps most important, the researcher will usually have to strive for a low refusal rate by prospective interviewees, especially in oligopolistic markets. Since there are so few companies that comprise the vast majority of the market, even a single refusal could create an important "hole" in the marketer's knowledge. Exhibit 6–5 shows several suggestions for improving cooperation from interview respondents.

Addressing the Tougher Issues   To summarize so far, having a network of customer contacts throughout the buying center—and periodically interviewing them, formally or informally—addresses several of the problems we have noted. The marketer will be able to

◆ Obtain market research data from all of the relatively few customers that exist in an oligopolistic market.

◆ Obtain information across the buying center.

◆ Better translate the complex or technical nature of the respondents' information, as long as she has done the homework.

EXHIBIT 6–5   Improving Cooperation from Interview Respondents

- ◆ Demonstrate an understanding of the respondent's organization.
- ◆ If necessary, reassure confidentiality of source.
- ◆ Ask open-ended questions—have questions prepared to serve as an outline.
- ◆ Have some follow-up probe questions scripted and ready, as well.
- ◆ Lead in with an easy question or two to break the ice.
- ◆ Ask the important questions early in the interview; then, if you run out of time, you will still have obtained the important material.
- ◆ Do not overstay your welcome; if you run out of time, ask to finish up over the phone or by e-mail.

To help get the most out of the interviews:

- ◆ Ask essentially the same questions of everybody interviewed.
- ◆ Take care to ask for what you need to know, but be flexible—be a sponge.
- ◆ Take good notes; write up a summary of the interview immediately after the interview, while it is fresh in your mind.

◆ Obtain data more quickly, because much of it has already been gathered through repeated, ongoing contacts; the marketer needs to only ask for quick responses to a limited list of questions.

◆ Avoid much of the problem with respondents' time compression because respondents know the marketer and trust that their time requirements will be honored; also, less information is sought at any one time, so quick responses are all that is usually necessary.

Three problems remain. What do you do in markets that are less concentrated, where more customers exist? What do you do about heightened uncertainty? And what do you do about anticipating the interactions within the buying center?

When a market looks more like monopolistic competition, with many customers of varying sizes but no customer that dominates its market, it becomes more difficult for the marketer to have a network of contacts that covers the market. The marketer should still strive to establish a network of contacts among the largest firms in the market but should develop contacts in other parts of the market as well. Size of market participation will likely end up as a segmentation variable, as behaviors are not likely to be consistent over the entire range of the market. The network should be built to represent the market as best as possible. This means that the marketer should try to develop contacts in firms that are *not* customers or even near-term prospects. They are cultivated for information purposes. The marketer can use the noncustomer contacts to verify segmentation and targeting ideas. Also, it is often useful to have the perspective of someone who knows the market but who sees the market as an objective third party.

In markets in which many prospective customers exist, the distinctions between exploratory and conclusive research become pronounced. While exploratory research takes the form of qualitative interviews as with oligopolistic markets, conclusive research generally involves surveys of one sort or another. Market research for such markets resembles research in consumer markets.

When the marketer must rely on surveys to obtain representative data, the problem of cooperation becomes prominent again, since the marketer will not use a network of personal contacts predisposed to cooperation. Providing **incentives for participation** is one approach to obtaining respondent participation. Very often, though, participants view a small monetary incentive with disdain. Recently, researchers have turned to charitable donations made in the respondent's name as an incentive. Researchers receive high rates of cooperation when the donation is large enough and the respondent is given a choice of recipients.

Managing heightened uncertainty remains a concern. Often the answer lies not in better research but in strategy designs that maintain flexibility and that have data collection and interpretation spelled out as strategy elements. On the research end, often care given to the research design can obtain information that is more useful for peering into the murky future. For instance, a researcher may face the task of thinking ahead beyond eighteen months in the future to what product configurations will be most attractive. Respondents will likely give spurious answers if asked about such features directly—they simply do not know what they will want that far into the future. How-

InsightExpress: Do-It-Yourself Market Research

Take a look at InsightExpress (http://www. insightexpress.com). This is an example of a do-it-yourself market research service.

Suppose you had a customer list of 500 people and you wanted to do a periodic cus-

tomer satisfaction survey. Could you do it through InsightExpress? How much would it cost?

ever, by asking respondents about the problems they face and the trends in those problems, rather than whether a respondent has a need for particular new product features, the data gathered are likely to give the marketer more foresight into future needs.

The issue of time compression, discussed previously, can be minimized through the use of market research companies. National and international research companies recruit thousands of respondents to serve as respondent pools. When a project comes along, a sample is selected from the pool to reflect the population that needs to be represented. These people receive the questionnaire and generally return it in a timely manner—all with a low refusal rate. When this process is managed over the Web, the speed and quality of the data are stunning. Results and data interpretation can be obtained within days or even hours. In a world where decisions must be made quickly, having real data from which to work, instead of questionable assumptions, can give the marketer better plans and better outcomes.

Interactions of the Buying Center

Finally, we address the problem of the buying center interactions. Research on the outcome of past interactions may shed light on possible future outcomes. In other cases, the marketer will have to address the variations in outcomes caused by such interactions as simply another source of uncertainty—all the more reason to create strong relationships with all elements of the buying center.

Participation Exercise

For practice in designing questions for a personal interview, choose a business for which you would like to learn more about how it markets. Do a preliminary investigation of the business by viewing its Web page and any newspaper, magazine, or trade journal articles you can find. Formulate a series of questions for an interview with a marketing executive at this company.

If you are so inclined, go ahead and interview a marketing executive from this company. What did you learn from the interview?

Summary of Market Research

As we have seen, market research in business-to-business markets has the same general purposes and follows the same general process and guidelines as market research in consumer marketing. However, the execution of market research in business-to-business markets is often very different than market research in consumer markets. As the opening vignette points out, Lou Gerstner took a typical approach to learning about IBM's markets when he first took the reins at the large computer maker. He talked directly with a relatively small number of customers and used this information as the basis for revisions of IBM's strategies. Business-to-business market research often involves a great deal of person-to-person contact, open-ended questions, and a lot of listening. While competitors were important, the effort to understand the markets started with an understanding of customers.

The limitations imposed by small numbers of buyers, the need for fast decisions, and the high levels of uncertainty make managerial judgment a valuable asset. The marketer's experience gives insight and makes decision making more effective; but managerial experience cannot operate alone. Marketers need good information about their customers.

Adobe, the marketer of publishing and image-handling software, came to this conclusion rather painfully in the middle of the 1990s. Accordingly, establishment of a proactive marketing research department became an important part of Adobe's reorganization. The results of the reorganization have been exceptionally successful. Industry watchers once speculated that Adobe would be acquired by Quark, a smaller competitor. They now acknowledge Adobe as one of the most astute companies in adapting to a software market heavily influenced by the Internet.[4]

Obtaining good customer information was the topic of this first section of the chapter. Once the marketer finds out how customers perceive and pursue value, she can move on to gaining an understanding of the competition, the standard against which customers judge what will be *superior* value.

COMPETITIVE ANALYSIS

Customer analysis is the place to start when doing an analysis of the business environment. There are two reasons for doing this. First, the point of competing is to create value for customers. Understanding how they perceive value gets the marketer started in designing the offering. Second, customers can tell you who your competitors *really* are. All you have to do is ask. If you want to know who your competitors are likely to be in the near to intermediate future, ask them who they think will likely have an offering. If you are looking far into the future, ask your customers and prospects what kind of characteristics a strong competitor would be likely to have. Of course, the farther into the future you are looking, the less likely you are to be right about who to be watching for, but at least this information from customers can help you start being vigilant.

---

[4]Kennedy Grey, "Rekindling an Old Spirit," *Marketing Computers* 20, no. 8 (August 2000): 64–70.

Before getting into the nitty-gritty of competitive analysis, we need to say a few words about the nature of competition. We have already described competition as competing to provide superior value to targeted customers, but this does not convey a sense of the dynamic nature of competitive markets.

We can think of markets as seldom, if ever, reaching an equilibrium state.[5] Rather, markets strive for equilibrium but are routinely upset by the innovation process. In Chapter 9, we discuss the innovation process thoroughly. For now, though, we note that the marketer must expect innovation to occur whether it comes from known competitors, new competitors, or even from within the marketer's own company.

Innovation has the effect of changing market dynamics, sometimes radically. At other times, it merely continues the progression of the market with few changes in competitive positioning.

Markets evolve, sometimes in revolutionary ways. Current competitors are always a concern; even if they are weak, they can reinvent themselves in the future. New competitors are likely to spring up as existing companies diversify and entrepreneurs attempt to pursue the opportunities they perceive. The Internet makes many kinds of new-venture competitors instantly viable. So the business marketer must anticipate abrupt changes in the competitive environment and try to prepare for them. Competitive analysis is a large part of this. However, in today's turbulent environment, competitive analysis must be done somewhat differently than it was done a decade ago. Many of the same ideas apply, but much more emphasis must be given to anticipating new competition from new ventures.

The Six Sources of Competition

Porter[6] characterized the several **sources of competition** that a company can face. Exhibit 6–6 includes the five sources that Porter suggested can offer competition: existing direct competition, competition from channels, competition from upstream suppliers, competition from new entrants, and competition from substitutes. As has already been described, in the last decade competition from new entrants and from substitutes has become more widespread and more viable more quickly. Hence, such competition is potentially more dangerous.

We have added a sixth source, partners through value networks. In today's business environment, partnerships are formed to provide the pieces that complete the whole offering. In many cases, the partners are already competitors in other markets. Value networks are often temporary alliances of convenience in which either party or both intend to sever relationships after more is learned about the market and internal strengths can be built. Technically, these partnerships are neither upstream nor downstream channel relationships, so we show them as a separate source of potential competition.

---

[5]This section is based on Peter Reid Dickson, "Toward a General Theory of Competitive Rationality," *Journal of Marketing* 56, no. 1 (January 1992): 69–83.

[6]Michael Porter, *Competitive Strategy* (New York: Free Press, 1980).

EXHIBIT 6–6   Six Sources of Competition

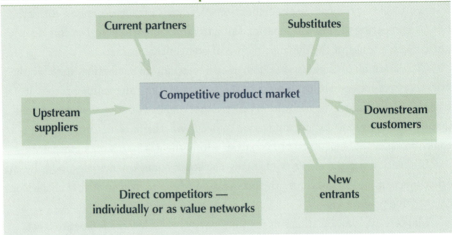

To start identifying competitors, then, the marketer must identify who the direct competitors are, either individually or as opposing value networks. Current partners must then be examined for their competitive potential. The marketer must also look upstream and downstream for any signs that existing suppliers or channel members have potential to become competitors. Next, the marketer must scan for indications that major companies from other industries are looking to enter the market (new entrants). Finally, the marketer should search for potential substitutes that could disrupt the existing industry. This disruption may come from some surprising sources. (See the boxed discussion, "Unexpected Competition—Antimatter Propulsion?") Substitutes usually come from competing technologies, but not necessarily. The innovation could come in the form of a channel design substitute, making existing products more available or less expensive. Dell Computers offered such a channel design innovation in personal computers. By offering computers through direct sales rather than going through VARs or dealers, companies could buy computers more cheaply and easily than they could from vendors such as IBM and Compaq.

After these real entities are examined, then the marketer can turn to building hypothetical configurations of start-ups or substitutes that might disrupt the marketer's place in the industry.

The marketer often knows direct competitors simply through experience. This may not be the case in emerging markets or when the marketer contemplates taking the company's offering to new markets. If the marketer knows who the direct competitors are, she can begin working on collecting data on them. In any case, though, the marketer must begin talking to customers and prospective customers as soon as possible. (Other sources for identifying potential competitors are discussed in the next main section, "Sources of Competitive Information.")

Information to Collect on Individual Competitors

The main idea is to anticipate competitors' future actions and reactions. In particular, the marketer wants to identify threats and opportunities that emerge due to

> ### Unexpected Competition—Antimatter Propulsion?
>
> A few years ago, Technology Strategic Planning, Inc., a technology consulting firm, was performing competitive research for a client that makes chemical engines for space vehicles. NASA's mission to Mars was the subject of the research. Instead of investigating future advances in chemical technologies, the consultant examined large companies that were pursuing any kinds of propulsion systems. They found Mitsubishi working on antimatter technology. Antimatter subatomic particles are created in particle accelerators and can be trapped and stored. Recombining antimatter with matter releases a great deal of energy.
>
> Competition from this unexpected technology achieved higher credibility when Technology Strategic Planning calculated the amount of antimatter produced in the world's particle accelerators. It would reach the amount needed for a round trip to Mars about the year 2016, the same time as NASA had scheduled for the Mars mission.
>
> *Source:* Based on Christopher A. Sawyer, "The Case for Antimatter," *Automotive Industries* (February 1996): 61.

competitors' perceptions and activities. To find opportunities and threats, the marketer wants to first understand the direction that a competitor will take if the marketer's company does not change its strategy or tactics. Next, the marketer wants to understand the competitor enough to anticipate how the competitor will react to strategies, programs, and tactics that the marketer may take in the foreseeable future.

Porter, again, offers a framework for understanding individual competitors. There are four areas in which the marketer will want to collect information: goals, strategies, capabilities, and assumptions.

Goals

Goals, of course, refer to the levels of performance the competitor wants to achieve. Often the competitor has a desired market position it wishes to obtain, for example, *dominance* or *largest market share.* The marketer should not assume that the competition always wants to achieve market leadership or dominance, though. Large companies are often satisfied with merely being a major player in a market. Smaller companies are often satisfied with having a small share of a market or an ownership position in a small niche. The goals of the competitor give the marketer an idea of how hard the competitor will fight to pursue its strategy and how vehemently it will react if its market position is threatened.

Strategies

Strategies are the means that the competitor uses to achieve its goals. We can cast these in terms of target segments, desired responses in the marketplace, value offered, marketing mix employed, core competencies employed, and core competencies being acquired. This is the crux of the marketer's understanding of how the competitor will behave and react.

Capabilities

Capabilities are the resources, both financial and organizational, that can be brought to bear in pursuit of the competitor's strategies. A good reading of the competitor's financial statements may give clues to its future ability to fund major initiatives. The marketer also wants to gain an understanding of the competitor's culture and core competencies. Such issues as how flexible the competitor's organization is, how creative they are in designing new strategies, and how effective they are in implementation all give the marketer a sense of the competitor's tendencies and limitations.

Another indication of changing capabilities of competitors can be their activity at the patent office. New patents can be a major indication (though potentially late in the game) of the research and development (R&D) focus of the organization. Naturally, this focus will be a result of how the company sees the future of the markets and how it expects to leverage its capabilities.

Assumptions

Assumptions are the most difficult dimension of competitive information to access. Executives of competitors have mental models of how their markets work. These models drive their choices of strategies and tactics. Seldom do competitors state their assumptions outside of internal business plans (although today more companies are publishing their views of the market mechanics on the Web—see the next section). Sometimes a CEO or other company executive explains her vision of the market in an article or interview for the trade or business press or she gives a presentation at a conference or trade show. More often, the marketer must infer a competitor's assumptions from the behavior of the competitor.

This is when competitive analysis becomes an exercise much like solving a jigsaw puzzle. The marketer must gather bits and pieces of evidence. A competitor's actions and reactions to competitive dynamics need to be studied over time. The marketer needs to think about why the competitor did what it did. Over time, the competitor's motives and beliefs may become evident. Often, the marketer never will get to the root of what drives the competitor. The marketer must remember that strategy is emergent as well as purposeful; often, something that looks purposeful was unintended. Also, competitors learn from their mistakes and successes, leading their belief systems to change. Accordingly, the marketer faces a moving target when trying to fathom the competitor's assumptions.

If the marketer learns that the competitor's assumptions are wrong, this knowledge can become a powerful lever. For example, a small printing company with three local weekly newspapers found that a regional chain of newspapers had acquired its principal competitor. The chain was purportedly offering advertising rates that the small printing company could not easily match. By quietly talking with its most important advertiser, the printer learned that the competitor was assuming that important accounts would want combination ads—ads that would run in several of its newspapers simultaneously. Advertising rates for ads that run only in a single newspaper were much higher. The printer, though, relied mostly on single-site retailers for whom the combination ads were of little or no use. The

printer did not have to lower its rates and was actually able to take some business away from the chain, whose management was slow to learn about the true nature of the local market drivers.

Sources of Competitive Information

While competition has intensified over the last decade, the amount and quality of competitive information have kept pace. Some new sources of competitive information have even emerged.

The Customer   The first source for competitive information, as was suggested earlier, is the end-use buyer. Customers and prospective customers can give anecdotal data on all four dimensions of competitive information: goals, strategies, capabilities, and assumptions. However, customers' perceptions of a competitor's capabilities may be somewhat myopic. The best way to acquire the data from customers is through normal cultivation of individual contacts. In the course of other discussions, the marketer can ask about comparisons between the marketer's offering and the competitors' offerings.

The Internet   The obvious new source of competitive information is the Web. Most companies now have Web sites, even if these are only on-line "brochures," Web sites with basic information and little else. Competitors' own Web sites make it possible to quickly find information about all four dimensions of competitor analysis. Even capabilities can often be determined from a company's Web site. If the company is public, it often shows all its Securities and Exchange Commission (SEC) filings and recent quarterly and annual reports. In addition to capabilities, companies often publish material describing their goals and strategies. This information helps prospective customers determine whether they are in the target segments and what the offerings for them are. Many companies also publish their mission statements for the same reason. Also, companies often publish their views of the industry and the market. This is done to give prospective customers

167

© JACK DEMPSEY/AP/WIDE WORLD PHOTOS

and partners a sense of how they can work together into the future. It also gives insight into the company's beliefs about the market and, as previously discussed, can provide a competitive lever if the marketer believes the competitor is wrong about the workings of the market.

Business and Trade Press   A third good source of competitive information is the business and trade press. The business press includes articles written about a wide range of industries; the trade press sticks closely to one industry or set of related industries. Articles based on interviews and analysts' interpretation can give insight into all four dimensions of competitive analysis. In addition, the press can provide a history of past events or actions, which may also shed light on the competitor's tendencies.

Trade Shows   Trade shows, a fourth source, can also provide a great deal of information to marketers. The trade show has booths and displays for any company of note within an industry. The marketer, or another person operating on the marketer's behalf, can make the rounds and get a close look at current products and programs. In the speaker sessions that also are part of the show, competitors' executives or managers may give talks or make announcements that define or give clues to the competitors' goals, strategies, and assumptions. (Chapter 13 discusses the use of trade shows and the trade press to establish a corporate image.) The hallways and bars in and around the conference hall and surrounding hotels may also have revealing conversations that are easily overheard without being nosy.

Other Sources   Other sources also provide insights into the four dimensions of competitive analysis. Many of them can be seen as outward indicators of trends and facts that lie beneath the visible surface. The business-to-business marketer may watch competitors' advertisements and publicity announcements. Classified advertising having to do with employment or real estate may also indicate changes in strategic directions.

Participation Exercise

Suppose you are the marketing manager for IBM's WebConnections. You want to analyze your competition. List the kinds of information you would want to collect and the sources for this information.

One common way of gathering and sifting through competitive information is to hire a consultant who does this on contract. Some consultants maintain extensive networks of contacts within their industries. Others have no immediate contacts but have good methodologies for obtaining information. As with any vendor, the marketer must check the credentials of such consultants to ensure that the consultant is not feeding more information back to some of the marketer's competitors. (Chapter 14 discusses some of the ethical implications involved in the collection of competitive information.)

All in all, there are many sources of information on competitors. Again, the marketer needs to realize that competitive information is like a jigsaw puzzle in which many small pieces are assembled into a larger picture.

Summary of Competitive Analysis

In a volatile, competitive environment, business-to-business marketers will want to learn as much as possible about competitors after they have come to understand something about their own customers. Competitive analysis sets the standard for customer value, which the marketer's firm must exceed. Competitive analysis is forward-looking. The marketer tries to anticipate competitors' future moves and reactions. The goal is to anticipate the threats to the marketer's strategy posed by competitors' strengths, as well as to identify opportunities presented by the constraints they face, their predisposition to certain behaviors, or other weaknesses in their offerings.

FORECASTING MARKETS

So far in this chapter, we have addressed the question "What's out there?" with discussions of market research and competitive analysis. All of this information is of little use if it is merely a snapshot of today. Markets change. The organization would prefer to have this information about the future. Predictions of the future or, as business organizations prefer to describe the practice, forecasts, are created

---

What Can We Say about Forecasts and Forecasters?

We do not believe forecasts are often fun to prepare. The very act of forecasting asks the forecaster to make claims about things that cannot possibly, without the capability of time travel, be known. Forecasting, then, sets us up to be wrong. In the context of forecasting, however, wrong can be acceptable.

Consider the following "rules" of forecasts:

1. Forecasting is difficult, especially if it is about the future.
2. When completed, all forecasts are wrong; you just cannot know by how much and in which direction.
3. State all forecasts to the third decimal place to prove you have a sense of humor.
4. When presenting data, provide either volume or timing, never both.
5. Compensating errors can make your day.
6. The best defense is a good offense, so, if you have to forecast, do it often.
7. If you get it right, never let your manager forget it.

Source: Adapted from Paul Dickson, *The Official Rules* (New York: Dell, 1978), 53–55. Dickson credits Edgar R. Fiedler with Fiedler's 25 Forecasting Rules, appearing in the June 1977 issue of *Across the Board,* the magazine of The Conference Board.

---

more often than they are believed. How often do you listen to a weather forecast with the idea in mind that it will influence what you will do the next day, then completely forget it and do what you want without consideration for the forecast? The same could be said for market forecasts. The credibility and reliability of forecasts are directly dependent on the quality of the information used to create the forecast (naturally) and whether or not the creator is invested in the forecast being "good" (as opposed to useful).

Notwithstanding the lighthearted (but usually accurate) view of forecasts and forecasters presented in the box—"What Can We Say about Forecasts and Forecasters?"—the usefulness of forecasts depends on recognizing many factors that contribute to the qualitative rather than the quantitative nature of the forecast. The marketer must recognize the value of applying managerial judgment that comes out of experience and familiarity with the market. When the person charged with doing the forecast has little experience in markets like the one being forecast, she would do well to seek the opinion of those who do have such experience. Experienced forecasters try to account for the following factors that will cause markets to change direction:

◆ *Technological change.* Can this be accurately forecast? Certainly Moore's Law is a forecast of growth. Most forecasts of technology incorporate growth, often based on the philosophy of Moore's Law. But, Moore's Law is a forecast of growth, *not* change. Did prognostications about the vacuum tube industry forecast the demise of that technology as the mainstay of electronic signal processing, or was the growth of solid state electronics as a replacement technology myopically ignored?

- *Time horizons.* The longer the time frame of the forecast, the less accurate and less useful the forecast is likely to be. How far into the future should a forecast look? What is the nature of change in your customers' markets? Does the market embrace new methods and technologies, or is it resistant to change? How quickly can customers react to changes in the market? If your offering is part of an enabling technology (a technology that makes possible your customer's next generation product/offering), what delivery time frame is required to meet your customer's development and production schedules? In this context, it may be appropriate to develop timing parameters in terms of the development needs or life cycle of your customer's products rather than your organization's product life cycle or calendar.

- *Barriers to entry/exit.* Never assume that the barriers to entry in your business will prevent another competitor from showing up in the market. Breakthroughs happen: How did your organization get in the market? Also, never minimize the staying power of a competitor, particularly one who has a significant investment (financially, culturally, image, etc.) in serving the market need.

- *Elasticity of demand.* Directly associated with technology replacement, demand in business-to-business markets is somewhat volatile. As discussed in Chapter 2, this volatility can defy conventional wisdom. Changing technology forces offerings through the adopter stages more rapidly as early adopters embrace newer technologies. Demand for offerings is influenced by changes in target markets, as technology products move from early adopters to markets whose participants are more closely associated with "proven" rather than "new" technology. This can be viewed as the dramatic increase in demand, as demonstrated by increased growth rate in the product life cycle and the shift from visionaries to pragmatists in the technology adoption life cycle (see Chapter 2, Exhibit 2–5).

- *Forecast expenditures.* What level of resources (how much time/money/energy) do you want to spend to improve accuracy? While this is not a factor having to do with the specific content of the information used in the forecast, it can have a bearing on how accurate a forecast will be. Conditions in developing markets demand rapid decision making. Committing greater financial resources to obtain more accurate information also often creates an additional expenditure of time. The market opportunity may slip away before enough data is accumulated to enable a comfortable decision. Our experience—reinforced by opinions we have heard from many managers—tells us that often the best decision is to do anything rather than standing still. Here again, experience can provide a sense of when it is worth it to gather more information. It pays to recognize when wanting more data is just another way to avoid making a decision.

> ### What Makes a "Good" Forecast Different from a "Useful" Forecast?
>
> Forecasting is sometimes considered one of those unavoidable "nasties" of business. At best, a forecast can be in the ballpark—close enough to be an aid in making business decisions. A good forecast is one that was created through generally accepted methods. Procedures were followed. Good forecasts can be wrong but are defended as good because they were done the right way. A cynic might say that this is a somewhat bureaucratic approach, focused on process rather than results. Good forecasts can be good and still be inaccurate.
>
> A useful forecast is a forecast that contributes data to decision making. There is a temptation here to use the term *accurate* in place of *useful*. Experienced forecasters know that forecasts are, at best, useful and, by their very nature, not exact.

Forecast Types and Techniques

Ways of performing forecasts differ according to the type of forecast. Some different types of forecasts, as well as some forecast techniques often encountered in organizations, follow:

- *Strategic forecast.* Generally a long-range business forecast associated with macro planning efforts. Strategic forecasts usually have a stronger element of "top-down" input, with a major effort to reconcile reality with the strategic direction. These forecasts usually involve three- to five- (maybe ten-) year periods, reviewed and revised annually. Chapter 5 deals with strategic planning on the macro level.

- *Marketing planning forecasts.* Usually associated with a particular product or market, these forecasts are the ones with which we are most familiar. Marketing planning (a plan to determine needs and satisfy wants generated from those needs) often has significant data inputs from market research and competitive analysis, while attempting to project what customers will do. These plans usually involve one- to three-year periods, with annual review and revision, though quarterly and semiannual reviews are not uncommon.

- *Marketing operation forecasts (MOFs).* The least formalized but often the most discussed operational forecasts are usually the responsibility of the field operation, sometimes in conjunction with brand/product/market specialists from headquarters. Under many themes, operational forecasts, tactical in nature, are an ingredient in sales forecasts for territories and the tool used to judge performance for missionary sellers/field marketing operatives. These forecasts usually involve one- to three-year periods, reviewed and revised monthly, and include major elements of market research and intuition (based on knowing your market) in their development. The actual length of the one- to three-year period is influenced by the product/technology life cycle and the rate of new product adoption.

- *Sales forecasts.* Shorter range than marketing operations forecasts, sales forecasts are valuable for logistics, manufacturing, and material resource planning.

While marketing operation forecasts and sales forecasts may at first glance seem very similar, major distinctions include the way data is collected and the techniques used in analysis. Sales forecasts include a stronger element of history; they more often are used to track existing sales patterns and apply those patterns to the future. As a result, statistical data manipulation plays a major role in development of useful information. Predictive models (i.e., rolling average, econometric models)[7] are used to develop data of value not just to sales management but to logistics, manufacturing, and materials requirements planning (MRP) managers as well. Herein lies a major difference between MOFs and sales forecasts. Very little history or statistical manipulation is used in MOF development. While "no statistician should ever undertake analysis of a market without drawing fully and continuously on the knowledge of the marketing management,"[8] marketers must realize that sales forecasts are not good substitutes for MOFs. A brief summary of a few predictive models,[9] used for sales forecasting, appears in Exhibit 6–7. Note the quantitative rather than qualitative nature of several models.

---

[7]E. J. Davis, *Practical Sales Forecasting* (London: McGraw-Hill (U.K.) Limited, 1988), 203.

[8]Ibid., 128.

[9]Ibid., 203–222.

EXHIBIT 6–7 Predictive Models

Rolling Averages

Forecast for the next period is a weighted average of a preset number of prior periods.

- Data: existing sales figures
- Averaging decreases impact and awareness of turning points
- Not predictive of turning points
- Appropriate for large-volume, low-value markets; ineffective with low-volume, "lumpy" markets (large single purchases—facilities, infrastructure, etc.)

Econometric Models

Forecasts are based on relationships derived through statistical analysis.

- Useful for coverage of several years
- Requires prediction of many independent variables
- A study of history applied forward
- Lumpy markets can be modeled
- Provides information about broad categories; not effective for single brands or share data

Delphi Approach

Forecasts are from a panel of experts who are systematically polled.

- Executive opinion polling with feedback provided to respondents to enable "correction" to the mean
- Selection of respondents critical to validity of results; stability over time improves usefulness of predictions
- A qualitative, intuitive model, useful for trends, not specific brands or offerings
- May have value in business-to-business marketing because of the oligopolistic nature of markets, ability to acquire informed respondents

Source: E. J. Davis, *Practical Sales Forecasting* (London: McGraw-Hill, U.K., Limited, 1988), 203.

Marketing Operations Forecasts in Depth

What are the data that make up a good *marketing-based* operational forecast? Let us create an ideal list of the types of information a marketer might want to see when she picks up a forecast developed by the field marketing operation and obtained at the customer level.[10]

Marketers would like to know answers to the question "How much?" about current business—much the same as a sales report:

◆   How much will customers buy of what they are now buying? What customers currently buy is part of internal sales data. How the volume of their regular purchases will vary, based on factors in their market, is information usually available from customers. This business volume is usually referred to as the **core business** at a particular customer.

◆   How much will customers pay for it? If selling price is not fixed, marketing will be interested in any changes in the customers' value perception of the offering.

Timing of purchases is important to marketing, not because a particular sales quota must be reached but because marketing and support resources have to be allocated to obtain the purchase and enable delivery. The ideal MOF answers the "When will . . ." questions:

◆   When will customers buy the noted volume?

◆   When will customers' purchases peak? Declining purchases could be a sign of a change in the customers' market, leading to new product introductions by customers that may or may not continue existing purchases. Business volume that was previously considered core may begin to erode.

◆   When will customers consider new technology? If the marketing organization has a new product or offering, when are customers likely to entertain a change in the current offering? What is the life cycle of their existing offering, and when will they be in the next design cycle to replace the offering?

◆   When will customers start buying from a competitor (or from us)? Have the customers re-bid the business? If your organization is the existing source, will they purchase from another supplier to avoid dependence on one source, or has your organization been able to capitalize on another defending supplier's difficulties and will now be a second source for the purchases? Your sales force, by the way, usually answers these questions, but the answers should be independently confirmed by marketing.

◆   When will customers buy new technology? Incorporating new technology into the next generation design is one step; when will customers actually require delivery of production volumes of the new technology? Purchases of new

---

[10]"Field marketing operation" personnel titles vary by industry. We have seen missionary sellers, market development specialists, customer and product evangelists, customer engineers, and so on. What is important to recognize, as is discussed further in Chapter 11, is that this individual is delivering value to the customer, is compensated by a relatively stable salary (with some bonus potential), and is part of the marketing organization.

technology offerings are often referred to as "new business." The net business to customers is not entirely new, as they are reducing purchases of what was previously considered "core."

♦ When will customers stop buying the existing stuff? If customers are introducing a new offering to their market, how long will the existing offering be continued? There is likely to be an overlap as the new product ramps up and the old product winds down. Replacing the old core business with new business is often referred to as **core churn.**

Many customer organizations are spread around the globe. It is not unusual for design and development operations to be in one location while manufacturing is at remote sites where costs are lower. If the customer organization uses contractors for manufacturing, locations may be more volatile as changes are made to accommodate decreasing volumes of older products and increasing volumes of the new offering. Marketers will want to know:

♦ Where will the existing stuff be shipped (stored, consigned, etc.) if a change occurs as a result of the new manufacturing plan.

This leaves a set of "Who" questions that will be asked by marketing. The customer contacts that provide most other pieces of the MOF can also provide these answers:

♦ Who will actually manufacture/incorporate your products? (Do they use contract providers? Will the contract providers have favorite sources other than yours?)

♦ Who are the primary specifying and buying influences, and where are they?

♦ Who are the customers' competitors?

Additional "What" questions that need to be answered for the MOF include:

♦ What are the customers going to use the product for/in?

♦ What is the customers' market like? Does your organization understand it?

New Business, Translation, and Core Churn

Real new business is the result of a major R&D, product development, and/or marketing effort, if done from a marketing viewpoint, in conjunction with the customer. This partnership with the customer results in first-time applications or adoptions of technologies.

Translation business occurs when the customer specification is not a first-of-a-kind application. Though it may be new in the view of the customer, it is not "new" to your organization; it is merely a translation of a previous success.

Core churn occurs when the translation business at a customer replaces an application of your older technology. This "new" business certainly required an effort by the team to get the business; however, it should not require as large an effort—assuming the translation tools were adequate. Unfortunately, the organization does not experience an increase in business equal to the sales of the replacement. The organization realizes the net of the old and new volumes.

- ◆ What R&D is necessary on your part to satisfy needs?

- ◆ What kind of new business is this to the vendor? Is this business a translation of an existing success? A new market? A new product? Both a new market and a new product? Can other opportunities be located that this success can be translated to? This translation is a particular function of the field marketing specialist/missionary seller.

- ◆ What else might be unusual about this business?

Consider the power of this level of information. Remember, this is a tactical forecast. This can be organized on a spreadsheet with monthly input/revisions and additions by the field teams. With this level of tactical information, bottoms-up forecasting for strategic purposes becomes not only less cumbersome but more accurate. The real power of this information, though, lies in the planning that it facilitates. Once the marketing manager knows what, when, and how customers will be considering, buying, ordering, and using the manager's products and services, the manager can direct the marketing effort. If more resources are needed, the manager can begin the process of obtaining the authority and funding to hire new employees, hire consultants or agencies, and schedule customer visits or whatever is required.

Several groups within the organization will find this information useful: manufacturing, R&D, scheduling, logistical support, customer service, and so on. If the supplying organization is engaged in a business that markets products to companies that use contract manufacturers or have several geographically dispersed manufacturing locations, they are likely to have such a logistical tracking system already. To clarify and perhaps simplify the nature of the MOF, consider the scenario in the box, "Back to Pacific Drives. . . ."

Operational forecasts of this detail can be difficult, not because the necessary information is not available but because obtaining it can be time-consuming and will be viewed by a field seller as getting in the way of selling. This will be aggravated if there is no formal missionary sales structure. If there is an existing missionary sales structure, they will need to be motivated to contribute to the MOF, probably through compensation based on their participation. (A review of the philosophy of compensation—you get what you reward—is included in Chapter 11.) However, a field marketing team is in the best position to gather and organize this information.

Exhibit 6–8 is an example of a concise way to handle all of this market information so that it is useful to many company entities. Enterprise software now exists to do "automatically" what was a once-a-month computerized report. With the advent of corporate Intranets, this data can be readily updated and available. Market factors that impact forecasts, such as regional economies, world economic conditions, interest rates, and other factors that can impact business levels, can be added to the report, but these factors are beyond the scope of this analysis.

First-of-a-Kind Application, Translation of a Previous Success, or Replacement for Existing Business? All new business is good—right?—but what kind of new business is it? Different types of "new

Back to Pacific Drives. . .

The missionary seller, working over a period of eighteen months, develops a major piece of business with a Silicon Valley computer company. Pacific Drives brand is specified on the drawings for new models of the computer company's network servers, though the "or equivalent" phrase follows the specification.

Over this eighteen-month period, many company disciplines will want to be notified of what is going on. Manufacturing will want to plan resources and schedule manufacturing. Logistical support will want to plan when and where to ship. Your missionary seller (a marketing position) has done an exemplary job. Except . . .

Like many companies, your customer has remote manufacturing sites. If the customer's new server line is successful, production will start in Ireland six months after initial manufacturing. Perhaps your sales team in these sales territories would like to know what is going on. They may have some interesting information to contribute to a better plan to serve this piece of business.

For instance, one of the potential contract manufacturers contemplating a bid for the business has a cozy relationship with your major competitor, DynaDrives, who has extended special credit terms.

Oh, by the way, two years ago, during a shortage, you cut off the contract manufacturer because of slow payment. How does this change the business and, hence, the forecast? Can you influence who/what/where/when? You can only if you know about it.

EXHIBIT 6–8   Data Chart for Marketing Operations Forecast

Customer Name	Application	Our Product	Annual Vol.	1st Year Vol.	Close Date	Run	New/ Trans.	Comp.*	Comp. Product	Ship/ Mfr.	Threat Assess.
Ajax Computer	Printer	MX272	35,000	4,000	7/02	24 mo.	Trans.	Zigma	Z-44	Ajax/ Mexico	70%
Widget Inc.	Step driver	PX401	100,000	45,000	4/03	48 mo.	New	UniMem	UM503	tbd	60%
Palo Alto Computer	Desktop computer	PD1000	60,000	30,000	4/03	18 mo.	Trans.	UniMem	UM300	Palo Alto/ Texas	60%
NBM Computer	Notebook computer	PDN1005	75,000	20,000	4/03	24 mo.	New	Coastal Drives	CDX	NBM/ Sinapore	20%
Spartan Computer	Internet appliance	PD1000	6000	5000	1/04	24 mo.	Trans.	UniMem	tbd	tbd	50%
.	.	.	.	.	.	.	.	.	.	.	.
.	.	.	.	.	.	.	.	.	.	.	.
.	.	.	.	.	.	.	.	.	.	.	.

*Comp. = competition

business" require different resources of the organization. Note the eighth column of Exhibit 6–8, "New/Trans." This is where the marketer indicates what category of new business the application falls into from the marketer's perspective. Is the application new business, a translation from a previous success, or incremental business as the application is a replacement for an existing piece of core business? In other words, beyond the actual sales volume, what qualitative value does the application have to the selling organization and how should the marketing effort be managed?

Real new business is the result of a major R&D, product development, and/or marketing effort if done from a marketing viewpoint in conjunction with the customer. This partnership with the customer results in first-time applications or adoptions of technologies. Many parts of the organization are involved. Can it be manufactured? Can we support the volume? The missionary seller gets a lot of help. The organization is going to want to brag about this piece of business after the customer introduces its product to the market, hoping to attract additional customers interested in the same value statement. These are the applications and efforts that everyone in the organization finds the most exciting. Most "new business" however, is not *real* new business.

What if the new customer specification is not a first-of-a-kind application? This is true for the majority of new business. While a partnership with the customer may have developed a specification for your company's product, and it may be new in the view of that customer, it is not "new" to your organization; that is, it is not a new technology, product, or use of a product. It is merely a **translation** of a previous success. As an example, let us say that working with Hewlett-Packard, you develop a *new* high-capacity disk drive for HP's personal computers. Business with HP (in this instance) is real new business. Your headquarters disk drive product specialist (or whatever title is used) develops a set of marketing tools for the field team to take this success and translate it to other customers. Missionary sellers eagerly take these **translation tools** to their other customers in the PC business—Sony, Compaq, Dell, and so on. Soon, these other PC manufacturers begin to use the new disk drive. While new business to the missionary seller and the customer, these applications are translations of the HP success.

What if the translation business at Compaq replaces an application of your older technology disk drives? Is this business still considered new? It certainly requires an effort by the team to get the business; however, it should not require as large an effort—assuming the translation tools were adequate. Unfortunately, the organization does not experience an increase in business equal to the sales of the new disk drive at Compaq. The organization realizes the net of the old and new volumes. This replacement business, core churn, is necessary, important, and critical to market ownership but not as glamorous to the team as "real new business." The organization needs all three types of new business, real, translation, and churn. Each type has different implications for margins, customer support, and product development—the entire marketing mix.

Summary of Forecasting

We have focused on the forecasting effort meant to support marketing operations. This forecast, the marketing operations forecast, is done yearly and updated monthly. It forecasts more than sales: it provides estimates of purchases from major customers and customer groups. It also forecasts the activities that customers will go through to make these purchases. Such forecasts give the marketing manager the information needed to deploy marketing resources and give direction to the sales force. The detail required is voluminous, and the integration of the data into usable forecasts requires experience and insight on the manager's part. Once the forecasts are operating, though, they provide a template for the marketing manager, allowing a truly organized effort to follow.

Learning about your business environment is much like your education process. You have to do a great deal of studying early in the process, and then you must engage in continuous learning. In this chapter, we have discussed the early studying that must be done, focusing on customers and competitors. Remember that all of this learning helps create and manage value for customers, so customers are the starting point in the analysis. Just as Lou Gerstner did when he started at IBM and just as Adobe did when it reorganized its company, everything starts with learning about value from the customer's perspective.

In this chapter, we have also presented one of the uses of this information, conducting forecasting. We have focused on the practical aspects of forecasting, particularly the construction of a marketing operations forecast. The marketing operations forecast starts with customers and what they are likely to do in the near future: how much they will buy of what kinds of products, when they will buy, when they will need delivery, and when they will need support. This provides information sufficient for planning the execution of marketing programs and tactics.

In the next chapter, we show you another major use of the information gathered in the analysis of the business environment. Information gathered about market segments and competitors that address them leads to decisions on choice of target segments and positioning. Then, in Chapters 8 through 13, the detailed information on customer needs and buying behavior obtained in the analysis helps in forming the marketing strategy, programs, and tactics.

Key Terms

alpha test	exploratory research	response rates
assumptions	focus groups	sample
beta test	goals	secondary data
capabilities	go/no-go decision	sources of competition
conclusive research	incentives for	strategies
core business	participation	targeting decision
core churn	market intelligence	time compression
design decision	personal interviews	translation
e-business	primary market research	translation tools
evidence seeking	real new business	

Questions for Review and Discussion

1. Why is market research needed in business-to-business marketing? Why can't decisions always be made based on the manager's experience and intuition?
2. What factors make market research in business-to-business markets different from research in consumer markets? What are the resulting characteristics of business-to-business market research?

3. Compare the data requirements for go/no-go decisions, targeting decisions, and design decisions.

4. What are the differences between exploratory and conclusive research? When could exploratory research be used effectively without progressing to the use of conclusive research?

5. Why do the authors assert that research for segmenting markets and research for designing offerings aimed at target markets should be kept distinct, instead of run in the same research study?

6. In what kinds of markets would you want to use quantitative research similar to that often used in consumer research?

7. Why is it more difficult to do competitive analysis in today's market than it was a decade or so ago? Explain in terms of the six forces of competition.

8. From a general viewpoint, what are you trying to determine about competitors when doing competitive analysis?

9. How would you go about collecting information on each of the following competitor characteristics: goals, strategies, capabilities, and assumptions?

10. Describe how competitive analysis is like doing a jigsaw puzzle or creating a mosaic. Why is it like this?

11. List the uses for forecasts in business-to-business marketing.

12. What are the different kinds of forecasts used in business-to-business marketing?

13. Who has primary responsibility for developing the marketing operations forecast? Why?

14. How is a marketing operations forecast used differently than a sales forecast?

Internet Exercises

Go to the Web site for InsightExpress: **http://www.insightexpress.com** Review the demonstration and descriptive material concerning its services. For what marketing research purposes in business-to-business marketing would surveys done through InsightExpress be well suited? Not well suited? Find another vendor of on-line, do-it-yourself market research (by using a search engine, for example). How does this service compare, apparently, to InsightExpress?

Suppose you were the strategic marketing manager for Insight Express. Use a search engine to identify competitors. (Try Google if you have never tried it: **http://www.google.com**) By visiting their Web sites and comparing to the information you found on Insight Express's Web site, characterize the major competitors that you find. How much can you piece together about their goals, strategies, capabilities, and assumptions from just their Web sites? How much more can you learn from on-line business and trade magazines and other on-line sources you can find (by using that search engine again)? What kind of information do you wish you were able to find? What is your overall evaluation of the usefulness of the Web for competitive intelligence gathering?

Go to eMarketer. **http://www.eMarketer.com** Find a recent forecast reported by eMarketer (recent press releases or eStats articles are a good place to start looking). How would a company in the industry being forecast use the forecast reported by eMarketer? What further data would you want to obtain? How would you go about getting such data?

Suppose your business school or marketing department wants to establish closer ties with the businesses in the local business community. Pick a business with which you think your school would like to establish closer ties. Do a preliminary investigation of the business by viewing its Web page and any newspaper, magazine, or trade journal articles you can find. Formulate a series of questions for an interview with a marketing executive at this company. Keep in mind that you want to learn what value the marketing executive might see in a closer relationship with your school. If you are so inclined, go ahead and interview a marketing executive from this company. What did you learn from the interview?

Staying with the example of building closer ties to the business community for your business school, think now about your competition. Examine the Web sites of your potential competitors (and other material you may have reasonable access to). See what you can determine about the goals, strategies, capabilities, and assumptions of other business schools that are also establishing ties to the business community. Use any information you got from the above to help you interpret the competitive information you obtain. Try to anticipate threats and opportunities.

APPENDIX 6–1

Typical Research Problems to Be Overcome by Attention to Good Research Methodology

Some typical problems in the use of market research that we have seen include the following:

◆ Misspecifying the problem. This usually comes from misunderstanding the general nature of the market or how the strategic management process (see Chapter 5) should progress. For instance, one of the authors was involved in a project in which managers in a company wanted to "fine-tune" their targeting and positioning. The research revealed that their beliefs about market structure and customer needs were inaccurate and that they were launching a product into a nonexistent market. Needless to say, fine-tuning was not the managerial issue in this case. If the problem is misspecified, everything that comes after this, then, has limited value.

◆ Designing a study that does not provide enough of the right kind of information to inform the decision maker.

◆ Choosing the wrong kind of data collection method or analytic tool. This is often the "kid with a hammer" problem: give a kid a hammer and he will find a lot of things that need pounding.* Many business marketers, particularly in the high tech and Internet realms, have fallen in love with focus groups. Often this is the wrong type of research for the issues under scrutiny.

◆ Choosing the wrong respondents. Very often in business marketing only one person in the buying center is queried.

◆ Drawing conclusions that are not supported by the data collected.

◆ Using the results of a study to draw conclusions about another problem altogether. Granted, there may not be enough time to do another study, but the limitations of the study must be clearly recognized.

APPENDIX 6–2

Useful Sources of Customer Information

In the new on-line environment, marketers can find several tools that can help in understanding customers, users, channel members, and even competitors. Some of these resemble off-line tools that do the same thing. Usually, the on-line form of the tool tends to work better or faster. Others have no off-line counterparts; they are simply something that is unique, that can only be done on-line.

---

*Attributed to Abraham Kaplan in Paul Dickson, *The Official Rules* (New York: Dell, 1978), 96.

User groups have been around for years (for a sampling of business-to-business user groups, go to http://groups.yahoo.com and view the list of product user group discussions that Yahoo hosts). In their off-line version, a marketer, customer service specialist, or technical specialist would set up the group, recruit its members, and manage the interactions through mailings, phone conferences, yearly conference meetings, and, often, e-mail. As proprietary on-line services such as CompuServe and Prodigy came into use, companies started to move more and more of their user group activities to these new "communities." Their proprietary nature, though, kept many users from participating. Similarly, many companies used "listserve" e-mail communities for their user groups or "UseNet" news groups. Both of these required the users to have Internet access and to be somewhat computer/Internet literate. Listserves and UseNet groups generally limited the nature of interaction among users and customer service people to text-based communications. On-line services had a little more flexibility in the use of graphics but were still somewhat limited. The advent of the Web and html enabled user groups to have much richer interaction.

While user groups were principally used for customer service interactions, user group communications can also be used for exploratory market research. Marketers, or research companies they hire, can treat the user group as a large focus group. The researcher asks questions and analyzes the answers. The researcher may set up the sessions in such a way that other user group members may or may not be able to read everyone's responses, depending on whether the researcher wants discussion answers or not. User groups may also be used as a panel of respondents for surveys. These are still exploratory in nature, because the generalizability of the data is unknown.

While user groups have fairly restrictive entrance requirements (e.g., members have to be users), a similar kind of on-line organization can be constructed using *on-line discussion groups* or *discussion boards*. For companies that do not want to incur the IT cost, or who want set up a discussion group quickly, several Web sites exist (e.g., eGroups, Topica, and eCircles, at the time this is being written) that allow a company to create discussion groups. The cost is free, and administration is straightforward. The company must be careful, though, to offer participants real value in exchange for their participation. Such value might be given to participants in the form of useful information, collections of links to other resources, presentation of research results, or monetary compensation. These discussion groups could be run as on-line focus groups. They would, of course, have most of the problems of focus groups, particularly the uncertainty as to whether discussions are being driven by people who are not representative of real prospective customers.

Advisory boards are another variant of the kinds of groups already discussed. Advisory boards of various kinds have been around for a long time. Advisory boards would tend to have more permanence in their membership than discussion groups. Advisory boards would tend to deal with topics more far-ranging than user groups and more decision-oriented—particularly with respect to strategic decisions—than would be discussion groups. Advisory boards would generally have a limited number of members as well. Accordingly, advisory board members can be asked to provide some big-picture views of buying behavior. While they provide useful information on the detail of buying behavior, most advisory boards would not feel well used for such purposes.

The company's own *sales force* is usually a good source of information. The marketer or researcher has to be careful in using this source, though. Most sales forces are heavily incentivized, both positively and negatively. Consequently, salespeople tend to take actions when it is clearly in their interest—often only their short-term interest—to do so. Consequently, it is important for the researcher or marketer to keep information requests to a minimum, both in frequency and level of effort required. If the marketer has enough budget to sweeten the pot, to provide some incentives such as a sweepstakes or other premium, the level of cooperation should rise. Finally, the marketer or researcher should be careful to clarify that sales quotas are not set based on the salesperson's predicted sales levels. If the salesperson believes this is the case, the results are likely to be skewed.

The marketer may also be able to collect customer data informally in ways that may not be entirely apparent. One such method is to *collect data when entertaining customers or prospects*. Often, marketers take customers to dinner or to sporting events, host parties at conventions, or provide other entertainment events. This may afford the marketer the chance to ask a few casual but well-thought-out questions. The answers in the casual setting may be more frank than they would be in the everyday business environment.

SOURCES OF SECONDARY DATA

A significant amount of decision making for business marketers derives from interpretations of secondary data. In this section, we give a brief review of some of the most prevalent and useful sources of such data.

Trade organizations often conduct good research of general interest and make the results available for members. Often the data are also available to the general public, either on a paid basis or for free. The quality of such research varies tremendously. As always, the marketer must look closely at the methodology employed before interpreting the results.

Subscription services provide detailed information to companies who subscribe. The analysis is provided in depth, usually concerning a single market or industry. The data and analysis are provided periodically, anywhere from weekly to quarterly or biannually. Information may include updated statistics on the performance of a market or industry. Many subscription services also include ad hoc reports on current issues and trends. In many services, the subscribers are permitted to submit several of their own questions to be included in the data collection. While this source gives more detail than is found in the public arena, it still has the drawback that it is collected and interpreted by a third party. Hence, except for the few questions that subscribers contribute to the questionnaire, it is still secondary data, albeit focused and usually useful secondary data. Another drawback is the price of subscription, which is often prohibitive for smaller companies.

In contrast to subscription services' reports, many *research vendors* perform other studies that constitute secondary data. These vendors create special reports on topics of interest and offer them for sale for a one-time fee. These are usually much more extensive than the special reports provided to research subscribers. These are very often timely and useful. Marketers must pay close attention to the definitions and methods used, though. Often research vendors studying the same issues come to strikingly different conclusions. The differences often arise from differences in approach.

The *federal government* is one of the best sources of data on domestic industries. The Bureau of the Census, the Department of Commerce, the Department of Labor, the Small Business Administration, and all of the bureaus and agencies with special commercial jurisdictions create a mountain of information. Two of the most useful for business marketers are from the Bureau of the Census. These are *County Business Patterns* and the *Annual Survey of Manufactures. County Business Patterns* provides a count of the number of companies, sorted by the size of company as measured by the number of employees. Reports are generated for each county in the United States and aggregated into data by standard metropolitan statistical areas (SMSAs), by states, and for the United States as a whole. The *Annual Survey of Manufactures* provides estimates of revenues and line item expenditures for companies in all the manufacturing standard industrial classification (SIC) codes for each state, each year. The problem with most of the federal government data is that it is usually about two years old before it comes out in a report. Some of the national-level economic and labor data are reported more quickly, but this information is usually not useful for specific industry analyses.

Two Web sites are particularly useful in finding federal government statistics. The first—http://www.fedstats.gov—is devoted solely to government statistics. The second—http://www.firstgov.gov—is a portal for finding anything governmental, including statistics, but also other kinds of research.

State and local governments produce research reports on similar economic and business issues for their own states. Often, the data reuse federally reported data. However, they may collect their own data and report it as well. For a regional or single city—focused business, these local sources may prove to be the most useful sources of all. Economic development agencies often are the best sources of this local information.

International trade organizations, such as the World Trade Organization, often have good sources of data on international trade. For someone that is used to looking at domestic data presented by the federal government, the availability of useful data on international markets will prove a letdown. The international trade organizations are just not as well organized for this as the federal government is.

APPENDIX 6–3

Working with Market Research Vendors

Market researchers often need help from outside agencies. Market research vendors come in all shapes and sizes. Large ones often can provide resources to support integrated marketing programs. Smaller research firms often specialize in types of information collection, types of problems addressed, or markets studied. In working with market research vendors, common sense will go a long ways toward getting the most from the relationship. There are, however, some special circumstances that need to be kept in mind when dealing specifically with research vendors.

Research, by its nature, is a process of discovery. When negotiating a contract, enough flexibility needs to be built in so that the process can be changed as required. By the same token, the researchers need to understand that deadlines for decisions must be met. Early in the process, the client and the researchers should discuss what dimensions of the research are the highest priorities.

Then potential trade-offs between the dimensions of the research should be agreed upon. For instance, a potential trade-off may exist between level of uncertainty and the time required for data collection and analysis. The parties should discuss what levels of uncertainty are acceptable and preferred. They should also discuss the consequences if the research schedule should slip, as well as the advantages gained if the research is completed early. This will give the researcher a good sense of context so that the researcher can adapt the study design appropriately as events unfold. The parties may decide to build incentives into the research contract so that the research vendor will have good reason to strive for the preferable levels of uncertainty and timeliness, rather than settle for the merely acceptable levels. By talking about the trade-offs, the parties will tend to have more open communications as the project progresses, which also leads to better project outcomes.

From the vendor's perspective, such an approach will produce a process that is easier to live with. Having a sense of the client's level of flexibility and sense of urgency helps the vendor gauge the budget requirements. It also gives the vendor a chance to describe the methodology and why its costs need to be incurred.

Finally, marketers seeking the services of a research vendor usually need to specify the problems that need to be addressed rather than the specific tasks of the project. Professional researchers usually have a better understanding of the latest methodology than do marketing managers. Once vendors have submitted proposals, the managers can seek explanations from the vendors as to the advantages and disadvantages of the methods proposed.

7

Segmenting, Targeting, and Positioning

© ANDY WONG/AP/WIDE WORLD PHOTOS

overview. . . In this chapter, we examine the process of segmentation, a process that partitions a market into subgroups based on similarities and differences in customer needs and perceptions of value. We then see how segmentation affects the marketing strategy of the business-to-business firm through, "targeting," a process of selecting the best segments for the success of the organization, and through "positioning," the establishment of competitive differentiation within targeted segments. We consider segmentation in terms of value and the value chain, discussing how such a method allows the formation of effective strategy. Two approaches for determining market segmentation are explored, an analytic approach and a discovery approach; and we discuss how these two approaches can work together to find useful segmentation frameworks.

Once segments have been identified, the marketer can choose target segments—those segments to be directly addressed with specific offerings. To choose targets, the marketer evaluates the likelihood of success within each segment based on the competencies of the firm and the willingness to commit resources to that market segment. We discuss the criteria for prioritizing segments and an approach for determining the number of segments to target.

Once target segments have been chosen, the process begins for designing strategy and offerings to engage each segment. The structure for this effort is the determination of positioning relative to competition.

The opening example shows how marketers at Panasonic positioned their offering for a segment of the larger market.

PANASONIC TARGETS THE RUGGED LAPTOP SEGMENT*

In 1996, four Japanese personal computer makers, Fujitsu, Hitachi, NEC, and Sony, "invaded" the U.S. PC market. Unlike these four, Panasonic did not address the U.S. consumer market, even though Panasonic's parent company, Matsushita, had a successful consumer offering in Japan. In the United States, the Panasonic Personal Computer Company targeted organizations that needed durable, portable computers. This market focus kept Panasonic's sales numbers down—in 1999, it only sold 400,000 units worldwide. Panasonic margins, however, were among the highest in the industry at a reported 30 percent gross margin per unit. In addition, the market Panasonic chose was growing at over 40 percent per year in 2000.

Panasonic's focus on the "rugged notebook" allowed it to have a clear, concise message and to structure distribution channels that provide value while not competing or conflicting. The segment consisted of organizations that deployed significant numbers of notebooks to employees in the field. These could be employees performing on-site customer service, field repairs, field sales, or other active duty as might be encountered in police or military uses. In these applications, customers wanted good performance that was not interrupted by frequent breakdowns. Panasonic's durable construction met this requirement. Additional features, such as wireless operation and touch-screen interfaces, honed the value of the equipment for the kinds of situations customers faced.

When Panasonic launched the line in 1996, the communications messages all revolved around the durability of the machines. The notebook line is named Toughbook, which of course immediately communicates the key core benefit. Print advertising was simple, elegant, and pointed, with the notebook sitting on an anvil or shown in some other industrial-strength pose. It received a great deal of publicity from a well-designed promotional event in which one of the hosts of a television network morning show drove a Hummer over a Toughbook at the Comdex trade show. The advertising campaign "Own the Road" won an EFFIE award (from the New York American Marketing Association for effective advertising) in 1998.

The channels for Toughbook involved two distributors. One distributor, Pinacor (a subsidiary of MicroAge), was aimed at Fortune 1000 firms. The second distributor, Government Technology Services, targeted government

*Based on Geoffrey James, "Standing Tough," Marketing Computers 20, no. 3 (March 2000): 34–42.

PANASONIC TARGETS THE RUGGED LAPTOP SEGMENT (CONT'D)

sales. Panasonic did not offer direct or Internet sales. Because the distributors did not compete against Panasonic or each other, and because customers were willing to pay for the value of product, fair margins were maintained for both Panasonic and the channel.

This strategy stands in sharp contrast to the strategies pursued by the four Japanese companies, who all attempted to enter the broader consumer market. Products were generally mismatched to consumer preferences (and often inferior to competitors' products), communications messages were diffused, and channel programs created conflict. All this occurred just as the consumer market for PCs became extremely competitive, driving prices and margins downward. Hitachi, Fujitsu, and NEC have essentially minimized or curtailed their PC operations in the United States. Only Sony has managed to thrive with its well-designed, premium positioned, Sony Vaio line of notebooks. Toshiba is the only other Japanese company performing well in the U.S. market, substantially based on its early entry into the portable computer market and its largely autonomous U.S. operations.

Panasonic is well positioned to defend this market segment. The segment is small enough that few of the larger competitors see it as attractive. Panasonic is already well known and well liked within this segment. The company continues to innovate to improve its offering. While it does not own the PC market as a whole, Panasonic continues to own this segment and it continues to be profitable in doing so.

introduction . . .

LEARNING OBJECTIVES

Three of the most important concepts in marketing, whether in business-to-business marketing or consumer marketing, are **segmenting**, **targeting**, and **positioning.** The process of **segmenting** markets makes it possible to know a market well enough to tailor an offering to the specific needs of a few customers rather than creating an offering whose attributes are compromised (e.g., too little, too much, or not exactly as desired) in an attempt to appeal to a broad market. The process of **targeting** involves choosing segments to address based on matching the firm's strengths to the segments that will place the greatest value on these strengths and yield the greatest

- ◆ Reinforce the student's understanding of segmentation as a tool to manage markets and resources.
- ◆ Develop an understanding of segmentation based on the concepts of value and the value chain.
- ◆ Understand how segmentation supports business-to-business marketing decisions.
- ◆ Understand when and how an analytic approach to segmentation is useful.
- ◆ Understand customer involvement in business-to-business segment discovery and evolution.
- ◆ Understand segment evaluation and the targeting process to maximize market opportunities.
- ◆ Reinforce market-positioning philosophy through an understanding of its importance as a tool to enhance both customer and vendor value.

success. **Positioning** is the creation of greater value for targeted customers than is offered by competitors and the communication of that difference relative to other offerings aimed at the target market segment. In this chapter, we show how segmentation and the choice of target segments works when based on the concepts of value and the value chain, discussed in Chapter 1 and Chapter 2. From these concepts, the criteria for a good **segmentation framework**—a method of segmentation used in understanding a given market—are derived, as well as criteria for the choice of a good set of target segments. Once target segments are chosen, the marketer determines how the offering for each of these segments ought to be positioned.

THE RELATIONSHIP BETWEEN SEGMENTING, TARGETING, AND POSITIONING

Recall that in business strategy, discussed in Chapter 5, the organization decides in what business to compete and how, generally, to compete. Whether it is done during the analysis of the business environment for corporate strategy or when analysis is done for business unit or product strategy, the analysis of markets, customers, and competitors (as discussed in Chapter 6) often reveals segments of potential buyers. Market segments are distinct from each other in what they need or how they buy. Within each segment, the needs or buying behavior of individual buyers are very similar to those of the other members of the segment. In other words, it is desirable to create segments whose members tend to have homogeneous needs or buyer behavior within the market segment and distinctly different needs or buyer behavior when compared to members of other segments. Though sometimes cumbersome in development, a good segmentation framework can simplify the approach to a market by reducing the variability of needs and behaviors across that market's members, allowing marketers to select segments for targeting where the firm can have the best advantage for success. Customers are also better served through the creation of offerings whose value is more closely aligned with their needs.

The Panasonic example illustrates these ideas well. The market segment that Panasonic discovered has only one primary value dimension, the need for durability. There is little variation within the segment on this dimension. The simplicity of the segmentation structure makes it easy to target and straightforward in providing the required value.

After alternative segments have been identified and understood, choosing target segments follows. It involves combining information about the opportunity within each segment and information about the organization's capability and desire to pursue each of the opportunities. The analysis creates a measurement, or at least a sense, of the overall attractiveness of each segment. The marketer chooses the most attractive segments that the company can address.

In the Panasonic example, the durability laptop segment was chosen because of four main attractiveness factors. First, the need was obvious and it was important. Second, no competitor was doing a good job of meeting this need and none was expected to do so in the near future. Third, this need matched well with Panasonic's capability. Fourth, the segment was projected to grow quickly. The only drawback was the relatively small size of this segment, but even this worked in Panasonic's favor. Because Panasonic did not set out to dominate the entire U.S. market for laptops, the size of the durable segment was acceptable. Meanwhile, it *was* too small for the major competitors who wanted to dominate the entire market. This gave Panasonic a competitive edge.

Once segments are targeted, the marketer analyzes the value sought within each target segment, as well as the value provided by the principal competitors, and determines how to create a competitive position to address each targeted segment. The positioning of an offering for a segment is the definition of which dimensions of value will be emphasized. The purpose is to offer more value than competitors on some key dimension or dimensions. Positioning establishes the framework for the marketing strategy. It defines the product or service features to be emphasized, the general message to be communicated to selected audiences, the channels that will be used to create value for the buyer at the point of sale, and the price level that the customer should see.

Panasonic positions itself well for the durable laptop market. First, the product is well suited to this market. Second, Panasonic has done well in communicating its message through advertising and publicity. Third, Panasonic has done a solid job in supporting the channels who carry its products. And fourth, the price tag meets expectations without charging too much of a premium. We now explore additional details of the relationship of segmenting, targeting, and positioning.

MARKET SEGMENTATION

The concept of market segmentation has been around for a long time.[1] In practice, there is much confusion surrounding the idea.[2] This is unfortunate, as the segmentation process is intended to reduce confusion and assist marketers to better understand how to serve particular markets. In business-to-business marketing, there are some special aspects to segmentation that make it even more perplexing. In this section, we develop the basic ideas of segmentation, then we examine segmentation in the context of business marketing, along with the most important implications. We then present ideas on the practical aspects of measuring and analyzing segmentation.

Basic Ideas of Segmentation

Finding Groups with Similarities in What They Buy or How They Act

As described earlier, segmentation involves dividing a market into subgroups or categories of customers in such a way that the marketer gains a competitive advantage. When defining segments, marketers must recognize that very broad segments, such as those in consumer mass markets, require products that appeal to the large population of the segment. Selecting smaller segments, either through a more detailed analysis of the market as a whole or as subsegments within the broad model, reduces the number of potential customers that one offering must satisfy. The offering may then be defined with more specific attributes that have value to that customer group rather than with a compromise that almost satisfies the members of a larger market. This is not intended to imply that a greater number of smaller segments is always better than a few large segments. Markets can become oversegmented. The fragmentation and diversity that result make it difficult to profitably serve the smaller markets.

Generally, marketers strive to create segments that have characteristics of **measurability, accessibility, substantiality,** and **actionability.** In business-to-business markets, *measurability* is important because marketers need to understand the size, value needs, and purchasing characteristics of a particular segment. If such measurements cannot be made, it becomes difficult to choose among alternative segments and to design offerings that provide superior value for members of a segment. *Accessibility* is a measure of the marketer's ability to communicate with the market segment in a manner that makes serving the segment possible. *Substantiality* implies a market segment that desires the particular value offering an organization presents, such that the segment is profitable enough to serve differentially from other segments. *Actionability* is a measure of the capabilities of the offering organization to create a competitive advantage with respect to the specific needs of the segment.

---

[1]Wendell R. Smith, "Product Differentiation and Market Segmentation as Alternative Marketing Strategies," *Journal of Marketing* 21, no. 1 (July 1956): 4.

[2]See Peter R. Dickson and James L. Ginter, "Market Segmentation, Product Differentiation, and Marketing Strategy," *Journal of Marketing* 51, no. 2 (April 1987): 1–10; and John Berrigan and Carl Finkbeiner, *Segmentation Marketing* (New York: HarperBusiness, 1992).

Targeting some segments and not targeting others may achieve such a competitive advantage. As Porter has pointed out, there are essentially three strategies for addressing market segments and achieving a competitive advantage.[3] In the first, the company that addresses segments may achieve a competitive advantage by obtaining a low-cost position and putting competitive-pricing pressure on competitors. A second strategy is to provide products or services that are differentiated; yet, they appeal to broad, mass markets. A third strategy is to target a niche or segment, providing exactly the right product or service at a reasonable price, thus differentiating the offering from competitors' in that small market space. Accordingly, the choice of general business strategy, as well as the marketing strategy to implement it, depends on an understanding of how the market is segmented and how the segments behave.

Typical Bases for Business-to-Business Segmentation

There are many **bases for segmentation,** some straightforward, some obtuse. A business must choose the segmentation strategy that makes the best use of its strengths and positions it effectively against competitors. Exhibit 7–1 shows the typical bases for segmenting business-to-business markets.

In the preceding chapter, IBM's WebConnections service was examined. In this instance, IBM chose to identify a market segment that was based first on the size of the organization, that is, smaller organizations with small-sized local area networks (LANs). They went farther than this, of course, and targeted the segment that was also defined by some special needs. These needs were to move into conducting business via the Web, yet without incurring a huge cost in adopting new information technology. Similarly, in the opening example, Panasonic identified a segment based on preferences of the customers, borne out of a special need. The common need, of course, was for portability and durability of the computers. While other potential customers in the market had a need for portability, their need for durability was not so acute as it was for those targeted by Panasonic. It turns out that, no matter how

[3]Michael Porter, *Competitive Strategy* (New York: Free Press, 1980).

EXHIBIT 7–1   Common Bases for Segmentation of Business-to-Business Markets

- *By product offered.* A company may treat all customers who offer the same kind of product as a market segment.
- *By geographic region.* Customers located in the same geographic area may be treated as a market segment.
- *By industry in which the customer participates.* All companies in the same industry group may be treated as belonging to a market segment.
- *By size of customer's company.* Companies of the same general size may be treated as belonging to a market segment.
- *By size of account.* A company may treat all its customers who order roughly the same amounts from the company as a market segment.
- *By buying behavior or preferences.* Segments may consist of companies whose buying centers act in similar fashions or whose needs are very similar.
- *By technology used by customer.* All companies that use the same general product or process technology may be treated as a segment.

segments are initially defined, the marketer should almost always be looking for special, common needs that can be addressed by the marketer's company.

Value-Based Segmentation

No matter which of the segmentation bases in Exhibit 7–1 is chosen by a business, business-to-business marketers, like consumer marketers, should target segments that have similar needs or buying behavior among their members. It makes sense that, if most companies in your target market want the same thing, you can save a great deal on costs by providing one product that is well designed and offering it with efficient and appropriate communications and sales methods. If, on the other hand, every company in your target market segment were to think and act uniquely, then it would be very costly to meet the needs of multiple customers within this segment, suggesting that a new segmentation strategy should be investigated.

A more complete way to think of segments is to say that segments should be based on differences in value sought. While simply defined—value is the sum of the benefits minus the sum of the costs—the perception of value will not remain constant across many customers. Exhibit 7–2a and Exhibit 7–2b show the value chain concept again. However, they also show the difference between two combinations of value chains and offerings. The first combination addresses a second segment whose members vary considerably in the kinds of value they seek. The second combination is built to provide value to a segment whose members all seek similar sorts of value. The offering and value chain for the first combination display considerably more complexity and, hence, will be more difficult to construct and probably will be more costly to execute. The implication is simple. Companies should try to choose and address segments that are homogeneous in the kinds of value sought rather than heterogeneous. The marketing organization will then find it easier to discern the needs of the customers and translate these into an offering that provides superior value, enabling the organization to be better able to manage their costs and their businesses.

EXHIBIT 7–2a   Value Chain and Offering for a Segment with Heterogenous Needs

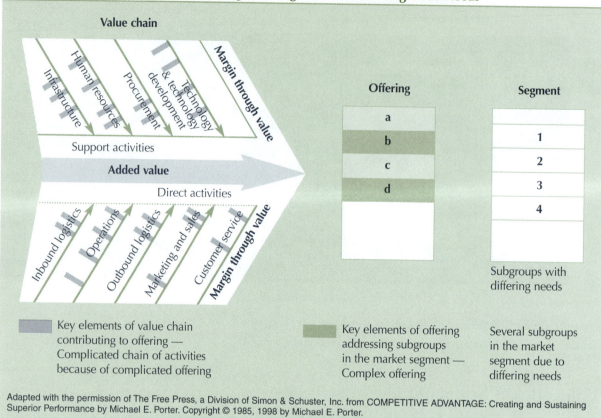

Adapted with the permission of The Free Press, a Division of Simon & Schuster, Inc. from COMPETITIVE ADVANTAGE: Creating and Sustaining Superior Performance by Michael E. Porter. Copyright © 1985, 1998 by Michael E. Porter.

EXHIBIT 7–2b   Value Chain and Offering for a Segment with Homogeneous Needs

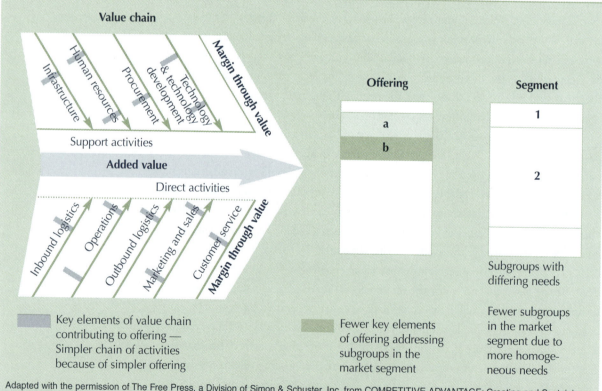

Adapted with the permission of The Free Press, a Division of Simon & Schuster, Inc. from COMPETITIVE ADVANTAGE: Creating and Sustaining Superior Performance by Michael E. Porter. Copyright © 1985, 1998 by Michael E. Porter.

The Process of Determining Segmentation

Two useful ways of determining a segmentation framework to employ are in general use in business-to-business marketing. They are, first, an analytic approach and, second, a discovery approach. The approach to use depends on the situation that the company faces. Marketers tend to use an analytic approach when they face a market with many customers or an unfamiliar market they are trying to enter. When a marketer has only a few large customers and is looking to extend its existing offering into new customer groups, the marketer often takes a discovery approach. Both approaches work well under the right circumstances. We feel that using a combination of the two approaches often would improve the segmentation and, hence, the positioning and strategy that results.

Analytic Approach to Determine a Segmentation Framework

An **analytic approach** employs research and data interpretation to derive a segmentation framework.[4] The approach attempts to develop two sets of information. The first set has to do with segment size and growth. These data help support decisions of which segments to target and whether or not it is a good idea to proceed. The second set of data has to do with an individual segment's needs and buying behavior. These data are much richer in terms of the value sought by segment members. Combined, these two sets of data support design decisions on products, services, communications messages, media choices, selling approaches, channel design, and pricing.

The first type of information—having to do with segment size and growth—must often be gathered quickly, particularly for decisions made early in the planning process on likely target segments and go/no-go decisions. To aid in quickly analyzing segments and making these decisions, the marketer must often rely heavily on secondary data. As can be seen in Appendix 6.2 (at the end of Chapter 6), government or trade organizations collect much of these secondary data. These agencies collect data so that many people and organizations can use them for various purposes. The data are usually arranged by the **Standard Industrial Classification (SIC)** or the **North American Industry Classification System (NAICS)** code, by geographical location, and perhaps by size of company (i.e., the data are usually arranged demographically). The marketer, however, would usually like to have the data arranged in more fine-grained fashion so that they are closely linked to differences in value sought. Consequently, to use the data quickly, the marketer will need to make some reasonable assumptions to convert the demographic data to estimates he can actually use.

> The **Standard Industrial Classification (SIC)** code is a scheme of industry classifications designed and used by the U.S. government. It is being replaced by the **North American Industry Classification System (NAICS)** that better reflects the distribution of industries in modern-day Canada, Mexico, and the United States. To see a comparison, go to http://www.census.gov/naics/

---

[4]See Peter Doyle and John Saunders, "Market Segmentation and Positioning in Specialized Industrial Markets," *Journal of Marketing* 49, no. 2 (Spring 1985): 24–32, for an illustration.

Before discussing the second type of data, let us look at a hypothetical example to show what the marketer might have to do.

Suppose the marketer was investigating entering the market for on-line surveys for small businesses to assess customer satisfaction. The marketer's company provides on-line surveys for larger companies for various kinds of market research. He has gotten wind of this potentially unmet need among smaller companies. In initial talks with CEOs of small companies, the marketer believes that several possible segments exist among companies who recognize that they have a need:

◆ Companies that are receiving frequent customer complaints and that are losing occasional customers; let us call this *Segment 1: Major turnaround.*

◆ Companies that believe their relationships with customers are generally weakening and are seeking to stop the deterioration before it is too late; let us call this *Segment 2: Stopping deterioration.*

◆ Companies that have high levels of customer satisfaction but that believe they are facing increasingly competitive markets in which they must achieve ever-higher levels of customer satisfaction if they are to remain competitive; let us call this *Segment 3: Competitive improvement.*

◆ Companies that believe they have problems in specific areas, such as meeting delivery schedules or performing effective customer training, and that seek to improve performance in these specific areas; let us call this *Segment 4: Specific area improvement.*

It should be obvious from the foregoing listing of categories that it is unlikely that the marketer will find secondary data that will break out the numbers of small companies into these groupings. The marketer may be lucky and find a research report done by a market research company that examines how well small businesses are performing and gives data that roughly approximates the size of the groups listed. If not, the marketer will need to find a way to make reasonable assumptions about how large each of the groups is and how fast they are growing. One way might be to talk with several small business consultants to get their opinions of how large these segments are. Another might be to examine Dunn and Bradstreet data (see Appendix 6–2 for an explanation of Dunn and Bradstreet) to get a breakdown of financial performance categories and use these as rough approximations of sizes for the segments.

Suppose that the marketer finds data on the number of small businesses from the U.S. Bureau of the Census and performs a Delphi forecast of segment growth by pooling estimates provided by a group of small business consultants. (See Chapter 6, Exhibit 6–5, for a description of Delphi forecasting.) The marketer believes that the relevant size range for small businesses is 50 to 500 employees: below 50 and they are not large enough to see the $5,000 per year price as worthwhile; above 500 and they are already likely to have a customer satisfaction tracking solution in place if they desire one. The hypothetical data are shown in Exhibit 7–3.

EXHIBIT 7–3   **Hypothetical Data for Segmentation for On-line Customer Satisfaction Survey Service***

From secondary data:	
Number of U.S. businesses with more than 50 and fewer than 500 employees	375,000
From quick survey of consultants:	
Segment 1: *Major turnaround.* Assumed percentage of small businesses with customer satisfaction problems	10
Segment 2: *Stopping deterioration.* Assumed percentage of small businesses seeking to stop deterioration in customer satisfaction	20
Segment 3: *Competitive improvement.* Assumed percentage of small businesses seeking to improve competitive performance	30
Segment 4: *Specific area improvement.* Assumed percentage of small businesses seeking to improve specific functional areas contributing to customer satisfaction (can overlap with above categories)	50
From a Delphi estimate of a small business consultants:	
Segment 1: Assumed percentage increase in *major turnaround* segment by year 2002	100
Segment 2: Assumed percentage increase in *stopping deterioration* segment by 2002	100
Segment 3: Assumed percentage increase (decrease) in *competitive improvement* segment by 2002	(50)
Segment 4: Assumed percentage increase in *specific area improvement* segment by 2002	150

*Number of businesses is projected from United States Bureau of the Census, *U.S. County Business Patterns* (1997, 1998). Other data are hypothetical.

On the basis of data in Exhibit 7–3, the marketer estimates that by 2002, the *stopping deterioration* segment will become the largest of the first three segments, at 150,000 companies (.2 × 375,000 = 75,000 companies in 2000; +100 percent = 150,000 companies in 2002). In addition, the *specific area improvement* segment of the market will increase to 281,250 companies (.3 × 375,000 = 112,500 companies in 2000; + 150 percent = 281,250 companies in 2002). This information and the resulting calculations give the marketer an estimate of relative segment size, both now and in the future. The segment sizes for 2000 and 2002 are shown in Exhibit 7–4.

With these estimates in mind, the marketer can evaluate the segmentation framework with respect to *measurability, accessibility, substantiality,* and *actionability.* First, concerning measurability, the estimates shown in Exhibit 7–4 illustrate that the segments in this framework can be measured. The estimates could be refined with more primary research, if need be. In terms of accessibility, let us assume in this hypothetical example that the segments as defined can be reached through normal distribution and communications channels. Small businesses, whether financially well off or financially strapped, can be contacted through mail, print, and Internet media; data can be provided to them through physical or digital distribution channels (further research may show preferences for certain types of media and channels within the segments). With respect to substantiality, let us assume that the sizes of these segments are large enough to warrant consideration, given

EXHIBIT 7–4　Hypothetical Sizes of Market Segments for On-line Customer Satisfaction Survey Service

Segment	Number of Small Businesses in 2000	Number of Small Businesses in 2002	Percentage Increase (Decrease) from 2000 to 2002
Segment 1: *Major turnaround*	37,500	75,000	100
Segment 2: *Stopping deterioration*	75,000	150,000	100
Segment 3: *Competitive improvement*	112,500	56,250	(50)
Segment 4: *Specific area improvement* (can overlap with above categories)	112,500	281,250	150

the goals of the research vendor. The marketer will later need to examine more closely the sustainability of profits within segments that are chosen. Finally, concerning actionability, let us assume that the needs of each segment can be met by an offering that the marketer feels his company can provide. Accordingly, the segmentation framework is one that is viable for the software supplier.

This simple example shows how an analytic approach might be used in making quick estimates of segment size and growth. This is not enough information for choosing segments, but it is a start. The marketer will need to develop and use information on needs within the segments, competitors' offerings and strategies for addressing the segments, and his own company's strengths and weaknesses in providing value to the segments.

The second type of data—data on the needs and buying behavior exhibited within individual market segments—needs to be mostly primary data. These data are used early in the planning process to suggest the bases for segmentation. They are also used for suggesting assumptions the marketer might apply to secondary data to determine market size and growth, as was done in the preceding example. For these two purposes, data gathering can be fairly quick, particularly if the marketer has a good network of contacts in the relevant market (as discussed in Chapter 6). However, data on needs and buying behavior are also used for design decisions, starting with decisions on positioning. These decisions require the development of in-depth information and, hence, require more time. The decisions themselves, though, also take some time to reach a conclusion, so there generally is more time for acquiring and digesting primary data (though this is still subject to pressure from the time compression trend, discussed in previous chapters).

Using the techniques described in Chapter 6, the marketer can obtain data on the prospective customers' needs, buying center behavior, reactions to messages, reactions to pricing options, and channel preferences. During this data gathering and analysis, the marketer may discover information that calls into question the original choice of target segments. Such discoveries ought to be anticipated; the decision process should allow for performing some reiterations that change the emphasis among target segments or even discard a segment from consideration. Before the investigation starts, the manager needs to predetermine what kinds of negative information will trigger reconsideration of the targeting decisions. If such

> ### New Business, Translation, and Core Churn
>
> *Real* new business is the result of a major R&D, product development, and/or marketing effort, if done from a marketing viewpoint, in conjunction with the customer. This partnership with the customer results in first-time applications or adoptions of technologies.
>
> *Translation* business occurs when the customer specification is not a first-of-a-kind application. Though it may be new in the view of that customer, it is not "new" to your organization, it is merely a translation of a previous success.
>
> *Core churn* occurs when the translation business at a customer replaces an application of your older technology. This "new" business certainly required an effort by the team to get the business; however, it should not require as large an effort—assuming the translation tools were adequate. Unfortunately, the organization does not experience an increase in business equal to the sales of the replacement. The organization realizes the net of the old and new volumes.

controls are not in place, too much effort may be spent in unnecessary reconsideration of prior decisions, rather than in proactive problem solving.

Before we follow the example to the stage of choosing target segments, let us take a look at the other approach to segmenting markets, the discovery approach.

Segmentation by Discovery

In markets in which only a few customers exist, a company may provide an offering to only one or two large customers. In time, the company may decide to look for additional customers who are attracted to the offering or to an offering that is similar to the original. In the process of looking for these new customers, the marketer may "discover" a market segment.

In Chapter 6, we discussed the marketing operations forecast (MOF) and gave the descriptions *new business, translation,* and *core churn* to three different scenarios by which business can be classified. These are briefly described in the adjacent box for your review. The idea of translation has relevance for understanding how segmentation by discovery works.

When a supplier's technology or offering is familiar to a market, customers may find new uses for the product or service without additional assistance from the supplier; or the supplier and customer together may find a new use through collaboration with each other. This new use may or may not be pursued as a new market segment for the supplier. The supplier can undertake a market development effort to determine the validity of the new segment. Stated another way, the supplier will need to validate the new use of the product by translating the new use to other customers with similar needs. Hence, a successful *translation* of new business can create a new target market. It has been our experience that many new market segments are discovered through this exact process. Segmentation by *discovery* emphasizes the nature of many business-to-business market segments—they exist because a customer pulled technology through a relationship with a supplier rather than a supplier having pushed a new offering to the customer.

The marketer, with the help of field marketers (i.e., missionary sales people) and their headquarters counterparts must be well coached to recognize the importance of information about how their products are being used, as well as to recognize new business opportunities that may be discovered in those applications. Once the opportunity is recognized, the headquarters marketing team should develop a marketing plan focused on serving the newly discovered segment. This plan should, of course, develop translation tools that expand on the distinctive features or competencies that make the offering the ideal choice in this new market, as well as further defining potential players in the market. These translation tools (data sheets for new product variations, examples of the "new business" application, press releases, collateral materials, etc.) should aid the field marketing team in implementing the translation of the application to new customers. Ultimately, should the new segment progress in a manner that the supplier's offering "owns" the market, customers automatically know the offering as the standard.

One barrier to discovering new segments that may have to be overcome is the resistance encountered from new customers who are wary of the marketer's prior relationship with one of their principal competitors. In markets with a few large players, success at one customer may not lead to success at another, even if the rational needs are similar. In oligopolies, players in the market often resist ideas and developments that have their beginnings at a direct competitor. This resistance can result from an extreme concern about proprietary information. If the offering is well tailored to the competitive need, the customer who is the target of the translation may be suspicious of the level and type of communications that take place between the suppliers and the first customer. Cultural and competitive factors can also play a large role. Some oligopolistic competitors avoid any sign of imitating major competitors, particularly if customers can discern who was "first" in the market.

Obviously, such resistance creates an additional burden on the field market development team or missionary sales force. Before they can assess whether a market segment can be developed, they must overcome the second customers' reservations. This is another reason for establishing a strong field market development organization so that the preparatory work for such translation efforts has already been done when the marketer decides it is time to attempt a translation.

Essential to the discovery segmentation process and the missionary sales approach to market development is an understanding of the role of **field market development (FMD) personnel** and their relationship to direct sales, end users, and headquarters marketing personnel. This marketing effort requires a value-added or value-based price approach to be margin supportable. We have found that suppliers whose offerings require significant customer education to take full advantage of the value offering will employ a field marketing team whose compensation and position structure enables the team to spend the time with customers in the education process. This is significantly different than the role of a direct sales team. As these issues relate to field sales and other aspects of business-to-business promotion, we deal with them in greater detail in Chapter 11 and Chapter 13.

Summary of Segmentation

We have seen two approaches to segmentation, the analytic approach and the discovery approach. To review, the analytic approach seems to emerge when the marketer faces a market with many customers or when the marketer is looking to enter a new market in which his company has little or no experience. We believe that the analytic approach can be helped by introducing some elements of discovery, particularly in developing in-depth information on value sought and buying behavior within segments. Discovery can be helped by some analysis, as well. The marketer and the field missionary sales force may want to collaborate on gathering data from the field and on interpreting the data to suggest possible new market segments. This analysis may lead the missionary sales force to target high-potential segments even though these might not be the easiest for gaining initial access. Whether the marketer uses a process that is largely analytical or largely discovery, the next step is to choose target segments.

CHOOSING TARGET SEGMENTS

Once segments are defined, the process of identifying the best opportunities for the organization begins. Of the segments chosen to address, the marketer may decide that one or a few should be targeted as primary, that is, they receive emphasis. To make these choices requires application of criteria in two stages. First, the marketer makes a judgment of how attractive each segment is; then a group of segments is chosen that allows organizational objectives to be met.

Attractiveness of Segments

Exhibit 7–5 shows the factors to be taken into consideration in determining the attractiveness of each segment. Notice that attractiveness is determined from information that comes from all the elements of an environmental analysis.

Attractiveness is obviously not a concept that can be easily quantified. Some organizations may want to allocate weights to the various factors and then assign attractiveness scores based on a qualitative assessment for each segment.

EXHIBIT 7–5   Factors in Assessing Segment Attractiveness

- Size of segment
- Growth rate of segment
- Intensity of unmet need(s)
- Reachability of segment through communications channels
- Readiness of segment to seek and adopt a solution
- Likelihood of competitive intensity
- Sufficiency of channel reach
- Likely value contribution by channel(s)
- Match between segment needs and supplier's strengths
- Differentiability of supplier's offering
- Opportunity to achieve strategic goal by addressing segment
- Opportunity to achieve learning goal by addressing segment

<u>Market Attractiveness</u>   Segments that are large and growing fast are obviously more attractive than smaller or slower-growing segments, all other things being equal. As part of the effort made in "knowing the market," the marketer can estimate the size and growth rates of various segments. At this point, qualitative judgments about the priority of needs as seen by the market segment are appropriate. In other words, how important is the marketer's offering when compared to the other opportunities or solutions under consideration by the customer? The answer to this may show up in the level of urgency displayed by the customer, whether or not the customer is willing to take the lead in a new development or application, and/or whether the customer is likely to outsource solutions to difficulties or develop its own solutions.

Boeing has faced this kind of a consideration in competing with Airbus in the "superjumbo" commercial airplane market segment.[5] The question is not so much whether a market exists for super jumbos—jumbo jets with 500+ seats—but whether the market is large enough to warrant design of a new plane instead of simply modifying the existing jumbo jet design. Boeing is modifying the existing 747 design to create a 522-seat 747X. Airbus, on the other hand, has committed to designing a 600-seat new jet, called the A3XX. With a projected price of $225 million and projected development costs that could reach $15 billion, Airbus will need to sell more than 600 of the planes over 20 years if the plane is to be a financial success. Boeing believes the airlines will not perceive their need to be strong enough to justify purchasing a new plane for a relatively high price tag. Airbus is taking the risk that, in the future, the airlines will see a need strong enough to justify such purchases. This illustrates the problem that many business-to-business marketers have in trying to anticipate the future. Time horizons are often so long that research data only provide a glimmer of what will occur in the future.

Adaptability may be very important when considering market segments for a new product or service. If potential customers are able to easily adopt a new product or service because they already have in place the required infrastructure for adoption, they are more likely to act on an intention to buy. Related to this may be the existence of relationships with existing buying center members. Again, potential customers are able to act more quickly if the participants already understand their buying center roles and are used to fulfilling those roles.

As an example, consider the customer that has its own manufacturing facilities that produce

© SVEN KAESTNER/AP/WIDE WORLD PHOTOS

---

[5]Andy Reinhardt, John Rossant, and Frederik Balfour, "Boeing Gets Blown Sideways," *Business Week*, 16 October 2000, 62.

components for some of its products. Some of the other components that are incorporated into those same products are sourced from other vendors. The customer would like to stop the outsourcing, but the current technology used in the outsourced components is an industry accepted standard. As a supplier to the customer, you realize that your capabilities can assist the customer to combine your distinctive competence and the manufacturing technology and skill of its facilities to replace the outsourced components with equivalent products. The customer is likely to listen to the joint development proposal as it coincides with its own goals.

Available budget also adds to attractiveness of a market segment. A prospective customer may indeed want the product, but, if the buying center cannot access available funds, the intention to buy may go unfulfilled.

Competitive Attractiveness—Choosing Your Battles

A good competitive analysis will provide the marketer with information on the existence or likely existence of strong competition vying for business from segment members. The marketer must think ahead to how strong the competition is likely to be. Just because a competitor's offering to the market segment is currently weak does not mean that this will remain the case. Also, a market segment that is currently unaddressed by a competitor may be pursued vigorously once the competitor realizes there is potential in the market.

A segment is competitively attractive if there are significant barriers to entry for other competitors. For instance, suppose it is apparent that the first company to enter a market segment is likely to acquire critical mass of customers quickly, leaving little room for new competitors to enter. This market would then be competitively attractive to the first entry only, as the marketer should recognize the "first" in a market could create a substantial defense from competitive intrusion.

Channel Attractiveness

The ideal situation is to find segments that are already served by well-established marketing channels. The next best situation would be segments that could easily be addressed by existing channels that could be adapted. Segments are least attractive when no suitable channels address them currently and development of new channels would be difficult.

When there are not any obvious suitable channels, a market view of competition may be necessary. Even when the offering is new to the market, customers will have been satisfying the existing need with less than ideal solutions and may be in the habit of seeking these solutions through particular channels. The appropriate channel may be the one in which customers expect to find solutions rather than the channel that is readily accessible or available.

Internal Attractiveness—Playing to Your Strengths

The marketer's environmental analysis identifies the company's current core competencies and those that it is building for the future. When a segment's most important needs can be met by using the company's core competencies, then the segment is more attractive. The Panasonic example at the beginning of the chapter illustrates this point. Panasonic was very good at creating sturdy portable computers. It also had proprietary technology for a touch screen interface. This interface proved to be very useful in field-use situations where ruggedness was also needed. Accordingly, Panasonic was well matched to the market segment it identified.

Attractiveness—Other Considerations

Other parts of the environmental analysis may lead the marketer to rate a segment higher or lower in attractiveness. The analysis of public policy, for instance, may lead the marketer to downgrade the attractiveness of a segment because meeting the segment's needs may encounter more government regulation. In the forestry industry, for instance, addressing a market segment focused on using high-quality wood for high-end interior designs may have become less attractive with more regulation. The high-quality wood tends to come from old-growth forests, which are being increasingly protected.

The organization's goals may have a significant impact on how attractiveness is assessed. Suppose a company's goal is to be the leader in its industry. Then the segments addressed will probably either have to reach a minimal size or be the market leaders/owners in the segments they serve. The industry also probably has one or more closely watched segments that reflect the health and direction of the industry. If a company wants to be recognized as the industry leader, it must participate in those segments, even if doing so is not particularly attractive strictly on profitability grounds. For instance, to be recognized as a leader in the automotive tire manufacturing industry, a company such as Goodyear or Michelin must be a major supplier of original equipment tires to vehicle manufacturers. Since this is a rather closed, oligopolistic market with significant entry barriers, some tire manufacturers, such as Cooper Tire, will not be recognized as leaders as they do not participate in the OEM market but focus on the second tier or aftermarket for replacement tires.

Choosing Targets

Once segments have been assessed for attractiveness, segments need to be chosen to target. If the marketer takes the analytic approach, a rational approach for choosing must be followed. If the marketer takes a discovery approach, based on translating existing business, some analysis can aid in the selection of the next trial customer or customer type. In either case, the marketer needs to take a careful look at the objectives that he is attempting to meet. The choice of segments must at least allow those objectives to be met.

Process for Choosing Target Segments Analytically

The main idea for choosing segments analytically is to start with the most attractive segments and to target as many as are required to assure that you will meet both financial and nonfinancial objectives. Most sets of objectives include a desired sales level and a desired growth rate in sales. The objectives include a profitability level and a growth rate for profits, as well.

Nonfinancial goals such as recognition as the market leader, learning about a line of business that is new to the company, reduction of risk by spreading the sources of revenue, or achieving synergy across other marketing programs may be relevant to the rank and attractiveness of segments. The marketer should rank attractiveness by choosing the most attractive segment and any others that are relevant for special reasons such as those already noted. The marketer should then ask whether the company could meet its goals by targeting only these segments. If the marketer does not believe that the company stands a reasonable chance of meeting its objectives, the marketer should look to the next most attractive segment on the list. After adding this segment (or perhaps a group of related segments), the marketer should again determine the likelihood of meeting the stated objectives. This process should continue until the marketer is satisfied that the objectives will be met or until there are no more attractive segments.

Let's return to the example of the on-line customer satisfaction survey service. Exhibit 7–6 shows the factors contributing to the attractiveness of the four segments we discussed earlier. The first three variables concern customer and market considerations. The next one concerns competitive attractiveness. Then come variables concerned with channel reach and communications reach. We have combined all the considerations having to do with the match between customer needs and company capabilities into one variable. Last we have included a variable concerning sensitivity to price. For each variable, a score has been assessed on a 5-point scale, with 5 being most attractive and 1 being least attractive.

EXHIBIT 7–6   Segment Attractiveness for Hypothetical Example*

Attributes	Segments			
Scores on 5-point scale†	Segment 1: Major Turnaround	Segment 2: Stopping Deterioration	Segment 3: Competitive Improvement	Segment 4: Specific Area Improvement
Potential size year 2000 (in $ million)	2 $187.5	3 $375.0	4 $562.5	4 $562.5
Growth, percent increase by 2002	4 100%	4 100%	1 (50%)	5 150%
Need strength	5	4	3.5	3.5 (high variance)
Competitive strength	3	3	4	3 (high variance)
Channel reach	5	5	5	5
Communications reach	4	4	4	4
Capability fit	2	5	5	2
Price sensitivity	2	3	4	3
Overall attractiveness (sum of attribute scores)	27	31	30.5	29.5

*Based on Peter Doyle and John Saunders, "Market Segmentation and Positioning in Specialized Industrial Markets," *Journal of Marketing* 49, no. 2 (Spring 1985): 30, table format.
†5 = most attractive; 1 = least attractive.

The scores are summed and listed at the bottom of the table. Notice that each variable was weighted equally. A marketer might weight the variables differently depending on how important each is judged to be to the selection of target segments. Realize that a marketer could create and analyze other variables, as well, depending on the situation.

In this hypothetical example, the second segment receives the highest score, followed closely by the third segment, the fourth segment, and the first segment, in order. To pick target segments, the marketer would first select the second segment, comprised of small businesses whose managers are seeking to stop deteriorating customer satisfaction. The marketer would then compare the size of this segment to the company's objectives. In this case, let us say that the company is seeking $2 million in operating profits per year. If the company's operating profit margin on its services is typically 20 percent of the price paid by ultimate customers (assumed to be $5,000 in this case), then sales must be $10 million per year ($2 million divided by .2). The marketer compares the $10 million needed to the $375 million current market potential, which is expected to grow to $750 million within two years.

Let us say that the marketer is uncomfortable with the prospects of obtaining 2 to 3 percent of market potential during the first year of addressing this market segment. The marketer does not know how fast customers in this segment will adopt the new service and how quickly competition will enter the market. On the basis of prior product introductions, he may feel that 10 percent of the market potential is the maximum sales that will be realized in the first year of an early market. If competitors enter the market, the chances of reaching the target profit level may dissipate quickly as competitors take part of the business and price competition erodes margins. The marketer would then be left addressing only one segment and not reaching desired profit levels (even if sales levels are reached). Accordingly, the marketer would probably decide to address the second most attractive segment as well, the segment of small companies seeking to improve competitive performance. Together these two segments represent about $984 million in market potential for 2001 and $1.031 billion in 2002. The marketer would probably be much more comfortable that the objective of $10 million annual sales could be reached.

At this point, the marketer would probably stop adding segments to be targeted. Objectives are reachable with the targets already chosen. The other two segments, while attractive, still have some major drawbacks. Both the specific area improvement segment and the segment needing a major turnaround in customer satisfaction present problems in the fit with the company's capabilities. For whatever reasons, the marketer has scored this category as a 2. Given the offering that can be provided, the value that can be delivered will probably not satisfy these customers. Accordingly, in this hypothetical example, the company will probably target only the two most attractive segments.

Looking at the process again in general, if a marketer reaches the point at which there are no more attractive segments and objectives still appear unreachable, then the process reverts to an earlier decision point. The marketer may try defining segments differently. Alternatively, the marketer may seek to change the objectives.

Changing objectives may be difficult if upper-level management is unwilling to alter the objectives. The part of this process that is most problematic may be assessing whether objectives can be met or not. At this point in the analysis and planning process, there is probably not enough information to do a good forecast of revenues, let alone of profits. There is probably a great deal of uncertainty in anticipating sales and profits that are likely from any given segment. Also, without a strategy and offering fully defined, it will be difficult to get an accurate idea of what market response the company can expect in each segment. Accordingly, this assessment will probably need to be done qualitatively by examining the market potential for each segment and by making reasonable assumptions about the level of market response and the costs involved. This analysis can be refined later, after more data are gathered about the segments chosen and after the offering is fully developed for each segment. Again, the marketing operations forecast can provide significant insight to market conditions and the likelihood of succeeding with trans-lations of the new offering.

It should be noted that the actual design, development, and commercialization of the total offering are taking shape at the same time as, and with significant input from, this market segmenting/targeting effort. This luxury—developing the offering as more is learned about specific target markets—is afforded only those organiza-tions that operate from a marketing concept. Organizations that develop a new offering from the point of view of their needs and then look for customers to fit to the offering have no such luxury.

Uncertainty and Time Compression—The Need to Use Analysis and Discovery Together

The problem in choosing target seg-ments based on reaching these objectives is that we do not really know whether our best offering will meet the objectives. We do not know at this point in the analysis whether we can grow fast enough to reach target sales growth, sales lev-els, and profitability. To compound this problem, the marketer generally will not have enough time to perform the analysis necessary to remove the uncertainty.

Accordingly, a decision-making approach must be used to make choices quickly and at least somewhat accurately. Whether the marketer uses an analytic approach or a discovery approach, some conscious effort needs to be spent on choosing seg-ments to meet goals if the outcome is to be good. We believe that either approach—analytic or discovery—can be improved under conditions of heightened uncertainty and time compression by adding elements from the other approach. So, if a marketer gravitates toward the analytic approach, he will benefit from adding elements of discovery into the choice of target markets. Similarly, if the marketer tends to use a discovery approach, the choice of target markets will improve with the addition of some analysis into the process. Neither process can operate alone as effectively as they can operate together.

In the first instance, the marketer takes an analytic approach, but time com-pression does not allow much collection and analysis of data. Also, it is highly likely in fast-moving, emergent markets that the nature of likely competition will be largely unknown. So, it is not certain the extent to which competitive action in the segment will allow large market share or high profitability. Instead of trying to obtain more data when there is not much good data to be found, the marketer can make the targeting decision by choosing tentative target segments. This would probably involve more segments being targeted than might have been chosen otherwise. In addition, the strategy and offerings chosen may involve some investment in flexibility until results of the strategy implementation indicate which segments are likely to be better performers. The strategy would involve reassessment of segment attractiveness after six months or so. At that time, the company might invest more heavily in pursuit of some segments and pull out of others.

Suppose a marketer uses a discovery approach. The company has developed a product that works for one large customer. The marketer is now looking to translate this business into other segments, usually within the same industry initially. A close look at which elements of value are best addressed in the relationship with the first customer—that is, by analyzing the value obtained by the first customer—may give some clues as to which types of customers or customer situations to look for as the next best translation. Then the discovery process of the missionary sales force can be more closely directed in market segments that are more likely to bear fruit.

POSITIONING

For each target segment chosen, the members of that segment will have one or more value dimensions that are most important to them. Recall that in the Panasonic case the targeted customers had "durability" as their most important value dimension. The marketer designs an offering for each segment that creates superior value for segment members, thus differentiating the offering from competitors. Panasonic created the ToughBook, which is more durable than other laptops. Through **differentiation** and communication, the marketer attempts to obtain the segment members' perception that his offering is better than the competitors' on one or more key value dimensions. Panasonic used a combination of ads and other publicity to get across its message of superior durability. The perception that prospective customers (and existing customers, too) have of the competitive offerings, in relation to each other, is the positioning of the offerings. In the Panasonic case, customers see the Panasonic as more durable than the competing brands.

Positioning, then, is foremost something that occurs in the mind of the prospect or the customer. Marketers attempt to influence this positioning, but, ultimately, it is the customer that creates "position." Marketers need to understand the very real limits they have on "positioning" their products and offerings. The prospect's perception of position is influenced by many factors: articles in trade journals, discussions with other buyers, discussions with salespeople, advertising from all relevant competitors, presentations at trade shows, and product trials, just to name a few. The marketer must grasp the fact that prospects will perceive the marketer's communications with a skeptical eye. Seldom would they consider the marketer an objective source of evaluative information about his own product. If

---

Participation Question

In the hypothetical situation of the research company launching a survey service for small businesses, the marketer chose the deteriorating performance and the competitive improvement segments. Assume you are the marketer, and for each of these segments, develop a set of important needs. Make some assumptions about the core strengths of your company. Define positioning statements for your offerings for these two targets. Position yourself relative to InsightExpress' offerings (visit their Web site at www.insightexpress.com to see their offerings).

---

credibility is required for the prospect to accept a communicated message, then the marketer must find ways to build that credibility.

The situation is somewhat different for the existing customer. Positioning, ultimately, depends on the customer's own experience with the product, the service, and all other dealings with the vendor and the vendor's agents (such as resellers). Communication can help the customer pay attention to important aspects of his experience. Communication can also help customers set expectations and interpret results of their usage of the product or service. In the end, though, customers' beliefs depend on the value they perceive that they have received; so, good positioning comes down to some very simple principles:

◆ Provide better value than competitors on one or more key dimensions of value, as perceived by your prospects and customers.

◆ Communicate the differentiation that you provide in such a way that the prospect and customer have high but reachable expectations.

◆ Deliver on your promises and occasionally find ways to surpass your customers' expectations.

These sound simple but, in reality, are difficult to execute. To be successful, marketers need to find what their companies do best and focus on building superior value from those strengths. The execution of this positioning begins with a **positioning statement,** which is the succinct statement of the positioning the company hopes to achieve in the minds of its target customers. In Chapter 9, we discuss business-to-business branding and its relationship to value, positioning, and image.

FURTHER ISSUES IN SEGMENTATION, TARGETING, AND POSITIONING

The basics of segmentation are mostly straightforward; yet, applying them is difficult because market structures are seldom simple. This complexity arises because customers are trying to differentiate and adapt themselves to their own complex, changing markets. The business environment that both marketers and their customers face also presents complexities and turbulent changes. Accordingly, when marketers develop segmentation frameworks, choose target segments, and develop their positioning strategies, they often have to adapt to this complexity and accommodate this turbulence. In this section, we discuss two situations that influence marketers to think and act beyond the realm of simple, static segmentation.

Segmentation and Positioning Based on the Technology Adoption Life Cycle

As discussed in Chapter 2, propensity to adopt innovations underlies the new technology adoption curve.[6] Moore's ideas about propensity to adopt have implications for identifying segmentation, choosing target segments, and positioning. Moore suggests that business-to-business companies can divide their markets into adoption groupings, as discussed in Chapter 2. The box—"Adoption Categories . . ."—presents the adoption categories for your review.

Moore observed that markets evolve in such a way that the segments follow each in order. Early in the life cycle for a product category based on an innovative technology, customers always come from technophiles and visionaries (innovators and early adopters in Rogers' terms). After visionaries have been buying the product and the infrastructure has been developing to support it, pragmatists begin to enter the market. Once the market has been established and specialized uses have emerged, the conservatives enter. Laggards may enter the market after prices have come down for specialized uses or costs of not adopting have risen so high that laggards can no longer afford not to adopt.

All of this suggests that a marketer needs to have a sense of where the offering is located on the technology adoption life cycle (TALC). The kinds of segments to address derive from the TALC. Given a type of buyer being targeted, the offering needs to be positioned for that type of buyer.

---

[6]Geoffrey Moore, *Inside the Tornado* (New York: HarperCollins, 1995).

Adoption Categories in the Technology Adoption Life Cycle

Technophiles adopt the very newest technologies, just to try them out and experiment. These adopters do not require a fully developed product or offering.

Visionaries see the competitive advantages they can build in their organization with the new technology. They buy before the product or offering is standardized and require a custom offering built around the new technology.

Pragmatists want to gain competitive advantage through new technology but will not buy until they believe the product is easily adopted with minimum upheaval. They will distrust the references from visionaries. They need a fully developed offering.

Conservatives tend to adopt only when it costs them not to adopt. They need to be convinced that the offering is exactly what they need.

Laggards will find reasons not to adopt, even when all evidence says they should.

For instance, Commerce One is a company that offers electronic commerce soft-ware. The software allows customer companies to establish their own electronic commerce operations, integrating them with much of the customers' existing opera-tions. Commerce One is the software vendor selected as one of the suppliers for Covisint, the e-commerce joint venture of the major U.S. automobile manufacturers.[7] The purpose of the joint venture is to establish an electronic marketplace for parts supplies. Covisint represents a "visionary" customer for Commerce One. As such, the offering for Covisint needs to be collaborative and customized. Commerce One must work with partners such as SAP, who provides many of the auto manufactur-ers' existing systems. The system delivered to Covisint must be customized, because nothing quite like this has been done before. As Commerce One looks for other visionary customers, it will create unique combinations of products and services to create unique value for each one. It will translate what it learns in working for Covisint and adjust and tailor it to the specific needs of additional customers.

As Commerce One looks to "cross the chasm"—to enter a **niche** within the segment of pragmatist buyers—Commerce One will need to design the more standardized offering sought by pragmatists. Because the pragmatists tend to want assurance that the offering works with minimal trauma, Commerce One must seek a niche whose need is so strong that, with the evidence of visionaries' success, the buyers' natural resistance to adoption is overcome. What is more, that segment must be a good candidate to provide references to other niches among pragmatists; it must be a niche that others can see as similar to themselves so they will believe Commerce One's solution will work as well in their own situations.

> **Niche** is a segment that is relatively small with fairly well defined bound-aries. The term is often used in a way that suggests that the niche can be served mostly or entirely by a single supplier.

If a marketer wishes to use the TALC as a guideline for segmenting, targeting, and positioning, the marketer probably needs to be analyzing and discovering at the same time, particularly in the stages of the life cycle prior to reaching the "tornado"—the period of rapid growth in sales. Analysis will help identify candidate niches. Discovery—employing a missionary sales force (probably falling under the title of "business development")—will help qualify and educate the candidate niches and may unearth other candidates not apparent from analysis. Using the TALC as a guiding concept forces the marketers and business developers to think about how the market will evolve and how their efforts will influence that evolution.

Positioning a Product Line

Product lines are groups of products that are sold together or that address similar market segments. For instance, a machine tool manufacturer may have a line of products that perform related functions, such as tools for cutting sheet metal, stamping patterns or holes into the sheet metal, and shaping the sheet metal by bending or twisting. The same manufacturer may have different models of each

---

[7]Edward Robinson, "Battle to the Bitter End," *Business 2.0* (July 25, 2000), 135–149.

tool, as well. At one end of the line may be machine tools with less throughput and fewer computer-controlled features. At the other end of the line may be high throughput, multifunction computer-controlled machine tools. These various models allow the tool manufacturer to address many different segments. In each segment, the buyers are looking to obtain machine tools that fabricate parts out of metal or plastic. However, the uses of the tools are different, requiring different combinations of features and differing purchasing criteria.

In most cases, the supplier will want to maintain consistency in the brand's image and positioning across most or all of the segments. There are several reasons for this. First, many of the competitors will be the same from segment to segment. Each of these will have fairly consistent strengths and weaknesses, allowing the supplier to occupy similar positions relative to these competitors in all the segments. Second, efficiencies can be obtained in product design, manufacturing, communications, training, service, and other elements if positioning is similar across all segments. Third, customers in closely related segments communicate with each other and pay attention to the same media. In many cases, the same buying center may be buying different products for differing situations: the people doing the buying are the same; the difference in the segments comes from the usage situation. Maintaining consistency in positioning across segments then makes it easier for customers to understand the supplier's position and to reinforce the positioning among each other. Indeed, many buying center members go to other companies in other segments as their careers progress. As they move from segment to segment, they take their beliefs along and expect suppliers to provide similar types of value from segment to segment. As long as all this "cross fertilization" is occurring, the supplier is wise to use it to advantage rather than create confusion.

Accordingly, the marketer needs to think about positioning a line of products rather than positioning the individual products. In most cases, a supplier company will have a few value dimensions that are common differentiators for all its products. These usually derive from the company's distinctive competencies. For instance, the manufacturer of the machine tools may differentiate its products on lowest cost of ownership and flexibility in application. Obviously, this gives the manufacturer the opportunity to make this a common theme in its communications for the entire line of products (similar to Panasonic's use of durability as the common theme for its line of notebook computers).

IBM, as discussed in the opening example of Chapter 6, is another illustration of the idea of positioning the company as a whole. To support positioning of offerings targeted at specific segments, IBM maintains consistent positioning based on good technology, good products, and superb customer support. As noted in the last chapter, IBM has renewed focus on building relationships with its customers, starting at the top with CEO Gerstner. This message is consistently communicated no matter what the line of business, and IBM's rebuilt capability to deliver on its promise reinforces this message.

In some cases, the supplier will want to establish a **<u>flagship product</u>**—a product in the line that is well known and conveys the positioning for the whole line.

A marketer would find this useful when the company has an initial product that can serve as a flagship. An example would be Hewlett-Packard's Laserjet product for small business. The product produces high-quality output and is easy to use. The product name has become a brand name that extends over several models. This positioning has become a central theme for all of HP's laser printers, for its inkjet printers, and for its accessory products such as scanners, as well.

This approach is possible when an initial product has achieved notoriety. A company might establish a flagship product after the product line has been established, but this is more difficult to do. It requires the existence of a large segment that can be addressed by the flagship and a clear and enduring advantage that can be embodied by the product and its offering. If the advantage is transitory, the flagship will not obtain the credibility to assume the positioning mantle.

This discussion of product line positioning demonstrates the concept of market ownership noted by McKenna.[8] Setting a high standard, continuous innovation, thoroughly satisfying a particular niche market segment, and creating credible dominance are factors that help define ownership.

---

[8]Regis McKenna, "Marketing Is Everything," *Harvard Business Review* (January–February 1991).

In the first part of this chapter, we discussed two approaches to determining segments—an analytic approach and a discovery approach. The analytic approach involves the use of secondary and primary research, plus the judicious application of informed assumptions. A marketer is most prone to use it when the market has many customers or when the marketer is entering a market in which he has little experience. The discovery approach involves efforts to find new segments based on translating an offering that has already been aimed at one or a few customers. It involves the use of missionary salespeople or business development specialists to look for and validate new market segments. We make the argument that, because of time compression and uncertainty, the processes can be melded to improve the segmentation, targeting, and positioning outcome.

Once segments have been identified, the marketer chooses some of them to target. This is done by determining how attractive each segment is and then choosing the most attractive segments. Ideally, the marketer continues to add segments to the list of targets until he feels certain that the organization's objectives can be met. If the marketer does not reach such a point, then objectives or the segmentation framework needs to be rethought.

Once the target segments are determined, the marketer needs to determine the positioning for each. Ideally, the positioning for one segment should not conflict or undermine the positioning for any other segment. Positioning is in the mind of the customer. The marketer attempts to aid the customer in establishing this position in the customer's mind. The marketer does this by first making sure the offering delivers superior value to the targeted customers. Second, the marketer communicates a message to targeted customers that emphasizes the key dimensions of value that create the desired position relative to competitors.

As noted in the introduction to the final section of this chapter—Further Issues . . .—markets are complex and everchanging. The process of finding a segmentation framework, choosing target segments, and developing positioning is difficult to do well but is rewarding when accomplished, as illustrated by Panasonic in the opening example.

Key Terms

accessibility	field market development	product line
actionability	(FMD) personnel	segmentation framework
analytic approach	measurability	segmenting
(to segmentation)	niche	**Standard Industrial**
attractiveness (of segments)	**North American**	**Classification (SIC)**
bases for segmentation	**Industry Classification**	substantiality
differentiation	**System (NAICS)**	targeting
discovery approach	positioning	
(to segmentation)	positioning statement	

Questions for Review and Discussion

1. Consider the following segmentation basis variables and note potential strengths and weaknesses of employing each in a segmentation framework:
    a. Demographics
    b. Technology
    c. Culture of technology adoption
    d. Perceived value subject to industry standards
2. How do the concepts of value and the value chain define how marketers should try to segment markets?
3. What is the difference between the analytic approach to segmentation and the discovery approach to segmentation?
4. Discuss how the marketing operations forecast (MOF) from Chapter 6 is of significant importance in the validation of segments developed through discovery.
5. What factors do you think will influence how strong the airlines' perceived need will be for super jumbo jets seating 600+ passengers in the year 2010?
6. Why would you say the market for super jumbo jets is a *market segment*, even though the customers—the airlines—are the same customers who also buy jumbo jets and other kinds of airliners?
7. In Exhibit 7–6, the last column of the table shows that there is a lot of variation in the strength of the need perceived by segment members and in the strength of competition in meeting functional improvement needs within this segment. Why would these observations argue against choosing this segment as a target segment?
8. What should a marketer do if, in choosing target segments, he runs out of attractive segments to add to the list of targeted segments and it does not appear that objectives can be met?
9. Why can marketers only hope to influence positioning and not create it?
10. Compare the importance of positioning in business-to-business markets with positioning in consumer markets.
11. How is positioning an offering for new customers different from positioning for existing customers?
12. Explain why mass markets require offerings with fewer distinctions than niche markets.
13. What is the difference between a niche and a market segment?
14. How is McKenna's philosophy of market ownership, discussed in Chapter 2, reinforced by the TALC positioning strategies suggested in this chapter?
15. Define the business segments addressed and positioning of your business school or marketing program. What could your school do to change or improve your target segments chosen? Your positioning?

Internet Exercises

Go to VerticalNet's Web site: **http://www.verticalnet.com** How many markets have "vertical portals" or exchanges created for them? Examine a sampling of these portals/exchanges. Are they all the same or tailored to the industry? Are segments within each industry addressed in some way? What sort of positioning does Vertical-Net.com try to accomplish? How?

Go to Kovair's Web site: **http://www.kovair.com** Gain an understanding of the service offered. How could a marketer use the shared Web site idea to obtain information useful in searching for new segments (i.e., translating an existing offering into new business with similar kinds of customers)?

Go to IBM's Web site: **http://www.ibm.com** Explore the Web site. Look at different parts of the site targeted to different kinds of IBM customers. Does IBM maintain a consistent corporate positioning across these different parts of the Web site? Do you think IBM should try to maintain more or less consistency in positioning? Why?

8

Planning and Positioning the Value Offering

overview. . . In the first four chapters, we discussed the context, market environment, and behavioral aspects of business-to-business markets. In Chapter 5 through Chapter 7, we examined the elements of corporate and marketing strategy, and market research. Many of the elements of these prior

© PATAGONIK WORKS/PHOTODISK

chapters can be regarded as the tools of the trade. In this chapter, you will begin to see how many of these elements pull together into a plan to develop, position, and manage the product and offering. In this chapter, we will also look in greater depth at the product life cycle (PLC), briefly introduced in Chapter 2, as a tool to gain insight into the management of offerings at various stages of the life cycle. The concept of the value network, also introduced in Chapter 2, is further examined.

The development process for new products and offerings is examined. Product and offering positioning in the market is discussed as an integral part of the development process.

In the following examples, the focus is on product failures. Very large organizations still make product development and commercialization mistakes. Students will recognize some of the consumer failures as "icons" of business history, while the business-to-business failures may be more obscure. Regardless of the market, many of these examples, though complex offerings, are in hindsight a failure of one of the basic tenets of new product development. The examples start with, appropriately, the Edsel, probably the best-known product failure, albeit a consumer product. An old example by today's standards, the Edsel set a standard by which many other "failures" are measured. Every company, business-to-business or consumer oriented, has had its Edsel. The Edsel is an icon.

THE BEST AND THE BRIGHTEST STILL HAVE PRODUCT FAILURES

In August 1957, Ford Motor Company introduced a car from an entirely new division of the company to the American market—the Edsel. The vehicle was conceived as a mid-priced vehicle slotted above the Mercury but below the Lincoln, aimed at the General Motors Buick and Oldsmobile line. The vehicle had been conceived in the early 1950s and developed through the middle of the decade. The mid-priced market was growing when it was conceived, but, by the time the car was introduced, the economy had taken a dive. The mood in America was hardly upbeat. On the day that the Edsel was introduced, the Soviet Union announced that they had a missile that could reach America.* By the end of 1960, the Edsel was gone, never to effectively compete in a mid-priced market that evaporated with the declining economy. The Edsel, a $350-million loss for Ford Motor Company, was to become an icon for failure. As early as the 1960s, a cartoon of the SST, the American response to the supersonic passenger aircraft, the Concorde, was shown attempting to take off with a "horse-collar" grill.†

Not to be outdone in the product failure game, in the 1960s RCA decided to take on IBM in the mainframe computer business. Codenamed "Project Intercept," the effort was the largest ever undertaken by RCA. In Sep-

tember 1971, after a loss of $500 million, RCA eliminated 8,000 jobs, backed away from an installed base of about 500 customers and ended the computer effort. RCA stock rose on the news. The Edsel had been replaced, if not in the minds of consumers, at least in the dollars-lost competition.‡

In the early 1980s, Apple Computer introduced the Lisa, a new desktop system aimed at business-to-business markets. Probably put off by its $10 thousand price tag and ineffective business-to-business channel, business users were not impressed and stuck with IBM, the established business supplier with the relationships and service they expected.

In an attempt to translate success in business-to-business markets into the consumer market, IBM introduced the PCjr. The IBM keyboard, once the standard by which others were measured, was not included. Instead, the "Chiclet" keyboard, with oval, rocking keys was the standard. Also, the computer was not expandable—a benchmark feature of previous IBM desktop computers. Dead wrong for the market, this product cost IBM $100 million. A pittance.

*Robert Lacey, Ford, The Men and the Machine (New York: Ballantine Books, 1986), 513.
†Ibid., 516.
‡Isadore Barmash, Great American Business Disasters (Chicago: Playboy Press, 1972), 241.

THE BEST AND THE BRIGHTEST STILL HAVE PRODUCT FAILURES (CONT'D)

In the late 1970s, a recognized leader in plastics introduced a new high-performance thermoset product into the engineering plastic market. The hope was that this new product would be a natural extension of an existing product that was in decline, soon to be discontinued. Recognizing that the product was significantly different from existing products and would likely have a different customer base, the company hired an entirely new sales and market development team. After two years, the new product was withdrawn and most of the staff was laid off. The product was never adopted by a significant commercial customer.

In 1981, Xerox, the recognized owner of the office copier market, introduced the Star System—a desktop computer system that used little graphic images as symbols of functions and a small palm-sized device to move the curser around the monochrome screen. The system received little support—after all, Xerox was a copier company. Who could be bothered with a "little" computer with a graphical user interface and that silly mouse to navigate around those little images?

New Coke, DuPont's leather substitute Corfam, RCA videodisc players, the Susan B. Anthony dollar coin (even the federal government gets in on this), the Apple Newton—the list goes on. How do so many companies with access to the best resources create such money losers?

introduction. . .

Each of the product failures noted in the opening example has an element of marketing failure associated with it. Whether an obscure business-to-business product that few consumers have heard of or a well-known failure icon, research has shown that the largest single reason for the failure of new products in the market-place is a lack of a thoroughly developed and executed marketing plan.[1] In this chap-

◆ **Understand the product life cycle—PLC—and its implications for the successful management of products and offerings.**

◆ **Understand the importance of customer and supplier involvement in the development of new offerings.**

◆ **Know the role of marketing in the development process, particularly in a market-driven firm, as the source of direction and definition.**

◆ **Recognize the concept of the value network as a powerful tool in creating market ownership.**

LEARNING OBJECTIVES

ter, we look at the relationship between technology, products, and marketing. As we proceed through this chapter, remember that, in most cases, customers seek solutions, not technologies or products. Offerings are perceived by the value they deliver, not by the specific technology that makes them work. However, products, technology, and marketing are significantly woven together in business-to-business markets.

Business-to-business marketing organizations are influenced by the technology of the products they offer and the longevity, or survival, of that technology in the market. Succeeding technologies as well as multiple product life cycles (PLCs) must be measured and planned to ensure the ongoing nature of the organization. While, at first glance, a particular technology may be viewed as the mainstay of an organization, long run successful organizations recognize that the customer acquires the technology for its solution value, not for the technology itself. The supplying organization then must recognize the value that the technology provides *from the customer view.* New product development should focus on the market of the customer, not the current product or product line of the supplier.

THE PRODUCT LIFE CYCLE

The generalized product life cycle, shown in Exhibit 8–1 (modified slightly from Exhibit 2–4), is useful as a device to relate many concepts of marketing. Life cycle management makes some basic assumptions about offerings.[2] These assumptions vary from the generalized case depending on changes in the market environment and the pace of innovation:

◆ All products and offerings have a limited life.

◆ All products pass through different stages of evolution. For each of these stages, there is an idealized marketing mix that best fits the environment in that stage when the life cycle is viewed from the viewpoint of a product category.

[1]Robert G. Cooper, *Winning at New Products* (Reading, Mass.: Addison-Wesley, 1993).

[2]Phillip Kotler, *Marketing Management: The Millennium Edition,* 10th ed. (Upper Saddle River, N.J.: Prentice-Hall, 2000), 301–304.

EXHIBIT 8–1   The Product Life Cycle

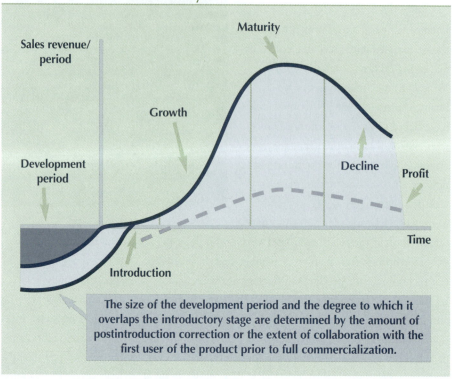

The size of the development period and the degree to which it overlaps the introductory stage are determined by the amount of postintroduction correction or the extent of collaboration with the first user of the product prior to full commercialization.

♦   The different stages offer the organization different opportunities and threats, and market segmentation and targeting should reflect the changes.

♦   Profits vary over the life cycle, contributing to the need to modify the market-ing mix. Profits classically peak in the late growth–early maturity time frame.

With our understanding of business-to-business markets and market environmental factors, let us consider the implications of these assumptions.

In markets that are slow to change, accepted products have longer periods of viable application, passing through the stages more slowly. Basic commodities fit the generalized life cycle with a greatly elongated maturity phase, potentially many years long; while products in fast-paced markets, such as computer processors, experience a full life cycle in a much shorter time.

Within market segments, products and services evolve through the use of new technologies, materials, and manufacturing methods. This may not change the functionality of the product offering but may change the costs to provide it. These lower costs may be passed on to users as improved value in response to competitive actions or through **negotiated price reductions.** These price accommodations, as well as competitive changes, impact the cus-tomer base along with the marketing mix. Different adopters con-sider use of offerings at different times, based on their own markets' ability to support the value of new versus proven technologies.

Suppliers are often expected to pass on to customers a part of cost improve-ments in the product. Multiyear supply contracts often include these **negotiated price reductions.** Suppliers are asked to share productivity improvements with customers. Chapter 10 addresses these situations in greater detail.

EXHIBIT 8–2   The Technology Adoption Life Cycle

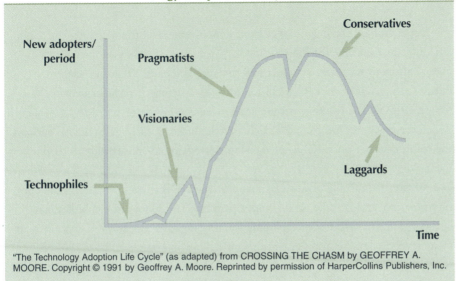

"The Technology Adoption Life Cycle" (as adapted) from CROSSING THE CHASM by GEOFFREY A. MOORE. Copyright © 1991 by Geoffrey A. Moore. Reprinted by permission of HarperCollins Publishers, Inc.

New technologies are accepted at a different pace by different market segments. This can cause discontinuities such as those demonstrated by the technology adoption life cycle, Exhibit 8–2, repeated here from Exhibit 2–5 for convenience.

THE PRODUCT LIFE CYCLE AND LIFE STAGES OF OFFERINGS

The generalized marketing mix implications of the product life cycle (PLC), familiar to many students, are discussed here (keep in mind that we are discussing the PLC at the product category level—the life cycle for a type of product or product category). Within this framework, this discussion is treated from the view of business-to-business offerings. Note that, as shown in Exhibit 8–1, *five* stages of the PLC are considered: development, introduction, growth, maturity, and decline. Also note that, while in Exhibit 8–1 a line distinguishes all borders between stages except the development/introduction boundary, these transitions are more likely to be "fuzzy" in application.

Offering Development Stage

While not always shown in exhibits of the PLC, the **development stage** as shown provides a visual reminder of the complexity and potential need for collaboration in the development of new offerings. During this period, the organization spends research and development, prototyping, field testing, and trial use resources (dollars, personnel, opportunity costs, emotional investment, etc.) to prepare the offering to correctly address the customer need. This investment does not necessarily end with the introduction of the offering.

The marketing mix in the **development stage** requires some attention. The *product* is not completely defined, and profits do not exist; though a target price/value point is being considered. Promotion, beyond the selling effort at the customer, may be oriented toward publicity about technological development. If the product development is a result of a significant collaboration with the customer and involves elements that the customer considers proprietary, the customer will have a voice in any promotional efforts.

Depending on the degree of customer involvement in the development, a specific introduction time for the offering may not exist. If the development is a mutual effort of both the customer and the supplier, as is often the case in business-to-business markets, inclusion into the customer's product may occur before introduction to the general market. This can be the result of an agreement in which the customer has exclusive rights to the offering early in its life or, perhaps, the result of other potential users developing a wait-and-see attitude toward a new technology.

With high-learning products, those that require the customer to rethink current practices and/or take on new manufacturing techniques, the supplier may spend significant resources developing the training and education of customers at many levels. Manufacturing operations of the customer need to learn the techniques and nuances of the new offering, and the customer's product service organization may require training to adequately satisfy field service requirements. Potentially, all elements of the buying center may require a break-in period to make using the new offering a routine event. The corresponding elements of the supplier value chain become a major part of the training process as different portions of both organizations adapt to the new situation.

Unlike education and training of various parts of the customer organization as just described for high-learning products, low-involvement or low-learning products are more likely to follow a more traditional path. Resource commitments to training will likely end at the start of the product introduction stage of the PLC, the assumption being that, for low-learning products, the customer and the general market will adapt more quickly.

Offering Introduction Stage

Many decisions about the offering (its flexibility for translation to other market segments, the ability to incorporate additional product attributes in future versions, the commitment of manufacturing resources, and so on) are made through the development stage and into the introduction stage of the PLC. The **introduction stage** of the PLC is one of low sales volume for reasons on both sides of the supplier-customer relationship, and many of these factors become key elements in how the new offering is positioned in and priced to the market. During this stage, the supplier experiences the growing pains of commercial manufacturing and/or mainstream involvement of the supply chain. If many of the elements of the new offering have been outsourced or are the result of a **unique or first-time value network,** the logistical process experiences a significant learning curve. The customer faces the same learning curve as it incorporates the offering into its operations.

Contextually, the management of the supplying organization must make a conscious decision about market ownership. If the new

During the **introduction stage,** profits are negative or, at best, break through to the positive side near the end of the stage. The product is somewhat basic, as competition has yet to force a need for differentiation. Price and positioning are strongly related. Promotion is used to build awareness, and distribution is necessary for other than large OEM customers.

offering is consistent with previous offerings in that it is the next generation that satisfies an evolving need in the market, then the concept of market ownership is likely recognized and pursued. (See Chapter 5 for a discussion of the strategic implications of market ownership.)

If the offering is independently developed and presents a high-learning situation to the market, early users are limited to innovators/technophiles who are willing to accept change and are attracted to innovation. Under these circumstances, price strategy is more about positioning in the market than about profitability. Certainly, price should not be dictated by early manufacturing or delivery costs. During the introductory stage, profits are unlikely or may experience a breakthrough to the positive side. This is dependent on many factors, not the least of which is how the pricing scenario is expected to play out through the life cycle, as well as the potential threat of competition in the market.

During the introduction stage, promotion is used to "announce" the offering. If the development was the result of a collaboration, then promotional tools that feature the customer's use of the offering, with the customer's consent, are appropriate. If the product is an innovative effort and the customer owns its market, promotion certainly wants to build awareness among other members of the market. Field marketing/missionary sales efforts should be focused in this area. With low-learning offerings, it may be appropriate to use sampling to encourage trial.

During the introductory stage, the place element of the marketing mix is influenced by whether the offering is collaboratively developed and introduced or is an individual development. If it is a collaboration between supplier and customer in an OEM relationship, product distribution and channel design have likely been part of the development process. As the offering is translated to other users and market segments and the market "knows" the product, additional marketing channels evolve. Late majority/conservative adopters who are not likely to have the learning needs or volume to justify a missionary or direct sales effort will seek channels more likely to provide inventory and ordering convenience.

In circumstances in which the product does not have a preestablished customer or is not the result of a collaborative effort, the development of distribution channels targeted at potential market segments may be the only means of product delivery. The circumstances surrounding these decisions are discussed in Chapter 12, "Channel Relationships."

> Just as members of the customer organization must learn about the new product, supplier personnel also must understand any new portions of the value network. If, in the development process, designers in the supplying firm elect to outsource elements of the product in a different manner than previous offerings, **a unique or first-time value network** is created, associated with the new offering. Members of the new value network experience a learning curve as they may not have delivered an offering to this particular customer as a part of this team before.

Offering Growth Stage

The good news: your offering has arrived—it is accepted by your target market. The bad news: you are now likely to attract competition, and your organization must get through the transition from introduction to growth or, as described by

Moore, cross the chasm.[3] Recall that in Chapter 5 we developed an analogy between the stages of the PLC and the stages of the growth-share matrix (Chapter 5). The transition to the growth stage is not unlike the successful development of a *question mark* into a *star*. As with a star, significant investment is required to grow with the market, including the investment required to keep ahead of new competitive entries, meet new supply and manufacturing demands, and meet price challenges to the value position of the product.

An offering that grows from the introduction stage to the **growth stage** crosses several boundaries. The early majority/pragmatists have accepted the product, economies of scale in manufacturing may be realized, product differentiation will now require distinctive attributes, and profits are rising. Let us look at the implications of each of these crossings.

> In the **growth stage,** profits increase rapidly as new customers accept the product. More adopter categories accept the offering. The need for product differentiation becomes apparent, as competitors seek to distinguish offerings. Market penetration pricing may be appropriate as competition puts pressure on high margins. Distribution channels, particularly for low-learning products, become important in the training and education of customers. Promotion is used to remind and reinforce purchase decisions.

Product Acceptance

When a product enters the growth stage, it is an indication that the market recognizes and accepts the value offering as a legitimate proposition. Customers who had taken a wait-and-see approach (i.e., pragmatists) now recognize that benefits outweigh the risks associated with use of something new. Often, in business-to-business markets, the new product has been incorporated into the offering of a competitor of the pragmatist and the market has recognized the increased value. The pragmatist must now play catch-up with the visionaries. The pragmatist may seek a way to leapfrog (i.e., jump ahead of) her competition through application of the next generation evolutionary product. A supplier firm should anticipate the translation/new business opportunities present in these situations with next generation offerings that capitalize on the learning curve of the original innovative offering.

Product Differentiation

That next generation of offering evolution may very well be offered by your direct (new or otherwise) competitor. Market entry, including the development of additional attributes ("bells and whistles") is easier for the competitor. While it may not be known as the market owner, the competitor has a competitive offering that costs less to develop (used your development curve); the offering likely is differentiated from your offering with features and attributes (though still compatible with your established standard); and the competitor has a proven market (your risk taking).

At this point, total offering attributes become increasingly important. The relationship that the innovative firm has with the technophile/visionary customer base contributes to market ownership—the reputation for innovation has value in the marketplace. Warranties, services, design assistance to incorporate the offering into customers' products, and experience in the market segment all add to the value of the offering.

---

[3]Geoffrey Moore, *Crossing the Chasm* (New York: HarperCollins, 1991).

Economies of Scale

Success in the growth stage is as dependent on the ability to supply in large quantity as it is on the acceptance of the offering in the marketplace. Recall that business-to-business demand is leveraged and volatile. The rapid growth of sales in the growth stage is not the result of many small users accepting the offering, as it would be in consumer markets. Growth is likely the result of the business-to-business customer specifying the new product for inclusion in its own offering. This specification creates a sudden jump in volume coincident with the start of production by the customer of its new product. The existing manufacturing capacity, style, or culture may not be able to handle the resultant increase in volume.

To further examine the complexities of this situation, consider the PLC for silicon pressure sensors as described in the following example:[4]

> As a major innovator and developer of the micromachining process, Sensacon Corporation has successfully developed a growing market for the micromachined pressure sensor. Sensacon, a high-technology, start-up operation, has begun to deliver on the profitability promises that management made to investors. By avoiding large-scale manufacturing, fixed costs were kept relatively low throughout the introductory period. Sensors were etched and assembled without much automation. Labor was added or reduced through the use of an agency that provided skilled temporary assembly workers. Users of the sensors were technology-oriented themselves, and volumes were such that the inconsistencies that resulted from hand assembly could be adjusted in the users' operations. Sensacon's annual production was in the range of five thousand units. Most applications of the sensor had been in SCUBA diving equipment used to measure pressure underwater and in medical devices used to measure blood pressure.
>
> The Sensacon breakthrough came when the sensor was selected for use in an automatic tire pressure monitor. Automobile and truck manufacturers had been looking for a cost-effective system to monitor tire pressures for some time, and the recent controversy over tire failures on sport-utility vehicles (SUVs) had prompted two manufacturers to specify systems for all of the SUVs they produce. The combined volume of the two companies was forecast to reach over one million vehicles. With four sensors on each vehicle, the sensor volume would be over four million units. Sensacon had been selected to supply approximately 50 percent of this volume. The remaining volume was divided up among three competitors. Sensacon monthly sales volume at the start of tire monitor production would exceed the most recent annual volumes experienced by the company and was expected to reach an annual rate of approximately two million units. Initial shipments were to begin in four months. Sensacon employees and investors were ecstatic.
>
> To be sure, Sensacon was not selected automatically by the SUV manufacturers. Competitors were entering the sensor market as the potential profitability was a very

---

[4]We believe some explanation is necessary here. Silicon pressure sensors are produced through a process called micromachining, similar to the process that makes integrated circuits. This process is used to manufacture many types of microstructures, referred to in the industry as micromachined electromechanical systems—MEMS. Without belaboring the technology or the jargon, these products are arguably at the chasm. This example is a compilation of the experiences of more than one company in this market. Simplifications have been made for academic clarity, and care has been taken to prevent any direct relationship with any single market participant.

attractive lure. Sensacon executives were aggressive in the price to the SUV manufacturers as they wanted to establish a leadership position in this new market segment. Recognizing the newly arrived competition, Sensacon had started development of the next generation offering, SensorSUV. The aggressive price to the manufacturers did not concern Sensacon as it was believed that the experience curve combined with economies of scale in manufacturing would create the necessary low cost position.

About three days after the new contract was announced, manufacturing management attempted to scale up production of the existing sensor. In anticipation of a production tryout, additional space had been leased and temporary skilled workers were added to the regular workforce. Unfortunately, even with added automated etching and manufacturing for the brass enclosure and increased facilities and labor, the tryout could not meet anywhere near the volumes hoped for. In addition, the part-to-part variability of the sensors was outside of the SUV manufacturers' specification. While Sensacon technology was up to the challenge, manufacturing was not.

A task force of key Sensacon personnel was assembled. It soon became obvious that the sensor would have to undergo a complete redesign to enable high-volume manufacturing. The necessary changes in the sensor included redesign of the sensor itself for automated handling and insertion into the enclosure; redesign of the enclosure and investigation of new materials, likely plastics, to replace the brass; new manufacturing expertise in high-volume plastic molding and assembly; and new high-volume, production-capable sealing techniques to protect the sensor core from the environment. Sensacon management began the search for a qualified contract manufacturer, hoping to eventually develop its own capabilities later in the contract period.

In this example, the impact of the new business extends not only to manufacturing and product design but to the culture of Sensacon as well. What was once a small specialty product company now must redesign itself organizationally. Crossing into the growth stage can be traumatic.

Offering Maturity Stage

Offerings that move from the growth stage to the **maturity stage** usually have become "standards" in business-to-business markets. While manufacturers work to maintain distinctions from their horizontal competitors, the market owner is already beginning the replacement of the offering with the next generation product. This is not, however, to say that maturity is an undesirable stage of the life cycle. In terms of the growth-share matrix analogy, a business in maturity, a cash cow for the successful market participant, is often capable of generating significant cash for development of other opportunities.

During early maturity, profits may continue to rise slightly and the competitors who are in the market have **economies of scale.** Proliferation of new product versions usually declines and, depending on the market circumstances, domestic manufacturers may be faced with foreign competition. Because competitors have

During the **maturity stage,** profits will have peaked and competition may begin to fight over market share. Promotion is used to reinforce buying decisions and often focuses on supplier reputation and value. Distribution efforts intensify to reach all possible subsegments of the market. New customers will not replace the volumes lost as old customers move to newer offerings. Price is a major part of the marketing mix.

economies of scale and the market is no longer growing as it had been, price becomes a significant part of the marketing mix as manufacturers attempt to keep their facilities operating at the most profitable volumes. Promotion stresses the reliability and reputation of the supplier as well as unique product attributes. When overall sales stop growing, if any one participant in the market desires increased sales, it will have to come at the expense of another participant.

Recall that business-to-business demand is more volatile than consumer demand. This places added pressure on markets in the maturity stage. Early adopters of the initial product begin to replace it in their next generation product with newer generations of the offering or, quite possibly, new offerings with significantly different capabilities. Suppliers must continue after initial specification and purchase to make the entire relationship routine so that they are already in a collaborative role when the product they supply is upgraded or replaced by the customer design process.

During maturity, marketing may focus on protecting market share. While this is a desirable strategy in the short term, it is not a substitute for innovation and self-initiated offering development and replacement programs. Sales volume lost as old customers (pragmatists and early majority) discontinue use and move to newer offerings is not replaced by conservative/late majority adopters. Sales volume declines rapidly during this period unless business lost (core churn) is replaced by new business or translations of other successes.

Offering Decline Stage

As an offering transitions to the **decline stage,** less-productive or weaker competitors drop out of the market, either through consolidation or by leaving the industry. A few competitors with highly efficient manufacturing capabilities or large commitments to customers may actively seek acquisition of the other players. For those competitors that remain in a declining market, efforts become focused on keeping manufacturing facilities running at productive utilization rates. Price, particularly associated with long-term contracts, becomes a major part of the marketing mix. Many of the relationship-derived product enhancements that were the difference between the core product and the total offering are reduced or eliminated. The product line is reduced to minimize production variation and improve economies of scale. Promotion is generally reduced to minimal levels necessary to satisfy existing customers. Depending on the circumstances of the company, a business in decline is often viewed as a dog and is either harvested or divested.

> When an offering or business enters the **decline stage,** promotion is reduced to the minimal levels that will accommodate existing customers. Consolidation usually occurs among suppliers, and price becomes a major part of the marketing mix.

Knowing Where a Product Is in Its Product Life Cycle

The preceding discussion assumes that marketers actually know where the offering in question is in the life cycle. Many management decisions are made with assumptions about the product/market cycle. Without the luxury of this knowledge, maturity or decline can become self-fulfilling prophecies. While not precise, here are some methods to help determine where an offering may be in the PLC:

- Develop and review trend information for the past three to five years or business cycles. As part of the review, include sales revenues, profits, unit sales, unit price, margins, return on investment (ROI), and market share. While all of this information may not be immediately available, get as much of it as possible. With this data, consider that profit ratios tend to improve as products enter the growth stage, begin to deteriorate as they move through maturity, and drop rapidly as they approach obsolescence in the decline stage.

- Examine any apparent changes in the number and nature of competitors. How has their market share changed relative to yours? If the market is still viewed as a growth opportunity, there will still be interest from new competitors. Do new competitors have an inherent advantage, such as low-cost labor from other countries? Will this advantage be significant when viewed by the market? Stated another way, will the low-cost labor advantage translate immediately to price reductions in the market or are other portions of the marketing mix still of value?

- Review short-term competitive tactics. Have recent contract opportunities been lost unexpectedly to competitors? If so, are competitors pricing to move volume short term (dangerous in a contract situation)[5] or are they trying to create volume to utilize new capacity or plant expansions?

- Have there been any new product introductions from competitors aimed at any of the market segments now served by the existing offering? Are these **evolutionary product introductions** or **discontinuous replacement technologies**?

- If reasonable, estimate the number of profitable years or business cycles remaining before a major consolidation among competitors. When consolidation begins, a planned strategy should be in place to position the organization where it wants to be at the exit of the consolidation period.

- Examine replacement technology and the timing of its market introduction. Will your organization be the "parent" of the new offering? The most serious concern should be whether a competitor will innovate your organization out of the business. Remember, it is better to obsolete yourself than to have it done to you by a competitor.

In the context used here, **evolutionary product introductions** are those new offerings that continue or sustain a market or product category. These changes may include small-step improvements to the original design that will not greatly influence the PLC. **Discontinuous replacement technologies** are changes in the offering such that the product category or market segments are redefined. These may be either breakthrough innovations or disruptive innovations. For a complete discussion of innovation and its role in competitiveness, see Chapter 9.

---

[5]Using price as a major element of the marketing mix is not unusual in contract negotiations when offerings face homogeneous competition. However, in situations in which new capacity is available, it is reassuring if the capacity is committed to a customer prior to its availability. Also, solving short-term capacity utilization problems with long-term commitments is dangerous in all but the most stable of markets.

THE PRODUCT LIFE CYCLE FROM THE VIEWPOINT OF AN ESTABLISHED OFFERING

Before we leave the PLC-based discussion and move on to the analysis and practice of new product development, we examine marketing alternatives for an offering that is in maturity or decline. While managing a mature product may not seem as exciting as new products and markets, remember that mature products usually provide a very important ingredient to the organization: cash.

The first alternative to consider for a product headed toward the end of the PLC is to maintain the current product and strategy: do nothing. This is an attractive alternative for market owners who have introduced or are ready to introduce the next generation offering. Strong brands are able to survive profitably into the decline stage long after competitors have left the market.

If the product has a solid customer base but is in the process of being replaced by new offerings, it may be appropriate to change the nature of product support. The market will understand the product well enough such that support can be reduced to a customer service operation. Design assistance and customer education may no longer be necessary, but a selling effort may be. The lower overhead will assist in maintaining profits for as long as possible. The low-cost producer has an advantage in this situation. This alternative usually involves a redesigned marketing channel, particularly for lower-volume customers whose buying habits will be better served by distribution. Such changes also require the acceptance by the supplier that the offering has reached the commodity stage. In this situation, the quality of the relationship with remaining customers is a significant factor in the acceptance of the change. Business-to-business marketers should anticipate the reaction of established customers. Customers may be concerned about the level of service they may receive under the new organization or may be concerned that they will be required to obtain the product through alternative channels. Large, direct customers should continue to receive the same level of selling and administrative service. Smaller customers may require assurance that, though they will receive the product through distribution rather than directly from the manufacturer, service and support for the product will be available directly from the manufacturer. If the organization does not have replacement offerings to maintain sales volumes, accepting the commodity status of the product may be the most difficult part of this transformation.

Another possibility is to change the product and alter the marketing strategy. This can breathe new life into a product in decline. This assumes that the product line or category is still viable. This alternative would be accompanied by approaches to market segments not previously interested in the product or expanded use by existing customers. The technology of a product, if not the form, may be applicable to other markets and applications. See, for an example, the box "Golf Balls and Wipers" on the following page.

When other alternatives either will not produce desired results (or have been tried and are no longer effective), dropping the product/line is a normal course of

---

Golf Balls and Wipers

A golfing equipment manufacturer undertook the development of plastic and rubber materials as part of the design and development of golf balls. The golf ball became a standard in the industry, partially because of the unique properties of the materials used in its production.

The R&D effort had been expensive for the company, so there was an interest in using the expertise in other areas; particularly as golf ball design was considered by some to be as much art as science, users could be a fickle market. At the same time, a major OEM windshield wiper supplier was looking for improvements that would hold off an onslaught of new competitors whose products were equal in performance but offered at a lower price. Sure enough, the golf ball material technology made an excellent windshield wiper blade—outperforming all competitors. A deal was made that gave the wiper supplier exclusive, proprietary rights to the golf ball material for wiper blades. The wiper supplier kept most of the OEM business, and the golf ball manufacturer found another use for the maturing materials technology!

---

action. If the customer base that relies on the product can be converted to a newer offering, the business can be maintained within the firm. In some instances, it may be beneficial to exit the business even though a core group of customers rely on product availability. If this is the case, the customers should be given adequate notice of the product elimination decision. If a replacement is not available within the supplier product line, the supplier should assist in an orderly transition to an alternate supplier. If there are no alternatives and the core customers still require the product, a price increase is usually appropriate. The increase will make previously undesirable alternatives appear in a better light, and, if you are to stay in a declining business, it may as well be profitable. Eventually, the customer base will find alternatives, motivated by both efforts to market new products to replace the old and the higher price for the old product.

Adding one or more new items into a mature or declining line or adding new product lines to a category can be successful if synergy can be obtained with other offerings in the portfolio of the firm. Maintaining an offering may assist sellers to provide a complete product line approach to customers. Older, established products can be the "entry ticket" to customers, providing an opportunity to develop interest in newer products and offerings.

Product Elimination Decisions

It is often necessary to consider discontinuing a product. However, this consideration goes beyond the profitability of the product in question. Marketers must consider the ability of the new or replacement product to maintain the revenue stream generated by the old offering. Customers may not have alternatives, and relationships may be jeopardized by the elimination decision.

The product to be discontinued may impact the sale or profitability of other products or entire product lines. Marketers need to look beyond their own immediate market to the entire firm and existing synergies between business groups.

How will corporate image be affected? Eliminating a product from the portfolio of offerings can raise doubts about the reliability of supply of related products and create concern about future employment among the supplier employees. Competitors are also likely to react, not just by pursuing your customers but by attempting to see the strategic motivation behind the decision. All of this assumes new product opportunities are available; or merger, acquisition, or end of business may be the only alternative.

BASIC NEW PRODUCT DEVELOPMENT PROCESS

Most readers are probably familiar with the basic concepts of the steps of the new product development process. To review, the stages and a brief explanation of the traditional new product development model follow:

♦ *Stage 1: Idea generation.* New ideas come from many sources. The organization must collect these and bring them to consideration, at least periodically. Ideally, an organization operating under the marketing concept looks to customer needs for new product ideas. Unfortunately, this is not always the case, though in business-to-business markets, the highest percentage of new product ideas originate with customers.[6] This should not be a surprise when the relationship-based nature of the organizational buying process is compared to the consumer process. The business-to-business marketer is much closer to the needs and wants of the customer and more able to anticipate the customer need for new offerings and solutions.

Companies with a successful track record of new product idea generation and subsequent product development usually have a culture and style that foster idea generation. Employees are encouraged to seek new ideas that improve offerings, both from an internal perspective, such as productivity improvements, and an external perspective, through seeking new uses for existing capabilities.

♦ *Stage 2: Product screening.* A select, multidisciplinary team reviews descriptions of potential projects to determine those that warrant continuation. While business literature provides several models for the makeup of the team, the primary concern is to select members who are at ease with change. Each new product idea usually needs a product champion/intrapreneur/evangelist to successfully get beyond this second stage.

Criteria for screening new ideas generally include the nature of the opportunity weighed against the organization's capabilities and the expected costs. A "ballpark" estimate of market needs and the capability of the new idea to meet those needs is performed.

[6]Kottler, op. cit., 335.

♦ *Stage 3: Business case analysis.* Ideas that survive the second stage must have the business plan developed more fully. The business plan must have both a market and a technical assessment. Later in this chapter, we discuss the high failure rate of new projects that do not have a complete market assessment associated with the business plan. The probable revenues and costs are analyzed to determine the likely financial contribution of each project. If it appears likely that minimum financial targets will be met, the project continues. The organization begins to consider additional attributes that will comprise the total offering.

When products are the result of collaboration between supplier and customer, the initial market application is usually assured. The design process integrates the product into the offerings of the customer. If the collaborative nature of the product has led to a design considered proprietary by the customer, the supplier may be limited from taking the product or its technology to other potential customers, at least for a period of time. Should this occur, translation to other customers and segments is delayed and the business case analysis must consider that the product is a custom design for one customer, at least for the specified time period.

♦ *Stage 4: Product/strategy/plan development.* In this stage, after the business analysis has shown a justifiable case for further expenditures, the product technology is further developed and refined. Meanwhile, the product's strategy and implementation plans are developed. The market assessment developed as part of the previous stage becomes the starting point for the detailed marketing plan. The ability to have several levels of offering, depending on customer need, may be considered at this point.

In the generalized case, at this point, operations plans are made, coordinating various functional areas. As part of the expanded technical assessment, numerous prototypes are developed and tested. Marketing programs and materials are developed and tested; the channel(s) is (are) prepared; manufacturing is "ramped up"; sales and service are trained; the press is prepared.

In many business-to-business product development efforts, the collaboration between supplier and customer results in a custom product unique to the needs and circumstances of the customer. The scenario under which this collaboration operates is one in which the supplier performs most of the research and development while the customer provides input to the operational needs of the product, testing various iterations of it in the process. The outcome of this effort is a well-defined product specification written by the customer that is well matched by the custom offering of the supplier. The early supplier collaboration gives it a competitive advantage. The specification, influenced by the collaborating supplier, is written to the supplier's competencies and technologies. Competitors must be willing to match the specification as an "or equivalent" offering. Recall from the discussion of buyer behavior in Chapter 3 that this is exactly the intended outcome of the four stages in the process flow model (Exhibit 3–3) of the buying decision evolution.

◆   *Stage 5: Test market.* If the new product is intended for a broad market, a limited release of the early product is trial launched in a "beta" test or the final product is released into limited markets or with selected prime customers. The purposes for doing these full-scale tests are to fine-tune the product, fine-tune the strategy, build the market's early awareness, and get final feedback on the product's viability in the marketplace.

In most business-to-business collaborative relationships, the summary in the previous paragraph is not a likely scenario. If the offering is the result of an ongoing relationship with a major customer, the first-use testing is limited to that customer. As noted earlier, there may be proprietary customer features that have been incorporated into the offering. The customer organization may have objections if features of its new product, contributed by the supplier product, become known to the market prior to market introduction. While some collaborative efforts include **proprietary disclosure agreements,** many collaborations are less formal. Suppliers should proceed with any market testing or awareness efforts with extreme caution. Inadvertently disclosing the product plans or technology of a customer can lead to an end of a business relationship.

◆   *Stage 6: Product launch.* If the new product is intended for a broad market, it is fully released once all the fine-tuning is complete. Promotion efforts aimed at target markets may be used to create awareness, interest, and early trials. Depending on the degree of newness to the market (from a market perspective), the education portion of the marketing plan should begin just prior to the launch. A public relations effort coordinated with the preparation of articles and features in technical journals should be considered as a start of the customer education process. (Chapter 13 addresses the effective use of public relations in business-to-business promotion.)

If the new product is a customized, collaborative effort with a particular customer, an introduction to the market is still possible. The timing of such an introduction, however, should be determined by the launch of the customer's product and be done with the customer's concurrence. A well-timed and targeted promotional effort that features the customer's offering should be well received by the customer. A premature promotional effort has all of the same risks as those discussed for beta testing fine-tuning.

◆   *Stage 7: Hand off to the translation/customer education team.* Once market introduction is complete, full-scale customer education can begin. With a high-learning or custom product, significant missionary effort is required to assist

> **Proprietary disclosure agreements** aid both the supplier and the customer. Customers working with suppliers in development of new products want assurance that the supplier is not taking any product or market information to competitors. With this assurance of nondisclosure from suppliers, customers are able to exchange proprietary data during the development process. In reciprocation, suppliers are often assured of receiving 100 percent of the business for a period of time. Suppliers are aided by disclosure agreements as they allow the supplier to be on the cutting edge of offerings in its customers' markets. After the agreed-upon period of time, the supplier may translate the product application to other potential customers.

Chapter 6 discusses the **discovery approach** (to segmentation). This approach is used to validate a new market segment. When new business is realized as a result of a collaboration with a customer, the product is a customized offering. Translation to other potential customers validates the existence of the market segment. Without this process, the new business is an isolated application of the design and development efforts of the supplier. Translation activities are usually the responsibility of missionary sellers/market development specialists.

the customer base in achieving maximum value from the offering. Utilizing the **discovery approach** (to segmentation), marketers attempt to translate the success to other potential customers.

With low-learning products or those introduced to a broad market, customer education efforts are not as extensive. Because of the more rapid adoption of the low-learning product by the market, product management specialists become involved more quickly. Once customer demand patterns have been recognized, management of the ongoing operations of offering the product can incorporate the new offering into the routine with the specified customer base.

Customer/Market Orientation

There are generally two approaches to effectively developing new products or services. One way to is to focus on the technology or the product first. In this approach, the product is developed with little or no customer input and introduced to the market. The second way is to extensively involve existing and prospective customers throughout the process. It would appear that these are two ends of a continuum. However, the amount of customer input usually represents a philosophy. An engineering-driven philosophy tends to minimize customer input; a customer orientation tends to maximize it.

This is not to say that the first approach is without merit; this approach has many supporters, particularly in high-technology organizations. In many circumstances, a customer orientation resides just below the technology-oriented surface or can be adapted to it. Consider this example: Suppose members of an engineering team require a particular type of design software but cannot find a suitable vendor. The alternatives are to settle for what is available or develop the software themselves. The internal development leads to a recognition that they are not the only engineering team that has a need for such software. Members of the team split away from the original engineering group and start their own company to provide such software. These engineers have been customer-oriented, even if they are not likely to recognize it! Though they have not performed any extensive market analysis, as long as there are other potential customers like the engineers, they understand customers already.

It is critical for the engineer/entrepreneur to maintain a customer-oriented approach when new markets are addressed. One of the comments we hear most often from business-to-business marketers is about the frustration they experience in dealing with engineering staffs that have little, if any, customer focus. We have also experienced this with many technically oriented students. Ironically, many first-time marketers that are initially product driven become customer-oriented over time. This transformation can occur suddenly and with some difficulty when a product is unsuccessful in the market and they decide to talk to potential customers to see what went wrong. In other circumstances, an evolutionary process takes place. Customer oriented marketers may purposely launch a new product with little customer input, just so they can get something quickly into the marketplace. After launch, which is typically small in scale, they obtain a great deal of feedback from users and nonadopters. They quickly come out with succeeding versions of the product. Each version more closely conforms to the desires of prospective customer market segments. This approach may be used in emerging markets where little is known about how customers will react to the new product. Competitors have not yet emerged, so there is some time for quick adaptation. Perhaps market segmentation has not yet become evident. Unfortunately, the customer may resent being used as the beta test site. The principal implication here is that paying attention to customer needs makes for better products.

Team Approach

About ten years ago, strategic management visionaries began decrying the "silo" approach to the management of the firm. The functional approach to management, in which marketing, engineering, product research, manufacturing, customer service, sales, and so on operated separately in "silos," was seen as particularly dysfunctional when it came to generating and launching new products. To break down the silos, small, cross-functional teams were espoused as appropriate for managing both the creative effort and cross-functional coordination required in new product development, launch, and management. Indeed, many companies have found this team approach beneficial. Recent examples can be found in such companies as Cisco Systems, IBM, Chrysler, and others.

There are some problems with the team approach. As noted, a new idea seldom survives the hurdles of repeated business metrics without a champion to father it. There is less short-term risk in slowing or ending a new product development as each development stage is exposed to measurements of business potential. Also, depending on the type of idea and eventual new offering, different management levels may require input or sign-off. If the new offering involves many new ways of doing business on the part of the organization, executive involvement is extensive. If the offering is closer to a derivative of existing offerings, a different approval dynamic exists. Products that are more likely to disrupt conventional processes and thinking in the firm require support at higher levels with each succeeding stage of the development process. This is understandable, as greater disruptions may strike at many levels in the organization. Individuals may feel that their current jobs are threatened or that they will have to learn a new technology or way of doing things. The composition of the new product development team should reflect these different demands and recognize the need for an internal marketing program. One of the ways to help with this process is to use rigorous market-driven standards early in the development process.

Invest in the Early Stages

Cooper[7] lays out the rationale and research findings relevant here. He explains that the idea of the staged approach to new product development (NPD) is to identify and weed out likely new product losers early in the process. The early stages are relatively less expensive than the later stages. Accordingly, if a bad fit is identified early on, the heavy expenditures for development and launch of a product failure can be avoided. By the same token, if a company is willing to take on high levels of failure risk, it may decide to pursue one or more projects with potentially high payoffs. Early stage analysis can help the company make such choices with a better idea of the risks, the potential losses, and the potential payoffs.

Stage Gates

Stage gates are simply checkpoints after each stage of the product development process. The ongoing NPD process is interrupted at certain milestones to ensure that the original goals and objectives are still viable and that the development is still forecast to meet the expectations that were created as a part of its initial approval. The stage gate process is a fairly rigorous but flexible process to keep NPD on track. While a development may not continue to meet initial expectations, continuous marketing input may point the NPD team to additional or substitute opportunities.

Cooper's conclusion is that progression from stage to stage ought to be governed by use of carefully constructed **stage gates.** These gates are pre-specified milestones that must be reached—and approved by a high-level manager or executive—before the project can continue. The gates have two qualitative aspects: technical milestones and market/business milestones. Again, Cooper has found that adherence to such stage gates produces superior performance.

Our experience suggests that such rigorous adherence to stage gates is practiced much less often than we would desire, particularly on the market/business side. The principal reasons for this are uncertainty and scarce resources. Given limited budgets, it is very tempting for the NPD manager to put as much effort into R&D as possible. The firm has much more control over technical developments. Also, the market is usually more difficult to interpret than is the technical performance of a product. Consequently, higher priority is placed on what can be influenced directly and budgets for market analysis go wanting. Later in this chapter, we make the argument to try to combat this pervasive belief.

Whenever we encourage the use of lists or stages in business, we are concerned that they will be applied as a recipe or prescription, without consideration for the context or intent of the process. It should be emphasized that the stage gate system is a process to facilitate new product development. It is not a checklist of functional items that must be done by each department before the project is handed off to the next group. The process is multidisciplinary, requiring the use of cross-functional teams in the development effort. Each stage is market driven but includes technical, financial, and production activities. With a strong focus on quality in each element of each stage, the development team stays in touch with the changing market and customer needs.

[7]Cooper, op. cit.

Concurrent Development

Another area where large strides have been taken is in improving "time to market" for new products. First to market, often key in market ownership, has advantages that can be exploited. The first entry into a new market often is able to define the parameters of the market, setting the standard for others who follow. Accordingly, creating products quickly has received a high priority in recent management thinking and development.

Concurrent development is simple in concept but hard to do. The idea is to identify activities that can be done simultaneously, in parallel rather than serially. This requires breaking the product into modules that can be developed separately. The notion of teams is also critical to doing concurrent development effectively. Interfaces between the modules are worked out ahead of time and updated dynamically if changes require. Obviously, the more simple and robust the interfaces, the easier the integration of the modules. Communication and coordination between the teams working on the modules must be maintained during development.

When a new product idea presents relatively high development risk but relatively low **opportunity costs,** it may not be particularly advantageous to speed up the development process.[8] Stage gate management can become particularly important as a way to ensure that development criteria are met.

When development risk is low, such as in a situation where there is a high correlation to existing offerings or ways of doing business, and the market opportunity costs are high, it is imperative to speed up the development process. Because the risk of development failure is low, the accelerated development process does not present the same degree of additional risk as it would if the risk of failure were high.

> **Opportunity costs** are the measurements of those business opportunities that are not pursued because resources have been committed to the new product development. NPD teams may use several different criteria to make these judgments, such as internal rate of return, net present value, and market scenarios.

---

[8]V. Kasturi Rangan and Kevin Bartus, "New Product Commercialization: Common Mistakes," Harvard Business School Note 594-127 1994, 63–75.

No Shortcuts

One of Cooper's primary conclusions is that effective NPD relies on doing the right things right. There are no shortcuts to be taken, no activities to be ignored. The chance of catastrophic failure can be minimized by enlightened application of the preceding principles. Failure likelihood goes up as "rules" are broken.

THE ROLE OF MARKETING IN THE PRODUCT DEVELOPMENT PROCESS

Ideally, in a market-driven organization, marketing is responsible for the definition of new offerings based on a continuous review of customer needs. As customer needs evolve over the period of the product development, the goals of the development evolve. Thus, marketing is responsible for the direction and outcomes of the product development process.

The responsibilities of marketing go far beyond the customer interface. Unfortunately, many new product development efforts minimize the resources committed to marketing while maximizing product and technology development. Research has shown that the marketing effort is often the most deficient part of the new product plan.[9] In 22 percent of development projects studied (including firms that considered themselves "market driven"), there was no detailed marketing study at all. In another 46 percent of the projects, the marketing plan was considered to be poorly done. In all projects analyzed in the study, a full 74 percent had no market study or plan or had a plan that was judged as seriously deficient. This deficiency in marketing effort continued through the development process to the product launch, where, even in a sales- or product-driven organization, you would expect significant input from marketing. Test marketing or trial selling efforts were deficient or omitted in 58 percent of the studied projects. Also, 52 percent of the projects failed to have adequate business or financial plans. However, technical assessments, in-house testing, and pilot production efforts were judged to be sufficient for the task.

Where should the marketing effort, particularly in "market-driven" firms, show up? In the first chapter, we characterized marketing as the driving force, the "heart and soul" of the organization. In this context, marketing has a responsibility to drive the new product development process.

Marketing Defines the Outcomes

To more closely examine this responsibility, we return to Sherlock.[10] There are several ways that marketing must serve the organization. Marketing must

◆ *Understand the technology in depth.* This is meant to imply not that marketers must have technical degrees but that they must know the value of the technology, its

---

[9]Cooper, op. cit., 24.

[10]Paul Sherlock, *Rethinking Business-to-Business Marketing* (New York: The Free Press, 1991), 84.

strengths and weaknesses, from the viewpoint of the user. Marketers need to know the science.

♦ *Define and redefine current and future customer needs.* The continuous evolution of customer needs creates a dynamic, sometimes volatile environment. An offering cannot be accurately defined at the beginning of the process and, without modification to the definition, be correct for the market at the end of the process. The quality of the information about customer needs is a reflection of the quality of the relationship with the customer.

© CHRISTOPHER PFUHL/AP/WIDE WORLD PHOTOS

♦ *Motivate other company departments and organizations.* The marketers most closely associated with the customer, whether headquarters or field personnel, should champion the development effort toward the best interests of the customer. To the rest of the organization, the marketer should "be" the customer! Business-to-business customers expect this, and the degree to which the development effort meets specific customer needs is evidence of the success of the effort. Marketing can make progress toward this synergy by involving as many corporate technology and development participants with the customer as possible. This not only establishes direct communications between members of the value network and the buying center but also instills a sense of ownership of the effort to satisfy customer needs in the participants.

♦ *Screen and select ideas from all sources.* Marketers should know their own companies well enough to know their strengths and weaknesses. The strengths are tools that can be used to bring value to customers. Marketers should also know the intricacies and nuances of their customers. What businesses are they in? What synergies are possible? What competencies of the customers can be matched to strengths of the marketers' companies to create distinctive offerings?

♦ *Guide the new product development with the continuous redefinition of current and future customer needs already noted.* Accomplishing this step is far easier when the organization is contextually prepared for the redefined parameters. This will be assisted significantly by the participant ownership already described.

♦ *Reward the efforts of the technical and support staff.* When the new offering is introduced and perhaps at milestones along the way, reward the participants. Have a party. Get a wall plaque. Create an event. Positive exposure and association with the current success bode well for cooperation in the future. Also, make the reward known to the customer, not only elevating the work of the participant but demonstrating the importance of the customer in your organization to your customer. If there was significant collaboration with participants from the customer, reward them too!

♦ *Catalyze company resources to get the right talent on the job—be willing to cross traditional company boundaries.* Marketers should cultivate relationships throughout their organization. Each of these relationships can become a positive igniter in the search for the best result for customers. Having working relationships throughout the organization is another resource the marketer can bring to bear on customer needs.

The level of responsibility prescribed here for the marketing organization is difficult for an organization that is not truly market driven. Firms that operate under the product or sales concept[11] often have an internal culture that views the marketing effort as an expense rather than a defining paradigm.

REDUCING THE RISK OF NEW PRODUCT FAILURES

New products have an element of risk associated with them. To reduce this risk, firms can utilize many of the development tools described here or any number of other processes described by a large body of research about new product development. Unfortunately, even with careful planning by organizations that engage in new product development, there are still product failures.

Why Do New Products Fail?

If the marketing effort in the organization is responsible for the process outcome, as we have described, then responsibility for the failure of the process also rests with marketing. Indeed, poor marketing (or no marketing effort at all) is a major cause of product failures. Consider the study by Cooper, noted earlier, that found that 22 percent of new product development projects surveyed had no detailed market study performed. While this may be a frightening prospect for true marketers, many managers do not even realize that they have missed a part of the development process. To improve the chances of new product success, let us look at some causes of new product failures.

The Missing Marketing Plan
At the outset of many new product development projects, assumptions are made about technology, manufacturability, and markets. These assumptions are often necessary to get the project off the ground, to get resources committed to begin the first stages of investigation and development.[12] These assumptions—market size, value as perceived by the customer, growth rates, desirability of features—that are often used to justify the initial effort can become ingrained in the project. Studies have shown that, once approved, project funds are most often used to validate technological assumptions, not market assumptions. In fact, 78 percent of total resources expended go to technological

---

[11]Kotler, op. cit., 25.

[12]Cooper, op cit., 25.

and manufacturing activities.[13] Note the following potential reasons for failure that could be avoided with an adequate marketing effort.

No Real Need Exists

Some products are the answer to a question that nobody has asked. These types of failures are often associated with executive attachment to a technology or idea. The development proceeds in isolation, with little attention to the real needs of the market. With strong executive attachment, market research results can be overlooked or interpreted to support the opinions of management. Cooper reports that this accounts for 28 percent of product failures.

The Market Size Is Overestimated or a "Me Too" Product Fails to Penetrate the Market

Few marketing efforts can maintain an exclusive hold on a market. In oligopolistic late growth/maturity situations, expecting much more than 30 percent market share can be overly optimistic. In new markets, once the offering is successful and competition seeks a piece of the action, the innovator that had "all" of the (small) market during introduction is certainly faced with losing share—while gaining volume as the market grows.

Overestimating market size has implications beyond lower-than-expected sales revenues. Initial market estimates are used throughout the organization. Whether to attract investors, plan facility development and expansion, or staff the organization, inflated estimates lead to unfulfilled expectations. Even if the offering is successful beyond the introduction stage, less-than-anticipated sales results tarnish the entire project and, in the case of a start-up, the entire organization. "Me too" products face a double whammy: market leadership is usually not an attribute associated with followers. The inability of "me too" products to significantly penetrate existing markets contributes to 24 percent of new product failures, second only to there being no real need for the product.[14]

The Offering Fails to Meet Needs Adequately

Accounting for 15 percent of new product failures,[15] products that do not work right can be the result of poorly defined needs—a marketing deficiency; poor product performance—a technology flop; or a combination—the product technology would have worked but the offering was rushed to market before all the bugs were worked out. Timing linked to competitive product launches can suffer in this manner.

In high-technology industries, technophiles and innovators are usually quite forgiving with regard to new product ship dates. These market segments recognize that the offering is new and subject to a slow and possibly cumbersome introductory period and are able to adjust the timing of their own offering to meet supplier schedules. They are usually not dependent on economies of scale, while their product is likely dependent on the new technology.

---

[13]Ibid., 26.

[14]Ibid., 27.

[15]Ibid., 28.

> ### Participation Exercise
>
> Return to the examples of product failures in the opening of this chapter. For each of the well-known examples familiar to many consumers, research the dollars for-feited by the firm and the year the product was discontinued. In today's dollars, what do the losses total up to? What are the elements of marketing missing from each failure?

High-volume industries, particularly those that serve consumer markets and have major economies of scale and high fixed costs, usually can tolerate neither inadequate product performance nor inexact delivery schedules. These industries (e.g., consumer electronics, automotive) adopt technologies later in the life cycle. Only proven technologies are incorporated into their value network.

Market Will Not Pay   Thirteen percent of product failures are the result of a price squeeze[16]—either the costs of development and marketing were higher than expected or the market price adjusted to the new supply. What is important to recognize is that a price that the market is unwilling to accept is a symptom of other problems. Had there been an effective marketing plan, the market price of the offering would have been studied such that the change as a result of the increased supply— the market elasticity—would be anticipated. Competitive reactions should also be anticipated. It is not unusual for existing suppliers to a market to adjust price downward when faced with a new competitor.

Contrary Perceptions of Innovation

The degree to which a new offering is an innovation impacts the positioning of that offering in the market. When the supplier perceives the offering as a break-through innovation but the customer perceives the offering as an incremental product, there will be a mismatch of perceived value, unlikely to result in an adoption of the product by the customer. When the opposite is true, the supplier regards the innovation as an incremental product but the customer perceives a breakthrough innovation, there is still a mismatch but one of significant value to the customer. Unfortunately, unimpressed supplier management may not provide the necessary resources to the product to enable it to fulfill its potential in the market. The contrary perception of the level of innovation and, thus, value in the market creates shadowed and delusionary products,[17] further discussed in Chapter 9.

COLLABORATORS

Fans of old war movies probably have a negative impression of the word *collaborator*. **Collaborators** were those who worked with the enemy for their own

---

[16]Ibid., 28.

[17]Rangan and Bartus, op. cit.

(perhaps) short-term benefit. The second meaning of *collaborate* in the dictionary is "aid or cooperate traitorously." However, developing a collaborative relationship in business can be very positive—if you are the successful collaborator.

We have discussed the total effective value of the firm as viewed by the customer or client. Sherlock's term, appropriately, is "value image."[18] Value image, similar in concept to market positioning but with a much broader vision, can have a great impact on the likelihood of success in business-to-business relationships. Let us take this concept one step further.

Delivering customer value encompasses more than providing the latest technology, though continuously providing adequate customer value assumes that the technology envelope is expanded by innovators. Successful technology companies, such as Cisco Systems, 3Com, and others, were founded on technology but, as we have said, cannot rely on technology to maintain a market advantage. As these companies establish successful markets, competition increases, tightening margins and forcing a closer look at research and development funding. What are the alternatives? Why not have someone else fund and manage your early-term, high-risk research and development (R&D)?

Enter the high-technology, start-up company. As companies like Cisco Systems develop market ownership, they attract a cadre of smaller companies (satellites? corporate groupies?) that follow their market. Some of these smaller companies are satisfied to pick up a few crumbs along the way, while others invest (emotionally and financially) in the next generation technology that will replace/threaten/enhance the Cisco portfolio. Cisco is faced with a dilemma. These satellites provide real value to Cisco's customers. They can fill in the gaps in Cisco's product line, and they often rely on Cisco to help establish customer contact. At the same time Cisco is partnering with the smaller company, the smaller company is hoping to gain a foothold in Cisco's market and, with its new technology, capture market share. While all this is going on, Cisco must continue to invest in R&D—if not to push the technology envelope, then as a defensive measure. Collect enough satellites in your market, and the situation can be downright threatening. The answer: Cisco reduces R&D expenditures and encourages R&D by the smaller companies through their partnering. Part of the attraction for the small company to become involved is encouragement from Cisco that, when proven in the market, Cisco would be interested in an acquisition. Cisco gets to select from an array of new technologies that impact its market without the associated development costs or introduction risks.

The result? One (or a few) of the satellite start-up companies gets acquired by Cisco. The start-up goes the way of many high-techology start-ups—acquisition. The other satellites go the way of many other start-ups—out of the market. For the winner(s), this collaboration has been successful. They partnered with "the enemy" and, over the long term (for a start-up), won. For the other companies, the collaboration held a context closer to that traditional old war movie.

---

[18]Sherlock, op. cit.

In this narration, the customer for the satellite was, tactically, the Cisco customer and, strategically, Cisco. The value of the satellite to Cisco had to be marketed in such a way that Cisco had confidence in the long-term relationship. From an investor view, the customer was always Cisco. In a new venture, a large company with coattails to success may be a greater asset than a marketing partner or a customer partner. They can be a **collaborator.** Not all collaborators win.

Collaborations or partnerships are not new to business. Different patterns of mutual development between organizations have always existed. The patterns, or business models, have changed with changing market conditions. In the next section, we compare the concept of value networks introduced in Chapter 2 with the more traditional vertical integration model of creating value as we discuss the "make-or-buy" decision.

MAKE-OR-BUY DECISIONS

Closely related to the product development process and marketing's role in it is the "make-or-buy" decision. The degree to which an organization incorporates new or unique components into its products, combined with the potential proprietary nature of those components, creates the need for a sourcing decision. When market conditions allowed it, many organizations preferred to vertically integrate back into the manufacture of parts and materials. Early in the twentieth century, Henry Ford manufactured his own steel, glass, and tires for his company's vehicles. The advent of electronics and home electrical products in the 1920s demonstrated the need for plastic materials, not just for insulators but also in radio cabinets and the bases for vacuum tubes. The volumes associated with these consumer applications justified the backward integration into the manufacture of circuit board and plastic materials by General Electric. During the period of rapid growth of the automobile market, General Motors integrated into the manufacture (often through acquisition) of many vehicle components.

Market conditions during this period of heavy vertical integration may not have given these early pioneers much choice. Many of the products that were the subject of the integration were not available from another source, or, if they were, **proprietary information** considerations prevented the company from outsourcing the components. Both of these factors remain a consideration in vertical integration versus outsource decisions in today's market.

Vertical integration has attributes that speak in its favor. An integrated supply chain provides assured sources for components and materials. The development back into the manufacture of components and materials can also lead to profitable business opportunities.

Proprietary information is data that, while not protected by patents, is not available to the general public and has significant value to the owner. Trade secrets, process techniques, formulas (think Mrs. Fields Cookies and Coke syrup) are a significant part of the value of organizations. Maintaining the secrecy of proprietary information can be a significant motivation in make-or-buy decisions. Organizations that outsource part of their offering to another firm risk the loss of this secrecy.

It can happen. Polaroid, faced with significant capital investment resulting from the success of its "instant" camera, contracted production of film to a reputable source for photographic supplies—Eastman Kodak. Later, Kodak entered the market with their own instant camera. Polaroid claimed that Kodak used proprietary information learned from the manufacture of Polaroid film in the development and manufacture of the Kodak camera. The courts agreed, and Kodak was forced to leave the instant camera market.

Today, GE Plastics is one of the preeminent suppliers of engineering plastics (though they have left the circuit board material business). However, vertical integration can also lead to the development of large, sprawling organizations. The GE multifactor portfolio matrix (Chapter 5) is used to manage diverse, separate businesses. To many, large size implies bureaucracy, and bureaucracy implies slow movement, often devoid of innovation. While this is not meant to imply that very large organizations cannot respond to rapidly changing markets, it does indicate the involvement of a different decision-making process.

Large, vertically integrated organizations have an investment in the current form and method of conducting business and manufacturing products. New technologies, while not overlooked from an R&D perspective, may not survive the internal standards of the business model if they do not utilize existing facilities or "fit" the current idea of what business the organization is in (defined by what the organization produces). This myopia has been demonstrated countless times[19]— from ice houses to refrigerators, from vacuum tubes to solid state devices. Investment in infrastructure can slow the response to change.

Factors in the Decision

Let us return to the Sensacon example (earlier in this chapter) to demonstrate some of the factors in a make-or-buy decision. Keep in mind that a make-or-buy decision has greater implications than just attempting the lowest production cost. The development of a successful value network may include many make-or-buy decisions:

> Sensacon has invested in new technology to create the next generation sensor, to be called SensorSUV. The new technology gives SensorSUV a faster response time and greater resistance to shock and vibration, both features that the market has expressed interest in. This new distinction is primarily the result of the incorporation of a new component into SensorSUV. While the technology of the component is not, by itself, new, it is the first time it has been used in the sensor market and Sensacon has modified the component somewhat. Should Sensacon manufacture this "new" component itself or purchase it from an outside source?

First, Sensacon must assess the component's contribution to SensorSUV's value as perceived by the customer. (See Exhibit 8–3, Make-or-Buy Decisions.) If the component has only a minor role in the value of SensorSUV, Sensacon then must decide if it is unique to the sensor market. If the component is unique, it is in the best interest of Sensacon to either develop a partner relationship with qualified suppliers to produce the component or encourage potential collaborators to develop the market for the component. In either case, the partner or collaborator will have to be assured of purchases from Sensacon and an opportunity to further develop, with other sensor manufacturers, market applications for the component after a specified period of exclusive use by Sensacon. Because the component's role

---

[19]Theodore Levitt, "Marketing Myopia", *Harvard Business Review* (July–August 1960).

EXHIBIT 8–3   Make-or-Buy Decisions

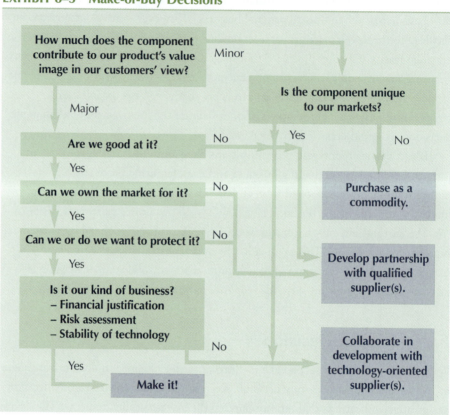

in the value of Sensacon's product is minor and technology based, it would not usually be a good decision for Sensacon to make the component itself. If the component plays a minor role in the value of SensorSUV and is not unique to the sensor market, Sensacon should treat the component as a commodity purchase.

If Sensacon determines that the component plays a major role in the value of the SensorSUV, an entirely different decision path is necessary. Since the component contributes significant value to Sensacon's end product, it may be in Sensacon's best interest to manufacture the component itself. Sensacon is, however, in the sensor business, not the component business, and may not have a distinctive competence in the manufacture of the new component. If Sensacon is not good at the manufacture of the component, then the sourcing alternatives become the same as the *Minor/Yes* decision flow in Exhibit 8–3—either source from a partner or encourage a collaboration.

What if Sensacon decides that it has the unique competency required to manufacture the component successfully? This may be a diversification decision. Using the parameters of market ownership,[20] Sensacon must now decide if it can "own" the market for the component and if it wants to protect the proprietary nature of

---

the component (patents, trade secrets, etc.). If either answer is "no," Sensacon should look to outsource the component through a supplying partner. It is only at this point that Sensacon should fully examine the business case for manufacturing the component itself.

Supplier Role in the Decision

Throughout this make-or-buy decision process, the potential supplier (either partner or collaborator) should be involved with Sensacon to determine what value it can provide as a supplier that will exceed the value that Sensacon can produce for itself. This level of supplier-delivered value will

- Allow Sensacon to invest in other areas closer to its main business

- Be recognized as a resource by the customer (Sensacon)

- Develop a business opportunity for the supplier

- Create or reinforce a potentially strong relationship between supplier and Sensacon

The supplier who knows the culture and competencies of its customer can create win-win situations for both organizations.

In this chapter, we have looked at the product life cycle as a tool to better understand the pressures placed on offerings by different aspects of the market environment and the methods by which the marketing mix can be used to respond. While the PLC is a generalized case, it provides a framework around which to build product management theory. The PLC may be used as a representation of sales revenue over time for individual products or product lines but is most often applicable to product or market categories. Through this view, an analogy to product categories as strategic business units in portfolio management is possible. Buying behavior, profitability, and competitive threats, as well as perceived value, vary over the life cycle.

The new product development process has been discussed in what we hope is not a bureaucratic context. Marketing is the defining force in new product development and thus bears significant attention in the review of why new products fail. New ideas must be considered from the view of the market and not be just a good idea for the offering firm. The failure to apply adequate marketing practice in new product planning is the single largest factor in new offering failures. The value of the offering *as perceived by the customer* cannot be overemphasized.

In the next chapter, we examine entrepreneurial orientation and the innovation process and their impact on the competitiveness of the firm. The pace of innovation contributes to the trend away from vertical integration and toward the application of the value network concept in offering development. The "make-or-buy" decision is crucial to the long-range planning of innovative organizations and requires marketing's insight and knowledge of customer perceptions of value. In Chapter 9, the management of innovation and the importance of business-to-business brands in the creation of industry standards are discussed.

Participation Exercise

Consider the complexity of the new product development process, particularly the levels of coordination required as firms develop value networks through collaboration with other firms. What unique management challenges are presented by value networks when compared to the vertical integration alternative? How does the "make-or-buy" decision further complicate the management process?

Key Terms

collaborators

decline stage

development stage

discontinuous replacement
  technologies

discovery approach

economies of scale

evolutionary product
  introductions

growth stage

introduction stage

maturity stage

negotiated price
  reductions

opportunity costs

proprietary disclosure
  agreements

proprietary information

stage gates

unique or first-time value
  network

Questions for Review and Discussion

1. Review the generalized product life cycle as shown in Exhibit 8–1. How well does the PLC model work for rapidly changing technologies? Markets? Why?

2. At what point in the PLC are the following product categories?

   Railroads   Gasoline   Commercial aircraft

   Desktop computers   Genetic engineering

3. What are the possible pitfalls in the elimination of business-to-business products or product lines when they reach the start of their decline in the market?

4. Under what circumstances would a product category that is in decline and barely profitable be kept as a part of a firm's business-to-business offerings?

5. How can executive attachment to a technology lead to product failure?

6. How does the fast pace of markets impact make-or-buy decisions?

7. What are the implications of outsourcing significant parts of an offering that will have a very long maturity stage in its PLC?

8. What are the implications of vertically integrating to provide most all of the elements of value for a product category that competes in a highly competitive technology market?

9. What role does marketing play in the new product development process? What are marketing's responsibilities?

10. How are the attitude and culture of the new product development team related to the number of successful developments?

11. Is it better to invest heavily in the early stages of NPD or toward the end of the process? Why?

12. If misunderstood or misapplied, what are potential pitfalls of the stage gate method of managing NPD?

Internet Exercises

Go to the System Administration, Networking, and Security (SANS) Institute site: **http://www.sans.org** Start with the link for "About SANS" and browse the site to get a sense of what it is about. Suppose you are the marketing manager for a small company developing network security products. How could you participate in the SANS network to build your value network? What limitations or drawbacks do you foresee in SANS involvement?

Choose a business-to-business industry in which you have an interest. Using your favorite search engine (e.g. **http://www.google.com**, **http://www.altavista.com**), obtain information on that industry (articles, research, etc.) and identify two or three of the key categories of products or services in that industry. Using the information you find, determine what stage of the PLC these categories are in. Explain how you made your determinations.

In the same industry you identified in the last exercise, find an established company and a new entrant company. Use their Web sites to identify the key partnerships they have formed. What role or roles do these partnerships play in their offerings? What differences do you see between the partnerships of the established company and the entrant company? Explain why the differences occur.

Innovation, Branding, and Competitiveness

overview. . . In this chapter, we address two methods by which marketing creates competitive advantage for the business-to-business firm: innovation and branding. We separate these out from other chapters because too often they are thought to be part of a single element of the marketing mix—

© DOUG KANTER/AP/WIDE WORLD PHOTOS

innovation as part of new product development and branding as part of either product management or business-to-business communications. We wish to emphasize that innovation and brand building need to extend across all elements of marketing.

Indeed, new product development is extremely important in getting a key portion of value right for customers. In new product development, marketing can and should add its own innovative contribution to the structuring of the product and service portions of the offering. However, the more we, the authors, view the successes and failures in business-to-business marketing, the more we have come to believe that broad-based innovativeness holds the keys to performance. Maintaining or increasing a degree of differentiation from competitors can be accomplished through innovating in the channel structure, the pricing structure, or even the communication strategy, as well as in the product. As we saw in the last chapter, the opportunity for product innovation becomes reduced during the mature portion of the product life cycle. If the company is not careful, it resorts to shaving margins to maintain competitiveness. Finding a way to innovate elsewhere in the offering, away from "product," may be the only way to maintain margins.

Innovativeness can be viewed as the key element of an entrepreneurial orientation; so, in this chapter, we discuss innovation in the context of marketing entrepreneurially. Entrepreneurial orientation includes proactiveness, controlled risk taking, and opportunity seeking, as well as innovation. In this chapter, we discuss how the marketing function of the firm can approach all elements of marketing with an entrepreneurial orientation.

We include brand building in the chapter because it can also be a key source of competitive advantage and requires attention across all the elements of marketing. Branding is just as important in business-to-business marketing as it is in consumer marketing. Business-to-business companies with strong brands receive favorable treatment in the customer's buying decision process. However, to create a strong brand goes far beyond building awareness for the brand name; rather, it takes mastery of all the elements in the offering that contribute to value for customers, which of course takes time to establish. A strong brand is something for new companies and new market entrants to strive to build; it is something for established companies to nurture, protect, and use with care. The discussion addresses methods of making a brand into a standard and generally building brand strength.

As you progress through this chapter, keep in mind how the concepts discussed contribute to a company's competitive strength. The methods discussed in this chapter build sustainable competitive advantage deep within the company's inner workings. Competitive advantage in the company's offerings comes as the result of attention paid to building these links in the company's value chain.

In the opening example, we show how Sun Microsystems created a platform for generating new initiatives that address emerging needs in new markets. The innovative effort actually has two stages: the building of the partner community framework and the formation of new marketing programs. Innovation at both levels involves much more than product innovation; the whole effort is very entrepreneurial in character. Notice, too, that branding plays a role in this innovative effort. If you read between the lines, you can anticipate what needs to be done to build both the partner community network and the new initiatives into strong brands.

SUN CREATES AN INNOVATIVE PARTNER NETWORK*

In March 2000, Sun Microsystems launched iForce, a networked community of Sun partners, including software developers, VARs, systems integrators, and peripheral equipment vendors. The idea was to provide business customers with a single entity to go to for e-business or other network systems. iForce is a good illustration of a nonproduct innovation.

The principal benefit provided by iForce is a one-stop shop for enterprise or service provider customers. Because all the elements of the offering are "under one roof," and are marketed together as a bundled offering, the customer saves time and some expense in acquiring and using a customized solution. Sun provides services and facilities that make it attractive for partners and customers to participate. Sun provides financing, operations services, and global marketing for Sun business partners. It provides discounts and consulting services for start-up Internet companies. Sun has also built test and proving facilities, called iForce Ready Centers, where partners, customers, and Sun technicians can experiment with and build customized systems for cus-

tomers that can then be scaled and translated to the customer's own facilities. Customer problems are addressed by all parties concerned using Sun methods or development approaches created by other Sun integrator partners, if more applicable.

Much of the revenue and margin produced in sales generated by iForce goes to the partners. Sun makes money on sales of equipment, operating systems software, some consulting, and eventually on returns from venture capital activity associated with the initiative.

Sun made an apparently wise move by not overspecifying the nature of the partnership program at the outset. Over a six-month period after launch, the partnership framework evolved and eventually produced a specific initiative focused on wireless systems called, appropriately enough, iForce Wireless. This initiative targets telecommunications companies and wireless service providers, offering combined packages of hardware, software, applications, and integration services.

*Based on H. M. Fattah, "Second Rising?" Marketing Computers 21, no. 3 (March 2001) 34–36; and on iForce Web site: http://www.iforce.com

introduction. . .

The nature of the business environment in business-to-business markets is constant change. Customers constantly want new and better products and services from their suppliers. Competitors are constantly trying new strategies and tactics for winning over customers. As Dickson notes,[1] there is no equilibrium; some competitor will always come along with something better that changes the relationships in the market.

To cope with this dynamic frenzy, business-to-business marketers must either find market niches that they can lock up so tightly that they face no significant threat of competition or they must compete just as hard as the other businesses in the market. The first alternative is at least limited in scope, if it exists at all. This means that marketers must compete by continually trying to create more value for both existing and new customers. In this chapter, we discuss a way to do this by acting entrepreneurially.

LEARNING OBJECTIVES

♦ Understand the application of entrepreneurial marketing and innovation in order to compete in business-to-business markets.

♦ Obtain an understanding of how innovation relates to entrepreneurial marketing.

♦ Gain a sense of how innovation can be accomplished in all elements of the offering.

♦ Understand how to implement innovation and entrepreneurial marketing in business-to-business marketing.

♦ Understand the concepts of competing over a long time frame through building and managing brand strength in a business-to-business environment.

♦ Obtain an understanding of how to implement brand-building efforts.

♦ Gain a sense of how current trends in business-to-business markets are affecting the concepts and implementation of innovation, entrepreneurial marketing, and building brand strength.

An entrepreneurial approach to competing involves four key elements: seeking opportunities, innovating, acting proactively, and taking controlled risks. In the second part of this chapter, we go into some depth on the why and the how of innovating. Continuing with the theme of competing over time in a changing environment, in the last section of this chapter we discuss the use of branding as a key competitive tool in business-to-business marketing. Brand building is a way to create competitive strength that endures, despite the progression of product life cycles.

In the opening example, Sun Microsystems noticed that its customers were becoming overwhelmed with the intricacies, choices, and uncertainties involved in building e-commerce systems. To bring all the pieces together in one place, Sun formed the iForce partner network and developed programs to support it technically and with marketing assistance. This example illustrates some of the key ideas in this chapter. Sun acted entrepreneurially through nonproduct marketing innovation. They controlled the risks involved by innovating in steps, obtaining feedback, and revising the innovation. Finally, while still early in the life of the initiative, they

---

[1] Peter R. Dickson, "Toward a General Theory of Competitive Rationality," *Journal of Marketing* (January 1992): 69–83.

gave it a brand name. As the initiative builds new aspects (e.g., the iForce Wireless program), the iForce brand will acquire a stronger reputation and help Sun compete against the likes of IBM and Hewlett-Packard.

MARKETING ENTREPRENEURIALLY

There is evidence that the methods of the entrepreneur add more to organizational performance than just energizing it through an entrepreneurial vision. Company executives can enhance performance by fostering an environment in which the organization does **entrepreneurial marketing**. Even if the company's upper level management does not create such an environment, the individual business marketer can still improve performance by incorporating entrepreneurial methods into his approach (within the constraints imposed by the organization).

What does it mean to market entrepreneurially? We generally think of entrepreneurship as the act of starting a new company. However, this is perhaps too simplistic a view. People within a company can act as if their organization is a high-growth start-up with the result that their organization shows at least some of the flexibility and boldness of a start-up. Accordingly, we can identify characteristics that indicate that an act is more or less entrepreneurial. Research done by marketing and management scholars has come to the point of defining entrepreneurial activity as having three or four dimensions.[2] For our purposes, the key dimensions of entrepreneurship can be thought of as *innovation, proactivity, controlled risk taking,* and *opportunity seeking.*

Innovation is creating something new and making it useful. The fact that somebody uses the new thing for some particular purpose distinguishes an innovation from an invention. Innovation can also be taking something that already exists and making it better, so that it provides more value to customers than it did before. **Proactivity** is doing something before others do it. Innovations, by their nature, are proactive, but entrepreneurs can do things that are not necessarily new. They might do something before their competitors do it, and this by definition is also being proactive. **Controlled risk taking** is a combination of knowing what the risks really are, taking moderate risks in which the worst case is survivable, and finding ways to manage the risks to increase the chances of success

Innovation is the creation of something new and commercially useful or the improvement of something to make it more useful. It might involve the application of science or technology but does not have to.

Proactivity is doing something before others do it. Taking the lead in a market or in a new development, even when the offering that will become obsolete by your action is your own, is a key element in market ownership.

Controlled risk taking is not "bet-the-farm" risk taking. Rather, entrepreneurial risk taking is knowing what the risks are and doing something to control the risk.

[2]Danny Miller and Peter H. Friesen, "Innovation in Conservative and Entrepreneurial Firms: Two Models of Strategic Momentum," *Strategic Management Journal* 3 (1982), 1–25; Michael H. Morris and Gordon W. Paul, "The Relationship between Entrepreneurship and Marketing in Established Firms," *Journal of Business Venturing* 2 (1987): 247–59; Jeffrey G. Covin and Dennis P. Slevin, "Strategic Management of Small Firms in Hostile and Benign Environments," *Strategic Management Journal* 10 (1989): 75–87.

An Entrepreneurial Offering

Go to the following site: http://www.sun.com/dot-com/tools/index.html What is Sun offering here? Why? Is Sun acting entrepreneurially by offering these tools?

and reduce the consequences of failure. Finally, **opportunity seeking** is largely self-explanatory. Note that people and companies that are more entrepreneurial tend to actively look for opportunities and are constantly evaluating how attractive prospective opportunities are.

With this in mind, we can begin to see what entrepreneurial marketing is like. For any one entrepreneurial event, there is a cycle of activity. The cycle begins with opportunity recognition (Exhibit 9–1). Then an initial design is produced to address the opportunity. The design is developed and tested on prospective users and customers, and their reactions are evaluated and incorporated into the design. Meanwhile, the resources for pursuing this opportunity are being gathered. The project grows; choices are made; the capability to produce and deliver is ramped up; and the product, service, or program is launched. After launch, feedback is received, analyzed, and acted upon. In the feedback, new opportunities are sought and can trigger the cycle anew.

EXHIBIT 9–1   Entrepreneurial Progression

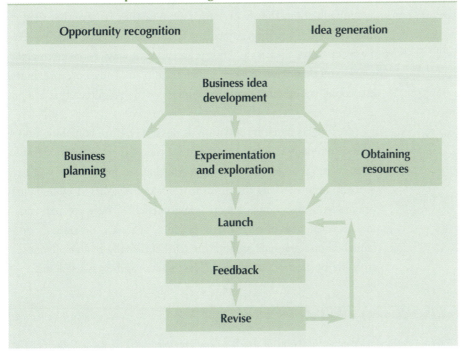

For this event to be successful, certain things must be done. First, the opportunity must be kept firmly in mind. The vision of the opportunity may change as feedback is received, but realization of the opportunity is the goal. Too often, new ventures lose focus as the team members start seeing new opportunities galore and trying to find ways to pursue them. Second, producing a successful design involves combining existing "technology" with new "technology" (*technology* is in quotes because we use a broad definition here: *technology* is any way of doing something; it is not just hardware or software—see the discussion later in this chapter). The new technology may take a fair amount of creative work. The mind-set here must be a willingness to change or do things differently in order to pursue the opportunity. "Whatever it takes" must be done to make the opportunity "happen."

Obviously, these first two strictures or guidelines connote the "opportunity seeking" and "innovation" portion of entrepreneurial orientation. Innovation without proactivity, though, can drag on forever inside the organization without ever seeing the market. The entrepreneur or marketer has to get the innovation into the market, first to test it, and then to pursue the opportunity full bore. Taking too long can kill momentum; the development team gets comfortable (or bored) with tweaking the product or program to "get it right." Taking the new design to the market becomes a psychological hurdle that is too high to get over easily. Taking too long can also lead to being preempted by competition or by the customers themselves. The window of opportunity may close for a number of reasons.

Proactivity, then, involves doing things to reduce the time to market. Once in the market, proactivity involves doing things to rapidly improve the offering before the competition can improve theirs.

Though risk taking is often seen as the ultimate role or characteristic of the entrepreneur, most entrepreneurs do not see themselves as taking huge risks. Either they do not know enough about the chances for failure or they believe that they have enough control over the situation to manage the probability that their project will fall short of expectations. Successful entrepreneurs find ways to make things work, and they trust in their abilities to do so. Thus, entrepreneurial marketing is done in a way that minimizes the resources that are put at risk.

Entrepreneurial marketing is the undertaking of a marketing strategy that actively pursues a new opportunity and has relatively high levels of innovation, proactivity, and controlled risk taking.

Getting as much information as possible before launching full scale is one way that marketers reduce the chance of failure. However, waiting too long can create a risk that an opportunity will be missed.[3] Another way that information can be gathered while being proactive is to run one or more "experiments."[4] These are trial runs in which the new business, new product, or new program is launched on a minimal scale in the market, usually in a small, controllable portion of the market. The results can be assessed and a

---

[3]Peter R. Dickson and Joseph J. Giglierano, "Missing the Boat and Sinking the Boat," *Journal of Marketing* (Summer 1986).

[4]Thomas J. Peters and Robert H. Waterman, *In Search of Excellence* (New York: Harper and Row, 1982).

revised offering launched into the larger market, eventually. In many cases, this can produce a full-scale launch faster than a launch based on extensive research.

Changing the Rules

The ultimate way of reducing risk, or at least changing everybody's risk, is to change the rules of the market, as discussed in Chapter 5. Recall that Hamel and Prahalad argued for competitive strategy that changes the relationships among the participants in a market, so that the "rules" determining competitive advantage are changed.[5] However risky, changing the rules is almost always entrepreneurial on the other three dimensions (proactivity, innovation, and opportunity seeking), as well, and can thus have a substantial payoff. It is usually very proactive in that action is taken before other competitors act. If the new rules come to be adopted by the market, the action may have the effect of upsetting the current competitive balance, starting the process of being recognized as the market owner. As for the innovation dimension, changing the rules almost always involves an innovation of some sort, whether it is innovation in the product or elsewhere in the offering.

Entrepreneurial marketing, then, is the undertaking of a marketing strategy that actively pursues a new opportunity and has relatively high levels of innovation, proactivity, and controlled risk taking. It stands to reason that it improves the marketer's chance of success because it creates new value that tends to be higher than the value offered by competitors.

Practical Aspects of Creating an Entrepreneurial Orientation

Over the past decade or so, many companies have said they wanted to "be more entrepreneurial" but have not gotten beyond paying lip service to the concept. The question arises of how an entrepreneurial orientation should be fostered, particularly in business-to-business marketing. We discuss four key elements to inducing an entrepreneurial way of doing things within the marketing function: hiring the right kinds of people, directing the right kinds of activities, removing impediments, and providing the right incentives.

Hiring the Right Kinds of People

Hiring people who are comfortable acting entrepreneurially means looking for many characteristics that are common for most management or professional positions in today's business world. Good communication skills and an ability to work well with small, diverse teams are valued skills in most career positions. They are equally important for implementing an entrepreneurial orientation. Three key traits stand out, though, as likely indicators of someone who will be comfortable in an entrepreneurial environment. First is the

---

[5]Gary Hamel and C. K. Prahalad, *Competing for the Future* (Boston, Mass.: Harvard Business School Press, 1994).

> ### Participation Exercise
>
> Examine your own background. What evidence can you discuss that would convince a hiring manager that you had entrepreneurial attributes (even if you do not have any direct start-up experience)? What might you do if you want to improve your "entrepreneurial profile"?

ability to persistently pursue a passion. The marketer will want to be surrounded with team members who can get excited about business, treat it as a venture, and work hard to make it succeed. The second trait is a comfort with trying new things, making mistakes, and learning from them. This does not mean that the person is careless or sloppy. Complete learning comes in part from a comparison of expectations to actual results and trying to understand why there is a variance. This means that the person will be comfortable with the detail of setting objectives and then measuring results against those objectives. The important aspect, though, is that the person will not see mistakes as personally threatening. The third trait is a bias for action. Proactivity requires taking action in a quick but prepared way. Unprepared action tends to be reckless; overpreparation, of course, creates delay. The characteristic required strikes a balance between the two.

Directing Appropriate Activities

We discuss innovation at length in the next major section of this chapter, so here we discuss activities that identify opportunities, create proactivity, and take controlled risks.

Opportunity recognition comes in part from formal activities to analyze potential markets and match unmet needs to a company's existing or expected core competencies. These are similar to the kinds of activities we discussed in Chapter 5 through Chapter 7. Specific analytic methods for opportunity recognition can also be found in trade and research journals.[6] An adjunct to analytic techniques is an opportunity-oriented way of looking at the world. This involves cultivating a constant sensitivity to unmet customer needs and possible partnership combinations that can create new kinds of value. Managers can help their less-experienced marketing staff learn how to build a network of contacts for information collection (see Chapter 6).

Marketers should also develop contact networks aimed at facilitating execution of marketing activities (see the box, "Contact Network for Execution"). This will help in instituting proactivity as a way of doing things. Controlling the results of planning activities also enhances proactivity. Plans should seldom be more than a few pages in length and should have a series of action items specified.

The key activity for controlling risks is to establish learning mechanisms. This means trying new initiatives on a limited scale and assessing the results. Such assessment should be directed both at internal operations and at customers' perceptions of value. The Sun iForce program illustrates this kind of learning. Sun was

[6]Thomas C. O'Brien and Terry J. Fadem, "Identifying New Business Opportunities," *Research Technology Management* (September–October 1999): 15–19.

> ### Contact Network for Execution
>
> Just as marketers develop a network of contacts for information collection, they will need to form a network of contacts for getting things done. It pays to determine ahead of time who within the organization is responsible for such things as graphics design, support of missionary sales, sales training, and document production. These contacts will be internal to the firm but may also include outsiders such as consultants, ad agencies, and contacts among distributors. By cultivating these contacts during planning, the marketer can make execution go smoothly when the time comes.

able to observe the effects of its actions in setting up the community of partners and learned what worked and what did not. Sun also learned what was valuable both to its partners and to customers, and this led to the Wireless iForce initiative.

Removing Impediments

Two principal impediments are often imposed by existing organizations. The first is a requirement for extensive justification. The second is a tendency to punish failure.

Opportunity seeking and proactivity are obviously hindered by a requirement for overanalysis. Controlled risk taking—and, hence, learning—is stifled if the organization demotes, ostracizes, or fires individuals who take risks that fail. These impediments need to be addressed by company executives. A marketing manager can do his best to shield employees from shortsighted company policies, but these policies would eventually limit the manager's ability to operate entrepreneurially.

Providing Incentives

Over the past decade, companies have gotten used to providing incentives to employees through profit-sharing bonuses and stock options. The economic slowdown of 2001 has shown the downside (literally) of these types of incentives. Accordingly, a range of incentives needs to be considered, including cash, equity, and nonmonetary rewards. The keys, as always when providing incentives, are to provide appropriate incentives, to award the incentives for doing the right things, and to provide the rewards soon enough after the actions to be real reinforcement for the desired activity.

COMPETING THROUGH INNOVATION

The entrepreneurial element of innovation is central to the continuing ability of the company to win customers and reap financial performance benefits. In the last chapter, we discussed product innovation through the new product development process. A point we want to emphasize in this chapter is that innovation in the nonproduct elements of the offering can be just as important—sometimes even more important—than product innovation.

Value comes from all elements of the offering. Maintaining or increasing a degree of differentiation from competitors can be accomplished through innovating in the channel structure, the pricing structure, or even the communication strategy surrounding the product. As was shown in the last chapter, the opportunity for product innovation becomes reduced during the mature portion of the product life cycle. If the company is not careful, it will resort to shaving margins to maintain competitiveness. Finding a way to innovate elsewhere in the offering, away from "product," may be the only way to maintain margins.

Innovation can be viewed not just as the creation of new things but also as new and better ways of doing what has been done before. Depending on viewpoint, all the following can be legitimate innovations:

Designing for more efficient production

Less use of raw materials

Reduced environmental impact

More effective marketing

More effective distribution systems

From this view, innovation is a significant contributor to productivity and, thus, is a significant contributor to our economic well-being and growth. In fact, at the macro level, innovation drives a free market economy. New products, services, retailers, other channel intermediaries, communications methods, and forms—all come from innovation. Innovation also gives us new government services, charitable organizations and services, publicly supported infrastructure, and elements of our culture. New ideas are the outcome of innovative effort. Our society "makes progress" through innovation. The long period of sustained economic growth in the United State during the 1990s came about because of innovations that gave us new products and improved productivity.

Innovation across the Offering

So, managing innovation is an important function of the firm. In the prior chapter, we discussed new product development and product management at length. New product development is extremely important in getting a key portion of value right for customers. We also discussed how the product and offering needed to be managed to address the realities of the product life cycle.

The last chapter discussed a new product development process that moved from idea generation through several steps to arrive at a commercially offered product, managed on an ongoing basis. We can think of this process being extended to the other aspects of the offering. Our experience, though, tells us that companies rarely spend the same kind of effort—nor do they have the same kind of process—for innovating in the other elements of the offering and value chain.

Before getting started, some definitions are in order. First, we want to be clear on what we mean by **technology**. As defined earlier, technology is a way of accomplishing something. Accordingly,

For our discussion, **technology** is not limited to items that comprise a manufactured product or those tools used in the performance of a service. Technology is a way of accomplishing something.

technology is not limited to the mechanisms that comprise a manufactured product or the code that comprises a software program. We can think of the marketing activities chosen by the firm as a technology to perform marketing. Similarly, innovation is not limited to changes of products or services. *Innovation* is a change in any technology. Further, the innovation must be useful and potentially commercialized to be an innovation—innovation is invention in commercial use.

With these definitions as background, consider what is required for building a process that will facilitate and drive innovation across the offering(s) of the company. Recall from Chapter 5 that the firm must have a clear mission and goals, and executive management must recognize the necessity of change to meet those goals. In other words, executive management and strategy makers must recognize a need to be innovative and must make a conscious choice to do so. Innovation is so important for the long-term health of the company that top-level management must drive it. This strategy decision must cover what technologies to pursue, what kind of innovation will be pursued to address these technologies, and how to pursue this innovation.

If the company is going to pursue innovation—and it is a rare company that would not—the company must adopt a predisposition for trying new things. The culture and reward structure must accommodate and assist people who seek to innovate, whether they succeed or fail. Failure in innovating is positive, as long as (1) something valuable is learned and (2) it does not kill the company. Most innovations can be tried initially on a small scale without pursuing "bet-the-company" risks. Without adoption of policies that reward innovation and support "useful" failure, creating a culture of innovation is an uphill battle. This inclination to innovate must extend beyond the R&D part of the organization, because R&D only addresses part of the offering.

Once the organization is on its way to instilling an innovation inclination, executive management and strategy makers must choose where and how to innovate, as already mentioned. In Chapter 5, we stated that company executives make the strategic decision to pursue major business opportunities. Given the choice of business, innovation initiatives to pursue these will probably be obvious; and, indeed, the expected contributions of innovation were considered in the choice of opportunities. Given the innovative directions and businesses to pursue, strategy makers then determine "how innovative" the company needs to be.

Over the past twenty years, researchers and practitioners have observed that "big" innovations differ greatly from "small" innovations.[7] The field has come to distinguish two ends of the spectrum in terms of *radical innovation* and *incremental innovation*. **Incremental innovations** take the existing product and offering and make small-step improvements to the original design. Incremental improvements add up to produce a great deal of change in an offering over time. **Radical innovations,** on the other hand, can produce large changes in the functions and performance of a product or offering. Radical innovations can be so radical

---

[7]c.f. James M. Utterback, "Radical Innovation and Corporate Regeneration," *Research Technology Management* 37, no. 4 (1994): 10.

that they create an essentially different kind of product or offering with a new combination of types of value produced. These have come to be called **breakthrough innovations,**[8] although common usage of the term is used inconsistently. Sometimes *breakthrough* is used to mean any extreme change in performance or costs, including a large improvement in existing benefits or costs, without changing the product's basic architecture or the offering's principal benefits. At other times, usage of the term means strictly that the technology architecture has changed drastically or that benefit structure is essentially different and vastly better. No matter how the terms are defined or used, the implication is clear: different kinds of innovation behave differently and require different kinds of organizational treatment.

A way of thinking about innovation with useful implications has emerged over the past seven or eight years. Christensen distinguishes between *disruptive innovation* and *sustaining innovation.*[9] He describes **disruptive innovation** as introducing offerings based on technology that is substantially different from the dominant technologies in use in a market. The benefits that are offered by the new technology are different from those offered by the dominant technology and offering, and so they may not even compete directly. While the different technology may start out as inferior to existing technology, it is still appropriate for new uses and different users in the market. Eventually, though, the new technology supplants the old as rapid technology advancement on the newcomer technology outstrips the capabilities of the established, mature technology. **Sustaining innovation,** by contrast, is innovation that improves the existing dominant technology and offerings.

Christensen argues that existing market leaders find it very difficult to pursue disruptive technologies. The leaders' infrastructure and operations are all geared toward pursuit and support of the existing direction in technology. Even the leaders' customers are all invested in receiving benefits from the existing technology; if a supplier produces an offering based on new technology, the customers will tend to redirect the supplier back to the established technology. Suppliers of the new technology target different customer groups than the current leaders. These market segments, though, may outgrow the earlier segments, completely shifting the power structure of the market.

Christensen, in his analysis of the disk drive industry, has shown that disruptive technology is *not necessarily radical innovation.* Incremental innovation may be the initiator of the disruptive innovation. Similarly, radical innovation does not have to be disruptive. It may simply improve the performance and benefit package of the existing architecture and offering but do so in one large leap. Take word processing in the early 1980s, for example. One might argue that the introduction of electronic, stand-alone word processors was a radical innovation over the electric typewriter. The word processors offered by Wang, Olivetti, Xerox, and IBM were far better and more useful than the standard IBM Selectric, but they were

[8]c.f. Gina Colarelli O'Connor, "Market Learning and Radical Innovation: A Cross-case Comparison of Eight Radical Innovation Projects," *Journal of Product Innovation Management* 15, no. 2 (1998) 151–66.

[9]Clayton M. Christensen, *The Innovator's Dilemma* (New York: HarperCollins, 1997).

still, after all, typewriters. Meanwhile, word-processing software was offered as a product to be used on the desktop personal computer, linked by printer cable to a dot matrix or daisy-wheel printer. It was not as versatile as the trained typist with the stand-alone word processor, but it worked and gave the amateur typist the ability to create a usable, changeable document without burdening the administrative assistant or going through the typing pool.

Word-processing software was not a particularly radical innovation. It had been around for years, making it possible to write documents using your company's mainframe or minicomputer. The initial market was not in the office products market; it was the individual professional (or even the student) who wanted to write his own documents. Over time, the software got better through incremental innovation. As professional staff learned that they could write, edit, and print their own documents faster and better than sending repeated drafts through a typing pool, the typing pool went away. As the remaining office staff started using the other mainstay programs of the PC—databases, graphics, and spreadsheets—and as offices invested in relatively expensive laser printers, administrative staff made the switch to multifunction PCs from their old, single-function word processors.

The heyday of the stand-alone word processor was over within a few years. One can still find one or two IBM Selectric typewriters in the office, kept under a desk or hidden away in a back room, used for typing the occasional envelope address. It is unlikely that there is a stand-alone word processor in that office. It is difficult to get support or supplies, and no one remembers how to program them.

The disruptive technology was the word-processing software; the innovation was incremental. The effect on the office products market was far-reaching. The radical innovation was probably going from the electric typewriter to the electronic typewriter. This was a sustaining innovation in Christensen's terms.

Accordingly, the firm needs to decide to address disruptive innovation if it is to survive in the long run. Without doing this, a new entrant will eventually replace the old technology for most of the market. The decision is not *whether* to pursue disruptive technology. The decision is *how* to pursue it and *to what extent.*

The company must also determine whether the innovation it will pursue is radical or incremental. Whether disruptive or sustaining, radical innovation requires a different kind of development and commercialization effort than does incremental innovation.[10]

A corporate or business strategy that intends to "change the rules of the industry or marketplace," as discussed in Chapter 5, almost always needs to pursue breakthrough or disruptive innovation and to be proactive rather than reactive. The goals of the strategy makers and the circumstances of the business environment dictate how aggressive the company needs to be in this pursuit. In any case, the business strategy sets the innovation context within which the marketer has to operate.

---

[10]V. Kasturi Rangan and Kevin Bartus, "New Product Commercialization: Common Mistakes," Harvard Business School Note 594–127, 1994. 63–75.

Pursuit of Disruptive Technologies

Assuming that the executive management of the firm decides to pursue disruptive technology to some extent, the question becomes "what does this mean for marketing?" within the firm. Christensen makes a compelling case that implementation of such a directive involves five things:[11]

1. Separate the project or business unit responsible for pursuing disruptive innovation from the existing company with its established customers and business model. Find new customers who really want the offering.
2. Address the new business with a small business unit appropriate in size for the small market size of the initial opportunity.
3. Use an iterative, exploratory approach for finding the right market and the right way of addressing the market.
4. Use processes and decision-making rules appropriate to the new business model; do not use the processes and rules of the existing organization, as these were not likely designed for an emerging business, nor will they facilitate changes.
5. Develop the markets that want the offering; do not try to find the breakthrough technology advance that makes the disruptive technology competitive in the old mainstream market. Eventually, the new markets will evolve together into a new mainstream of their own.

These prescriptions suggest that the business-to-business marketer who finds himself in the pursuit of disruptive innovation (whether in the product, service, or in other elements of the offering) should be in a small business unit pursuing an uncertain opportunity (if it is not an uncertain opportunity, the innovation is probably not disruptive). If the marketer observes that his organization lacks autonomy from a large organization, then he should start looking for ways to change this situation. The large organization will usually impose its systems, values, and metrics on the new venture and unwittingly kill it. Even a supposedly enlightened organization that gives the new venture its own criteria for support will be tempted to change its mind later and impose revenue and profit objectives that are impossible to meet.

The box "From Pistons to Fuel Cells" describes the innovative effort of Kolbenschmidt Pierburg AG. Notice that the kind of innovation pursued will probably involve a changeover in the infrastructure, that is, the innovation pursued is probably disruptive. Kolbenschmidt Pierburg AG will have to be careful how it manages its efforts, or it may be tempted to stay with the old line of business and lose out to the new, even though it has addressed the new technology directly.

A case might also be made that a portion of the e-business-to-business (eB2B) meltdown of 2000–2001 grew out of a wholesale violation of Christensen's prescriptions. The IPO-oriented venture capital imposed upon eB2B start-ups the values and rules appropriate for larger, more-developed markets. The size of the real opportunities was still too small to earn a reasonable return on the amounts of money invested. In addition, the companies needed more time for trial and error to get the technology,

---

[11]Christensen, op. cit.

From Pistons to Fuel Cells

Kolbenschmidt Pierburg AG is the world's second largest supplier of pistons to manufacturers of internal combustion engines—auto and truck, gasoline and diesel. Annual sales are $1.8 billion, with revenues forecast to hit $3 billion in 2005. Because of demand for products in North America, the company will build a new U. S. production line, part of a $50 million capital investment.

How does this company spend research and development dollars? Certainly to maintain the position that its internal combustion engine components command in the market, but also by anticipating the future needs of the market. Kolbenschmidt has established a new business segment within its organization devoted to the development of clean, efficient fuel cells. Dr. Dieter Siepler, chairman of the Kolbenschmidt executive board, thinks it makes good business sense. Siepler says that Kolbenschmidt is confident that, by 2010, fuel cell powertrains will be a viable alternative to traditional systems, with annual revenues forecast to start at $140 million.

Kolbenschmidt is a stakeholder in the future of the internal combustion engine. More importantly, the company's management recognizes that that stake is not in the product form but in the satisfaction of customer needs.

Source: Lindsay Brooke, "Piston Supplier Invests in Fuel Cells," *Automotive Industries* (April 2001).

strategy, and business models designed right. When it became obvious that these start-ups would not be able to meet the over-inflated expectations of the public investment markets, investment money sources dried up, cash ran out, and companies failed. Several companies could probably have developed into sustainable market leaders if they had been brought along more slowly, with more time to make mistakes and learn. The lucky companies are the ones with more patient venture capital investors or even the ones who had not issued an IPO and who now find themselves with a little more time for introspection and revision of business models.

If the marketer is indeed located in an autonomous venture with a cost structure and reasonable revenue targets of its own, then the question becomes how to accomplish the innovation required. One key is to take a *learning* approach. This is very different than an approach to execute a marketing plan. The premise of the learning plan is that uncertain markets are unknowable at first. Resources have to be allocated to trial, error, learning, and reconfiguration.

There are two important parts of this learning approach—called **discovery-based planning** by Christensen.[12] The first is gathering as much market and customer data as possible. In Chapter 6, we discussed establishing a network of customers and industry contacts that become the sources for a large part of the customer data that need to be collected. This needs to be done in this case as well, but it is a network of different kinds of contacts that must be built. In particular, current customers in an established business are generally poor information sources about future direction. They are often focused on the day-to-day effort of maintaining the existing

---

[12]Christensen, op. cit.

offering. They tend to not see the innovative uses of new products or the value of new services or other changes in the offering. For disruptive technologies, most of the customers emerge in new markets and segments; and the marketer will not have a good idea of what these segments are. Consequently, the marketer needs to cast widely for new, useful contacts. These contacts should be similar to the kinds of people von Hippel calls **"lead users."**[13] These are not necessarily the market leaders. Rather, they are users who have vision, who can anticipate what kinds of needs will arise among potential customers in the future. In this case, though, the lead user has to be someone who can anticipate what kinds of users will even exist in the future. Customer organizations that rely on innovation as a driving force in the competitiveness of the firm will have separately managed and rewarded groups in their organizations. These groups will have a different focus, interested in changing rather than maintaining the status quo. When presenting innovative offerings, marketers will find these parts of the customer organizations their strongest ally.

The second important part of discovery-based planning is the judicious use of trial and error. Many users will not be able to give usable information on the nature of their needs and buying behavior until they become familiar with the offering and have had a chance to see how their organization would benefit from it. Consequently, the innovating company must run a sequence of trial offerings. In each one, user feedback is sought on the value provided by all aspects of the offering. It is important to systematically collect this feedback and learn as much as possible about what will best provide value to the customers. Firms that recognize the need for continuous innovation, both as suppliers and customers, will have these relationships as part of an ongoing effort.

Pursuit of Sustaining Innovation

Most innovation is what Christensen calls **sustaining innovation.** Such innovations are changes, radical or incremental, that make somewhat predictable improvements to existing technologies. *Radical sustaining innovation* increases performance or costs dramatically but within the same technology direction. *Incremental sustaining innovation* makes small changes along predictable vectors. While most innovation is sustaining innovation, most sustaining innovation is incremental in nature. To compete for any length of time within an industry, a company must pursue sustaining innovation.

When the marketer is in the situation of competing through sustaining innovations, a rigorous and disciplined process of managing innovation is possible and necessary. The principal characteristic of this situation is that customers can provide a good idea of what they want, how it will be used, and how they will acquire it. Value is provided to customers through a well-established extended value chain.[14]

---

[13]Eric von Hippel, "Lead Users: A Source of Novel Product Concepts," *Management Science* (July 1986): 791–805.

[14]Christensen calls this a value network. His idea is similar to our notion of a value network but is more limited. We also see the partners who are contributing something to the offering, rather than just the vendors who make materials and components that are aggregated into final products.

With this in mind, the process for preparing the periodic marketing plan can be used as the framework for instituting innovation throughout the offering. Just as the company has a process for development of new products, the annual marketing plan (or plan done on some other periodic basis) can be treated as the process for marketing's R&D. The purpose of the planning process should be to evaluate the market, evaluate past marketing efforts, recognize evolutionary developments, and find new ways to create value for customers.

The periodic nature of the planning process is important. **Time pacing** of planned organization change—setting strict timetables for new versions of products, operations, strategies, and so on—has been found to work well in fast-paced business environments in focusing the company's efforts and setting expectations for customers.[15] It has been found to be extremely useful in dictating the rules of engagement in a competitive market, particularly from the point of view of the market leader or owner. Business-to-business marketers can use time pacing in their attempts to achieve incremental innovation across all elements of the offering. The rules for doing periodic marketing plans should state that each plan will include improved value in all elements of the offering. Not only will customers come to expect periodic improvements in the value they receive from such things as service or pricing plans, but the sales force, channels, and partners will learn to expect new programs and support as well. Too often, business-to-business marketing planning focuses innovative attention on products and markets to the exclusion of innovation in the other elements of the offering. Time pacing of nonproduct innovation will take the marketers out of product-centric marketing planning and refocus them on pursuing multiple avenues to improved value for customers.

Practical Aspects of Accomplishing Innovation

In this discussion of innovation so far, we have described the need for the company's strategy makers to decide what businesses and technologies to pursue and to decide whether they are working on disruptive innovation or sustaining innovation. Disruptive innovation requires an autonomous organizational unit with its own mission, processes, and metrics. Sustaining innovation requires attention to constant customer inputs and time pacing applied through the marketing plan. Just as was done in the first section of this chapter, we turn now to some practical aspects of implementing innovation across the offering. Again, we will discuss this in terms of obtaining the right people, directing the right activities, removing impediments, and providing incentives.

Obtaining the Right Kinds of People   Innovation occurs in either a project format or through ongoing management of the marketing function of the company. Projects often result in special purpose teams assembled for the duration

---

[15]Kathleen M. Eisenhardt and Shona Brown, "Time Pacing: Competing in Markets that Won't Stand Still," *Harvard Business Review* (March–April 1998): 59–69; and Connie J. G. Gersick, "Pacing Strategic Change: The Case of a New Venture," *Academy of Management Journal* 37, no. 1 (1994): 9–45.

of the project. If upper-level management assembles the team, then the marketer may have no choice of with whom he must work. If given the choice of people for the team or when hiring for the ongoing marketing function, it is important to match the type of person to the type of innovation being pursued.[16] Someone that takes a visionary, extensive redesign approach to every problem would not be appropriate for incremental innovation. Someone that takes an impatient, results-oriented approach may become frustrated in a setting with so much uncertainty and uneven progress as displayed by disruptive or radical innovation.

Other than this distinction, the marketing manager will want to include (hire, if appropriate) people who are creative and innovative. Note that innovativeness is focused on usefulness or value for the customer. This is not "variety seeking" for its own sake. Another trait to try to avoid in team members is a strong tendency toward being territorial. Because of the fluid nature of innovation and the tendency to change directions if needed, a strong sense of territory can be detrimental. A new offering will need a champion to gain adoption within the organization. However, when the feelings of ownership become too strong, the person will stand in the way of adapting the innovation or even scrapping it when the need arises.

Directing the Right Activities

We have already discussed ways to obtain customer information when working on disruptive innovation or sustaining innovation. Both involve establishing networks of relationships with people who can supply information. The biggest difference is who is included. In a disruptive innovation effort, the network must be broad and focused on insightful customers and industry watchers. In a sustaining innovation effort, the network is focused more on customers, partners, and channel members within the markets of interest.

A current trend in innovation efforts is the use of collaborators and partners in innovation efforts. The opening example describing Sun Microsystems' efforts to develop the iForce initiative is an example of collaborative development, all under the directive efforts of one company. It should be noted again that this innovative effort extends across the entire offering; it is not limited to innovation in product, service, channels, or any other part of the offering.

Cisco Systems is in the forefront of developing another variant of this innovation approach. It involves investing in many smaller, young companies who are working on new technologies. The companies that create breakthroughs will be acquired; the ones that are less successful may be directed in other areas or cut loose. This approach amounts to outsourcing one's R&D. It has the advantage of improving the larger company's technology portfolio without having to fully fund the development. The young companies benefit in that they do not have to invest in much more than the R&D. Their founders and employees become wealthy much more quickly than they would if they were to pursue the development as an independent company. While the Cisco example focuses on product technology innovation, the same approach can be used in the other elements of the offering. For

---

[16]Rangan and Bartus, op. cit, 70.

instance, in the Sun Microsystems example, venture capital is a part of the iForce initiative, which may result in the eventual acquisition of some of the partners.

A key aspect of getting the activities right is matching the activities to the type of innovation. We have mentioned that the distinction between sustaining and disruptive innovation makes a difference in how the innovation is addressed. Radical innovation needs autonomy and constant updating of the vision of the future market.[17] This is particularly true when the radical innovation is disruptive. Even when the radical innovation is a sustaining innovation, there is still considerable uncertainty in how the configuration of the offering will eventually stabilize. Indeed, market uncertainty exists as well, although not to the extent of market uncertainty under disruptive innovation. Accordingly, there is probably good reason to address radical sustaining innovation with an autonomous business unit. While the relationship is not perfect, there tends to be more incremental change associated with sustaining innovations; and disruptive change has more radical innovation (see Exhibit 9–2). Hence, the autonomous units tend to be associated more with disruptive change than with sustaining change. The applicability of time pacing for radical innovation, even when the innovation is sustaining, is questionable. There are just too many uncertainties about how long it will take to configure the new offering.

Rangan and Bartus point out that a large problem in product commercialization is the match between the company's beliefs about the innovation and customers' beliefs.[18] They say that mismatches occur when marketers believe the innovation to be radical while the customers believe it to be incremental, and vice versa. When the market sees the innovation as radical while the company sees it as incremental, the company is likely to miss a major opportunity. Rangan and Bartus call these

---

[17]O'Connor, op. cit.

[18]Rangan and Bartus, op. cit., 71.

EXHIBIT 9–2   Interaction of Types of Innovation

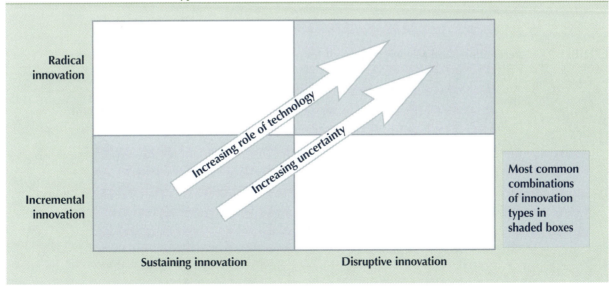

products "shadow" products because they hide in the shadows of the products the company feels are more important. When the market sees the innovation as incremental while the company sees it as radical, the company will spend too much on promoting it and will lose credibility in the eyes of the customers. These products Rangan and Bartus call "delusional."

While these are useful characterizations, we need to break down these mismatches and misperceptions further, because the way to address the problem depends on the source(s) of the misperception. First, the innovating supplier and the marketer working for the supplier can misread the importance that customers will place on the innovation. The marketer can also misread the customers' ease or difficulty in adopting the innovation. The innovating supplier is not the only party that can misperceive importance or ease of adoption: the customer can have misperceptions as well. Pragmatist or conservative customers may not believe that an innovation can change their competitive advantage as much as it really can. Also, they may have misgivings about adoption that are really quite easily handled. Exhibit 9–3 shows these different sources of misperceptions and some differences in how a company might try to overcome them.

The current sluggishness in the adoption of services from "application service providers" (ASPs) is at least partly due to innovators misperceiving the ease of adoption. At the same time, potential adopters may be misperceiving the potential costs—actually the risks—of adoption. The marketers for ASPs believe that it is easy for a customer to adopt the services of an ASP. Instead of customers running a software program on their own systems, customers "outsource" the operation of the product to the ASP. They just access the application through a Web browser. While this is easy to accomplish, the barrier to adoption has been the customers' uneasiness with the workings of the ASP model. First, they are worried that the ASP may have a systems outage just when they need to use the application. Second, they are worried that the ASP may not handle their data successfully or securely. This could result in lost data or the loss of information to competitors.

EXHIBIT 9–3   Perceptions and Misperceptions of Innovations

Type of Innovation	Supplier Perception/ Misperception	Customer Perception/ Misperception	Approach to Solving
Radical	Accurate	Inaccurate—not radical	Education, demonstration
	Accurate	Inaccurate—difficult to adopt	Education, demonstration, target by TALC
	Inaccurate—not radical	Accurate	Listen to customers and prospects; reposition
	Inaccurate—easy to adopt	Accurate—hard to adopt	Listen to customers and prospects; create rest of offering that eases adoption
Incremental	Accurate	Inaccurate—hard to adopt	Education, demonstration, target those with greatest need
	Inaccurate—not incremental	Accurate	Listen to customers and prospects; reposition; scale back effort

Marketers have probably correctly assessed the importance of the innovation—the ASP model holds a great deal of promise for reduction of information technology costs. However, ASP marketers are now recognizing the higher level of resistance to adoption from customers than the marketers expected. Marketers must treat customers' concerns about the risks of giving up control of their applications to the ASP as both real and perceptual. Accordingly, they must handle the real risks through better security and reliability features—these must be tangible to reduce risks. To handle the perceptual part of the risk, the marketers must focus on customer education—probably through communication of security and reliability test results and through publication of customer testimonials.

Impediments and Incentives   The impediments to instilling innovation in an organization are similar to the impediments we discussed for the rest of entrepreneurial marketing. One impediment is holding managers accountable for justifying their projects when there are no results data available or secondary data that are usable. A second is overzealous punishment of failure. Upper-level management must set the guidelines and the tone for removing these impediments.

Similarly, incentives need to be provided for being innovative. In the entrepreneurial marketing section, we mentioned that the incentives need to be set at the right level, using the right forms, and delivered in time to reinforce the right behavior. These statements are equally applicable for instilling innovation in the offering.

COMPETING BY BUILDING A BRAND

The unifying theme in this chapter is that marketing can create competitive strength in a business-to-business environment. We have so far discussed creating superior value to customers through innovation and entrepreneurial activity. Market ownership, though, has a perceptual dimension, as well. Being recognized as the leader or owner of a market conveys a competitive advantage whenever a customer is trying to decide whose offering to choose or whether to purchase the next offering from the same supplier as the last purchase. We tend to think of **branding**—establishing a strong, positive reputation—as a consumer marketing phenomenon, but it has relevance and importance in business-to-business marketing as well. As was noted in Chapter 3, business buyers are people, too. They develop beliefs (associations) and preferences. They remember some things and do not remember others. When they lack information and do not have time to search, they fill in the blanks from what they already know.

The trends in today's business environment are also working to make branding even more important. We noted earlier in this chapter and earlier in this textbook that competition has become fast paced. One result is that customers tend to make buying decisions under a great deal of time pressure. A way for buyers to short-circuit the pressure is to only evaluate and choose from among known suppliers. In other words, there is emerging a more powerful role for branding among business-to-business markets.

© RIC FELD/AP/WIDE WORLD PHOTOS

In general, building strong brands requires time to establish trust and confidence. Brands usually cannot be built overnight. There are certain circumstances in which a vendor's product can quickly become a standard, but the general case requires time for extended interaction between customer and supplier. In this way, brand building in business-to-business marketing differs somewhat from branding in consumer markets—strong brands are built one customer at a time. Marketing communications has a role in business-to-business brand building, but it is not nearly so important a role as in consumer marketing. Another difference between consumer branding and business-to-business branding is the importance of company name versus product name. In business-to-business marketing, the name of the company comes to stand for many kinds of assurances associated with a product or service: assurance of product quality, assurance of service availability and dependability, assurance of timely and reasonable upgrades, and assurances of priority attention to a relationship, for example. This is often a rich fabric of beliefs about the brand built through numerous interactions. By contrast, consumer brands are often product specific, built around a smaller set of customer-vendor interactions, and involve a less-complex network of brand beliefs.

In this section of the chapter, we first walk through the buying decision process and show why branding plays a key role. Then we discuss how a vendor obtains the status of a standard for its products or services under certain circumstances. Then we discuss how strong brands can be built in circumstances not conducive to standard setting.

Importance of Brand in Business-to-Business Buyer Behavior

Reexamine the buying decision process discussed in Chapter 3 and repeated in Exhibit 9-4. As the following discussion illustrates, a recognized brand name with positive associations attached has an advantage at each stage of the decision process, even under high-learning (high-involvement) purchase situations.

♦ *Determine that a need exists.* Missionary salespeople from a well-known and well-respected company may have entry into the buying center to discuss new products, which triggers the buyers' recognition that they indeed have such a need. Missionary salespeople from an unknown or start-up company may not be given such an opportunity or may have to work harder to obtain entry.

♦ *Determine product specifications.* The designers for the customer may design around component products from a well-known supplier; thus, the recognized brand may be the standard by which the specifications are set. Assistance and design input from missionary sellers of the known brand will be strongly considered. The

EXHIBIT 9–4　Stages in the Process Flow Model of the Buying Decision Process

Process Flow Stages	Buying Decision Process Steps
Definition Stage	
◆ Problem definition ◆ Solution definition ◆ Product specification	◆ Problem recognition ◆ General need description ◆ Product specification
Selection Stage	
◆ Solution provider search ◆ Acquire solution provider(s)	◆ Supplier/Source search ◆ Proposal solicitation ◆ Contract for supplier(s)
Deliver Solution Stage	
◆ Customize as needed ◆ Install/Test/Train	◆ Make the transaction routine
End Game Stage	
◆ Operate solution ◆ Reach end result ◆ Evaluate outcomes ◆ Determine next set of needs	◆ Evaluate performance ◆ Resell the job

*Also shown as Exhibit 3–3.

well-known supplier often has permission to participate at a more intense level than the unknown supplier. An unrecognized brand will probably have to go through extensive testing and competition against other products before the designers feel secure in specifying it as a standard.

◆ *Acquire solution providers.* The list of vendors from whom to invite bids will most likely include the well-known companies; if the list of proposals does not include a branded player, the buyer may specifically request a bid from a brand name player so that a benchmark is established or so that upper-level management will sign off on the proposals allowing the selection process to proceed.

◆ *Cull the bids/proposals to a short list.* The well-known supplier gets the benefit of the doubt for inclusion on the short list or may be included for comparison purposes; if a choice exists between a recognized brand and an unknown vendor, all other things being equal, the name brand will usually get the nod.

◆ *Evaluate the short list, or get revised proposals/bids.* Evaluations of name brands are given more weight or are trusted more than proposals from lesser-known companies.

◆ *Cut the short list to finalists.* Again, the name brand may be included for comparison, may get the benefit of the doubt, may be evaluated higher because its figures are better known or trusted, and may win any ties. The brand name may be included to give the lesser-known brands more legitimacy (it is easier to explain the list to upper-level management if it includes at least one name that is known).

- *Presentations.* The name brand may be treated with more deference or respect; holes in the presentation may be assumed away. The claims from lesser-known companies may be subjected to closer scrutiny.

- *Final evaluation and choice.* The well-known company wins ties; higher price for name brand may be tolerated if the brand means higher value to customers (e.g., Intel); the name brand may have more negotiating power to obtain various concessions from the buyer; trust of the name brand will be a factor to consider.

- *Postpurchase relationship.* If satisfaction is good with the well-known company, there is no reason to switch; if there is minor dissatisfaction with the name brand company, the customer may doubt whether the situation could be improved with another vendor. For a lesser-known vendor company, the customer may be inclined to seek outside help or switch vendors entirely more quickly if results do not live up to the customer's expectations.

In each stage, in each instance of a customer decision, the advantage for a well-known vendor may be small. The accumulated effect in any one customer decision, though, can add up to a sizable advantage. Over time, too, having a slight advantage in a large number of customer decisions will result in a sizable number of wins for the well-known company.

In the preceding discussion of the decision process, the ideal state for a marketer to reach is to have his product or service specified as the **standard.** Every other potential competitor then has to show that it meets or exceeds the specifications and that its overall offering has better value. Even if the brand has not been attributed standard status, having a known and respected brand brings competitive strength into the buying process.

Branding as a Standard

Industrial products are often established by initial users as a defacto standard for that product type. Just as we say "make a Xerox" when we actually mean make a *copy* (using equipment from Canon, Kodak, or another manufacturer), brands such as Loctite (anaerobic adhesives), Velcro (plastic hook fasteners), Plexiglas (brand of acrylic sheet), and others have set industrial standards. While generic forms of these products exist, the brand itself has become jargon for the type of product and the expectation for product performance.

Under these circumstances, brands become a specification standard, often noted in "engineering call-outs" as "Velcro #XXX or equivalent" or "Lexan 500 or equivalent" (*engineering call-outs* is a "shorthand" term simply referring to design engineers' specification of materials and parts on the engineering drawings of devices). The use of the brand as the standard creates shortcuts for purchasing and engineering. (All trademarks, such as Xerox, Velcro, Plexiglas, and Lexan, are owned by their respective companies.)

How does a manufacturer's brand become a standard? The following discussion offers some possibilities.

First with New Technology

A new technology often requires extensive manufacturer assistance for application (the role of missionary sales is critical to the product's success). Branding of the product at this point reinforces its use as jargon (what else will the customer call it—manufacturer X new product number XXX?) The customer needs to be told what to call the thing. Future similar or copycat products will be called by the first manufacturer's brand. (At this point, it becomes critical for the first manufacturer to take steps to formally and legally protect the brand, while not discouraging its *informal* use in discussions. Note that many of the product names mentioned here are trademarks of their respective manufacturers.)

Return again to Sensacon and the supply of the SensorSUV to sport utility vehicle manufacturers (Chapter 8). Customer laboratories, or an independent investigatory body as selected by design engineering, will be asked to verify the performance of SensorSUV, based on samples and performance data supplied by Sensacon. The lab will work with the manufacturer to develop the standard, based on the accepted performance of the sensors as previously approved. Once this standard specification is completed and accepted, copycat products will be required to meet it. This standard is "owned" by the first manufacturer—Sensacon. The copycat manufacturer will always be faced with the question "Does your sensor do everything that SensorSUV does?" (Important even if the customer does not necessarily need all the things that SensorSUV can do, tailoring of the product—also known as cost reducing—occurs later in the life cycle and is motivated by a customer need to reduce the manufacturing cost of the product that has had the sensor incorporated into it.)

Being Best with Service

When it absolutely, positively has to be there overnight, we "FedEx it"—whether it goes via Airborne, Emery, DHL, or some other carrier. Establishing a service niche that is not questioned under any circumstance helped create this standard. This level of commitment must also be applied to tangible products, parts, components, and so on. Sensacon must realize that the technology edge does not suffice to create the brand. Market ownership is necessary. (Market share *does not* equal market ownership.) Why did the customer specify Sensacon? Without excellent service, product education, application assistance, and general application development hand-holding, the customer would find other devices (not copies or direct replacements for Sensacon but devices that can fill the need when included as part of the design process) that meet the requirements.

The danger of a customer using alternative devices in the design of its product is particularly acute when the alternative is a proven product in the eyes of the designer. Whenever there is any doubt, the customer is likely to use what it is already familiar with. A new adhesive may be entirely appropriate (e.g., less costly, lighter weight, etc.) to hold an assembly together, but it is only as good as the confidence that the customer has in it.

Innovating the Need, Not the Technology   As SensorSUV matures and becomes known throughout the customer base, less application development is necessary on the part of Sensacon. However, users of SensorSUV will begin to look to the next generation of *their* product and how it can be enhanced. This enhancement can lead to a need for a next generation sensor. This next generation product, if it is to be truly new, may require new technology, style, and materials and/or have different performance requirements. By serving the need and not the product, the SensorSUV brand becomes known as a solution rather than a component part.

   Note: If your company is strictly known as a technology company, technology innovation is necessary, though not sufficient, for success. The argument that "we are focused on our high-technology product—that's why customers buy from us" is a dangerous position. In fact, the technology-oriented organization will have branding as a more important task, as their product is expected to make a value statement rather than be a "me-too" product. The "me-too" organization can focus on manufacturing efficiencies, distribution economies, and alternative cost (read "lower") positions with purchasing departments. Ironically, the technology-oriented company must establish a brand position or become a low-cost producer of maturing products.

Defending the Brand

Obviously, if SensorSUV is a profitable item, there will be imitators, either copycats trying to be the low-cost producer or modifiers trying to slightly move the technology envelope—at least enough to meet all the properties of SensorSUV while enhancing their own product's attractiveness. Some ideas on how to make defending the brand easier follow. Reach out and touch *everyone*—at all levels of the customer organization:

♦   *Market up.* As the specifying influence moves through the process of establishing SensorSUV as the product of choice, the missionary seller should build relationships with management above the influencers to reinforce the decision process (as well as to learn more about what is going on at the customer—but that is another topic).

♦   *Market down.* SensorSUV will have to pass several hurdles in the customer's organization. Laboratories will test the product; manufacturing will manipulate the product; and purchasing will, eventually, buy the product. Technicians in the lab will appreciate attention from the missionary sellers. The lab personnel are often ignored, not only by specifying influences but by suppliers. Yet, lab people can make or break a product. (Do you test that fabric horizontally or vertically for the flammability test? Does color make a difference? What is the value image of this supplier? Who are they? How long did the samples take to get here? etc.)

♦ *Market sideways.* The first specifier of SensorSUV should not be the only specifier. If SensorSUV is used in a breakthrough (or otherwise significant) customer product, that customer product should (with the customer's concurrence) be used as a demonstration of SensorSUV's capabilities. This translation of an initial success should be featured in print promotion, at trade shows, and at any other promotion opportunity in which influencers at other potential customers can be exposed. Make SensorSUV a wagon that people want to ride. ("Nobody ever got fired for specifying SensorSUV.")

The SensorSUV example operates in a market where the customers are manufacturers of SUVs. The customers' market is an oligopoly, so there are only a few customers. Specification of a component part in the design for a new vehicle almost automatically makes that brand a standard. Becoming a standard when the customers' market is characterized by monopolistic competition is more difficult and time-consuming. Because each customer is looking for unique ways to differentiate itself and because there are a lot of customers, it is difficult to get agreement among the industry participants to declare something as a standard. In many industries, there are standards bodies comprised of customers and vendors. To avoid accusations of antitrust collusion, these standards groups work hard to create standards that do not convey monopoly status or unfair advantage to any of the participants. Very often, standards bodies will continue to confer until the market has largely declared a winner. At other times, standards are written so that only product interfaces are standard; the product itself can be unique. In other cases, a standard must be declared before the industry can move ahead. In such cases, a neutral solution is usually found in which all participants can choose to participate.

Building a Strong Brand

Strong brands take time to build unless special circumstances prevail. A start-up or young company without a brand reputation has the opportunity to become a standard in markets like the one faced by Sensacon. In other markets, principally early markets, in which there is no established competition, a young company can also build market ownership and brand reputation quickly. VerticalNet, the purveyor of industry-focused Internet exchange Web sites, is a good example of this. In the early market, it was able to build many exchanges and became well known and well respected, before sizable competition developed at least until the Internet business collapse occurred. Without special circumstances like the ones just mentioned, the company must expend considerable effort to build a strong reputation. In established markets in which young companies compete against companies with strong brands, young companies are at a disadvantage because they have no brand recognition or reputation. Consequently, from an early point in time, the young company needs to think about whether and how it should build its brand. In general, unless a company is going to be a low-cost, low-price vendor, a strong brand reputation will translate into competitive advantage.

For established companies, strong brands are an asset to be enhanced and supported. A company with a poor reputation will find it difficult to overcome that reputation for two reasons. First, proposals offered will be discounted in the minds of the buying center. Consequently, even if the company has solved the problems that have led to a poor reputation, it will receive relatively few chances to prove its mettle. Second, when it does obtain the chance to prove it has solved its problems and it performs well, the customer may be inclined to diminish the positive results based on past history. It will take a series of positive outcomes before the blemished reputation of the past dissipates.

Brand strength is generally made up of brand recognition or **awareness,** quality of the products or services, and the customers' positive beliefs—**associations**—linked to the brand.[19] In business-to-business markets, awareness adds little until the company's value chain is established so that superior value is created for customers.[20] So, building brand strength is a relatively long-term process that revolves around building value for customers first, from which come positive associations about the product and company, and then building broader awareness.

Note that positioning is a particular aspect of brand building. It involves matching the product and directed message with the most important needs of the target market segment (see segmentation, Chapter 7). It is a position that is maintained for a temporary period of time and evolves into a set of associations linked to the brand. The essentials of brand building include creating strong products and communicating this to the appropriate target markets.

Building Associations

Brands are basically symbols. People use symbols to represent clusters or bundles of information that are related to the things the symbols stand for. They can then efficiently compare and evaluate alternatives by considering the symbols that represent those alternatives. People in a buying center tend to make holistic judgments concerning the entity represented by the symbol, based on all the associations attached in their minds to those symbols. The most powerful associations come from customers' direct experiences. If these are numerous and positive, the holistic evaluation will be positive. The ideal situation is for everyone in the buying center to have at least a few positive experiences with the company and its products or services. If the experiences of the people in the buying center have not been uniformly positive, then the political dealings within the buying center can be detrimental. This suggests that the sales team and service personnel have an important impact not only on the immediate outcome of a customer's buying decision but on the outcome of future situations as well. The effect of advertising and other less-personal communications has an impact on brand perceptions but without the robust and durable character of personal contacts.

---

[19]David A. Aaker, *Building Strong Brands* (New York: Free Press, 1996).

[20]Kathryn Dennis, "A Q&A with Regis McKenna," *Marketing Computers* 20, no. 12 (December 2000): 38.

Brand associations are not so hard to create as they are to control. Every time customers interact with a supplier, use its product, or interact with a customer service person, impressions are formed. Every time they see an advertisement, hear a news story, or talk to someone who has an opinion, impressions are formed. However, memory is selective. They may not remember what the marketer wants them to remember, so the marketer has to try to be as consistent as possible in all the messages delivered. These messages also have to be consistent with the customers' own experiences. Ultimately, customers' experiences with the product or service will be the things that they will remember most. Accordingly, making those usage experiences as positive as possible is critical for the marketer.

The communications part of association building, then, has to do with managing expectations. Too much hype can create expectations that are hard to meet. This is one of the problems that Apple faced with its Newton. Everyone was expecting this wondrous device, when wondrous was not about to be delivered until version 3 or so. Underplaying the value created by the company's new product is also problematic. If customers do not believe they will get much value, then few will be inclined to try it. This is not as bad as overblown hype where the aftereffects of unmet promises can live on for years. However, mediocre sales results have been known to kill products, too.

In planning the effort to build a strong brand, then, the marketer must first understand what associations customers currently have about the company and its offerings. Then, the marketer must decide what associations the company would want customers and prospective customers to have in the future. The marketer must then determine what combination of experiences and messages is most likely to achieve the desired change in the customers' and prospects' minds.

Quality   One of the key associations is the **quality** level of the company's offering. The reason it is singled out here is that quality is the only type of association that is directly related to profitability, as determined by researchers in the area of strategic management.[21]

Quality has special meaning: it is *perceived* quality from the point of view of the customer. Further, quality can be thought of as the ability to provide appropriate value from the customer's point of view. Hence, "durability" when durability is not needed is not quality; "aesthetically pleasing" when aesthetics are not valued is not quality; and so on. So, "high quality" means having the ability to perform very well on the most important dimensions as determined by targeted customers.

To create quality, companies must know their targeted customers very well to understand what it is that means quality to them. Second, the company must have a fair amount of creativity to be able to turn the customer's vision of quality into a product or service while being able to keep costs under control.

[21]c.f. Robert D. Buzzell and Bradley T. Gale, *The PIMS Principles* (New York: Free Press, 1987).

If the marketer wants to create associations that denote quality, it is important that the company communicate this; and the product has to perform when the customer uses it, or the service must provide superior satisfaction.

Obtaining Awareness

Obtaining awareness is generally thought to be fairly straightforward. However, a principal question arises whether simple *name* awareness, with no substantive associations, is useful. For example, 3Com bought the rights to name Candlestick Park in San Francisco. Now 3Com is imprinted in the consciousness of a much broader range of individuals. Has 3Com gained anything in the process?

An argument can be made that now many upper-level managers who have no special knowledge in the IT field have heard of 3Com and it is in their memory at some level. If you look back at the buying decision process, there are a number of points where it helps to have upper-level management aware of the brand. If members of upper-level management approve the request for proposal (RFP) list, or the short list, the list of finalists, or the final choice, they tend to give special attention to the companies whose names they recognize. If they recognize 3Com, then 3Com tends to get the benefit of that special attention.

If a marketer is attempting to get simple awareness, there are many creative ways to do this. Getting the company's name put on a baseball/football stadium is one example. The question arises, though, of what associations are built up in the minds of prospective customers, perhaps even inadvertently.

In 3Com's case, one wonders whether managers and staff involved in purchasing IT equipment might think, "It's pretty silly for 3Com to put its name on a stadium," or even "Candlestick is a much better name for a stadium than 3Com." If these thoughts cross the minds of managers and staff, and even upper-level management, 3Com may have created negative memory associations in the minds of its intended target. On the other hand, 3Com's purchase of the naming rights for Candlestick Park may create associations of "innovative" and "I wish I'd thought of that." These would tend to enhance upper-level managers' evaluation of the brand.

Planning and executing the marketing activities that create an offering can be competitively impotent if the marketer treats it as only a cookbook exercise. To make the offering competitive on an ongoing basis, the business-to-business marketer needs to attack the competition with several tools. We have discussed some of the most important concepts and tools in this chapter.

Innovation gives the marketer the opportunity to produce more value for customers and to continue to do so over time. As markets mature, it becomes more and more important for marketers to look for nonproduct ways to innovate. As discussed in this chapter, it is necessary to have a sense of what kind of innovation is being pursued. This dictates the approach to the development of innovations in the offering.

Innovation is a key part of marketing entrepreneurially. By marketing with innovation, proactive efforts, controlled risktaking, and attention to opportunities, marketers should be able to compete on both value and time. Adopting an entrepreneurial orientation involves setting the expectations for the marketers that they will need to act entrepreneurially and then setting the structure and incentives so that marketers will be motivated to be entrepreneurial.

Finally, marketers have a powerful tool at their disposal for competing over the long term. Brand building helps build a strong reputation that gives the marketer a competitive edge. Brand building is dependent on providing superior value to customers and reinforcing their beliefs through consistent performance and appropriate communication.

As you go to Chapter 10 and beyond, be thinking about how to innovate and act entrepreneurially in the particular element of business-to-business marketing addressed in each chapter. When it comes to competing through brand building, we want you to be thinking about how each chapter contributes to the development of the brand. Too often, observers forget that brand building involves more than integrated marketing communications.

Key Terms

associations

awareness

brand strength

branding

breakthrough innovation

controlled risk taking

discovery-based planning

disruptive innovation

entrepreneurial marketing

incremental innovation

innovation

lead users

opportunity seeking

proactivity

quality

radical innovation

standard

sustaining innovation

technology

time pacing

Questions for Review and Discussion

1. Why would taking an entrepreneurial orientation in business-to-business marketing yield better competitiveness for a company than would a more reactive, risk-averse approach?

2. How does innovation differ from proactivity?

3. Why is controlled risk taking more competitively attractive than strictly risk-averse behavior?

4. What is the difference between radical innovation and disruptive innovation?

5. Why is an autonomous organizational unit the appropriate way to pursue disruptive innovation?

6. Why should a marketing manager try to enhance and direct incremental, nonproduct innovation? Since it is incremental, why not just let it happen on its own?

7. Why should a business-to-business marketer care about building a strong brand?

8. Why is it advantageous to have your brand designated as a standard by a customer's purchasing process?

9. How are positive associations for a brand established in the memory of persons in the customer's buying center?

10. Can a business-to-business marketer be innovative in the way a brand is built?

11. Compare the marketing mix and customs of an innovation-oriented firm and a market share–driven firm. What prevents a share-driven firm from also being a leader in innovation?

12. Referring to Question 11, what suggestions could you make to a share-driven firm that also wants to be known as the innovator in the market?

Internet Exercises

Go to Sun Microsystems' iForce Web site: **http://www.iforce.com/wireless/** Compare the services offered under the Wireless initiative to those offered as individual iForce solution sets at: **http://www.sun.com/iforce/solutions** What is the difference? Does the difference represent an innovation? Can you find other Sun iForce initiatives comparable to the Wireless initiative? What does this say about what Sun has learned from the Wireless initiative experience?

Go to Hewlett-Packard's support program for partners: **http://www.hppartners. com/garage/partners-overview.php3** How does this program differ from Sun's iForce program? Suppose you were a wireless service provider wanting to go into a new venture that facilitates business-to-business wireless e-commerce. Who would you be more inclined to choose as your solution provider—HP or Sun? Why? What does this say about how each of them has innovated in this area?

Use your favorite search engine and locate some business-to-business branding consultants. Pick one, and evaluate how what they purport to do to help business customers build strong brands. Do you think they are taking a good approach? Why, or why not?

10

Pricing in Business-to-Business Marketing

overview. . . Price is a key component of value. Customer-oriented pricing involves setting prices that reflect the customer's perception of the worth of the offering. This is set by the customer's own value chain and cost structure. Prices charged by competitors influence the perceived maximum that customers will pay.

This chapter first reviews some basic ideas about setting prices in light of maximum prices that can be obtained for a given offering and costs that must be covered to make a profit. Basic concepts of demand, supply, and price elasticity of demand are reviewed in light of their contribution to pricing.

The next sections discuss the management of pricing as part of the marketing mix. Strategic aspects of pricing include objectives of pricing, price development for new products or services, and price throughout the product life cycle. Tactical pricing includes pricing of bundled products (bundles of several products for a single price), competitive bidding, and changing prices.

The next section concerns negotiated price. In the final section, the general trends in business-to-business markets and how marketers must adapt their pricing efforts are discussed. We revisit the trends of time compression, hypercompetition, and the growth in the use of the Internet.

© EYEWIRE COLLECTION

INTEL CHANGES ITS COMPETITIVE PRICING FOR MICROPROCESSORS*

In the past, Intel Corporation had used a price-skimming approach for microprocessors. New processors would be introduced and offered at a high price level. The OEM buyers—Compaq, Dell, IBM, and so on—would buy relatively few processors for a relatively few computers that would be offered to high-end users—corporate specialty users in finance, engineering, network serving, and Web hosting. After these first needs had been fulfilled, and as software development was catching up to the capabilities of the new processor technology, Intel would drop prices and the OEMs would offer computers to users whose need for speed was not so immediate as the first users, but who were willing to wait for lower prices and more functionality. As prices came down, Intel would also drop prices on its prior processor version, to the point at which late majority and laggard buyers of low-priced computer equipment would purchase.

Meanwhile, competitors, principally Advanced Micro Devices (AMD) and Cyrix, were introducing compatible processors priced under the Intel price points. Since competitors were playing catch-up, Intel was able to minimize the competitive influence of these low-cost alternatives by continuing to enhance the speed and functionality of their processors. This market ownership by Intel controlled the pace of innovation to maximize Intel profitability while squeezing the competition.

At the end of the decade (1990s), AMD processors reached (and, in some views, surpassed) the performance levels of the most capable Intel chips. AMD began a brand identity program, and the Athlon processor became a viable alternative at the premium end of the market. AMD had solved some earlier production problems to reach the point where competitive processors could be shipped in quantity and on time, giving the OEMs a solid second source of microprocessors. The significance of this should not be minimized; AMD was able to price Athlon processors for the premium market, greatly improving the company's overall financial performance.

As Intel introduced the Pentium 4 in late 2000, the U.S. economy and much of the world economy were entering a slowdown. Sales of workstations and personal computers slowed considerably, causing inventories to escalate and PC makers', as well as chipmakers', earnings to fall.

Intel is using the downturn as an opportunity to rejuvenate its competitive advantage. It is dropping prices

*Based in part on Cliff Edwards, "Intel Inside the War Room," Business Week (30 April 2001): 40.

quickly on its high-end processors. Prices on its 1.5 GHz Pentium 4 processor were dropped from $795 in December 2000 to $519 in April 2001. Similarly, the 1.4 GHz Pentium 4 was priced at $574 in December and reduced to $300 in April. Meanwhile, the price of an 866 MHz Pentium 3 fell from $241 in December to $150 in April. AMD, of course, followed suit with similar reductions in its line of processors.

Aggressively lower prices were not Intel's only strategic move made to improve competitive position. Intel, like most other technology companies during the period, actively cut costs. A program to trim the workforce by 5,000 employees through attrition had to be enhanced with a "voluntary separation program" in which workers were offered incentives to depart (it seems that during a downturn workers want to keep their jobs and not feed the normal attrition rate). Even while earnings were declining, though, Intel announced that it would not reduce R&D spending, nor would it slow its capital spending plans. Because it has the resources, Intel wanted to be ready with new products when the economy rebounds. Also, during a downturn, capital projects, such as new plants and equipment, can be obtained for lower cost than during boom times. So, when the economy improves, Intel can produce product with a cost advantage, which will allow it more price flexibility while maintaining higher profitability.

The pricing aspects of this scenario raise the question whether aggressive pricing is necessary for this strategy or merely a discretionary move for Intel to follow in an economic downturn. Does Intel even have a choice in this instance?

introduction. . .

In the Intel example, we can see some of the common aspects of pricing in business-to-business markets. Intel uses price as part of a broader strategic initiative that includes elements of product strategy and communications. Intel counts on customers to respond to the price reductions it makes. Intel expects its competitors to react but to not have the financial stamina or the extensive product line to profit as much from current conditions as will Intel. As we discuss pricing ideas throughout this chapter, some of the nuances of Intel's strategy will come more clearly into focus.

LEARNING OBJECTIVES

- ◆ Reinforce the basics of pricing from your marketing principles course.
- ◆ Understand the relationship between perceived value and price.
- ◆ Understand the relationship between cost and price.
- ◆ Gain a sense of what aspects of business-to-business pricing are strategic and which are tactical, and how to address these aspects.
- ◆ Understand how negotiated pricing works; gain a sense of strategies for maintaining margin and customer relationships in negotiated pricing.
- ◆ Learn how to avoid handling uncertainty by dropping price.
- ◆ Gain an appreciation for the effects of current trends on pricing.

Price makes it possible for transactions to take place. The customer receives benefits from the product or service offered in exchange for the exchange price. The supplier receives the price paid by the customer in exchange for the product or service offered. Both parties expect that the outcome of the transaction will enhance their total value. Neither the customer nor the supplier will act unless the price makes it worthwhile for both parties.

For the marketer, pricing is situational and depends on strategic purposes and the business environment. Pricing generally involves the setting of prices for business-to-business offerings. It also involves changing these prices, just as Intel did, as the marketing strategy is implemented and as the business environment changes. In many cases, the price element of the offering includes such things as providing financing, setting financing terms, allowing for several methods of payment, establishing payment terms and schedules, allowing price adjustments for activities performed by the customer or services provided by the vendor, or calculating exchange rates to allow for payments in any of several currencies.

Business-to-business pricing differs considerably from pricing in consumer marketing. When consumers make purchases, price is a deliberate contributing factor to the final decision and is usually a predetermined suggested list price. The elements that contribute benefits beyond the core product, such as a convenient retail location, adequate product assortment, and an easy payment method, may be part of the shopping experience but are not usually foremost in the decision process. In business-to-business markets, however, all costs (indirect and direct) and the benefits from the offering are considered.

Price levels for business-to-business products and services can be evaluated objectively in light of the customer's value chain, while consumers evaluate prices and costs in light of their perceptions of acceptable price levels—often determined by the relative position of competitive offerings. Pricing in business-to-business markets must deal with professional purchasing people who are skilled at extracting value from transactions. Business-to-business pricing involves competitive bidding and negotiating much more than does pricing in consumer markets. The psychological aspects of pricing in business-to-business marketing are certainly subdued when compared to consumer marketing.

Pricing is one of the easiest marketing variables to change and one of the most difficult to do well. Too often, cutting price becomes the "magic word" that allows the marketer or seller[1] to sell a mismatched product or service to an otherwise unwilling customer. As you have no doubt gleaned from the preceding chapters, this is not the kind of strategy we want you to regularly pursue. While the short-term consequences may be positive—the company gets the business of a new customer or keeps the business of a dissatisfied customer—the long-term results can be bitter. Recall the discussion of the misuse of the value chain concept from Chapter 1. Recognizing value from the supplier point of view can lead to a failure to see what customers perceive as value. Constantly giving price concessions to win over customers undermines margins, which in turn means few resources for investing in the growth of the business.

What is just as bad is that cutting price is habit forming. Sellers start to see it as a first resort instead of a last resort. Marketers start basing their marketing programs on elaborate, costly, and ever-more-frequent promotion plans, built around price reductions, used to support channels or "incentivize" customers (who, predictably, stockpile enough product to see them through the period during which no promotion is run). Customers become addicted, too. They get to the point where reduced price always becomes a major concession sought in negotiation; and, once the precedent has been established, it has become the benchmark to which future negotiations refer. Recognize also that business won primarily through price concessions can be lost the same way.

In this chapter, we discuss concepts and methods in pricing that, hopefully, can avoid pricing that results in prematurely collapsing profits. Note, though, that understanding customers, their needs, and buying decision processes and preparing good offerings for them go a long way toward supporting prices that lead to profitability. Good pricing depends on doing a good job in the rest of the areas of marketing.

One key idea we want to stress in this chapter is that setting prices is often caught up with the supplier's efforts to build a relationship with customers. Setting prices, then, has to address the competing interests of establishing goodwill with customers (a pressure to give the customer price breaks) and extracting the maximum profit from transactions (a pressure to charge as much as "the market will bear"). Balancing these two competing forces is where creativity comes into play. This becomes particularly necessary when sellers are negotiating with customers and a concession on price seems to be the thing that will close the deal. We discuss at length how good pricing can be achieved and maintained in negotiated pricing.

---

[1] We use the term *seller* for efficiency's sake instead of using the generic, and more awkward, *salesperson*.

> ### Participation Exercise
>
> Do you think Intel's price cuts will (a) induce customers like Dell and Compaq to buy more chips and (b) have a negative impact on prices for future product introductions? Why, or why not?

Finally, this chapter discusses some of the effects of our three current trends: time compression, hypercompetition, and the Internet. Time compression does not allow companies to fully understand customers and markets and how they respond to price levels and changes. Time compression also places a great deal of pressure on marketers, sales people, and business development people to negotiate and reach closure quickly. Hypercompetition makes it difficult for companies to maintain differentiated positioning. Without differentiation, and with low-price–oriented competitors working hard to win customers, business-to-business marketers face increased pressure to lower prices.

PRICING BASICS

At its most basic, a price is an indicator of the worth of the offering. A customer looks at the price of the offering and asks three general questions: "Are the benefits worth the price being charged?" "Can we obtain the same benefits for a better price?" and "Can we obtain the same benefits at a lower cost by producing them ourselves?" If the customer has a budget constraint, which is usually the case, an additional question is "Can we pay the price?" In simple terms, the marketer's job in pricing is to set a price that obtains positive responses to the questions about whether the benefits are worth the price and whether the customer can afford the price. The marketer must also set the price so that the customer cannot obtain more value from some other supplier's offering. As market conditions change, the marketer may have to change prices for existing offerings to maintain or improve the attractiveness of the offering. This is what Intel did in pricing its processors as economic conditions changed.

Setting and changing prices, when done well, involves a combination of analysis and creativity. The analysis part must address both customers' perceptions of value relative to competition and the supplier's cost structure. We have observed that, too often, the analysis is incomplete, focusing solely on internal costs and profits. To really understand a customer's perceptions of value, including the perception of price, marketers often need to understand the customer's own cost structure.

The creativity part is often incomplete itself. The marketer must use all the elements of pricing as part of the jigsaw puzzle of the offering (Exhibit 10–1) to create superior value for customers. Xerox's pricing in its early days is a classic example of how creative pricing can add to value instead of subtracting from it. To overcome customers' negative reaction to the purchase price of the first

EXHIBIT 10–1   Components of the Offering

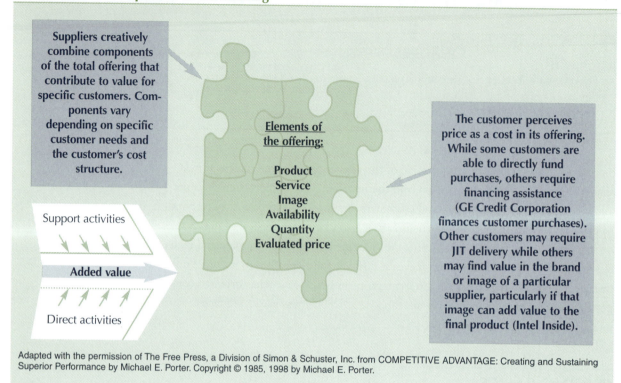

Suppliers creatively combine components of the total offering that contribute to value for specific customers. Components vary depending on specific customer needs and the customer's cost structure.

Support activities

Added value

Direct activities

Elements of the offering:

Product
Service
Image
Availability
Quantity
Evaluated price

The customer perceives price as a cost in its offering. While some customers are able to directly fund purchases, others require financing assistance (GE Credit Corporation finances customer purchases). Other customers may require JIT delivery while others may find value in the brand or image of a particular supplier, particularly if that image can add value to the final product (Intel Inside).

Adapted with the permission of The Free Press, a Division of Simon & Schuster, Inc. from COMPETITIVE ADVANTAGE: Creating and Sustaining Superior Performance by Michael E. Porter. Copyright © 1985, 1998 by Michael E. Porter.

Cost-based pricing is the determination of price by figuring costs of offering a product or service and then adding on a standard percentage profit. An alternative method is to determine a price that will yield a targeted rate of return on capital invested in the offering. Several problems arise with either procedure. First, costs per unit usually depend on volume and the volume is set arbitrarily. Second, many cost categories are added based on a "standard rate" that may have no relationship to actual costs required or incurred. Third, and most important, the price has no relationship to customers' perceptions of the worth of the offering. Customers might be willing to pay much more for the offering or much less. Either way, the marketer loses.

photocopy machines, Xerox provided a leasing option for the equipment. The reduced cash flow burden at the time of acquisition made the cost more palatable and reduced the customer's risk; if they did not like the new technology, they could return it without having tied up a significant amount of cash. Of course, customers found that they soon relied heavily on photocopying and adopted the technology wholeheartedly.

Pricing based on customers' perceived value—**value-based pricing**—is not the easiest way to set prices but creates prices that are consistent with the marketer's strategy. This stands in contrast to **cost-based pricing,** which is often used in business-to-business marketing. Cost-based pricing runs the risk of losing profits or pricing too high for the market.[2] Costs are important in determining profit levels from different pricing alternatives, and they matter when downward pressure on prices puts price level in jeopardy of falling below costs. Beyond these considerations, cost has little to do with price.[3] When profitability is threatened, marketers need to understand what costs are relevant and what consequences will result from setting prices at levels near cost levels; but, different stakeholders within the supplier organization may

[2]Michel H. Morris and Gene Morris, *Market-Oriented Pricing: Strategies for Management* (New York: Quorum Books, 1990), 87–93.

[3]Paul Sherlock, *Rethinking Business to Business Marketing* (New York: The Free Press, 1991).

have different perceptions of what those costs levels actually are. Usually, though, costs should have nothing to do with setting price levels.

Pricing to Reflect Customer Value

To set prices, the marketer must understand the way customers perceive value. This is more complex than simply charging what the market will bear. It involves balancing the concerns of customer value, supplier profitability, customer goodwill, and long-term relationships. At the core of these considerations are the customers' perceptions that there is a price that is appropriate for the benefits customers will receive from the offering and that there is a maximum price that they will be willing to pay for that offering.

Recall that customers evaluate the value of an offering by considering both the benefits they receive and the costs they incur from acquiring something offered. Part of the cost consideration is the price paid for the **total offering**. The other part is the cost of acquisition and use of the product or service that is acquired in the offering. We have combined these two elements of cost into what we call **evaluated price**. Evaluated price can be very different from the price that is charged. Exhibit 10–2 describes a situation in which a comparison of the charged prices of two raw materials shows a big advantage for the first material. However, when the evaluated price of the two materials is compared, the second material comes out the clear winner.

The customer considers value to be the difference between benefits and evaluated price. For the customer to continue to consider the offering as a viable alternative, the difference between benefits and evaluated price must be positive; the evaluated price cannot be considered to be more than the benefits.

Exhibit 10–3 shows the evaluated price compared to the benefits and how customers make choices from competing alternatives based on value. After the customer determines the value of each offering, she makes a selection based on which alternative she perceives to offer the most value. Suppose a company was considering contracting with a computer systems vendor for an automated ordering system; the company's employees could order their own systems interactively through an on-line catalog. The customer has the option of installing a system in which users can order from a constrained list of options. Alternatively, the vendor can establish an ordering process in which users have far more choice in the hardware and software they can order. The benefits of the second option—the one with more choices for users—make it appear to offer more benefits than the first. However, the evaluated price of the second option might be high enough to make the first option more attractive; in the second option, users might order desktop systems with such a wide array of hardware and software that the customer's information technology department would incur a huge cost in integrating all the systems into its network.

> The **total offering** is the offering that provides a complete solution to the buyer's needs. This may include financing, delivery, service, or, based on the buyer's preference, only the core product.
>
> —*From Chapter 1*

> The **evaluated price** is the price of the offering, from the view of the customer, after all costs associated with the total offering are evaluated.

EXHIBIT 10–2　Evaluated Price—Where Does Value Come From?

How do you convince a customer to substitute a higher-priced product for a low-priced product? Value.

Consider the experience of manufacturers that use small motors in their products—in particular, small appliances and power tools. Historically, these small motors were manufactured with die-cast metal frames. Simply stated, die-cast metal parts are essentially the result of molten metal poured into a mold, cooled, and then removed from the mold. The metal raw materials used often cost very little, say, $.50 per pound.

Suppose you are the field marketer for a company that makes engineering plastics. (Engineering plastics are not like the disposable "picnic" plastics. Engineering plastics have physical properties that make them a viable substitute for metals in many applications.) Your next development effort is to work with a major manufacturer of small appliances to convince the manufacturer to switch from metal, at $.50/pound, to engineering plastic, at $2.50/pound. How are you going to pull this off? The place to start is by knowing your customer's business and having a credible relationship with stakeholders in the buying center. You see, when the total offering is examined, the plastic is cheaper than the metal. How?

When die-cast metal parts come out of the mold, they have a very rough surface. Motor frames require smooth bearing-like surfaces at many points. This means the metal part must be put through a machining step to make each critical surface smooth. Motor frames also must have ways to attach other parts to them—casting cannot produce the necessary holes with screw threads; another machining step is required for each hole/screw thread. The metal part still is not ready to be a motor frame. Many metals rust. (Even if a zinc alloy, corrosion may be a problem in some applications.) A surface treatment may be necessary to prevent rust or corrosion. If the design is such that the motor frame is part of the appliance housing, it will require an aesthetic coating or paint to match the design of the appliance. Several steps are necessary to create a usable motor frame.

Plastic parts are made by melting the plastic and injecting the plastic, under pressure, into a mold. The nature of the engineering plastic is that it will flow into tiny details in the mold. Intricate designs are possible, reducing the number of other parts that must be attached; they get molded as part of the motor frame. What screw holes are still required are molded in at the same time. Engineering plastics will not rust and can be colored before molding; no painting of finished parts is required. The motor frame is finished when it comes out of the mold.*

The $2.50/pound material creates a less-expensive part than the $.50/pound material, though a view based strictly on material price would have never recognized the possibility. The total offering approach builds real value for the customer and new business for the supplier.

Today, the majority of all small power tool and appliance motors are made with engineering plastic frames. That new business was translated to many manufacturers and is now the accepted way to build small motors.

*Apologies to engineers familiar with these manufacturing processes for our simplification to create academic clarity!

The end result would look very much like the situation depicted in Exhibit 10–3, in which the option with the lower benefits might have the higher value. If the marketer understands the customer's situation, then she can structure the offering so that benefits minus evaluated price works out best for the customer.

So what is the maximum price that a marketer can charge for her product or service? If there is no competition, it is the price at which benefits are just noticeably more than the evaluated price, that is, the point at which there is a noticeable value for the offering. If the marketer wishes to establish or maintain a relationship with customers, then she will probably charge a price at a level where customers believe they are getting a "fair" price and are willing to work with this supplier in the future. This "fair price" level may be somewhat nebulous, but, if the marketer knows the customers well, she will have a sense of where this price stands. If there is some sort of competition—and there usually is—the customer will likely use the price charged by competitors as a reference point. If the marketer's offering creates

EXHIBIT 10–3   Customer's Perception of Value and Evaluated Price

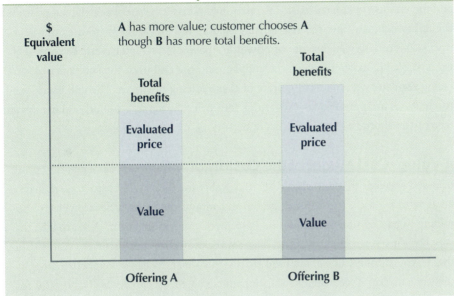

more benefits than the competitors' offerings, then customers will be willing to pay a premium; if not as much as competitors' offerings, then customers will be only willing to pay a discounted price. Again, the marketer must have a good understanding of customers' perceptions to know how much premium or discount is appropriate.

In many circumstances, customers have a preconceived idea of what something should cost, which has the effect of limiting the price that can be charged. Sometimes this preconceived price is based on what value the customer places on a solution and has the effect of becoming a defining parameter of the segment for the supplier. At other times, the preconceived price is based more on what the customer can afford rather than the value received. For instance, market research vendors often encounter customers that believe that a market research study should cost just "a few thousand dollars." The reality is more likely to be that the market price of such a study runs tens of thousands of dollars, and the economic value to the customer may be millions when the costs of launching a poorly positioned product are considered. Even after showing the value to the prospective purchaser of the research, the marketer will find that those prior expectations and what the market has been willing to accept hold down the price that can be asked.

Obviously, most pricing situations involve setting prices below the maximum that can be charged, but not all situations. Whenever a supplier is engaged in a single transaction in which future relationship is not an issue, or when the supplier is expected to extract maximum revenue from a transaction, the supplier can maximize profit by charging at the point where value is zero. The electric power market of the early 2000s illustrates both the situation and the limits of this practice. The United States' power-generating capacity had reached a point where spot shortages occur. Distribution systems must buy power on the wholesale spot market, and prices for this power can be extremely high. No relationship between the supplier and the end-use customer exists. A relationship may exist between the supplier and the utility company, but the relationship seldom has a bearing on spot market prices. Accordingly, high costs of power are passed on to ratepayers. Even though no relationship exists between the supplier and the end user, the supplier is now facing regulatory and judicial review of these pricing practices. The end users' representatives are pursuing investigations into price "gouging"—unfairly taking advantage of the shortage—that might have been done by some suppliers.

A Value–Cost Model of the Customer

Business customers buy products and services to aid in the creation of value for their own customers. A marketer working for a supplier can better understand the price the customer will be willing to pay by understanding the customer's own value chain. Accordingly, the supplier's marketer might want to diagram the way that the customer creates value, that is, to map the value chain used by this customer. When several customers in the same market have a similar value chain, a value map can be used as typical for that segment. If the customers in the market vary considerably in their value chain configurations, the marketer may want to map out typical configurations for the market segments that are identifiable and, to whatever extent is possible, understand why participants in the same market have dissimilar value maps. The main idea is to understand what activities are done by the customers that are linked together to create value.

> **Revenues** are simply the actual price received for the product multiplied by the number of items sold.

Once the marketer has a sense of the customer's value chain, the marketer needs to overlay the costs that customers incur by performing these activities. Working backward from the **revenues** obtained by customers, the marketer can see what activities subtract the most from the customers' profitability. By paying particular attention to the point in the value chain at which the marketer's product or service enters into the customer's value chain, the marketer can approximate how important the product or service is to the customer's creation of value. The level of importance in the overall customer value map will be an indication of what the customer can afford and how sensitive the customer is likely to be to changes in the supplier's price.

Exhibit 10–4a and Exhibit 10–4b provide an example of such a **value-cost model** for hypothetical small market research firms. Suppose that these are research firms that have special areas of expertise, such as qualitative research, customer satisfaction research, or new product concept tests. The model shows that the principal benefits offered by the research firms are their expertise in obtaining and analyzing data, the relevance of their analyses to their clients, and their adaptability to pursue questions that their clients want answered. This value is produced chiefly by their systems for collecting and analyzing data and their client relationships built up through long experience with their clients. The value from these relationships comes from the quality of their account managers and analysts.

EXHIBIT 10–4a   Value-Cost Model for Analyzing Customers

	Management and infrastructure	Value score:	FC%
	Technology development	Value score:	FC%
	Other overhead	Value score:	FC%

Value for customers: Characterize important elements of value.

Delivery & customer service	Sales	Marketing	Operations	Supply logistics	Materials
Value score:	Value score:	Value score:	Value score:	Value score:	Value score:
VC%	VC%	VC%	VC%	VC%	VC%
FC%	FC%	FC%	FC%	FC%	FC%

Value score: Contribution to value for customer's customer
1 = Key component of value
2 = Significant component of value
3 = Minor component of value

Cost percentage: Percentage of either fixed (FC) or variable costs (VC)

EXHIBIT 10–4b   Hypothetical Example of Value-Cost Model for Specialty Market Research Firms

	Management and infrastructure	Value score: 1	FC% 15%
	Technology development	Value score: 3	FC% 5%
	Other overhead	Value score: 3	FC% 20%

Value for customers:
• Quality of analyses
• Relevance of analyses
• Flexibility

Delivery & customer service	Sales	Marketing	Operations	Supply logistics	Materials
Value score: 1	Value score: 3	Value score: 3	Value score: 1	Value score: 2	Value score: 3
VC% 10%	VC% 0%	VC% 0%	VC% 70%	VC% 10%	VC% 10%
FC% 25%	FC% 10%	FC% 5%	FC% 20%	FC% 0%	FC% 0%

Value score: Contribution to value for customer's customer
1 = Key component of value
2 = Significant component of value
3 = Minor component of value

Cost percentage: Percentage of either fixed (FC) or variable costs (VC)

Suppose a marketer for an on-line e-mail/Web questionnaire research service is analyzing this segment of market research firms as customers. A large part of both fixed and variable costs of the market research firms comes from operations—the collection, analysis, and interpretation of the data. This activity is also a key contributor to value for the clients. An on-line questionnaire system would significantly reduce the cost of data collection and analysis. It would also reduce the cost of the supply logistics and materials. An analysis of actual cost reductions would give the marketer for the on-line service a sense of the economic value of the service. This would give an approximation of the maximum evaluated price that could be charged.

Let us say that a key benefit from the on-line research is time savings. This would affect operations, but the research firms' operations already provide a key component of value for their clients. More time might make it possible for the analysts to do a more thorough analysis, so there might be a moderate benefit to the research firms from time savings. This might increase the price the on-line service could charge, but probably not by much. In general, though, in this hypothetical market segment, savings in time is not highly valued, so most of the benefit that the market research firms would be willing to pay for would be the cost savings.

In summary, customers' perceived value, relative to competitors' offerings, establishes the appropriate price to be charged. Customer-oriented pricing, then, is based on an understanding of these perceptions held by the customer. The lower the price charged, the higher the value as perceived by the customer.[4] However, there is a **minimum price** that can be charged. In the long run, the minimum price is a price that covers the supplier's relevant costs (see Exhibit 10–5). Contribution to profitability comes from setting a price higher than the level at which relevant costs are just covered. The question becomes, then, what costs are relevant?

---

[4]There may be a point at which the price is so low that the customer does not find the offering believable. This is more of a problem in consumer markets, where consumers use price as a proxy for product quality. There may be instances, though, in which a business buyer would see a low price as "too good to be true" and would require extra documentation to prove that the offering is legitimate.

EXHIBIT 10–5   Maximum and Minimum Price

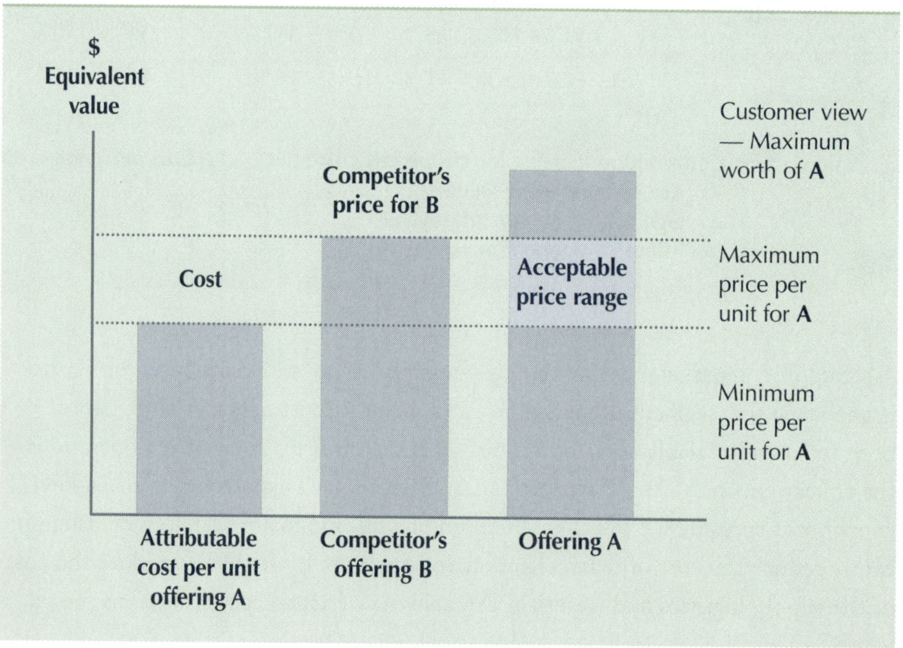

Relevant Costs

The supplier must see price charged as the mechanism for making a profit. To understand which costs are relevant in the calculation of profitability, the marketer must think in terms of paying for **ongoing costs** out of **ongoing revenue.** It also helps to think of the act of setting price as a decision. In thinking about costs, we are only concerned with the costs that are consequences of that decision. Thus, the timing of when pricing decisions are made has much to do with what costs are relevant. Relevant costs are those that meet the following criteria:[5]

> Resultant
>
> Realized
>
> Forward-looking incremental
>
> Avoidable

> Think of **ongoing costs** and **ongoing revenue** as the cash flow associated with the incremental activities required specifically to offer the product or service in question. Revenues from the product are reduced by only those costs directly attributable to the product.

Resultant costs are those costs that result from the decision. Pricing is often part of a decision that affects two or more of the four Ps. For instance, pricing may be part of the launch of a new product, so a pricing decision is part of a decision to pursue development and launch of a new product. In this case, the relevant costs are those associated with the development, manufacture, marketing, operations, and partnerships done or formed because of the new product.

Realized costs are actual costs incurred. Not included are costs that are allocated for accounting reasons but are not directly traceable to the decision being made. Thus, overhead costs allocated based on accounting averages are not "real" costs and are not relevant. However, actual increases that are attributable, such as the number of staff, production equipment, office space, and utilities, are relevant as long as they are attributable to the decision being made at that time (note that once these things are committed and become part of ongoing fixed costs, they may not be relevant for future decisions on price changes related to the same product; see the discussion of *avoidable costs*).

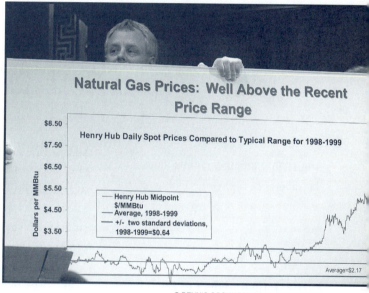

© DENNIS COOK/AP/WIDE WORLD PHOTOS

Forward-looking incremental costs are the costs that will be incurred (forward-looking) for the next unit or units of product or service that will be sold when the decision is implemented (the costs of the incremental units); that is, they are the next costs to be incurred. For instance, suppose a new product has been on the market for six months when the competition drops its prices significantly. If we dropped our price to match the competitor's, the price would drop below the level

[5]Based on Thomas T. Nagle and Reed K. Holden, *The Strategy and Tactics of Pricing: A Guide to Profitable Decision Making,* 2d. (Upper Saddle River, N. J: Prentice-Hall, 1995), Chapter 2.

where it is recovering each new unit's share of the R&D previously expended on the product. This R&D cost would not be relevant for decision making because it is not forward-looking. Consideration of incremental costs defined in this way ensures, again, that the actual costs resulting from the decision will be considered.

Avoidable costs are those costs that would not be incurred—that is, costs that would be avoided—if the decision were not made, for example, if the product or program were not launched. Avoidability becomes a concern when the marketing manager is considering a price reduction. The manager must determine at what point the price does not cover costs. Suppose that a product manager is considering matching a competitor's price reduction on certain product models. In calculating the price at which the revenue does not cover cost, the manager's salary is unavoidable; if the product models were to be dropped in price, the manager would still be employed and the cost incurred.

This may seem counterintuitive, because any manager wants to cover all costs. Think about it this way, though. Even if the price on a particular model drops below the level at which sales do not contribute fully to their share of the manager's salary, they still contribute something to cover it, as shown in the left-hand bar in Exhibit 10–6. If the price were dropped below the level required to pay for the variable costs associated with the product models, as shown in the right-hand bar in Exhibit 10–6, then the manager would be better off not offering the products at all, as, with each additional unit produced and sold, the losses mount.

Contribution margin can be viewed as the difference between ongoing attributable costs and ongoing attributable revenue.

Contribution Analysis   From the supplier's point of view, price needs to be set in such a way that contribution margin is positive. **Contribution margin** for a product (this could also be for an offering, for a new marketing program, or for a customer) is the revenue less the avoidable costs that are directly attributable to the product in question. It is called contribution margin because it repre-

EXHIBIT 10–6   Effect of Price Reductions on Cost Coverage

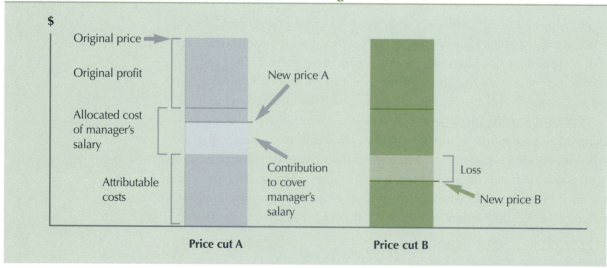

sents the portion of revenue that "contributes" to coverage of fixed costs, indirect costs, and profit. Marketers need to be careful in deciding which costs are relevant and which are not, as discussed earlier. If, for instance, the accounting department has given you a standard percentage that is "your share" of overhead costs or indirect costs, it is not a relevant cost to contribution margin calculations. For more discussion, see Appendix 10–1.

Demand Functions and Pricing

All of the preceding discussion has dealt with pricing on a "per unit" basis. The marketer is interested, though, in the effect of the offering and marketing program on total sales and profits in the market. (Will sales be high enough to cover fixed costs and contribute to profitability?) We find the concepts of demand, equilibrium prices, and elasticity—often presented as the foundations of pricing management—conceptually useful but largely impossible to quantify and use in real-life situations. In practice, marketers generally do not have enough time or data to fully analyze demand-price effects and so must use assumptions and quick approximations to make informed decisions. The theory does generally help understand market behavior, even if exact forecasts cannot be made.

Recall from your economics principles course that a **demand curve** shows what quantity of products or services will be sold in a market at different price levels. An industry **supply curve** shows how much product will be produced in an industry at different levels of price (see Exhibit 10–7).

In theory, the intersection of a demand curve and a supply curve (the sum of individual supply curves for firms in a given market) gives the equilibrium price

EXHIBIT 10–7　Demand and Supply Curves

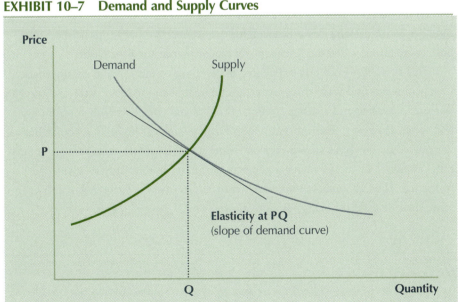

and quantity of products in that market.[6] This equilibrium point is a theoretical state or condition that markets will tend to move toward. When a marketer is looking to set prices for the first time for a new product or for a product entering a new market, an estimated demand curve could, in theory, help assess what sales to expect. An estimate of market share would give the marketer a projection of the revenue the company can expect. Given this level of activity, the marketer could then, with an estimate of costs at that particular level, estimate profits. Profits at different price levels can then be compared and an optimum price level chosen.

The problem with this approach is that demand curves and supply curves are abstractions that often defy estimation. Because demand is derived in business-to-business markets, forecasting demand at different market prices is a Herculean task. Supply curves are difficult to forecast as well, due to the complex interplay of input costs and the uncertainty about what competitors will actually participate in a market. Instead of estimating a demand curve, it is probably best to get a sense of what a majority of the customers project they will buy in the foreseeable future and to further get a sense of how sensitive to price they are. This provides a "limited version" of a demand schedule over a narrow range; this is about the best a more rigorously estimated demand schedule would contribute to decisions on pricing in any case.

The usefulness of demand and supply concepts lies in the relationships they describe. The concept of *elasticity* is useful when thinking about the effects of a price change; however, the context of business-to-business markets must be kept in mind. **Elasticity** refers to the tendency of demand to react to changes in price; generally higher prices yield lower demand, and vice versa. In business markets, there is likely to be a significant difference between short-term and long-term demand. In the short run, a customer may have little choice but to stay with its initial order because products and services purchased are so dependent on one another. Thus, when a marketer raises prices, the customers are not likely to change their demand level much in the short term. They suffer lower profits for the time being. However, in time, a customer's product and production plans can be changed to revise their input combinations. This, then, results in lower demand (or no demand) for the marketer's offering. In the short term, business-to-business demand is inelastic; in the long term, it is very elastic.

This is what is currently happening in response to increases in energy costs. Companies can find ways to conserve a little energy and reduce costs—less travel, less use of heating and cooling, turning off lights and computers when not in use, and so on. However, their current ways of doing business leave little choice but to use power as they have and to take on the higher costs. Over time, though, companies can invest in energy-saving equipment and new, more energy efficient processes. Thus, their short-term reaction to higher costs is fairly inelastic; longer term, their demand for energy is more elastic.[7]

---

[6]See, for instance, Jack Hirshleifer and Amihai Glazer, *Price Theory and Applications* (Upper Saddle River, N.J.: Prentice-Hall, 1992).

[7]Paul Raeburn, "Don't Write Off Energy Conservation, Mr. Cheney," *Business Week* (14 May 2001) 46.

Another difference between short-term and long-term elasticity occurs because of switching costs and derived demand. Think back to the example in Exhibit 10–2. Suppose the manufacturer of small motors was faced with a sharp price increase in metals. In the short run, it might be very difficult for the manufacturer to switch from zinc to plastic as the material for the motor frames. Accordingly, the manufacturer would pay the increased cost of the zinc. The manufacturer would probably not reduce its quantity purchased either, since that amount depends on the demand for small motors. In the short run, the manufacturer will most likely absorb the increased cost of the materials but begin seriously looking for alternatives. The price of the metal has approached the maximum price that the manufacturer is willing to pay. After an investigation of the price and costs of alternatives—in this case, the evaluated price of the plastic alternative—the manufacturer undertakes the switch. So, while the short-term reaction to price is inelastic, in this case, the long-term elasticity reflects "on-off" demand. Once the evaluated price has exceeded the relevant maximum, the buyer simply "turns the buying switch to off," ceasing its demand for the product.

A short-term reaction to a price decrease followed by a long-term reaction may be just the opposite effect. Suppose an office supply dealer reduces prices on printer paper (passing through a reduced cost from paper suppliers). The dealer's customers may react quite noticeably, buying large quantities of paper, particularly if they believe the price will increase again in the near future. They are simply stockpiling extra paper when it can be purchased at a low price. The customers still use the paper at the same rate, or nearly so, even if the price remains low. Just because the price of paper is lower does not mean customers will write more or longer documents.

In addition to concepts of demand and elasticity, it is important for the marketer to consider competitive reactions to price changes. Just as it may be easy for a company to change its prices, it is probably equally easy for competitors to do so. A price cut to take away business from competitors may simply be matched or exceeded by the competitor, resulting in lost margin for all with little shift in market share. Firms are particularly susceptible to this trap when a product has passed through the maturity stage of the PLC and market sales volumes decline. Cuts in price may have little effect on overall number of units sold. Any increase in sales will come at the expense of a competitor, which can be expected to vigorously defend its market share. The lower price means that revenues will drop accordingly.

To anticipate competitors' price reactions requires an understanding of their cost structures and their tendencies to participate in industry price changes. In the Intel example, Intel is anticipating that competitors may not be willing to fully match price cuts. If the competitors do match them, Intel is counting on them to suffer more than Intel from the lost profitability.

In summary, there are several lessons that the marketer can take away from the economic fundamentals of price:

1. Demand levels will be different at different levels of price; different market segments will have different price sensitivity based on segment members'

perceptions of the benefits from the product or service in question: in most markets, one price does not fit all segments.

2. Changes in price yield reactions from customers, which are different in the short term from their long-term reactions: short-term reactions are usually constrained by customers' situations; longer-range reactions allow greater flexibility. In other circumstances, customers may shift the timing of their expenditures in response to short-term price changes; their longer-term reactions may show less elasticity.

3. Changes in price will yield reactions from competitors: it is important to pay attention to their communications as well, since these may give clues to how they are viewing the market, prices, and other pressures that may influence future actions.

MANAGING PRICE AS PART OF MARKETING STRATEGY

These ideas form a framework for thinking about pricing, but at some point the marketer must take what is known and what is assumed about customers and competitors and must make price decisions. Again, the principal price decisions are what prices to set, how to change prices when necessary, and what the other elements of pricing should be—payment terms, financing, and so on. Pricing is situational, depending on strategic purposes and market circumstances.

Internally, price is a part of positioning, so the marketer must set prices to be consistent with the other elements of the offering for positioning purposes. Beyond its role in positioning, there are several strategic purposes for which pricing is a crucial element. The marketer will want to use price to obtain specific reactions from customers, competitors, distribution channels, or from the direct sales force. The instances we discuss are pricing to introduce a new product, pricing to use the experience curve or learning curve to achieve advantage, and pricing when engaged in discovery. Before we get into the discussions of these circumstances, though, it is necessary to discuss the strategic context for pricing decisions. Accordingly, we first discuss pricing to achieve marketing objectives and pricing in the context of the product life cycle and the technology adoption life cycle.

When the marketer makes price decisions to address a change in competition, to win over certain customers, or to achieve some other short-term objectives, then pricing becomes tactical in nature. Price is a marvelous (and dangerous) incentive for motivating customers to take action. As a tactical decision, marketers will need to decide what discounts will be given, to whom, and how. Other price conventions also need to be observed. In many markets, customers will choose vendors based on competitive bidding. To be successful at competitive bidding, the marketer must have a good sense of how to prepare a competitive bid. We also examine how to approach changing prices to reflect market conditions. These tactical issues in pricing are discussed in the section of this chapter that follows managing price as part of marketing strategy.

Strategic Context of Pricing

Setting prices to achieve strategic purposes takes place within the context of the business environment and the strategy chosen to address that environment. As we have done in prior chapters, we examine pricing through the product life cycle and the technology adoption life cycle. The environment, however, does not fully define the strategy to be taken. Companies have choices of what sorts of strategies they will follow. Accordingly, we examine how pricing contributes to different kinds of purposes or objectives.

Pricing Objectives   As discussed in prior chapters, the strategic management process sets out objectives and strategic purposes for the firm to address. In setting objectives for marketing strategies and programs, the marketer will realize that some objectives are addressed directly with pricing strategies. These objectives have come to be called *pricing objectives* but are really broader objectives in which price plays a key role; other marketing elements are usually key components as well. Exhibit 10–8 shows several objectives whose achievement depends on pricing.

The marketer must address the first two strategic purposes no matter what. First, the marketer needs to address profitability targets set by the company. Price levels must obtain enough revenue volume and margin to satisfy the company's strategic concerns. Second, the marketer needs to determine pricing that is consistent with a desired level of goodwill or relationship building. As noted earlier, there is a maximum price that customers will accept for an offering. Generally, though, even though customers agree to pay this price, they will not subsequently enter into a close relationship with the supplier that charges such prices because they believe the supplier is exploiting their need. If the marketer wishes to develop relationships with customers, price levels must fall within ranges that are acceptable or attractive to the customers.

EXHIBIT 10–8   Several Marketing Objectives Addressed by Pricing

Strategic Purposes
◆ Achieving a target level of profitability
◆ Building goodwill, or relationships, in a market or among certain customers
◆ Penetration of a new market or segment
◆ Maximizing profit for a new product
◆ Keeping competitors out of an existing customer base

Tactical Purposes
◆ Winning the business of a new, important customer
◆ Penetrating a new account
◆ Reducing inventory levels
◆ Keeping the business of disgruntled customers
◆ Encouraging customers to try a product or service
◆ Encouraging sales of complementary products

For each of the purposes listed in Exhibit 10–8, it is obvious that there are other elements of the marketing mix involved. For instance, in encouraging the sale of complementary products, the supplier must communicate so that the customer will know that the complementary products are available and why together the products provide more value. Also, the complementary products must work well together, implying that product design and execution are also necessary. Availability implies some sort of channel support. In fact, for most of these objectives, addressing them with price alone is usually inadequate, leading to lost sales and lost profitability. Objectives must be set in designing strategy and tactics. The role of pricing in accomplishing those objectives then needs to be understood. In the following sections, we examine situations where price plays a key role in achieving a strategic purpose.

Pricing throughout the Product Life Cycle and the Technology Adoption Life Cycle

Pricing is situational, depending on strategic purposes and market circumstances. Both of these parts of the situation are heavily influenced by market evolution as the PLC and TALC progress. Customers' perceptions of needs and value change during this market evolution. Concurrently, the competitive environment changes as well. Strategies—and the role of pricing in those strategies—should evolve as the markets evolve.

Recall that we are most concerned with life cycles for a product category, not for individual models or incremental innovations within that category. When a new product category is introduced, only the innovators will be interested in adopting so early. When offering a new technical product, the marketer is trying to obtain adoption from technophiles, who usually do not have big budgets and who do not really *need* the product anyway; they just want to try it to see what it will do. At this early stage, few if any competitors exist, so pricing can be set commensurate with perceived value. However, value may not yet be readily apparent. (Recall the discussion of shadow and delusional products in Chapter 9; value must be understood from the customer's viewpoint.) At this early stage, pricing is constrained more by customer perceptions than by competitive pressures and the objectives pursued by marketers may focus more on learning about needs and building early references than on creating cash flow. Price may be more of a way of getting customers' reactions to price levels than anything else.

In the next stage, when early adopters, or visionaries as Moore calls them, are targeted, the offering is usually custom-built and is still undergoing rapid improvement in design and performance. Pricing has to accommodate several competing purposes. To some extent, the vendor will probably try to obtain trial and will want to price for penetration. In these circumstances, customer organizations will usually provide a forecast of usage that the supplier can use in financial and capacity planning efforts. The vendor is also trying to pay for ongoing R&D costs, plus customization costs and training costs. If the design and development process has not been part of a collaboration or partnership between the supplier and the customer, R&D, customization, and customer training will tend to push the price up. Unfortunately, if this occurs, the development may have occurred in isolation, away from a continuous feedback process described in Chapter 8 as necessary for successful new product development. Visionaries will also see the new product as something that provides a competitive advantage and so will tend to place a high value on it, justifying relatively high prices. Still, there is often a desire to learn something about the technology and the market, so the marketer may be asked to reduce price in exchange for learning (see Pricing in Discovery Mode, page 315). In general, whether the product is a system, a component part, a material, or a service, volumes will be low and development costs will still be high. Pricing at this early stage will tend to be relatively high.

In getting across the chasm, or the market development gap, the first pragmatist buyers may need additional incentive to spur adoption of the product. Beyond these initial pragmatist buyers, though, the dynamic interaction of market segmentation, price sensitivity, innovation, competition, and marketing strategies can send pricing in many different directions. In some markets, rapid growth may be spurred by reductions in pricing. In segments where the marketer encounters competition, price will have to be set to reflect the competitive pressures, pushing price levels down. In technology markets during the growth phase, as standards emerge, the dominant players will be able to price their products at a premium, since their products will have more value. In other market segments, growth may be so rapid that even with several competitors, there is no great pressure downward on prices, at least until growth slows. Marketers facing a growth phase will need to examine their targeted segments, their positioning, and their strategies and set prices accordingly.

At the end of the growth period, but before maturity, competition will generally become more intense and will tend to drive prices down. During this period, product differentiation opportunities begin to disappear. Bloomberg is a company offering a service that seems to be reaching this stage of the life cycle. See the description of their situation in the box, "Bloomberg's One Size Fits All," and consider whether they will have to change their strategy, including their pricing.

Two key drivers are at work: the drive to integrate features to improve performance and the drive to reduce costs. Intel is a good example of a company that has pursued both improvement directions simultaneously. They have built communications, graphics, and memory cache capabilities into their chip sets. Meanwhile, they have pursued production efficiency improvements and labor cost savings to drive costs down. This approach worked very well for the market segment of customers who were not likely to upgrade their computers but were more likely to purchase a complete replacement. This segment consisted of high-volume, low-cost, but with poor upgrade capability/flexibility, computers.

As the market evolves into maturity, there is often a consolidation among participants. The structure of the supply base begins to appear oligopolistic. A few dominant players begin to exercise the ability to control (or, at least, strongly influence) the market. The dominant suppliers control pricing and often they do so by investing in cost reductions so that they can drive prices lower. A current trend in

Bloomberg's One Size Fits All

Bloomberg LP is a private company that provides financial information to the investment community. Money managers, corporate financial managers, investment advisors, and Wall Street brokerages all obtain detailed analysis from Michael Bloomberg's empire. Bloomberg started the business in 1981 and has built it into the leader in the industry.

Bloomberg's clients have a private connection to the financial network. The data and analyses are displayed in real time on a personal computer at the end of the network wire coming into the business. Pricing is a flat $1,285 per month fee per terminal. Competition from net start-ups and from Reuters has arisen, for which the prices are generally lower than Bloomberg's, but the quality of the information still makes Bloomberg the preferred alternative.

Participation Exercise

Why can Bloomberg price at a flat rate? As competition from Reuters grows, will Bloomberg have to change its pricing method? Why, or why not?

Source: Based on Tom Lowry, "The Bloomberg Machine," *Business Week* (23 April 2001), 76–84.

business markets to accomplish this is the outsourcing of technology development. Companies will find low-cost sources of undifferentiated product or service modules. While cost leadership is important, there is a danger of losing control here, perhaps outsourcing a process or technology that should be incorporated as a distinctive competency of the firm. Performance improvement through technology integration is an important source of competitive advantage at this point in the PLC. When a company outsources a portion of the technology, even if it is not core technology, it runs the risk of losing its ability to fully integrate the technology with other parts of its products and, hence, it loses a portion of its unique value. Also, since it does not have direct control over product development, the company may lose its ability to react quickly as the market changes. This is essentially what happened to Lucent, a leading vendor of telecommunications equipment. As the data communications market moved from analog to digital technology built around Internet protocol networks, Lucent turned to outsourced product development (through acquisition of technology companies) that did not integrate well into their corporate culture. Companies like Cisco Systems and Juniper Networks, who were newcomers to the market (minimizing integration problems), were able to create a better offering and win the business of the new Internet service providers.

Pricing during maturity depends upon how much the supplier can differentiate its offering. Since product features offer little chance for differentiation, much of the possible differentiation arises in the relationship between the supplier and the customer. This is discussed at length in the next chapter. If the supplier can create this nonproduct differentiation, it can charge a price that earns something of a premium. If its relationships are not strong or cannot be strengthened, the supplier needs to be able to drive costs down to stay competitive and profitable.

As the market moves into decline, pricing depends upon the market segments still served and the number of suppliers still competing for a piece of the pie. Because of unique switching costs, some users may continue to use old equipment or supplies from an earlier era. A premium price may be possible for such customers, but there is an upper limit set by the switching costs. Other customers will stay with older products as long as they can get a low price. Depending on the supplier's cost structure, it may still be profitable to serve these customers.

Penetration Pricing and Price Skimming

The PLC and the TALC will define the business environment the marketer faces and will influence the purposes the marketer pursues. When a supplier is introducing a new product ahead of the competition, marketers have a strategic purpose in mind for which price plays a key role. The product introduction may be aimed at maximizing profit in the short run until competitors overcome the supplier (which would be a purpose pursued by a nondominant competitor in the earlier stages of the PLC); or it may be aimed at maximizing profit segment by segment as the product achieves wider adoption (a purpose pursued by a dominant competitor in the late growth or maturity stages of the PLC). Alternatively, the marketer may want to achieve a rapid adoption by customers in which the supplier obtains a large, defensible market share (a purpose pursued by a company in the growth stage hoping to become a dominant competitor).

Price skimming is charging relatively high prices that take advantage of early customers' strong need for the new product. Since the benefits of the product are so important to them, customers are willing to pay higher prices. Without competitors offering similar products, the supplier can charge a skimming price and these first customers will pay the premium. **Penetration pricing,** on the other hand, is charging relatively low prices to entice as many buyers into the early market as possible.

With the range of pricing options so wide, it is important for the marketer to understand what circumstances favor the differing approaches. Suppose a marketer is about to launch a new offering that provides superior value to competitors' current offering and believes that competitors will not be able to match the new offering for several months at least. Penetration pricing would make sense if the marketer further believed the following:

1. The market can be dominated by gaining early customer commitments.
2. Key large customers will commit early rather than waiting for a competitor if they believe that they are getting the best price now.
3. A learning curve effect will result from early adoptions all coming to the marketer's company, allowing cost or quality improvements that give the marketer's offering a competitive advantage over forthcoming entrants.

Penetration pricing requires that a large group of customers are sensitive to low prices. This is most prevalent in markets that have evolved enough for customers to understand the value of an offering. In early markets, this may not be the case (see the earlier section on pricing throughout the PLC).

If the marketer already dominates the market and serious competition is not likely to materialize—either because of a dominant lead in technology or airtight patent protection—then the marketer can set skimming prices that obtain purchases from the early price-insensitive customers. After this segment has been largely sold, the next highest price-insensitive segment may be addressed with a lower price; then the next, and so on, as if peeling the layers of an onion. This is a profit maximization approach followed by many market leaders in the past. It has an element of risk, though, if the market leader does not realize that some unforeseen competitor is going to undermine this strategy. AMD was able to take advantage of Intel in the market for low-end microprocessors in this way. Intel did not realize that the market would be so strong and allowed AMD to undercut its pricing on the Pentium II and Pentium III with powerful but inexpensive Athlon processors. Intel countered with newer Celeron processors, but only after AMD was able to establish a beachhead in the market.

Another circumstance calling for skimming prices is when the company wants to maximize short-term profits. It has a temporary lead in the market but does not expect to be able to compete over the long term. This would be the case with a small company entering a market ahead of the market leader, who is likely to be in the market within, say, six months. The small company could make as much profit as possible by charging a skimming price for the most price-insensitive customers. In the meantime, it is looking for the next market opportunity because it knows the current situation will not last once the leader enters the market. In many circumstances, this company may end up selling the product technology or even the company to the market leader.

Learning Curve Effect   A special case of penetration pricing occurs when management in a company believes that competitive advantage can be achieved through running down a **learning curve.** The learning curve concept says that as more product units (or service units) are produced and sold, unit costs can be reduced through the learning that has occurred. As they obtain experience, companies learn how to produce products with more quality; they learn how to handle inputs more efficiently; they learn how to distribute products more efficiently; and they learn how to provide service more efficiently and effectively. To obtain this experience, the supplier sets a relatively low price for its new product or service. Price sensitivity in the market, if it exists, will drive higher sales volumes, and the supplier will gain the experience that much faster.

The conditions for effective use of this strategy are fairly restrictive and relatively rare. The marketer must have a good sense of whether *all* these conditions are met before attempting to pursue a learning curve strategy. First, there must be enough prospective customers, with high

> Repetition leads to learning more efficient ways to complete the same task. This is the principle behind the **learning curve.** Just as with individual tasks, the more you do something, the better you get at it (if not, why practice?); organizations (teams) will improve performance through learning.

enough quantity demand, who are price sensitive and who will adopt if the price is right. If these companies do not exist, or if they are not willing to purchase large volumes, then the strategy will not produce enough learning to drive down costs. This suggests that pragmatists must be ready to buy; any earlier in the PLC or the TALC, there may not be enough buyers.

Second, there must be ample opportunity for learning to occur. The marketer needs to poll the relevant managers in other parts of the firm to determine whether they believe more units made and sold will indeed contribute significantly to improved operations. If this strategy is pursued too late in the product life cycle, all the learning may have already been done.

Third, there must be sufficient time to learn. Learning is a function of both volume and time for assimilation of new knowledge. If the volume of demand comes too quickly, assimilation may not occur.

Fourth, there must be a sufficient lead over the competition to avoid direct price competition. If a competitor can match price, then learning will not occur as fast and the competitor will learn just as quickly.

Fifth, there must not be a competitor who will come along in the near future with a process innovation that will start a new learning curve. If this occurs, the cost savings may not be enough to match the unit costs for the competitor, no matter how much learning has occurred. Meanwhile, the supplier on the original learning curve may have built up switching costs to the point that it cannot easily adopt the technological innovation of the competitor to pursue the new learning curve. The marketer might take a quick poll of technologists in the company and a few external experts in the field to see if they believe such an innovation is likely. If the marketer believes there is a good chance that such an innovator-competitor will emerge, the safe course may be to avoid investment in the learning curve strategy.

If conditions are ripe for a learning curve strategy, the marketer must ensure that the learning takes place. It is not enough just to set the low price and then sit back and wait for nature to take its course. The marketer must meet with the relevant managers in the areas of the firm where learning is to occur and obtain their cooperation in pursuing the necessary process improvements.

Pricing in Discovery Mode

One of the key ideas discussed in earlier chapters is that business-to-business marketers learn about new segments through a process of discovery. When a new customer comes along with an apparent need for a new or revised product, the supplier may work with the new customer on a trial basis. The supplier and customer will embark on a process of discovery to see whether the needs of the customer can be met reasonably and profitably. The marketer will need to negotiate a price for the product and for the service of developing it. The customer will want to be credited for the assistance it provides to the supplier in specifying the product, trying it and testing it under varying conditions, and generally in providing the platform for launching a successful new business.

Perhaps the best way to price this type of activity is to separate the components. First, the development activity should be treated as a consulting service. However, the service cannot be charged at a full consulting rate since the customer is, in effect, consulting back to the supplier developing the product. Consequently, the development time should be charged on an hourly or daily basis and the customer's assistance should be charged back against this at a reasonable rate. The product itself can then be charged on a value basis. The price could be set initially at a preliminary rate when the contract is first signed and then adjusted based on value at some specified future date. Some part of the deal might be structured in a way that pays the customer a royalty on future sales of the product to new customers.

Pricing for International Marketing Efforts

A key trend over the past twenty years has been the move to marketing of products across national boundaries. Several hundred of the world's largest firms conduct business globally. Thousands more sell their products and services in more than one country. Such international or global reach raises some interesting pricing challenges, including how to set prices in different currencies and whether to charge global prices or prices that differ by region or country.

The problem faced by companies operating internationally is that customers, competition, and channel structures differ greatly from country to country. Market conditions may call for lower prices outside the company's home country, or the competitive situation may be such that the company can charge higher prices and make more profit. Often, the costs incurred in opening foreign markets reduce contribution margins to the point where prices must be raised to make any contribution at all; and, of course, these higher prices may or may not reflect the value perceived by customers in the new market.

As a company does more and more business in foreign markets, it will face increasing pressure to regularize its prices from country to country. If the company has global customers, they will look to minimize their costs by buying products wherever the price and shipping costs are the least in combination. They may negotiate to conduct a transaction for products or services in one country and receive delivery at the location of usage. Smaller companies may also take advantage of this cross-border arbitrage by buying through global distributors who accomplish much the same purpose.

The problem faced by the marketer is similar to the problem of addressing multiple market segments. Maximizing profit by addressing the segments separately only works when segments can be separated from each other. If they cannot, then the marketer must decide how to address the combined segments as one market. To do so, the marketer needs to address the portion of the market that is most important, given the company's competitive position and its goals. If this makes the price too high for other segments (geographic segments, in this case), then the company must live with the meager earnings from these other segments. When conditions change and the company can address the segments differentially, then the pricing strategy can change accordingly.

MANAGING PRICING TACTICS

Companies face changing business environments that require fast reactions. Often, pricing is the first thing that can be changed to fend off a competitive threat or take advantage of an opportunity. Business-to-business marketers need to keep in mind that the tactics employed must be consistent with overall positioning and must still reach a balance between value for customers and profitability for the company. As you read the sections that follow on pricing tactics, note that, in certain circumstances, tactics when generally applied may be strategic. The issues discussed here, though, usually arise in business-to-business marketing as a way to implement some strategic direction or to obtain a short-term reaction from customers, competitors, channels, or the company's own sales personnel and, thus, are tactical in nature.

Bundling   In business-to-business marketing, bundling is principally a tactical pricing move, rather than a strategic one. Price **bundling** is when several products or services are sold together as a package for one price. The reasoning behind bundling in consumer marketing is to create the impression that the bundle has value and is a good bargain. It induces consumers to buy products, services, or features that they would not buy when sold separately. In business-to-business buying, the customer usually has information and professional purchasing personnel who know what the bundled products are worth individually and who will attempt to bundle or unbundle purchases as fits their need. Bundling is a way to sweeten a deal to close a sale or to move some old inventory while minimizing transaction costs. In other circumstances, bundling of materials, parts, or components can lead to serious price-discrimination issues. Suppliers who consider bundling to close a deal may find that, in the long term, they have compromised the price structure integrity of one or more product lines.

Discounts and Allowances   Discounts and allowances are reductions in price for some special reason. Discounts are usually given as a reward incentive for some action taken by the buyer during the transaction. Thus, a discount may be given for paying promptly in cash or buying in quantity. An allowance is a credit against price given to channel members in exchange for some logistical or marketing activity that they perform. For instance, an allowance may be given for prospecting new accounts, for providing after-sale service, or for advertising. The key is determining what needs to be done to influence the final customer's buying decision and then providing sufficient incentive for the channel intermediary to perform the necessary activities.

The problem with discounts and allowances is that customers and resellers get used to them and expect them. Communication that accompanies such reductions in price must be clear that the reductions are offered only for specific purposes. Even so, powerful customers and resellers may insist that the reduced pricing should be the norm.

In the box, "Airbus Tries to Enter the Japanese Market," a description of the current competition between Airbus and Boeing, Airbus is offering significant price breaks to obtain adoption of the A380 aircraft. Airbus's action raises questions of future profitability, particularly in light of Boeing's obvious desire to defend this market.

Airbus Tries to Enter the Japanese Market

Boeing has a long-standing relationship with Japanese airlines. Fully 84 percent of the fleets of Japanese commercial airlines—including JAL and All Nippon Airways, the two largest airlines—come from Boeing. But now Airbus Industrie sees an opportunity to break into this market with its A380, the super jumbo jet currently in development. The opportunity stems from the congestion at Japan's major airports. The A380, which will seat 550 to 800 passengers, offers the chance to reduce the number of airliners traveling the most heavily traveled routes.

Boeing has its own version of a super jumbo jet on the drawing board. However, Boeing does not believe that the market for true super jumbo jets is large enough to justify developing a new airliner from scratch. Its version is a redesigned 747 that will carry about 500 passengers—dubbed the 747X. The 747X is scheduled to be ready in 2005, a year before the A380, and is list priced at $200 million, just below Airbus's price of $220 million.

This competition goes beyond the head-to-head battle over super jumbos. Boeing is concerned that, if Airbus obtains a foothold with super jumbos, it will begin getting more Japanese business for smaller jets. This is not just a market share contest: smaller jets flying longer routes are seen by the air travel industry as a way to relieve pressure on the hub-and-spoke system of airline route design. As airline traffic continues to grow, the number of passengers is rising to levels justifying nonstop trips between destinations without going through overly congested hub airports, such as Narita Airport in Tokyo. Industry executives think that jets about the size of the 300-seat Boeing 777 would fit the requirement for this shift in route structure.

In a nutshell, Airbus has an intriguing option but does not have the relationships. Boeing has well-established personal and corporate relationships with the Japanese (extending back almost fifty years), for whom relationships are so important. Boeing understands the nuances of maintaining and nurturing relationships with the Japanese, while Airbus is just beginning to form closer ties. Airbus is increasing the size of its office in Tokyo, spending more effort on personal contact at the executive level with the Japanese, and offering price incentives up to 40 percent off. Boeing is stepping up its own executive-level contact; lining up Japanese contractors, such as Mitsubishi Heavy Industries, to produce parts for the 747X; and seeking special treatment from the Japanese government for the 747X that would include financing assistance.

The stakes are great. At the core of the competition are two competing views of the future—one in which super jumbo jets play a key role (Airbus) and the other in which super jumbo jets play a niche role (Boeing). The direction taken by the Japanese market may well prove to be an indicator for other parts of the industry.

Source: Stanley Holmes, "Rumble Over Tokyo" *Business Week* (2 April 2001), 80–81.

Competitive Bidding

In many markets, the method of choosing suppliers is through competitive bidding. Participation in markets that buy through bidding is a strategic decision for the supplier. This is based on the factors discussed in Chapter 5 and Chapter 7: market potential, competitive intensity, ability to provide superior value, and expected profitability. Once the decision has been made to participate in markets where competitive bidding is done, then the actual preparation of bids is tactical in nature.

Bidding can be arranged in a number of different ways, but two main types of competitive bidding are common: **sealed bid** and **open bid**.[8] Sealed bid, or closed bid, pricing involves placement of private bids by prospective suppliers. Usually, the lowest bid wins the contract but not always. In many cases, the customer evaluates the total offering and chooses the vendor it considers to offer the best package. In some cases, the customer provides feedback to bidders and accepts revised bids. This begins to look a lot like open bidding; however, the customer may allow significant time for revisions between bidding rounds.

In open bidding, competing suppliers see each others' bids. The idea, of course, is to let competition drive the offered price to its lowest possible level (or to drive the package of product and service benefits to its highest possible level for a relatively low cost). If the bidding is limited to price offers and little time is allowed for revised bids, the process begins to look like an auction. In a real-time auction, the customer also benefits from the competitive emotions that build as the bidding

---

[8]Morris and Morris, op. cit., 119.

Participation Exercise

How do you think Airbus's offer of price incentives will affect the competition with Boeing? What do you think will be the effect on long-term prices for the A380 and the 747X?

Defending Supplier Advantage

In many industries, it is common practice that when a new supplier has bid below a current supplier for a piece of existing business, the current supplier—the defending source—gets a "second look." This is an acknowledgment of the costs involved for the customer in switching suppliers for an existing piece of business. Many of the initial start-up concerns related to logistics, invoicing, JIT services, and even the packaging methods of shipments will have to be reestablished with the new supplier. Recall the "make the transaction routine" portion of the buying decision process; the more comfortable a customer is dealing with the friendly routine of a competent supplier, the less likely that supplier will be faced with a price threat. If the current supplier has not put a "friendly routine" in place, things could be much different.

progresses. (Recall the opening example from Chapter 2. United Technologies received lower price opportunities but price was not the only deciding factor.) The customer may actually get a sizable discount that results from a supplier's desire to beat a major competitor in a public forum.

In sealed bid pricing, the marketing manager needs to do significant analysis in preparing a bid. Since the customer usually specifies the amount of business they wish to acquire, the sales volume is usually a given. The supplier's costs are usually a straightforward calculation based on this volume. However, the marketer needs to be careful to consider ancillary costs, such as the impact on production schedules or special training costs for service people. The creative part of preparing the bid comes in determining the price level. This requires understanding the customer's perceptions of value to ensure that a reasonable price is bid. More important is having a sense of how the competitors will bid. Past experience in bidding against competitors will provide some sense of their proclivities in bidding relative to costs and perceived value. From this information the marketer can construct a table of probabilities of the likelihood of winning the bid at certain prices. Exhibit 10–9 shows a table of possible bids, probabilities for winning, and expected profits in a *hypothetical* proposal and bid situation in which a bid is being prepared for, say, a market research project.

The basic idea in determining a bid price is to find the price at which the expected profitability is maximized. Expected profit at a given price is calculated as:

$$E(PF) = PW(Pr) \times PF(Pr)$$

where

$PF(Pr)$ = Profit at price Pr

$PW(Pr)$ = Probability of winning the bid at price Pr

$E(PF)$ = Expected profit

In the example in Exhibit 10–9, the probabilities of winning the bidding are shown as low at very low bids, since the credibility of the project being successfully completed is likely to be questioned by the customer at these low levels. In

EXHIBIT 10–9   Hypothetical Example of Profit Expectations in a Competitive Bidding Situation

Cost	Bid	Profit	Probability of Winning Bid	Expected Profit
$20,000	$20,000	$ 0	.2	$ 0
20,000	22,000	2,000	.5	1,000
20,000	24,000	4,000	.7	2,800
20,000	26,000	6,000	.5	3,000
20,000	**28,000**	**8,000**	**.4**	**3,200**
20,000	30,000	10,000	.3	3,000
20,000	32,000	12,000	.2	2,400

Source: Based on table construction shown in Morris & Morris, op. cit., 120.

this hypothetical situation, the highest expected profit is at a price of $28,000. This would be the bid price to use. Managerial judgment, of course, may adjust this up or down for any of several reasons. The marketer may believe that this particular instance is unique and that the competitor will bid higher (or lower) than usual. Perhaps the marketer believes that this particular request for bid will draw entrants into the market that do not usually participate, requiring a higher (or lower) bid to win. In any case, the determination of a best bid based on the calculation of a highest expected profit at least provides a place to start.

Competitive bidding purchase processes vary considerably from situation to situation, so we have only given a general sense of what is involved. It should be noted, though, that the work of the sales team and missionary sellers might favorably influence the request for bids. If a relationship between supplier and seller is in operation, the supplier's team may help the buying center to specify a solution that closely resembles the offering of the supplier. The request for bid, then, would ask for bids on a project that the supplier is well prepared to provide; other competitors will probably be less able to meet the requirements sought. Thus, even though the project goes out for bid, the customer has largely already made the decision of which supplier will be chosen.

Initiating Price Changes

Once the marketing plan has been finalized, the company will implement the plan and price levels will be set. As events unfold, the business-to-business marketer will need to react and change the marketing activities to match changes in the market and to take advantage of opportunities that arise. Price levels will need to be reviewed, and, at times, prices will need to be changed. The key thing to keep in mind is that changes in prices induce reactions from customers and competitors.

Events that would change the structure of demand or the nature of competition, and that might cause a marketer to reevaluate prices, include: competitors' changes in prices; changes in customers' perceptions of the value of an offering, either positive or negative; entrance of a new competitor into the market; introduction of the next generation of products, making the current generation less valuable to customers; and exit of a competitor from the market, which in turn changes customers' perceptions of the relative value of the remaining offerings in the market. Events that would change cost structures in such a way that prices might be affected include: the introduction of new process technology that reduces the supplier's costs, allowing reduction of prices; and increases in costs for all competitors such that the industry's supply curve shifts (see Exhibit 10–10 in which an across-the-board increase in costs shifts the industry supply curve to the left). Notice that an increase in costs that affects only the marketer's company will generally not have an effect on prices because the industry supply curve is not affected. No other competitors see the increase, and so they will continue to compete at what was a competitively set price. In time, there may even be a price shift downward as market shares redistribute and some competitors realize cost reductions from

EXHIBIT 10–10   Effect of an Industry Increase in Costs

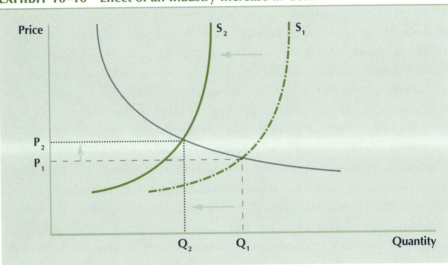

higher volumes. In a competitive market, these cost savings may be passed on to customers. However, the effect is not likely to last long. As other factors in the dynamic market shift, the effect of the unique cost increase will likely be superseded by other changes.

Summary of Managing Price

Pricing needs to be consistent with both business unit strategy and marketing strategy. In certain circumstances, pricing is a key component of strategy in that it builds and uses competitive advantage. General price levels are set when business unit strategy is designed; specific price levels and price schedules are set in the design of marketing strategy and tactics. As the marketing strategy is managed, the marketer must monitor competitive prices and the reactions from customers. Price changes will usually need to be considered as the business environment changes.

One of the key purposes of pricing is the creation of profitability. Prices are set to achieve profits, but the implementation of those prices needs to be done so that desired profit levels will indeed result. In many business-to-business markets, prices are negotiated at least to some degree. The next section discusses the negotiation process and how it can be managed to maintain profitable prices.

PRICING IMPLEMENTATION: THE CASE OF NEGOTIATED PRICING

In many instances, the development of a price list, along with a set of consistently applied price discounts and allowances, represents the whole of the implementation phase in the management of pricing. This is especially the case when prices are implemented through an established network of distributors. Very often, though, for large purchases, customized offerings, and for new products or services, the final price of an offering will be negotiated between the two (or more) parties. This, of course, happens much more frequently in business-to-business marketing than it does in consumer marketing. Another large difference between consumer and business-to-business situations is that most business-to-business negotiations occur within the context of a relationship between buyer and supplier, or at least they have the potential of becoming a relationship. As already stated, the difficulty in dynamic pricing, that is, pricing through negotiation, is that it must address both the goals of building relationships and building profits *simultaneously.*

This takes a great deal of skill and usually falls to the seller to implement, at least in part. Some companies give their sellers complete authority to negotiate and agree on prices. Other companies give their sellers limited authority, requiring price approval from a sales manager for larger deals. Still other companies require sellers to obtain approval on all prices. In certain other situations, higher-level executives for both the supplier and the customer complete the negotiations.

A problem that can arise is that sellers think of negotiation as part of "closing the sale." The temptation for the seller is to cut price to close the deal.[9] This may significantly improve the value provided to the customer but can play havoc with meeting profitability targets. With attention to some basic ideas in negotiation, the marketer can implement pricing through negotiation such that both a price associated with the customer's perceived value and the supplier's margin can be maintained.

Effective negotiating boils down to two key processes: matching the negotiating style to the type of negotiation situation and thoroughly preparing for the negotiation.

Two Types of Situations

Sellers and marketers face two general types of negotiating situations, based on the extent to which a relationship with the customer is involved. As seen in Exhibit 10–11, when there is no relationship, nor even a slim chance of one developing, the situation can be treated as a stand-alone transaction. When the supplier has a relationship with the customer or has a reasonable hope of building a relationship, then negotiation must be done while balancing the concerns of profitability and enhancing the relationship.[10]

---

[9]Nagle and Holden, op. cit., 190–91.

[10]G. Richard Shell, *Bargaining for Advantage: Negotiation Strategies for Reasonable People* (New York: Penguin Putnam, 1999).

EXHIBIT 10–11   Two Types of Negotiating Situations in Business-to-Business Sales

	Situation	
	Stand-Alone Transaction	**Balanced between Transaction and Relationship**
Effective Bargaining Styles	Competitive; problem solving	Problem solving; compromising
Effective Approach	Use of leverage	Seek common interests

The first situation, the stand-alone transaction, occurs when a company is making a one-time unique offering, such as selling off excess inventory of discontinued product. Another common stand-alone transaction occurs when a vendor attempts to get the business of a company whose primary objective is always price.[11] To be chosen by the customer, the supplier must meet minimum quality and delivery requirements and then is expected to offer as low a price as possible. The buyer generally is in a position of leverage, usually as a high-volume purchaser with multiple sources of supply. This would typically occur when the offering is in the mature phase of the product life cycle. The customer uses professional buying expertise and often "hardball" negotiating tactics to push the price as low as it can.

In the stand-alone transaction, a negotiator with a competitive style or one with a problem-solving style would best represent the prospective supplier. The negotiator with a competitive style will tend to extract as much profit out of the deal as possible and will be able to match any hardball tactics used by the customer. There is always the risk that a clash of competitive styles will kill a potential deal; upper-level management of the supplier company will have to decide whether it can tolerate this risk and any potential adverse outcomes. Even if the deal is signed, there may be little goodwill left between the parties. Since this is a single transaction, though, this should not matter.

A problem-solving approach may also work well in this situation, particularly if the customer's negotiator also takes a problem-solving approach. Problem solvers tend to think beyond the surface issues of the negotiation and look for unique solutions that improve the benefits received by both parties. Even though the situation is a single transaction, the result can be unexpectedly positive for both the buyer and the seller.[12]

The other kind of situation involves a transaction with long-term consequences. In the best of circumstances, it involves a customer with a different attitude than the price-oriented customer just described. In general, this is a customer that wants to receive the best value package possible but that also sees the potential benefit from establishing a lasting relationship with suppliers, so that the suppliers know the customer's business and can be proactive in providing value. This situation can occur in any stage of the product life cycle, including maturity. Even though a customer has leverage through volume purchasing and multiple sources of supply, this does not mean that the customer will use this leverage to press for price concessions. The customer may compete in its own markets on quality or innovativeness or may have a social agenda; thus, the customer will be interested in suppliers that contribute to these distinctive competencies.

A problem-solving approach works best in the second situation, where transaction concerns are balanced with relationship concerns. Good creative problem

[11]Nagle and Holden, op. cit., 193.

[12]Roger Fisher and William Ury, *Getting to Yes: Negotiating Agreement without Giving In* (New York: Viking Penguin, 1981); and Shell, op. cit.

solvers will find ways to enhance the relationship with each successive negotiation session. A compromising style and approach will also tend to produce positive out-comes but may not produce the unique outcomes of the problem solver.

The marketer must be cautious to correctly identify the situation. We have known of customers that sought value and seemed to want to pursue long-term rela-tionships. However, as negotiations developed, it became clear that lowest price was an overriding concern. Such customers really want the benefits of both high value from a relationship and low price. This is a dangerous sort of relationship in which to become involved. The switching costs for the supplier become too great to easily leave the relationship, while the profit from a long-term relationship never materializes.

Preparation for Negotiation

Obviously, to do a good job of negotiating, the company should prepare as much as possible. It helps to think in terms of the stages involved in a negotiation and to do what is necessary in each stage to make a favorable transition into each subsequent stage. Negotiation involves teamwork in most instances. At a minimum, the negoti-ating team includes a marketing role and a seller role (which may be called *business development* in many cases). Often in small companies, the same person fulfills both roles, but this is usually suboptimal because too much responsibility for prepara-tion will fall on the shoulders of a single person. Exhibit 10–12 shows the stages and substages of the negotiation process.

Most companies do a reasonably good job of preparing their sales teams to present the offering and show its benefits. This requires understanding of the cus-tomers' needs, buying center interactions, and the buying decision process. Some of this preparation serves the price negotiation process as well. Knowing customers' needs and their relative importance gives the sales team an idea of what issues the

**EXHIBIT 10–12   Stages in the Negotiation Process
in Business-to-Business Sales**

Preparation
- Data collection and analysis
- Determination of negotiation strategy

Information Exchange
- Elicit information not yet obtained
- Test hypotheses about nature of situation

Engage in Negotiation
- Opening
- Discussing positions
- Concessions
- Closing

Obtain Commitment

customer will bargain hardest on and the ones on which they will be most likely to make concessions. Other kinds of preparation items include:[13]

- Who has the authority to make a final decision?

- What are the bargaining styles of the individuals most likely to participate in the bargaining decision process?

- Will the situation be perceived as a transaction, part of a relationship, or a balanced combination of the two?

- What evaluated price range is the customer expecting?

Data about the customer can be obtained using the methods described in Chapter 6. Whatever is not known can be obtained through contact with customers during the prenegotiation period. In addition, the marketing analyst's cost and value model of the customer's business will have been used already to set price levels for the product and offering. This same model can give the sales team an idea of what the customer's acceptable price range will be. The newer the market or the newer the customer, the more general will be the cost/value model. In any case, though, it can give the sales team a starting point from which to negotiate.

The second part of the preparation phase involves determining the negotiation strategy. The first part of the strategy-making stage is framing of the negotiating situation, estimating the objectives of the other side, and determining the likely negotiation style to be employed by the other side. Once the nature of the transaction has been recognized, the negotiating team's goal should be to bring the most appropriate bargaining style to bear.

Determining goals is the next step. If the marketing analyst has done the homework, an acceptable price range should be laid out—from the supplier's viewpoint as well as from the customer's. Also, the homework should indicate what issues are likely to be key for the customer and on which issues the customer is likely to be willing to compromise or make concessions. With this in mind, the supplier's negotiating team needs to determine what issues—including price—are most important and how these issues are prioritized.

The team then needs to determine where it has leverage and where the customer has leverage. A party in the negotiation has **leverage** when it has the power to get the other side to accede to its position. Leverage comes from an unequal distribution of importance or need—one side needs the deal more than the other side. For instance, if the customer has alternative suppliers available, the customer tends to have leverage. If the customer needs immediate delivery so that it can meet a tight production deadline, the supplier tends to have leverage. Even if the negotiating team decides that it has some leverage, it may choose not to use it for reasons of enhancing a relationship.

---

[13]Shell, op. cit.

The bargaining strategy may even extend to anticipation of the kinds of concessions that will be attempted. Concessions work best in an "if . . . then" format, such as "if you are willing to wait an extra month for delivery, then we can come down in price per unit by 5 percent." This is called **integrative bargaining,** an approach in which multiple dimensions are considered simultaneously.[14] The negotiation team may want to identify important issues for the customer that can be easily accommodated. They can then offer concessions on these issues to obtain reciprocal concessions from the customer in areas that are important to the supplier.

In preparing for the closing stage, the supplier's negotiator avoids the temptation to give in on price to complete the contract. The negotiation team may prepare one or more final "pot sweeteners" that can be reserved for deployment to close a deal. These are based on the customer's important nonprice needs that the negotiating team has discovered. Ideally, these are high value for the customer and low cost for the supplier. If the deal closes before these concessions are reached, the negotiator can add in one or more of them as a special bonus (especially if they are low cost). This could help cement a relationship with the customer.

The outcome of all this preparation is a game plan for undertaking the bargaining. All of the participants on the negotiation team now have an idea of what they are trying to accomplish and what their roles are. The plan helps the team to concentrate on reaching their goals rather than on simply achieving the minimum deal they will accept. Lastly, it sets out information areas that need to be filled in with information from the customer. After the negotiation team goes through an information-exchange stage, the negotiation plan is updated to reflect new information.

Last Thoughts on Negotiation

Note one last piece of preparation: when involved in a stand-alone transaction—particularly with a large, leverage-holding, price-oriented customer—the negotiator needs to know when to walk away from a deal. With the price-oriented customer, the negotiator should not fool herself into thinking that a contract taken now at minimal profit or even a loss could build into a relationship in the future. The purchasing department will always push for price concessions, even if the supplier has a relationship with other members of the buying center. When dealing with a price-oriented customer who has leverage, the supplier should have a cost structure that creates profit; this is the only way to consistently win in this situation.

Finally, it is important to recognize the need for finishing the negotiation process by gaining commitment. Sales contracts usually have a section on remedies for nonperformance. However, suppliers and customers do not want problems to progress to the point of having to use these remedies. The negotiator chooses some method to get the customer invested in receiving and paying for the final product. In some circumstances, this may be providing incentives for early acceptance and

---

[14]Shell, op. cit., 169.

payment, such as a discount for early payment. In other circumstances, a simultaneous exchange of payment and product will occur by placing the payment in escrow, with orders to release the payment at the time of successful delivery. In circumstances in which a contract concerns completion of a project or delivery of a service, the supplier attempts to fairly closely match payments and costs incurred. In such a case, a sizable down payment may need to be included, both to fund the early activities of the supplier and to raise the commitment level of the customer. In any case, the requirements for the customer's acceptance of the product should be clearly stated and understood by both parties, so that costly disagreements later can be avoided.

PRICING AND THE CHANGING BUSINESS ENVIRONMENT

Throughout this text, we have explored how the trends occurring in the business environment are requiring business-to-business marketers to change and adapt. In particular, we have examined the effects of time compression, hypercompetition, and the growth in use of the Internet. In this concluding section of this chapter, we again examine these trends. We also examine the increased use of on-line auctioning and its effect on pricing. Auctioning arises again in Chapter 12 when we discuss supply chain management, but at this juncture we raise the issue of when it is appropriate and what its effect on relationships can be. Despite the changing nature of the environment, we believe the fundamental principles of pricing we have discussed still hold; they just need to be adapted to the new dynamics.

Pricing, Time Compression, Hypercompetition, and the Internet

Time compression affects the time that marketers have for analyzing industry conditions and customer reactions. It also puts pressure on marketers, salespeople, and customers to negotiate quickly so products and services become available before market conditions change. Obviously, pricing is not done as well as it could be when time compression prevails. When time compression interacts with the ease that prices can be changed, the effect is insidious.

Under time pressures, marketers are forced to try to react to quick-changing customer needs or rapidly developing competitor actions. Product features and channel programs take time to develop, so a quick reaction is difficult. Changes in sales force methods take time to disseminate within the organization, but these can probably be done more quickly than product changes. Promotional messages delivered over the Web can be changed fairly quickly, but messages going out through other media take time to develop. Price changes can be implemented very rapidly, though. If a marketer believes that a response to a competitive move must be immediate, the quickest way to respond is to drop prices.

Related to time compression are the trends of hyper-competition and increased use of the Internet. Hypercompetition increases the number of competitors to price against. It also means having to compare the marketer's value against some very different value packages involving substitute products or services offered by competitors (for instance, a company such as EMC that offers high-end data storage systems may find itself competing against a company that provides similar storage capability on an outsourced basis; so EMC must compete against a service rather than a systems vendor).

The question becomes how to deal with such problems. The answers are not easy. A marketer can address time compression and hypercompetition through more attention to constant preparation. This means, in part, constantly collecting information about customers' value-cost models and paying constant attention to the customers' customers and their perceptions of value. As much as possible, the analyses we have discussed needs to be done on an ongoing basis rather than as ad hoc analyses. This allows setting of prices more quickly and gives negotiators more information when they begin the negotiation process. This may seem to the marketer like overattention to tactical information. However, time compression is so prevalent and pricing is so crucial to profitability that constant preparation is truly a strategic activity. Also, both quicker price quotes and better presentation of value for customers relative to competitors help address the problems of hypercompetition.

Adoption of a constant preparation attitude probably extends to the operations of the company, as well, not just to information collection and analysis. If all negotiating sessions occur under constantly increasing time pressure, one way to buy more time is to design the product, service, and logistics systems for quick deployment. This may add additional costs to the offering, but the effects might more than offset the costs. First, rapid deployment is a benefit in itself, particularly when in a high-growth period and when high-need products are in short supply. On its own, rapid deployment is likely to give the supplier a leg up on the competition. Second, the additional time for negotiation allows the buyer and the seller to explore some more creative solutions to problems, which is also likely to deliver more value to the customer. Part of the negotiator's attention can also be spent on finding creative solutions that provide enough value to support higher margins.

Increased use of the Internet has both beneficial effects on pricing and some drawbacks. Internet communication through e-mail and shared Web sites can increase the buyers' and marketers' communication and preparation. In collaborative circumstances, in which both the transaction and the relationship are important to both parties, increased sharing of information facilitates more creative solutions. In the situation in which three or more parties are involved and relationships are important, such communication facilitates better coordination.

A major trend facilitated by the Internet is the use of auctions, particularly in supply chain transactions. Auctions are a two-edged sword, having both benefits and drawbacks. The key to maximizing benefits for all parties and minimizing the drawbacks is to use auctions in appropriate circumstances. Auctions are good for transactions involving undifferentiated commodities. Used outside this context, the benefits of relationships become minimized or circumvented.

Auctions can be used by marketers in offering their products or services. Marketers may also encounter auctions used by buyers to obtain products or services. When a buyer-seller relationship already exists and one party or the other begins using an auction, the trust in the relationship is called into question. The buyer or seller using an auction is saying, "We think we can get a better price; you've been holding out on us." An auction is better used for one-time transactions or for obtaining a first supplier (buyer) in a new line of business that may develop into a relationship. An example of a one-time transaction might be the case of a supplier with excess or obsolete inventory. Rather than contacting individual resellers or customers, the marketer may announce an auction and direct the inventory to the customer or reseller who values it most. An analogous situation from the buyer's side might arise when a company has a one-time need to purchase a standardized component part for use in a customized product. The customer is not likely to need such a product again, so it runs an auction to get the best price for this one-time purchase.

If marketers are tempted to run an auction, they need to think about the potential deterioration in relationships that might result. There may also be times when marketers decide an auction is needed to demonstrate to a recalcitrant partner that it is being unreasonable in its requests.

If the marketer is an existing supplier to a customer and finds that the customer wants to run an auction to choose suppliers, the marketer must think about what leverage she has. Individually, the supplier may not have enough leverage to get the customer to abandon or modify the auction idea. However, as a group, the suppliers may be influential enough to do so. If the marketer is not an existing supplier to the customer, the auction may offer a way to obtain an entry into the account. The marketer must be very careful, though, to determine what the minimum affordable entry price is and *what price is likely to prevail in the future.* The idea is to avoid getting business that will prove to be unprofitable in the long run as well as in the short run.

In this chapter, we have espoused value-based pricing. The key idea is to set price level in such a way that superior value is created for customers. Recall that value is composed of benefits received by customers, less the customers' costs. These costs include the price of the product or service. The marketer tries to set the price and structure the customers' costs so that customers receive more value than they would receive from the marketer's competitors. On the other side of the transaction, though, price must be set so that the supplier establishes profitability. Price must be set to cover the relevant costs and contribute to profit. To accomplish value-based pricing, then, the marketer needs to understand both the customers' perceptions of value and the marketer's own costs.

We have discussed ways for managing prices in a competitive environment that changes as the supplier's market evolves. We have discussed how the marketer's pricing must be consistent with business and marketing strategies pursued by the marketer's company. In some instances, as with penetration pricing and price skimming, price plays a key role in accomplishing strategic purposes. Pricing tactics also play an important role in implementing marketing strategies.

In business-to-business markets, marketers must often face the prospect of implementing their pricing through price negotiations with customers. We have discussed the importance of preparation for such negotiations as the core means of ensuring that negotiation is successful in creating customer value and supplier profitability.

As you move into the next chapter concerning selling and relationships, keep in mind the negotiating role for sellers described in Chapter 10. In many cases, the seller is the primary person for maintaining profitable pricing in the presence of the customer. Think about how the marketer, the missionary seller, and the sales representative can work together to build relationships with customers and still manage to create a strong negotiating position.

Key Terms

avoidable costs
bundling
contribution margin
cost-based pricing
demand curve
elasticity
evaluated price
forward-looking
  incremental costs

integrative bargaining
learning curve
leverage
ongoing costs
ongoing revenues
open bid
penetration pricing
price skimming
realized costs

resultant costs
revenues
sealed bid
supply curve
total offering
value-based pricing
value-cost model

Questions for Review and Discussion

1. In general, what is the maximum price that can be charged for a product or service?

2. What is the maximum price that can be charged for your product when you have direct competitors but your product is differentiated, that is, it provides more benefits than competitors provide?

3. Under what kinds of circumstances would a marketer want to charge a price less than the maximum price possible for the offering?

4. In general, what is the minimum price that can be charged for a product or service?

5. When would R&D costs be a relevant cost to consider in pricing decisions?

6. Suppose you were considering a price increase. What kind of difference would you expect between short-term elasticity and long-term elasticity in response to your price increase?

7. Under what general conditions would you want to use a price skimming strategy? A penetration price strategy?

8. Under what conditions would you switch from a skimming strategy to a penetration strategy? What elements of the marketing mix other than price would be involved?

9. Suppose your company is the market leader in a fast-growing market. Your product is differentiated in that it provides more and better benefits than your competitors'. How would you price your product?

10. In competitive bidding, what factors would enter into your determination of a bid to offer?

11. Why is preparation for negotiation so important to effective pricing?

12. Explain the major differences between negotiation in a single-transaction situation and negotiation in a balanced-concern situation.

13. Explain why time compression causes problems for price negotiations even when both parties have an interest in enhancing a relationship.

Internet Exercises

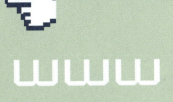

Go to the Web site for Luminate: **http://www.luminate.com** Browse the site and determine what kind of service Luminate offers. How is the service priced? What problems does this offering, including the pricing, solve? If Luminate were to offer a packaged software product instead of a service, how would the pricing have to change? Suppose Luminate is targeting large companies with large networks of servers. What advantages and disadvantages does the service approach have compared to the packaged software product approach?

Go to the Web sites for Intel and Advanced Micro Devices: **http://www.intel.com** and **http://www.amd.com** Find pricing information on the two most recent versions of their microprocessors. Try to find pricing for the OEM market. You may have to go to an article in an industry trade magazine to get a summary of this pricing. How is AMD responding to competitive moves by Intel? Explain why it is responding the way it is.

Use your favorite search engine to find the most recent news on Boeing and Airbus and their marketing efforts for super jumbo airliners in Japan. Have Airbus's efforts, particularly their "introductory pricing," paid off? Why, or why not?

APPENDIX 10–1

Contribution Analysis

In evaluating alternative marketing programs or actions, a useful way to make comparisons is to analyze the contribution to fixed cost, overhead, and profit from the alternatives presented. *Contribution* is the expected revenue less the costs that can be attributed to the action taken, as shown in the following equation:

$$TC = [(P - VC) \times Q] - AC$$

where

> TC = Total contribution to fixed costs, overhead, and profit
> P = Price
> VC = Variable cost per unit
> Q = Quantity sold
> AC = Other attributable costs (costs incurred by undertaking the action)

Often one will see contribution presented as revenue minus the variable costs. The problem with this is that variable costs are not the only kind of costs that are caused by a particular action. For instance, launch of a new product may require the hiring of a product marketer and involve retaining advertising and public relations agencies. These are not variable costs, but they are attributable to the project and they are avoided if the decision is to not launch the product. So, in essence, these costs must be paid for out of the proceeds from this product if the product is to be deemed profitable. Let us take a simple example to illustrate.

Suppose a marketing manager for a manufacturer of commercial pizza ovens is considering launching a new service program for resellers. The program will involve hiring three marketing specialists who will help resellers analyze their markets and plan and execute marketing programs. The program is supported by a 10 percent allowance on product purchases for resale. The marketing manager has forecast that product sales will increase by 80 units in the next year due to the new program. It is expected that the dealers who participate in the program would have sold 120 units without the new program. The pizza ovens wholesale for $25,000; variable cost on the ovens is $7,500. The marketing specialists cost $100,000 per year, each, including training and benefits. The manager estimates that support costs will run $50,000 per year.

Accordingly, the contribution is calculated as follows:

$$TC = [(P - VC) \times Q] - AC$$
$$TC = [(\$25,000 - \$7,500 - \$2,500) \times 80] - (\$120 \times \$2,500) - \$300,000 - \$50,000$$
$$TC = [(\$15,000) \times 80] - (\$300,000) - \$350,000$$
$$TC = [\$1,200,000] - \$650,000$$
$$TC = \$550,000$$

This has a positive contribution, so the company would be better off if the manager pursued this program. We can also see what the break-even volume would have to be for this program. If we set $TC = 0$, which is breakeven, we can solve easily for Q:

$$\$0 = [(P - VC) \times Q] - AC$$
$$AC = (P - VC) \times Q$$
$$Q = AC/(P - VC)$$
$$Q = [(120 \times \$2{,}500) + \$300{,}000 + \$50{,}000]/(\$25{,}000 - \$7{,}500 - \$2{,}500)$$
$$Q = [(\$300{,}000) + \$350{,}000]/\$15{,}000$$
$$Q = \$650{,}000/\$15{,}000$$
$$Q = 43.3 \text{ units}$$

So the break-even number of pizza ovens needed to be sold under this program is 44. The expected total of 80 is considerably more than the break-even number, so there would seem to be ample room for uncertainty. The manager should probably go ahead with this program. The final decision will depend on other alternatives and what their total contribution figures are. Any projects that return a positive contribution would improve the profitability of the company. However, there may be projects that are incompatible. If two projects are incompatible, the manager would choose to do the project with the higher contribution.

11

Business-to-Business Selling: Developing and Managing the Customer Relationship

overview. . . In previous chapters, we have stressed the importance of relationships and the value they add to business-to-business offerings. In this chapter, we focus on the seller,* who performs the sales function of the firm, making that relationship a reality. The discussion concentrates on the different roles that sellers can play, depending on the culture of both supplier and customer and the level of involvement of the buying center.

© EYEWIRE COLLECTION

The business-to-business selling process is more time-consuming and, ultimately, more personal than the consumer process. In business-to-business selling, the complexities of successful selling require the buyer and seller to develop mutual respect and trust, a luxury that sellers in consumer markets seldom have the opportunity to achieve.

The role of the business-to-business seller changes with the expectations of different customers and the nature of the offering. Throughout this chapter, we reinforce the notion that there is not necessarily a "way to sell," but there is certainly a way that customers want to buy. Ultimately, the most successful way to develop a sales organization is to match the way the customers want to buy.

The opening example tells the story of how Kinko's, the well-known chain of quick copy shops, created a program to increase its business-to-business sales by more than 50 percent, primarily through the power of relationships.

---

*The term "seller" is used often in this text to simplify "salesperson" nomenclature. While not used in this text as an exclusive replacement, "seller" is interchangeable with "saleswoman," "salesman," and "salesperson." We have seen this simplification used in industry.

KINKO'S PRINTS A BUSINESS-TO-BUSINESS PLAN*

In 1998, Kinko's, the 24-hour copy shop for business travelers who lost their luggage and students whose dog ate their homework, obtained approximately 20 percent of revenues from business clients. Efforts to attract business customers were largely left to the discretion of each local copy shop. Kinko's headquarters provided little assistance for business-to-business selling efforts. There was no clear vision, no common marketing plan, nor any common compensation process for efforts in the business-to-business market. As a result, sellers were little more than order takers, an extension of the retail shop, waiting for customers to come to them. Business-to-business sales were small, one-time corporate deals. There was little repeat business, and new business was difficult to forecast.

Kinko's management recognized that it had to turn its sales force from a collection of hardly managed order takers into a team of relationship-creating, problem-solving sellers. Business-to-business sales were reorganized. Management created a focus and goals. Sellers were encouraged to find long-term, profitable relationships with large customers. Marketing tools were created that helped sellers approach higher levels of management in potential customer organizations, enabling discussions of continuous duplicating services, rather than overflow copy making. A new Intranet site was developed with information on the new sales process, frequently asked questions, customer case studies, and aids for new employees approaching unfamiliar customers and customer types. To effectively use these new tools, the newly created 500-person sales organization was trained in a seven-step sales process that focused on building value for customers. Key to the success of the process was continuous communication with customers. They were no longer to be treated as "some people who need a rush set of copies" but as business partners who had selected Kinko's as the provider of choice for their copying and duplicating needs.

The results? Not only have sales increased more than 50 percent but sellers report that the new process, with common measurements, procedures, and more clearly defined offerings, assists in creating lasting relationships. Having gone from order takers to relationship builders/problem solvers has proved very satisfying. Turnover is lower, and sellers are excited about future prospects. Sales? Results are 110 percent of plan. Not bad for an organization that had not met its sales targets for the three previous years.

*Based on Andy Cohen, "Copy Cats," Sales & Marketing Management (August 2000): 50–58.

- Understand the roles of sales and the seller in business-to-business organizations.

- Understand the differences between selling in business-to-business markets and selling in consumer markets.

- Understand the basics of business-to-business sales force organization.

- Recognize the different types of sales representation that are most appropriate for offerings under different customer buying patterns.

- Understand the internal and external relationships necessary for successful sales and market development personnel.

- Recognize the different levels of selling associated with product types, rewards, and seller performance.

- Reinforce the necessity of understanding customers' needs and preferences in the building of a sustained organizational relationship.

introduction...

The seller in business-to-business markets plays a much larger role in the sales process than the seller of consumer products. In consumer markets, relationships between sellers and customers are usually brief, one-time events, with little personal information exchanged between the participants in the transaction. While some consumer product sellers may develop a clientele who return for repeat purchases, the relationship is sporadic. In business-to-business selling, however, the nature of the purchase and the characteristics of the process require an ongoing relationship between the seller and all of the stakeholders in the buying center. As discussed in Chapter 3, the buying process in business-to-business markets evolves through more intricate phases than the consumer purchase process; but, before we get involved in the specifics of business-to-business selling, we take a step back and look at the role of selling in general.

THE NATURE OF SALES AND SELLERS

Everyone has an idea of what sales "is." When the word *salesperson* is heard, most people have an immediate image of a sales stereotype based on individuals' experiences with salespeople they have dealt with or have heard about. The car salesperson, the insurance broker, the real estate agent—almost every entity we deal with will have a selling role associated with it. The diversity of these roles and the skills required to be successful make it almost impossible for any particular stereotype to accurately reflect the reality of the profession. However, we form our impressions from a limited sample and then generalize these into our stereotypes. Unfortunately, this leaves most people with a far too narrow view of selling.[1] Let us examine some broadening perceptions of the sales function.

Selling is a natural function. We all sell. In social situations, we find ourselves trying to "sell" to the rest of the group where to go to party that night; we see children trying to "sell" parents on why they need that new bicycle; and, at work, we

---

[1]Gilbert A. Churchill Jr., Neil M. Ford, and Orville C. Walker, *Sales Force Management,* 2d ed. (Homewood, Ill.: Richard D. Irwin, 1985), 4–7.

see coworkers selling their skills and accomplishments to the boss. At its most elementary level, selling is persuading.[2]

The form the persuasion takes and the style with which it is applied determine the success of the effort. Customers resent "pushy" sellers who they believe are attempting to force something on them that they do not need. Whether the resentment is the result of a seller who does not regard the needs of the customer as most important (fit the market to the product—a sales era strategy; see the later discussion on the evolution of sales philosophies) or whether there is a mismatch in acceptable persuasion techniques, the customer still feels resentment toward the seller. Better sellers, then, attempt to understand customers' personality and behavior variables and work to satisfy the intangible as well the tangible needs of the buyer.

Selling creates value for both the buyer and the seller. The principle of exchange, in which both the buyer and the seller possess greater value after the transaction, is instigated by the sales process. While at first appearing elementary, the review of this concept can be a grounding force for sellers and their managers who get caught up in the "meet the quota at any costs" short-term sales approach. In fact, in relationship-based sales organizations that operate with a strong sense of partnering with customers, the seller's role is often viewed as that of a value creator.[3]

Sellers are the front-line personnel, the first line of one-on-one communication with the prospective customer. The seller is an important part of the organization's value image.[4] Beyond "first impressions," the customer makes many judgments about the selling organization based on the image and presentation of the seller. In the customer's eyes, the seller is the selling organization. Conversely, if the seller competes well for organizational resources for his customers, the seller is the customer in the eyes of the selling organization. Sellers, particularly in partnering roles, are often called upon as the liaison to manage both intrafirm and interfirm conflicts.[5] Sellers, thus, are often in the role of **boundary personnel,** the diplomats of the organization.

> **Boundary personnel** is the term given to individuals in the organization who operate, as a significant part of their responsibilities, spanning the boundaries of their own organizations and those of customers. Both buyers and sellers have boundary roles. Actual job titles and levels in the company can vary, but the function of liaison and/or diplomat can be a major asset to the relationship between buyer and seller and, in some instances, across internal boundaries in the customer buying center.

CHARACTERISTICS OF BUSINESS-TO-BUSINESS SELLING

As summarized in Exhibit 11–1, business-to-business selling situations are different from consumer selling in many ways. As consumers, we seldom experience the level of professional selling necessary for survival in business-to-business markets. In business-to-business markets, the seller spends time building and nurturing

[2]V. R. Buzzotta, R. E. Lefton, and Manuel Sherberg, *Effective Selling through Psychology* (Cambridge, Mass.: Ballinger Publishing/Harper & Row, 1982), 3.

[3]Barton A. Weitz and Kevin D. Bradford, "Personal Selling and Sales Management: A Relationship Marketing Perspective," *Journal of the Academy of Marketing Science* 27, no. 2 (1999): 241–54.

[4]Paul Sherlock, *Rethinking Business to Business Marketing* (New York: The Free Press, 1991).

[5]Weitz and Bradford op. cit., 244.

EXHIBIT 11–1   Business-to-Business Selling Characteristics

- ◆ Repeated, ongoing relationships
- ◆ Solution-oriented, total system effort
- ◆ Long time period before selling effort pays off
- ◆ Continuous adjustment of needs
- ◆ Creativity in problem solving often demanded by buyer of seller

the personal and business relationship with several individuals throughout the buying center.

Repeated, Ongoing Relationship

The relationship between the seller and buying center members is often a series of **dyadic interactions.** The seller builds the enhancing elements of the relationship and minimizes the threats to the relationship over the course of these interactions, not unlike the way personal relationships are built over time through a series of get-togethers. As the duration and complexity of the relationship grows, the seller must convince the buyer of the seller's interest in the success of the buying organization and of the buyer as an individual. The repeated, ongoing nature of the relationship can eventually permit the seller to be a motivator (though not necessarily the prime mover) in new solutions for the buying organization.

Dyadic interactions are one-on-one meetings or sessions between stakeholders in the buying center and the seller or other individuals in the selling organization's value chain. A typical "sales call" by a seller on a buyer would qualify as a dyadic interaction, as would a meeting between a field marketing representative and the project manager of a new development effort in the buying organization.

Solution-Oriented, Total System Effort

A natural outcome of the seller's focus on the success of the buyer and the buying organization (though cause and effect could probably be argued) is a solution-oriented, "total system" effort or total offering approach. As repeated throughout and a major theme of this book, customers buy solutions, not technologies or core products. This approach, of course, requires the seller and the selling organization to fully understand the customer, including the customer's market environment and culture, as well as every facet of the differing needs of the buying center. The successful seller also understands the different motivating elements between members of the customer buying center. These factors contribute to a level of "knowing" that reinforces the relationship with the customer and assists the seller to develop and nurture an appropriate solution.

Long Time Period before Selling Effort Pays Off

In most consumer selling situations, the seller will know in a matter of minutes whether the sales effort has been successful. In business-to-business sales situations, the outcome of the effort may not be known for months or even years. For example, the complexity of decisions in the design of a new electric power facility may extend the period for selecting turbine suppliers for several months or longer. As described in Chapter 3 from a behavioral context and again in the discussion of the Marketing Operations Forecast in Chapter 6, the solution provider selection process is time-consuming. Astute sellers use the development period to reinforce the value of their offering versus potential competition throughout the development period. The level of risk associated with the selling organization's commitment of resources to the buying organization over this development period can be greatly reduced through effective reinforcement of the total value of the offering.

Continuous Adjustment of Needs

Sellers and selling organizations must be flexible and responsive to the changing needs of customers, particularly if the selling organization has joined with the customer in a mutual development effort. The next generation solution that results from the application development process may not be what was initially envisioned. The specific needs of customers evolve as they learn more about the product and how it can be applied to their needs. The development process is usually an education for both the buying and the selling organization.

Creativity Demanded of Seller by Buyer

Business-to-business customers, particularly large ones who may specify the use of significant quantities of the selling organization's products, expect an innovative and creative approach to their needs. They do not appreciate being offered the exact same solution as another customer, even if the success of the offering at the other customer is what attracted them to the supplier in the first place.

Approaching each customer's problems in a way that can be recognized as unique has subtle advantages to the seller. Unique offerings to customers who are in competition with each other can relieve the seller of many concerns regarding pricing and price discrimination. Unique offerings may very well have different costs associated with them. The supplier should also look to each new application of its capabilities to push the envelope into new areas.

THE ROLE OF SALES IN A MODERN ORGANIZATION

"Nothing happens until somebody buys (sells) something." This statement, and variations on the theme, are as true today as they have ever been. While new communications technologies such as the Internet and new management tools such as customer database management software have the capability to make the task more productive, buying and selling are still at the heart of business. This is probably the only constant in selling and sales management.

Relationship Sales and Marketing

The term *relationship selling* has been used frequently in recent years to describe the context of business-to-business selling. Unfortunately, there seems to be no clear definition for the term. In our experience, we have found that the "relationship" between seller and buyer is sometimes considered to be far less important in low-involvement, low-technology sales than it is in more involved situations. We do not necessarily agree with this position. In fact, given homogeneous products late in the product life cycle, the case could be made that the buyer-seller relationship is one of the important differentiators between competing suppliers. We believe that "the relationship" between buyer and seller is always important but that the nature of the relationship and the expectations of the parties involved change under different circumstances.

Defining What a Relationship Is
Successful relationships between suppliers and business customers involve mutual respect, trust, and authenticity. At this level of relationship, the business-to-business seller must demonstrate an authentic interest in the success of the customer as an individual and the customer's organization. Customers who place a high value on business relationships reciprocate in kind.

As is true with all marketing, relationship marketing is based on the concept of exchange. The intricacy and complexity of the exchange directly impact the nature of the relationship. We can then think of different levels of relationship associated with different levels of intricacy or complexity.[6]

> **Switching costs** are the costs to the buying organization of changing suppliers after an initial selection has been made and supply has begun. Switching costs result from, among other things, changes in logistical requirements, engineering and design, and services. Switching costs can create barriers to exit for firms, contributing to a customer feeling locked in to a particular supplier. Appropriately, incurring high switching costs should be mutually beneficial to both parties.

◆ *Discrete exchange.* Interaction is of a short duration, with a minimum of involvement. Applicable in one-time-only exchanges, these transactions have very low **switching costs.** There is little reason or motivation for any loyalty. Economy or necessity is often the primary motivation, with little interest by either party in an extension of the relationship. Sellers need not be much more than order takers.

◆ *Differentiating an undifferentiated product.* In competitive situations with homogeneous products, vendors seek to differentiate the total offering with the strength of the relationship between individuals and organizations. In these circumstances, the relationship often involves a greater degree of social interaction rather than collaboration or partnering in a new development. Ownership of the relationship is at the individual level, often fostered by the seller. The seller is in the role of a persuader or, in the case of continuing existing business, a sustainer.

---

[6]Michael H. Morris, Janinne Brunyee, and Michael Page, "Relationship Marketing in Practice," *Industrial Marketing Management* 27 (1998): 359–71, 361.

◆ *Multiple transactions.* Interaction is repeated, and individual transactions tend to merge into an ongoing **relational exchange.** In these situations, there is usually mutually high investment by supplier and customer. Both social and economic interaction occurs, and both parties see strategic implications in continuing the relationship. Mutual benefits exist. The goals of the buying and selling organizations have evolved to be interdependent. Beyond persuasion, sellers become problem solvers and effective resources for the customer. The seller in this role has opportunities to encourage and motivate customers toward processes, technologies, and techniques that reinforce the use of its offerings.

> **Relational exchange** is the term given to customer-supplier relationships where the interaction recognizes the long-term benefit of the combination. Interdependence is an accepted, even fostered element of the relationship.

◆ *Collaboration/partnering.* A level of intimacy is proactively sought by both parties. In business-to-business markets, organizations interested in obtaining the best value from their suppliers view the suppliers' representatives, whether sellers or marketers, as resources. The parties involved work toward bringing the capabilities of the supplying firm and the customer firm together to provide value for each party. Both buyer and seller view the relationship as a potential element in their competitive advantage.[7] These relationships are strategic in nature, fostered by senior management in both organizations. The relationship is dynamic, with each organization actively seeking opportunities for the other. In many cases, these relationships lead to joint operations or ventures that are mutually beneficial. At the extreme, this level of collaboration can lead to acquisition of one party by the other.[8] The selling role in this context is one of relationship/value creation.

Relationships and Attitude   In practice, a major element of many relationships is attitude rather than behavior.[9] The attitude and culture of the organization and how they are reflected in the attitude of individual sellers and marketers will imply certain behaviors toward customers. All relationships are not of the partnering level, nor should they be. Relationships imply investment by both parties, and not all suppliers or customers will perceive the other party as a viable investment. Many sales and marketing relationships, while having elements of both social interaction and partnering, are haphazard rather than planned. The costs and benefits of complex relationships vary and are often very difficult to quantify. Like any relationship, both parties must want the relationship to work. In some instances, buyers will not want any type of relationship other than that which is purely transaction-based. Though this is not the norm, selling organizations must be willing to accept this view.

---

[7] Arun Sharma, Nikolaos Tzokas, Michael Saren, and Panagiotis Kyziridis, "Antecedents and Consequences of Relationship Marketing," *Industrial Marketing Management* 28 (1999): 601–611.

[8] Morris et al. propose a *common* working definition for *all* relationships, defining relationship as "a strategic orientation adopted by both buyer and seller organizations, which represents a commitment to long-term mutually beneficial collaboration." This is similar to the collaboration/ partnering definition discussed here, but we do not concur with its universal application.

[9] Morris et al., op. cit., 369.

The Philosophies of Marketing

Different eras in business history have spawned different marketing eras/philosophies. These eras or philosophies assist in the understanding of marketing and its role in business and society. All organizations, however, have not moved on to the marketing or societal marketing theme. Depending on corporate culture and marketing environment, some firms continue today to embrace earlier philosophies.

- *Production era and product era.* Management focus is on maximizing consumption, making sales the objective of sellers. Production efficiency has high value, while, with little or no effort to understand customer needs, customization is almost nonexistent. In the production era, supply is not always able to keep up with demand. Early beginnings of product differentiation occurs in the product era. Sellers are order takers.
- *Sales era.* Sellers still focus on making sales, and maximizing consumption is still important, though some attention is paid to customer needs. "Fit the market to the product." Sellers use persuasive techniques, often interpreted as a hard-sell approach.
- *Marketing era.* The primary objective of the sales force is satisfying customer needs. Conceptually, this marketing philosophy works to maximize choice in the market. Differentiation efforts extend to the total offering.
- *Societal/partnering/value network era.* (Many terms have been used to describe this era.) The sales force objective is to build stable, long-term relationships. Conceptually, this marketing philosophy works to maximize relationship/ life quality.

Relationships and Loyalty   The basis for long-term relationships is satisfaction with prior experiences between the parties. (Note that this relationship can be either individually based or organizationally based. Obviously, organizations will seek to ensure that the relationship grows beyond the individuals involved to protect the firms from employee job changes.) The longer the relationship has had to mature, the greater its stability. Loyal customers remain loyal after an unsatisfactory experience.[10] (Recall the relationship of Ford Motor Company and Firestone, used in Chapter 1, Exhibit 2. The relationship between Ford and Firestone dates back to a close friendship between each company's founder. The recent severing of the relationship as a result of the Firestone tire debacle is surprising, and Firestone tires are not likely to be found on many new Ford products in the near future.)

Relationships and Corporate Culture   Increases in competition and the ever shorter life span of new technology are contributing to the evolution from product selling to offering selling (i.e., transaction-based to relationship-based sales). The diversity of choices available to customers makes it more difficult to be the seller of the customer's choice. Depending on the philosophy of marketing or culture under which the firm operates (see Chapter 1 and box above, "The Philosophies of Marketing"), sellers will be focused on different objectives and be expected to perform

---

[10]Sharma et al., op. cit.

different tasks.[11] Corporate culture and the level of importance in the firm's marketing mix given to customer relationships will determine the approach of the seller. In product- or sales-driven organizations, sellers are measured and rewarded by the short-term results obtained. Seller objectives are focused on meeting the needs of the selling organization—selling more now. If the organization is truly customer/market driven, the seller is measured and rewarded with longer-range goals in mind. Seller objectives are focused on satisfying customer needs. Recall the success of Kinko's business-to-business sales force when management transformed order takers into relationship-creating sellers. One of the key things that Kinko's management did was change the nature of the objectives that sellers were accountable for.

Four Forms of Seller Roles

Given the preceding discussion on the components of and types of relationships, we can define seller role patterns for different organizational cultures and types of offerings.[12] These roles vary by complexity of skills required of the seller, proactivity, and the degree to which the relationship is transactional or value creating. The names we have assigned to the different seller roles, depending on organization and offerings are:

1. The order taker
2. The persuader/sustainer
3. The motivator/problem solver
4. The relationship/value creator

The Order Taker   The **order taker's** primary role is taking orders and ensuring timely delivery of the correct products. The buyer's need for product and the seller's need for short-term sales results are the driving factors in the relationship. Most selling efforts are concentrated on making potential customers aware of stable product offerings. A major part of the marketing mix is place, providing locational convenience and timely delivery. Product types associated with this type of selling are usually in the late maturity or decline stage of the product life cycle. Users may be conservatives or laggards as described by the technology adoption life cycle, generally avoiding risk associated with innovative offerings. Little if any customer education is required to obtain maximum value from the product, as the market is familiar with the technology. Sellers are rewarded based on short-term results. Product- and sales-driven selling organizations that rely on this type of transactional selling are unlikely to have the skills or approach to handle more sophisticated, innovative offerings.

---

[11]Weitz and Bradford op. cit., 242.

[12]Sherlock suggested three "levels" of selling, A, B, and C, in *Rethinking Business-to-Business Marketing*. C level was doing everything right but just maintaining the landscape, B level was all of C level plus the ability to establish and maintain the customer relationship, and A level was all of B level plus the ability to live up to the customer's archetypical model of seller. This description has proven useful to demonstrate some of the psychological aspects of selling but does not consider all of the factors noted here.

Participation Exercise

Look in the yellow pages or the business directory for your area. How many business-to-business service organizations have names that creatively (or not!) put them at the beginning of an alphabetical list of providers? What type of customers might these providers be looking for?

At first glance, it may seem like the order taker can be replaced to a large extent by an Internet Web site. In many instances, this may be possible. Certainly, a well-developed Web site can prove a valuable productivity-enhancing asset to both buyers and sellers. However, this works as long as the Internet-based relationships are primarily transactional. When there is an element of personal service required, Web-based systems have not yet proven to be good substitutes. The quality and depth of the selling relationship become major differentiating elements of the marketing mix.

In the opening example about Kinko's, the company business-to-business sales organization, before the change described, was made up primarily of order takers. As described in the opening, this reactive sales model can make repeat business subject to significant reselling effort. If the buyer feels that it has been the proactive party in the transaction, it is more likely to seek assistance from any number of homogeneous providers.

One type of the order taker role is the inside sales/customer service specialist. The individual in this position seldom meets customers in person. The relationship is usually over the telephone or via e-mail. The primary functions of the position are to administer the sales order system of the supplier and to facilitate the logistics needs of the customer. Many of the commitments related to availability and delivery made by the field selling organization are satisfied by the efforts of the inside sales team. Known by many titles (sales service specialist, order facilitator, customer service representative, etc.), these individuals are often the backbone of internal customer order handling. In the case of routine purchases, the inside sales team is often the direct contact for the customer. Once a customer buying pattern is established, a proficient sales service specialist anticipates orders and proactively solicits routine business buyers in the customer organization. The inside sales team serves the field seller by freeing time for relationship building and value creation and serves the customer by always being available to take, track, and expedite orders.

The Persuader/Sustainer
The development of the order taker relationship into a major differentiating element of the marketing mix leads to the **persuader/sustainer** role for the seller. In this role, short-term results are still the primary sales orientation. However, the seller takes a more proactive role in the relationship.

As a persuader, the seller continuously informs and updates customers about products and offerings. The persuader attempts to convince the customer of the value of the product versus the competition's, though the focus is still on the needs of the selling organization. (Fit the market to the product.) Though we believe a hard-sell approach is of diminishing value in business-to-business sales, the persuader often resorts to such techniques to obtain orders now rather than later. In this selling situation, product types, though similar to the order taker scenario, are still evolving and thus have an added degree of heterogeneity. Some customer education may be necessary. The product is likely in the maturity stage, and differentiation from horizontal competition does not rest solely on price.

As a sustainer, the seller has a responsibility beyond that of obtaining short-term sales to include maintaining and nurturing an existing relationship with established customers. In the circumstances described here, customers look to the supplier for help in making the best selection among heterogeneous offerings. As described in Chapter 6 and in the box, "New Business, Translation, and Churn," this sales role is most likely to deal with business that would be described as core churn. Because of the differentiable nature of the product and the variety of alternatives, the sustainer must actively recognize the role of sales in maintaining the positioning and image of the selling organization.

The Motivator/Problem Solver

Customers rely on sellers for advice, particularly as product offerings become more innovative and complex or require a significant degree of customer education to obtain full value. Under these circumstances, the persuader/sustainer evolves into the **motivator/problem solver.** This is not, however, automatic. The selling organization must be market driven—sensitive to customer needs. The type of offering described (complex, innovative) and the need to assist customers in maximizing the value received would seem to naturally apply to products in the introduction or growth stage of the product life cycle. Depending on the level of customer education necessary and the level of customer interest in new and innovative offerings, typical customers are visionaries or pragmatists. In this scenario, the selling organization has a much different task than in prior role descriptions.

The motivator/problem solver is part of a sales force whose primary objective is satisfying customer needs. This is accomplished less through short-term sales goals and more through the ability to create unique customer solutions through matching of supplier capabilities with customer needs. The seller is expected to fully understand the customer organization, its culture, buying habits, processes, and its customers. This level of knowledge assists in anticipating customer needs or recognizing problems where seller solutions can be applied. This type of business often fits the description of translation business—often proving the segment through discovery.

The motivator/problem solver is most certainly considered a resource by the customer. Customers, as described earlier in this chapter, demand creativity and commitment on the part of the seller. The motivational aspect of this selling role consists of the seller's ability to encourage customer product development personnel to incorporate the offerings of the supplier. Involvement begins early in the

---

New Business, Translation, and Churn

Different types of "new business" require different seller resources. *Real* new business is the result of a major R&D, product development, and/or marketing effort, usually in conjunction with a customer. This results in first-time applications or adoptions of technologies. Many parts of the organization are involved. These are the applications and efforts that everyone in the organization find the most exciting. Seller resources required for *real* new business include training with the product, training on matching customer needs to product capabilities, prospecting assistance, and other market intelligence. *Real* new business produces new revenue but usually incurs greater selling costs than either translation or core churn.

Most "new business," of course, is not *real* new business, not a "first-of-its-kind" application of new products or technologies. While a partnership with the customer may have developed a specification for your company's product, and it may be new in the view of that customer, it is not "new" to your organization. It is merely a translation of a previous success with another customer. In translation business, sellers must be accustomed to the new products and uses among prior customers. Some prospecting assistance may be required. The revenue is new to the company, and the costs will not be as great as with real new business.

What if the translation business replaces an application of your older technology product? Is this business still considered new? It certainly requires an effort by the team to get the business; however, it should not require as large an effort—assuming the translation tools were adequate and the customer relationship has been at least sustained. Unfortunately, the organization does not experience an increase in business volume equal to the sales of the new product. The seller realizes the net of the old and new volumes. This replacement business, core churn, is necessary, important, and critical to market ownership but not as glamorous to the team as *real* new business. Such selling effort requires some new resources in terms of product and usage knowledge but usually generates the lowest level of the three in the way of additional selling costs.

The organization needs all three types of new business—real, translation, and churn. Each type has different implications of margins, customer support, and product development—the entire marketing mix.

---

new-task buying process. The closer the relationship between supplier and customer, the earlier in the buying decision process this influence can be applied.

For the motivator/problem solver approach to be successful, the seller must expand the sphere of influence to a greater number of stakeholders in the buying center. This is a major distinction between this role and the role of the persuader/sustainer. This proactive approach begins to take on the appearance of field market development. Sales management, recognizing that compensation must be tied to results, is challenged as a larger quantity of seller resources become committed to development of solutions rather than maintaining existing sales. (Compensation is discussed later in this chapter.) When the supplier has a line of products that require significant customer education, the likelihood increases that the customer development process will require considerable attention.

The complexity of motivator/problem solver objectives has led management in many organizations to recognize the value of splitting the functions into a sales role and a missionary sales/field marketing role. When this occurs, it is important that the field marketer reporting arrangement is to the marketing organization, freeing the individual from short-term sales objectives. (In our experience, the title of the field marketer position varies and sometimes holds little descriptive evidence of the job function—i.e., customer engineer, product evangelist, etc. See the later "Missionary Sellers/Field Marketers" section.)

The opening example about Kinko's readily demonstrates the value of the motivator/problem solver role even with products and offerings that, at first glance, may seem generic. Since the rebuilding of Kinko's business-to-business sales force, new business-to-business customers are not likely to see the service provided as generic, particularly since the offering has been tailored to the individual needs of the customer.

The Relationship/Value Creator

In the **relationship/value creator** role, sellers are expected to build and maintain relationships with all elements of the customer buying center. The relationship between supplier and customer develops into a partnership that it is mutually inspiring and stimulating. Both supplier and customer recognize an equity in each other where their success is tied to the other party's success. Rather than an individual seller effort, these relationships are often built by sales and marketing *teams.*[13] Value is created by both customer and supplier teams, and each appreciates the value of the other. In this role, the selling objective is to creatively join supplier capabilities with customer needs. The outcome of this effort would be "new business" development (as opposed to translation or core churn).

The partnering role of value creation adds many different tasks to the responsibilities of the seller. The seller becomes a liaison between elements of the supplier value chain and the customer buying center. In this role, the seller is a diplomat, a manager of conflicts, a resource allocation expert, and a director of a team whose mission it is to provide value to both organizations. There is no mention of maximizing short-term sales or persuasion tactics.[14] In fact, short-term results are often sacrificed to build the relationship and the associated long-term benefits.

At this level of relationship, there is not anything that is not the seller's job. A crucial element of success in this type of customer-supplier relationship is the commitment of senior management of *both* firms. Customers must be equally interested in relationships at this level. It is important that all members of the team, both customer and supplier, understand the nature of the relationship.[15]

The relationship/value creator is a more sophisticated sales approach than other role models described here. The seller must be solution oriented, for the needs of both the customer and the supplier. This more sophisticated approach requires a more complex set of seller and selling organization skills. This context is not served

[13]Weitz and Bradford, op. cit.

[14]Weitz and Bradford, op. cit., 244.

[15]Sharma et al., op. cit., 605.

Knowing Your Markets

Knowing your markets includes knowing and understanding:

- *The customers' technologies.* Learn how your customers' technology and willingness to apply it impact the application of your products.
- *The customers' products.* What is your customer going to use your product or service for? What will be expected of it? By understanding your customers' products and their fit in the market, you can better anticipate needs and head off problems—and competitors.
- *The customers' markets and customers.* Your distinctive competency may well provide an opportunity for your customers in their market—but first you have to know what they are attempting to achieve. Know where their next opportunity is and make it your next opportunity.
- *The customers' competitors.* This should not be a surprise, but your customers' competitors either are your customers also or should be.
- *The customers' channels.* How do your customers reach their customers? What level of missionary sales effort, such as customer education and inventory assistance, do your customers provide? Can you assist with channel logistics in any way? Are there buying habits in the end-user market that dictate a particular channel behavior that is not ordinary (i.e., accompanying a companion offering or a channel dictated by the way customers buy related products)?
- *The customers' buying center and buying patterns.* How do your customers make decisions? Do they have several levels of decision making, or are decisions made quickly with little oversight?
- *The customers' culture.* Just as you may treat a market or technology differently from your competitors in an attempt to differentiate yourself, your customers are doing the same thing. "Certain companies buy from certain companies." Tradition, long-term relationships, logistical considerations, common enemies, and many other factors make up your customer's culture.

Chapter 6 discusses *knowing your markets* in greater detail.

by the typical sales training advice on selling tactics. Suppliers and their sellers must have a strategic vision of the customer's industry and the customer's fit in it.[16]

Knowledge of the customer's market environment, an understanding of the nature of the customer's business and the customer's approach, is also important. (See Chapter 6 regarding *knowing your markets,* summarized in the box above.) Individual seller capabilities should also include strong interpersonal skills, business analysis skills, and problem-solving skills.[17]

Other Types of Selling Roles

As we have discussed throughout this text, the customer decision process and usage situation for many business-to-business products and services are so complex

[16]Todd Kulik, "Forging an Effective Sales Organization," *The Conference Board* (1999): 13.
[17]Ibid.

that several other selling-related roles are needed to successfully deliver value to the customer. The two most important of these are the missionary sales person and the post-sale customer service provider.

Missionary Sellers/Field Marketers

The four models of seller roles we have described evolve from simple order taking into complete immersion in the internal organization of the customer. When the supplier/customer relationship is complex—such that significant sales and business development are ongoing or when the development period is significantly long, regardless of the existing sales relationship—it is inappropriate to expect sellers, compensated on commission with a short-term focus, to be responsible for the development effort. In these cases, creation of a *field market development* (FMD) team can separate the long- and short-term efforts into more appropriate field functions. Missionary sellers/field marketers (MS/FMDs) are known by several position titles (customer engineers, product evangelists, market development specialists, to name a few) but are best categorized as field marketers.

Field marketers are critical in finding new prospective customers, finding and testing new market segments to address, and in developing new business within existing customer accounts. As we discussed in Chapter 3, the initial phase of the customer's decision process may extend over a relatively long period of time, particularly when the product or service includes significant learning or represents a significant departure from the way that the customer is used to operating. The missionary sales person then must be adept at building relationships and participating with those relationships to create value for both parties.

Recall that, as footnoted in Chapter 3, missionary sellers are part of the marketing organization. Exhibit 11–2 shows a typical organization that uses the dual field approach of sales and marketing. The field marketing team, consisting of MS/FMDs, reports to the marketing manager through a field manager. The MS/FMDs can be located in headquarters but are more effective as field positions, sharing regional facilities with the field sales team. The MS/FMDs' primary functions are as relationship/value creators, working with members of the buying center at the specifying customer.

The field sales organization shown in Exhibit 11–2 has a primary role of either motivators/problem solvers or persuader/sustainers. Purchasing influences in integrated customer organizations that buy directly from the seller, as well as influences at contract providers who supply to the specifying customer, make up the primary field sales relationships.

As described in Chapter 6, these field marketers are often the individuals who are responsible for the marketing operations forecast (MOF). As part of the marketing operation, these marketers can rely on the entire marketing management chain to reinforce value creation efforts at various levels of the customer organization, leaving the sales organization to concentrate on short-term revenue generation. Regardless of level, the purposes pursued are the same: to obtain information, establish rapport, to educate, and to explore ways that the supplier can create

EXHIBIT 11–2   Organizational Relationship between Field Sales and Field Marketing

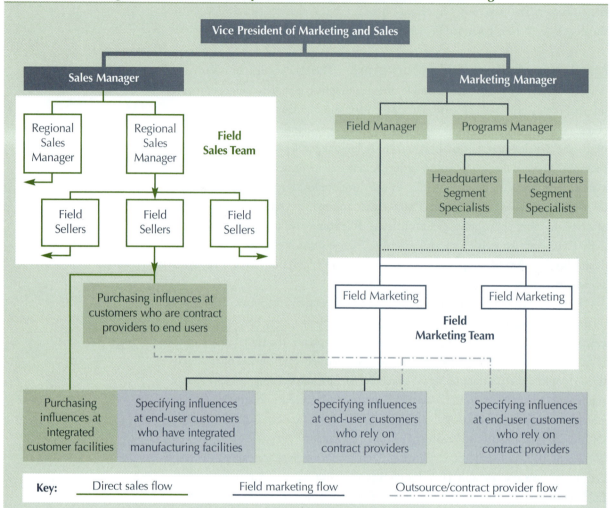

value for the customer. These activities can begin the establishment of an ongoing partnership and insert the supplier into the customer's decision process for future purchases.

Post-Sale Customer Service

For many relationships, the customer organization needs considerable attention and assistance from the supplier organization to effectively use the products or services it purchases. Effective customer service can make the difference between delivering superior value to the customer and having a customer that is not fully satisfied. Obviously in the latter case, the relationship may be degraded or even terminated. Accordingly, it is important to provide the right kind of service and to do so effectively.

Customer service done right is expected; done wrong is a disaster. Service requirements can cover a range of needs, including product or process design assistance, marketing planning and execution assistance, installation, training, troubleshooting, repair, and upgrades. In some cases, suppliers provide customers with assistance in product design and management.

Two principal problems must be addressed to provide good customer service in business-to-business markets. First, the service has to be useful and appropriate for the customer. In many business markets, the customers are few in number and their needs unique. Accordingly, the customer service staff must be skilled in tailoring its service to the customer's special needs—major customers may be provided with dedicated, specialized service personnel within the supplier organization. In other markets, the customers are numerous and varied. Customer service personnel must be able to handle service requests quickly and appropriately.

© EYEWIRE COLLECTION

The second principal problem to be addressed is that service must be provided in a cost-effective manner. Service costs are usually imbedded in the price of the offering, unless the customer specifically declines that level of packaged value. When service is sold as a separate offering, that offering can be subject to close scrutiny by the customer. Still, the service organization must be able to manage costs in such a way that profitability is maintained.

Customer service situations are opportunities to build and reinforce the customer relationship, not cost-based situations to be avoided. A product problem that could become a major issue can be transformed into a service success, creating "a fan" of the customer. Poor customer service only reinforces the initial difficulties that caused the customer to seek aid in the first place. Because customer service can be so important to providing value to customers, the marketer should be involved in the design of the service offering or in directing the personal interaction required between service provider and customer. Service should be provided in a way that furthers the relationship with the customer.

This task of building customer relationships through service is made more difficult when the service delivery model does not provide for continuity of contact between the customer and individual service personnel. It is important that the service organization have some sort of institutional memory in such cases. Suppose, for example, a technical problem arises at a customer site. If the service organization has a database of interaction histories, the service person that gets the call can see the service history and have more information on which to base a solution.

Customer relationship management (CRM) software and services have been developed and deployed in recent years that have greatly improved suppliers' ability to deliver good service. The software keeps track of all orders and service provided. It gives any service personnel updated information on the complete history of every customer. It tracks current order progress and current service progress. It further gives callback schedules and reminders.

Good service people can also initiate the customer decision process for future purchases. A good CRM system (automated or not) prepares the service people to recognize opportunities through observation of other customer problems and to begin the collaboration between customer and supplier toward finding a solution.

Management Perspective

In all of the roles we have discussed, management must consider what the selling organization is trying to accomplish and match that with what the best information available says that the customer organization is trying to accomplish. The most sophisticated seller role does not automatically work with all customers. Developing a sales force and establishing the context for the sales relationship require an understanding of what is seen as having value by both the supplier and the customer.

Exhibit 11–3 generalizes the correlation of value and relationship complexity. While this summary is a generalized case, it does illustrate that the appropriate sales force design is dependent on many factors, often situational.

In Exhibit 11–3, the shading of transactional sales and relationship sales bars is not intended to imply that relationships have no significance in transactional sales. In fact, a strong case can be made that the buyer/seller relationship may be one of the strongest factors by which the product is differentiated from the horizontal competition.

The increasing complexity of the buyer-seller relationship can be based on many factors, such as the size of the buying center, the need for customer training, design assistance, and the overall attitude and approach to relationships by the customer organization. Responsibilities and coincident training needs of the seller will vary with the expected role type the seller will play. Different customers and organizations place different performance and relationship expectations on the seller. As the sales relationships depicted in Exhibit 11–3 become more reliant on a value orienta-

EXHIBIT 11–3   Correlation of Value and Complexity of Relationships: A Generalized Case

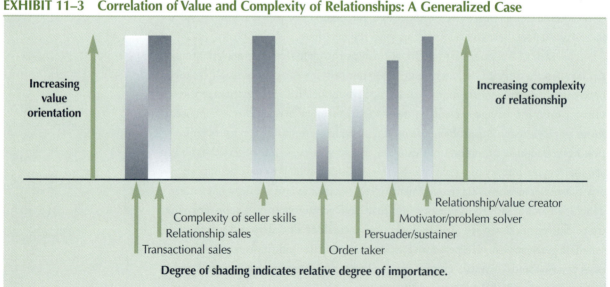

Increasing value orientation

Increasing complexity of relationship

Complexity of seller skills
Relationship sales
Transactional sales
Order taker
Persuader/sustainer
Motivator/problem solver
Relationship/value creator

Degree of shading indicates relative degree of importance.

tion and an increasing complexity of the buyer-seller relationship, the demands on the skills of the seller increase. The seller roles will be a reflection of management commitment and support. Based on the commitment of senior management in both the supplier and customer organizations, the relationship/value creator role is far more likely to create value with technophile and innovator customers and sellers.

THE MUTUAL NEEDS OF BUYER AND SELLER

In effective dyadic relationships, the creation of value is not limited to the immediate task at hand. Both buyer and seller will have expectations of the role each will play and how individual and organizational needs will be met. The most effective relationship is one in which the individuals involved recognize the factors that make each other a success. What defines success, however, is broader than satisfactorily completing the immediate task and varies with the individuals involved. With this in mind, consider that organizational buyers and sellers have three needs to satisfy:

1. The needs of the job function
2. The needs of the organization
3. The individual needs of the buyer and seller

The Needs of the Job Function

At the most elementary level, each member of the buying center in the customer organization, as well as each member of the value creation team in the supplier organization, has a specific, short-term job to perform. Tactical sales trainings and purchasing seminars cover the necessary content of "good selling and buying." It is not our intention to elaborate in this area. Our emphasis is with the context or attitude of the effort. In most selling efforts, it is no longer adequate to "just sell" and not be concerned with satisfying customer needs beyond the immediate trans-action, just as in buying, it is not wise to leverage a supplier in a manner that threatens long-term survival. Exhibit 11–4 takes a look at some of these issues.

Both sides of the relationship have job-related tasks that must be performed to achieve a minimum degree of success. Other members of each organization rely on them to meet day-to-day expectations associated with the job function. Within the

EXHIBIT 11–4   Relationships Have to Work Both Ways

Though the relationship has received attention lately, the automotive industry has always talked of the Tier 1 supplier base as a group of critically important suppliers. To reduce their own design and development costs, the auto makers have encouraged suppliers to take on development of vehicle modules—entire suspension systems, interior seating systems, climate control, and other subsystems. Though major suppliers would incur higher costs as a result of these modular design efforts, they were assured that their efforts would be considered at price-setting time. In other words, the ideal partnership is building relationships that create value for both parties.

There have been a few problems. It seems that as soon as the overall automotive market turns down or one auto maker gets into a profit squeeze, suppliers are asked to make up the difference. The first episode was in 1992 when Jose Ignacio Lopez, then purchasing chief for General Motors, forced, with the threat of losing the business, suppliers to cut costs. This began an all-out war between GM and suppliers that lasted through much of the 1990s. Supplier relationships crumbled. GM never realized the savings that Lopez projected, and supplier quality and performance declined. Even after Lopez left GM for VW, his name became an icon for relationship busting and price cutting.

During the period that GM was damaging relationships, Chrysler had come from near-bankruptcy into a period of prosperity. Chrysler insisted that it knew the value of supplier relationships, as suppliers could make or break the company. Suppliers were encouraged to work with Chrysler to find cost savings, and both suppliers and Chrysler shared in the outcome. Suppliers rated Chrysler as their favorite customer. In 2000, however, Chrysler, part of Daimler-Chrysler since 1998, was in trouble. Group CEO Dieter Zetsche announced that, effective immediately, Chrysler would reduce all purchasing contract prices by 5 percent. Under the new rules, if a supplier shipped goods, they were agreeing to the new terms. In effect, Chrysler "did a Lopez." In fact, trade press editorials soon had headlines like "Lopez All Over Again." Some industry commentators called it extortion. Suppliers, however, sent their own shock back to Chrysler. Seventy percent of Chrysler suppliers said no. Supplier commentary was similar: "They can't say partnership in good times when we spend development funds and then say cut margins when they have a problem. We can't afford it. It does not benefit us in the long run. Quality and warranty costs will suffer."

The debate over long-term relationships versus transaction-based relationships goes on. Will Chrysler benefit from the arbitrary price cut? Maybe a little in the short term. However, GM is still haunted by supplier memories of Lopez. It is unlikely that either company will recover good working relationships with suppliers as long as they treat them as commodities. Customers, too, must be responsible for the long-term benefit of supplier relationships. GM found out. Kinko's figured it out. It is now Chrysler's turn.

Sources: Based on several reports: Mark Yost, "Suppliers Say Ghost of GM's Lopez Haunts Online Auctions," *The Wall Street Journal/Dow Jones Newswires* (March 8, 2000); Lindsay Brooke, "It's Not Business, It's Extortion," *Automotive Industries* (March 2001), 7; Ron Harbour, "Nothing to Give Back," *Automotive Industries* (March 2001), 16; Maryann Keller, "Lopez All Over Again?" Automotive Industries (March 2001), 19; and Gerry Kobe, "Supplier Squeeze," *Automotive Industries* (March 2001), 26–30.

selling organization, these expectations depend on the type of seller roles employed. Within the buying organization, role types are determined by the complexity of the purchase, from new task to routine repurchase. The number of participants in the buying center and the value creation team will change, depending on the purchase complexity and frequency of the purchase. In a customer-sensitive organization, the selling team becomes a mirror of the buying team. In other words, sellers will sell the way buyers want to buy.

The Needs of the Organization

As previously stated, it is no longer adequate to "just sell." The needs of the supplier and customer organizations extend beyond the short-term needs of the job functions

---

Fruits, Flowers, Potted Plants, and Chocolate

A substantial part of relationship building is getting to know the customer beyond the work environment. Still an accepted part of the sales relationship is business entertainment. Entertainment can take the form of meals, attendance at conferences, tickets to sporting events, and similar gratuities. Many companies have policies that limit the extent of these events to prevent abuses from either buyer or seller.

Sellers often find that they have pulled customers away from their families with business-related meetings, trips, or occasional sporting events. This does not help the customer with their family relationship. In an effort to turn the home conversation from "Are you going to the baseball game with those business buddies again tonight?" into something positive, many astute sellers reward the home environment with delivery of flowers, candy, fruit baskets, or other tokens of appreciation. The intended message is "We recognize your sacrifice for our business—we just wanted to let you know we appreciate it." Hopefully, this turns the conversation into something like "You're going to the conference with them—hey, the flowers they sent were beautiful."

Some care should be taken in this venture. Do not send house plants to people who have serious allergies, and avoid candy if someone is on a diet. Most of all, be sure to let the business associate know that the gesture will happen. A few years ago, a major airline forgot this part. As part of an effort to lure more business travelers, the airline offered a "spouse flies free" to business travelers. They thought they had a very successful promotion until they mailed "Thank you for flying with us" cards to the homes of business travelers. Rumor has it that not so many spouses had actually made those trips!

---

of buyers and sellers. Members of the buying organization will place demands on the selling organization that will be focused by the buying center through the seller. Sellers, then, not only need to be competent in representation of their product or offering but also must represent the image, culture, and value potential of all elements of the company they represent. Sellers have an obligation to their organization on a day-to-day basis, to be goodwill ambassadors and crisis management specialists. In the eyes of the customer, the seller is the selling organization.

Just as customers place demands on sellers that are beyond traditional transactional roles, the supplier expects its sellers to have an extensive familiarity with the backgrounds of their customers. Sellers are the first source of information about the customers. Sellers have an obligation to their own organization not only to know what the customers buy and how/when they will use it but also are expected to understand the customers' businesses well enough to anticipate, with an adequate degree of confidence, how decisions will be made (refer again to box "Knowing Your Markets" on page 350).

Buying activities of customers also extend beyond just a transactional nature. It is up to the seller to recognize the organizational demands placed on each stakeholder in the buying center and to be a part of the resolution of those demands. As discussed earlier in this chapter, attitude is a major factor in the successful relationship. Both sellers and buyers need to recognize that they are the first level of interaction in the business-to-business relationship.

The Individual Needs of the Buyer and Seller

Beyond job function and organizational needs, individuals in buying and selling roles have career, personal, and professional needs that are part of their goals. Sellers that recognize the mutual nature of these needs can be far more effective in building relationships and creating value for both organizations.

For professionals, rewards and goals go beyond monetary compensation. Individual needs related to career advancement, recognition, professional organization membership, and office holding and authoring of journal articles and features are all possible goals or needs felt by different members of the organization. Particularly in situations in which the offering is a result of a joint development effort by supplier and customer, there are opportunities to recognize individuals in both organizations. As the new business is prepared for translation through the discovery process, contributors can be acknowledged by sponsorship of technical papers featuring the participants as authors.

Buyers may also have aspirations that are related to how they are perceived in their roles ("make me a hero in my organization") or how they are perceived by family and personal relationships. Suppliers have opportunities to play a role in the attainment of these goals. There may even be opportunities, within the bounds of ethics and good taste, to impact perception in the home environment (see box, "Fruits, Flowers, Potted Plants, and Chocolate").

SELLING—THE STRUCTURE

Should the business-to-business supplier employ its own **direct sales force**, establish an agreement with a **manufacturer's representative**, or rely on **distributors**

Selling Structures

A *direct sales force* consists of personal field sellers directly employed by the supplier of the offering and support staff and resources. Sellers' responsibility may be defined by product or customer type, geographic region, or another segmentation scheme that meets customer needs and creates a manageable workload for the seller. Direct sales is the most costly type of selling structure.

Manufacturers' representatives are independent businesspersons who act as a supplier's agent or representative in a particular market segment. Manufacturers' representatives usually represent several noncompeting manufacturers who rely on the "rep" for account coverage. Reps do not take ownership of the goods they represent. Reps are compensated by commissions on the products they sell.

A *distributor* represents manufacturer's goods by taking ownership and providing local inventory to businesses in the region. Distributors provide many other business services involved with form, time, place, and possession—the four types of economic utility. Distributors make money by buying products from suppliers at wholesale prices and reselling them to final customers with distributor's markup (added margin).

for sales coverage? The answer to this question depends on the nature of the offering, the concentration of customers, and the manner in which customers want to buy the product or service. Chapter 12 focuses on the rationale for using distributors and the development of various types of marketing channels. In this chapter, we examine the underlying principles behind the use of either direct sellers or manufacturers' representatives or, in some circumstances, a combination of both.

Sales Force Organization

The direct sales force can be organized in several different ways. This brief summary describes only the most common types of organization. The most common sales force organization is by geographic territory. Firms with multiple products may organize by product, particularly when different products do not have the same customer base or **call pattern.** When a firm has a large concentration of customers in a particular area, such as the automobile industry in Detroit, the computer industry in Silicon Valley, or the oil and gas industry in Houston, the sales team may be organized to focus on that particular customer type. An extension of this type of organization may be the "national accounts" or "account manager" position. This is useful when one customer has many locations that are served on a daily basis by many different sellers. Such a situation would occur with a customer like IBM, with major facilities and buying centers throughout the world. An account manager is the coordinator of all the individual efforts. Of course, depending on the collection of products and offerings, different suppliers may elect to use any combination of these types of organization. Whatever sales organization structure is used, firms must recognize that the organization should match the buying habits and patterns of customers, not the convenience of the firm.

> A sales **call pattern** is dependent on the type of selling involved with a product and the type of customer base. Products with similar buying styles, habits, customer types, and selling intensity may be grouped together and represented by the same seller. An equipment product line that is a new task purchase, possibly requiring a capital investment decision by the customer, would not fit the same call pattern as items that are routine purchases such as supplies and materials. Matching call patterns is an important consideration in sales force design.

All of the factors already mentioned that differentiate sales organizations can be used to determine the correct manufacturers' representative for a supplier. When the firm cannot afford a direct sales force, when call patterns for a new product are significantly different from existing patterns, or when customer facilities are not concentrated in a manageable geography, contract representation may be the best alternative. Often, firms that have sales teams serving concentrations of customers utilize manufacturers' representatives in other market areas with few customers, ensuring complete coverage for the firm's products.

DIRECT SALES FORCE

We will start with an in-depth discussion of the direct sales force. Manufacturers' representatives are discussed later in this chapter. We discuss distributors in-depth in Chapter 12.

For purposes of this discussion, a **sales call** is an in-person meeting between the seller and stakeholder(s) in the customer buying center. The meeting may be dyadic or involve several members of each organization.

The average value-added sales call costs the seller's company over $200.[18] The approximate number of in-person **sales calls** that a professional seller makes in a day is four. This is down from almost five calls per day twenty years ago. What contributes to these numbers?

While the cost of sales calls varies greatly, depending on the type of product or service, the travel involved, and many other factors, the $200 previously noted considers the costs of putting a direct sales force in the field. Costs such as the purchase/lease and operation of a company-provided vehicle, travel expenses and expense accounts, cellular phones/faxes/laptop computers, and, of course, the seller's compensation. The average cost of each in-person meeting with the customer is further influenced by the fact that sellers, on average, spend slightly more than a third of their time with customers. The same study notes that sellers spend approximately one quarter of their time performing administrative duties (paperwork, meetings, etc.) and almost one third of their time traveling or waiting to see customers.[19]

Sales managers are always in search of methods to improve the statistics we have quoted. One of the numbers noted, four sales calls per day, may at first look to be moving in the wrong direction. Quite the contrary; through the more effective application of widely available communications capabilities (phone, fax, e-mail, teleconferencing, and etc.) and the availability of large quantities of standard information from electronic sources such as the Internet, sales force productivity has improved.

Sales Force Deployment

A **top-down forecast** is often the result of research efforts to forecast market potential, starting with a "whole market" forecast and reducing it to the specific segment(s) in question. A **bottom-up forecast** starts with an analysis of how much product can be sold to each customer in a particular region or territory. The forecasts are rationalized with the business objectives of the organization.

Effective deployment of a company's sales force requires knowing the market sales potential, compiling these estimates into sales estimates for specific customers in specific territories, and evaluating trends that may impact this forecast. Knowing the market potential is often the result of a **top-down forecast,** while market estimates for individual customers, if the territories are already staffed, are usually the result of a **bottom-up forecast** such as the marketing operations forecast discussed in Chapter 6.

Some trends can be anticipated; others cannot. Natural disasters, wars, political crises, financial market upheaval—all of these can impact the design of the sales force structure. The newness of the offering—its distinction or degree of innovation in the market—and the existence of ongoing relationships with potential customers can impact the outcome. Smaller organizations placing new technology in the market may not have an extensive relationship base. Managers

---

[18]Michele Marchetti, "What a Sales Call Costs," *Sales and Marketing Management* (Bill Communications, Inc.: www.salesandmarketing.com, 2001).

[19]Philip Kotlor, *Marketing Management: The Millennium Edition,* 10th ed. (Upper Saddle River, N.J.: Prentice-Hall, 2000), 620–632.

will have to estimate the acceptance of the offering as it moves through the adopter categories. (A more in-depth discussion of forecasts can be found in Chapter 6.)

The next step is to determine how many sellers will be needed to bring about the sales forecast, consistent with the resources of the firm. The nature of the offering, the learning curve, and the required level of customer education to get maximum value from the offering will have significant influence on the **intensity of territory design** and skill levels of the sellers. Managers will be expected to estimate the average length of sales calls, travel time between calls, and the number of calls per customer per sales period (customers must be prioritized). The offering position in the PLC will influence the length of each sales call and the number of missionary or development sales calls that will be necessary to turn potential customers into buying accounts.

This last factor, the amount of missionary or development effort required to create a success, has significant influence on seller selection and compensation. Organizations that require a significantly large missionary effort from their sales forces but still need day-to-day short-term sales results may find it appropriate to split the responsibilities between a short-term–focused seller and a long-term–focused field marketer. This "double field team" can be costly. Small or start-up organizations without a strong base of core business may find it more appropriate to focus on the missionary role, regardless of position title, and provide appropriate compensation.

> **Intensity of territory design** refers to the number of sellers in a given region. If customer education is a major consideration, sellers will be required to spend greater amounts of time with each customer. As the customer base learns how to use the full value of the offering and the purchase becomes routine, less attention to each account will be required. While this can appear as an opportunity to increase seller productivity, it may be a false indication; in most instances it would be preferred to have new, additional offerings rather than change the nature of the seller relationship.

Sales Force Compensation

Our focus in this section is on seller compensation programs. Rewards for sellers take various forms as part of an overall motivation package. Rewards can include sales contests, better territories, higher salary, better company car, and similar monetary and personal/ego gratification. Different activities of the seller will be pursued with different levels of enthusiasm depending on the expected reward. Studies have shown[20] that sellers' motivation is derived from their beliefs about whether an expended effort will lead to a given amount of improved outcome (expectancy); their belief that an improvement in a particular area of performance will lead to a corresponding increase in a given reward (instrumentality); and the desirability of the offered reward, relative to other levels of achievement and reward already obtained by the individual seller (valence perceptions). At the risk of oversimplification, a summary of the preceding statement could be that, generally, *you get what you reward*. Thus, in the process of designing a compensation plan for sellers, managers must assess the job performance and behavior that will most benefit the overall marketing and sales objectives of the firm.

---

[20]Churchill, et al., op. cit., 434–50.

Straight-Commission Compensation Programs
Many managers believe that sellers are primarily motivated by money and, thus, will favor compensation plans that are directly tied to sales obtained *and paid for.* While money is a major motivator, this style of compensation must be consistent with the objectives of the organization and fit with the type of product offered.

Commission-only plans are most appropriate for products and services where repeat efforts are necessary to sustain customer purchases. Frequently ordered items (routine rebuy), such as consumables and other supplies, and materials and parts easily replaced by horizontal competition are such items. These are low-involvement, low-learning offerings, often in the maturity or the decline stage of the PLC. The selling role is order taker or persuader/sustainer. Referring again to Exhibit 11–2, the value of these sales roles is correlated to products with few if any adoption issues, late in the PLC, with the least complex product-related value statement. "Product-related" is an important distinction. As described in "Four Models of Seller Roles" earlier in the chapter, the buyer-seller relationship can be a major differentiating factor in these sales.

With commission-only compensation plans, rewards are linked to short-term, repeated performance. Sellers most likely will concentrate their efforts with customer accounts that have a pattern of frequent and substantial purchases. If the seller is meeting organizational and personal objectives, there will be little incentive to develop new accounts or introduce new innovations to existing accounts. Sales managers find that they have little leverage or control with which to persuade sellers to engage in sales development efforts or even perform routine administrative tasks. Any diversion from the time spent with preferred customers is considered an opportunity cost by the seller. In an attempt to exert some level of control, at least with regard to the attention paid to different products in the product line, variable commission rates are used. More profitable products have higher commission rates, hopefully encouraging sellers to focus on those products. Offerings that require a significant time period for adoption or customer learning may be inappropriate products for a full-commission sales force. The amount of missionary time required to create results may be viewed as an opportunity cost and discourage sellers from giving any attention to more sophisticated products.

Straight-commission plans can also be a problem for sellers. Consistent with the personal needs of the seller, the variability of compensation may not fit well with personal income requirements. Negative changes in the economic climate will also cause instability in the income stream. In an effort to reduce this variability, firms will allow sellers to borrow, or draw, from future commissions, providing a stable income stream.

Concerning straight-commission programs, with financial rewards tied directly to sales volume, straight-commission compensation is inappropriate during the initial period of sales training and new seller familiarization with customers and territories. Unless coming from an identical position with similar customers and products, new sellers should be given time to acclimate to the position.

Straight-Salary Compensation Plans

Straight-salary plans overcome many of the disadvantages of straight-commission plans. Management has significantly greater influence and control over the activities of the sales force, because how the seller spends time will not directly impact compensation. Managers can direct sellers to develop new territories or broaden their customer bases without impeding the ability of the sellers to earn a living. The time-intensive efforts associated with relationship building, market research, sales promotions and publicity, and solving customer problems do not get in the way.

Selling roles that are required to provide design and engineering assistance are more appropriately compensated with salary plans. The motivator/problem solver and the relationship/value creator are roles typical of straight-salary compensation. Appropriate offerings for straight-salary plans are products and services that have long gestation periods, high learning, and are in the introduction and growth stage of the PLC. An increasing value orientation and complexity of the customer relationship also increase the need for additional management control and stability. Salary plans are also appropriate where management cannot reasonably determine the direct impact of individual sellers on sales results.

The most significant objection that sales managers have to salary plans is the lack of financial rewards tied directly to sales results. Straight-salary plans create stability. Straight-salary plans may attract sellers who are security oriented rather than achievement oriented. Sellers who are compensated by straight-salary plans will not always see a direct link between specific sales performance and reward. As with commission plans, the style of compensation must be consistent with the objectives of the organization and fit with the type of product offered.

Combination Compensation Plans

Combinations of salary and bonus or commission are the most frequently used and popular of seller compensation plans.[21] Properly designed, they can deliver most of the advantages of both straight-salary and straight-commission plans while avoiding most of the disadvantages of both. Whether the plan uses a salary plus commission or a salary plus bonus depends on the degree of flexibility and control desired by management.

Salary-plus-commission plans operate much the same as straight-commission plans with compensation tied directly to sales outcomes. The salary portion of the plan validates management direction with regard to administrative duties and customer problem solving and service, while the commission portion provides the seller with an opportunity to increase compensation through increased levels of effort. The commission portion of the package is usually paid as earned and is part of the seller's regular income stream. The ratio of salary to commission in the total compensation package should reflect what management believes to be the objectives of the organization and the territory.

---

[21]Churchill et al., op. cit., 467.

Bonus plans provide management with an increased degree of flexibility. Bonuses are paid for exemplary performance, meeting specific goals (sales, marketing, or administrative), and reaching specific levels of performance. A bonus is paid when the benchmark is surpassed rather than on a continuing basis. The bonus, then, is an additional incentive rather than a regular part of the compensation plan. The ratio of salary to bonus in such plans is usually greater than the ratio of salary to commission in those plans. Bonuses are paid only when a specific goal is reached and then usually at the end of the measurement period—quarterly or annually.

A final note about seller compensation is appropriate. There are many myths associated with seller compensation and its relationship to performance. Compensation plans are not the only motivational tool available to managers; not all sellers prefer high-risk or leveraged compensation plans; and sellers are not motivated only by money. Professional sellers are results oriented but not just short-term sales results. Successful sellers are oriented toward commitment and accountability.[22] As with other employees in different roles, sellers will be motivated by effective leadership, acknowledgment, and reward.

MANUFACTURERS' REPRESENTATIVES

The "rep," in business-to-business marketing jargon, is an independent business person who has specialized in a market segment or collection of segments that have common users or call patterns. Reps act as agents for firms in particular markets or regions. They carry no inventory and take no ownership of the goods they represent. The firms they represent are known as their principals. When the rep's customer makes a purchase, the terms of sale are often between the principal and the buyer. From a transactional viewpoint, the rep is not in the middle of the sale. The rep is compensated for the sale by the principal after the sale is culminated or **"booked."**

When is a sale **booked?** Many organizations will have different policies regarding when a sale is "booked" for commission purposes. In most instances, a sale is not considered complete until the customer has paid the invoice. Reps, then, just like direct commission sellers, must wait for all terms of a sale to be concluded to receive their compensation.

The value of a good manufacturers' representative is in existing relationships with customers. Established reps have ongoing, successful relationships with buying organizations in the market segments in which they specialize. In selecting a rep, suppliers seek out those who already have good relationships with potential customers—often determined by asking the customers who they might recommend as the local rep for the product or product line.

Because reps have an ongoing, established business relationship with potential customers, they already understand the nature of the markets in which they compete. Little time is needed to get "up to speed," except possibly with the principal's product line. Since it is in the best interest of the rep to keep the

---

[22]Kulik, op. cit., 18.

lines of products represented current, the rep may solicit a new principal for a potential relationship as a way to complete or extend an existing product line. In these circumstances, little time is required to explain the supplier's product line. The rep usually has a target buyer already in mind.

In the short term, there are few costs associated with the use of manufacturers' representatives. Since all compensation is commission related, all selling costs are variable. The **fixed costs of sales** are covered by the rep, spread out over the commissions earned from all products represented. Thus, adding another product is efficient from the perspective of the rep when call patterns required by the new offering match those of existing products. From the perspective of the principal, no investment is necessary to establish a competent sales force. The lack of any significant fixed costs makes the use of manufacturers' reps very attractive for small firms that cannot afford full-time sellers, firms who may have full-time sellers in areas of customer concentration but require coverage in territories where sales volume does not warrant a direct seller, and firms introducing new products or entering new territories.

> The **fixed cost of sales** includes administrative overhead and field selling expenses. Administrative overhead includes all management and administrative salaries, the salaries of planners and sales support people, the cost of sales literature, and other special costs that cannot be linked directly to an individual transaction, such as prospect seminars, sales meetings, attending industry conferences, and so on.

Over the long term, particularly when a rep is very successful with the products of the principal, the mutual advantages of the relationship change. When sales volumes increase, the principal does not recognize any economies of scale in the selling process. At some point, selling costs associated with using the rep will exceed the costs of placing a direct sales force in the same territory. When this becomes significant, sales managers often believe that a direct sales force will better represent their products because they will be focused solely on their products and will more aggressively represent the firm. Many reps half jokingly say that they want to be successful for the principals they represent but not so successful that they lose the product line to a direct sales force! Suppliers that rely on reps as the primary sales force often must be reminded about the reason they selected to use reps in the first place. The principal is compensating the reps for their knowledge of the industry and their relationships with customers. While responsibility for sales in a territory may be transferred with the termination of the rep's contract, relationships are not so easily transferred.[23]

---

[23]The termination of the manufacturers' representative contract does not terminate commissions to the rep. The rep is usually compensated for ongoing core business and also receives a portion of the commissions on new business that will close shortly, the presumption being that the business would not have happened if it were not for the efforts of the rep. We know of one situation in which a rep developed a very lucrative business for a principal, the business becoming the largest single contributor to the rep's sales volume. The principal noted that the commissions paid to the rep were multiples of the costs that were forecast if a direct sales office, fully staffed, were placed in the territory. The rep lost the product line. To achieve the same level of coverage, the principal hired two full-time sellers and administrative help and transferred two design engineers from headquarters to the sales office. The principal may have failed to recognize that the rep had a very productive and efficient relationship with the customer base.

Market Conditions That Favor Either Manufacturers' Representatives or a Direct Sales Force

Exhibit 11–5 compares the market conditions that tend to favor either manufacturers' representatives or a direct sales force. While much of this information is a summary of the information already discussed, let us examine a few situations and the trade-offs involved.

Technically Complex Products
Products, services, or total offerings that are complex favor the use of a direct sales force. Whether because of the need for integration into other products or a steep learning curve associated with a new technology, reps will be more successful with standardized or generic products. This can lead to undesirable trade-offs.

Suppliers of high-technology, high-learning products are often small companies that may not have the financial ability to invest in a direct sales force. Using manufacturers' representatives may not be ideal but may be the only choice because of the low fixed costs. When reps are to be used to represent these types of products, a technical background or education is very important. The culture and environment of the rep and the target market must be supportive of new technology.

Long Lead Times
Whether because of the technically complex nature of the offering or the time to actually build and book the offering, long gestation peri-

EXHIBIT 11–5 Comparison of Appropriate Market Conditions for a Direct Sales Force and Manufacturers' Representatives

Appropriate for Direct Sales Force When	Manufacturers' Representatives When
◆ The product is technically complex.	◆ The product is standardized or generic.
◆ The selling situation requires a specialized background that reps do not usually have (e.g., scientific or special technical).	◆ For technical products, a general technical education or background is important.
◆ Control of the seller is important—the organization selects, trains, and controls personnel.	◆ Control of personnel is less important—reps are independent business people.
◆ Long lead times for results are common—direct sellers have more patience (and more budget) through the long sales cycles.	◆ Short sales cycles are common or long sales cycles without much pre-sale service required.
◆ Significant missionary work is required to build relationships.	◆ The reps have other complementary lines.
◆ Significant prospecting for new customers is required.	◆ Reps have established relationships with target customer segments.
◆ The customer base is highly concentrated.	◆ The selling effort required for the product matches reps' existing call patterns.
◆ Explicit customer feedback is desired for Innovations New products Competitive information	◆ The market is dispersed and/or the market consists of many small customers. ◆ Customer feedback is less critical (can stand the filter/time delay).
◆ High fixed costs exist but with economies of scale.	◆ Low fixed costs are required.

ods tend to favor a direct sales force. The selling organization must have the financial wherewithal to support fixed selling expenses incurred during the period between customer specification and sale of the product. Manufacturers' representatives are not likely to be interested in waiting through long design, development, and build cycles to realize any compensation for their efforts.

If the selling organization finds that reps are to be used under these conditions, compensation becomes less straightforward than straight commission. Variations based on when a sale is booked or payments based on progress or goals reached are among the alternatives. The selling organization is at risk as funds will be expended before an actual sale is made. Reps are a last resort in situations with long lead times.

Selection, Training, and Control

A manufacturer selects, trains, and has direct control over its own sales force. Sellers can be selected who become aligned with the goals of the organization and "fit" with the culture and environment. Sellers are trained at the discretion of the manufacturer, not only in particulars of the offering but in the internal relationships, behaviors, and expectations of the organization. The sales manager, to the extent allowed by the compensation plan used, has significant influence and control over the activities of the seller. Such is not the case with reps.

Reps are independent business people, either in business for themselves or part of a manufacturers' representation firm. They are directly responsible for their success or failure. Their efforts are spread over many products or product lines. The time spent with the products of any particular manufacturer is directly dependent on what they believe will be a short-term success.

Missionary Work Required

If a missionary selling effort is required to educate customers or build relationships in a new market segment or territory, a direct sales force/field marketing organization is almost always required. Few reps are likely to take on new markets or building new relationships unless long-term benefits will accrue to the rep. Keep in mind that reps are selected in large part because of their existing relationships. If a principal finds that the manufacturers' rep is often asked to approach new markets, it may be appropriate to question the process that selected the rep in the first place.

Explicit Customer Feedback Desired

Collaboration with customers, whether as part of a value network or an individual effort, requires explicit communication between supplier and customer. Situations that would normally require motivator/problem solver or relationship/value creator sales roles usually require the use of a direct sales force.

There can be alternatives. If the supplier can accept less timely or filtered customer feedback, using a rep may still be possible. This is not likely in the development of first-of-a-kind new business. A more likely scenario would be the use of the manufacturers' representative for direct selling and a direct field marketing/ missionary sales effort for joint development efforts.

Combinations of Representation

The "explicit customer feedback" scenario leads into a representation pattern that occurs often. Many firms use manufacturers' representatives or, as described in the next chapter, industrial distributors for their products. These relationships are focused on the short-term selling needs of the firm, usually fitting the role descriptions of order takers or persuader/sustainers.

How do these firms partner with customers to develop new products or "push the envelope" in their markets? Does the use of reps preclude a firm from taking an ownership role in a market? Firms that rely on reps and distribution for selling support usually have a direct field marketing or missionary sales organization. This releases the missionary seller from day-to-day sales and account maintenance responsibilities to focus on longer-term research and development issues with customers. The selling effort also benefits because sellers have been freed from development responsibilities. A typical example of this type of arrangement can be seen in the sales arrangements of manufacturers of communication equipment (e.g., telephone switching devices), computer workstations, and other products that have quick product delivery, installation, service, and training as part of the offering. Sales and local inventory are accomplished by the distributor while installation, training, and service are provided by the missionary seller.

Basic selling is persuasion. In this chapter, we have presented the basic role of selling and several levels of complexity that become the selling model we have named the relationship/value creator. Throughout this text, we have focused on the value network and the total offering that can be provided to the customer buying center. Elements of the value network, when brought forward to the customer by the seller, represent the supplier's approach to satisfying the needs of stakeholders in the customer buying center. The seller represents the different solutions to the different stakeholders and returns the feedback about each value element to the appropriate part of the supplier network.

Based on the complexity necessary to create a successful selling situation, a direct sales force or a manufacturers' representative is used. The greater the complexity of the offering and the greater the collaboration between supplier and customer organizations, the more likely a direct sales force will be used. We have also discussed the role that missionary sales/business development personnel can play in complex relationships, relieving the seller, either direct or rep, of the need to be concerned with longer-term developments. Also discussed were the types of compensation appropriate in these different circumstances.

A direct sales force to handle short-term situations combined with a missionary seller for a long-term focus is just one marketing channel design that can be successful when it matches the way the customer organization works. Chapter 12 examines marketing channels and, more generally, value networks and their appropriate design and development and looks at a variety of business-to-business channel and network designs that may be appropriate in certain circumstances. Different types of channels, channel intermediaries, and partners are discussed, and their role in long- and short-term relationships is examined. As you go forward, consider the three needs that buyers and sellers work to satisfy—the needs of the job function, the needs of the organization, and personal needs. All must be considered, not only in successful relationship selling but also in value network development.

Key Terms

booked sale	fixed cost of sales	persuader/sustainer
bottom-up forecast	intensity of territory	relational exchange
boundary personnel	design	relationship/value creator
call pattern	manufacturer's	sales call
direct sales force	representative	switching costs
distributor	motivator/problem solver	top-down forecast
dyadic interactions	order taker	

Questions for Review and Discussion

1. Compare the role of a seller in consumer markets with a seller in business-to-business markets.

2. How is the repeated, ongoing relationship in business-to-business selling an advantage for both the seller and the buyer?

3. Explain why a dyadic relationship between buyer and seller may be of value to order takers.

4. As a product moves through the product life cycle, how do the nature and complexity of customer support change?

5. Characterize the differences between a motivator/problem solver and a relationship/value creator.

6. Many sales managers claim, "Our sellers are the first line of defense and the first line of offense in the supplier-customer relationship." What is meant by this statement? What role types are the sellers likely operating in?

7. Suppose you are the marketing manager for a small company marketing a new product that requires extensive collaboration with the customer before the customer will adopt it. What are the advantages and disadvantages of selling your product through manufacturer's representatives?

8. One-to-one marketing has been a goal for marketers since Peppers and Rogers popularized the idea.[24] One-to-one marketing is, in essence, treating each customer as a segment of one and marketing directly to that customer. In business-to-business marketing, how close do you think most companies can come to implementing one-to-one marketing?

9. What risks must be considered when changing representation from manufacturers' representatives to a direct sales force?

10. At what level of sales success would you consider making the switch described in Question 9? What are the factors you must consider to make such a decision?

11. Consider the relationship between Daimler-Chrysler and its suppliers described in Exhibit 11–3. Chrysler was in trouble and needed cost reductions. Think of some ways that Chrysler could have obtained the reduced costs and maintained a strong working relationship with its suppliers.

---

[24]Donald Peppers and Martha Rogers, *The One-to-One Future: Building Relationships One Customer at a Time* (New York: Doubleday, 1993).

Internet Exercises

Revisit Siebel Systems and E.piphany. How well do each of these two products support a sales effort that must work with a protracted customer decision process?

Go to Kinko's Web site and examine the different ways that consumer services and business-to-business services are presented. Is the importance of ongoing relationships with business-to-business customers apparent from the design and layout? Are there clear distinctions between consumer and business-to-business markets?

Go to the Web site for UpShot **http://www.upshot.com** What does this company offer? How important is it for a sales force to improve its efficiency the way UpShot offers? Explain.

12

Channel Relationships

overview. . . Previous chapters have discussed buyer and seller behavior in business–to–business relationships, market research and competitive analysis, and new product development and pricing—all in the context of delivering value to the customer. This chapter focuses on that delivery function. In your marketing principles course, you learned that it is often necessary

© RYAN McVAY/PHOTODISC

to have marketing intermediaries make the connection between customer and supplier. Whether done through intermediaries or directly between supplier and customer, the functions and activities that form this channel comprise the "place" component of the marketing mix. This chapter's examination of the complexities of marketing channels and how the different elements come together includes an emphasis on the development of networks of partners to create value for customers. The concept of "value networks," first introduced in Chapter 2, is further developed.

Effective marketing channel designs and efficient business logistics systems are often the elements of an offering that provide the winning edge in competitive situations. A well-designed and well-developed marketing channel effectively provides offering attributes beyond the core product in a manner and form acceptable to the customer. The logistics system, part of the channel design, delivers the core product at the right time and place, again as determined by the customer. Customers in different target markets require different combinations of channel services. As a result, unique channel designs are often required to effectively satisfy different markets. The opening story, a classic example, demonstrates how a successful company targeted a new market but did not develop a new marketing channel to reach that market.

THE APPLE LISA

In 1983, Apple Computer introduced the Lisa computer. This new desktop computer was the first major new product to follow the successful Apple II line of personal computers. The Lisa initially had a $10,000 price tag. Priced at this level, the system was obviously meant for large commercial/business users. Apple introduced the Lisa through the same channel that had been successful with the Apple II computer line.

The Lisa was a major sales disappointment. Apple, the company that earlier had successfully introduced the personal computer to an embryonic market had now failed with its first premium, business-oriented computer. While Apple enthusiasts were stunned, potential business customers seemed uninterested.

What happened? Among other problems, Apple failed to recognize that the business target market would have a different set of needs and expectations associated with the purchase of a computer.* Different target markets usually demand a different set of services and, thus, a channel design focused at providing those services. The marketing channel for the Apple II line of computers, comprised of independent computer dealers, had contributed to the success of the product. The target markets for these early computers were schools and, to a large extent, home users. The home Apple user was likely to be more interested in the computer as a technology device in itself than in the functionality of the device. This hobby or enthusiast attitude—from the technophiles of the home computer market—was well served by the independent dealer network as many had entered the business as would-be "hackers" themselves. Business users, however, want the computer itself to be "invisible" while accomplishing the required business support tasks. Differences from the home market in user training, product information, product support, financing, delivery, and many other facets of the total offering, combined with a lack of awareness or ability of independent channel members to satisfy these needs, contributed to this major product failure for Apple. Had Apple recognized this difference, it should have been obvious that its current channel design was ill-equipped to approach the business market. Was the Lisa a "good product"? Because of the poor channel design, we will never really know.

*Louis W. Stern, Adel I. El-Ansary, and James R. Brown, "Instructor's Manual Discussion," chap. 8 in Management in Marketing Channels (Upper Saddle River, N.J.: Prentice-Hall, 1988).

LEARNING OBJECTIVES

- ◆ Understand the principles of market channel design and the delivery of economic utility—form, time, place, and possession—to customers.

- ◆ Understand value networks and the relationship to marketing channels.

- ◆ Understand classical vertical integration patterns and the value network alternative.

- ◆ Understand the fundamentals of business logistics.

- ◆ Recognize the importance of building channel relationships from the view of providing economic utility and developing sustainable value networks.

- ◆ Gain an understanding of how the Internet can enhance the value that marketing channels can provide to customers.

- ◆ Obtain an appreciation for the limits of applying information technology to enhance marketing channels.

- ◆ Know when and how the Internet can provide competitive advantage by enhancing marketing channels and when application of Internet technologies will not provide a competitive advantage.

introduction. . .

Marketing channels comprise the *place* element of the marketing mix. A **marketing channel** is the means to manage the presale contact, transaction, and fulfillment activities between the supplier and the final buyer. The original supplier of a product or service can provide the value provided by the channel, or the value may be provided through one or more channel intermediaries—organizations that perform channel functions between the original supplier and the final buyer. Without the place element of the four Ps—whether supplied directly or through intermediaries—the customer cannot realize the value contained in the supplier's product or service.

Place is the most difficult element of the marketing mix to change. It involves many organizations—**primary channel participants** and **ancillary channel members**—that are independently owned and operated. These organizations, while participating in the channel, may very well have internal goals that are not always consistent with the goals of the channel leader. Combine this with a natural resistance to change among well-established operating organizations, and *place* becomes a very difficult part of the marketing mix to alter.

The channel is usually direct in supplier-customer relationships in which the volume of business is large, particularly in relationships between a supplier and an original equipment manufacturer (OEM). The sales force, market development, customer service operation, and the delivery system of the manufacturer form a **direct channel** with appropriate corresponding parts of the customer organization. For instance, Dana Corporation, a major manufacturer of transmissions and chassis components to the automotive industry, does not go through intermediaries to supply automobile parts to General Motors. Rather, they form a direct channel in which Dana sales and marketing personnel work directly with GM engineers, buyers, and other stakeholders in the buying center. General Motors places orders directly with Dana; Dana manufactures

Primary channel participants in the marketing channel are those intermediaries, such as wholesalers, distributors, retailers, agents, and brokers, who are part of the proactive *marketing* design of the channel. These intermediaries can have responsibilities associated with presale customer contact, sales, customer service, and transactions in the channel. Primary channel participants form a vital link between the supplier and the final user of goods and services.

and ships the parts directly to GM; and Dana personnel handle the GM account.

When the target market segment is not oligopolistic—not dominated by a few, large participants—suppliers may not be able to provide the total offering desired by the market and still provide superior value. The costs associated with serving the many dispersed customers in such a target market at the same intensity level as that of serving a major customer with a direct relationship will not be recovered by the orders of smaller quantity and high handling costs. In such circumstances, channel designs other than direct channels are necessary.

THE RATIONALE FOR MARKETING CHANNELS

Why have channel intermediaries? Couldn't the supplier do everything that channel members could? The answer lies partially in the economic theory of division of labor. A specialist is usually more adept at providing a service when that service is the mainstream offering of the business. When serving dispersed customers who buy a large assortment of goods associated with the market segment but buy in small quantities, intermediaries often have efficiencies, special skills, or special circumstances that upstream suppliers do not have.

Another example of the value of intermediaries is the reduction in transaction costs and complexity. As shown in Exhibit 12–1, the number of transactions is cut considerably by selling through a distributor,

> **Ancillary channel members** are those businesses and service providers whose efforts have been traditionally viewed as somewhat generic but without which the channel could not work. Marketers often do not consider *which* trucking company products will be shipped on, just that the channel design will include trucking as part of its logistical requirements. A similar approach is used regarding financing, storage, promotion, and other facilitating services. Marketers specify the function in the channel design, not necessarily the specific provider.

> A **direct channel** is formed when the supplier markets and sells directly to the buying organization. No additional primary intermediaries are involved.

EXHIBIT 12–1   Channels Can Create Efficiency

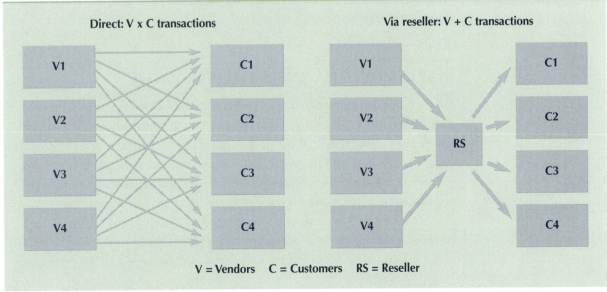

V = Vendors   C = Customers   RS = Reseller

reducing overall selling costs and the opportunities for error. The ability of the intermediary to purchase in quantity to serve a bundle of small users, rather than each user making a direct purchase, lowers costs to users because the intermediary can take advantage of quantity-scaled pricing.

Customers in different market segments may have different expectations about the level of services that are provided with purchases. As a result, different target segments may require differing channel structures. The opening example of the Apple Lisa illustrates what can happen when the target segment wants and expects services that the channel is not able to provide. The existing Apple channel served home users who usually purchased individual units, but the target market for the Lisa was large- and medium-sized businesses more likely to purchase in large quantities. The home user was likely an innovator or early adopter of home computers, somewhat enamored with the technology. The institutional buyer, however, was likely far more pragmatic, requiring functionality and ease of use instead of hot technology.

Apple's existing consumer product channel was not particularly well suited to the value sought by the target market. We can see how this might be done better, though, using the Dana example. The relationship with large customers—the OEM market—requires a particular set of services and is identified as a separate target market in the Dana segmentation scheme. The product is custom tailored to the specific customer application. While Dana may supply, for instance, the four-wheel drive transfer case for sport utility vehicles to both GM and Ford, the designs are the result of collaboration with each customer and are unique. However, these transfer cases are not only delivered as components to the vehicle manufacturers, but enter the service market—repair shops—as well. The service segment has very different demands related to economic utility. Repair shops want one component, locally available for quick delivery. Thus, the marketing channel for these two segments—the OEM segment and the service segment—must deliver different levels of form, time, place, and possession value (see "dual distribution" later in this chapter).

MARKETING CHANNELS DELIVER VALUE

Successful marketing plans require significant channel development and planning, if they are to provide superior value as perceived by the final customer. As we have seen in the Apple example, the importance of "how the customer gets the product" is often overlooked by both novice and experienced marketers, and the recognition that different parts of the offering (services, financing, etc.) may require separate and unique channel activities is often ignored.

In the rest of this section, we examine more closely the value generally provided by channels. This reinforces why channel design and management are so important to the marketing strategy and its execution. Channels principally provide the four kinds of economic utility that we have discussed many times throughout this text. Channels also create costs, both for the supplier and for the customer, in the creation of this utility. Supplier- and channel-incurred costs must be recouped from revenue in a way that they have a minimum effect on the price that can be charged. Customer costs subtract from the value realized by the customer. Accordingly, channels must be designed and managed in a way that controls channel costs and allocates the savings among customers, channel members, and suppliers.

Economic Utility

The ideal product not only satisfies core customer needs but also is part of a total offering that is provided in the correct quantity, at the right time and place, and in a manner that fits the routine of the customer. This sort of value provided by the offering has been called *economic utility* and has four parts—*form, time, place,* and *possession.* Often, the supplier can create differentiation by uniquely providing these four kinds of value through the marketing channel. At a minimum, all four elements of value must be created for the marketing strategy to succeed.

Form   **Form** utility is the usable quantity or mode of the product most preferred by the customer. This may be an individual item on a retailer's shelf in the consumer market. In an industrial setting, it might be a specified lot size of industrial components with convenient packaging, containerization, or **palletizing** to accommodate the operations of a customer's manufacturing facility.

Time   **Time** utility describes the availability of the product when the customer needs it. In the consumer market, this may be reflected in a retailer's store hours. In business-to-business markets, just-in-time (JIT) delivery service aimed at minimizing raw materials inventory at the customer is an example.

Place   **Place** utility, also known as *locational convenience,* is provided in the consumer market by retailers as several stores in a region or stores clustered with similar outlets of competitors, as demonstrated by the clusters of competing automobile dealers at various "auto rows." In business-to-business markets, place may be demonstrated by rapid and frequent delivery associated with JIT inventory services or may result in the development of supplier manufacturing facilities adjacent to customer sites.

Form, **time**, **place**, and **possession** in business-to-business markets are described subsequently. Economic utility is part of *place* in the four Ps of marketing. The relationship between the four Ps, the total offering, and economic utility is discussed in Chapter 1.

Palletizing is the arranging and securing of products on pallets—platforms that can be easily stacked and moved by forklifts—so that the products can be handled, shipped, and deployed for use quickly and easily. Many customers have a particular style or design of pallet that works with the material-handling equipment in their facilities. Suppliers are required to provide shipment of goods on compatible pallets.

Possession   **Possession** utility is the methodology by which the customer obtains ownership or the right to use of the product or service. In consumer markets, possession may be the variety of methods a customer may pay for an item—cash, check, credit card, or retailer-provided financing. In business-to-business markets, the financing of customer purchases can be a major part of the total offering.

While each of these four types of utility can vary in complexity and degree of intricacy, provision for them must be in every marketing channel. The responsibility for satisfying customer needs associated with form, time, place, and possession may be shifted to other channel members (distributors, wholesalers, manufacturers, etc.), but the functions cannot be eliminated from the channel; chaos in the delivery of value would result without performing them.

Channel Flows and Activities That Create Value

How are these economic utilities—the aspects of channel value—created? Suppliers or channel intermediaries may provide one or more of the following services in their effort to provide economic utility:

Marketing and sales flows

♦ Creating product assortments aligned with customer demand rather than with the manufacturer's product line

♦ Communicating with customers in both a sales role and as a communication channel between customer and supplier (in the Apple Lisa example, the Apple retailer was unprepared for the buying culture of large institutions)

♦ Setting and negotiating prices

Product and ownership flows

♦ Taking temporary ownership, transferring title, handling government documentation and registration, and so on

Installation, training, and service flows

♦ Providing before and after sales services to customers (the Apple dealer's role in the education process for home users was quite different from the training needs of institutional buyers who would need basic training for actual users of the computer)

♦ Installing and maintaining complex systems (the institutional buyer would expect installation and on-site testing for all locations)

♦ Providing systems and services support to channel members (the independent dealer is unlikely to have the staff to support ongoing inquiries from the numerous users of the institution's systems)

Ancillary flows

♦ Providing financing for customers or for suppliers (the institutional buyer would have different finance needs than the usual Apple user)

Contracted transportation, handling, and storage services

- ◆ Contracting promotion services
- ◆ Arranging for insurance, financial protection
- ◆ Managing information gathering, analysis, and dissemination

These services, shown in Exhibit 12–2a, exist to a varying degree in most channels, but the **channel pattern** that performs the service changes. In the Dana example earlier in this chapter, sales and marketing would flow through direct sellers for very large accounts (e.g., GM, Ford), while the service channel would use distributors able to provide the specific needs of repair personnel. Missionary sellers assist the distributors in assortment and quantity decisions and provide product training to distribution personnel.

In the Dana direct channel, customer-specific product flows from the manufacturer (Dana) to the customer (GM, Ford) directly. Shipments are likely in large quantities, palletized per customer requirements, and are aided by a contract transportation services provider—an ancillary channel member. Ownership transfers directly between Dana and the end users (note that, in the interests

> The **channel pattern** is the particular design or arrangement of various intermediaries that perform channel functions. Different circumstances in the target market environment may call for different channel patterns (i.e., different types of intermediaries) to meet specific requirements. Different types of channel patterns are discussed in the "Channel Design" section.

EXHIBIT 12–2a   Marketing Channel Flows Supplier to Customer

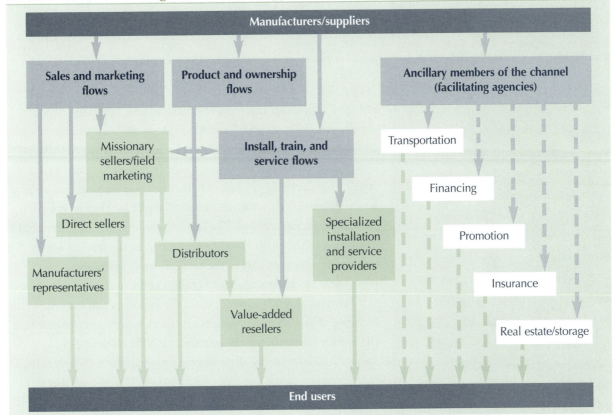

Note: This exhibit is not intended to imply that all channels contain all flows shown or that all possible flows are shown here.

EXHIBIT 12–2b   Marketing Channel Flows Customer to Supplier

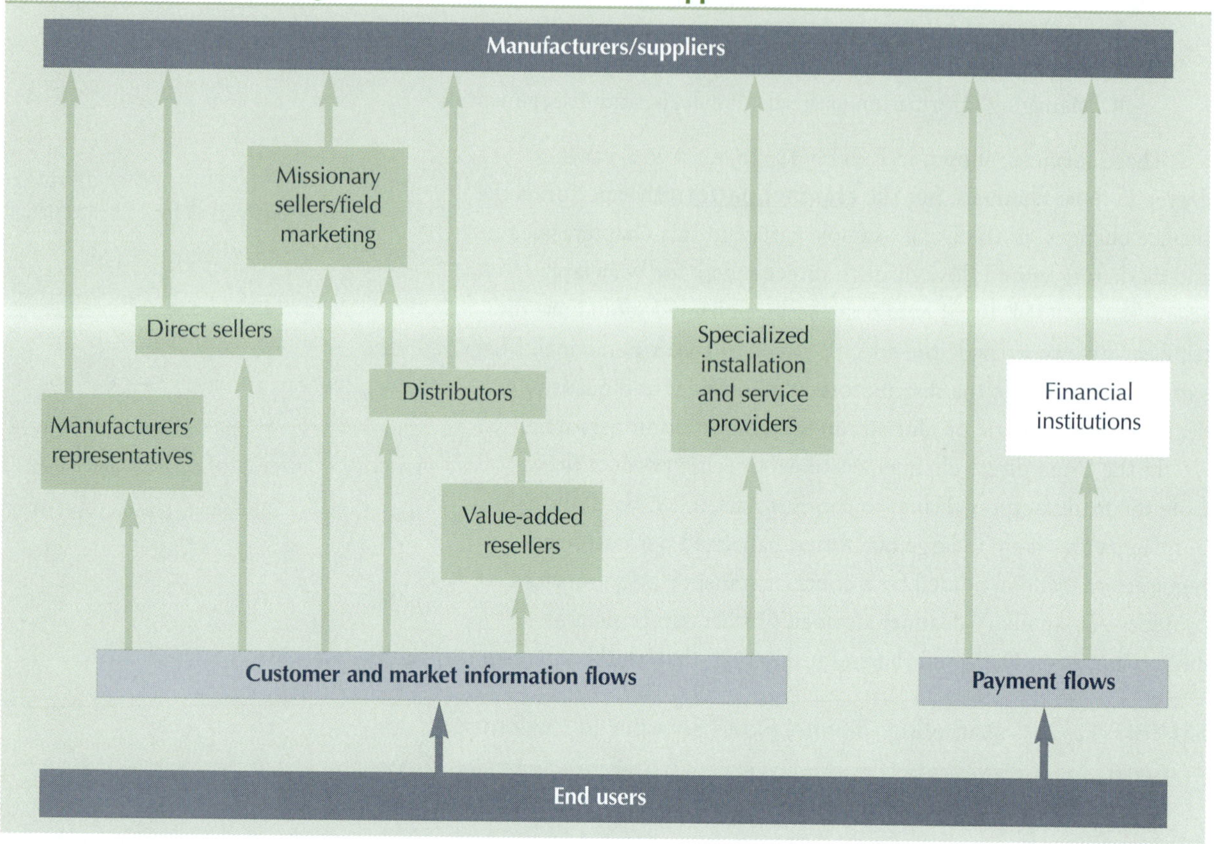

Note: This exhibit is not intended to imply that all channels contain all flows shown or that all possible flows are shown here.

Trade credit is the payment term provided to end users by distributors and other channel intermediaries to finance purchases. Particularly in the purchase of components and materials, small business-to-business customers rely on trade credit as a way to finance operations.

Different target markets have different expectations regarding the availability and duration of trade credit. Channel members should be aware of market expectations with regard to credit services, and manufacturers should be prepared to grant terms to distributors that aid in this part of the total offering.

of legibility, a direct line from "ownership" and "end user" is not shown in Exhibit 12–2a). Exhibit 12–2b shows various flows from the customer to the supplier. Naturally, payment flows are of great importance. Payment does not necessarily follow the same path (albeit, in reverse) as product, whether the manufacturer has an in-house financing operation or uses ancillary channel members who provide financing services. The level of importance of the financial institution in the channel is directly related to the level of importance of financing as part of the total offering. Many small businesses rely on the availability of **trade credit** to finance operations.

Previous chapters have discussed the importance of marketers knowing all aspects of the markets served. A major source of customer and market information is the participants in the marketing channel. As shown in Exhibit 12–2b, *all* participants, not just those directly related to the supplier, can be a source of information. Channel members' proximity to customers provides a direct source of potentially detailed information that contributes to "bottom-up" market analysis such as the marketing operation forecast (MOF) discussed in Chapter 6.

Dana Corporation: Aftermarket

Go to the Web site for Dana Corporation (http://www.dana.com). Examine the Aftermarket part of the site. How does this part of the site target the repair service segment?

Marketing Channels Meet Customer Needs and Expectations

Marketing channel flows of possession, ownership, promotion, negotiation, financing, risk taking, and market information are organized by intermediaries comprising marketing channels so that goods and services are provided to customers in the form and at the time desired. Just as consumers have favorite methods that meet their particular needs to purchase products and services, businesses have a preferred way they "buy." While the core product may be similar in many cases, different target markets have different expectations of the total offering, as shown in the example of the Apple Lisa.

Depending on the resources of the firm and the needs of the target markets, channel designs may include a direct sales force, the use of independent intermediaries (wholesalers, brokers, distributors, manufacturers' representatives, etc.), or any combination of these options, as previously shown in Exhibit 12–2a. These options, often referred to as *channel patterns,* include dealer networks, franchise systems, Internet broker systems, and other various forms of contractual relationships beyond the scope of this discussion. Additionally, there are ancillary functions that every channel design must provide, including but not limited to transportation services, insurance, and other financial services. A very large firm with an established channel infrastructure will often elect to perform all of these ancillary services in-house. While this may have significant economies of scale, this **vertical integration** limits flexibility. Today, companies desiring greater flexibility often seek specialists to perform ancillary tasks, allowing the firm to concentrate on development of its markets. In the last ten years, we have seen the emergence of "business logistics" providers—grown-up transportation companies who realize that they have more to offer than just moving goods (see Exhibit 12–3 for a discussion of services provided by UPS and FedEx). This channel design technique, called **functional spin-off,** assumes that ancillary services are provided most efficiently by experts in

Vertical integration, as used here, refers to the degree of ownership a firm has of its marketing channel. The firm may own distributors of its products and may actually own the organizations that provide ancillary services, such as transportation, inventory control, and financing. Ownership of these facilitating agencies can be efficient through economies of scale but "expensive" when a change in channel design or services are required.

EXHIBIT 12–3   UPS Competes with FedEx through Focus on Logistics

Two key logistics-driven initiatives developed by United Parcel Service (UPS) have put increasing pressure on FedEx, formerly Federal Express, in two areas in which they compete. First, UPS has been slowly building its capability for providing overnight delivery. The improvements to UPS's system involve integrating overnight airfreight with short- to medium-haul ground transportation via UPS's ubiquitous brown trucks. FedEx still has 39 percent of the overnight express market, but UPS has grown to about 29 percent (in 2001). Meanwhile, UPS's costs run about two thirds of FedEx's costs per package.

The second initiative, begun in 1994, is a logistics services line of business offered for medium- and large-sized companies. Logistics services include supply chain and distribution systems design and management. The group applies new technology where needed but focuses on achieving desired results with whatever methods are appropriate. This line of business has landed several major global companies as customers and produced dramatic cost and time savings for them. Meanwhile, FedEx has had to revamp its logistics service operation.

FedEx is building out its ground delivery system and its special overnight services, such as extended pickup hours and Saturday delivery. It has also struck a deal with the U.S. Postal Service to share shipping space so that FedEx planes fill up unused space. It is further strengthening its overseas capabilities.

The lessons from this rivalry include the following:

♦ Core competencies in logistics can produce competitive advantage.
♦ New competitive strengths can be built through patient development of new core competencies.
♦ Traditional markets must be actively and creatively defended.

Source: Charles Haddad, "Ground Wars," *Business Week* (21 May 2001): 64–68.

each service[1]—a basic application of the principle of division of labor. For many small firms, using a service provided through functional spin-off allows a lower capital investment, greater flexibility, and a broader range of long-term options.

Industrial Distributors Serve Industrial End Users

Why would an industrial end user want to purchase from a distributor? Wouldn't products cost less by purchasing directly from the manufacturer? For very large customers, when the supplier/manufacturer has the advantage of logistical economies of scale, this is likely true. Suppliers, however, are often unwilling or unable, at a reasonable cost, to provide many services for medium or small customers or those who have irregular usage patterns. Distributors fill the gap, giving attention to and building relationships with medium and small users. These industrial distributors develop an understanding of the smaller customers' business that the supplying manufacturer could not achieve through the relationship possible within the profit margins provided by the small purchase volume. The distributor spreads the costs associated with the relationship over several products and product lines, often from many different suppliers. Small- to medium-sized purchasers (these may be large organizations that purchase small volumes of certain items) can

---

[1]Louis W. Stern, Adel I. El-Ansary, and James R. Brown, *Management in Marketing Channels* (Upper Saddle River, N.J.: Prentice-Hall, 1988), chap. 8.

receive better customer service from a modern industrial distributor. Within this context, distributors can serve customers in many ways:

◆ *Provide fast delivery.* Distributors maintain a local inventory of the products from suppliers they represent. Arrangements can be made with customers to provide regular JIT deliveries, allowing the customer to avoid a large resource commitment to incoming inventory. The particular *physical distribution* philosophy (see "The Physical Distribution Concept" later in this chapter) employed by the distributor can impact the distributor's ability to create a competitive niche in this area.

◆ *Provide segment-based product assortment.* Distributors can provide "one-stop shopping" to small- and medium-sized industrial customers. A small electronics assembly company may need a variety of components, from circuit board materials to computer chips and all the ancillary components in between. The distributor maintains a product line focused on the needs of its served markets, creating product assortments from many sources.

◆ *Provide local credit.* Small businesses often find it difficult to obtain financing, particularly during periods of tight money. Most distributors provide trade credit for established customers. It is not unusual for unique payment terms to be a significant part of a distributor's total offering. In many instances, the credit-granting capability of the distributor becomes a major competitive feature.

◆ *Provide product information.* The electronics assembler in the earlier example may require advice on the application of components or may need instruction of the proper use of supplies. The assembler might be switching to a new soldering method that requires the handling of new solvents. The distributor not only will be a source for the solder, solvents, and ancillary equipment but also will be able to advise regarding their proper use.

◆ *Assist in buying decisions.* Our electronics assembler may need assistance in the selection of technically equal components from two different manufacturers. The distributor can assist in this selection process. The assembler will seek well-known industrial brands at the inception of a project but may seek an alternative supply as production increases. This not only helps to develop lower cost alternatives but also provides the assembler with a second source of goods should a calamity befall the manufacturer of the industry standard. Distributors of well-known industrial brands seek to include a generic equivalent in their product line. The distributor can then provide both products to the assembler, preventing the assembler from obtaining the generic product from another source. Manufacturers of industry standard products attempt to dissuade their distributors from offering an alternative but often have little choice in the matter. (In consumer markets, distributors often advise retailers regarding "hot sellers" and avoiding "turkeys" from a manufacturer's line. It is in the best interest of the distributor to have profitable, successful customers—that is how the distributor can be sure of getting paid!)

◆ *Anticipate needs.* By maintaining a close relationship with customers, the distributor can anticipate future needs and have inventory available in a timely manner.

Through the relationship with a customer, the distributor can know new business opportunities that the customer is pursuing and, in a coordinating effort with the customer, have the necessary materials and supplies available at the right time. The distributor essentially becomes the materials-handling specialist for the customer—another example of functional spin-off, this time by the customer.

Industrial Distributors Serve Industrial Suppliers

Manufacturers benefit from distributor channels, particularly when the manufacturer recognizes the proactive role distribution can play in a well-designed marketing channel. Distributors perform many functions for manufacturers that enable the manufacturers to reach market segments that would be prohibitively expensive to reach otherwise:

◆ *Buy and hold inventory.* Distributors purchase goods from manufacturers. In this context, distributors are customers of the manufacturers, selecting, buying, and *paying* for goods. With the purchased goods, the distributor provides local inventory for the manufacturer's smaller customers whose order volume and frequency make them too costly to serve directly. The manufacturer is relieved of the financial and logistical responsibility of holding local inventory in the form required by these customers.

◆ *Combine manufacturers' outputs.* The customers served by distributors usually purchase products of more than one manufacturer from the distributor. The distributor serves many manufacturers by providing assortment and selection to customers based on the needs of the customer segment, not the product line offering of any one manufacturer. In our earlier electronics assembler example, the distributor provides products related to the assembler's business. This may include supplies, such as solder and solvents, worker protective clothing, and electrical components, such as computer processors and memory chips. Manufacturers with narrow product lines may find that distribution with complementary products is the only way to gain exposure with potential customers.

◆ *Share credit risk.* Manufacturers often provide credit terms to their distributors to enable them to carry and hold inventory. This actually becomes a service to the manufacturer. The risk associated with credit terms extended to the distributor (assuming an ongoing relationship between the manufacturer and the distributor) are significantly less than the risks associated with extension of credit to the many small customers who rely on the distributor for trade credit. The credit granted to the distributor is a significant factor in the distributor's ability to grant credit to its customers.

◆ *Share selling risk.* Though distributors are often independent businesses who are customers of the manufacturers via the purchase of goods, there is also an underlying assumption that the goods purchased are marketable by the distributor and that marketability has been developed in large part by the manufac-

EXHIBIT 12–4   Enhanced Customer Service—Distributors Serve Both Buyers and Sellers

Seller Benefits	Buyer Benefits
◆ Buy and hold inventory.	◆ Provide fast delivery.
◆ Combine supplier outputs (reduce discrepancy of assortment).	◆ Provide market segment-based product assortment.
◆ Share credit risk.	◆ Provide local credit.
◆ Share selling risk.	◆ Provide product information.
◆ Forecast market needs.	◆ Assist in buying decisions.
◆ Provide market information.	◆ Anticipate needs.

turer. The manufacturer is served by this shared risk and partnership; both parties have a stake in the success of the product.

◆ *Forecast market needs.* Since distributors are much closer to the markets they serve, they are able to provide manufacturers with realistic forecasts of business activity. This enables the manufacturer to better schedule its own production activities.

◆ *Provide market information.* Beyond market operations forecasts, discussed in Chapter 6, distributors can have a better understanding of unmet customer needs. Working with the manufacturer, new products and services can be devised that enhance the value of both parties to the ultimate customer.

The factors just described and summarized in Exhibit 12–4 point to the partnership between distributors and manufacturers. When both sides recognize the possibilities that a strong partnership can create, the customer wins.

Value Networks Are Marketing Channels

We can think of a value network as encompassing a distribution channel, as shown in Exhibit 12–5. The key thing to recognize is that the distribution channel is only a portion of the value network in most cases. The value network includes the supply chain feeding into the supplier, the partners providing product and service components of the offering, and the distribution channel reaching the final buyer. All of these elements combine to form a final offering for the final customer, as well as having a role in contributing value for the final customer.

Recall that value for customers is the sum of the benefits minus the sum of the customer's costs. The incorporation of channel elements into the offering creates certain benefits and imposes certain costs upon customers, which, of course, they evaluate when choosing among competitors' offerings. Before designing channels and determining how channels will be managed, the marketer must understand how channels contribute to value in the offering.

Return to the opening example of the Apple Lisa and the ways that the existing Apple channel could not provide value for the intended target market—corporate buyers of computer systems. Apple Computer's independent dealer network was

EXHIBIT 12–5   A Value Network

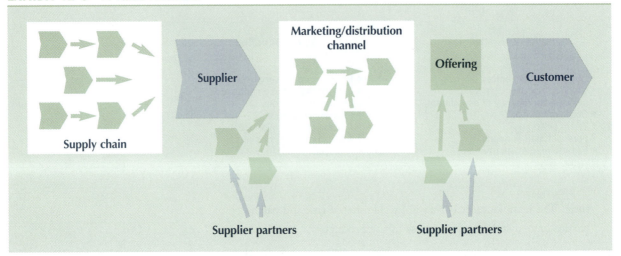

adept at providing support and services of the Apple II target market but was unable to satisfy the *same needs* of a larger, more intricate target market.

The same needs? Generally speaking, yes. The same expectations and demands, no. Just as consumers have favorite methods that meet their particular needs to purchase products and services, businesses have a preferred way they "buy." While the core product may be similar in many cases, different target markets have different expectations of the total offering. Look at each of the following channel activities.

User Training   The home computer buyer most likely purchases a computer for individual use or use within the immediate family. This user seeks out the computer dealer to discuss the features and capabilities of the product. The user does not need a "computer for dummies" training. The corporate customer, however, is unlikely to go to the independent computer shop to discuss the purchase. More likely, the institution's buying center has a diverse set of needs and the actual users of the computer want to know how to use "this thing" (remember, this was 1983). The computer systems supplier is expected to go to the institutional customer. Training in computer fundamentals is necessary on a large scale.

Product Information   The home user's enthusiasm for the computer is accompanied by a knowledge of the computer obtained from magazines, user groups, and other sources. At the time of the Lisa introduction, the home user was likely an early adopter of home computing technology. The dealer's role in the education process was probably limited to product technology alternatives and options. An institutional buyer, however, likely expresses needs in terms of what the computer can accomplish, rather than how it accomplishes it. This is an important distinction. While technophiles purchase technology just because it is new, business users are far more pragmatic, requiring functionality and ease of use over technology.

Product Support and Delivery   For the home market, the dealer is likely to discuss the product technology with the customer and provide one-on-one technical support. Outside of making sure the buyer leaves the shop with all the necessary cables and computer accessories, the dealer usually does not play a large role in the computer installation. The institutional buyer, however, expects installation and on-site testing for all locations. This is a different expertise and service context than the technical product support at the shop. Often, channel designs for products that require on-site installation and service have separate channel flows to accomplish these needs. Exhibit 12–2a, previously discussed, shows some of the possible channel flows and participants. Additionally, the independent dealer is unlikely to have the staff to support ongoing inquiries from the numerous users of the institution's systems.

Financing   A large purchase by the home computer user might include a printer and an external storage device. The extent of financing provided by the independent dealer might be the acceptance of third-party credit cards (Visa, MasterCard, American Express, etc.).

The institutional buying center may have particular finance needs. The acquisition of many computers may be more acceptable as a lease rather than as a purchase, or the buyer might want a payment plan spread over several years. The independent dealer is unlikely to have the financial capability to support the financing portion of the offering.

Apple's existing consumer product channel was not particularly well suited to the value sought by the target market. The product itself may have been very well suited to the target market (debatable, but possible in this case). The different types of value discussed, though—the other kinds of value sought by the market segment—could not be delivered by the channel and so the marketing of the Lisa was problematic.

BUSINESS LOGISTICS MANAGEMENT

Up to this point in this chapter, the discussion has been focused on the rationale, economic utility, and design of marketing channels. The actual movement and storage of goods, major ingredients in the marketing channel, have been relegated to the mention of ancillary members of the channel. The management of the movement, sorting, and storage of goods in the marketing channel is called **logistics.** Actual design of a logistics system should be done with the aid of professional logisticians. Marketers, though, should have a sense of the basic goals of logistics design and management, because logistics can add so much to customer value and to competitive advantage.

The economic utilities discussed earlier in this chapter comprise the kinds of objectives that must be met in performing logistical operations: meeting customer form needs, meeting customer time needs, meeting customer place needs, and meeting customer possession needs. The logistics system must get the right products to customers, in the right quantities, in the right place, at the right time. Logistics must do this in ways that transfer ownership to customers (and to channel intermediaries) at the appropriate time and place.

The Physical Distribution Concept— A Cost-Service Relationship

Logistics systems design includes decisions on inventory placement and management, transportation modes and scheduling, warehouse size and location, physical handling systems, and information handling systems. System design is aimed at minimizing costs while maintaining a given level of customer service. In this effort, managers are concerned with the simultaneous management of three elements:[2]

◆   Inventory

◆   Transportation

◆   Warehousing

The lowest system cost of these three elements combined will not necessarily be a result of the lowest possible cost of each element. The balance of these three elements to minimize costs at a given level of customer service is called the **physical distribution concept**.

Inventory Management

Inventory management is often the largest cost associated with any logistics system. Channel members have significant investment in inventory, and that investment usually implies carrying and finance charges as well as the costs associated with storing and assorting the inventory. Recognizing the high costs associated with large quantities of inventory, tools to minimize these costs are used. Tools such as just-in-time inventory management, just-in-time manufacturing and facility location, and electronic data interchange (whether in private networks or facilitated by the Web) are employed. Obviously, the lower quantity of inventory that can be maintained at any time leads to lower inventory costs. However, lower inventory levels often lead to more frequent and thus more costly transportation.

Transportation

Transportation decisions traditionally have involved the choice of water, air, rail, truck, or pipeline utilization, depending on the nature of the product to be moved. Slower transportation methods usually have lower costs, with airfreight the highest cost method. Slow transportation methods imply that safety stocks—the amount of inventory available between the time of reordering and the arrival of new inventory—must be of larger quantities than with rapid transportation methods. While other factors can impact lead times, such as particular product and manufacturing circumstances and optimal quantity order sizes, if transportation costs are minimized without regard for the impact on the total system, inventory carrying costs increase.

---

[2]Lou E. Pelton, David Strutton, and James R. Lumpkin, *Marketing Channels, A Relationship Management Approach* (Chicago: Irwin, 1997), 301–311.

Warehousing

Warehousing   As the level of inventory increases, so does the cost to store it. If low-cost transportation leads to an increased inventory level, then warehouse costs are also increased. If warehouse costs are minimized, transportation costs increase, particularly as suppliers attempt to avoid "stockouts"—running out of goods just as a buyer may require delivery.

Depending on the nature of the products and the goals of the channel design, channel management focuses on two functions of warehousing. The first of these is product flow/movement, and the second is product storage. Channel designs that focus on rapid movement of goods rather than on storage of large quantities of goods use facilities optimized as **distribution centers.** Channel designs that accept slow movement and focus on storage of goods use facilities optimized as **warehouses.**

Distribution centers are optimized to move product through the facility, creating assortment in the process. Materials flowing into the center are immediately redirected to customers. The discrepancy of assortment is reduced, and goods are held for a minimal period of time. Depending on the nature of the goods and the lead times associated with their creation, rapid transportation may be used to replace the need for significant safety stocks.

Warehouses are optimized as storage and assortment creation facilities. If the nature of the goods is such that long-term storage creates an optimal logistical pattern, warehouses are employed. Because inventory quantities are usually larger when the longer-term storage is used, transportation costs can be reduced.

Material Requirements Planning

Material Requirements Planning   The storage, movement, and assortment of goods in business logistics systems are part of the **material requirements planning (MRP)** effort, which is now often subsumed within enterprise resource planning (ERP) systems. While an extensive discussion of MRP practice is beyond the scope of this text, business-to-business marketers should understand the goals of MRP and how suppliers can create value for customers in this area.

Material requirements planning efforts involve many stakeholders in the organization, often some of the same stakeholders that contributed to the buying decision in the buying center. MRP requires forecasting demand on an ongoing basis, aimed at minimizing business logistics costs and the impact of the bullwhip effect while maximizing customer service. Purchasing, manufacturing, transportation, and marketing contribute information to synchronize the various needs of each part of the organization. MRP responsibilities usually reside in the purchasing department of the organization. Successful MRP efforts involve purchasing professionals in the management of the entire supply chain. This presents another opportunity for the supplier to influence the specification and selection process of the buyer.

Logistics as a Competitive Edge

Logistics as a Competitive Edge   Logistics have become an important part of competitive advantage in most product-oriented industries. Getting the product to the customer faster means that needs of end users can be met more quickly. In the case of component parts, getting the products into the production process faster means that supplier production schedules can more closely match end customer demand, thus reducing inventories, carrying costs, and waste. Even in industries in which documents are the only part of the offering moved from place to place, such as in insurance or commercial real estate, logistics management means closing deals faster and more accurately, which can translate into time and money saved for the final buyer of the policy or property. The discussion of the rivalry between FedEx and UPS, shown in Exhibit 12–3, illustrates the importance of logistics in building or maintaining competitive position.

Economic Utility of Business-to-Business Markets

The examples noted demonstrate the broad array of methods that can be used to provide economic utility in a channel. Note also how different the methods are for business-to-business markets versus consumer markets. In mass consumer markets, economic utility is provided, with much speculation, by a channel design that attempts to anticipate consumer needs. In business-to-business markets, economic utility is often the result of a specific demand by a particular customer—part of "the way a customer buys."

Chapter 3 discussed the process flow model of the buying decision process. The *Deliver Solution Stage* and the *End Game Stage,* as shown in Exhibit 12–6 (repeated from Exhibit 3–3), contain elements related to the transactional aspects of the process, shown as analogous to *Make the Transaction Routine* and *Resell the Job* of the classical industrial buyers' decision process. The marketing channel design is a direct result of recognizing and accommodating the materials planning, handling, inventory, scheduling, and invoicing needs of the customer. Part of building a long-lasting relationship with customers is developing a marketing channel that is **differentially invisible** to the customer. A differentially invisible channel meets all of the logistical parameters of the customer. The merging of the two systems is so smooth that the customer does not recognize any differences in operation or style. This can be a significant advantage should the customer ever consider changing suppliers, as customers can incur significant costs associated with changing or adding suppliers. In oligopolistic markets, a supplying firm may have a different customized "routine" for each major customer, as well as a standardized routine for smaller customers. Each of these parts of the total offering is an opportunity to create value for the customer while demonstrating a differential advantage versus the competition. It should be noted that the "invisibility" of the interface between customer and channel is often done in physical handling of products. Ideally, a supplier would want to accomplish this with the administrative aspects of transactions, as well. Information technology has not developed to the point, yet, where such invisibility is indeed achieved. IT systems compatibility between customer and supplier still requires a degree of systems matching.

Customers should not be required to match the channel and logistics design of the vendor. Vendors should develop channel designs that seamlessly match the operation of customers. For small customers, this usually involves the use of industrial distributors. For large customers, this involves matching delivery time and methods, palletizing, and other requirements. We use the term **differentially invisible** to imply that the customer should not be required to adapt to the vendor—the process should be invisible. This level of service, part of the total offering, can be a competitive differentiating factor.

EXHIBIT 12–6   Stages in the Process Flow Model of the Buying Decision Process

Process Flow Stages	Buying Decision Process Steps
Definition Stage	
◆ Problem definition	◆ Problem recognition
◆ Solution definition	◆ General need description
◆ Product specification	◆ Product specification
Selection Stage	
◆ Solution provider search	◆ Supplier/Source search
◆ Acquire solution provider(s)	◆ Proposal solicitation
	◆ Contract for supplier(s)
Deliver Solution Stage	
◆ Customize as needed	◆ Make the transaction routine
◆ Install/Test/Train	
End Game Stage	
◆ Operate solution	◆ Evaluate performance
◆ Reach end result	◆ Resell the job
◆ Evaluate outcomes	
◆ Determine next set of needs	

CHANNEL DESIGN

With value for customers firmly in mind, the business-to-business marketer must design a working channel structure as part of the marketing strategy and plan. Sherlock suggests that the marketer must start with an understanding of the final customer and determine what channel-provided value the customer wants.[3] Then the marketer can begin to design the channel that delivers this value. This sounds like an obvious, even trivial, approach. Too often, though, the marketer begins at the doors of her own company and designs forward to "reach" the customer. Taking this approach, as we saw with the Apple Lisa, can have damaging results.

As we just said, the marketer must know what the customer wants. The marketer must extend this analysis upstream as well. The environmental analysis must also include an analysis of existing and potential marketing channels. The information desired is similar to that collected for customers—their needs, their buying behavior, how they view value, the nature of their buying centers, and so on—but includes an analysis of the value they provide and their internal value chains that produce that value. Accordingly, an analysis of channels is akin to an analysis combining the methods of customer analysis and competitor analysis.

In designing the channel, the marketer must decide whether to go through intermediaries or to go through a direct channel. Other decisions include the level of **intensity of distribution** (how many distributors within a territory), the kinds of channel partners to obtain, how the channel flows will be structured, and, most

---

[3]Paul Sherlock, *Rethinking Business-to-Business Marketing* (New York: The Free Press/Macmillian, 1991), chap. 10.

importantly, how competitive advantage will be built. Recall from Chapter 10 that we suggest that marketers innovate across the offering to create competitive advantage. Designing channels is one area where large advantages can be created.

Dual Distribution and Multidistribution

Dual distribution is a channel pattern that uses more than one channel design, each intended to reach a different target market. Incorporation of dual distribution is a decision to reach multiple market segments with different economic utility needs. The Dana example earlier in this chapter is an example of dual distribution. Two different channel designs—one direct to the OEM market, the other through intermediaries that reach the service parts market—provide coverage to market segments based on the buying requirements of each segment.

Suppliers work with one or more channel intermediaries to provide the value required to serve different market segments. When a supplier uses different channel designs to reach different markets—as Dana does for OEM and service markets and, perhaps, Apple should have for the Lisa—it is called **dual distribution.** Dual distribution, then, is a decision about providing desired services to differentiated markets. Dual distribution usually does not create horizontal competition in business-to-business markets, as it is unlikely that the high-volume, direct Dana channel described earlier in the chapter would express any interest in the service channel.

When a manufacturer selects more than one channel intermediary at the same level—such as two industrial distributors in the same market—horizontal competition is created. This channel pattern is called **multidistribution.** The multiple distributors serve the same market segment and compete for the same customers. Manufacturers selecting multidistribution are increasing the **intensity of distribution** for their products. Recall from your principles of marketing course that intensity of distribution refers to the degree to which a product is available from one (exclusive), a few (selective), or several sources (intensive distribution). Multidistribution occurs later in the life cycle of a product when generic forms may be available in the market and locational convenience is of prime importance in the marketing mix.

Multidistribution is the deployment of multiple channels of the same design in a given territory. Multidistribution is a decision about the intensity of product placement or distribution.

Intensity of distribution refers to the level of locational convenience required by the target market. Specialty products are usually in exclusive distribution while mature, generic products (whose marketing mix puts more emphasis on convenience factors) are usually in intensive distribution, creating horizontal competitors in the channel.

Reduce Discrepancy of Assortment

Another service provided by channel intermediaries is the creation of assortments based on customer needs rather than on manufacturer product lines. Industrial end users who purchase through channel intermediaries select the intermediary that has a product line representative of the needs of the end-user business. A nursery supplying landscaping services businesses purchases supplies—fertilizer, soil additives, agricultural chemicals, and flower pots—from a distributor who has specialized in supply to the nursery market. It is unlikely that the nursery buyer could find a manufacturer with a product line that included all of these items. Most manufacturers produce a large quantity of a few items, and most end users purchase a small quantity of a diverse set of goods that serve many aspects of the business. The distributor has sought to create an assortment of goods needed by the nursery market segment. By carrying the products of several producers, the distributor creates a "one-stop shop" for nurseries. This effort transforms *the manufacturers' assortment* into a *market assortment.* By reducing the **discrepancy of assortment,** the distributor has saved the end user the cost and time of dealing with multiple vendors.[4]

The creation of market-based assortments serves producers and users. Suppliers seek channel members that carry complementary product lines. The value of a single product is enhanced by the availability of associated goods from a single source. Producers also seek intermediaries that have product lines that include goods from recognized market owners or well-known industrial brands. The association with the market standard bearer becomes a positive attribute for the producer of the lesser-known product.

When Use of Distributor Channels Is a Good Channel Design

When is it appropriate to use a distributor, and what products are good candidates for distributor channels? Distribution, as part of the "place" of the marketing four Ps, does not stand alone but must be fully integrated with the other parts of the marketing mix. The previous discussion centered on the four economic utilities and how manufacturers and distributors can serve each others' needs. The following discussion examines other factors that are necessary and appropriate for successful distributor channels.

Marketing Mix Issues   Obviously, some products are appropriate for distributor channels while others would be unsuccessful in the market if distributor channels were selected. Traditionally, products that favor the use of distributor channels require local stock, are somewhat generic, and have very low unit value. This traditional view of distribution can be limiting, and there is often a predisposition against distributors by manufacturers as low tech or unqualified. Customers in each market segment will have an expected channel of delivery for product, service, and all other marketing channel flows. Competitor efforts will also influence channel design. With this in mind, let us examine when use of distributor channels is appropriate. In the following discussion, while each factor is discussed individually, they are seldom solitary influences in the marketplace.

Factors Favoring Use of Distributor Channels

◆   *Product requires local stock.* Certain products require local and immediate accessibility. Certainly this is the case with food stuffs, but it also applies to certain industrial chemicals, components used in construction trades, and any product (or service) for which shelf life or perishability is a consideration.

---

[4] Louis W. Stern and Adel I. El-Ansary, *Marketing Channels,* 4th ed. (Upper Saddle River, N.J.: Prentice-Hall, 1992), 5.

◆ *Small product line, unable to support a direct sales force.* Regardless of other factors involved, companies with limited product offerings just may not be able to afford their own sales force. Distributors who have compatible product lines and established relationships with appropriate customers will be sought out to carry the limited line.

◆ *Product is somewhat generic.* While few marketers relish admitting that their product is substitutable, those who are in such markets should realize that they can be the substitute for the competitors' products. Goods in the maturity stage of the product life cycle (PLC) are often sold based on the most accessible and/or available. Local stock and established distributor/customer relationships are the deciding factor in these sales. Margins on generic or easily substitutable products may be insufficient to support a direct sales force.

◆ *Product has low unit value.* Similar to generic products, items that are relatively inexpensive on a unit basis and are sold to many customers but seldom in high volume are likely candidates for distributor channels. Office supplies are an example of this category.

◆ *Product is near the end of its product life cycle.* Beyond availability issues, products that are in the mature or decline stage seldom need significant customer education for proper application. As a product matures, channel redesign is often an important tool to maintain profitability. It is easier to place a product into distributor channels as the need for customer education/missionary sales lessens.

◆ *Customers are widely dispersed.* The logistics expense of serving customers who are geographically spread out can be a real problem. Depending on the volume of purchase by each customer, distributor channels are usually a more effective channel design. Often, a manufacturer will have overlapping channel designs— distributor channels for small-volume, dispersed customers and direct sales for the few very high volume accounts in the same geographic region.

◆ *Local repackaging, sizing, or fabrication is required.* The steel industry relies on steel service centers to cut, blank, and perform some first-stage processing on products shipped to the centers in very large rolls. Customers of the service centers are able to purchase custom-formed components that are more readily incorporated into their operations. Many chemical and plastics manufacturers ship their products to distributors in bulk railcars where the distributor repackages into 25 kg to 500 kg packages (solids) or large drums or gallon containers. These smaller sizes allow customers to purchase in smaller lots and lower their investment in inventory and risk from spoilage and obsolescence. A significant portion of distributor margins are derived from the different prices for the bulk versus packaged products.

◆ *Market has many small-volume buyers.* Similar to the situation with geographically dispersed buyers, many small-volume buyers will create a transaction nightmare for a volume-oriented manufacturer. Distributors can take over the small but frequent transactions on a routine basis.

Factors Not Favoring Use of Distributor Channels

◆ *Product is highly customized.* When individual customer applications of products require customization, shorter channels are more appropriate. Close contact by design, manufacturing, and engineering personnel in both the supplier and customer organizations is essential to application success. Distributor channel services like local inventory and rapid delivery are more suited to products that have a more generic nature.

◆ *Product is new or innovative.* The application of new products often requires that customers be educated in the most efficient use or service. The role of missionary sales is very important. While distributors can be used for logistical needs, the application development efforts necessary to deliver full value to the customer are best handled directly by the supplying firm.

◆ *Product is technically sophisticated.* Complex or technically sophisticated products, similar to the situation for new or innovative products, require advice and counsel in their correct application (see the subsequent glazing example).

◆ *Significant missionary selling is required.* If part of the total offering involves a high service and design assistance profile, distributor channels may be suitable only for the logistical needs of the product. Many of the product types already noted fall into this category, but the list is not exhaustive. Regardless of other factors, a manufacturer may elect to promote products through missionary sales while spinning off logistics to independent distributors.

◆ *Manufacturer requires control over product application.* Regardless of the degree of innovation, some manufacturers may not be comfortable with leaving application counseling about their products to third parties. Pharmaceutical companies' use of "detail persons" calling on physicians is an obvious example. Prescription drugs are specified for patients by physicians, requiring the "detail" person to provide up-to-date and accurate application information. The product flows to pharmacies through distributors who maintain local inventory and provide timely delivery. Even with recent innovations in delivery, such as centralized health maintenance organizations' mail delivery and Internet pharmacies, the physician, as the specifying influence, must be made aware of product features. Other products that have significant liability issues that manufacturers wish to control also fall into this category. Consider manufacturers of bullet-resistant glazing (better known as bulletproof glass—only their legal counsel will not let them say "proof"). Application of these products in banks, gas station kiosks, and similar locations requires careful product specification and installation to be fully effective.

Manufacturers wish to reduce their vulnerability through control of all aspects of the product application.

♦ *Large buyers are geographically concentrated.* Regardless of other product characteristics, when the customer base is made up of a few geographically concentrated large users (typical oligopolistic markets), shorter channels better meet customer needs. Large-volume deliveries, price structure, and other service factors favor direct relationships. The same product may be represented by independent distributors in areas of lesser customer concentration.

Other Circumstances   There are many less obvious but equally important possibilities favoring the use of distributors. When an offering requires extensive sales effort directed at buying professionals (purchasing agents, buyers) because there are many direct competitors, existing buyer/seller relationships may be critical in gaining acceptance by the customer. If sourcing decisions of a product type or within a particular market segment rely primarily on the relationship aspects of the total offering, it may be necessary to use distributor channels to penetrate the market. In these circumstances, the existing relationship between the industrial end user and the distributor becomes the primary competitive feature of the distributor.

Another possibility that seems to defy the logic of when to use distributor channels is the case of a new business. Whether offering an innovative new product or a product with several substitutes in the market, new companies without the resources to place their own sales team in the field may find that a distributor channel is the only affordable way to reach certain segments. Similarly, an existing business-to-business manufacturer about to enter a new market may find distributor channels particularly attractive. Customers in the new markets may have significantly different buying patterns than existing customers. The direct sales force of the business-to-business manufacturer may be well trained and organized but only in relation to the existing products and markets. Placing the new product in distributor channels avoids distracting the direct sellers from their normal call pattern and customer base.

When customer buying patterns indicate that customers expect to find the offering in distributor channels, it is necessary to also use distributors. If known competitors use distributor channels and your company expects to reach the same market, it may be necessary to use distributors. The channel relationships for the product or service type may be already established, and customers are unwilling to establish different habits. Even if the product is the next-generation innovation targeted to replace existing offerings in the segment, users of the established product expect their needs to be satisfied by the same distribution pattern.

Often, particularly with smaller customers, purchases through distributors are preferred. The smaller industrial end user may be taking full advantage of the inventory services and trade credit available from the distributor, taking advantage of the complete solution offered. To penetrate this customer, it may be efficient to join the buying pattern rather than compete with it. Exhibit 12–7 summarizes factors favoring or not favoring the use of distributor channels.

**EXHIBIT 12–7   Factors Favoring Use or Not Favoring Use
of Distributor Channels**

Favoring	Not Favoring
◆ Product requires local stock. ◆ Product line is small, unable to support direct sales. ◆ Product is somewhat generic. ◆ Product has low unit value. ◆ Product is near end of PLC. ◆ Customers are widely dispersed. ◆ Local repackaging, sizing, or fabrication is required. ◆ Market has many small-volume buyers. ◆ Product requires extensive sales effort directed at buying professionals. ◆ Start-up venture or established company is entering a new market. ◆ Competition uses distributors. ◆ Customers prefer distributors.	◆ Product is highly customized. ◆ Product is new or innovative. ◆ Product is technically sophisticated. ◆ Significant missionary selling is required. ◆ Manufacturer requires control over product application. ◆ Large buyers are geographically concentrated.

DISTRIBUTION AND THE PRODUCT LIFE CYCLE

The preceding factors address a combination of marketing mix variables and how they can impact the use of distribution. These factors may exist alone or in combination with others. Consider these factors as they relate to the PLC.

Introduction

Early in the product life cycle (introduction), a start-up with a new product may not have the resources to fund a direct channel, though use of a manufacturers' representative is more likely if the product is new as a category and requires some customer education for use. A start-up organization may often be the least able, from a marketing view, to use a distributor for many of the other marketing mix variables previously noted. While contrary to conventional wisdom, it may be appropriate that start-ups in this position seek additional financing from their investors to build the appropriate sales force.[5] This sales force will most likely take on the organizational style of missionary sales or an application development team while business logistics functions can be handled by independent distribution. As already noted, an established manufacturer may also use distribution for a new product if the target market is not consistent with the existing markets served by the manufacturer's sales force.

Promotion as it relates to marketing channels during the introductory stage consists primarily of establishing brand awareness. New brands must prove viable not only in the market but also to channel intermediaries. Listing allowances and discounts may be required to gain acceptance among intermediaries.

[5]Sherlock, op. cit.

Growth

Once an offering has proven its worth in the marketplace, obtaining distribution is much easier. Distributors want successful products and will readily accept an offering that their customers are likely to want. During this period, missionary sellers can help establish the product in distribution and build loyalty with the distributor sellers by providing customer and seller training and sales leads, particularly with high learning products. When the supplier goal is to position as the industry standard, loyalty built by a strong missionary effort at this time will help fend off imitators in the future.

In technology markets, the marketer may enlist the services of value-added resellers (VARs) during the growth phase. VARs have established relationships with technology buyers and provide technology and integration services that are needed to complete the offering. One problem that can arise with VARs is that, as the market begins to expand rapidly, the VARs may want to continue to participate as high-volume resellers. This is fine as long as they have the capability to do so, but VARs may not have the ability to handle large volumes, the desire to open new markets, nor the willingness to reduce prices. Consequently, they may be a bad fit for fast-growing markets yet not want to face the fact that the fit is poor.

Handling this systematic channel conflict requires some delicate negotiations early in the process. One thing that the marketer might try is to specify in the contract with the VAR that, as the market changes, the VAR can be designated a high-volume distributor if it meets certain criteria. Then the channel manager or marketing manager must continually communicate with the VARs to let them know how the market is evolving so that changes in channel patterns do not come as a surprise. The wise manager will continue to work with the best VARs, setting them up for the next set of new products coming through the pipeline as they become ready to market to the VARs' traditional target segments.

Maturity/Decline

A product that has reached the maturity/decline stage of the PLC may require an entirely redesigned marketing channel. A product that has moved into the low-learning stage as customers become more familiar with its use and no longer need applications development support may be placed in distribution for the first time. If the product has become an industrial commodity (with several "or equivalents"), margins will be less than during its added-value stage, possibly not able to support the development effort employed during higher learning periods. Distribution will be able to handle the new buying criteria more efficiently than direct sales. (New buying criteria may relate to locational convenience, JIT, low cost in small volumes, etc.)

During maturity and decline, particularly when there are a number of alternative products, suppliers use a number of trade promotions to keep products in the forefront of seller efforts. Rebates to channel members, special volume discounts, and sales incentive contests are all used to attract and keep sellers' attention.

MANAGING CHANNELS OF DISTRIBUTION

Once the channel strategy has been designed, the marketer must execute the plan. The kinds of activities included are selection of channel partners and building relationships with them, running channel programs to keep them motivated and performing to the plan, and reshaping the channel strategy as the market changes.

Selecting and Caring for Distributors

Selecting distributors has some of the same elements as selecting manufacturers' representatives (see Chapter 11). Like manufacturers' reps, distributors—even those that are part of nationwide distribution companies—are designed to have regional impact. Nationwide distributor organizations need to be examined region by region. It is rare to find a national distributor who is equally strong in all regions where they compete. Regionally based distributors or a combination of national and regional players may be better able to serve your particular needs. In any event, here are some basic points to remember:

♦ Ask potential customers who they recommend. Who better to recommend a distributor with successful relationships?

♦ Determine which distributor fits marketing plan goals. While logistical concerns may be a perfect match, the goals and aspirations of the distributor should be aligned with yours. Contextual differences may not surface early in the relationship but will be difficult to resolve later. A simple example, particularly for aggressive, growth-oriented companies, is a distributor who is willing to sacrifice growth to maintain higher margins.

♦ Make calls with them. This can be part of the selection process as well as part of the relationship building process after selection. If acceptable to the distributor, make customer calls with some of its sales force before the contract is signed. Remember that your distributors are both customers and sales assets. Making customer calls with them, often in a missionary role, is an essential part of building the relationship and protects your company from being isolated from your ultimate customers. (Many distributors will be cautious about letting the customer—manufacturer relationship get too cozy.)

♦ Make calls on them. As we have said, your distributors are also your customers, particularly if they distribute products for your competitors. Build the relationship at all levels.

♦ Train and support them well and often, at both your facilities and theirs. Your training and education of your distributor can increase the comfort level with your products and your organization. Show them your facilities, not only to provide product and service training but also so that individuals from each organization can develop connections beyond e-mail and telephones. Make them feel like a part of your team.

Superordinate goals are those goals that go beyond a single intermediary, are desirable to many of the channel members, and are unobtainable through the effort of a single channel member. Cooperation and mutual understanding between intermediaries are necessary to achieve these goals. Since the goals are considered laudable by many of the channel members, the process of obtaining them fosters teamwork and cooperation.

Team Players   Different channel designs exist for different markets. Some are the result of years of unintentional channel design that has become customary in a particular market, while others are tightly designed with significant (and sometimes resented) control at many levels. Regardless of the details of the channel design, channel members must recognize that they are part of a team whose individual goals can be enhanced through agreement with the system goals. Any channel member at any particular level can maximize profits/performance as an individual entity. Successful channels are the result of teamwork—the creation of a win-win situation. Channel performance that is consistent with the needs and wants of the target market and internally consistent with the goals and objectives of members requires a contextual approach that recognizes and develops both individual member and **superordinate goals**.

To understand this dual-purpose goal setting, students must recognize and understand the channel from the perspective of each member. Factors that can improve the performance of a retailer are often costly to manufacturers and wholesalers (increased promotion, local inventory, rapid shipping, etc.). While acceptable to the retailer, these factors decrease the profitability of the channel for other members. Thus, channel management must include a balance that is acceptable to all members.

Power and Conflict in Marketing Channels

Power in marketing channels usually results when one channel member (Member A) is dependent on another member (Member B). The dependent member, A, is not completely free to select its own direction on all issues. Member B then has influence and control over Member A with regard to the issues in which A is dependent on B. The dependence may not be just monetary but may include specialized knowledge, skills, and market access. Thus, the portfolio of resources and skills that a channel member commits to the channel effort can have a significant impact on how the channel relationship is managed and controlled.

Bases of Power   Power can be classified as deriving from bases of resources and skills. The *bases of power*[6] include reward, coercion, legitimate, expertise, identification, and information power. For discussion purposes, these bases are broken into categories. *Soft* bases are comprised of expertise, identification, and information power; and *hard* bases are comprised of the remaining reward, coercion, and legitimate bases.[7]

---

[6] Stern and El-Ansary, op. cit., 268–83.

[7] The first three bases—reward, coercion, and legitimate—are often referred to as *mediated* power bases, while the remaining are called *nonmediated* bases.

Hard power bases are usually quantifiable and specific. Rewards can be margin rates, incentive programs, and special monetary promotions through the channel. Rewards may be specifically related to performance in product sales results or territory coverage. Coercive power, effective only when there is a significant imbalance in the channel, often takes the form of punishment for a lack of performance or results. Legitimate power stems from a contractual agreement that is enforceable by a third party or, in highly intraorganizational channels (i.e., a corporate or contractual vertical marketing channel), a strong feeling of obligation or commitment. Continuous use of hard power bases often leads to greater conflict as members feel *required* to perform rather than *invited* to perform.

Soft power bases are more qualitative in nature than hard bases. Product and market expertise and information are shared between channel members in the recognition that improved channel performance can be of benefit to all members. Identification power exists when one channel member possesses an image, reputation, or position in the market that makes belonging to that channel system a positive asset. This association may be related to brands, channel support, or prestige market positioning. In business-to-business markets, identification power can be associated with exemplary assistance provided to channel members by a manufacturer's missionary sellers as well as a manufacturer's brands being the industry standard in target markets. Agreement on goals and the understanding of win-win outcomes are important in the effective application of soft power bases.

As is often the case, mutual dependence exists between members such that an imbalance that leads to conflict can be avoided. Many marketing channels are often combinations of independent businesses attempting to meet channel goals while also meeting the goals of the individual business. Unfortunately, these goals are not always in complete alignment. Goal incompatibility and its variants are among the primary causes of channel conflict. Older, established channel members who have "proven their mettle" may have as a primary goal stabilizing profit margins at the highest level, while newer, less-known intermediaries have a more-aggressive posture in the market. Other conflict igniters are territory issues, where suppliers may reserve **house accounts** for a direct selling function, and **product line maintenance** issues, where suppliers try to force a full line of products or prevent channels from carrying competitive products. The scenario of adding a second source for a product type, discussed in this chapter, can lead to conflict between channel members if there is an expectation of loyalty that has been lost or not earned. While many conflict resolution techniques are available, their details are generally beyond the scope of this text. The following discussion looks at channel design, leadership, and control as elements in channel power and conflict.

Channel Patterns and Control

Traditionally, channel power was the realm of the large manufacturer at the top of the channel. Manufacturers who desired greater power and control over channels would either forward integrate into corporate vertical marketing systems or enter into

© PHOTODISC

contractual relationships in which goal setting included superordinate goals. As manufacturers moved to establish control of channels, economies of scale in buying were created that began to influence intermediaries who were not aligned with a vertical marketing system. The outcome was the joining of **horizontal competitors** (intermediaries at the same level in a channel, usually existing in multidistribution) into buying groups to create the scale necessary to compete with corporate systems.

Exhibit 12–8 shows the organization of several traditional **vertical marketing systems (VMSs)** and the addition of value networks, arranged in order of dependence on or degree of supplier control (increasing left to right) and dependence on mutually beneficial relationships (increasing right to left). The following discussion characterizes these channel patterns from the viewpoint of channel control and the importance of mutually beneficial relationships.

Historically, a large manufacturer's size and financial power gave it the privilege to strongly influence, if not control, the marketing channel. Manufacturers that desired greater control or were unable to achieve distribution goals through independent intermediaries would integrate operations, forming a **corporate vertical marketing system (CVMS).** This provides centralized control but limits flexibility and requires a significant capital investment.

Contractual systems aim at control through binding agreements with otherwise independent intermediaries. Of these systems, probably the greatest control exists with franchisors in franchise systems. However, even with the significantly controlling contractual agreements that exist in franchises, franchisees are independent business owners, not employees of the franchisor. (Among the most interesting contractual channels are the farm producer co-ops—see "Finding More Uses for Cranberries"). Contractual systems are voluntary; there is no unified ownership. Most contractual arrangements were created to develop competitive buying positions. Faced with competition from large vertically integrated organizations, independent channel members formed voluntary chains. (Voluntary chains were started at the wholesale level as well as at the retail level. The main difference is where the motivation for the cooperative effort came from and is not significant to this discussion.) In the grocery industry, the Independent Grocers Alliance (IGA) is among the best-known systems, while Ace, Tru-Value, Pro, and Sentry Hardware are all types of voluntary chains. Toro, the outdoor equipment manufacturer, uses contractual channels (franchises) for commercial outdoor equipment; and McKesson, the pharmaceutical wholesaler, has over 3,300 independent retailers that are part of its voluntary chain.[8]

Because of their voluntary nature, contractual channels require a greater degree of cooperation and mutual goal setting to be effective. This is more true with administered channels, whose composition and level of commitment by intermediaries are not legally binding. **Administered channel intermediaries** are inde-

---

[8]Stern and El-Ansary, op. cit., 331–34.

EXHIBIT 12–8 Control and Cooperation in Vertical Marketing Systems

Increasing centralized control →

Value networks	Horizontal sprawl	Conventional systems	Administered systems	Contractual systems	Corporate vertical marketing systems (CVMS)

Value networks are almost totally dependent on relationships that create cooperation and win-win scenarios. The assembled team creates a solution to a particular customer need. The team will be unified in the approach at that customer, but there is not necessarily any agreement to participate together beyond the immediate collaboration. Today's partner may be part of a competing network tomorrow.

Conventional systems, not vertical channel patterns, are similar to administered channels but without agreement on goals. Intermediaries are independent businesses with concerns only for their own operations.

By most traditional views, administered marketing systems are the closest to conventional systems. Independent intermediaries agree on goals related to a particular administrative leader's market segment while maintaining disparate goals associated with their own operations.

Contractual systems include wholesaler- and retailer-sponsored voluntary chains and franchise systems. Ace and Tru-Value Hardware and IGA are voluntary chains. New car dealers and fast food restaurants (e.g., McDonalds, Burger King) are franchises.

CVMSs were likely developed when there were no other channel alternatives. In a CVMS, all functions and flows are performed by (or contracted by) the integrator. CVMSs have the greatest degree of centralized control but less flexibility. Many Goodyear tire dealers are forms of a forward integrated CVMS; Sears is a backward integrated CVMS.

Horizontal sprawl is a term applied to the Japanese keiretsu channel pattern. A keiretsu is a group of loosely associated companies that may have many ties at the ownership and management level. A keiretsu is often a complete supply chain with many buyers, sellers, and ancillary service providers. There is significant sharing of goals, risks, and benefits among members of the chain.

← **Mutual goals** ← **Increasing voluntary cooperation** **Directed goals** →

pendent businesses who have agreed to marketing goals and programs developed by other companies. General Electric used administered channels for major appliances in consumer markets and industrial components and motors in industrial markets. Owens & Minor, Baxter, and several other hospital supply distributors provide JIT "stockless" inventory services to their customers. A sophisticated refinement of JIT systems, stockless systems provide supplies in quantities as small as single units to care stations within client hospitals.

Known for the implied business camaraderie that exists between suppliers and customers, **keiretsu** systems often have little contractual control. Sometimes called **horizontal sprawl,** the keiretsu consists of a very flat channel pattern, with few, if any, vertical layers. Each supplier has a direct relationship with the customer.

Finding More Uses for Cranberries

Imagine that you are the owner of a cranberry bog. Your big market consists of one day a year—Thanksgiving—and not everyone likes cranberries on turkey. You dream of cranberries on cereal in the morning, cranberry-apple juice as a breakfast drink and a cocktail mixer. As the owner of just one bog, you might find it difficult to develop new uses for cranberries, but as a member of a consortium of bog owners, resources could be pooled and risks minimized in a way that you could afford product and market development efforts.

Your dream is the vision that many farm producer cooperatives have been built on. Ocean Spray, Sunkist, LandO'Lakes, and others are co-ops established to expand the markets for basic commodities and establish quality standards that could be reflected as premium brands in the market place.

To be part of the co-op, growers must meet certain quality standards associated with their particular produce and agree to certain resale terms. At the inception of many co-ops, growers were very interested in joining as there was significant upside potential—more markets would be available, and price and quality would be stabilized. With time, the co-ops developed channel power positions that benefited their members both in the markets for their products and the markets for farm equipment and supplies. Farm co-ops are big business. Consider this the next time you have whipped cream and cranberries on your ice cream. A farm-producer co-op may have marketed all three products!

Ancillary providers in the pattern are also members of the keiretsu, such that shipping, financing, and other services are available to members at favorable terms. The favorable consideration is part of the relationship; members recognize that what is good for other members will be good for the entire group, strengthening the keiretsu for all. Operating without centralized control, the composition of the keiretsu is dependent on members recognizing the value of long-term cooperative relationships and win-win attitudes.

Value networks are similar to the keiretsu at any given customer or solution development. However, members of value networks are often part of a specific network for only that development program or customer application. The success of the network rests on members understanding that they must respect and value other members' positions; they could very likely be competing with others as members of different networks. While sometimes appearing ad hoc, value networks provide ultimate member flexibility; particularly important are face-changing, high-technology markets.

CHANNELS AND THE INTERNET

Throughout this text, we have explored the effects of the Internet on business-to-business marketing. One of the areas being most affected by rapid adoption of Internet technology is the area of business-to-business channels. Web technology has the potential to bring significant portions of business transactions on-line in a very short period of time. At the extremes, Forrester Research has predicted that $6.3 trillion of global business-to-business transactions will occur on the Web in 2004 and International Data Corporation (IDC) projected $2.2 trillion.[9] Forecasters at eMarketer created a composite forecast of $2.8 trillion in business-to-business Web transactions in 2004, with $1.8 trillion in the United States.[10] A sizable portion of this on-line activity would be channel transactions.

Over the second half of 2000 and into 2001, the promise of conducting business-to-business marketing on-line has suffered a series of setbacks. Many of the new forms of Web-based business have not proven successful. Within existing supply chains, automating via the Web has often taken longer to implement than hoped. This does not mean that business-to-business marketers should ignore the adoption of Internet technology. Indeed, many established companies have successfully employed such technology in streamlining their supply chains, enhancing the value provided through channels, and improving their communications. This area continues to hold promise, though planners and pundits now take a more realistic view of it. Later in this section, we examine reasons for the disappointments and we look ahead to the changes, opportunities, and threats that adoption of the new technology holds. In the earlier part of this section, though, we explore some of the factors that give impetus to these changes and some of the conceptual underpinnings of new forms of channel business.

The Internet's Potential Role in Business-to-Business Marketing

If we look at the Internet and the Web as enhancements to information flow, we can then think about how the new technology can affect channels. As we noted earlier, channels provide value for business-to-business customers by creating form, time, place, and possession utilities. All of these utilities can be enhanced through better and faster channel flows. Rapid flow of order data between resellers and suppliers can closely track demand patterns for different product models. This allows the supplier to create better forecasts of demand for different models and thus provide better product assortments in real time. Better information flow also allows the execution of just-in-time manufacturing and supply. This improves time utility for end-use customers, since they can receive a product in days or even hours from the time they ordered it, instead of waiting weeks or months. Real-time information can give suppliers more information about geographic demand patterns, allowing more inventory to be placed downstream near locations where customers actually need the product. Thus, place utility is improved (and time utility as well); and, of course, this gets products into the possession of customers earlier.

---

[9]As reported in *eMarketer*, "The eCommerce: B2B Report," *eMarketer* (February 2001): 11.

[10]*eMarketer*, op. cit., 10.

In addition to these ways of creating value, the Web also reduces transaction costs and other channel costs. Management of channel relationships using Web applications squeezes costs out of the channel in several ways. First, the accuracy of Web ordering, inventory tracking, billing, and payment reduces a great deal of the costs associated with error checking and corrections. The time spent reworking incorrect information flows can be very costly and happens frequently when the process is not automated. Second, better information makes forecasting more accurate, reducing inventory costs. Better information also makes timing of orders more manageable so that quantity and payment discounts can be obtained on a higher proportion of orders.

Companies are also learning that value can be produced for customers by reducing customer costs through the use of Web-enhanced order processing and fulfillment tracking. For instance, four oil pipeline companies in the United States have formed a joint venture project, called "Transport4." This effort, headed by Colonial Oil of Atlanta, created a Web-based ordering and scheduling facility for shipments of oil products. Oil producers, industrial oil buyers, oil distributors, or any other institutional customer can go to the password-protected site to schedule and route oil shipments from point of origin to any destination served by the four member pipelines. Prior to the existence of the joint venture, a customer would have to arrange such a shipment by EDI, phone, fax, or mail. The worst part of the old system was that each pipeline company was a separate entity with its own product codes, data interchange protocols, and ordering/scheduling procedures. The joint venture allows the customer to order and schedule across all four pipelines in one step. Confirmation is immediate. In the past, a complicated order might take a week or more to finalize. Now it can be done in a matter of minutes.[11]

Thus, companies are discovering that Web automated channels provide better value to the end customer. Lower channel and inventory costs, plus an ability to forecast demand more accurately, mean that fewer stockouts and back orders occur for products moved through the channel. Customers may benefit directly through reduced transaction costs. They may benefit directly through reduced variation in costs, meaning that they do not have to carry a heavy load of slack resources (for instance, more people in the purchasing department, in the oil shipping example). Reduced channel costs can also produce value to customers if suppliers or resellers turn cost savings into lower product prices or lower charges for shipping and handling. Value to customers may also be enhanced from channel cost savings that are reinvested in such things as filling out product lines and increasing inventory of complementary products; this results in customers receiving more value from product availability. Suppliers or channel members might also invest cost savings into enhanced customer service.

---

[11]Sean Donahue, "Pipe Dreams," *Business 2.0* (January 2000): 90–95.

Explorer Pipeline: Transport4 System

Go to the Web site for Explorer Pipeline (http://www.expl.com). Go to the part of the site that explains the Transport4 system. In

what direction do you believe this system will evolve in the future?

Development of New Types of Channels

New channel structures are emerging as more companies obtain experience with the Web and with automating their channel transactions and as more entrepreneurs are exposed to Web-enabled commerce. All of the new channel arrangements described in subsequent paragraphs have the same general purposes as traditional channel structures: providing the appropriate selection of the right products and making them available to end-use buyers, efficiently handling ordering and order processing, and facilitating fast delivery at the lowest cost possible. Following are some of the new structures that have emerged or are emerging.

Affiliates   An **affiliate** is anyone who has a special link on its Web site that refers a viewer to a product or service supplier's site. The affiliate has downloaded a special piece of code from the supplier's Web site. This special code creates the referral link on the affiliate's site and allows the supplier to track referrals coming from that affiliate's link. Any sales resulting from a referral from the affiliate produce a commission that is paid into an account that has been set up for the affiliate. This is attractive to prospective affiliates because any organization with a Web site has the potential to be an affiliate and can easily earn extra income. It is attractive to the supplier because it is an easy way to establish a network of sites that will "drive traffic"—send many prospective customers—to the supplier's Web site. This idea started in the on-line consumer market. It apparently originated with Amazon.com and quickly spread to other retailers. It was not long before on-line business-to-business marketers caught on, as well, particularly among small businesses.

Affiliate programs run by companies doing e-commerce are, in many respects, very similar to networks of sales agents. However, there are some important differences that make this "sales channel" unique. Manufacturers' representatives, who are independent sales agents, are generally professional sales people who sell manufacturers' product lines to customer companies with whom

407

they have established relationships (as described in Chapter 11). A large network may have a hundred or more "reps." Reps usually do not represent products that compete against each other. On-line affiliates, on the other hand, are generally at a lower level of expertise in selling (or on-line marketing) and can be much greater in number.

While affiliate networks are appealing for their simplicity, business marketers have learned that managing affiliate networks takes time, effort, creativity, and investment. The box titled "Making Affiliate Networks Effective" lists ideas to keep in mind when establishing and running a network of on-line affiliates in a business-to-business market.

If the business marketer handles this correctly, the affiliate network will be a good source of qualified new customer leads. It should be obvious, though, that running an affiliate network well is not a trivial exercise.

Hubs   New intermediaries are emerging that "make markets"—bring buyers and sellers together to facilitate transactions—in a business-to-business context. In general, these new intermediaries are called portals, or **hubs**,[12] but they can be one of several types: catalog, auction, exchange, or barter. **Catalog hubs** serve as agglomerators, in which the products from several vendors' catalogs are combined in a searchable database. **Auction hubs** match buyers and sellers in an on-line analogy of real-world auctions. **Exchange hubs** act as clearing centers for bringing buyers and sellers together. Commodity-like products are offered in a setting where buyers and sellers indicate the products (or services) they want to trade and the prices they seek. **Barter hubs** act like exchanges, except that "prices" are nonmonetary. Buyers and sellers each exchange something of value (the exchange may involve a bartered service or product, plus some amount of money). This may be particularly attractive for small businesses with constrained cash flow. Hubs make money by charging processing, handling, and marketing fees. They may also take a commission or transaction fees. Hybrid hubs have emerged as companies have learned how to manage these businesses better and as it has become apparent that these businesses often need multiple revenue streams to survive and prosper.

In all of these business models, the hub marketer must understand the vendors and buyers in its market. Especially important is gaining an understanding of buyer motivations, decision and purchasing processes, and expectations. The hub marketer can then structure the hub so that products and services are offered in such a way that buyers receive superior value. Of course, the business model must have value for the sellers as well. In this regard, hub marketers must view both their vendors and buyers as customers.

---

[12]A good early description of emerging models appeared in an article by Don Tapscott, David Ticoll, and Alex Lowy, "The Rise of the Business Web," *Business 2.0* (November 1999): 198–208.

Business.com: Becoming an Affiliate

Go to the Web site for Business.com (http://www.business.com). Click through on the link for becoming an affiliate. What does it take for a company to become an affiliate?

What sorts of Web sites would be good candidates for becoming affiliates of Business.com?

Making Affiliate Networks Effective

♦ Be careful how affiliates are selected; make sure they attract the right kinds of prospects and will properly position the supplier's offering.

♦ Offer the affiliates attractive incentives for participating.

♦ Assist affiliates in positioning and marketing; if they do not attract prospects to the affiliate site and to the link, then few real prospects will be sent to the supplier's Web site.

♦ Set up the supplier site to give affiliate referrals special treatment; this will help sales.

♦ Make the affiliates happy, and help recruit new affiliates from the referred prospects.

♦ Be careful in budgeting for this expenditure; compare the costs of affiliate marketing to costs of other sales channels.

What Went Wrong

All of the potential contributions mentioned so far are nice in theory. Since April 2000, however, Internet businesses have run through a series of problems. Business-to-business marketers have faced problems related to—but not identical to—problems faced by consumer businesses. Both sectors faced dramatic shrinkage in funding as the investment community reevaluated the future profitability of Internet and Web-based businesses.

In business-to-business markets, two interrelated problems emerged.[13] First, relationships require more off-line attention than on-line business models assumed. It is not enough to cut transaction costs if barriers that arise in supplier-customer relationships detract more from the value produced. Second, because relatively few

---

[13]Elise Ackerman, "Businesses Hit Rough Spots on Internet Journey," *San Jose Mercury News* (26 February 2001): 1E, 10E.

potential users actually used the on-line market exchange sites, volume has not risen to levels that produce profits for the market exchange companies. New companies found low entry barriers in the technology: almost anyone could set up a market exchange site. As a result, too many exchanges were chasing too few transactions. Chemdex, as an example, hoped to "make a market" in the life sciences industry. While it was one of the first, it soon found thirty-seven other companies competing for the same business. Ventro, the owner of Chemdex, decided to close down the site in December 2000.[14] To add to these problems, many businesses have relied on advertising to supplement their on-line revenue streams. Over the past year, advertisers have come to realize that the returns from on-line advertising often do not warrant the expense.[15] A combination of declining returns from advertising and reduced advertising as the economy slowed has produced a precipitous drop in advertising revenue.

The end result has been that new on-line businesses, the different kinds of hubs mentioned earlier, often have not fared well. They have not acquired enough participants to reach critical mass, that is, enough transaction volume to create profitability for the on-line businesses. Many are out of business or running at greatly reduced activity levels. The business models in which a single company runs an automated supply chain or distribution system have fared better. However, even these have proven to take longer and involve more investment than was originally anticipated. The companies that began investing in such systems in the 1996–98 time frame are seeing their efforts rewarded. Companies that waited are scaling back their expectations.

Future Adoption of Internet Technology for Channel Management

Internet and Web-enabled businesses and supply chains still hold promise. However, the adoption rate of the new technology will not likely proceed as fast as originally predicted. All of the key ideas from traditional channels apply when channel relationships are created or enhanced through the use of the Web. Improved information flow reduces costs, improves inventory management, and boosts channel support. The idea is to produce superior value for customers and to enhance the profitability and competitiveness of suppliers.

Risk and uncertainty involved in adopting Web technology are probably managed best by taking a two-pronged approach. First, marketers should be talking extensively with their end-user customers and with their existing channel members to learn about their emerging needs and concerns. Secondly, the development of new systems and models is probably best managed with small experiments. User

---

[14]Cecelia Kang, "On-line supply exchanges refocus their strategies," *San Jose Mercury News* (26 February 2001): 1E, 10E.

[15]Jennifer Rewick, "Beyond Banners," *The Wall Street Journal* (23 October 2000): R38.

feedback can be obtained rapidly and adjustments made, allowing the marketer to adapt quickly and actually push the direction of some of the change.

These trends are coming, of course, whether the business marketer wants them to or not. If the marketer wants to build a competitive advantage, she will already be adopting new systems and adapting as more is learned. As more and more companies obtain the benefits of adopting the new technology, the competitive advantage will dissipate and adoption will be necessary just to maintain competitive parity.[16] Business marketers need to address the change proactively rather than waiting to see what direction change will take. Much learning needs to be done if the marketer is to compete effectively. This learning can only be accomplished through trial, obtaining feedback, and paying close attention to the results.

---

[16]Michael E. Porter, "Strategy and the Internet," *Harvard Business Review* 79, no. 3 (March 2001): 62–78.

Channels create and enhance value for business customers. They provide value in terms of making the right products and services available, by giving buyers an appropriate level of choice, by providing products and services in the appropriate quantities, and by doing so at appropriate levels of cost. To do this, channel members perform a variety of tasks. The combination provided by any individual channel member is dependent on the nature of the product and the way that customers expect to obtain it. The combination may include such activities as forecasting market needs, performing market research, buying products that create a selection, holding inventory, creating product bundles or performing final assembly, providing service, setting or negotiating prices, communicating with and selling to buyers, facilitating transactions, moving products, providing financing, and establishing relationships with customers.

To create value for final buyers, suppliers need to understand those buyers, understand the perspective of potential channel members, and then design a channel structure that is as appropriate as possible, that is, that provides superior value to final buyers and that makes appropriate profit levels for channel members and for the supplier. Once the design is in place, the marketer must recruit and choose individual channel members to implement this design. In most cases, the marketer must then work to establish a relationship with channel partners. In that relationship, the marketer must adjust to partners' goals and needs and provide them with the tools and incentives they require to enhance the value provided to the customer. Over time, the environment will change and the marketer must adapt the relationship accordingly.

One of the most pressing environmental changes that must be addressed today is changing technology. As the Web changes the way that business channels are structured and managed, the business marketer must adapt. A proactive rather than reactive approach is called for. The risk of "missing the boat" is too great otherwise.

Key Terms

administered channel intermediaries	contractual systems	exchange hubs
affiliates	corporate vertical marketing system	form
ancillary channel members	differentially invisible	functional spin-off
auction hubs	direct channel	horizontal competitors
barter hubs	direct channel participants	horizontal sprawl
bases of power	discrepancy of assortment	house accounts
catalog hubs	distribution centers	hubs
channel pattern	dual distribution	intensity of distribution
		keiretsu

logistics

marketing channel

material requirements
  planning (MRP)

multidistribution

palletizing

physical distribution
  concept

place

possession

product line maintenance

superordinate goals

time

trade credit

vertigal integration

vertical marketing system

warehouses

Questions for Review and Discussion

1. Does a company that markets directly to other companies have a channel? Why, or why not?

2. Why can channel structure differ between segments, even though the products are the same?

3. Explain the four kinds of economic utility.

4. When a channel provides financing to customers, what kind of economic utility is it providing? Explain.

5. When a channel provides training for the customer's personnel, what kind of economic utility is being provided? Explain.

6. What does it mean for a channel to "reduce the discrepancy of assortment"?

7. Why is carrying extra inventory so costly for suppliers or channel members?

8. What are three reasons that a business-to-business marketer may want to market through channel intermediaries rather than market directly?

9. Review the opening example of Apple and the Lisa computer. Using Exhibit 12–2a, determine what path Apple used to get the Lisa to its market. Compare that to the path you think may have been more appropriate.

10. What sorts of risks does an industrial distributor share with the supplier?

11. Suppose that a start-up company is offering an innovative product that management hopes will establish a new product category. What forces will tend to lead the company to market the product through channel intermediaries? What characteristics of an early market will tend to lead the company to market the product directly to final customers?

12. What are key causes of channel conflict?

13. What are the chief differences between an administered channel and a value network?

14. What kinds of value can be provided by Web applications that manage channel transactions?

15. What kinds of value would channels provide that cannot be substantially enhanced through Web applications?

16. Why did so many Web-based market exchanges go out of business during the economic slowdown of 2000–2001?

Internet Exercises

Go to the sites for Oracle and SAP: **http://www.oracle.com** and **http://www.sap.com** Examine the parts of their sites having to do with e-business systems or products. Evaluate the differences between the two. To what extent do they target the management of distribution channels? Compare and contrast their approaches.

Pick a business-to-business industry that interests you. Using your favorite search engine, see if there is a market exchange hub for this industry (if you have difficulty, try VerticalNet: **http://www.verticalnet.com** or Ventro: **http://www.ventro.com** or a site like these to see if they have an exchange in your industry). How does the exchange provide value to vendors and customers? If there are multiple exchanges, how do they compare? If there are no exchanges, why do you think this is so?

Go to the web sites for FedEx and UPS: **http://www.fedex.com** and **http://www.ups.com** Examine the portions of their sites that discuss logistics services. How do the two compare? Most likely, they will have summaries of customer case histories. Compare several cases, and compare the kinds of value they report having provided for customers. Are these two companies competing head to head? Why, or why not?

13

Communicating with the Market

overview. . . All relationships depend on reliable and timely communications. Throughout this book, we have stressed the importance of building customer relationships at many levels. In Chapter 11, we emphasized the importance of the personal selling portion of the promotion mix. While personal selling plays a critical role in communication with customers, the other three elements of the <u>promotion mix</u>—<u>advertising</u>, <u>sales promotion</u>, and <u>public relations</u>—are required for the specialized role that they play in the communication process. In this chapter, the discussion focuses on these three elements and their value in business-to-business markets. Not only does each element of the promotion mix have a specialized role, but the synergies between the elements combine to provide a unified message to the marketplace.

This chapter starts with an overview of promotion and the differences between consumer products promotion and business-to-business promotion. A typical communications process is reviewed. After the overview of promotion, the discussion turns to achieving different outcomes with combinations of the elements of the promotion mix. There are some forms of business-to-business communication that defy categorization into only one of the elements of the promotion mix. In discussion of the management of promotion, this chapter examines how definition of outcomes desired rather than process employed is more likely to provide insight to the promotion needs of the situation.

Implementation of positioning and differentiation strategies determined by the strategic plan of the organization is, in large part, the purview of the promotion effort. Discussion of the value creation elements of promotion is followed by an examination of the Internet and its role in business communications.

© RICHARD VOGEL/AP/WIDE WORLD PHOTOS

ANDERSEN CONSULTING DOES A QUICK TRANSFORMATION TO ACCENTURE*

After nearly three years in a courtroom squabble, on August 7, 2000, the arbitrator finally ruled that Andersen Consulting could split from Arthur Andersen, the accounting firm. The $1 billion price was deemed reasonable, but one condition seemed a monumental challenge: Andersen Consulting could no longer use the Andersen name (not too bad, so far: they were already moving to change the name), and the name had to change by January 1, 2001. The split meant Andersen Consulting had to change its name in 129 days and not "disappear" in the process.

Arthur Andersen had had an excellent reputation as a business consulting organization, when in 1989 the partners decided to institutionalize the consulting arm of the firm with a separate public identity. The consultancy was still a part of the firm, contributing to the firm's overall financial performance. Disagreements arose concerning the strategic directions of the firm, allocation of resources, and clashing cultures; and Andersen Consulting filed for arbitration in 1997.

Over the years, Andersen Consulting had redirected its consulting efforts from general management consulting to focus more on enterprise-level IT consulting. As client companies changed over to business operations that relied on information technology and enterprise resource planning systems, Andersen Consulting became the integration engine that accomplished the restructuring. Now Andersen Consulting was faced with the task of continuing in this business, building on its past success and reputation, without losing its identity when the name changed. And it did not yet have a new name.

The task was Herculean on three fronts. First, a new name had to be found that conveyed the strengths and vision of the new company. Meanwhile, the name had to be available; the URL—the Web address—had to be available; and the name had to have no negative connotations in any of the sixty or so countries in which Andersen Consulting did business. Second, the logistics of changing the name on all the company's materials was enormous: business cards, letterhead, brochures, paychecks, and signage, as well as all the company's advertising and corporate communications materials. Third, the changeover had to be communicated to customers, prospective customers, and the world at large in such a way that all these audiences would take notice and maintain positive memory associations with the new name. The changeover had to be done well, too. If the

*Based on H. M. Fattah, "A Giant's Rebirth," Technology Marketing 21, no. 6 (June 2001): 44–47.

ANDERSEN CONSULTING DOES A QUICK TRANSFORMATION TO ACCENTURE (CONT'D)

changeover was managed poorly, people would notice and Andersen Consulting would have to begin life as a new company digging its way out of a credibility hole.

Andersen Consulting started by seeking suggestions for names from its executives and employees, as well as from hired consultants. By October, after culling 2,677 entries, the partners and their hired consultants, Landor Associates, chose the name Accenture. The name was originally the suggestion of a senior manager in Oslo, Norway.

Andersen Consulting launched an advertising campaign that "teased" the audience, suggesting a name change was coming. The name officially changed on January 1, and Accenture launched an extensive campaign to make the change very visible. It involved advertising in several media, a public relations campaign, and the culmination of the physical changes to identity materials throughout the company. The logistics campaign had been implemented by fifty employee teams. To accomplish all this, Accenture employed the project management skills that were the core of its consulting business.

The results, of course, will not be fully known for a while, maybe for years. The early results, though, indicated that Accenture was on the right track. A majority of target audience members realize that the name has changed, and the Accenture name is gradually acquiring memory associations. In all, Accenture's efforts stand as a good example of what it takes to accomplish such a name change.

Introduction. . .

In Chapter 11, we discussed personal selling, which is, of course, face-to-face communication. Business-to-business marketers also use communication in which other media are used to transmit messages. All forms of communication, called the **promotion mix** in most marketing principles texts, are generally grouped into four categories: personal selling, advertising, sales promotion, and public relations. In business-to-business marketing, there are some forms of communication that defy such categorization. The communication effort does not fit nicely into any one element of the promotion mix. For instance, participation in industry trade shows and conferences employs all four categories of communication: sales people are on duty at the booth and interact with customers, and brochures on products and marketing programs are given away (advertising); other sales premiums—promotional items such as T-shirts, coffee mugs, and so on—are given away to provide incentives for customers to visit the booth (sales promotion); and the company president, wearing the company's T-shirt and sun visor, sits on a discussion panel in a seminar session to expound on the company's vision of the industry's future (public relations). At the same time, company technical professionals are presenting a paper on the company's newest technology breakthrough at the conference that is a part of the trade show. The object of all this communication is to help the members of the buying center move through their buying decision process.

This chapter concerns all the methods of communication that are not personal selling. In many organizations, these promotional efforts are known as **marketing communications,** (marcom) or, in large organizations when public relations are handled at the corporate level, advertising and sales promotion (A&SP). For brevity, the term **nonpersonal communications** is used to describe these promotional efforts.

In the opening example, Andersen Consulting was faced with a monumental communication task as it moved to quickly change its name to Accenture. In doing so, Accenture and its consultants followed the main guidelines for good communications. They started by choosing a name that would communicate a desired message.

LEARNING OBJECTIVES

- ◆ Understand the distinctions between personal selling and the nonpersonal types of promotion.
- ◆ Understand the differences between promotion in consumer markets and promotion in business-to-business markets.
- ◆ Understand the role of promotion in providing value to customers and influencing the buying decision process.
- ◆ Become familiar with the kinds of promotion used in business-to-business marketing and their uses.
- ◆ Gain a sense of how to manage promotion in conjunction with the other elements of marketing strategy and the offering.
- ◆ Understand how promotion can assist the development of a firm's strategic positioning.
- ◆ Gain a sense of how publicity and Internet communications can play special roles in business-to-business marketing.

The term **nonpersonal communications** refers to the elements of the promotion mix other than personal sales, such as advertising, sales promotion, and public relations. Depending on organizational structure, nonpersonal communications may be known as marketing communications (marcom) or advertising and sales promotion (A&SP).

© STUART RAMSON/AP/WIDE WORLD PHOTOS

Then they used multiple methods to deliver the message that the name was changing. The campaign was sequenced in such a way that it got the attention of the target audiences and primed them for the name change. Repeated messages in differing forms reinforced the message so that audience members' memory would be enhanced. All the while, the company kept in mind the role of the company's name and the impact of these messages on the buying decision process.

Communications contribute to the marketer's delivery of value to customers. Without communications, the customer might not fully understand his own need. Also, he might not realize that the supplier has a solution for his problem or is willing to work with him to develop a solution. The customer might not fully understand how much value the supplier's solution truly provides.

A COMMUNICATIONS MODEL

There are three key ideas in providing value through communications. First, the members of the buying center respond to messages; media are only *a means of delivering messages*. Second, messages must be crafted to assist members of the buying center to *progress through* the buying decision process. Third, messages must be crafted *to implement the positioning* chosen in the design of marketing strategy. Keep these three ideas in mind through the following discussion of the communications model, shown in Exhibit 13–1.

Losing Meaning in the Translation

The basic communications model, *sender-encode-medium-decode-receiver,* is familiar to many students. As shown in Exhibit 13–1, there are some areas of this model that require particular attention. Note that the sender and the encoding process are not separate. As the sender creates a message, that message is placed into "code" that has meaning to the sender as an accurate representation of the message. The message can be received accurately only by a receiver who has the corresponding correct "decoding" capability. In personal communications (everyday conversation), this is not *usually* a problem, though you can probably recall having asked someone to rephrase something they said because you did not understand it. While this sounds simple, many market segments have their own languages, usually referred to

EXHIBIT 13–1   A Model of the Communication Process

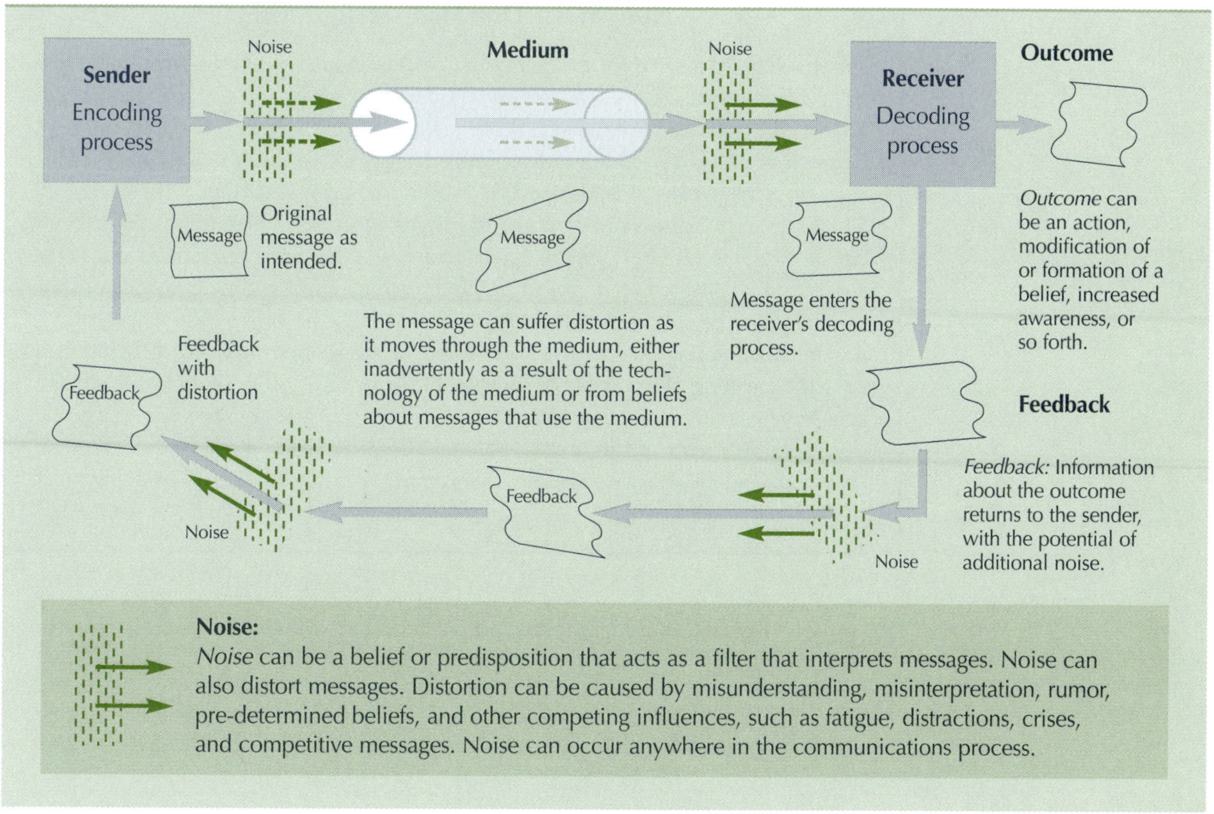

Noise:
Noise can be a belief or predisposition that acts as a filter that interprets messages. Noise can also distort messages. Distortion can be caused by misunderstanding, misinterpretation, rumor, pre-determined beliefs, and other competing influences, such as fatigue, distractions, crises, and competitive messages. Noise can occur anywhere in the communications process.

as the **jargon** of the market or discipline. Jargon improves communication efficiency within a group but tends to isolate the group from outsiders and may have the effect of intimidating non-group members. Jargon across industries may have the same alphanumeric form but mean something completely different, adding confusion to the isolation and intimidation (see box, "Now What Did That Really Mean?"). In business-to-business marketing, messages must be encoded in the language of the receiver/customer if the goal is to assist the customer through the decision process.

Jargon is any specialized language of a group that is used to improve the efficiency of communication among members of the group. A price paid for this efficiency within the group is to separate the group from nonmembers who may not have experience with or knowledge of the language.

Media Can Impact the Message

The means of transmission selected for the message will have an impact on how the message is received. Receivers may prejudge messages because of previous experiences, or beliefs about certain media or the medium technology may have a distorting impact on the message. The telemarketer whose call is abruptly cut short may have had the deal of a lifetime, but the receiver absolutely does not tolerate interrupting phone calls. Management perceives that time spent at conventions and technical conferences is not productive, so the engineering staff is

---

Now What Did That Really Mean?

Different things mean different things in different industries. In the chemical industry, ABS is *acrylonitrile-butadiene-styrene,* a widely used plastic for consumer products. In the automotive industry, ABS is *antilock brake systems.* Again, in the auto industry, rear windows are *backlites* (tail lamps *are* called tail lamps though). PC is a desktop computer but is also *politically correct* in social situations.

Colloquial expressions in some languages can cause communication difficulties. In the United States, we say that someone who has accepted responsibility for a situation has *stepped up to the bar.* And, of course, when a concept or idea is not anticipated to be successful, *that dog won't hunt.*

In common language, many words imply meanings not intended. When polled as to the meaning of the word *compromise,* students most often reply *to give up.* Yet, compromise is often the outcome of negotiations aimed at creating win-win situations that work for all involved, enabling all parties to commit to an agreed-on direction, goal, or *common promise.* Compromise can thus be defined as doing what works!

---

not provided with any budget to attend. Whether reasonable or not, different customers and markets have established methods by which they obtain information. The medium used in a market segment must be an accepted conduit for information and must be consistent with the positioning of the firm and its offering.

Feedback

Critical to any marketing communication effort is knowing whether the message was received as intended. In consumer markets, because of the heavy dependence on advertising (a monologue),[1] sales results are often the first indication of a message not performing as designed. In rapidly changing markets, the time lapse associated with waiting for sales results is too great to effectively add correction to the message. When advertising is a significant form of promotion, firms must use other means to solicit feedback. Still, even with the use of **direct response requests** inserted in promotions, feedback through the Internet, toll-free access to customer service, and other means, feedback is often only available through a proactive choice of the customer.

One of the advantages of the personal selling and strong relationship aspects of marketing in business-to-business markets is the opportunity for immediate, personal feedback through the field sales and marketing team. When the relationship is also the medium that carries the message, feedback is immediate. The ongoing dialog with customers reduces the opportunities for distortion and misunderstanding.

Direct response requests—reader surveys, questionnaires, and warranty registrations—are forms of customer feedback. The difficulty with these types of feedback is that they require an active interest by the customer in providing feedback. This implies that only a portion of the total market for the product is providing information. The behavioral aspects of those customers who will make an effort to provide feedback may be significantly different than the entire market segment.

---

[1]Regis McKenna, "Marketing Is Everything," *Harvard Business Review* (January–February 1991).

Customer Feedback Opportunities

Pick a consumer product company (CD play-ers, home appliances—you choose) and a business-to-business company you are familiar with, either through exercises in this text or through other means. Go to the Web sites for both companies and find ways that they allow or solicit feedback about their offerings through their Web sites. Compare the ease of use and apparent effectiveness of the two companies' feedback mechanisms.

Does the ease of providing feedback vary between consumer and business-to-business markets? Which site gives you the most confidence of a real interest in customer feedback?

Noise

Jargon and the other factors noted that create distortion or inac-curacies in messages are commonly combined into the category of **noise.** Noise can be a belief or predisposition that acts as a filter that interprets messages. Noise can also distort messages. Distor-tion is caused by misunderstanding, misinterpretation, rumor, beliefs, and other competing influences, such as fatigue, distrac-tions, crises, and competitive messages, and can exist at several different places in the communication process. Whenever the message is interpreted, either for transmission through media or creation of an outcome, the possibility exists that the message will be changed. As the target audience for many types of promo-tion, customers screen incoming messages based on timing, their individual interests, the needs of their job function, or the imme-diate needs of the task at hand. Other messages get screened out. Receivers, to protect themselves from message overload, only pay attention to useful information. Thus, noise in the communication process can be a situational factor. The successful message must be created to survive the influences of media, break through the screening process, *and* be accurately perceived by the receiver.

Customer perception, then, is both selective and subjective.[2] Message interpretation is subject to **selective exposure, selective attention,** and **selective retention.** Successful

Selective exposure, **selective attention**, and **selective retention** are *jargon* for different behaviors associated with mes-sage perception. As with any behavioral element, there is a degree of subjectiv-ity, based often on the receptiveness or attentiveness of the receiver.

Selective exposure refers to the actual media to which a receiver may be exposed. Different stakeholders in the buying center experience different types of media exposure. Just as McDonald's places commercials during Saturday morning cartoons focused on fun meals and Ronald McDonald and commercials focused on family relationships on the evening news, business-to-business mar-keters must recognize the media that the target audience is regularly exposed to (magazines, business press, etc.).

---

[2]Norman Govoni, Robert Eng, and Morton Galper, *Promotional Management* (Upper Saddle River, N.J.: Prentice-Hall, 1986), 53.

Selective attention is a protective method receivers use to prevent overload. Based on an individual's ability to process and store messages, only useful information is seen or heard. The successful message may be a reinforcement of a previous decision or may address an immediate need. Either consciously or not, receivers only take interest in information that has immediate value.

Selective retention is the measurement of the "storage function"—the quantity or portion of a message retained and the time span over which it is recalled. Because of timing or other circumstances, receivers will not recall messages that have no immediate use, though they may be of value at a later time. Several reminder techniques, such as leave-behind brochures and other sales paraphernalia (coffee mugs, pens, paperweights, etc.), are used to address this issue.

promotion, as in other parts of the marketing mix, requires business-to-business marketers to make judgments about the behavior of customers.

Capabilities of Promotion

In the next section, we examine the strengths and weaknesses of different elements of the promotion mix. Promotional efforts can accomplish a number of purposes that provide value, both short and long term. However, marketers must understand the limitations of promotion as well as its capabilities. Exhibit 13–2 lists purposes that can and cannot be pursued with most promotional efforts. As you study this material, recall that promotion must be contextually consistent with the overall marketing effort and support the positioning of the offering and the organization. Recognize that the promotion mix is the implementation of the communication strategy. Every part of the promotional effort should be designed to communicate effectively with the customer under specific circumstances. There are not good or bad elements of the promotion mix, just inappropriate elements or combinations of elements for the task at hand.

THE ELEMENTS OF THE PROMOTION MIX

How are messages delivered to audiences? A variety of methods exists. We start with general categories of the promotion mix from a marketing principles course—personal selling, advertising, sales promotion, and public relations—and then discuss common, useful methods, often a mix of elements, in business-to-business settings.

Personal Selling

Chapter 11 discussed personal selling in depth. Recall that personal selling is individualized communications, often a series of dyadic interactions—one-on-one conversations between the seller and customer. The seller's message can be tailored and adapted to the particular needs of the customer. Even beyond one-on-one communications where several customers are addressed at once, personal selling reaches a relatively small audience at any one time. Because of the closeness of the personal interactions in sales, personal selling is the primary driver in building effective relationships.

When the sales force consists of order takers or persuader/sustainers (see Chapter 11), relationship building is not necessarily a primary concern. Sellers are more often concerned with moving the customer to action or placing an order. This type of selling is most appropriate when the customer decision regarding brands or features can be influenced at the point of sale.

EXHIBIT 13–2 Capabilities of Promotional Efforts

What Promotion Can Do	What Promotion Cannot Do
◆ Inform about availability. ◆ Persuade trial. ◆ Encourage repurchase. ◆ Communicate advantages. ◆ Establish awareness. ◆ Aid in securing channels. ◆ Assist in creating brand preference. ◆ Build image. ◆ Move product to balance production. ◆ Support selling efforts.	◆ Sell products that do not meet needs. ◆ Convince customers that an inferior product is superior. ◆ Convince customers to go out of their way to purchase when comparable goods are more readily available. ◆ Convince customers to pay more than perceived value. ◆ Overcome a weak marketing strategy. ◆ Substitute for a bad product.

Regardless of the type of sales force employed, personal selling is the most costly communications method on a cost-per-contact basis. Many companies use nonpersonal communications in the early part of the decision process for prospective customers, because it is more cost-effective than contacting customers with sellers. Advertising, sales promotion, and publicity help make buying center members aware and interested in the supplier's offering and help draw them to contact the supplier to begin including the supplier in the buying decision process.

Advertising

As consumers, we believe we are experts in advertising, or at least in how to surf around or through it! While advertising is most important in consumer markets, it still has a role in business-to-business markets.

Advertising is a monologue—impersonal mass communication without any direct feedback mechanism. When mass communication is used, the message must be short, to the point, yet general enough to be understood by a broad range of recipients. Advertising is effective at establishing awareness in and providing general information to the target market. In both the consumer buying decision process and the business-to-business buying decision process, advertising's impersonal, nonspecific nature is not usually effective when the final purchase choice is made at the point of sale.

Initially, advertising costs can be high from both a production and a placement viewpoint. However, once created, advertisements are most often used several times, spreading the production costs over more than one use of the ad. Also, while the **media buy**—the cost of airing or placing the advertisement—can be expensive, the size of the audience reached results in a relatively low cost per exposure.

The **media buy** is the selection of where and when the advertisement will be distributed. Considerations should include not only how people are exposed to the message but whether they are the right people. Business magazines and trade journals track the decision-level authority and influence of the professionals who are regular readers and use that data to influence advertisers regarding the frequency and placement of ads in their publications.

Sales Promotion

Sales promotion is often considered the "all other" category in the promotion mix. Sales promotions are incentives that are used to enhance the value of an offering over a specified period of time. As consumers, we know sales promotions as coupons, rebates, point-of-purchase displays, samples, and contests. While these are the sales promotion focus of consumer markets and are also used in business-to-business markets, additional categories such as promotional allowances, sales meetings, conventions and trade shows, exhibits, and cooperative advertising are more often the focus in business-to-business markets.

Sales promotion can be divided into three general categories based on the results desired:[3]

- ◆ Sales promotion focused on sales team support
- ◆ Sales promotion focused on middlemen support
- ◆ Sales promotion focused on customers to shift the time of purchases, stimulate trial, or encourage continued use of a product

The discussion that follows focuses on the first two of these three categories. The third category—sales promotion focused on customers to shift the time of purchase, stimulate trial, or encourage continued use of a product—is contextually more consistent with consumer marketing. Consumer rebates encourage purchase during the period of the promotion, often borrowing sales from later periods. Samples or bundled products (e.g., a sample jar of a new jelly attached to a jar of peanut butter) seek to get customers to try new products. These direct-to-consumer sales promotion tactics have only limited use in business-to-business markets.

Sales Promotion Focused on the Sales Team

Company or organization internal marketing programs often have a large element focused on internal motivation and annual or seasonal themes. Annual sales and marketing meetings are often the kickoff events for these programs, aimed at bringing everyone together in support of the common theme. While a major internal promotion effort, the sales meeting affords the opportunity for all members of the field team to interact with headquarters counterparts and be a part of the planning of the strategy that they implement. It is at this time that many sales incentives and contests are introduced and training in new products, merchandising programs, and support materials takes place.

Sales Promotion Focused on Channel Intermediaries

The correct promotional allowance to middlemen can make or break efforts to get product through a distributor channel. Rewards to channel members for cooperation with seasonal promotion plans are essential to get middlemen focused on products. The necessity of these promotions is most often obvious very early in the product life cycle and again in the maturity and decline stages when a product is likely to face horizontal competition.

Early in the product life cycle, incentives to middlemen may be necessary to get new products accepted by the marketing channel. Listing allowances, incentives that provide for the costs associated with adding a new product to the industrial distributor's line, are common. Merchandising assistance and training for the distri-

---

[3]Ibid., 384.

bution sales force, particularly with new offerings, are important sales promotion efforts. Coincident with the push promotional effort through the channel must be the pull effort with end users of the product. Recall from Chapter 11 and Chapter 12 that distribution sellers, often more involved in transactional sales, most likely are rewarded on a short-term commission basis so they pay close attention to how they spend their valuable time. The distributors must be convinced of a ready market for the new product before encumbering their sellers with the additional time commitments of training and customer development.

As the popularity and profitability of the new product grows, competitors will be attracted to the market. Distribution will recognize the benefits of belonging to the channel for the product. It is shortly after this recognition that the distributor seeks a second source for the product in an effort to protect customers from relying on a single source or using other distributors for a second source of the product type. In these circumstances, when products face horizontal competition, sales incentives in the form of sales contests, volume bonuses, and rebates to the distributor or directly to sellers can maintain focus on the product. Firms that use distributors for products must recognize that, regardless of the product position in the product life cycle, the distributor and the distributor sellers are an extension of the sales team of the firm. Sales and marketing meetings at the distributor level provide an opportunity to develop and improve relationships with distributors while giving them the opportunity to feel a part of the organization. These meetings and seminars operate for the distributors the same as the national sales and marketing meetings operate for the firm's sales team. New products are introduced, and training in new products, merchandising programs, and support materials takes place.

Public Relations

The intent of public relations and publicity is to develop a positive image of the company or product line through nonsponsored (nonpaid) messages. Public relations covers all efforts to obtain the attention and favorable coverage of the firm's business by third-party media and publics. Companies engage in publicity to transmit a message that is viewed, interpreted, and retransmitted by news organizations, reporters, and media "luminaries"—news commentators that have developed reputations and are recognized personalities or expert authorities. Since the message has been digested by the media and **public stakeholders** and supposedly evaluated on its merits, the retransmitted message reported in the media gains credibility. Very often, the reach and attention-getting ability of the media extend far beyond the reach and impact that a company can buy with advertising. Well-executed public relations efforts, then, have the potential to obtain much higher levels of response than can equivalent expenditures in advertising. Within this definition, public relations is somewhat analogous to organized word of mouth!

Public stakeholders are those public entities that have a vested interest in the financial performance and/or social responsibility demonstrated by the firm. These **publics** or public stakeholders may be large retirement systems with significant financial holdings in the stock of the firm, mutual fund managers whose funds are invested, government agencies charged with regulating portions of the firm's business practices, and public interest groups whose agenda can be advanced or damaged by actions of the firm.

At times, management will need to be persuaded that publicity or an ongoing public relations effort has value. The results of these efforts develop over long time periods, making them difficult to quantify. In addition to the difficulties associated with measuring results, public relations efforts are difficult to control because so much of the message will be interpreted and reinterpreted by other parties who will have their own level of knowledge and perception and may have their own agenda regarding the message. These difficulties contribute to a lower regard for public relations among some business-to-business marketers. This is unfortunate, as publicity and public relations can serve the organization well, particularly during difficult times.

Public Relations Activities

Public relations (PR) activities include special events, press tours, public appearances by company executives and participation in media dialogue as industry observers and experts, participation in trade shows and conferences, and any number of other activities intended to obtain public recognition or notice (see **guerrilla marketing**). Note that we have included trade shows and conferences as, at least in part, a public relations activity. While this is not the traditional definition, the outcomes of trade shows and conferences contribute significantly to the corporate image/public relations effort. These events thus serve as an example of the overlap of different elements of the promotion mix. The purposes of these activities are to generate awareness, credibility, and reassurance of legitimacy and quality, as well as to convey differentiation on a few important dimensions. Messages to be conveyed through PR cannot be complex: media coverage and interpretation will tend to simplify the message transmitted from the company. The exception to this is evaluative expositions coming from media luminaries, who can go into great detail in examining a company and its offerings. However, so much evaluation and interpretation go into media luminaries' reporting that a company cannot count on a complex message to be retransmitted in whole.

Guerrilla marketing is the use of attention-getting small events intended to get the company noticed, to build small pockets of sales, and to obtain word-of-mouth diffusion of a message. It might involve passing out free samples or promotional merchandise in public places or engaging in small bits of "street" theater to attract attention. The idea is to generate grassroots-level excitement while spending a minimum amount of money. Small companies or start-ups often rely on guerrilla marketing.

Effectiveness in Public Relations

Two major dimensions of effort underlie effective PR. The first is effective management of relationships with the media. The second is creativity. In both areas, prudent management often looks outside of the organization to professional public relations agencies. A good public relations agency is "worth its weight in gold" for managing media relationships (i.e., it is worth the hefty retainer it will charge for its efforts). The right agency has established relationships with reporters and editors who influence the media that the target market is exposed to. The media editors who make decisions about the content of their reporting trust the agency to give them newsworthy information and rely on the agency to filter out unsupported "hype" (messages that are conveyed in consistently superlative language—hyperbole). Good PR representatives have nurtured the relationship with editors and reporters and know the customs and nuances of the market. They know how often they can contact editors without wearing out their welcome and know how to diplomatically introduce new ideas to the media. Good agencies have the contacts and the credibility to schedule press tours that draw the best reporters, industry analysts, financial analysts, and industry luminaries.

As previously noted, management can be reluctant to hire the services of a full-time PR agency. Too often, companies that are new to publicity underestimate the value of a good agency, believing that they do not need such relationships with the media or that a summer intern can come close to replicating an agency's efforts for a tenth of the cost. Many companies, large and small, have learned that the need for an existing positive public image can occur without warning. Then it is too late. Very few companies can ignore the need for a good public image. Those that do must have an unassailable market position.

When the Image Unravels   What happens when the firm is faced with a serious PR problem? While the management of crisis situations is a major focus of Chapter 14, an understanding now of the fundamental concepts of PR is appropriate. In the preceding discussion, public relations was defined as having a long-term focus with little management or control over the actual reporting of the news or event and a reliance on (or fear of) the trust and credibility of the secondary sources—the reporting media personalities. Recognizing these conditions should also foster the recognition that just handling a bad situation does not suffice; closing the barn door after the animals are already out does nothing to address the main problem! An ongoing PR effort that has built relationships with the media and established a positive corporate value image can create a significant predisposition to forgiveness from the market.

Knowing these fundamental concepts, why do some firms do so poorly when faced with a serious image problem? It has been our experience that, because of the long wait for a payoff (that may never be quantifiable), management spends promotion dollars on elements of the promotion mix that have immediate, measurable impact. This predicament is aggravated by the short-term business measurements used to reward many managers. Though a positive public image can contribute to, among other things, the recruitment of employees and location and development of facilities, these outcomes are seldom quantifiable. The PR effort may never be missed—until it is needed.

PROMOTIONAL METHODS IN BUSINESS-TO-BUSINESS MARKETING

The methods used most often in business-to-business marketing are effective because they are designed for use when there are relatively few people in the audience and the audience is looking for specialized information on several dimensions.

Nonpersonal communications—advertising, sales promotion, public relations—can have a positive influence on the way the buying center progresses through the buying decision process. Care must be exercised to ensure that messages are appropriate. This means that messages must be appropriate for the type of individual, appropriate for the role in the buying center, and appropriate for the stage in the buying decision process. There are two principal challenges in accomplishing this—aside from the *creative* challenge of creating compelling, effective messages. First, the marketer needs a thorough understanding of the customer, that is, what the behaviors of people are in the buying center, what their roles are in the decision process, and what motivates them. We have, of course, stressed this understanding throughout the text. The second challenge is to keep all these messages consistent. The marketer may be able to target certain roles in the buying center by placing communications in certain media, but this does not assure that people in one role are not reading messages aimed at someone else in the buying center. This is particularly true for print advertising, sponsored articles, or contributed material in trade magazines and for Web site content. People in many different roles read trade magazines: executives, managers, technical people, and purchasing managers. Web sites, by their nature, attract all sorts of viewers.

In business-to-business marketing, different types of nonpersonal communication can be designed to have a significant effect at several points in the buying decision process, as can be seen in Exhibit 13–3. The types of promotion used must have an order—a map—associated with their placement. A trade journal editor may be willing to mention a new offering in an editorial about changes in a particular

EXHIBIT 13–3   The Buying Decision Process and Potentially Effective Methods of Nonpersonal Communications

In the Process Flow Stages . . .	Nonpersonal Communications Can . . .
Definition Stage	
◆ Problem definition ◆ Solution definition ◆ Product specification	◆ Help identify problems ◆ Provide info for defining solutions ◆ Help customers remember vendors
Selection Stage	
◆ Solution provider search ◆ Acquire solution provider(s)	◆ Provide info on vendor ◆ Provide info on products and partners
Deliver Solution Stage	
◆ Customize as needed ◆ Install/test/train	◆ Deliver service and training info
End Game Stage	
◆ Operate solution ◆ Reach end result ◆ Evaluate outcomes ◆ Determine next set of needs	◆ Provide reinforcement ◆ Deliver service info ◆ Share performance data for evaluation

market or include the offering in the "new products" section of the magazine but would not consider either action if the offering had already been featured in a print advertisement. The news would not be new.

As Exhibit 13–3 shows, communications early in the buying process among the members of the buying center can influence and motivate to recognize a problem and to seek a solution. In earlier chapters, we have discussed how sellers and missionary salespeople can influence this aspect of the buying decision process. A coordinated effort of nonpersonal methods can also influence buying center members' perceptions. For instance, a print ad in a trade journal may catch the attention of a product designer, creating a level of awareness that assists the missionary sales effort and starting the process of thinking about embedding new capabilities in his product.

In the next stage of the buying decision process, nonpersonal communication can provide a great deal of information as members of the buying center collect information and compare offerings and vendors. During this information search phase, nonpersonal communication may influence the direction that the decision process takes. For instance, information on a Web site may be enough for a process engineer to make early comparisons among alternative system components and to decide to keep the vendor's product in his consideration set. The process engineer may have decided to look at the Web site because he received a well-designed direct mail piece or read a product review in a trade magazine.

During the next stage, in which selection of a vendor occurs, the participants may remember communications they have seen before; or an executive may remember an ad for one of the companies on the short list of suppliers that he is about to approve for final proposals for a project. In these instances, nonpersonal communications may not have access to decision makers *during the stage.* However, a well-designed ad that the decision maker has seen before may have created a high enough level of recognition in the decision maker's memory that it has a positive influence, small though the effect may be, on the decision. Also during selection, a sales promotion offering may induce the customer to try a product or service to see whether it holds value or not. For instance, an office supply dealer may send an e-mail coupon to an administrative assistant that provides a 15 percent discount for trying the dealer for next month's order, plus a "special gift" for the administrative assistant. This may be enough to induce the administrative assistant to make the decision to try the dealer (without feeling guilty about receiving the special gift, because the company has received a discount in the deal, too).

As Exhibit 13–3 shows, after a sale has been made, the supplier's communications could reinforce the idea that the customer made a good choice. Promotion that features a customer's new use of the firm's offering not only reinforces the customer's selection but also encourages other similar users in the market (often competitors of the first customer) to examine the value provided by the offering. This can lead to translation opportunities for the firm and good exposure for the customer's products—assuming the customer is amenable to having its products featured in the promotion. And, of course, nonpersonal information may be provided that helps the customer to use the product. For instance, a Web seminar that helps a customer learn to use a new software program he has just purchased and down-loaded may help the customer to realize the value in the product and also establish a relationship that makes it easier for the customer to find value in product upgrades that can be purchased later.

Convergence of the Promotion Mix

In the following discussion, the methods and devices of business-to-business pro-motion are discussed. Each of these methods or devices follows the basic tenets of the four variables of the promotion mix—personal sales, advertising, sales promo-tion, and publicity. However, it can be difficult to specify these efforts as fitting into only one of the promotion mix variables as they are a mix, or combination, of many different parts of the promotion mix. Therefore, the discussion of these meth-ods focuses not necessarily only on the process by which promotion mix variables are used, but on the desired outcomes of the promotional effort. After we discuss several of these important promotional tools, we return to the Sensacon[4] example, used in Chapter 8 and Chapter 9, to aid in understanding them.

Print Promotion

One of the key methods of communicating with customers in business-to-business markets is through printed promotion. In most industries, there are several trade publications that reach members of a buying center. When stakeholders in various positions find an ad for a product or service they like, they often save the magazine issue, download a file from the magazine Web site, or clip the ad. This provides extended memory beyond what can be kept in their heads.

There are other kinds of publications that run print advertising, principally business magazines and industry directories. Advertising run in these vehicles has slightly different purposes than ads run in trade journals, and, hence, the execution is different.

Advertising in Trade Journals
Most industry segments have several journals, magazines, or newsletters reporting developments, events, conditions, and trends in the industry. Audiences for the major publications cover large propor-tions of the membership of the major buying centers for companies within the industry. One of the difficulties with trade publications is that the audiences are diverse; executives, as well as design engineers and administrative staff, are likely to read many of the same publications. It is therefore difficult to create ads that appeal to all or many roles in the buying center.

In creating print ads, the marketer and his advertising agency should target specific members of buying centers and the stage of the buying process that most

---

[4]Recall that the Sensacon example is a composite of the experiences of more than one company in this market. Simplifications have been made for clarity, and care has been taken to prevent any direct relation-ship with any single market participant.

will be in at the time. The message should convey *key benefits* important to the buying center member at this stage in the process and should be delivered in language most compelling to those benefits. This means that product advertising does *not always convey product attributes*. This can be very difficult for technology-oriented product managers to accept. For instance, a small manufacturer of emission control equipment in a semiconductor industry was targeting process engineers with print ads that conveyed a great deal of information on product features, technology, and specifications—read: *boring*. They changed the ad design to focus on cost savings—a key benefit sought by process engineers when looking for system upgrades—and ran it with the headline "Be a Cost-Saving Hero"—read: *attention getting*. The company quadrupled their information inquiries from the engineers! Again, customers do not buy technology; they buy solutions, so doesn't it make sense to promote solution-creating capabilities?

In business-to-business marketing, careful consideration should be given to the amount of technical data that is included in the promotion. In making this decision, the marketing manager should be aware of the attitude and behavior of the individuals in the target audience. Complex data can be left to separate documents available on request, provided through toll-free assistance or "faxback" systems or on the Internet.

In general, advertising in trade journals requires some effort to break through the noise, but this noise level is usually only moderate. At times, though, the noise level can rise precipitously. During the Internet boom of 1999–2000, for instance, trade magazines such as *Business 2.0* and *The Industry Standard* greatly expanded the number of pages printed, mostly with more ads. This made it difficult for individual companies to get noticed in amongst all this noise.

Directory Advertising

Directory Advertising When members of the buying center are looking to build a list of vendors to approach for an **RFP**, **RFQ**, or **RFB**, they often turn to an industry directory. A well-placed ad in the appropriate directory for the marketer's industry can generate significant new leads. A clear statement of the principal products offered and the key points of differentiation attract more attention than a simple listing in the directory. A problem with directories is that they are usually compiled less frequently than product introductions, so the directory ad needs to be fairly generic, yet convey points of differentiation. Often this amounts to stating the company's general positioning, as well as pointing out the company's key product lines.

Consumer Media

Consumer Media Sometimes, important members of the buying center are not reachable through trade media or other traditional business-to-business media. In other instances, the marketer wants to reach a broad audience and convey a message in a way that evokes an emotional response. In such circumstances, advertising in consumer

RFP, request for proposal; **RFQ**, request for quotation; **RFB**, request for bid. These acronyms are industry jargon for the process of asking potential suppliers to submit their proposed solutions to the described customer need. Depending on the type of business (new business, translation, core churn) and the type of sales (transactional, problem solving, relationship based), the degree of importance in the supplier selection process of RFQ, RFP, and RFB will vary. Chapter 3 and Chapter 11 deal with these issues in greater detail.

media may be appropriate. Broadcast advertising—radio and television—may be the most effective way to reach a general business audience. Consumer media may also be appropriate when targeting small businesses that do not have a strong tie to an industry or to a profession, or, as described in the box, "Billboards in Business-to-Business Promotion," when a message that will be widely viewed will, in fact, have a narrow target audience.

A problem with consumer media that business-to-business marketers may not be used to encountering is the high noise level. Consumers have erected high barriers to attention and it is easy for advertisements to get lost in the clutter. The ad agency must work at producing ads that get attention.

At that point it is crucial to not get carried away in the creative effort and undermine the message or to convey unintended messages that undermine the company's positioning. There is a software company with a current ad campaign in which a flock of roosters runs around town "sounding the wake-up call." In this case, it is lucky, if somewhat expensive and wasteful, that the name of the company is not conveyed in a particularly memorable way. We can imagine that many company executives are quietly asking themselves "Who is this chicken outfit?"

Sensacon Applications of Print Advertising

To briefly review, recall that Sensacon is a company at the chasm of the technology adoption life cycle. It just completed a major development of its pressure sensor technology for application as tire pressure sensors on sport utility vehicles (SUVs). The size of this new business forced the remaking of the company. Sensacon has the opportunity to become the industry standard for tire pressure sensors but must first position its product and company as the market owner. The task is to communicate Sensacon technology and leadership beyond the SUVs and the two manufacturers that have specified its product.

Now, consider the communication needs of Sensacon. What advertising should Sensacon engage in? Recall that Sensacon is a new supplier to the vehicle industry—many participants may not be aware of Sensacon capabilities or presence. The first task then would be an awareness campaign in major trade journals. However, a review of exactly what Sensacon wants to accomplish and where it is now is critical.

Having a print ad is, in itself, of little use if it does not convey a well thought out, consistent message. Recall that management at Sensacon has named its new product

---

Billboards in Business-to-Business Promotion

It may not sound like a good idea at first, but billboards—outdoor advertising—can play a role in business-to-business promotion. When a principal stakeholder in the buying center is not reachable through other means and a thought-provoking message can be developed without complexity, billboards may be a good choice.

Located on major commuter routes, the billboards will be seen by all passers, but as long as that executive who is the target of the ad sees it, it has done its job. This is one time when a slow, congested commute is a good thing!

SensorSUV. While this *brand name* differentiates the product from other Sensacon products, it does little to identify the product with potential customers. What does the product do, sense the presence of SUVs? No, the device monitors tire pressure. This is not a feature that the industry is likely to limit to SUVs. By knowing the nature of the vehicle industry, Sensacon realizes that this feature is likely to be spread to other types of vehicles—sports cars, family sedans, and anywhere remote tire pressure sensing may be a desirable attribute or feature. The name needs to be changed to something more indicative of what customers will identify with.

Sensacon retains an advertising agency, and, among other tasks, the agency works to rename the offering. SensorSUV becomes *InflationGuard*. Print ads to broaden awareness among vehicle designers and engineers (a sizable group, who tend to pay attention to trade magazine advertising) are developed that focus on the ease of use, low cost, and safety advantages of InflationGuard. The ads feature scenes of vehicles that use Sensacon tire pressure sensors (with the concurrence of the vehicle manufacturer), perhaps SUVs in rugged terrain or loaded for a family camping trip, with a caption that reads, "Vacations are to get away from worries about pressure." Perhaps an inset picture of the sensor in a tire is part of the ad.

Which journals should the ad be placed in? What exposure does Sensacon want? Well, since Sensacon and its customers must prepare the tire service industry for these devices, print ads in service industry journals, in addition to vehicle and tire manufacturer journals, are appropriate. The tire service industry may also be an appropriate audience for direct mail (discussed subsequently), though with a different message. Service, repair, and replacement procedures and advice are distributed by Sensacon to all tire dealers on industry mailing lists, advising them of procedures and reassuring them that Sensacon will be available to assist in their service efforts.

Corporate Advertising

There is value for the firm to achieve an image distinct from competition. Corporate advertising is a promotional effort undertaken to enhance the value image or positioning of the firm itself. Corporate advertising is not specifically related to any product of the firm. In this view, corporate advertising is not unlike the institutional advertising done by many supermarkets in consumer markets. By advertising the store, the firm adds brand recognition to all of its house and private brands without the expense of specific promotions that would challenge nationally known brands.

The use of corporate advertising can provide outcomes that would be difficult for specific product-related promotion:[5]

♦   A company's reputation impacts the chance of getting a first hearing at a new account and can help overcome problems at an existing account; a degree of forgiveness can exist.

---

[5]Phillip Kotler, *Marketing Management*, 8th ed. (Upper Saddle River, N.J.: Prentice-Hall, 1996).

- ◆ Community concessions and subsidies, particularly when a firm seeks to expand or create new facilities, can be enhanced.

- ◆ All things being equal (such as "average" sellers from all competitors), the larger, well-known company will get the business over the lesser-known smaller competitor. Thus, a smaller company should spend what might be limited promotion dollars to select and train good sales representatives, to overcome the larger competitor's average seller, rather than spend money on advertising.

Company reputations help selling and marketing efforts most when the product/offering is complex or the risk to the customer is high. When either of these circumstances exists, customers seek suppliers who are willing to address needs in a collaborative manner. The customer seeks a partner to share risk and to be able to help with recovery if something should go wrong. Similarly, a customer favors the well-positioned supplier when it is less familiar with the technology or market or the task at hand is not well defined. All of these reasons were important for Accenture. When the name of the firm was changed, Accenture's management wanted to leverage the strong reputation they had as Andersen Consulting. To do this, they relied in part on corporate advertising to get the attention of buying center members and attach their beliefs to the new name.

Direct Mail

Direct mail advertising has several attractive features for the marketer. In many circumstances, it can be closely targeted to some important audience characteristics. Second, its effectiveness can be fairly easily measured by determining the proportion of targeted individuals who respond. Third, it is relatively inexpensive.

Direct mail also has its disadvantages. The most important of these is that a large portion of the target audience can easily ignore it. At its worst, direct mail is annoyance that undermines customer perceptions of the positioning of the offering. In general, though, direct mail is expected, and, while not exactly cherished by customers, it can be a good source of information when it is well done.

Sales and Support Literature

As has been mentioned before, much of the communication effort in business-to-business marketing centers around face-to-face personal selling and customer service. These efforts can be greatly aided with well-executed printed materials. Often called *collateral materials,* these materials are useful early in the customer's buying decision process, when buying center members are collecting and comparing information about several vendors; they are useful during the customer's review of supplier's proposals, since they help clarify and remind the buying center members of vendor's key differentiators; and they are useful at the end of the process when the buyers are considering their next purchases.

Good sales support literature serves two general purposes: it tells the customers about benefits they will receive, and it gives them enough information that they can determine how the product or service will work. This helps the buying center members think about how the offering can be integrated into their own operation. There are several types of printed materials that are lumped into this category. Each type has a particular function and capability suited to specific circumstances.

Catalogs, Product Brochures, and Data Sheets

The use of catalogs, brochures, and data sheets implies that the product or product line is relatively stable. Offerings that are evolving, either through research and development by the supplier or in conjunction with customers, are not likely to be featured in catalogs. As sales support material, catalogs, brochures, and data sheets provide excellent **leave-behind materials** for sellers but are most effective in transactional sales in which the seller role is that of an order taker or persuader/sustainer.

Capabilities Brochures

When the seller's role is that of a problem solver or relationship/value creator, standard products are less likely to be the focus of the sales effort. Catalogs and product brochures are less likely to be as valuable. This is similar to the situation faced by service companies. Collateral materials for service organizations focus on the capabilities of the firm and may include testimonials from satisfied customers. The relationship between customer and supplier in a collaborative development effort is not very different. The customer is not necessarily interested in a specific product form as he is in the capabilities of the supplier as a collaborator.

> **Leave-behind materials** are items that sellers can give to customers following an in-person sales call. Leave-behind materials do not necessarily have to stand alone; the seller explains the literature and the value points to the customer.
>
> Another very similar type of promotional material is called the seller stand-in. Seller stand-in materials are often used in direct mail campaigns. This type of material must be self-supporting; the seller will not be able to emphasize or explain its relevance to the customer's needs.

Technical Bulletins, Test Reports, and Application Histories

Technical bulletins, test reports, and application histories are excellent design guides and problem solvers for customers. Customers in collaborative relationships with suppliers are interested in information that will make their effort easier, more timely, and more productive. Technical information that assists the customer with integration of the product or design features into his product, best practices data, and application histories—case studies of other successful applications of the product or technology—can be very useful. For example, a paint manufacturer may have a specific treatment process to get certain paint grades to stick to otherwise unpaintable surfaces. The *best practices information,* the technical data relating to the chemistry and surface preparation, could be in a technical bulletin. Application histories show unique and notable applications of the technology. Printed advertisements used in trade journals, as previously described, that have been replaced by newer examples often become part of application histories.

The technical bulletin and the application history, though used in the same manner, usually are positioned differently. Traditionally, the technical bulletin is hardly ever a four-color glossy advertisement reprint, while the application history starts out as exactly that. With the advent of the Internet, technical bulletins and application histories are not only easily updated but are more readily available to customers. Technical bulletins on the Internet may feature *opt-in* capability, providing customers with immediate, up-to-date information. Opt-in features of on-line newsletters and customer information systems are discussed later in this chapter.

Sensacon Applications of Sales and Support Literature

InflationGuard is a new product with great potential but with only two customers—the SUV manufacturers who have awarded Sensacon the business. Marketing managers at Sensacon want to capitalize on this development effort in what they believe to be an expanding market. The Sensacon field team has the task of *translating* this *new business* success to other customers. (*New business, translation,* and *core churn* are discussed in Chapter 6 and again in Chapter 11.) The headquarters market segment specialists (see Exhibit 11–2 for a perspective of where the headquarters market segment specialist fits into the organization) are responsible for developing the translation tools that will assist the field team.

Appropriate translation tools targeted at vehicle manufacturers include a capabilities brochure introducing Sensacon; a technical bulletin focused on the ease of adaptability of InflationGuard to other tires and vehicles beyond SUVs; and an application history featuring the current SUV success story, partially culled from the print advertisement discussed earlier. As Sensacon adapts InflationGuard to more vehicles and tires, the updated data can be made available through the Internet.

Translation tools for the aftermarket—tire service and repair facilities and SUV dealers—require a different approach because these channels get information from different sources. Sensacon plans to develop an aftermarket version of InflationGuard. Individual customers will be able to have the product installed on their vehicles by a certified dealer. This is, however, several months away. In the meantime, Sensacon will seek one or more tire manufacturers as partners, training the field personnel to handle Sensacon inquiries.

Channel Promotions

When Sensacon does decide to enter the aftermarket, there may be several options. A collaboration with a company that already has established aftermarket channels—a tire manufacturer or automotive accessory company—may be the correct choice. Whichever channel design Sensacon pursues, an appropriate promotion plan will be necessary. Sensacon will need to consider various sales promotion techniques focused on middlemen, as discussed earlier in this chapter.

Promotional Merchandise

Premiums, as they are called, are merchandise items given away to customers, prospects, channel members, media representatives, and other stakeholders or interested parties. Premiums are a form of sales promotion, usually intended to augment other promotions. Sales promotions serve, in consumer marketing, as short-term inducements to purchase, while, in business-to-business marketing, they are intended to get action other than a sale. Most business-to-business transactions are too complex and valuable for a sales promotion incentive to provide much inducement. Rather, sales promotions are used to provide incentive for small, intermediate actions in the buying decision process, such as an incentive to visit a trade show booth, an incentive to fill out a questionnaire, an incentive to visit a Web site, or an incentive to remember a brand name when it is time to put together a list of vendors to invite to make a proposal.

Premium merchandise, something of limited but noticeable value, is provided, and some reciprocal action is expected or hoped for. Premium merchandise is given away at trade shows with the most interesting and unique items encouraging a lot of visits to booths. Sellers give out premium merchandise on customer calls as they make excellent leave-behind items. The incentive is for remembering the company and the seller and for establishing positive feelings about either or both. Often, a small premium is sent with a direct mail piece, providing incentive for the recipient to call for more information or to set up an appointment with a seller.

Premium merchandise should be chosen that is unique, to get attention and memory. However, the nature of the premium should, if possible, be related to the product or service offered and should provide value to the customers in their role in the buying center. This is often difficult to do and might require very different kinds of merchandise for, say, engineers and managers. More often, the marketer finds it necessary to simply find merchandise that is unique and valuable and has a clever use of the brand logo emblazoned on the merchandise.

PUBLIC RELATIONS, TRADE SHOWS, CONFERENCES, AND CORPORATE POSITIONING

Trade shows and conferences, usually considered short-term sales promotions, are great opportunities to initiate and reinforce the positioning of a firm relative to other industry participants. In this section, we examine how these promotional methods are used in an overall integrated corporate promotional plan. First, let us review the basics of trade shows and participation in them.

Trade Shows and Conferences

Trade shows are considered by some to be a great excuse to travel to a major city at the company's expense. They are much more than that. Anyone who thinks that is all trade shows are has never worked in a show booth or tried to absorb all that is going on at the show. Attendance at industry trade shows is expected of any serious player in the market segment. Also, all but the smallest companies are expected to exhibit. This is important. Without visibility at the industry show, it is far more difficult to build awareness among potential customers.

At times, it may be difficult to decide which trade shows to attend. In some industries, particularly if the industry is doing well financially, several shows spring up, each claiming to be "the" show to attend. Many large shows divide into regional shows, lowering travel expenses, making it possible for more people to attend. This, of course, means more shows for exhibitors who then experience increased costs. The process of selecting shows to attend and/or participate in includes but is not limited to an analysis of

- What shows are considered important by customers in their markets

- What shows are considered notable by industry and financial analysts who track the industry or firm of the marketer

- What shows are likely to have the best audience for announcements, conference presentations, and technical sessions

- What shows are likely to be attended by customer/industry luminaries who are part of the target audience of the firm

If a marketer's customers have trade shows, the marketer should also attend. The opportunity to see what the marketer's customers consider to be important, not only to their customers but also among their competitors, should not be passed up. If the marketer's customers in different segments have shows, he should attend and, maybe, exhibit. This sounds like a lot of trade shows. However, with all of the marketer's potential customers in one place, why wouldn't he attend and, possibly, exhibit?

Who Should Attend

The trade show is not a party for marketing and sales staff (even though trade shows, and their ancillary hospitality events, can be quite raucous) but is an opportunity to educate members of the firm about the business, particularly the new employees. Everyone that the organization can afford to send should attend the industry trade show. This includes support staff, technical staff, production staff, marketing and sales, and senior executives. Firms that operate under the marketing or societal marketing concept recognize the importance of all team members contextually understanding the markets in which the firm competes. Of course, attendance at the show helps cement relationships among the staff and with customers and distributors as well.

Individuals should have a plan of attendance that includes learning as much as possible about what impacts their role in the organization. Technical conferences or seminars usually occur simultaneously with trade shows. Advanced programs are available such that attendance at appropriate events can be scheduled. Traditional with many trade shows, particularly in the high-technology or consumer products arena, are press conferences about new product introductions or new business alliances. While the information presented at these events is not likely to be startling or reveal any proprietary information, the *spin* placed on the presentation can be telling.

Having an Exhibit

Why would anyone actually want to spend hours at a show booth at a trade show? As stated in the last paragraph, there will not be any new information that a well-informed marketer does not already know. However, in the industry trade show, current and potential customers visit the show to learn about suppliers and their offerings. If the tradeshow in question is the marketer's customers' industry trade show, the marketer's presence is noted as support and commitment to the segment. Besides, not all of the marketer's horizontal competitors recognize the importance of attending shows other than those in their own industry. The marketer's effort may be rewarded by having his customer base all to himself, avoiding comparisons with his competition!

Having exhibits at the customers' trade shows provides an opportunity to identify and start relationships with customers that may be new to the market, as well as to reinforce relationships with existing customers. If the marketer's company is entering a new market, an exhibit at that market's show is a good way to begin the market development efforts.

If the marketer's firm is about to announce a new product for a particular market segment or collaboration with a major customer that will result in a new offering, it makes more sense to do this at the customer's show. Consider that all of the potential customers will be there with an interest in what the marketer's company has to offer and what value it can contribute. This may make more sense than using the marketer's industry's trade show when all of his horizontal competitors will be present looking for potential weaknesses to exploit.

Staging the Exhibit

Technically competent people who can explain offerings *without relying on jargon* should be at the booth. The booth staff should be well coached so that they are aware of the goals of the exhibit and aware of what not to do—or reveal! Sales and marketing staff are naturally gregarious and enjoy engaging people in conversation, while technical staff may not be fully aware of the strategic importance of certain information. It is sometimes startling how much proprietary information can be obtained in a conversation with a poorly trained or poorly briefed person at a trade show.

In a well-attended, lively trade show, marketers find it difficult to obtain customers' attention and memory. This is a good place to consider well-done publicity events as part of the booth activities. Trade shows are a place where a good deal of silliness and drama can be staged to obtain attention. Marketers need to be mindful of the company's image and the positioning of its products. Too much silliness or the wrong kind can convey the wrong message if a marketer is not careful.

Whenever possible, products or applications of the company's technology or capabilities should be available to *touch and feel* in the booth. Just as with print advertisements in trade journals, featuring customer applications (with their concurrence) can be very effective. If the marketer's firm is the market owner in a segment, the product trade name should be prominently displayed and reinforced in conversation. However, if the marketer's company is not the market owner, use of the generic name for the offering may be more appropriate even if the firm has its own brand name. If there is little chance of establishing the marketer's brand, there is no reason to help with the reinforcement of the competitor's brand name.

When the Show Is Over, Capitalize on the Effort

When the show is over, everyone goes home, proud of a job well done; but, the effort is really only starting. The show will have generated many inquiries about the company's products and capabilities. These leads should be made available as soon as possible to field teams for appropriate follow-up. Unless contacts specify otherwise, "as soon as possible" should be measured in days, not weeks or months. As with any promotional effort that creates customer expectations, failure to respond to inquiries in a timely manner is more damaging than not accepting the inquiry itself. If the marketer's firm is unable to respond quickly due to anticipated inquiry volume of other planned events (i.e., the company's national sales meeting, etc.), individuals who have made inquiries should be advised of the delay. Those who cannot wait should get immediate attention.

Fulfillment firms specialize in timely response to customer inquiries. Requests for product literature and any other follow-up that can be handled through the use of printed materials or premiums are requests that can be appropriately contracted to fulfillment firms. In addition to trade show follow-up, fulfillment firms are often used to respond to "bingo card" requests (magazine reader response cards), create special promotions, and satisfy rebate requests. Should a recall or product advisory become necessary, fulfillment firms can be called on to handle the increased number of inquiries placed to company phones, e-mail, and Web sites.

To improve response time, many firms hire **fulfillment firms**. These organizations specialize in responding to inquiries. A direct mail response immediately after the show, handled by the fulfillment organization "buys some time," as well as serving as a reminder to keep the firm and its offering uppermost in the customer's mind until the field team can respond.

Shortly after the show is over, an evaluation of the costs per lead generated should be made. This evaluation should be performed again six months later, or at least before the next show. With the day-to-day pressures in many business environments, the six-month review of cost per legitimate lead may never happen. This is unfortunate, as this evaluation can provide guidance as to what to do, or what not to do, with the next show. If there were many leads, but very few proved legitimate, then an in-booth screening method may be appropriate. If the company is giving away a popular premium, the marketer may want to qualify recipients—but without denying the premium to someone who may not appear qualified. After all, who is to say who does or does not deserve a chair (see box, "Chairs as Baggage?").

Public Relations and Positioning

Press conferences and technical conferences coincident with trade shows are an excellent tool to build the positioning of the firm and the offering. Many of the promotional methods described here may seem focused at large,

Chairs as Baggage?

Premium merchandise items at trade shows can create interest in a show booth but can also create some interesting opportunities to study show attendees. In the early 1980s during the National Plastics Exposition at Chicago's huge McCormick Place (attended by industry professionals from all over the world), a foreign manufacturer of injection molding machines was demonstrating the dependability and capacity of its largest equipment by molding patio chairs. The machine, about the size of a highway bus, reliably produced a new chair about every thirty seconds. This created notable interest among attendees, as the line to receive a chair stretched almost the full length of the aisle.

One wonders how all those chairs got home on all those airlines.

---

financially capable firms well positioned to take advantage of the trade show environment. While that is not strictly the case, what alternatives are there for the small firm that is not yet established in the market or does not have the financial ability or the existing positioning to attract interest at a trade show? The careful use of publicity can help to overcome these limitations. First, management in the small firm must recognize that the firm cannot directly take on large competitors and develop appropriate strategy. A market niche must be developed in which the capabilities of the firm can be demonstrated. This can be particularly challenging for a small, high-technology company.

High-technology companies do not become high-technology companies by accident. Most start-up organizations believe they have a unique product. The challenge is to remake the positioning of the firm from one of offering a unique technology product to one that is known for applying technology to customer needs. Publicity and a good public relations consultant are the tools to accomplish this. Consider the assets of the high-tech company. What are they? The founders of the organization have—or at least believe they have and are able to convince investors that they have—a distinctive competence in their field. Usually, this competence is put to work developing the technology of the product. While this is necessary, it is not usually sufficient to position the firm as a leader in the market. Let us again consider the Sensacon example.

Sensacon Applications of Public Relations, Trade Shows, and Positioning

Prior to winning the InflationGuard business, Sensacon engineers and developers spent years developing the application in collaboration with customers. In the selection stage of the buying decision process (see Exhibit 13–3), manufacturers of SUVs had to find sources with the capabilities to solve the tire pressure monitor problem. These capabilities had to be not only in technology but also in the ability to support the SUV unit volume requirements and to work with the culture of a mass production–oriented customer—not something for which high-technology companies are known. SUV manufacturers had to believe that Sensacon was capable of meeting the standard. Among other factors, Sensacon management used publicity and corporate positioning to establish its positioning in the market.

Shortly after becoming established, it became apparent to Sensacon management that the company competency was in the application of very precise micromachining technology to large-volume applications. However, large customers were not likely to trust this capability without some tangible evidence. To support the business needs of the firm, management focused on two, low-volume but technically complex markets—SCUBA equipment and medical devices. In both markets, Sensacon could prove the technology without investing in high-volume manufacturing. With the assistance of a PR consultant, Sensacon developed a strategy to position the company as the technology leader in the market.

First, the founders of the company and a select set of technical employees were supported in active membership in all related professional societies. This support included both financial incentives and time commitments; the active membership became part of the job description for these individuals. Soon, Sensacon representatives were chairing technical committees and conferences. This was only the start. Technical papers were written for presentation at conferences focusing on Sensacon technology and its potential in the marketplace. Hypothetical examples of high-volume applications of the technology were demonstrated at associated trade shows. (A delicate balance was necessary between revealing proprietary information and presenting technically enlightening information.) Through the relationships of the PR consultant, Sensacon was able to get mentioned as an up-and-coming organization by editors of trade journals and magazines. Technical papers authored by Sensacon employees were accepted for publication in peer-reviewed professional journals. As momentum developed, Sensacon experts were asked to contribute signed articles about pressure sensor developments to trade journals in that market segment. In reprint form, the signed articles were used as leave-behind sales support items. After approximately two years, Sensacon was the technology icon in the pressure sensor industry.

Technical Papers   A comment about the use of technical papers for publicity and corporate positioning is appropriate. Creating technical papers implies writing ability, speaking ability (if the paper is to be presented at a conference), and technical capability. Without all three capabilities, the effort is not likely to create the intended results. Strategically, selection of authors to represent the firm in these endeavors must consider the capabilities of the individuals. The firm must provide adequate support or coaching of individuals, and the individuals must be willing to be coached. As we maintain from Chapter 1, in a market-driven firm, everyone is part of the marketing effort. Here are some simple guidelines for successful use of technical writing and presentations under the circumstances described here:

◆ As author or coauthor, the exposure within the company *and* the industry is a good career-enhancing opportunity. Give it the best effort possible.

◆ Recognize that conference presentations are not only about the technology. Keeping the audience awake and interested is also important. Also, be aware that the paper may be used as a leave-behind brochure or a signed article in a trade journal—more good career exposure, if it is done right.

◆ Avoid product claims that cannot be verified or accomplished within the parameters of the claim. Again, never create an expectation that cannot be delivered.

◆ Do not present the paper if any of the following circumstances exist:

  ◆ The product is still not ready for market.

  ◆ You do not want to stimulate the competition.

  ◆ The product is in joint development with a customer who considers the effort proprietary.

  ◆ The strategy is to target a small number of selected accounts.

  ◆ You cannot handle the volume of inquiries that may be generated.

  ◆ You are not a good speaker.

INTERNET AND WEB COMMUNICATIONS IN BUSINESS-TO-BUSINESS MARKETING

In Chapter 12, we discussed the transactional use of the Web in business-to-business marketing—how the Internet is being used to facilitate product sales and channel functions. Business marketers also make use of the Web for communicating with customers and channel members; this is the other major use of the Web. Even though many Web-only businesses failed or were acquired during 2000 and 2001, the Internet and Web still have appeal for these two uses. Many companies—both new Internet-oriented companies and established "brick-and-mortar" companies—make extensive use of the Internet and Web for these two purposes.

At this point, we need to make a distinction between Web communications and Internet communications. Web communications are communications messages and methods used through Web sites. Internet communications include not only Web communications but also e-mail and some other less-used Internet tools. Consequently, unless we are being more specific, we use the term *Internet communications* to include Web and e-mail communications.

For communicating with business customers, the biggest advantage the Internet offers is low-cost interactivity. Unlike other nonpersonal communications methods, Web sites and e-mail messages can quickly convey messages back and forth between sender and receiver. While not always as rich a communication medium as personal selling, Web sites and e-mail messages can address large portions of the customer's buying decision process for a lot less cost. In many instances, the buying decision process requires interaction with a seller, but Internet communications can effectively address other portions of the process at far lower cost than would have been incurred without the site.

In crafting Internet communications, marketers need to keep in mind three key ideas. First, as with all communications, the marketer needs to understand buyers, the buying center, and how decisions are made. The role of Internet communications can then be determined in assisting buyers in moving through the decision process. Second, Internet methods must be coordinated with other communications methods. Messages, most of all, must be coordinated so that target audiences receive the messages that inform and prompt the appropriate action. Third, marketers should track the relative effectiveness of the multiple Internet communications methods used so that the marketer can tell what methods are working and what ones are not. The Web, through the use of software for analysis of **server logs,** affords the ability to run experiments with alternative messages and presentations. After only a short period of time, the alternative that is most effective can be determined and fully deployed.

> A **server log** is a computer file that records every action taken by every visitor to a Web site. Analysis of a log file can tell the marketer what parts of the site get the most traffic, how long visitors stay on a page, and what patterns are evident in visitors' interaction with the site.

Marketers should follow the three aforementioned guidelines for all types of communications, but we reiterate them here for some special reasons. The first two guidelines—understanding customers' decision processes and integrating the communications methods—often get ignored or paid scant attention in Internet communications. There are systematic reasons—explained at the end of this section—that marketers need to be diligent with respect to these two guidelines. As for the third guideline, Web technology makes it so easy to track and analyze results of experiments that it changes the way that marketers think about communications methods. This, too, is addressed at the end of the section. First, though, let us examine some Internet marketing tools.

Web Site

Almost all business-to-business marketers will want to use a Web site in their marketing efforts. For many, it has become their core communications method, or at least their core Internet communications method. Not all customers use the Web for part of their buying decision process, but many do. In markets in which customers are large companies in oligopolistic markets, at least some of the members of buying centers use the Web extensively for information search and other activities in the decision process.

Companies learned very early that the Web was an efficient way to display and distribute brochures and product data sheets without incurring printing and mailing costs. Even today, many companies find that the best use of a Web site for them and for their customers is to provide basic information about the company with no further Internet activity or e-commerce capabilities.

Web sites today have far greater communicative abilities than this, though. A good Web site can address all the purposes and objectives we have discussed for nonpersonal communications in a business-to-business setting. By providing concise information about customer problems and solutions that are provided by the supplier, a Web site can help members of the buying center:

- recognize and understand their problems;

- collect and compare information about alternative solutions and costs;

- collect and compare information about alternative suppliers, their partners, and their successful delivery of value to prior customers; and

- easily and quickly obtain such things as training materials, user manuals, and troubleshooting guides for use during the installation, testing, and use of the supplier's product or service.

Many marketers have added **product configurators** to their sites over the past few years. A configurator is an interactive program that lets the prospective customer choose from among product attribute alternatives to configure a product that the customer believes will best meet his needs. The configurator then provides supporting information, such as system requirements, and quotes a price. For products that are relatively inexpensive, such as a laptop computer or a data router, the Web site often has a feature that lets the customer place an order for the product the customer just configured.

Marketers find it most difficult to provide value for different market segments. The promise of Web site design is to provide a uniquely defined user experience. In reality, this is still difficult to do, so marketers should try to determine what segment the site visitor is part of and offer appropriately targeted material. Two ways to distinguish market segments are by the viewer's industry or by the type of product that interests the viewer. Many Web sites do these quite well already. (Recall the Web sites for Dana, TRW, and Siemens that we have already visited in past chapters—http://www.dana.com; http://www.trw.com; and http://www.siemens.com)

Most companies do less well in trying to segment by type of buying center member or by the stage of the buying decision process in which they find themselves. Companies have often done well to distinguish types of customers by existing versus prospective customers, allowing access to a secured extranet that has more detailed information pertaining to their particular account. Prospective customers may be divided into segments by level of interest: site visitors with a higher level of interest sign up for a free "membership," which gives them access to a portion of the site that is for "members only." Another way of segmenting by level of interest is to have visitors that are more interested sign up for free e-mail newsletters or even free "Webinars"—Web seminars. These methods of addressing segments still do not distinguish by type of role in the buying center or situation in the decision process.

A Web site that is truly customer centric in its design would allow a visitor to enter a portion of the Web site based on his role or situation. For instance, suppose a vice president of customer service is exploring options for customer relationship management (CRM) systems. The vice president or his delegated manager looking for options has a different agenda in looking for information on CRM systems and providers than does the IT project manager who is involved in choosing and implementing a system. The VP wants to know about improvement in customer care; the IT manager wants to know about compatibility with existing systems and IT overhead costs. Both are concerned about ease of use and price.

In searching for information on CRM vendors, the vice president has to troll through several sections of each vendor's Web site. He has to look in the "Company" section of a Web site for information about the strengths of the vendor. He has to look through the "Products" section for a listing of features and maybe a description of specific benefits. He has to look at the "Customer Cases" section to see how other customers have deployed the systems and to get customer references. The "Partners" section lists various software, hardware, integration, and consulting partners; but, in most circumstances, he has to read between the lines in this section and the "Customer Cases" section to really understand which partners provide what pieces of the system that can best fit his situation. The IT manager probably finds a fair amount of technical information under the "Products" section of the project, but also needs to examine the "Partners" and "Customer Cases" sections to obtain a sense of what an implementation project will involve in his case.

If the site asks whether the visitor is a service executive, service manager, IT project manager, IT executive, or someone filling some other role in the buying center, then prepackaged groups of Web pages can be presented. In addition, the marketer can use a form to ask what else the visitor would like to see. A service rep can follow up with e-mail. The marketer can also collect these requests and build new pages in the site that can provide the commonly asked-for information.

In addition to targeting, other considerations must be kept in mind when designing Web communications. The Web site should be attractive without requiring annoyingly long download times. Many business-to-business Web sites are built with eye-popping graphics and animation, but the value of this is questionable for most companies. These generally take too long to load for someone who wants usable information quickly. Interactivity should be designed at appropriate levels. Product configurators give the buyer a great deal of flexibility; but, often, the buyer is looking for less flexibility and more speed in the transaction. A limited list of standard product models may be enough for targeted segments.

To create Web sites that provide superior value in their communications requires—just as we have stressed all through this text—a good knowledge of customers, their motivations, and their buying behavior. This includes an understanding of the roles and needs of the different actors in the buying center. Too often, Web sites are designed around the supplier's organization and offerings rather than around the customers' needs and buying behavior.

Attracting Visitors to a Web Site

A Web site has little impact if existing and prospective customers do not visit it. Consequently, a sizable effort must be made to bring the right kind of visitors to the Web site. These efforts usually require the marketer to combine and coordinate marketing communications efforts that include both on-line and off-line methods. The marketer has several communications techniques that can be used to contact and attract visitors to the Web site. Banner advertising provides a means to get a message in front of targeted prospective buyers. Clicking on the ad takes the viewer to the Web site, usually to a portion of the site that is related to the offer in the ad. The problem with banner advertising is that "click-through rates"—the proportion of viewers who see the ad who actually click through to the Web site—have declined to levels where banner advertising's effectiveness is questioned. Targeting, when done carefully, can increase banner click-through to rates above 10 percent of exposures. Too often, though, the targeting is too broad to be effective. Other means are usually required.

A common way for prospective customers to find a Web site is to use a search engine. Some, like Goto.com, are aimed at business users. Marketers can do three things to appear on the first page of search engine results. First, in some engines like Goto, the business actually bids for highest rankings, that is, higher bidders have their sites come up higher in rank on the search words they bid for. They then pay their bid for viewers who click through. Second, there are methods of Web site design that will obtain high rankings on relevant searches. The methods to obtain these rankings generally follow the guidelines for good communications—concise wording of Web site text, closely related to the purpose and message of the Web site. (More can be found at such Web sites as http://www.marketingsherpa.com or http://www.searchenginewatch.com) Third, a marketer can purchase key words on search engines. When the advertiser purchases a key word, his banner ad displays when a searcher searches on the key word. This is better targeting than simply placing ads on Web sites where viewers have a general interest in topics loosely related to the marketer's business. Finally, of course, the marketer should register his site at the search engines that are used most by his target audience.

In addition to these methods, other methods are described in the subsections that follow.

Opt-In E-Mail

E-mail has proven to be one of the most useful methods of Internet marketing communications in business-to-business marketing. When e-mail is unsolicited, it is called spam. Because the Internet and e-mail grew up as a communications medium with a strong anticommercial culture, spam is viewed as annoying by most recipients (perhaps more so than is direct mail "junk mail"). Accordingly, e-mail is best used when an interested person gives permission—**opts in**—to the marketer to send e-mail messages. Once permission is obtained, e-mail messages are sent often enough to be noticeable but not so often that they are annoying. This generally is about once or twice a month. The key is to have something of interest to say each time.

E-mail can then be used to provide product notices, notices of special events, or other short messages of interest. E-mail is attractive because it is quick, inexpensive to produce, and almost costless to add people to the audience. The downside of e-mail is that it can wear thin quickly. The marketer must truly have value for the customer in mind. Otherwise, it is too easy to turn good customers into sour excustomers.

Newsletters

Closely related to opt-in e-mail is the use of e-mail newsletters. These are specialized content news briefs, usually with links to full news stories located on a Web site. The reader signs up for a subscription, usually for free, and receives the newsletter in his e-mail mailbox periodically. Newsletters have proven to be very useful marketing tools for business-to-business marketers for several reasons. First, the content is valuable to the user—as long as the writer/editor is doing a good job of finding stories and reporting them well. Second, good newsletters usually are short enough to keep the reader's interest—they get read. Third, the newsletter is a good branding tool for the supplier. It keeps the supplier's name in front of prospective customers on a periodic basis.

Newsletter Advertising

Many newsletters are supported by advertising. Advertising on Web sites—banner advertising and other types of advertising—has not proven to be a good means of advertising a message to target audiences, as already noted. On-line newsletter advertising, though, has the advantage of reaching an audience with a predefined interest in the topic areas covered by the newsletter. If a marketer has an offering that matches well with these interest areas, then the marketer should find it useful to advertise in the newsletter. Newsletter advertising rates are generally less expensive than other kinds of advertising, both on-line and off-line. Further, newsletter ads usually are limited to four or five lines of text with no graphics, so the creative execution of the message is straightforward.

On-Line Seminars

Just as seminars can be useful in educating prospective customers and generating sales leads from the audience, business-to-business marketers can use on-line seminars to great effect. The Internet communications methods we have mentioned have, as their primary objective, attracting a prospective customer to a Web site. On-line seminars, though, seek to accomplish more: the establishment of a relationship with a prospective customer who is already very interested in the company's products or services. Seminars can be done in combination with a conference telephone call or can be done solely on the Web. They can involve self-paced Web presentations or elaborate combinations of broadcast video and audio delivered via the Web. The audience can range from one to thousands. The best Web seminars have relevant content that is well designed for Web delivery. The marketer has to be careful not to be too technologically adventurous. He must remember that many in the audience do not have the latest software and hardware available and that the company's server must be able to handle the interaction from the audience.

Effective Internet Communications

As we mentioned at the beginning of this section, good on-line marketing requires integration of Internet communications with other forms of communication. This is not as easy to do as it sounds. Companies typically have initiated their Web and e-mail marketing by launching semi-autonomous organizational units with dedicated budgets. Due to the specialized technical nature of Web site development, the differences between interactive communication and other kinds of nonpersonal communications, and the necessity of the unit manager to follow the dictates of his own budget, these Internet or Web marketing units have a tendency to maintain their autonomy and may create messages that do not reinforce the other messages promulgated by the company.

A further word needs to be said about the nature of Internet communications and how different they are from other marketing communications. Once the Web site is running, it is relatively easy to change messages and to experiment with new messages and presentations. This is very different from the development requirements for other kinds of communications. Trade advertising, publicity events, trade show booths, and the like do not lend themselves well to fast design and extensive testing. Designs take longer, and opportunities for testing are limited, if they exist at all. There is a natural difference in outlook between the people who work in either camp. This may create some operational problems—Web marketers who want more trial and error; traditional marketing people who expect a more formal design with less flexibility—as well as cultural problems. A marketing manager who has responsibility for Internet marketing, as well as other kinds of marketing, needs to recognize these differences and keep the two camps talking to each other.

PROMOTION AND THE IMPACT OF TRENDS IN BUSINESS-TO-BUSINESS MARKETS

As in prior chapters, we now address the two general trends affecting business-to-business marketing and examine how they are influencing nonpersonal promotion. The two trends, time compression and hypercompetition, influence both the purposes and the requirements for competent execution in promotion. Overcoming the problems that are caused relies upon recognition of these problems and adjusting, rather than on adopting new techniques intended to address the problems.

Promotion and Time Compression

The principal problem arising from time compression is the tendency to create "hype" to deal with short time horizons.[6] One source of this problem is the inability to rapidly achieve an understanding of customers. When the marketer does not have time to understand and develop appropriate communications, the temptation is to communicate in superlatives just to be sure that the offering is perceived as good enough. A second source of the problem arises from the time it takes to achieve the purposes of business-to-business nonpersonal promotion. Too often, the marketer is faced with the task of trying to establish trust and assurance of quality when the customer has little time to arrive at these states of mind. The tendency here is to try to come across as the best—again, the tendency to create hype—and to create memorability by using multiple kinds of media and a high number of repetitions. Marketers anticipate entering new markets and want to build strong brands in these markets quickly. As a result, they resort more and more to multiple advertising repetitions in consumer media hoping to reach at least some of the people in the right audiences with more exposures than can be achieved with trade magazine print ads. The results can be puzzling. We recently saw an ad for an IT services company appear on an obscure cable station at an obscure time during a five-year-old program on an unsolved murder case involving an obscure scion

---

[6]Lou Hoffman, "Haste Makes Hype," *Technology Marketing* 21, no. 6 (June 2001): 56.

of a not-so-obscure, scandal-prone family. The audience (if any) watching the program was not likely to be the audience sought by the marketer.

To address the time-compression problem, marketers first need to understand the limits of what can be accomplished in a short period of time. The fact that it takes time to build trust and it takes time to build a business should not be lost on the marketer or his hired agency. The problems created by the Internet companies' recent efforts to build businesses too fast should convince most marketers to consider building their own businesses for the long term. Perhaps a bit more emphasis on corporate image advertising would be useful to help set the stage for entry into new markets, but marketers should resist the temptation to rush into ridiculously misguided promotional excesses.

Promotion and Hypercompetition

As we have noted in prior chapters, hypercompetition and time compression often are related. In this case, time compression has induced marketers to increase their promotion efforts. In the recent past, the excess of investment money available to many companies created a lot of competitors with a lot of marketing money trying to obtain awareness and brand associations. All of this promotional activity created a lot of clutter—a lot of messages bombarding target audiences. The result of this activity made it more difficult for marketers to get the attention of target audiences, so they responded with more repetitions and messages that got more shrill or "edgier." Many marketers found themselves with campaigns that were so "edgy" that the message and the purpose of the ads were lost in the angst or weirdness. Too much clutter forced marketers to try too hard to get noticed.

When hypercompetition has this result, the marketer needs to focus on purpose, benefits of the offering, the buying decision process, and the segment, that is, get back to basics. The way to compete is not by being louder, stranger, or more ubiquitous. The best way is to understand the needs and decision process of the buying center. The marketer and his agency can then create and deliver messages that address the customers' needs that are most important in ways that help them through the decision process.

This chapter has discussed communicating with the market as part of a well-planned, purposeful effort. Communications, whether through personal selling or through nonpersonal promotion, begin with an understanding of stakeholders—most importantly, the buying center members, their roles in the buying decision process, and their individual motivations. The marketer must start by crafting a message that is intended to address specific kinds of people and to achieve some reaction from them. If the target audience is members of the buying center, usually the purpose is to help them progress through the decision process. Different variables in the promotion mix are best suited for different communication intentions. Just having an advertisement is not necessarily the answer, even though it may be the path of least resistance because it is what has been done before. Rather than focus on the process of promotion, the focus has been on the outcomes that serve the overall marketing plan.

If a company employs an agency, it is important that the agency fully recognize the marketing goals of the organization. One size does not fit all, and the firm should not be distracted from what the marketing plan needs to succeed.

In the development of promotional plans, consider questions like: What function will the promotional materials perform? How complex is the product? Does complexity prevent any brochure or advertisement from being successful? Is the promotional material consistent with the language and customs of the target audience? What combinations of promotion tools, in a fully integrated approach, are necessary to achieve the results desired?

Looking forward to Chapter 14, the role of promotion in corporate positioning, particularly in a crisis, is discussed. The fundamentals of promotion still apply, though with a sense of urgency not previously addressed. Also discussed are ethical issues that, beyond promotion, really involve the corporation as a citizen, a member of society, and a respected resource to customers. As you conclude this chapter, it is our hope that, with the foundation of the prior chapters, the ethical issues addressed will be a natural part of your approach to business-to-business marketing.

Key Terms

advertising	opt-in e-mail	RFQ
direct response requests	premium merchandise	sales promotion
fulfillment firms	product configurator	selective attention
jargon	promotion mix	selective exposure
leave-behind materials	public relations	selective retention
media buy	public stakeholders	server log
noise	publics	
nonpersonal communications	RFB	
	RFP	

Questions for Review and Discussion

1. Compare the relative importance of the promotion mix variables in consumer markets versus business-to-business markets. Why do these differences exist?

2. When would the use of industry-specific jargon be acceptable in the communication process?

3. What is the importance of the encoding-decoding process in message accuracy? How do individuals attach meaning to messages?

4. How will the communication capabilities of the Internet impact the ability of business customers to receive feedback from customers?

5. Explain what promotion can do and what it cannot do.

6. How are the promotion mix variables interrelated? Why is it necessary to coordinate efforts between the variables?

7. What types of promotion are most appropriate at the different stages of the buying decision process?

8. What are the promotional goals most desired at each stage of the buying decision process? How well does this relate to your answer to Question 7?

9. Trade shows have usually been classified as sales promotions. The text makes the case that trade shows are excellent publicity and public relations tools. Which is it? Are trade shows sales promotion or publicity? Does it matter? Why, or why not?

10. What communication purposes can be addressed in a business-to-business Web site? What purposes can be addressed by e-mail?

Internet Exercises

Go to **http://www.businesswire.com** Examine the services available. What are the advantages and disadvantages of using a service such as Business Wire? Suppose you are the marketing communications manager for Sensacon. You want to distribute a press release announcing that Sensacon has been selected as the major supplier of tire pressure sensing devices for sport utility vehicles. What constituents do you want to reach with the press release? What Business Wire circuits would be most appropriate? Would you target regionally? nationally? the general consumer media? news bureaus? trade journals? financial press? Explain your decisions.

Return to the TSNN Web site: **http://www2.tsnn.com** How does the Web site target different segments of prospective customers and existing customers? Would you do this any differently if you were the marketing manager for TSNN? Why, or why not?

Go to the Web site for eMarketer: **http://www.emarketer.com** See how many newsletters eMarketer offers. Consider the clutter created by all the newsletters available to marketers from all the many Web sites targeted at them. How do you think eMarketer, or a company like it, should get through this noise to get the right marketers to read eMarketer newsletters?

14

Business Ethics and Crisis Management

overview. . . This chapter discusses ethics in business-to-business marketing, followed by a discussion of crisis management. The second is often necessary when there is a lack of the first.

This chapter follows the chapter about publicity and public relations since

PHOTOLINK

these tools play a major role in crisis management. To fully understand ethical concerns in business-to-business marketing, an understanding of the many facets of these tools is necessary. Our discussions with associates and practitioners leads us to suspect an underlying sense of skepticism about business ethics. We do not agree with this; the term "business ethics" is not an oxymoron.

Business-to-business managers make many day-to-day decisions—some routine, some significant—that include application of an ethical standard. That standard can be a compilation of many inputs. Organizations may define and hold employees to a high ethical standard; professional associations contribute policy statements about what is (and is not) ethical behavior; and individual lifestyle and beliefs weigh in with distinctive influences.

In the first part of this chapter, we discuss different influences in ethical business decision making and examine the societal marketing concept that defines the "citizenship" of a firm. In the second part of the chapter, we discuss how, in the long run, ethical standards improve the chances of successful crisis management and organizational as well as individual success.

TWA FLIGHT 800: CRISIS MANAGEMENT AND ETHICAL CONCERNS

On July 17, 1996, TWA Flight 800 took off from New York bound for Paris. Thirteen minutes after take off, the Boeing 747 exploded, plunging into Long Island Sound, killing all 230 people on board. The crash of TWA 800 began an unprecedented investigation into the cause of the explosion that would involve the airline and its suppliers, Boeing (the aircraft manufacturer) and its suppliers, at least three government investigative bodies, and international safety advisory groups.

While airline travel is statistically very safe, crashes happen. As terrible and unthinkable as any airline tragedy is, airlines must think of them. Airlines have in place crisis response teams who are trained to deal with the complex personal, legal, and emotional issues surrounding such an event. They are expected to cope with such a tragedy in a professional and compassionate way. Anything less would not be acceptable.

Effective management of the crisis is not the end of the story of TWA 800. Travelers expect that whatever caused this mishap will be investigated and resolved— quickly. The National Transportation Safety Board (NTSB) has the responsibility to determine causes and recommend corrections to the Federal Aviation Administration (FAA). In December 1996, the FAA received

MAX NASH/AP/WIDE WORLD PHOTOS

NTSB's recommendations. The NTSB found that a combination of events, not any one single factor, likely caused the explosion aboard TWA 800. The recommendations included engineering design modifications to fuel tanks, air-conditioning insulation, and wiring (which would need to be addressed by Boeing); upgrading of fuel quantity indicating systems (to be addressed by Boeing & Honeywell); changes in refueling procedures and equipment to fill the area above the fuel level in tanks with inert gas (a process called "inerting," to be addressed by various ground facilities management and crews); changes in fuel composition (to be addressed by petroleum refining companies); and changes in flight procedures (to be addressed by airlines

TWA FLIGHT 800: CRISIS MANAGEMENT AND ETHICAL CONCERNS (CONT'D)

and pilots). The recommendations raised several issues, and before acting on them, in February 1997, the FAA took the unusual step of seeking public comment.*,†

The recommendation to fill the empty portions of fuel tanks with an inert gas caused the most comment. While used on many military aircraft, the procedure is considered cumbersome and costly. By mid-1998, the FAA issued directives regarding the inspection of wiring systems on existing aircraft and design changes in fuel quantity indicating systems and ordered further investigation into the fuel vapor problem.

In October 1999, it was revealed that Boeing knew about center wing tank (CWT) overheating as far back as 1980. At that time, Boeing had been investigating problems with the military version of the 747. NTSB was not informed of the results of that investigation at that time, nor after the TWA 800 explosion. Ironically, key findings of the Boeing study in 1980 are similar to those eventually determined by NTSB following the TWA 800 crash—that hot runways and air-conditioning equipment can overheat fuel tanks. It recommended that additional insulation be used to stop the heat from reaching the tanks. Boeing was somewhat embarrassed that the report did not make it to NTSB, but a Boeing official claimed that the study was about military fuel pump problems, different from those used in commercial aircraft.‡

In March 2001, a Thai Airways Boeing 737 burst into flames on the tarmac in Bangkok, Thailand. One crew member was killed; seven others were injured. The NTSB study said that the CWT, located adjacent to the air-conditioning system that had been running continuously, exploded.

On August 8, 2001, a special task force of an Aviation Rulemaking Advisory Committee (ARAC) submitted its final report to the FAA regarding fuel tank flammability. An ARAC is a committee of airline industry professionals, FAA representatives, and, often, their international counterparts. The report cites the benefits of work already underway to improve fuel tank safety (safer designs, better inspections, upgraded wiring systems), estimating that these steps have already eliminated approximately 75 percent of the potential risk through 2020. Without additional regulations, the remaining 25 percent risk is likely to result in two additional fuel tank

---

*Federal Aviation Administration, "Summary of FAA Actions on TWA 800/747s," FAA News (8 December 1997).
†Robert Davis, "FAA to Review Safety of Fuel Tanks," USA Today (16 December 1996). Available from http://www.usatoday.com
‡Deborah Feyerick, "Boeing Delayed Handing Over Study of Fuel Tanks to TWA 800 Investigators" (30 October 1999). Available from http://www.cnn.com/us/9910/30/boeing.report.02

explosions over the period between now and 2020. Contrary to the NTSB recommendations, the task force does not recommend inerting. In fact, the report states that none of the additional safety alternatives—all with a projected cost of $10–12 billion each over the next fifteen years and an economic benefit of $250–440 million—produced "reasonably balanced" results; they are not cost-effective.[§]

Here are excerpts from the statement issued by acting NTSB Chairman Carol Carmody after the report was submitted:

> The . . . report clearly demonstrates the significant benefits to . . . safety . . . provided by inerting. I am disappointed that their cost-benefit analysis leads them to not recommend inerting systems. . . . I am pleased that the ARAC Executive Committee

appears to share our concerns and has requested a further clarification of that analysis.

The recent destruction of a Boeing 737 in Thailand shows that center fuel tank explosions continue to occur, and likely will occur again in the future. This problem must be addressed if we are to maintain the confidence of the traveling public.[||]

How many ethical lapses or questions can you count? Are you confident that decisions have been made that will protect your safety? When lives are involved, cost-benefit analysis usually relies on the belief that "it will never happen."

[§]Andy Pasztor, "Plans to Avert Fuel-Tank Explosions Tied to '96 Jet Crash Called Too Costly," Wall Street Journal (8 August 2001), A2.
[||]National Transportation Safety Board, "NTSB Advisory" (8 August 2001). Available from http://www.ntsb.gov

- ◆ Understand that a good ethical foundation is a good business foundation.

- ◆ Recognize that ethics are, ultimately, an individual decision.

- ◆ Understand the source of ethics, both organizational and personal.

- ◆ Develop an appreciation for how differences in personal ethical standards versus organizational standards can lead to an uncomfortable environment.

- ◆ Recognize the role of publicity and public relations in crisis management.

- ◆ Become familiar with the elements of good crisis management.

introduction. . .

Many students and business professionals are skeptical about the value and sincerity of business ethics. Claiming that for-profit organizations have only one overriding goal—to maximize profit—the inexperienced or uninitiated give business ethics little regard. For whatever reason, stories about "bad" business behavior attract more attention than stories about "good" business behavior. Is this because "good" behavior is common and not as newsworthy as "bad" behavior? Perhaps. Mass news media report about a firm producing defective products and then resisting recalls, dumping hazardous wastes inappropriately, or conspiring with competitors to fix prices. Combined with reports of individuals engaged in stock fraud, swindles, and scams, it is not surprising that many people are skeptical.

Most consumers form beliefs—individualized truths—based on information from the news media, word of mouth, and personal experiences. These beliefs, or perceptions, form the public impression or **value image** of the firm much like product positioning attempts to create a product image. Once established, these "truths" can be changed only with an overwhelming amount of information, often involving personal experience. Value image, when positive, grants forgiveness in times of crisis or, when negative, will lead to a guilty verdict before trial. The importance of value image then, cannot be measured, at least in the short term.

Several factors contribute to value image. The attitude of a company toward its customers, suppliers, and employees and its approach to living in the community are major elements of the reputation of the firm. Employees who treat customers well and speak highly of the firm are goodwill ambassadors. Suppliers not only take more interest in working with customers who recognize the value of the relationship but will likely make judgments about resource commitments based in part on this recognition. How the firm addresses controversial issues and problems in its markets is also a major influence. The corporate "attitude" portrayed in these circumstances can be a reflection of the philosophy or culture of the company.

Value image, as described in Chapter 3, is the total of all impressions that the public will have of the firm. An individual's beliefs about a firm, situation, or occurrence are based on many inputs. The public reception a firm will receive can be impacted by the value image of that firm.

ETHICAL ISSUES AND THE MARKETING CONCEPT

The marketing concept, discussed in Chapter 1, says that the successful firm, while meeting corporate goals, should be market sensitive, understand customer needs, and meet those needs in a coordinated way that provides value to the customer. Without satisfying customers, the firm eventually ceases to exist. In a truly market-driven firm, all employees recognize that they contribute to the marketing effort. The marketing concept fosters competition and maximizes choice in the marketplace.

Consider the example of the McDonald's switch from plastic to paper packaging, cited in Chapter 2. McDonald's switched from plastic to wax-coated paper for its products because its customers perceived paper as an environmentally friendlier packaging material. A Florida state senator asked, "For a hamburger that lasts a few minutes, why do we need a package that lasts as long as the pyramids?"[1] Was McDonald's following the marketing concept in delivering the greatest value as perceived by its market? What other choices did McDonald's have? Well, they could have implemented a customer education program about the intricacies of recycling. However, they had some experience in this area—customers at its restaurants had not done a good job of separating plastics from paper in collection containers. If the consumers, who are ultimately responsible for their actions, did not respond well to the request to keep waste material separated, what responsibility does McDonald's have? Note that McDonald's is not alone in this quandary. Many organizations face the situation where customers' actions are not as environmentally committed (or ethically, or legally, or socially committed) as its own organization. What place does the supplier have in imposing standards on customers that the customers would not voluntarily adopt?

THE SOCIETAL MARKETING CONCEPT

Is the marketing concept a philosophy that is compatible with the complexity of the business environment? Throughout this book, we have endorsed the marketing concept and value creation as the criteria for success for business-to-business organizations. Critics of the concept say that (1) the marketing concept is unrealistic as it imposes ethical constraints on an organization that reduces its competitiveness—other firms will see an opportunity and exploit it; or (2) the marketing concept is inappropriate as it often allows satisfying customer needs without acting in the best interests of society. With today's resource limitations, degrading environment, world hunger, and neglected (or failed) social services, the marketing concept does not go far enough. Obviously, these two views are not held by the same critic.

[1]Moira Marx Nir, Department of Chemical Engineering, Massachusetts Institute of Technology, Cambridge, Mass., "Implications of Post-Consumer Plastic Waste," *Plastics Engineering* (September 1990).

We believe that marketers have a responsibility, as the defining function of a modern organization, to include society's interests in decision making. Perhaps the place to start the development of a greater view of marketing is with one of the tenets of the *American Marketing Association (AMA) Code of Ethics* and a basic paradigm of professional ethics—*not knowingly to do harm.*[2] The AMA *Code of Ethics* says that "marketers must accept responsibility for the consequences of their activities and make every effort . . . to identify, serve and satisfy all relevant publics: customers, organizations, *and society.*" [Italics added for emphasis] This expansion of the responsibilities of the marketing function leads to the **societal marketing concept**.[3] The societal marketing concept states that, in addition to being market sensitive, understanding customer needs, and meeting organizational goals, marketers must deliver satisfaction more effectively than competitors and in a way that considers the well-being of society. Operating under the concept requires that social, ethical, and community considerations are built in, rather than added on, to every marketing plan. The goal of the societal marketing concept is quality of life.

Organizations operating under the **societal marketing concept** meet organizational goals by understanding customer needs and delivering customer satisfaction more effectively than competitors and in a way that considers the well-being of society—not knowingly doing harm. Firms operating under this concept have several constituencies—stockholders and investors, customers and suppliers, and employees and community.

Critics of the societal marketing concept say that it blurs the separation of business, government, and individual responsibilities. How far should a firm be allowed to influence the quality of life of its customers, employees, and suppliers, beyond what is required to perform a narrowly defined business function? At what point does the good citizenship of the firm become advocacy for the agenda of the leaders of the firm? While much of the in-depth discussion is beyond the focus of this text, we believe that the marketplace answers many of these questions. As customers and customers' customers—derived demand—demand greater application of responsible and sustainable business practices, firms have little choice but to meet the standard.

Events of the 1990s serve as excellent examples of firms paying heavy prices for ignoring or denying the societal responsibility of the organization. Tobacco companies became the focus of consumers—not just smokers or former smokers—who were no longer willing to tolerate the marketing of tobacco products. Restrictions were placed on promotion of tobacco products, particularly those promotions that seemed aimed at children and teens. Local community groups placed initiatives on ballots to ban smoking from public-access facilities. As a result, many states now ban smoking altogether in enclosed facilities. The popular movement led to government action to recover healthcare costs allegedly attributed to smoking, and many lawsuits are still pending. Whether you agree with these actions or not, whether you are a smoker or not, it must be recognized that tobacco companies have paid a very high price for ignoring the potential hazards of their products.

[2]American Marketing Association, AMA *Code of Ethics.* Available from: http://www.ama.org/about/ama/fulleth.asp

[3]Philip Kotler, *Marketing Management,* 10th ed. (Upper Saddle River, N.J.: Prentice-Hall, 2000), 25.

The same type of grassroots effort and application of law that led to the tobacco companies' reduced market access are often considered as tools to approach the makers of alcoholic beverages and handguns and rifles. In narrower instances, manufacturers have been forced to answer for the performance of their products through product recalls and class action damage suits. Whether baby strollers, appliances, or tires for sport utility vehicles, product recalls are ever more frequent than many years ago. We suggest that the increased number of recalls is not a sign of lower product quality but a sign of increased awareness on the part of manufacturers as to how society will hold them responsible for the outcomes of the use (or in some cases, misuse) of their products. The organization that operates from the societal marketing concept will be proactive in ensuring the reliable and safe use of its products. We suggest that, in fact, the demands of the marketplace have led to products of greater quality, safety, and reliability for all consumers.

Societal Marketing as an Ethical Base

The societal marketing concept touches every part of the organization—recruiting, hiring, training, and retaining of personnel; contractual relationships with suppliers and service providers; and environmentally sound decisions regarding the use of natural resources. Many of these elements are visible, in part at least, in many organizations. The challenge—often called a dilemma—for an organization is to be at the forefront of societal marketing in every part of the firm. This level of effort starts with a well-defined and communicated mission statement that should encourage individual ownership at every level of the organization. Herein lie some problems. First, management that creates the mission statement (or its corporate culture substitute), either through ignorance or intention, may not define ethics as they are viewed at all levels of the organization. It is a challenge to develop ethical standards for an organization that will fit contextually with the standards of the many individuals who will work together toward common goals. This creates a gap between what is perceived as ethical by different members of the organization.

Second, reward systems must in fact support ethical behavior. Management that rewards short-term results and then advocates that those goals be met "at any cost" immediately widens the gap between the individuals' view of what is ethical and what is required to succeed. Employees may have personal economic needs, such as continued employment or meeting sales quotas, which dictate behavior inconsistent with what might be considered ethical.[4] What may begin as "minor" ethical discrepancies can bloom into major causes of stress and friction among participants.

A CLASH OF ETHICAL STANDARDS

The previous section hinted at a clash between the ethical standards of the individual and the performance standards of the organization. The clash also occurs

---

[4]Betsy Cummings, "Slowdown Effect: Lack of Ethics," *Sales and Marketing Management* (June 2001): 13.

between ethical standards at different levels in the organization and among different stakeholders in the situation. Let us consider the last clash first.

Ethical Standards among Different Stakeholders

Suppose you are the marketing manager charged with deciding the fate of certain products in the product line. The line has been expanded, and several earlier variations of the product are no longer competitive. The firm has successfully *crossed the chasm* with this product line, and the success of the product line has led to increased competition. As is its nature, competition "improves the breed" and your product is no exception. Improvements in your products have been encouraged by the desire to maintain a competitive edge—your goal has always been ownership of this market segment. Competitors have, of course, been able to use your product as a starting point and have added innovative product attributes to the mix. As the market has grown, competitors have relied on the low costs of offshore manufacturing facilities. While this has been a challenge, your product is recognized as the leader and has maintained the number one position in the segment, though not by the same lead as earlier in the product life cycle.

When the firm started large-volume production of the first-generation product (the one you are now considering eliminating), dedicated manufacturing facilities were built in a relatively rural section of the state. Because of high unemployment resulting from the decline of agricultural interests in the area, the region was more than willing to help with tax breaks, infrastructure improvements, and code variances in construction of the new manufacturing facility. The community has embraced the company, and the area has prospered compared to its previous economic climate.

Manufacturing management has informed you that the new products planned to replace the products to be discontinued must be manufactured offshore to meet cost targets. The facility built for the original product is not capable, with its existing equipment, of meeting productivity goals. Without replacement for the discontinued product, the workers will be let go and the facility idled. The alternative would be to increase the production of the old product at the facility to create a stockpile to meet customer needs, then shut down the facility for six months while upgrading its equipment. You like this idea, but it will delay the introduction of the new product by four months.

Who are the stakeholders in this situation? Of course, there is the community and its workers who will be impacted, directly and indirectly, by the shutdown. Manufacturing management, who are also stakeholders, want the lowest-cost, quickest way to produce product. Marketing and sales management are not very receptive to losing four months in the market, particularly since competition is increasing. The board of directors, made up of members from inside and outside of the company, question the ability to maintain continuously improving quarterly sales and profits by "losing" four months of sales. The media in the community where the facility is located have heard of the dilemma and are being critical of facility engineers who did not plan with enough flexibility in the building of the plant in the first place and are raising the issues of the company commitment to the community while workers are talking of forming a union. From their *individual* perspectives, do any of these stakeholders appear to be acting in an unethical manner?

Ethical Standards at Different Levels in the Organization

Frontline employees should not be asked to accept ethical standards different from those embraced by executive management; and, of course, no firm's executive management would create such an ethical standard. But, as the saying goes, actions speak louder than words. The existence of a common ethical standard does not ensure that all levels of an organization regard it equally.

Behavior of individuals in organizations is best influenced by leadership rather than by control. Executive management sets the context—the example or defining paradigm—for the rest of the organization by the standards it demonstrates. It is difficult for a regional sales manager to strictly enforce written policies regarding legitimate business expense account deductions with her sales team if she knows that the vice president of the organization has had his home landscaped at company expense or has committed price fixing or some other antitrust violation. Similarly, it will be difficult for the field seller to take seriously corporate policies related to bribery or collusion with unscrupulous buyers if she knows the firm is paying market access fees (read: bribes) to foreign officials.[5] The immediate management of the department or workgroup often defines what is acceptable in an organization, compared to what is written as acceptable. This institutionalized definition of what is acceptable moves through the organization and probably takes on different properties at different levels. Maintaining consistency throughout the organization then becomes an *individual responsibility* of managers and those they manage.

Another way that standards can mutate through levels of the organization is when executive management leads in a way that corresponds with the corporate standard but places performance demands on subordinates that may not be realistic. Individuals will work in their best economic interest. A corporate mantra of obtaining goals "at any cost" can encourage expedient but questionable practices. This scenario has often been accompanied by executive denial of any knowledge of a questionable practice at lower levels in the organization. In large organizations, the CEO cannot know the details of every transaction.[6] However, goal setting without knowledge of the markets, followed by rewarding the attainment of the goals without concern for how it was done, is, at best, conveniently naïve.

The implications of the preceding examples are that executives and managers should be clear and consistent as to what standards apply for everyone in the organization. Also, employees need to have a good sense of what degree of ambiguity they themselves can tolerate. If the organization creates more ambiguity than they would want, they must either work to obtain more clarity or decide that they need to work for a different organization.

---

[5]The Foreign Corrupt Practices Act (FCPA), passed in 1977, makes it a crime for a U.S. corporation to bribe officials of another government to obtain favorable business decisions. However, under the FCPA, *gratuities* are permitted. The dilemma is in defining the difference.

[6]Vernon R. Loucks Jr., "A CEO Looks at Ethics," originally published in *Business Horizons* (March–April 1987): 2–6.

Ethical Standards of the Individual and Performance Standards of the Organization

Individuals develop moral and ethical standards by which they make day-to-day decisions. While there is much debate over how and where these standards originate, the actual development of a personal standard probably varies. **Natural law,** developed or **positive law,** and religious beliefs are possible sources that contribute to the formation of a personal moral or ethical standard. For some, these standards are absolute; for others, they may be flexible. Individuals can have acceptable levels of application of their own standards depending on the demands of the circumstances. Sometimes this flexibility is a convenience, and sometimes it may be viewed as a necessity. When the mission of an organization or the context under which a firm operates sets an ethical tone different from that which an individual accepts or believes, the individual may develop a level of anxiety or unease in participating in the operation of the firm.[7] Note that we have said *different;* no judgment is offered at this point as to the relative *good or bad* of the individual or organizational ethical standard. As an alternative, the individual may choose to set flexible standards that allow departure from personal ethical levels in order to survive within the organization. Establishing standards based on the circumstances is often called **situational ethics.**

> **Natural law** is a term applied to the theory of ethics that holds that individual moral standards are derived from a higher, universal source. This is contrasted to a man-made, created, or **positive law** standard of moral or ethical behavior. Ethical standards derived from positive law are said to be determined simply by what is legal.

Situational Ethics   Day-to-day events provide many examples of flexible ethical standards. Often justified by "the greater good"—or maybe just convenience—situational ethics use ad hoc standards influenced by the circumstances of the dilemma. Small ethical choices are made on a daily basis: *it is okay to speed—you're late for an important meeting.* It would be truly difficult to find anyone who could positively say she had never exceeded the speed limit. Sometimes individuals justify ethical choices with larger consequences based on some consideration of relative right or wrong: *it's OK to cheat on income taxes because everybody does it and you probably will not get caught.* Exhibit 14-1 lists some circumstances in business in which situational ethics, perhaps better called ethical lapses, occur. In all of these examples, the ethical standard is lowered to accept a situation that may lead to a short-term gain. Depending on the extent of the ethical lapse, individuals in these situations can feel conflicted and uncomfortable. With the added pressure of creating results in the organization, employment can evolve into an unsatisfactory experience.

Often a situation arises in which ethics stand in opposition to costs or convenience. For instance, after two previous errors on a customer's orders, for which the customer's purchasing manager has rebuked the sales team, the marketer's company makes a minor mistake in the next order. There is a reasonable chance that the

---

[7]Marianne Jennings, *Business: Its Legal, Ethical, and Global Environment* (Cincinnati: South-Western College Publishing, 2000).

EXHIBIT 14–1   Situational Ethics: Ethical Lapse or Convenience?

How many times have you heard these justifications for less-than-exacting ethical behavior?

◆ *But everybody else does it.* This implies that statistics are a valid basis for ethical decisions.
◆ *This is the way we've always done it.* Either "it" was not previously significant or nobody has been caught yet. Compare this to the substantially test cited in Chapter 4.
◆ *I was just following orders.* Often heard in military trials, this implies that the individual does not have the power of free choice or an internal ethical standard. Being told to do something illegal or unethical does not make it okay to do it.
◆ *It is considered standard practice in that market.* This is often a rationalization for bribes, questionable gratuities, or other attempts to inappropriately influence a situation.

Note: Jennings discusses similar and additional phrases as early warning signs of ethical rationalization in Chapter 2 of *Business: Its Legal, Ethical, and Global Environment* (Cincinnati: South-Western College Publishing, 2000).

error will not be noticed, but if it is, the purchasing manager undoubtedly will be furious. While the marketer's company will not likely lose the account, even if the mistake is found out, the customer will have so much bargaining leverage that the account may not be profitable for some time to come. The marketer is tempted to pretend she had no knowledge of the mistake, hoping that the customer does not notice the mistake, and face the consequences only if the customer does find it and complains.

In practical reality, most ethical marketers will have occasional instances in which they take the easy route—usually when the trauma of doing the absolute right thing is substantially greater than the ethical price of not doing it. Caution should be exercised if occasional instances develop into ethical rationalizations— standard ways of doing business. Some indicators are listed in Exhibit 14–1.

On the other hand, some organizations have a culture in which little decisions continuously strive toward "seeing how much can be gotten away with," and the larger ethical decisions are made based on whether the organization can win in a court of law (or even based on whether a settlement after-the-fact is likely to be within a tolerable dollar range). These are organizations for which it is difficult for an ethical person to work. It is also difficult for an ethical company to do business with such an organization, except at an arm's length. Consider some of the following situations that occur often enough that questions of ethics may not be immediately recognized.

Ethics in Product Announcements   Failure to meet pre-announced
dates for product introductions may not, at first, seem like an ethical problem. Most common in consumer markets, these delays are acceptable only when there are no large investments relying on the availability of the delayed product. Consumers may be frustrated by waiting longer than expected for the latest version of that game software, but there is seldom any financial investment by the consumer that is put at risk by the delay. However, in business-to-business markets, many firms assess penalties for late delivery. In the extreme, some firms—particularly those that rely on closely monitored inventories and continuous production methods, such as the automotive industry—may assess fines by the minute or hour

whenever a supplier fails to meet a shipping commitment and shuts down an assembly facility.

A more obvious ethical dilemma is pre-announcing a new product, even though you know the product will be late or underfeatured. In markets where being "first" is important, pre-announcing might be done to match the timing of competitors' new products. Is it ethical to promise an offering to a customer within a certain time frame, knowing that the timing cannot be met, the real goal being to prevent the competitor from being successful (if I can't win, maybe I can keep them from winning)?

Ethics in Product Capability Claims
It is a fundamental principle in marketing that you never promise more than you can deliver. How is this reconciled with advertising claims that are unsupportable? Again, many consumers are skeptical of *any* advertising claims. In business-to-business marketing, exaggerated or false claims just do not work. Customers test the offering for its suitability to their needs before committing to large purchases. The most that the supplier can gain with exaggerated product claims is short term—early consideration in the decision process. When the exaggerations are discovered, the value image of the firm and the individual may be damaged and future dealings will be heavily scrutinized.

Ethics in Obtaining Competitive Information
What is ethical when obtaining competitive information? While many firms will zealously guard proprietary or competitive information from the marketplace, many opportunities exist for companies to obtain competitive information. Misrepresentation, taking the form of employees posing as customers of competitors or as student interns, among other circumstances, can abuse the good intentions of customer service organizations and willingness of companies to support academic efforts. Two interesting circumstances come to mind. In the first, many firms will offer internships to students from local universities, ostensibly to provide a real-world experience in the student's area of study. As an intern, the student is compensated for her effort, either by earning money from the firm or credits from the school. Once she is compensated for her efforts, is the student still a student or is she an employee? What position should she take if asked to identify herself as a student working on a project and calling competitors to obtain competitive information.

The second circumstance is probably one cause for the increase in sales of paper shredders and carbonless forms in recent years. Consider this scenario:

Newly hired into a field sales position, you complete the company's training program and are assigned to a field territory working with a senior seller for some on-the-job training. You feel really lucky because the senior seller you are working with has an outstanding reputation not only for meeting sales quotas but for having a thorough understanding of the territory and the competitive environment. This will be a great learning opportunity.

After a couple of weeks in the field, the senior seller tells you to meet her at a nearby office complex in the evening—"wear old clothes." When you arrive, she asks you to join her in some "dumpster diving"—explaining that your major competitor has offices in the complex and tosses out the carbon paper from computer output showing territory sales and targeted business activity. You participate but are uncomfortable as you think about it later. Was this ethical?

Basically, any information available *to the public* is fair game in a competitive investigation. Any discomfort felt regarding the preceding examples should be a tip-off of an ethical lapse. In either example, the uninitiated or inexperienced person can use the situation as a pattern for future acceptable behavior, or, if uncomfortable with the circumstances, take a stand to overcome the discomfort—avoid the ethical lapse. The choice is one the individual must make.

Other Questionable Ethical Choices and Opportunities   As you ponder your degree of discomfort with the examples you have just read, examine the following ethics dilemmas. Should you, or shouldn't you? *Would you, or wouldn't you?*

- Paying bribes to foreign officials (or to government officials in the United States) by having a consultant pay the bribe and reimbursing the consultant for "miscellaneous marketing costs"

- Charging an exorbitant price for your product at a time when your product is in a temporary state of shortage

- Taking marketing allowances or promotional money even though there is little likelihood you will perform the marketing activities required to receive such bonuses

- Posing as a prospective customer to obtain competitive information

- Favoring one distributor over another; creating an unfair advantage through sales promotions and incentives *designed for one of your distributors,* knowing that your other distributor in the same territory is not likely to participate as effectively

As this is written, three American companies stand out as examples of companies facing major crises. Microsoft has been found to be a monopoly and to have used that monopoly position to limit competition in the marketplace (see Chapter 4), and Firestone and Ford Motor Company are caught in a battle over responsibility for the failure of tires on sport utility vehicles. These are three very different companies, yet each faces a serious value image situation. Microsoft, with market dominance (monopoly, as determined by the courts[8]) is part of a growing industry that many pundits say is the future of American business. Firestone, once a major American tire manufacturer but now owned by Bridgestone of Japan, finds itself in a declining market and losing its largest OEM customers. Ford, under new chairman William Clay Ford Jr., is struggling through a cultural shift while in a mature market. However, none of the circumstances that each company faces provides permission for unethical behavior. Each crisis likely started as a much less

---

important ethical lapse that, at the time, did not seem to be of significant conse-quence. All three are interested in maintaining or improving the value image of the company, and each has chosen a different path of defense. Microsoft claims to have done no wrong; Firestone says the tires are fine—it is a problem with the vehicles; and Ford is recalling millions of tires claiming it is protecting its customers from potential catastrophic tire failures. Though the final episode of these dramas has yet to be written, the public images—and potentially the sales—of the companies suffer.

INDIVIDUAL ETHICAL BEHAVIOR

Students will often ask for advice when faced with these and similar situations, as they occur in group study projects, their careers, and life in general. The advice we usually give is that ethics are a self-realized code of behavior. Our experience is that many business students, operating from the skepticism fostered by media reports, are apprehensive of what they perceive as questionable ethics in business. We have found that the anticipated standards (or lack of standards) are actually worse than the reality. This is compounded by the fact that individual ethical stan-dards are internally generated.

Win-Win, Win-Lose, and Zero-Sum

The need to succeed, to win, is inherent in Western culture. Peer pressure, family responsibilities, and self-centered needs contribute to a win-at-any-cost attitude. When faced with winning or losing, most people elect to win. Built into the win-lose paradigm is the idea that, for there to be a winner, there must be a loser. Busi-ness schools go as far as teaching "zero-sum" management approaches in decision making. The concept of win-win gets lost in this shuffle.

How do individuals behave when faced with these choices? Our experience is that many people will rationalize ethical standards to fit the situation. If the organi-zation cannot win, actions are taken to ensure that there will not be a winner—keep the playing field level (lose-lose). This fosters individuals to suspect that oth-ers, either individuals or organizations, are playing to keep them from winning. Instead of "playing to win," a protective approach, "playing to not lose," becomes the operating posture.

Consider the preparation for a negotiating session. Good business practice would have participants learn as much as possible about the other party's position—strengths, weaknesses, likely negotiating strategies. Part of this analysis should include a reasonably good understanding of what the other party considers "a win." If, as shown in Exhibit 14–2, there are no circumstances in which a win for one party is also a win for the other party—each party's definition of a successful negotiation excludes the other party—then there is no chance for a "win-win" sce-nario. It may even be inadvisable to enter the negotiation process, as one side

Some More Ethical Dilemmas: What Would You Do in Each Case?

◆ You have started a new sales job with a successful telemarketing company. Pay is commission based. Your manager is reviewing calling tactics. She tells you to start each call by asking potential customer's if they are willing to answer some market research questions. The questions are about the discretionary income and credit cards used in the household. When it is determined that the household can afford your product, the sales pitch starts; otherwise, you are instructed to hang up.

◆ As field marketing manager, you are about to hire a new FMD for a major territory. Of the three top applicants, the best is a woman. You know that, even though it is the twenty-first century, some of the customers in the territory prefer dealing with men.

◆ You are the seller at a contract provider who just landed a big job from an end user where your product has been co-specified with a competitor's product. Closing this piece of business will put you over the top of your sales quota. The purchasing agent keeps saying things like "good sellers know how to land a big fish—they just use the right bait" while talking about a new video camera she's interested in.

◆ A good customer asks you for four tickets to a hockey game for himself, his wife, and another couple. You give him the tickets. The following week, he asks you for six tickets. You respond that you have only four and that you would like him and his wife to join you and your significant other at the game. He reluctantly says "yes" but then asks you to not mention the previous week's tickets as he was not there with his wife.

EXHIBIT 14–2 Circumstances That Are a "Win" for A and B

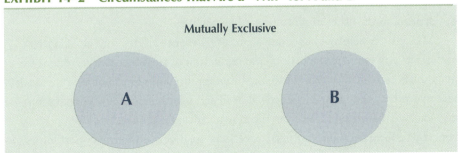

471

EXHIBIT 14–3   Circumstances That Are a "Win" for A and B

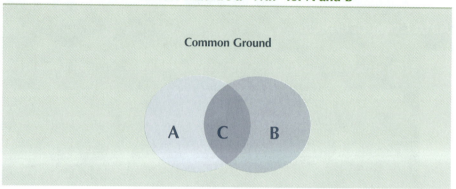

must lose for one side to win. If a long-term association is planned, another partner should be found, as the "loss" on one side may build resentment and a search for an opportunity to "get even." If, as shown in Exhibit 14–3, there are circumstances in which a win for one party is also a win for the other party—the area labeled as C bounded by the arcs from each circle—then there is a win-win scenario that should satisfy both parties. This becomes the foundation for future efforts as well as immediate success. Neither party need succumb to a defensive "playing to not lose" posture.

Readers ask about the portions of the circles that are considered a win by each party but do not fall in C—the mutually inclusive area. The inference is that these winning positions, A minus C and B minus C, are lost in the negotiation, the loss a result of a *compromise*. This is not the case. They could not be "lost" because they were never in consideration as a positive outcome by *both* parties. The winning opportunities represented by the areas that are not overlapped are still winning opportunities, just not immediately between these two parties.

Compromise and Win–Win

Recall the sidebar *Now What Did That Really Mean* from Chapter 13. When students are polled as to the meaning of the word compromise, the most frequent reply is *to give up*. Yet, compromise is the outcome of negotiations, area C in Exhibit 14–3, aimed at creating win-win situations that work for all involved, enabling all parties to commit to an agreed-on direction, goal, or *common promise*. Commitment to the common promise is important. Alliances are more likely to generate mutually beneficial outcomes when each party can depend on the other to work toward *mutual* benefits.

Markets' participants have long memories. Before entering into an alliance, each party will examine the history and reputation of the other party. Actions by individuals can reflect on the entire organization. Previous behavior by individuals that was other than mutually beneficial or raised issues of trust and cooperation may exclude the organization from the new alliance. Again, the long-term positive impact of ethical decisions and actions reflects positively on future opportunities.

EXHIBIT 14–4   Winning Common Ground for Three-Party Value Network

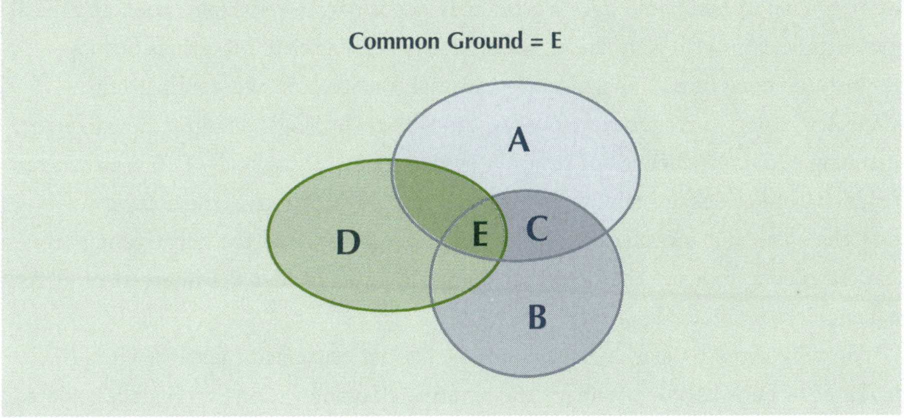

Common Ground = E

ETHICAL BEHAVIOR AND VALUE NETWORKS

In Chapter 2, the concept of the value network was introduced as different combinations of capabilities merged in alliances to serve various sets of customer needs. When a marketer seeks new customers, value networks may be formed to tailor the offering to specific customer criteria. Exhibit 2–3 attempted to show graphically the intricate web possible in the creation of a multidimensional value network. When two firms participate in value networks, they are working in an alliance to serve both firms as well as a specific customer. This is not unlike the relationship shown in Exhibit 14–3. The common ground, area *C*, is the offering created to satisfy the needs of the specific customer. For another customer, Firm *A* may combine with Firm *B* again or with a third firm or create a network of many value providers.

Exhibit 14–4 shows a value network of three providers. Intertwined relationships work in alliances to create offerings for specific customers. Not all participants engage in each creation. However, participants in other networks become aware of the reputation (value image) of each firm as an ally in the network. *A*, *B*, and *D* participate in a value network to create an offering comprised of the common area, *E*. A contributor's respect for proprietary information shared in each alliance, as well as even-handed, ethical treatment of each partner, improves the long-term outlook for that contributor.

The firms and individuals involved in the preceding scenario that have long-term value network opportunities are those who operate ethically as partners in previous networks. The win-win scenario, then, is determined not by size, technology, or leverage but through trust and regard for all members of the team.

CRISIS MANAGEMENT

Related to ethics is the management of crises in which the organization is involved. The relationship between ethics and crises is obvious in some situations; the crisis is the result, in part, of ethical choices made by the organization's executives, managers, or employees. Sometimes a crisis may occur because someone took an ethical stance in dealing with a situation. More often, a crisis related to ethics occurs because someone in the company has addressed a situation with subpar ethics. Many crises derive from other sources, though—technological failure, human error, unanticipated consequences of complex system elements, or really bad weather, for instance—and ethics are minimally involved in their creation. If the company follows the societal marketing concept, it will attempt to avoid the negative impacts that may occur, mitigate the ones that do occur, and consider the interests of all its stakeholders when dealing with crises.

So why should a marketer be concerned about crisis management? First, the marketer often is asked to manage the external communications with stakeholders. Even if the company has a corporate communications department, this department is often organizationally within the marketing organization of the company. Second, in a crisis, the whole company ought to be involved in dealing with it. Marketers and the sales force are charged with managing relationships with customers and channels during a crisis, just as they are during normal periods. Third, in preparing for a crisis, the marketers need to represent the needs and concerns of customers and channels as crisis plans are made.

At its core, effective crisis management depends on ethical attitudes and behavior. The two most important components of ethical attitude applied to crisis management are, first, a willingness to take an honest look at the organization and the possible consequences of its actions and, second, a willingness to feel compassion for those who are affected by the organization's actions. This means that an ethical company will take the effort to anticipate the negative effects of its actions just as it anticipates the positives. Some of the negative effects can be prevented or mitigated with proper safeguards, quality controls, incentives, and so on.[9] Complexity, though, creates unforeseeable effects. Crisis preparation can establish mechanisms for handling incidents and accidents, isolating them, and keeping them from growing into crises. Some events may become full-blown crises no matter how much preparation has been done. The ethical organization will have mechanisms in place for assisting those affected, minimizing the impacts, and learning from the crisis so that future crises can be better addressed.

Pauchant and Mitroff[10] describe four layers of crisis-related systems within an organization that must be understood and addressed *in specific order* to effectively manage crises, as listed in Exhibit 14–5. At the core are the people—particularly those in leadership roles—in the organization and their mental and emotional capabilities for addressing crises. The next level is the culture within which the people operate. The culture must be conducive to introspective and external learning and planning to avoid and manage crises. The third level is the organizational structure.

[9]Steven Fink, *Crisis Management: Planning for the Inevitable* (New York: AMACOM, 1986).

[10]Thierry C. Pauchant and Ian I. Mitroff, *Transforming the Crisis-Prone Organization: Preventing Individual, Organizational, and Environmental Tragedies* (San Francisco: Jossey-Bass, 1992).

EXHIBIT 14–5   Layers of Pauchant and Mitroff's Crisis Management Model

Level one. Character of the people in the organization—willingness to take responsibility and take corrective action.

Level two. Culture existing in the organization—supports appropriate preparation and response actions.

Level three. Organizational structure—crisis management structure in which all stakeholders are represented.

Level four. Plans and mechanisms for dealing with crises—crisis management team has fully prepared plans, disseminated them, and trained people in key roles.

Source: Thierry C. Pauchant and Ian I. Mitroff, *Transforming the Crisis-Prone Organization: Preventing Individual, Organizational, and Environmental Tragedies* (San Francisco: Jossey-Bass, 1992*).*

The structure must directly address crisis prevention and management if it is to be effective. The fourth level is the strategic integration of crisis management. The strategy and mechanisms pursued by the company must recognize negative impacts as possible and directly address crisis management.

Crisis Preparation

So let us assume that the organization has enlightened, open-minded management, unencumbered by neurotic defense mechanisms that prevent good crisis management. They have infused this thinking in the organizational culture (i.e., the first two levels of the crisis management model are successfully addressed). How should a company then prepare itself for crises, and what are the marketers' roles?

Four key aspects of crisis preparation are: establishing effective structures for planning and handling crises, assessing the elements of the company's operations that produce risks and working to reduce these risks, planning for procedures to follow as events occur to minimize the damage and isolate the effects, and inoculation against negative public attention that will occur during a crisis.

Organizational Structure for Crisis Management   An important organizational structure for crisis preparation and for handling crises when they occur is an established, ongoing crisis management team. The team has representation from inside and outside stakeholders. In an organization large enough, it may have its own full-time staff. It has the charge of assessing crisis threats, changing operations or recommending operational changes to head off crises, and establishing roles and procedures for dealing with crises when they occur. It needs to have top-level support if it is to succeed.

Assessing and Addressing Risks   Assessing crisis risk involves first asking the question, "What is the worst that could happen if we continue to do XX?" If the crisis management team represents the views of the major stakeholder groups, then a fair representation of potential crisis areas will emerge. For instance, the marketing executive's concerns that a new product platform will miss the market when

---

How Remote are the Chances of the Worst Happening?

Once in a thousand?
Once in a million?
Once in a Jurassic age?

Small actions can precipitate major situations. Crisis management teams should ask what series of events and interactions might produce the worst-case scenario. This exercise helps the team to understand the negative effects of current systems and the possibility for worst-case circumstances that would otherwise be seen as unlikely. Just as, in the novel *Jurassic Park,* park developers thought they had considered *every* possible *reasonable* circumstance to ensure the containment of the dinosaurs, Exxon officials apparently underestimated the likelihood of a major oil spill from a tanker mishap. Only months before the *Exxon Valdez* crash, an Exxon executive suggested that such an incident was a one-in-a-million likelihood event.

Source: Thierry C. Pauchant and Ian I. Mitroff, *Transforming the Crisis-Prone Organization; Preventing Individual, Organizational, and Environmental Tragedies* (San Francisco: Jossey-Bass, 1992).

---

it is introduced, causing major financial problems, will likely be represented. Concurrently, the concerns of users will also be represented. Let us say that the product platform is a new type of programmable manufacturing equipment. Users' concerns could range from labor unrest as a result of displaced workers to injury or death caused by machinery malfunctions. If the crisis management team had included representation of only the company's internal perspectives, the users' concerns about safety might be underemphasized.

Planning for Unanticipated Crises

Thinking through potential problems is not enough, though. The nature of complexity and chaos makes it impossible to foresee all potential problems that may arise. Consequently, the crisis management team must prepare procedures for handling the unanticipated events.

Crises come in stages:[11]

♦   Early on, there is a buildup period in which early signals indicating an impending crisis usually occur.

♦   The second stage depends on whether the organization has received and understood the signals. If so, the organization can go through a preparation period. If not, the crisis will be triggered by some event and will arrive on the organization's doorstep full-blown.

♦   If the organization has been able to prepare for but not head off a crisis, a trigger will occur that creates an incident or accident.

♦   A period of intense activity and public scrutiny will ensue. The organization must address the situation with "crash management" activities. The organization's

---

[11]Pauchant and Mitroff, op. cit.; Fink, op. cit.

EXHIBIT 14–6   Six Types of Crises

1. *External economic attacks.* These include such things as extortion, boycotts, and hostile takeover attempts.
2. *External information attacks.* These include such things as copyright infringement, product counterfeiting, and malicious rumors.
3. *Breaks.* These include such things as product recalls, product defects, plant defects, and security breakdowns.
4. *Psycho.* These include such things as terrorism, plant or product sabotage, and sexual harassment.
5. *Occupational health diseases.* These include such things as injury or death from occupational hazards, AIDs in the workforce, and other epidemic effects.
6. *Megadamage.* These include such things as major environmental accidents and economic impact of plant closings.

Source: Pauchant and Mitroff, op. cit.

experience during this period will be made more tolerable if good preparation has occurred.

◆   Following the disposition of the crisis, a lower-intensity period occurs in which the organization and its environment and stakeholders proceed to a new normalcy, which may be very different from "doing business as usual."

◆   The organization may take follow-up actions and may go through a period of serious learning. In most cases, follow-up and learning *should* be done or a new crisis may be brewing soon.

In a study of crisis types, Pauchant and Mitroff identified six clusters of crises, shown in Exhibit 14–6. For each type of crisis, a crisis management plan should be developed. The plan should identify who does what and at what stage of the crisis. Roles should be described for public relations and human resources personnel. A primary decision maker and a single spokesperson must be designated as well. The crisis management plans should be reviewed periodically. In companies in which the likelihood of crisis is relatively high, the company may want to periodically run crisis simulations so that key people have practice in performing their roles. Meanwhile, the crisis management team must collect and digest information on an ongoing basis that will provide early warning of trends and factors that could lead to the emergence of crises.

Inoculation against Negative Media Attention
Once a crisis occurs, the analysts working for the media will present their views on causes for the crisis, how well it is being handled, and what the future implications are likely to be. An existing relationship with the media will tend to set the context for such scrutiny. In the absence of a good relationship, media analysts may consider or even impute that unscrupulous motives are at play on the part of the company. However, if the company has established a good relationship with the media, displaying sincerity and good citizenship, this will set the context for the media analysis of the crisis. As we suggested in the discussion of branding, a good public image must be backed by substance; *the company must truly act in the public interest if the public image is to be believed.* This must continue during the crisis as well. The company must be cooperative and open to the media, providing useful, accurate,

and timely information. The media will eventually see through the efforts of a company that tries to project an image of openness and sincerity, when it really does not possess these characteristics. The negative media attention that will ensue will only exacerbate the crisis—and rightly so!

Media Relations during a Crisis

When the inevitable occurs (and it has been planned for), there are standard methods for handling the public exposure that will occur. The organization acting ethically will follow a few basic rules: give the media access, tell the truth, be proactive, and stay calm.

With these principles in mind, media relations should be managed a little differently in each stage of a crisis. In the pre-crisis stage, the organization is still unsure what early signals mean and has a good chance of heading off a crisis if it can be identified and addressed. Accordingly, the organization's crisis spokesperson will not want to be proactive with the media. Rather, if a reporter asks about a potential crisis, then the spokesperson can respond that the organization is paying attention and will take actions to avoid problems.

In the preparation stage, the media may be contacted to demonstrate how the organization is preparing for certain kinds of emergencies—those caused by sudden outside forces, such as natural disasters and so on. This may have some news value and help to establish relationships with the media. Other than this, the company's preparation efforts should remain mostly private and media relations should be reactive.

When a triggering event occurs and a true crisis begins to erupt, the crisis team will need to determine whether a response is actually needed. In some cases, the company may consider not responding to accusations of wrongdoing, figuring that a response would validate the legitimacy of the accusation. However, in most cases, a quick response is better than no response. If accusations are unfounded, a quick display of overwhelming facts should quell the problem. This means that the company's spokesperson should have access to executive management to learn what the company's latest information and decisions are. It also means that the company's information-gathering mechanisms need to activate at the first sign of a problem.

Early on, the crisis team and company executives should begin deciding what messages the company will communicate. The message may change as events proceed and as new information becomes available. The crisis management team should take steps to ensure that all messages emanating from the company are consistent with the current core message coming from the crisis management team. All communications efforts need to be sensitive to the needs of the audience. If the company is running an emergency hotline, the people answering the 800-number calls should be knowledgeable and helpful and have authority to make appropriate decisions for individual callers. If callers are likely to speak different languages, company representatives should be available who speak all the major languages that callers are likely to speak. Mechanisms for doing all this should have been established as part of general crisis planning.

> ### Here Comes the Goodyear Blimp!
>
> In September 2000, at the peak of the tire controversy between Ford Motor Company and Bridgestone/Firestone, the Goodyear Tire and Rubber Company released data on the performance of its tires that had been standard equipment on Ford Explorers in 1995–1997. The data showed virtually no failures of the Goodyear tires. This certainly helped Ford in its argument that the problem was with Firestone tires, not the vehicle, and it likely reinforced the relationship between Goodyear and Ford. An annoyed source within Ford who wished to remain anonymous commented with regard to the conflict with Firestone, "We just dropped the Goodyear blimp on them."
>
> *Source:* Robert L. Simison, Norihiko Shirouzu, Timothy Aeppel, and Todd Zaun, "Logistics of Tire Recall, Investigation Cause Increasing Corporate Clashes," *Wall Street Journal* (28 August 2000).

In many crises, the company may come under fire for its practices or ways of doing business. When appropriate, the company might ask for support (though not through coercion) from customers and partners; see the Goodyear blimp story. This may help sway public opinion and media attention. These partners may be waiting to be asked or may not want to interfere until the company has indicated a need for help.

In some circumstances, it becomes obvious that the company will not be able to "win" even though the company may be right in its position. The company may have to accept blame, apologize, and move on to the next stage. In such cases, the company may decide it is better to "lose" quickly than to get involved in a protracted public battle. It becomes difficult to make this decision, though, when the costs of "losing quickly" are not known and could potentially be catastrophic.

In the aftermath stage, the impact on the company's public image will already have been done. Any repair that needs to be done to the image of the company or the brand will take time and effort. If the relationship with the media has been fostered throughout the intense portion of the crisis, and the company has been sincere in its efforts to address stakeholders' needs and concerns, it will be easier for the company to do the image repairs necessary. As we have stressed all along, though, this means providing value for customers and behaving ethically in the company's relationships with partners and the community in general.

Minor Crises: Preparation for and Handling of Incidents

While the high-profile crises get all the attention, they only occur infrequently. Most companies deal much more with crises that are not going to kill or seriously impair the company (at least any time soon). These are minor crises, incidents, or fast-occurring problems that merely erode confidence among the company's stakeholders and reduce the company's financial performance. Some of these incidents may be quite public, but they usually do not last long in the public eye. The effect on customers and channels may be much longer lasting, or the effects combine with other minor crises to add up to major problems for the company. These minor crises range from handling the media attention when the company announces poor performance in its most recent quarter to dealing with the public attention associated with a major lawsuit or arrest of one of the company's executives for violating trade laws. If the company has several of these pile up, then it has long-term credibility or even viability problems. If these minor foul-ups occur fairly infrequently and they are handled well, then the company will face temporary embarrassment and perhaps some extra costs, but viability is never in question.

The principal objectives in handling day-to-day problems are similar to the objectives in handling major crises. The first is to solve the problems so that value for customers is not compromised and so that stakeholders' interests are protected. The second objective is to protect, repair, or minimize damage to the company's reputation. To address the first objective, anticipation of, early detection and diagnosis of, and quick remedy of problems are the desired way to maintain superior value for customers and stakeholders. For many of these situations, the actions to be taken will be quite similar—though, hopefully, not frequent. As we have stressed throughout this chapter, remedies for problems must be consistent with the company's value system.

To address the second objective, the company must maintain good relations with the media before and during problem episodes and deal with public issues in a *substantive* way. As we have noted throughout this chapter, real public image goes beyond superficial appearances; it depends on providing value and meeting societal needs. Interaction with media must coincide with real attempts to address problems, that is, to address the first objective. Again, all of this must be done in a manner consistent with the company's ethics and values.

Just as with major crises, avoiding problems is preferable to having to deal with them. Early detection, diagnosis, and corrective action are important. Some nasty surprises will always occur, and they must be handled appropriately. In such instances, it is better to have policies and mechanisms in place to deal with the everyday nasty surprises than it is to address them completely in an ad hoc fashion.

Handling Minor Crises in a Young Company
If the company is doing a good job of inoculation—preparing for a major crises—it will generally be in good shape to handle minor crises as well. Crisis plans and mechanisms will be in place. Roles will be defined and people will understand how to act.

There is one set of circumstances in which an ethical company will probably not be in a good position to handle minor crises. This is when the company is new. A young company may not have had the resources available for crisis planning. It is important, then, for the young company to retain a good public relations firm as soon as it reaches a size sufficient to be able to pay the retainer. Whether it is the same agency that handles promotion campaigns or a different one, the job is different from proactive marketing publicity. The crisis-related job for the agency should be to manage ongoing relationships with the media to begin the inoculation process we mentioned in the prior section. This is just as important for minor crises as it is for major ones.

The company should pay particular attention in the selection process to the PR firm's track record in dealing with negative public attention. Also, the company should be certain to try to find an agency with ethical values closely aligned to its own. The company's executives do not want to be in the position of arguing with their PR agency on what to say to the public media and how to say it in the middle of a crisis.

To facilitate clear understanding between the company and its PR agency, as well as between the company and its management and employees, the management of the young company should set out a policy of how it deals with public adversity. This written policy should reflect the company's core values and ethics. It should be done early in the life of the company, again because the company will probably face minor crises before a major one comes along. This policy will then form the basis for the company's attitude in addressing public adversity in a major crisis, as well.

Maintaining Vigilance while Marketing
Entrepreneurially   Monitoring threats and anticipating crises would seem to contradict and undermine the entrepreneurial efforts we espoused in Chapter 9. This is a real concern. The role of crisis planning and crisis management efforts

needs to be couched within an entrepreneurial context and not allowed to over-whelm it. The key to attaining balance between the two kinds of efforts is to first realize where the two coincide and then to coordinate the purposes of the two efforts.

Recall from Chapter 9 that an entrepreneurial orientation involves innovative-ness, proactiveness, moderate risk taking, and opportunity seeking. The principal point of intersection between an entrepreneurial orientation and crisis preparation is in the area of risk taking. Entrepreneurial marketers must realize that the kinds of risks they are willing to take relate to performance risks: can the new product or program generate the desired response? The marketing people charged with antici-pating major and minor crises have performance risks in mind when they look for threats. However, in the crisis management purview, this becomes a monitoring function coupled with planning for handling public relations when performance is subpar. The marketing organization with an entrepreneurial orientation should be willing to accept some risk of poor financial performance. Crisis management peo-ple can raise questions that can halt a marketing strategy or require substantial change when the strategy appears to create other kinds of risks, such as risks of harm to customers or other stakeholders. Entrepreneurial marketing does not mean that new ventures will be pursued when they create moderate nonfinancial risks for stakeholders or for the community at large.

In this chapter, we have presented the societal marketing concept and its relationship to business ethics and crisis management. We hope that you recognize that the societal marketing concept can significantly reduce the need for crisis management. We also hope that the material presented in this chapter demonstrates the dilemma many people face, both as professionals and as individuals in society. Ideal conditions do not exist, yet this is neither an excuse for less than ethical individual behavior nor less than an organizational commitment to ethical standards. Situational ethics (or ethics of convenience) permit a spiraling down of standards that lower the image and esteem of the people who make up the organization. Ethics are an individual choice. We hope that this chapter has given you some things to consider as you make choices in the professional world.

An ethical approach to marketing and to doing business in general also obliges the company to prepare for the crises that it cannot anticipate and avoid. The societal marketing concept requires businesses to prepare for times when they have negative impacts on society, mitigate the problems that arise, communicate with all stakeholders honestly, and to take responsibility for the company's actions and their impacts. The marketer's role in crisis management is to manage the relationship with channels and customers even during these periods of stress.

This is the last chapter in the book but what we hope will be the beginning of your continued interest in business-to-business marketing. The differences between business-to-business marketing and consumer marketing have been discussed. The creation of the total offering based on customer perceptions of need and value has been strongly advocated. Process and methods to influence business buying decisions have been described, based on the establishment of long-term relationships, partners, and value networks. Revisit these concepts after you obtain more experience in business-to-business marketing. We think you will recognize the real value of what you have learned when you apply it "in the real world."

Key Terms

natural law	situational ethics	value image
positive law	societal marketing concept	

Questions for Review and Discussion

1. Discuss consumer attitudes toward business ethics. Why are so many people willing to accept business ethics as an inconsistency in terms?
2. Are ethical marketing practices more important at the business-to-business level or at the consumer level? Is there a difference?

3. Considering the nature of relationships in business-to-business marketing versus consumer marketing, are ethical lapses more likely to occur in consumer markets or in business-to-business markets?

4. Select a recent crisis faced by a prominent member of society—politician, statesman, community leader, and so on; how well was the crisis handled with regard to the principles discussed in this chapter?

5. What ethical factors can contribute to individual discomfort in a position in an organization?

6. Do all crises, big and small, involve ethics? Briefly explain.

7. Can all crises be averted with good crisis planning? Why, or why not?

8. What should an organization look for in a PR agency to handle the company's public crises? When should the PR agency be hired? Why?

9. Think about the emotions experienced by TWA's stakeholders (both internal and external to the organization) during the Flight 800 crisis. If you were the spokesperson for TWA, whose emotions would you be expected to address? How might you, in your role as spokesperson, address these emotions?

10. How can a business-to-business marketing organization be watching for the sources of minor crises without becoming too conservative in its strategies and actions? How can marketers stay entrepreneurial while still proactively managing crises?

Internet Exercises

Based on your exposure to recent business news, choose a company that you believe is in a major crisis (remember, this could be a long-term drawn-out crisis; it does not have to be a short-term acute crisis). Go to the company's Web site, view its recent news releases, and determine how well you think it is handling the crisis. If there are inadequate resources on its Web site, go to the Web site for a trade publication in the company's industry. Review the news stories about the company and its crisis and make your determination.

Again, based on your exposure to recent business news, choose a company that is being accused of antitrust violations or that is in court over antitrust issues. Go to the company's Web site or business press news stories and see what the company's stance is relative to the accusations or charges. Do you think the company was acting ethically? Is it acting ethically now? Would you approach the company's situation any differently if you were one of the company's executives?

1

LastMile Corporation: Choosing a Development Partner

overview . . .

In this hypothetical case, LastMile's CEO is faced with a decision on whom to partner with for development and launch of LastMile's new product. LastMile has two offers on the table and is trying to decide how to proceed.

In this case, you will be asked to determine the best approach, given the company's situation.

LASTMILE'S DILEMMA

Stepping out from a meeting that just ended, Tom Sherman, the president and CEO of LastMile Corporation, is reviewing the main points discussed. This was an internal meeting with LastMile directors and executives, in which alternatives for LastMile's strategy were discussed. LastMile has two proposals on the table for strategic partnerships. One is a proposed technology licensing agreement from Midwest Technologies, Inc., a large defense contractor and advanced technology vendor. The second is an acquisition proposal by ANZ Investment Group, who has offered LastMile a substantial funding offer in exchange for a significant ownership share of LastMile. The meeting reached no conclusions but raised a number of issues pertinent to the decision the board of directors will have to make. Tom, who as CEO is a member of the board, is trying to make up his mind on the position he will take tomorrow when the board next meets in a conference call.

Tom still remembers the early days of LastMile when he and nine others gave an idea a definite shape, which resulted in what the company is today. They have come a long way since those endless hours of constant struggle. The effort paid off, and the company, LastMile Corporation, is a pioneer in technology for wireless broadband access. They are very proud of their achievements.

However, Tom realizes that now, in 2000, the company might do better with closer ties to a larger company with more resources and complementary technology products. The business environment is fast changing, and new technologies are coming up much faster than in the earlier years. The gestation period for new technology has been rapidly cut down. The market environment is promising, with money pouring into new ventures. New companies are springing up, and more and more players are entering the wireless communications industry. Being a privately held, small company, LastMile does not have the financial resources to invest enough in its future technological developments. The company is facing financial problems that need to be addressed immediately.

Industry analysts predict that the broadband wireless communication industry will experience a growth rate in the next couple of years that will be four times the present rate. This is largely attributed to the exponential growth of the Internet and e-business. The broadband wireless communications technology is relatively inexpensive and quick to install, with a high data-transmission rate, more than 2,700 times faster than that of the fastest dial-up modem used in personal computers. The transceiver technologies for broadband access systems are also used for wireless infrastructure connectivity in cellular networks. As the density of cellular users continues to increase, broadband wireless communications promises to be a strong growth area.

The Internet has revolutionized the way businesses communicate and exchange information, becoming a crucial factor in the success of any business. The products that LastMile Corporation manufactures will help businesses overcome problems that are encountered when trying to connect to the local switching office or Internet access point at broadband frequencies.

Midwest Technologies, Inc., provides advanced technology products and services to the automotive, aerospace, and information technology markets worldwide. Having annual sales of about $20 billion, the company employs more than 115,000 employees with primary locations in more than 35 countries. Founded early in the twentieth century, it has been at the forefront of some of

> *Monolithic microwave integrated circuit (MMIC) is a generic technology that is used in the amplification of microwave frequencies. It is a low-power-consumption device, which is used in all high-frequency-transmission devices like cell phones.*

the significant technologies of the last hundred years. Micro Manufacturing, a fully owned subsidiary of Midwest, is the company's telecommunications systems development and manufacturing unit. It develops and produces telecommunications equipment, including MMIC modules, for Midwest's contract customers. The mission of Midwest Technologies is to accomplish a leadership position in the automotive, aerospace, and information technology markets by serving the needs of its customers in innovative ways—by being the best in everything it does. One of the strategies that the company has adopted is to create value for its customers through the execution of alliances, new ventures, and mergers that bring an array of communications technologies to the marketplace.

LastMile Corporation is a privately held company, founded in 1992, with its headquarters in Santa Clara, California. LastMile's core competency is based on its innovative efforts in transceiver systems design and integration. This expertise has been used to develop low-cost microwave transceivers based on revolutionary MMIC design. It has over a dozen patents covering the core technology in its line of products. LastMile sells its subsystems directly to telecom equipment makers like Hughes Electronics, Nokia, and Nortel Networks. They, in turn, refine and sell the broadband wireless systems to the actual communication service providers. LastMile serves as a core building block vendor in the broadband wireless arena and is a crucial player in the build-out of the widely anticipated third-generation cellular networks. With the explosive growth that this industry is anticipating, Tom is thinking about what needs to be done, so that the company will be able to ride the tide. The need is for cash that can be used to support the rapid growth in response to customer demand.

ANZ Investment Group provides investment to companies to realize their financial goals and objectives. Established in 1983, it has its headquarters in Torrance, California. It emphasizes quality service and long-term client relationships. In its portfolio of investment companies are several young companies with technology related to LastMile. Together, the ANZ companies could approach the telecom equipment vendors with a fuller line of products, but these would still have to be made compatible with the products of other technology suppliers.

Since the end of December, Micro Manufacturing has been showing an active interest in LastMile and, together with Midwest's technology licensing group, has recently put forth the proposal to Tom Sherman. Micro Manufacturing is a leader in the manufacture of the kinds of transceiver modules made by LastMile but has only a rudimentary development capability itself in this area. It is looking for an increasing involvement in the broadband telecommunications marketplace. The VP of business development for Micro Manufacturing sees LastMile products as a perfect fit with Micro Manufacturing's products and its future plans.

The proposal is for a licensing agreement between the two companies. Midwest Technologies has also hinted at financial support for LastMile's technical research and development. The agreement would require LastMile to supply its technology to Micro Manufacturing. Micro Manufacturing would be able to provide this technology to its customers in return for specific royalty payments. At the end of the term of the license agreement, both Micro Manufacturing and LastMile could go their own way.

Some of the terms of the license concern Tom. As Micro Manufacturing used LastMile technology as its own with customers, Micro would have an opportunity to co-develop the next-generation offering with direct customer input, using the LastMile technology to establish a beachhead in the market segment. This could provide Micro with a strong presence with customers, as it would be the defending source. The agreement also implies that LastMile would modify the technology to suit the needs of Micro Manufacturing customers, which would result in

LastMile narrowing its market to Midwest Technologies only. Tom is wondering whether this might not be too large a hurdle in LastMile's progress and development of its new technologies. If and when LastMile decided to approach the marketplace directly with next-generation technology, the licensing agreement could have created a formidable competitor.

ANZ Investment Group has proposed a direct investment option. This would provide LastMile with the much-needed cash for further development, which would help the company keep competition at bay. The company faces competition from companies like Infineon Technologies, Raytheon, and Andrew Corporation. New competitors like Telaxis Communications and MTI Technology are also vying for a slice of the broadband wireless equipment market pie. A direct investment would give ANZ Investment Group a genuine interest in the future of LastMile Corporation. LastMile would also have total control over its products and would be free to choose which markets it would like to pursue.

Tom Sherman is leaning toward the offer from Midwest Technologies. It offers better access to the markets he wants to address. It also would be easier to co-develop compatible products with Micro Manufacturing, thereby reducing development costs and time. His principal concern is the loss of flexibility in pursuing technology directions, particularly if the market moves away from Micro Manufacturing's architectures. He is not too fond of the situation once the license period is over, either. The ANZ option, on the other hand, would provide money with few strings attached. Tom's concern, though, is that this option would do little to improve LastMile's marketing punch. Tom is wondering whether Midwest Technologies would be willing to consider an alternative proposal.

Questions

1. What are the other alternatives that LastMile could look at that would create a working relationship between Midwest Technologies and LastMile?
2. What are the advantages and disadvantages of these alternatives?
3. What are the objectives that LastMile would like to accomplish out of such a partnership?
4. What counter proposal(s) would you recommend? Explain.

Author note: Though based on real situations, individual and company names are fictional and several simplifications have been made, in the interest of academic clarity, to product and market information. For this reason, specific situations and factors mentioned herein may not recreate the actual circumstances experienced.

2

Automotive Headlamps

The paradigm shift from standardized glass-sealed beams to today's plastic custom designs

introduction and company background . . .

The General Electric Company Plastics Division (GEP) began as an internal supplier of *thermoset phenolic* molding compounds used in electrical components (such as vacuum tube bases and radio cabinets) and later sold these plastic materials in the general market to other manufacturers of similar devices. The need for plastic materials with improved physical properties led GE research labs to the development of new, *thermoplastic* engineering plastics such as *polycarbonate* (Lexan®) in 1959, *polyphenylene oxide* (PPO) in 1965, and PPO alloys (Noryl®) by 1966. With these materials, GEP, then led by Jack Welch who was eventually to become GE chairman, became a significant factor in the growing plastics materials industry and a star in the GE corporate portfolio.

The company served the automotive industry from a district office in Cleveland, selling its products to captive and custom molders. Early applications of GEP products included distributor caps and rotors and the plastic parts of many electrical devices. As the use of engineering plastics in the automotive market grew, GEP established a field office in the Detroit suburb of Southfield, Michigan. With a local manager, a small staff and three market development specialists assigned to the U.S. vehicle OEMs, the focus shifted to generating business through the development of automotive applications at the car companies. GEP annual automotive sales at the time were less than a million dollars, but destined to grow.

Thermosets and Thermoplastics

Simply defined, *thermoset phenolics* are those materials that undergo a chemical change when heat is applied in the molding process and, when reheated, do not melt. These materials are capable of withstanding high heats without deforming but usually have poorer physical properties than thermoplastics.

Engineering *thermoplastic*s are materials that can be melted again after the initial molding process, analogous to ice melting to water and then being cooled to ice again. Thermoplastics are easier to recycle and generally have better physical properties, making possible more complex part designs.

During the 1970s, the GEP product line, automotive application development efforts, applications, and sales started to take off. The market-development efforts of the GEP team established applications in several areas of the vehicle, including engine and body electrical components, interior and exterior trim, and lighting. With its higher thermal and impact performance offsetting higher cost, Lexan polycarbonate had replaced acrylic in lenses, as well as zinc and ABS (*acrylonitrile-butadiene-styrene*) in housings—in specific, demanding signal lighting applications. Tail lamp applications began in the commercial truck segment, then were translated into pickup trucks and other vehicles with bumper mounted lamps. Smaller signal lamps (park and turn, cornering, etc.) that required heat resistance also became selective applications of Lexan.

By the late 1970s, GE's automotive marketing team, in pursuit of new applications, wondered why headlamps would not also benefit from what their plastics could do. By this time, the quest for better fuel economy was a major factor in design and material selection decisions. Headlamps, made of glass, were very heavy when compared to other vehicle lighting applications made of plastics. Substituting Lexan for the glass was a natural fit. The GE team set out with a new goal: to convert headlamps to their plastics, worldwide.

THE HISTORY OF FORWARD LIGHTING—HEADLAMPS

In the 1930s, cars manufactured in the United States had glass headlamps of various shapes, such as the "teardrop" design on the Lincoln Zephyr and the rounded rectangular shape on the 1939 Plymouth. Because the construction of these lamps was typically comprised of a glass lens, a bright surface metal reflector, and a separate incandescent bulb, sealing, corrosion, and resultant lower performance of the headlamps over time became an issue.

As a result, the "sealed beam" came into use and became the standard of headlamps for many years. The term *sealed beam* was used to describe a hermetically sealed, all-glass lens and reflector unit that contained filaments in an inert gas atmosphere—similar to an incandescent light bulb. From their inception in the 1930s until 1957, they were available in one round size: seven-inch diameter, usually with two filaments to provide both low- and high-beam lighting. Becoming standard on every car, they were readily available—at low cost and easy to replace.

By the 1957 model year, styling trends of "longer, lower, wider" led to the advent of the five-inch, four-lamp system, with two outer high/low beams and two inner high-beam units. This system was first seen on such cars as the 1957 Mercury Turnpike Cruiser and the 1958 Edsel—with most other 1958 models adopting the

Captive and Custom Molders

A manufacturer that makes plastics components itself at its own plastic manufacturing facilities is said to have *captive facilities*—manufacturing facilities that produce plastic parts strictly for that manufacturer. When outsourced, plastic components are produced to the manufacturer's specifications by *custom injection molders*—contract providers that produce plastic parts as designed and specified by the manufacturer.

Acrylic versus Polycarbonate

Acrylic, best known as Plexiglas® from Rohm & Haas Chemicals, and *polycarbonate* (Lexan from GE), are two of the most widely used plastic materials when optical-quality transparency is required. While both exhibit excellent optical properties, acrylic is considered to have poor impact and less high temperature capability when compared to the polycarbonate. Products molded from polycarbonate are often considered to be "virtually unbreakable" and are able to perform in higher-temperature environments.

Why not use polycarbonate all the time? Cost. Polycarbonate is 50 to 100 percent more expensive than acrylic. As a result, polycarbonate gets used only in the more demanding applications.

same configuration. By the mid-seventies, rectangular sealed-beam headlamps also became available in 4″ × 6″ four-unit systems and 5″ × 7″ two-unit systems.

During most of this time, headlamps in Europe evolved differently. The sealed-beam phenomenon never became a major factor. Instead, headlamps continued to evolve in shapes designed to fit the vehicle design, and construction continued to evolve and improve. Typical units were comprised of a glass lens, a metal reflector, and one or more replaceable bulbs, with an industry-standardized connection and mount design. Bulbs evolved from standard incandescent to halogen cycle units, typically exemplified by the H4 two-filament high/low beam design in the main headlamps, with single filament bulbs used for long-range driving, front fog, and other forward lighting applications. European models sold in the U.S. had their designs modified to incorporate the United States sealed-beam units—often to the detriment of the vehicle appearance.

In the early 1980s, the domination by the conventional incandescent sealed-beam in the United States was challenged by the desire for better lighting and the availability of European halogen-bulb replacement units in the aftermarket—the consumer replacement and retrofit market. As a result, halogen bulbs were added to standard-shaped, glass-sealed-beam headlamps, resulting in a premium range of products, producing a whiter, brighter light.

At this juncture (with the exception of headlamps), all exterior lighting on modern vehicles had evolved to all-plastic units, designed to fit the style and shape of the car, using replaceable, standard bulbs and connections. Acrylic plastics were typically used for lenses, with various other plastics and metals competing for the reflector/housing and trim components.

THE SITUATION

When GEP began to approach car companies with the idea of plastic headlamps, it encountered many objections. Some of those objections were that plastic head-lamps would not work because

- Compared to glass-sealed-beam units, they will be unable to maintain a hermetic seal, thus causing premature filament failure.

- They will be insufficiently resistant to weathering and abrasion over the life of the vehicle.

- Engineering *says* they are not legal or not approved by the U.S. Department of Transportation (DOT), the National Highway Traffic Safety Administration (NHTSA), or the Society of Automotive Engineers (SAE).

- They will cost more and, therefore, offer no incentive to change.

- Some car company captive manufacturing divisions (e.g., GM's then Guide Lamp Division) and some independent suppliers that made glass headlamps (e.g., GE) have considerable investment and vested interests in conventional glass-sealed-beam lamp manufacturing. Therefore, they will not be receptive to change.

Faced with these objections, a few members of the GEP marketing team felt that the project was not worth pursuing. The time spent marketing the plastic headlamp could be better spent on less complex applications (read: easier). Still, GEP wanted to move forward and develop business in plastic headlamps, and a few people were prepared to bet their careers on it.

THE MARKETING PLAN

Benefits

GEP marketing people began analyzing and developing ideas about the benefits of plastic headlamps to OEMs. They concluded that the primary benefits of plastics were

◆ Plastics allowed the creation of unique designs with easier optical detail reproduction than glass, allowing vehicle manufacturers to design a more modern, smooth, streamlined front end, with the headlamps integrated into the overall vehicle shape and mounted flush to adjacent surfaces.

◆ The plastic/halogen bulb combination could reduce the risk of fire in a rear-end collision—since the Lexan was virtually unbreakable; and, even if broken, the bulb filament was separately encapsulated. Therefore, the risk of fire was reduced, compared to the glass-sealed-beam unit, with its incandescent filament exposed when broken.

◆ The Lexan lamp would be significantly lighter than a glass-sealed-beam lamp, contributing to need for lower vehicle weight.

These benefits, when combined into a package, could provide a method for manufacturers to make their cars look better and different and have that advantage over their competitors, potentially reduce collision hazards, and contribute to the overall goal to produce lighter vehicles. Indeed, at that time, there was a heightened concern for safety, since a spate of sensational rear-end collisions and resultant fires had occurred coincidentally. In addition to the safety aspects, GEP noted the proposed shaped-to-the-car flush designs as being more aerodynamic, thus contributing to less drag and better fuel economy. (The new concept was quickly tagged as the "aerodynamic headlamp" at Ford, and the term was used during development and application.)

Risks

The development project was not without risks, both for customers and for the GEP team. General Motors Guide Lamp Division (now part of Delphi Automotive) was the primary supplier of glass-sealed-beam headlamps to GM, while the GE

Lamp Division (a significant cash cow) was the largest supplier to the rest of the North American market. The Guide Lamp Division was unreceptive, and its general manager typified this by stating emphatically that it was not going to change from glass to plastic because "sand will always be cheaper than oil." The GEP program manager also recalls being practically thrown out of a meeting by the head of GE's then Miniature Lamp Department at Nela Park, near Cleveland. Fortunately, GEP's management at the Pittsfield, Massachusetts, headquarters backed the efforts in Detroit and provided political support within GE for its personnel.

Finding the Right Customer

The GEP approach to the customer then changed. Realizing that the potential "customers within the customer" were actually those who would value the benefits of styling differentiation, they focused on the design and styling organization, as well as managers in product planning and marketing. In other words, attention centered on the people at Ford who cared about the way a car looked and sold. The vehicle manufacturer customers were not the conventional engineering and purchasing people but really the marketing, styling/design, and product planning departments, with engineering as a necessary, if sometimes reluctant, ally. At the same time, GEP developed a champion within the Ford organization: an open-minded, creative manager in advanced engineering—who not only "got it" but wanted to see it happen himself. After taking its story to all the major car companies, GEP increasingly focused its efforts on Ford as the target—perceiving it to be the most likely taker.

Challenging the Standard

Though the effort was considered to be a waste of time by many Ford personnel, GEP marketing people started to politely but systematically question "legal" assumptions. They made some important discoveries. Everyone had assumed the incumbent designs to be necessary, but this proved not to be the case. The applicable SAE standard was in place primarily as a design guideline to describe the significant dimensions, mounting and aiming points, and so on of sealed-beam headlamps—but not outlining or determining performance. GEP also decided to question the "legal" assumptions at the external agency level. The GEP program manager contacted a senior DOT official in Washington, D.C., and arranged a meeting to discuss a new, safe headlamp idea. At this meeting, the official indicated that the government's only real concern was that headlights provided drivers consistent, safe illumination over the period of their life (or that of the car). In fact, the government did not care about the headlights' material or shape. The GEP representative cited the safety benefits of the plastic concept. The plastic/halogen bulb combination would reduce the risk of fire in a rear-end collision—since the Lexan was virtually unbreakable and, even if broken, the bulb filament was separately encapsulated. Therefore, the risk of fire was reduced compared to the risk with the glass-sealed-beam unit, with its incandescent filament exposed when broken.

Validating the Concept

GEP decided to make some prototype plastic headlamps and test them in simulated use to see if they would work over an acceptable period of time. The GEP team agreed that, if those tests went well, then the next step would be to further prove it out with a production vehicle trial. Until then, no one had questioned the prevailing assumptions.

Prototypes were designed, fabricated, and tested. Results were favorable and reviewed with Ford, as well as with the appropriate agencies. Ford and GE decided to further validate the concept in actual field use. The first polycarbonate headlamp to be used on a production U.S.-built vehicle was a two-piece, injection-molded version of the standard $4'' \times 6''$ rectangular, high-beam-only design—using a halogen capsule bulb as its light source. It used an injection-molded lens with a UV protective coating, bonded to an injection-molded, metallized, and coated reflector/housing. The vehicle application was the inner (high-beam-only) units on the 1980 Lincoln Town Car, of which approximately 60,000 examples were produced and sold that year. Conventional glass-sealed-beam units were used on the outer high/low beam pair of headlamps. The purpose was to gain production use experience and prove the durability of the plastic lamp in actual field use. These lamps were manufactured by GE's Miniature Lamp Division as part of a development project funded by GEP and Ford. This test application was deemed successful, paving the way for further use.

GEP hired an experienced automotive designer from Europe, where aerodynamic headlamps styled to fit the car were the norm. They developed "before and after" illustrations of existing and potential models, graphically showing the appearance advantage of smooth, new, flush plastic designs—compared to the upright, rectangular holes in the otherwise stylish front end of most vehicles. It worked.

At about this time, GE Lamp withdrew support of the development program. To say that both Ford and GEP were disappointed would be an understatement. While Ford was proficient at the manufacture of plastic parts with some of the largest captive molding facilities in the industry, it was convinced that the development required a cooperative lamp manufacturer. Over dinner with a GEP representative, the Ford VP of Car Engineering made the Ford position clear: Ford was going to go ahead with the aerodynamic lamp development. Ford preferred to partner with GE, as GE had both plastics and lighting expertise. However, it would not refrain from finding another lighting manufacturer and another plastics supplier and putting them together into a team (e.g., a value network) to make the project happen. The Ford VP asked the GEP representative to get that message back to GE.

ANALYSIS

This case represents a situation that is often associated with innovation. A few people within a company have a bright idea that would benefit the company if accepted and implemented. However, the current industry situation is characterized by a well-established technology combined with external, third-party government and industry standards developed around the incumbent systems.

Questions

1. What is your assessment of the situation?
2. What are the benefits of plastic headlamps? To whom?
3. How would you overcome the objections of Guide Lamp?
4. What is the rationale behind the GE Lamp decision to withdraw support from the development?
5. Does it make sense to innovate the offerings of a cash cow? Why?
6. How has GE Lamp impacted the GEP relationship at Ford?
7. What approaches would you take with other potential customers?
8. How would you address and overcome the issues regarding agency approval?
9. What are the key factors likely to determine success in this application?

3

Marketing Plastic Resins: GE and BW

overview . . .

Borg Warner Chemicals and General Electric Plastics, prominent suppliers in the engineering plastics markets, were facing increased competition and a changing market environment. Value as viewed by customers was evolving, and sales channels and field marketing organizational structure played a major role in the way each company elected to provide products and services to its customers.

In this case, you will be asked to determine an optimal channel structure for this market.

introduction . . .

Consumer awareness of plastics is usually limited to the final products manufactured from the plastics. Many consumer products either are enclosed in plastic cases or contain component parts manufactured from plastics. Manufacturers whose products include plastic components or cases must either manufacture the plastic parts themselves or outsource production to a contract provider. A manufacturer that makes the components itself at its own plastic manufacturing facilities is said to have *captive facilities*—manufacturing facilities that produce plastic parts strictly for the manufacturer. When outsourced, plastic components are produced to the manufacturer's specifications by *custom injection molders*—contract providers that produce plastic parts as designed and specified by the manufacturer. As contract providers, custom molders are often independent small businesses, engaged in the manufacture of plastic components on contract to the company who will eventually incorporate the components into its own product.

The term *injection* refers to the method of manufacturing plastic parts. Most plastics are supplied in pellet form. The pellets are heated to a molten state and *injected* by a hydraulic ram into a clamshell-like mold, much in the same way cookie presses squeeze dough to make holiday cookies. The mold cools rapidly and is opened, the part is removed, the mold is closed, and another "copy" is molded immediately. Depending on part size and design, this cycle may be repeated several times a minute.

As an example of this process, consider the design and manufacture of the water reservoir for a new home coffee pot. The coffee pot manufacturer, let us say Black & Decker (B&D) in this case, decides what features the reservoir should have. (Should it be transparent so the water level can be seen inside it? Will it look better with a glossy or satin finish? How high will the temperature get while the coffee is brewing? and so on.) The engineering staff then designs the water reservoir to meet these requirements, specifying the type of plastic material needed to meet the design standards. A custom molder is contracted by B&D to mold the plastic reservoir to the requirements specified by the engineering group—including the type of plastic materials to be used in the part. The manufacturer of the coffee pot, B&D, is the customer of the molder. The molder purchases the specified plastic raw material (usually supplied in pellets by a plastics producer) to make the reservoir. The molder is the buyer but not the specifier of the material. From the point of view of the molder or plastics material producer, B&D would be the end user, because B&D would be the final decision maker, or specifier, of what type of plastic material would be used. B&D retains control of the design and material specifications.

PURCHASING HABITS

Plastic materials are generally purchased by either very large companies who have captive molding facilities (e.g., General Motors, Ford, IBM, Rubbermaid) through volume buying agreements or by smaller custom molders, contract providers whose volume is significantly less. To take full advantage of the economies of scale, larger purchasers usually process very high volumes of just a few material types, in bulk quantities shipped in tank trucks (approximately 40,000 pounds) or railcars (approximately 250,000 pounds).

Custom molders manufacture a variety of parts for several different customers, often from several different types of materials, making large-volume purchases of any one material unlikely. Thus, they buy a larger assortment of both *engineering* and *commodity* materials (see the next section for explanations of these two material categories) in smaller quantities. Smaller custom molders purchase the specified plastic materials in pellet form, packaged in 50-pound bags or 1,000-pound boxes. Quantity-pricing policies exist, with higher unit prices charged for the additional handling and packaging required for smaller purchases. Plastic producers usually suggest quantity-scaled list prices from a full truckload, usually forty thousand pounds, also known as truckload (TL) pricing, down to minimum purchases of fifty to one thousand pounds, known as less-than-truckload (LTL) pricing.

THE PRODUCTS

While there are thousands of different plastics in the marketplace, there are two basic categories of plastic materials: *commodity plastics* and *engineering plastics.*

Commodity Plastics

Commodity plastics are used for consumer packaging, fast food and "throw-away" items, toys, and items that generally are not required to perform any mechanical or structural functions or demonstrate any long-term durability. These plastics are generally inexpensive, available from several sources, and most often known by their generic chemical names. A few of the generic names for these plastics are *polystyrene* (PS), *polypropylene* (PP), *polyethylene* (PE), and *polyester* (PET). Typical examples of products made from these materials are detergent and fabric softener bottles (PE); throw-away cups, forks, and so on (PS); and soft drink bottles (PET). The price range for commodity plastics—also known as commodity resins—is typically $0.60 to $1.00 per pound. Commodity plastics, generic in nature, are considered to be in the mature phase of their product life cycle. Little brand loyalty exists; selection is by generic type, with greatest attention paid to price and availability.

Engineering Plastics

Engineering plastics are used for components that are generally required to perform one or several mechanical or structural functions and/or meet durability and safety standards imposed by independent agencies such as Underwriters Laboratories, as well as by the specifying end user/manufacturer. A few chemical names for these types of plastics are *acrylonitrile-butadiene-styrene* (ABS), *polybutylene terephthalate* (PBT), *polycarbonate* (PC), and *nylon.* Many of these products are branded by their manufacturer (such as Lexan® polycarbonate from GE, Cycolac® ABS from Borg Warner, and Zytel® Nylon from DuPont), though comparable materials are usually available from at least one other source. These materials are considered to be nearing the end of the growth stage of their product life cycle, with the exception of nylon, which is a mature product. Typical application examples are computer cases (ABS and PC, with PC used where impact resistance, color stability and appearance, or transparency are critical), automobile bumpers (PC), plastic gears and other mechanical components (nylon and PBT), kitchen appliances (ABS and PC), and fibers (as in nylon carpets and rope). The price range for engineering resins is $1.50 to $3.00 per pound.

MARKET HISTORY

One of the first applications of plastic materials was the result of a quest to find a substitute for ivory in billiard balls. In the late nineteenth century, the game had become so popular that hundreds of elephants were killed each day to obtain ivory for the balls. In 1866, an American named John Wesley Hyatt discovered celluloid. After some trial (and error—the first billiard balls made with the material would disintegrate when hit), celluloid became the first substance molded under heat and pressure to retain its shape after the pressure and heat were removed. So was born the American Cellulose Chemical Corporation (later to become part of Celanese Corporation), a fledgling plastics industry, and greater safety for elephants.[1]

Initially, modern development of commodity plastic materials grew out of the improved refinement of petroleum by-products. Approaches to the marketplace varied by company, product, and life cycle. Producers of commodity plastics, usually large chemical or petroleum companies such as Dow Chemical, Arco, Mobil, Amoco, and so on, preferred to sell in very large quantities (truckload, railcar) on a contract basis to large molders. Many of these suppliers provided very little direct sales coverage, if any, at small custom molders. Because these products were commodities, profit margins and logistical costs often did not allow the luxury of significant sales attention to small accounts. Like many other products in the chemical industry, pricing was often based on the addition of a set margin to manufacturing costs. Price was strongly influenced by competitive supply in the market and the going rate for that particular product. Molders interested in purchasing these products in LTL quantities found that they had to pay a significant price penalty (per pound) for their low-volume purchases. Because of the lack of sales attention to these smaller customers, product information and assistance were often difficult to obtain.

The major oil and chemical companies had historically shown little interest in the engineering plastics, originally considering them small-volume niche products best handled by other companies.[2] Many of the engineering materials required additional manufacturing and processing steps to create "specialized" products. These low-volume refining operations did not suit the capabilities of the oil companies; nor were the volumes attractive to them.

Most suppliers of engineering plastics were not backward integrated in the supply chain for chemicals. Major engineering plastics suppliers were BW, GE, DuPont, Monsanto, Celanese, and Miles Chemical. (Note that a few companies—notably, Dow, DuPont, and Miles—participated in both the engineering and commodity materials market; see Exhibit C3–1.)

With the exception of nylon (which was commercially available after World War II), engineering plastics, whose development and commercialization followed commodity products by several years, did not gain significant market presence until the mid- to late 1960s. By the end of the decade, GE recognized that, while these

---

[1] *History of Plastics,* American Plastics Council, http://www.americanplasticscouncil.org (1 September 2001).

[2] Ibid. U.S. production of plastics in 2000 totaled 100,093 million pounds, of which only 5,732 million pounds (5.7 percent) were injection moldable engineering plastics. In the interest of academic clarity, the American Plastics Council classification of engineering materials has been modified with the addition of nylon and ABS, more closely reflecting market conditions at the time of this case.

EXHIBIT C3–1   Material Suppliers and Their Market Positions

Material Types	DuPont	Miles	Celanese	Monsanto	Arco	Amoco	Mobil	Dow	BW	GE
Commodity										
PS					□	□	□ #2	□ #1		
PP					□	□ #1				
PE					□	□ #2	□	□ #1		
PET	□ #1	□					□			
Engineering										
PBT	□	□	□ #2							□ #1
ABS				□ #2				□	□ #1	
PC		□ #2						□		□ #1
Nylon	□ #1	□	□ #2	□						

Note: An "□" indicates that the supplier has a share in that particular material market. A blank indicates that the supplier does not participate in that material market. A number following the "□" indicates the supplier's relative market position, based on sales volume, in that market such that "#2 indicates that the supplier holds the #2 market position. As an example, the table shows that Amoco is the largest supplier of polypropylene (PP), the second largest supplier of polyethylene (PE), participates in the polystyrene (PS) and PET markets (but does not hold the #1 or #2 position), and does not participate in any engineering materials markets.

advanced materials were capable of successfully performing mechanical and structural functions, making it possible to replace more costly materials and processes (e.g., many cast metals that required a large number of machining steps, sheet steel that required corrosion protection), traditional plastics sales techniques used by commodity producers as well as the consumer perception of "cheap plastics" would hinder the successful communication of these unique benefits. A new approach that more fully informed customers (designers) of how to take advantage of the benefits of these materials was needed. As a result, GE began to provide extensive services related to end-user education; plastic component design, development, and manufacturing; as well as product information intended to maximize the value potential of its products. The pricing of engineering materials became based on a "value-added" strategy, reflecting what the materials could do rather than what they cost to produce.

By the early 1970s, GE had extended the value-added sales approach through the use of field market development (FMD) personnel. FMDs, part of the GE Plastics marketing operation, complemented the GE field sales force by working with plastics specifiers and end users (*not molders*) to encourage the design and development of products that would rely on the properties of GE plastics. FMDs as relationship builders kept specifiers up to date on new product developments and design techniques, generally creating goodwill and an allegiance to GE products. FMDs generally did not call on custom molders and were not responsible for any direct sales, leaving the direct sales responsibilities to the field sales team. A large customer that had its own captive molding facilities would have two GE field representatives calling on it; a field seller worked with purchasing influences, and an FMD worked with design and specifying influences in the buying centers. Smaller

EXHIBIT C3–2   General Electric Plastic Field Organization

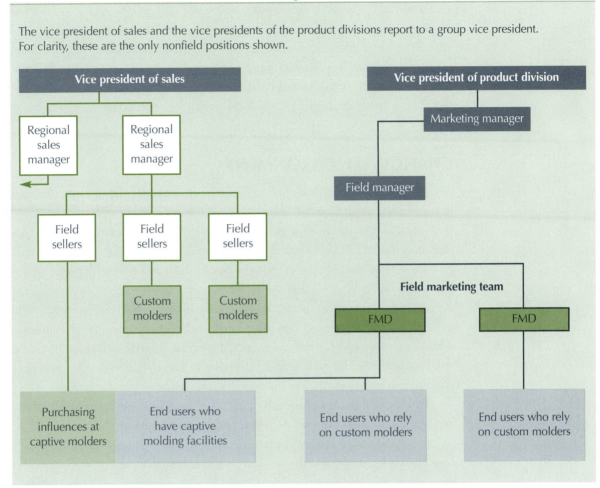

The vice president of sales and the vice presidents of the product divisions report to a group vice president. For clarity, these are the only nonfield positions shown.

end users might develop a relationship with just the FMD, while custom molders usually were the responsibility of the field sales team. An organization chart is shown in Exhibit C3–2. This field organization was initially viewed as a very expensive approach by plastic material suppliers who relied on a sales force for both sales and marketing efforts. The GE value-added pricing approach, however, allowed the FMD system to be margin supportable.

The FMD approach was very successful in the marketplace. GE gained a reputation as an aggressive innovator in the market and soon developed sales leadership in all product types it marketed. Through the FMD effort at the specifying influences, GE-branded materials were often pre-selected when custom molders were contracted to produce plastic parts. This success led other engineering plastics suppliers to begin to imitate the GE field structure. Borg Warner, the leading supplier of ABS, and Miles, the chief rival to GE in PC, were forced to adopt the FMD approach to the market to stay competitive, though account coverage and resource commitment were not as broad as those provided by GE. Other engineering material suppliers such as DuPont and Celanese found it necessary to provide some kind of design assistance to specifiers, but a formal field organization rivaling FMDs was not completely developed.

Engineering materials suppliers not using the FMD system soon found their sales efforts at molders much more difficult. Field sales personnel from GE's competitors found they were locked out of opportunities to pursue the business. Custom molders at times also resented the GE value-added approach because it took out of their hands the choice of where they could buy materials.

CHANGING ENVIRONMENT

The energy crisis of the 1970s had a major impact on the plastics industry. Cutbacks in the availability of crude oil meant that plastic manufacturers were not able to meet demand from molders for materials. Many molders who traditionally purchased their materials in LTL quantities found that available supplies had been purchased by large-volume customers who had previously established relationships with plastics companies. Smaller molders without consistent buying patterns or high-volume demands found themselves unable to obtain raw materials and meet the production demands of their customers. This was a particularly difficult position for molders whose customers (the plastics end user) had specified a particular engineering material, leaving the molder with very little alternative supply flexibility. The customer's specification limited the molder's ability to find a second source for material.

To lessen the impact of this situation, some specifiers developed new strategies. As an example, a specification that once required the use of "Lexan 500" would be modified to require "Lexan 500 or equivalent." This modification was time consuming, as the specifier would have to certify that the equivalent products from competing sources—in this case, other PC suppliers such as Dow or Miles— met the originally established standards required by the application. Where the materials were used in critical applications where failure of the alternate material could lead to injury or other harm, specifiers would be cautious about accepting a second (though theoretically chemically identical) material. This lack of flexibility led many large-volume specifiers (e.g., Ford and GM) to develop internal standards for engineering materials. By using the predetermined standard, engineers specifying a material for their designs would automatically allow the use of generic or other branded materials of like kind and quality, provided they had met the internal standard. While this helped with new designs, it was of little value in alleviating the immediate supply problem.

By the end of the seventies, BW concluded that a new approach was needed to serve small- and mid-sized customers. Market research commissioned by BW showed hundreds of small- and medium-sized molders who had much in common. They used small quantities of three or more kinds of plastics, required short lead times, and had limited cash flows and other special needs. Because most plastics companies' field sales forces concentrated on large-volume customers, these smaller users had not consistently been called on by representatives from plastics producers.

During this same time period, GE and BW (as well as other engineering material suppliers) were facing increased competition. Companies that had previously ignored the engineering plastics market were now attracted by the higher margins available and the expiration of many U.S. company patents. In addition to competition from U.S. firms, foreign companies, like Mitsubishi (Japan) and Lucky (Korea), were beginning to compete in the U.S. market. Without established channels in the United States, many of these new competitors used brokers and independent, regional resellers.

CHANNEL IMPLICATIONS

Recognizing an increased competitive threat and the need to distinguish itself from its new competitors, BW established Plastic Service Centers (PSCs) in 1981. Plastic Service Centers was a nationwide full-service distributor catering to LTL customers whose service needs were not fully addressed by direct representation from major plastics companies. While BW continued to maintain its direct sales force for its large customers, it turned over small account responsibility to the new PSC sales team—some of whom moved from BW to be part of the new organization. BW approached other plastics companies whose product types did not directly compete with its own. Several of these companies agreed to use PSC as their distributor, turning over their LTL customers to the PSC team.

The establishment of PSCs was a significant competitive development in the marketing channel for plastic resins. Critics of using distribution for engineering plastic resins (notably GE) responded by saying that using distribution was an admission by plastics manufacturers that they could not handle the needs of their smaller customers. In the February 1986 edition of a then major trade publication[3] GE and BW presented their viewpoints on the issue of using distribution versus using a direct sales force to meet the needs of plastics resin customers. Joseph Sakach, vice president and general manager of Borg Warner Chemicals, Inc., and Herb Rammrath, vice president, General Electric Plastics' plastics sales division, represented their companies.

The following is from "How Borg-Warner handles less-than-truckload customers" (sic) by Joseph Sakach, in the February 1986 edition of *Plastics Industry News:*

> Solid customer service had helped establish Borg Warner as an industry leader. . . . Borg Warner had the skills and the culture to assemble the kind of service package these LTL customers needed and the kind of distributorship our fellow resin producers needed.
>
> With all this in mind, we mapped out what we wanted the PSCs to be. To processors [custom molders], we're a one-stop shop for . . . [plastic] material in producers' standard packaging [e.g., fifty-pound bags], and at producers' quantity-scaled

---

[3]The trade publication was *Plastics Industry News,* which ceased publication several years ago. In this case, some individuals' names have been changed and market and product conditions have been simplified in the interest of academic clarity.

prices; we ship quickly, typically [from local inventory] within 12 hours; we give special assistance in emergencies; we eliminate the need for processors to keep large inventories; and we provide technical advice. The icing on the cake is that we provide the personal touch typical of resin-producer/large-customer relationships.

Meanwhile, resin producers themselves continue to concentrate on volume accounts that justify the high cost of sales and service calls. It was becoming a problem for us [BW], and we were confident other resin producers felt the same way. For those suppliers, PSCs provide an independent, nationwide distribution network for engineering . . . and commodity materials with a skilled sales staff.

Many molders in the target segment corroborated this view of the market. An Oklahoma City PSC customer stated that service from the PSC was much better than that received from large plastics companies such as Monsanto and Dow, as they were only interested in the larger accounts. The PSC seemed to fill a void in customer sales and service.

The advantages of the system were not lost on some plastic resin producers who, because of the high costs involved, did not have extensive sales coverage at smaller accounts or saw a way to more effectively organize their field sales. Management at one firm noted that the market was changing and that, without some accommodation, small volume purchasers would be increasingly ignored as competitive pressures increased. Senior management at DuPont, a producer of both commodity and engineering plastics, saw the PSCs as an opportunity to free up some field resources that could now be devoted to end-user assistance and application development efforts, better enabling them to compete with organizations that had large FMD organizations, such as GE.

An initial concern of the resin producers that would eventually sign up with the PSC to distribute their products was that the PSCs might give favorable treatment in sales and application development to the BW materials rather than the other product lines. PSCs took steps to alleviate this concern.

Sakach continues:

We [PSCs] offer the same culture and experience that made Borg Warner successful, yet [PSCs also offer the] independence to ensure the PSCs' credibility among other [resin] suppliers. The PSCs have been steadfast in a commitment to viewing Borg Warner as only one of their many quality suppliers [avoiding any possible claims of favoritism by other resin producers distributing their products through PSCs].

We at Borg Warner think of ourselves as good business persons with foresight, imagination, and an ability to serve a dynamic marketplace. That's what the PSCs are all about. Last fall we opened our 11th PSC location built on those principles. The PSCs offer a full range of products from producers including Borg Warner Chemicals, Gulf, Arco, DuPont, . . . and Miles[4]. . . The PSCs have more than 4,000 customers, and our projections of market potential were on the mark.

For Borg Warner, the PSCs are an important part of our service mix. For LTL customers, Borg Warner, and the PSCs' other suppliers, the PSC concept is an innova-

---

[4]In this case, the number of participating companies has been reduced. Also, names as used may not reflect current names as a result of acquisition, merger, or other corporate exchanges.

tive, effective, and cost-efficient way to address the former's needs in the context of a sound and profitable overall business strategy.

The suitability of using industrial distributors for engineering resins was not a universally agreed-upon idea. GE, which had grown to an industry leader through its market development efforts, did not necessarily see the fit. The following is from "Why GE Plastics relies on a direct sales force" (sic) by Herb Rammrath, in the February 1986 edition of *Plastics Industry News:*

> General Electric Plastics has taken a hard look at distributors and recognizes the needs they are satisfying in today's marketplace. The bottom line is that we have opted to continue selling our materials through [our own] direct sales [team].
>
> The most important reason for our decision to sell directly is our desire to help molders grow. We are investing a significant portion of our resources in the development of new applications, many of which involve a conversion from metal into plastics. As a resin supplier, we need to work closely with the companies who will handle that conversion. This is important to the industry as a whole, as there is a need to develop the molding capacity necessary to meet the demands all of us are generating for plastics. At GE, we believe that much future capacity will come from what are now small molders. We'd like to help them grow, and we can do a much better job of that by serving them directly.
>
> The move toward just-in-time delivery systems, plus the cost of carrying inventories, is forcing molders and resin suppliers to manage inventory differently and better. Distributors help meet that need by reducing inventory . . . of . . . molders. . . . They [distributors] are, in fact, inventory-management companies and have little to do with application development or technical service. At GE, we believe there are several advantages in using direct sales:
>
> ◆ While distributors may be able to handle commodity materials effectively, they are generally not equipped to handle engineering plastics. Engineering resins are not commodities and require sales support both before and after the sale.
>
> ◆ Engineering plastics also require much more technical support than the typical distributor can provide.
>
> ◆ We have found that our customers would rather deal directly with the prime supplier than with a middleman. The reasons are obvious, but crucial—they get better overall service, better response to their needs, and faster resolution of their questions and concerns. In addition, they know that all of the resources of a company like General Electric stand behind their resin purchases.
>
> I feel that using a distributor to handle our products is an admission that we are not able to serve customers ourselves. That's not an admission that I would like to make on behalf of GE Plastics. So, having decided not to use distributors, yet recognizing that they do serve some needs, we know we must manage our business to satisfy all of the needs our customers have. Among other things, we have done the following:
>
> ◆ We have put into place additional sales resources [more field sellers] so we can maintain our already high level of direct communication with customers and increase our contact with the smaller molders. In short, we've increased our capability to manage higher levels of direct contact with more molders by investing in an expansion of human resources.

◆ We have centralized our customer service efforts [across all of our plastic product lines] to respond more quickly and effectively to customer needs. This operation . . . enables us to provide improved order handling and better inventory management, develop just-in-time inventory management, and establish electronic order entry which we expect to be a major factor in customer service. We have taken the steps necessary to meet the whole order-entry/inventory-control challenge.

◆ We have established our first specialty compounding facility at our Indiana manufacturing site. This facility produces small lot quantities for both developmental and commercial use, giving us greater flexibility to meet special customer needs ["small order sizes"].

These systems we are putting into place will help provide many of the services that customers need in addition to a direct link to their material source—direct contact, instantaneous communication, and feedback. In taking this approach, we know we are bucking an industry trend. We stand virtually alone in this commitment to direct customer service. In a sense, we are "out of step" with almost everyone else, but perhaps that's what leadership is all about. We take our leadership role in this industry seriously and would relinquish that title if our service to customers were no longer second to none. We can only guarantee quality service when we provide it directly. . . .

In summary, we at GE Plastics are designing our business in such a way that we can service our customers—large and small, short term and long term—with the complete range of products and services they demand. We simply are not willing to compromise that objective. We call ourselves the "Strategic Supplier." We want to be a company our customers can call upon, can rely upon—directly—for all their needs.

ANALYSIS

This case presents two large, experienced and well-reputed firms who have selected two very different approaches to market similar products. BW formed Plastic Service Centers (PSCs) to handle smaller LTL customers, not only for its own products but also for other resin manufacturers, while maintaining its established direct sales force for larger customers. GE, on the other hand, relied entirely on its own direct sales force.

Questions

General questions. Given all the facts at your command, what is your recommended channel structure for plastic resins? What are the alternatives?

In the development of your case analysis, you should consider the following:

1. From the information provided, describe the market environment *as viewed* by GE and BW. Are both views the same (consistent with each other), or are they different? If they are the same views of the environment, why are the approaches to the market dramatically different? If they are different, which view do you feel is more useful?

2. Consider customer needs as viewed by GE and BW. Do they see needs as being the same? Are they segmenting the market the same? Have they targeted the same segments? Are they interested in the same market?

3. Does selection of target markets impact channel design?

4. From what you can discern in this case, describe and compare the goals of BW and GE.

   a. How do their goals impact their channel structure?

   b. Do their goals impact how they view the market? Are their views realistic?

   c. It may be of assistance to consider how their goals and market view compare to others in the market, such as DuPont. Are certain channel structures more suited to certain goals?

5. Consider the service mix BW and GE intend to provide. Relate these services to promotion strategy and marketing functions. Is the mix of services consistent with their and/or your view of customer needs?

6. What role does the FMD specialist play in the marketing organization of GE? What potential conflicts do you see in the dual field structure of GE (having both field market development personnel and field salespeople in sales territories)? Consider all viewpoints—the custom molder, the plastics end user, and the individuals serving as either FMDs or salespeople.

Author note: As described in the case, extensive use has been made of articles appearing in the February 1986 issue of *Plastics Industry News,* as well as the author's personal experience and discussions with professionals in this market. When quoting from the article, bracketed comments have been added for clarity while ". . ." indicates the deletion of parts of the article not considered germane to this academic exercise. Though based on real situations, some names have been changed and several simplifications have been made, in the interest of academic clarity, to product and market information. For this reason, specific situations and factors mentioned herein may not recreate the actual circumstances experienced.

More Case Studies on Book's Web Site!

For additional case studies, visit our Web site at **http://vitale.swcollege.com**

Glossary

accessibility in market segmentation, a measure of the marketer's ability to communicate with the market segment in a manner that makes serving the segment possible.

accessory equipment products that accompany or work with a core product or system, enhancing the offering.

actionability a measure of the capabilities of the offering organization to create a competitive advantage with respect to the specific needs of the segment.

administered channel a type of vertical marketing system where cooperation is based on agreement on goals rather than ownership.

advertising as part of the **promotional mix,** nonpersonal mass communication for which a company is paid to develop and place in specific communications media.

affiliate anyone who has a special link on its Web site that refers a viewer to a product or service supplier's site.

alpha test a test done with a product or prototype internally within the company developing it; **alpha tests** determine the viability of the product technology.

analytic approach (to segmentation) employs research and data interpretation to derive a segmentation framework.

ancillary channel members see channel facilitators.

associations customers' beliefs concerning a brand.

assumptions a strategist's mental models or beliefs about how a market operates.

attractiveness (of segments) the likelihood that addressing a segment will significantly contribute to the firm's objectives.

auction hubs on-line **portals** or **hubs** that match buyers and sellers in an on-line analogy of real-world auctions.

avoidable costs those costs that would not be incurred—that is, costs that would be avoided—if the decision were not made.

awareness recognition or recall of a brand.

balanced scorecard a tool for strategy content that focuses on the goals of the organization and quantifies these into specific performance targets.

barter hubs an on-line portal or hub in which "prices" are nonmonetary, i.e., the participants arrange to trade goods and services.

bases for segmentation those factors used for determining how business-to-business markets will be divided into segments.

bases of power bases of resources and skills from which power derives: reward, coercion, legitimacy, expertise, identification, and information power.

beta test a second test of a new product or technology, done at customer sites.

booked sale in most instances, when a sale is culminated i.e., when the customer has paid the invoice.

bottom-up forecast a forecast of sales based on an analysis of how much product can be sold to each customer in a particular region, territory, or market (compare to **top-down forecast).**

boundary personnel individuals in an organization who operate, as a significant part of their responsibilities, spanning the boundaries of their own organizations and those of customers; the diplomats of the organization.

brand strength the ability of a brand to have a strategic impact, generally made up of brand recognition or awareness, quality of the products or services, the customers' positive beliefs—**associations**—linked to the brand, and customers' loyalty to the brand.

branding establishing a strong, positive reputation; building strength and image around a name or symbol that represents a company, its products, and its services.

breakthrough innovation an innovation so radical that it creates an essentially different kind of product or offering with a new combination of types of value produced.

bullwhip effect wide swings in demand experienced by upstream suppliers resulting from the leveraged impact of changes in demand.

bundling when several products or services are sold together as a package, or "bundle," for one price.

business markets all organizations that purchase goods and services to use in the creation of their own goods and services.

business model a configuration of the elements of a business, how they work together, and how they produce profits.

business portfolio a collection of strategic business units that contribute toward the goals and objectives of the company.

business-to-business marketing the process of matching and combining the capabilities of the supplier with the desired outcomes of the customer to create value for the "customer's customer" and, hence, for both organizations.

buying center a collection of individuals and organizations with a stake in the buying decision, individuals who contribute to the final purchase decision.

C

call pattern a sequence of sales calls, either planned or evolved, that matches the seller's collection of offerings to the needs and buying habits of customers.

capabilities the resources, both financial and organizational, that can be brought to bear in pursuit of strategies.

capital goods those goods used by the customer to produce its own products; items that require expenditures as investments rather than expenses or variable costs.

catalog hubs on-line transaction facilitators that serve as agglomerators, in which the products from several vendors' catalogs are combined in a searchable database.

channel facilitators those service providers to the channel that are not necessarily part of channel design but who make possible the efficient operation of the channel; channel facilitators are financial institutions, transportation and logistics companies, third-party service providers, and so on.

channel pattern the particular design or arrangement of various intermediaries that perform channel functions.

chasm (pronounced kaz' em) in the technology adoption life cycle (TALC), a drop-off in the adoption growth curve for a new technology that occurs between stages of the TALC.

collaborators companies, both customers and/or suppliers that work together to produce an offering.

common law a method of interpreting law in which judges interpret any law based upon all case decisions already made about the same issue; this accumulation of decisions, called "precedence," was developed in England.

conclusive research research that tests hypotheses.

consent decree a written, negotiated agreement between an agency and a company.

consumer demand the quantity of goods or services desired to be bought by households or individuals, given market conditions (usually expressed as a function of market price).

contractual systems a type of vertical marketing system that aims at control through binding agreements with otherwise independent intermediaries.

contribution margin for a product, the revenue less the avoidable costs that are directly attributable to the product in question.

controlled risk taking a combination of knowing what the risks really are, taking moderate risks in which the worst case is survivable, and finding ways to manage the risks to increase the chances of success and reduce the consequences of failure.

copyrights the exclusive legal right to reproduce, publish, and sell original works of, among others, authors, musicians, and photographers; copyrights protect the expression of ideas, not the underlying ideas themselves.

core business the existing, ongoing sales volume at the particular customer in question.

core churn replacing the old **core business** with new business.

core competencies a company's skills, capabilities, and knowledge assets that are necessary to compete in its markets; they may be competencies that the company currently has or ones that it will need to obtain.

corporate vertical marketing system an integrated operation in which one company owns or controls all levels of the channel; formed by companies that desire greater control or are unable to achieve distribution goals through independent intermediaries (this provides centralized control but limits flexibility).

cost-based pricing the determination of price by figuring costs of offering a product or service and then adding on a standard percentage profit.

crisis management the process of anticipating negative trends or events, preparing actions to avoid as many events as possible, and managing those as they occur.

cross license permission used when two businesses each have patents or other intellectual property that is of value to the other; see also **license**.

culture all the symbols and themes that reflect a society's norms and values.

D

decline stage referring to the stage of the product life cycle during which sales levels decline as demand shifts to new technologies or offerings.

demand curve shows what quantity of products or services will be sold in a market at different price levels.

demographics the vital statistics that describe a population.

derived demand the demand experienced by the chain of suppliers and producers that results from ultimate consumer demand.

design decision the decision or the configuration of an offering.

development stage the period during which the organization spends research and development, prototyping, field testing, and trial use resources (dollars, personnel, opportunity costs, emotional investment, etc.) to prepare the offering to correctly address the customer need.

differentially invisible refers to a channel design that seamlessly matches the operation of customers; that is, the merging of two systems is so smooth that the customer does not recognize any differences in operation or style.

differentiation something that a company does better than its competitors on one or more key value dimensions; it must be something that provides superior value to customers.

direct channel that channel that is formed when the supplier markets and sells directly to the buying organization; no additional primary intermediaries are involved.

direct channel participants in the marketing channel, those intermediaries, such as wholesalers, distributors, retailers, agents, and brokers, who are part of the proactive marketing design of the channel.

direct response requests forms of direct customer feedback, such as reader surveys, questionnaires, and warranty registrations.

direct sales force personal field sellers directly employed by the manufacturer of the offering.

discontinuous demand the condition in which quantity demanded in the market makes large changes up or down in response to changes in market conditions; the transition from one market state to another occurs in large increments rather than small incremental changes in demand.

discontinuous replacement technologies changes in the offering such that the product category or market segments are redefined; these may be either through breakthrough innovations or disruptive innovations.

discounts and allowances reductions in price for some special reason, such as pre- and post-season discounts and promotional allowances; generally, discounts are given to customers while allowances are provided to channel members.

discovery approach (to segmentation) when a marketer "discovers" a market segment by attempting to translate a successful new offering from its initial customer to additional customers.

discovery-based planning a planning approach based on the premise that uncertain markets are unknowable at first and that resources have to be allocated to trial, error, learning, and reconfiguration.

discrepancy of assortment that situation that is reduced by channel intermediaries who create assortments based on customer needs rather than on manufacturer product lines, saving the end user the cost and time of dealing with multiple vendors.

disruptive innovation introducing offerings based on technology that is substantially different from the dominant technologies in use in a market.[1]

distribution centers used by channel designs that focus on rapid movement of goods through the facility, creating assortment in the process.

distributor the selling structure that represents manufacturers' goods by taking ownership and providing local inventory to businesses in the region.

dual distribution a channel pattern that uses more than one channel design, each intended to reach a different target market.

dyadic interactions one-on-one meetings or sessions between stakeholders in the buying center and the seller or other individuals in the selling organization's value chain.

E

e-business a business with the capability to perform some business activities electronically.

economic utility refers to customer preferences in locational convenience, required purchase quantities/sizes, temporal convenience, and acquisition convenience.

economies of scale reduction of per-unit costs as size and productivity of an operation increases; usually results from capital investment in facilities and equipment.

elasticity the tendency of demand to react to changes in price; generally higher prices yield lower demand, and vice versa.

electronic data interchange (EDI) a technology for exchanging information concerning ordering of goods; the information exchanged consists of order and fulfillment information as well as payments through electronic funds transfer; EDI is facilitated through *value-added networks,* which are private, secure networks, inaccessible to nonmembers of the network.

---

[1]See Clayton M. Christensen, *The Innovator's Dilemma,* (Boston: Harvard Business School Press, 1997).

emergent strategy a combination of intended strategy and ad hoc, unintended strategy.

end user (E/U) a customer that purchases goods and services for consumption, either as supplies, capital goods, or materials for incorporation into its products such that the identity of the purchased product is lost; also called **user**.

entrepreneurial marketing the undertaking of a marketing strategy that actively pursues a new opportunity and has relatively high levels of **innovation**, **proactivity**, and **controlled risk taking**.

equality/proportionately equal terms the requirement that a seller must provide to buyers in horizontal competition with each other substantially equal offers; the offers may differ in specific attributes but must be relatively equal in value; the offers may be proportioned by the volume of business received from each buyer.

ethics rules for distinguishing between right and wrong behavior.

evaluated price the total cost of owning and using a product; this may include transportation, inventory carrying costs, financing costs, potential obsolescence, installation, flexibility to upgrade, cost of failure, and obsolescence of existing products or equipment, plus the price paid to the vendor.

evidence seeking interpreting the data optimistically in a way that supports the conclusions the marketer wants to reach.

evolutionary product introductions those new offerings that continue or sustain a market or product category; these changes may include small-step improvements to the original design that will not greatly influence the **product life cycle**.

exchange hubs, on-line **portals**, or **hubs** that act as clearing centers for bringing buyers and sellers together; buyers and sellers indicate the products (or services) they want to trade and the prices they seek.

exclusive dealing when a seller sells to only one buyer in a region such that competition is lessened.

exploratory research the first phase of market research, in which the researcher obtains a sense of the issues and upon which hypotheses can be based.

F

field market development (FMD) personnel in those situations in which a supplier's offering requires customer education to take advantage of the value offering, the team of marketing personnel whose compensation and position structure enable the team to spend the time with customers in the education process.

fit referring to the relationship between the business strategy and the business environment, when the organization pursues purposes and takes actions that are consistent with the needs, perceptions, and behaviors of the other actors within the environment.

fixed cost of sales administrative overhead and field selling expenses.

form one part of economic utility, the usable quantity or mode of the product most preferred by the customer.

forward-looking incremental costs the costs that will be incurred for the next unit or units of product or service that will be sold once the decision is implemented.

four Ps in marketing—product, price, place, and promotion; the **four Ps** apply whether operating in a consumer or a business market.

free rider a retailer who, either through mail order, e-commerce, or other means, provides a reduced-service package to customers, enabling a lower sales price; this service package often takes the form of purchase assistance, product information, and customer education.

fulfillment firms hired organizations that specialize in timely response to promotional campaigns and customer inquiries.

functional spin-off the channel design technique that assumes that ancillary services are provided most efficiently by experts in each service.

G

goals usually the first quantification of a business mission statement, a general statement of desirable outcomes, directly supportive of and aligned with the mission.

go/no-go decision the decision made before launch of a new strategy, product, or program.

growth stage the stage of the product life cycle during which sales increase rapidly as new customers accept the product.

growth-share matrix a resource allocation tool developed by the Boston Consulting Group that uses categorizations of strategic business units as stars, cash cows, dogs, and question marks.

H

horizontal competitors intermediaries at the same level in a channel, usually existing in multidistribution.

horizontal sprawl also called **keiretsu**, referring to a system consisting of a very flat channel pattern, with few, if any, vertical layers.

house accounts customer accounts served directly by a manufacturer rather than the distributor that serves other accounts in that territory.

hubs online intermediaries that bring buyers and sellers together to facilitate transactions; also called "portals."

hypercompetition a heightened sense of competition occasioned by many competitors changing strategies quickly; includes new companies that emerge quickly or create new markets and industries.

I

incentives for participation rewards given to respondents in a survey for their cooperation/participation.

incremental innovation taking the existing product and offering and making small-step improvements to the original design; incremental improvements can add up to produce a great deal of change in an offering over time.

inelastic demand a characteristic of demand in which a price change produces a change in demand that is less in percentage than the percentage price change.

initial public offerings (IPOs) first offerings of a company's stock on a public exchange.

innovation the creation of something new and commercially useful or the improvement of something to make it more useful.

integrative bargaining an approach to negotiation in which multiple dimensions are considered simultaneously.

intensity of distribution ratio of distributors to prospective customers within a territory that distribute products of the same manufacturer.

intercorporate stockholding when one company controls the stock of another company and exercises control such that trade is restrained.

interlocking directorates firms that are in competition with each other but that have common members on their boards of directors.

internal brand branding carried out solely within a company for internal customers only.

intranet portals a site that operates on a company's internal Web network; it provides the employees with a personalized Web site from which they can access internal or external Web-based resources, such as news, employee benefits, and programs.

introduction stage the stage of the product life cycle during which the product is initially offered; (profits are negative or, at best, break through to the positive side near the end of the stage; the product is somewhat basic, as competition has yet to force a need for differentiation; price and positioning are strongly related; and promotion is used to build awareness).

J

jargon any specialized language of a group that is used to improve the efficiency of communication among members of the group.

K

keiretsu also called **horizontal sprawl**, referring to a system consisting of a very flat channel pattern, with few, if any, vertical layers.

L

lead users not necessarily the market share leaders, the users who have vision, who can anticipate what kinds of needs will arise among potential users in the future.

learning curve relationship between volume and unit costs, when, as more product units (or service units) are produced and sold, unit costs can be reduced through the learning that has occurred.

leave–behind materials items that sellers can give to customers following an in-person sales call; the seller explains the literature and the value points to the customer; not necessarily stand-alone items; compare to **seller stand-in materials**.

leverage when a party in a negotiation has the power to get the other side to accede to its position.

license permission to use an asset as one's own without any right of ownership, granted by the owner of the asset.

logical incrementalism the creation of the direction or strategy of the organization through a series of decisions that produce small changes; these small changes can add up to a very large change overall.

logistics the management of the movement, sorting, and storage of goods in the marketing channel.

M

macroeconomy the sum total of all economic activity in a region or jurisdiction and certain economic characteristics of note.

manufacturers' representative an independent businessperson who acts as a supplier's agent or representative in a particular market segment and who does not take title to a product as a reseller would.

market attractiveness–business strength matrix a business portfolio matrix model that helps the strategist determine whether to build, maintain, or harvest strategic business units based on market conditions and business strengths.

market development gap the gap in the product life cycle between the introduction stage and the growth stage, analogous to the **chasm** in the TALC.

market intelligence information collection and interpretation about markets, customers, prospective customers, the customers' markets and customers, and existing and potential competitors.

market ownership proactively leading a market by establishing standards and producing customer value that direct competitors will emulate and other companies will seek to be competitive with.

marketing channel the place element of the marketing mix, the means to manage the presale contact, transaction, and fulfillment activities between the manufacturer and the final buyer.

marketing concept the marketing philosophy that states that, to be successful, the firm should be contextually market sensitive, understand customer needs, meet those needs in a coordinated way that provides value to the customer, and do so in a way that meets organizational goals; a firm that is (or claims to be) a market-driven/customer-driven firm is applying the marketing concept, recognizing that every employee of the firm contributes to the marketing effort.

material requirements planning (MRP) a system for managing the logistics of inputs to production on an ongoing basis to optimize the purchase and inventory of materials.

maturity stage the stage of the product life cycle during which sales have peaked and competition may begin to fight over market share (promotion is used to reinforce buying decisions and often focuses on supplier reputation and value; new customers do not replace the volumes lost as old customers move to newer offerings; and price is a major part of the marketing mix).

maximum price the price at which benefits are just noticeably more than the evaluated price; the point at which there is a noticeable value for the offering.

measurability the extent to which a segment's size, value needs, and purchasing characteristics can be measured.

media buy an advertiser's purchase of the airing or placement of an advertisement, including the selection of where and when the advertisement will be distributed.

minimum price a price that covers the supplier's relevant costs.

mission the contextual definition of who an organization is and what it expects to accomplish; usually a qualitative description, it is further defined by **goals** and **objectives**.

modified rebuy a buying situation in which the buying center determines that the problem or solution is somewhat similar to past problems or solutions.

monopoly a market with one dominant supplier.

monopsony a market with one dominant buyer.

motivator/problem solver one of the four seller roles in business-to-business marketing.

multidistribution the deployment of multiple channels of the same design in a given territory, primarily a decision about the intensity of distribution.

N

natural law the theory of ethics that holds that individual moral standards are derived from a higher, universal source.

negotiated price reductions concessions in price that result from negotiated reevaluation of value as perceived by both the supplier and the customer.

new task a need that has not previously been faced by the organization; a buying situation in which the buying center defines the problem and the general nature of the solution as an unfamiliar task.

niche a segment that is relatively small with fairly well defined boundaries; often able to be served mostly or entirely by a single supplier.

noise factors that create distortion or inaccuracies in messages or that distract the receiver from the message.

nonpersonal communication the elements of the **promotion mix** other than personal sales, such as advertising, sales promotion, and public relations.

North American Industry Classification System (NAICS) a scheme of industry classifications [compare to Standard Industrial Classification (SIC)] that reflects the distribution of industries in modern-day Canada, Mexico, and the United States.

O

objectives specific, measurable expressions of the stated goals, with specific targets and time periods.

oligopoly a market situation in which each of a few producers affects but does not control the market.

ongoing costs the cash flow expenditures required to keep the company operating and offering products and services; compare to **ongoing revenues**.

ongoing revenues the cash flow income associated with ongoing operations.

open bid a bid that is seen by competing suppliers.

opportunity costs cost of not pursuing a business opportunity because resources have been committed to some other project, such as new product development; several criteria are used to make these judgments, such as internal rate of return, net present value, and market scenarios.

opportunity seeking proactive search for opportunities and constant evaluation of how attractive prospective opportunities are.

opt-in e-mail refers to e-mail messages that are sent by a marketer with the permission of the receiver.

order taker in selling, the person whose primary role is taking orders and ensuring timely delivery of the correct products.

original equipment manufacturer (OEM) a type of customer; a manufacturer who purchases goods to incorpate them into goods it produces and sells to its own customers.

outsourcing the purchasing of part of the company's continuing operations, such as recruiting or manufacturing, rather than investing in the infrastructure to accomplish the task internally.

P

palletizing the arranging and securing of products on pallets—platforms that can be easily stacked and moved by forklifts—so that the products can be handled, shipped, and deployed for use quickly and easily.

partnership in marketing, a business combination in which the businesses agree and act upon a vision that capitalizes on the strengths of the combination.

patents protection or ownership rights granted by government to inventors for their original products, processes, or composition of matter.

penetration pricing charging relatively low prices to entice as many buyers into the early market as possible.

persuader/sustainer one of the four seller roles in business-to-business marketing.

physical distribution concept the balance of the three elements of inventory management, transportation, and warehousing to minimize costs at a given level of customer service.

place one part of economic utility, also known as *locational convenience*.

portal a Web site that serves as a launch site for other sites or programs.

positioning the creation of perceived value for targeted customers compared to that offered by competitors; positioning is in the minds of customers, but can be influenced by the actions of marketers.

positioning statement the succinct statement of the positioning the company hopes to achieve in the minds of its target customers.

positive law the theory of ethics that holds that individual standards are man-made, created, or, simply, determined by what is legal.

possession one part of economic utility, the method by which the customer obtains ownership or the right to use of the product or service.

predatory pricing when a firm with a dominant position in a market, threatened by a new or smaller firm, changes its pricing structure, potentially incurring a temporary loss, such that the new firm cannot operate profitably.

premium merchandise something of limited but noticeable value given away by sellers at trade shows or on customer calls; some reciprocal action is expected or hoped for.

price discrimination when a supplier sells the same product to the "same class" of buyers at different prices such that the price differentials lessen competition.

price elasticity in demand, refers to the percentage change in quantity demanded relative to the percentage change in price.

price maintenance a manufacturer's attempt to dictate the resale price of an item; price maintenance is usually illegal.

price skimming charging relatively high prices that take advantage of early customers' strong need for the new product.

primary market research the collection of data directly from respondents in the population in question. The marketer determines what data needs to be collected and sets out to obtain it.

proactivity doing something before others do it; a key element in **market ownership** and entrepreneurial marketing.

product configurator an interactive software program often accessed via a Web page that lets the prospective customer choose from among product attribute alternatives to configure a product that the customer believes will best meet his needs; the configurator then provides supporting information, such as system requirements, and quotes a price.

product life cycle (PLC) the series of events or stages—referred to as "life stages"—that a product or category of products typically goes through.

product line a group of similar products with a range of product attributes that address similar market segments.

product line maintenance attempting to persuade a distributor to carry a full line of products or prevent the distributor from carrying a competing line of products.

promotion mix a configuration of the elements of communication in marketing—personal selling, advertising, sales promotion, and public relations—employed in a given marketing plan.

proprietary disclosure agreements the assurance of nondisclosure from suppliers that allows customers to exchange proprietary data during the development process.

proprietary information data that, while not protected by patents, is not available to the general public and has significant value to the owner.

public relations as part of the **promotion mix**, the activities that communicate with public stakeholders, the media, and the public in general.

public stakeholders those public entities and groups that have an interest in the financial performance and/or social responsibility demonstrated by a firm; see **stakeholders; publics.**

publics communities of interested parties who are not direct participants in a market as customers, channel members, suppliers, or competitors

Q

quality the ability to provide appropriate value from the customer's point of view.

R

radical innovation producing large changes in the functions and performance of a product or offering, often resulting in new types of value for customers.

realized costs actual costs incurred.

refusal to deal considered to be illegal if the motivation is to restrain trade or fix prices.

relational exchange in customer-supplier relationships, an interaction in which the long-term benefit of the combination is recognized.

relationship/value creator one of the four seller roles in business-to-business marketing.

resale restrictions when suppliers maintain house accounts (customers that, while they are located within a reseller's market area, remain a direct customer of the manufacturer) or when suppliers limit resellers to certain territories.

response rates the number of responses to a research inquiry, stated as a percentage of the total number of potential respondents contacted.

resultant costs those costs that will occur because a decision—e.g., launching a new product or establishing a new sales plan—will be made.

revenues the actual price(s) received for a product multiplied by the number of items sold.

RFB industry jargon for request for bid; see RFQ/RFP.

RFQ/RFP synonyms for the common business practice of asking a supplier to quote a piece of business; an **RFQ** is a **request for quotation;** an **RFP** is a **request for proposal.**

S

sales call an in-person meeting between the seller(s) and one or more members in the customer buying center.

sales promotion as part of the **promotion mix,** efforts intended to provide incentives for customers to take an action over a specified time period, such as to visit a sales booth or to consider a product or sales proposal.

sample the members of a population who are chosen to be respondents in a research study.

sealed bid a private bid by a prospective supplier.

secondary data market information compiled for purposes other than the current research effort; it can be internal data, such as existing sales-tracking information, or it can be research conducted by someone else, such as a market research company or the U.S. government.

segmentation framework a method of segmentation used in understanding a given market.

segmenting dividing a market into manageable elements whose members, based on the segmentation framework, are homogeneous.

selective attention in communication, a protective method receivers use to prevent overload; based on an individual's ability to process and store messages, only useful information or information that has immediate value is perceived.

selective exposure in communication, a receiver selects preferred media to which the receiver wants to pay attention.

selective retention in communication, the receiver remembers the portion of a message that reinforces pre-existing attitudes and beliefs.

seller stand-in materials stand-alone promotional materials for which the seller will not have an in-person opportunity to emphasize or explain their relevance to the customer's needs; compare to **leave-behind material.**

server log a computer file that records every action taken by every visitor to a Web site; analysis of the file can tell a marketer what parts of the site get the most traffic, how long visitors stay on a page, and what patterns are evident in visitors' interaction with the site.

situational ethics the flexible application of ethical standards based on circumstances; often becomes a post hoc rationalization of behavior based on questionable ethics.

societal marketing concept a marketing philosophy that maintains that in addition to being market sensitive, understanding customer needs, and meeting organizational goals, marketers must deliver satisfaction more effectively than competitors and in a way that considers the well-being of society.

spam unsolicited e-mail, viewed as annoying by most recipients.

stage gates checkpoints after each stage of the product development process to ensure that the original goals and objectives are still viable and that the development is still forecast to meet the expectations that were created as part of its initial approval; the **stage gate** process is a fairly rigorous but flexible process to keep new product development on track.

stakeholders the individuals and organizations that have an interest—a "stake"—in the company, its operation, and its performance; the interest may or may not be financial.

Standard Industrial Classification (SIC) a scheme of industry classifications designed and used by the U.S. government [it is being replaced by the **North American Industry Classification System (NAICS)**].

straight rebuy a buying situation that is routine and has established solutions; straight rebuys are "more of the same" and often involve simply the reorder of a previous product.

strategic business unit a business, department, organization, or possibly even a product line within the larger organization that has separate goals and objectives; these business units must be capable of being planned and measured separately from the rest of the organization.

strategic management process a stepwise progression of actions to conceive, implement, and adjust **strategy**.

strategy the determination of goals or objectives and the general means for reaching them; literally, the "art of the general."

substantiality a characteristic of a market segment referring to the sufficiency of its size and profit potential.

superordinate goals those goals that go beyond a single intermediary, are desirable to many of the channel members, and are unobtainable through the effort of a single channel member.

supply chain the chain of entities and activities that results in products provided to end users; it starts with raw materials and traces the flow of materials and subassemblies through suppliers, manufacturers, and channel intermediaries to the final customer.

supply curve shows how much product will be produced in an industry at different levels of price.

sustaining innovation changes, radical or incremental, that make somewhat predictable improvements to existing technologies.

switching costs the costs to the buying organization of changing suppliers after an initial selection has been made and supply has begun.

T

targeting choosing segments to address based on matching the firm's strengths to the segments that will place the greatest value on these strengths and yield the greatest success.

targeting decision the decision that is supported by an understanding of market segmentation.

technology a way of accomplishing something.

technology adoption life cycle (TALC) the series of events or stages that describe how certain kinds of customers come to adopt new technology.

time one part of economic utility, the availability of the product when the customer needs it.

time compression an increase in the "speed" of doing business; changing customer needs and competitive pressures cause companies to try to get new offerings out faster and to replace these products with succeeding generations of products even more rapidly.

time pacing in organization change, setting strict timetables for new versions of products, operations, strategies, and so on.

top-down forecast the result of research efforts to forecast market potential, starting with a "whole market" forecast and reducing it to a forecast for the specific segment(s) or products in question (compare to **bottom-up forecast**).

tornado in the TALC, a period of rapid growth in which most pragmatist buyers first adopt a product based in a new technology.

total offering the offering that provides a complete solution to the buyer's needs; this may include financing, delivery, service, or, based on the buyer's preference, only the core product.

trade credit the payment term provided by suppliers to distributors and other channel intermediaries to finance purchases.

trade secret a process, technique, or competitive advantage whose owner has chosen to not seek additional legal protection, either in an effort to maintain the secret by avoiding disclosure or because the secret does not meet legal tests for originality.

translation a new customer specification that is not a first-of-a-kind application; that is, not a new technology, product, or use of a product—rather, merely a **translation** of a success of a new offering.

translation tools a set of marketing tools for the field team to take a new success and translate it to other customers.

treble damages three times the actual loss incurred by the injured party as a result of a violation of antitrust law; the injured party must prevail in a civil court.

tying contracts requirements to purchase ancillary goods or services "in a bundle" to get the offering really desired.

user see end user.

value the sum of all of the benefits that the customer receives in the process of buying and using a product or service less the costs involved.[2]

value-added reseller (VAR) a reseller of information technology products who provides enhancements to manufacturers' products, usually in the form of software; a VAR typically provides integrated systems to its customers, tailored to a particular customer's needs.

---

[2]Michael Treacy and Frederick Wiersema, *The Discipline of Market Leaders* (Reading, Mass.: Addison-Wesley, 1995).

value-based pricing pricing based on customers' perceived value.

value chain the chain of activities that creates something of value for the targeted customers.

value-cost model the model of a business' value chain that shows how activities contribute to value and to costs.

value image the sum total of all impressions and experiences that the buyer has of the supplier, whether or not pertinent to the current buying situation.

value network a coalition of suppliers who contribute to an offering to satisfy specific segment needs.

vertical integration referring to the degree of ownership a firm has of its marketing channel.

vertical marketing system producer and intermediaries acting with common goals in a marketing channel.

warehouses facilities optimized for storage and assortment creation.

Subject Index

A

Accessibility, 193
Accessory equipment suppliers, 38–39
Actionability, 193
Added value, 48, 70, 80
Administered channel intermediaries, 402–403
Administrative agencies, 91
Advertising, 8–9, 91, 168
  See also Communicating with the market
  Advertising and sales promotion (A&SP), 419
  See also Communicating with the market
Advisory boards as source of competitive information, 183–184
Affiliates, 407–408, 409
After-market parts, 31
Aggravation costs, 18
Aggressive competition, 107, 108
AIDS, 477
Airline industry, 318, 333, 457–459
Alpha tests, 154
  See also Market research
American Marketing Association (AMA) Code of Ethics, 462, 471
Analytical approach to segmentation and targeting, 197–201, 206–209
Ancillary channel members, 374, 375
Annual Survey of Manufacturers (Bureau of the Census), 185
Antimerger acts, 95
Antitrust implications of intellectual property, 106
Antitrust law, 109
  See also Legal environment

Application histories, 437
Application service providers (ASPs), 156, 276–277
Archetypical roles, 83n.5
Asian economy in the 90s, 14
ASP. *See* Application service provider
Associations (symbols) and brands, 284–285
Assortment discrepancy, 392–393
Auction hubs, 408
Auctioning software, 25
Auctions, 329–330
Augmented product, 6
Authority, 79
Automotive industry, 356
Aviation Rulemaking Advisory Committee (ARAC), 458, 459
Avoidable costs, 304
Awareness and brands, 284, 286

B

Balanced scorecard in business strategy, 135
Barriers
  and network alliances, 48
  to entry, 50
  to entry/exit in forecasting, 171
Barter hubs, 408
Bases of power, 400–401, 401n.7
Beachhhead, 54
Belief systems, 79, 81, 82, 83n.5
Beta tests, 154
  See also Market research
Big ticket purchases, 38
Billboards, 434
"Bingo cards," 422
Binomial choices, 82
Booked sale, 364
Bottom-up forecast, 360
Boundary personnel, 339
Bounded rationality, 82
Boycotts, 477
Brand identity, 50
Brand image, 19
Brands, 257, 277–286
  building strong brands, 283–286
    associations (symbols), 284–285
    awareness, 284, 286
    quality, 285–286
  defending, 282–283
  importance of, 278–280
  internal, 68
  recognition of, 61

  as a standard, 280–282
    new technology, 281
    service, 281–282
Breaks (type of crisis), 477
Breakthrough innovations, 268
Bribes, 469
Bullwhip effect, 11–13
Bundled offering, 38
Bundling, 317
Business development, 325
Business ethics, 456–473
  American Marketing Association (AMA) Code of Ethics, 462, 471
  compromise and win-win, 472–473
  in different organizational levels, 465
  in different stakeholders, 464
  ethical dilemmas, 469–470, 471
  individual ethical behavior, 470–473
  individual ethical standards versus performance standards of the organization, 466–470
  and the marketing concept, 561
  in obtaining competitive information, 468–469
  in product announcements, 467–468
    in product capability claims, 468
  situational ethics, 466–467
  societal marketing concept, 461–463
  and value networks, 473
Business legislation issues, 96–102
Business logistics, 71, 72
Business marketing
  defined, 5
  financial publics, 40–41
  independent press, 41
  internal publics, 42
  public interest groups, 41–42
  trends and changes in, 23–26
    hypercompetition, 23–24
    information technology and the Internet, 24
    partner networks, 24
    supply chain management, 25–26
    time compression, 26
  vs. consumer marketing, 4–17
    market research, 154–155
    place, 7–8
    price, 6–7
    product, 5–6
    promotion, 8–9
    summary of differences, 10
  and Yahoo, 3
  See also Marketing
Business markets, defined, 5
Business model, 115
Business portfolio, 118, 125–126

Business regulation in a free market,
90–91
Business strategy, 110–142
culture within organizations,
125–126
entrepreneurial culture, 126–128
changing the rules, 115, 128, 142
mission of the organization,
127–128
ownership creation, 114, 115, 128
goals, mission, and objectives,
112, 113
hierarchy of, 115, 116
key concepts, 113
portfolios of business, 118, 125–126
cultures within organizations,
125–126
value networks, 114, 126
recent trends, 114–115
resource allocation, 115–116, 125
special issues, 136–139
the Internet, 114, 136–137
market ownership, 138
new businesses, 138
value networks, 137
volatility and uncertainty require
flexibility, 137
strategic business units (SBUs),
116–117, 118, 142
strategic management process,
129–135
balanced scorecard, 135
critique of the model, 134–135
step (1) develop goals and
objectives, 131–132
step (2) environmental
analysis, 132
step (3) strategy design, 132–133
step 4) implementation plan
design, 133
step (5) strategy
implementation, 133
step (6) monitoring of
environment and performance
results, 133
step (7) analysis
of performance, 134
step (8) adjustments, 134
theory versus practice, 130–131
tools for designing strategy,
117–125
growth-share matrix,
117–120, 142
market attractiveness-business
strength matrix, 122–125, 142
matrix analysis illustration,
120–122

Business and trade press, 168
Business-to-business marketing. *See*
Business marketing
Buyer decision making, 4
Buying center, 62–63
diversity of interests, 154–155,
154n.2
interactions of, 161

C

California State Employees Retirement
System (CalPERS), 41
Call pattern, 359
Candlestick Park, 286
Capabilities brochures, 437
Capital goods manufacturers, 38
Catalog hubs, 408
Catalogs, 437
Celler-Kefauver Act (1950), 95
Change
in markets over time, 50–55
predicting, 52
Changing the rules, 263
in business strategy, 115, 128, 142
Channel attractiveness
in targeting, 205
Channel facilitators, 24
Channel patterns and control, 379,
401–404
Channel relationships, 372–414
ancillary channel members, 374, 375
channel design, 391–397
assortment discrepancy, 392–393
distributor channels, 393–397
dual distribution and
multidistribution, 392
channel flows and activities,
378–380
channels and the Internet, 404–411
affiliates, 407–408, 409
future trends, 410–411
hubs, 408
problems with,
409–410
role in marketing, 405–406
customers needs and expectations,
381–382
direct channel, 374, 375
distribution and the product life
cycle, 397–398
economic utility, 377–378
efficiency, 375
industrial end users,
382–384
industrial suppliers,
384–385

logistics management, 387–391
economic utility, 390–391
physical distribution concept,
388–390
managing distribution channels,
399–404
channel patterns and control,
401–404
power and conflict, 400–401,
400n.7
selecting distributors, 299–400
primary channel participants, 374
rationale for, 376–377
and sales promotion, 426–427
value networks, 385–387
Charitable donations, 156n.3, 160
Chasm, 53–54
Classified advertising, 168
Clayton Act (1914), 92–93, 94, 95
Co-opetition, 114
Collaboration/partnering, 343
Collaborators, 246–248
Collateral materials, 436
Collective unconscious, 83n.5
Colloquial expressions, 422
Columbia (space shuttle), 31
Combination compensation plans,
353–364
Commercial enterprises, 35–36
Commodity markets, 47
Common law, 96
Communicating with the market,
416–455
communications model, 420–424
capabilities of promotional
efforts, 424, 425
feedback, 422–423
losing meaning in the translation,
420–421
media impacting the message,
421–422
noise, 423–424
Internet, 445–452
effective communications, 451
newsletters, 450
on-line seminars, 451
opt-in e-mail, 450
promotion and
hypercompetition, 453
promotion and time compression,
452–453
Web sites, 446–449
promotion-mix elements, 419,
424–429
advertising, 425
personal selling, 424–425
public relations, 427–429
sales promotion, 425–426

promotional methods, 429–439
  channel promotions, 438
  corporate advertising, 435–436
  direct mail, 436
  nonpersonal communications,
      419, 430–432
  premium merchandise, 439
  printed promotion, 432–435
  sales and support literature,
      436–438
public relations and positioning,
    443–446
technical papers, 444–445
trade shows and conferences,
    439–443
Communication among
    stakeholders, 61
Communications capabilities, 260
*Community Publishers, Inc. v. Donrey
    Corporation,* 98
Company protection, 90
Compensation for the direct sales
    force, 361–364
Competition
  aggressive, 107, 108
  hypercompetition, 295, 328–330
  inefficient, 51
  and innovation, 265–277
  in the market, 90
  and positioning, 188
  See also Branding; Innovation
Competitive advantage, 18
Competitive analysis, 144, 162–169
  information to collect on individual
      competitors, 164–167
    assumptions, 166–167
    capabilities, 166
    goals, 165
    strategies, 165
  sources of competition, 163–164
  sources of competitive information,
      167–169
    business and trade press, 168
    competitors' advertisements
        and publicity
        announcements, 168
    consultants, 169
    the customer, 167,
        182–185
    the Internet,
        167–168
    trade shows, 168
  See also Branding; Innovation
Competitive attractiveness in
    targeting, 205
Competitive bidding, 319–321
Competitive environment, 45–47

Competitive information
  and business ethics, 468–469
  sources of, 167–169
  See also Competitive analysis
Competitive pricing, 291–292
Complexity, 14–17
Component parts producers, 38
Component technology, 68
Compromise, 422
Compromise and win-win, 472–473
Concentrated markets, 154
Conclusive research, 151
  See also Market research
Concurrent development, 241
Conscious mind, 83n.5
Consent decree, 94
Conservatives in technology adoption
    life cycle (TALC), 212
Consultants for competitive
    analysis, 169
Consulting organizations, 417
Consumer buying versus organizational
    buying, 60–61, 80
Consumer demand, 9–10
Consumer Goods Pricing Act
    (1975), 95
Consumer marketing versus business
    marketing, 4–17
Consumer media, 433–434
Consumer Product Safety Commission
    (CPSC), 91
Consumer protection, 91
Contact networks, 264, 265
Containerization, 377
Contracts, 70
  long-term, 81
Contractual systems, 402
Contributing margin, 304–305
Contribution analysis, 304–305,
    334–335
Controlled risk taking, 260
Copying, 106
Copyright infringement, 477
Copyrights, 105
Core business, 174
Core churn, 175, 201, 348, 438
Core competencies, 113, 114, 115
Core products, 5–6, 22, 31–32, 38, 65
Corporate culture, 78–79
Corporate vertical marketing systems
    (CVMS), 402
Cost-based pricing, 296
Costing methods, 102n.11
Costs, 71
  aggravation, 18
  coverage and price reductions, 304
  of doing business, 19

hidden, 18
minimizing, 8
of mistakes, 18
switching, 15, 25
time, 18
transaction, 25
County Business Patterns (Bureau of the
    Census), 185
Crisis management, 456, 473–482
  assessing and addressing risks,
      475–476
  media relations during a crisis,
      478–479
  minor crises, 479–482
  negative media attention, 477–478
  organizational structure, 475
  planning for unanticipated crises,
      476–477
  types of crises, 477
CRM. *See* Customer relationship
    management
Cross licenses, 106
Culture of the organization, 125–128,
    148, 460
Customer relationship, 85, 336–371
  characteristics of business-to-
      business selling, 339–341
    continuous adjustment
        of needs, 341
    creativity demanded of seller by
        buyer, 341
    long time period before selling
        effort pays off, 340–341
    repeated, ongoing
        relationship, 240
    solution-oriented, total system
        effort, 240
  customer relationship management
      (CRM), 156, 353, 355, 448
  direct sales force, 359–364, 368
    compensation, 361–364
    deployment, 360–361
    and manufacturers'
        representatives, 366–368
  distributors, 358
  management perspective, 354–355
  manufacturers' representatives, 258,
      364–368, 365n.23
    combination
        of representation, 368
    explicit customer feedback
        required, 367–368
    long lead times, 366–367
    missionary work required, 367
    selection, training,
        and control, 367
    technically complex products,
        366

nature of sales and selling, 338–339
needs of buyer and seller, 62, 145,
    355–358
    individual needs, 358
    job function needs, 355–356
    organizational needs, 356–357
organizational model between field
    and field marketing, 352
post-sale customer service, 352–354
relationships, 341–355
    and attitude, 343
    and corporate culture, 344–345
    definition, 342–343
    and loyalty, 81–82, 344
sales force compensation, 361–364
    combination compensations
        plans, 353–364
    straight-commission
        compensation programs, 362
    straight-salary compensation
        plans, 363
sales force organization, 359
seller roles, 345–352, 345n.12
    missionary sellers/field marketers
        (MS/FMDs), 351–352
    the motivator/problem solver,
        347–349
    the order taker, 345–346
    the persuader/sustainer,
        346–347
    the relationship/value creator,
        349–350
selling structures, 358–359
See also Customers; Market
    research; Organizational
    customers
Customer relationship management
    (CRM), 156, 353, 355, 448
Customers
    and channel relationships, 381–382
    and classification of markets, 39–40
    education of, 20
    as sources of competitive
        information, 167
    value and pricing, 22, 297–302
    See also Customer relationship;
        Market research;
        Organizational customers
Customization, 71
CVMS. *See* Corporate vertical
    marketing systems

D

Data sheets, 437
Delivery functions. *See* Channel
    relationships

Delphi approach, 173, 198
Demand
    consumer, 9–10
    derived, 9–11, 14, 21
    discontinuous, 12, 14
    inelasticity of, 13
    leveraged, 10–13
    and pricing, 305–308
Demand and supply curves, 290,
    305–306
Demographics, 42–43
Derived demand, 9–11, 14, 21
Design decisions in market research,
    150, 152
Differentially invisible channels, 390
Differentiation, 46–47, 50, 210
    of an undifferentiated product, 342
    in business strategy,
        113, 114
Direct activities, 19–22,
    48–49
Direct channel, 374, 375
Direct response requests, 422
Direct sales force, 359–364, 368
Directory advertising, 433
Discontinuous demand, 12, 14
Discontinuous replacement
    technologies, 232
Discounts and allowances,
    317–318
Discovery approach to segmentation
    and targeting, 201–202,
    209–210, 238
Discovery mode and pricing,
    315–316
Discovery-based planning, 271
Discrepancy of assortment,
    392–393
Discrete exchanges, 342
Discussion boards as source of
    competitive information, 183
Disruptive innovations, 268
Disruptive technologies, 270–272
Distribution centers, 389
Distributor channels, 393–397
    See also Channel relationships
Distributor selection, 299–400
Distributors, 358
Downsizing, 23
Dual distribution, 392
Dyadic interactions, 340

E

E-business, 147
E-business-to-business (eB2B), 270
E-commerce, 89, 97, 109

E-mail, 57, 360
E/Us. *See* End users
EB2B. *See* e-business-to-business
Econometric models, 173
Economic environment, 43
Economic events, 13–14
Economic utility, 7–8, 19, 377–378
    and channel relationships, 390–391
Economies of scale, 11, 16, 90,
    229–230
EDI. *See* Electronic data interchange
Efficiency and channel
    relationships, 375
EFFIE award, 189
Elasticity, 306–307
Elasticity of demand in
    forecasting, 171
Electric power market, 299
Electronic data interchange (EDI), 25
Emergent strategy, 130
End users (E/Us), 36
Enforcement responsibilities in the
    legal environment, 91
Engineering call-outs, 280
Enterprise resource planning
    (ERP), 389
Entrepreneurial culture, 126–128
    See also Culture of the organization
Entrepreneurial marketing, 260–265,
    481–482
Environmental accidents, 477
Environmental analysis in business
    strategy, 132
Environmental changes
    and markets, 13
Environmental impact, 266
Environmental protection, 91
Epidemic effects, 477
Equality, 95
ERP. *See* Enterprise resource planning
Established products, 233–235
Ethical dilemmas, 469–470, 471
Ethics, 108
    See also Business ethics
Evaluated price, 18–19, 24, 297,
    298, 299
Evaluation of alternatives in consumer
    buying process, 61
Evidence seeking, 150
Evolutionary product
    introductions, 232
Exclusive dealing, 90, 93
Executive agencies, 91
Exchange hubs, 408
Exhibits at trade shows, 441–442
Expenditures in forecasting, 171
Exploratory research, 151
    See also Market research

External economic attacks, 477
External information attacks, 477
Extortion, 477
Exxon Valdez oil spill, 476

F

FAA. *See* Federal Aviation
    Administration
Facilitators, 24
Fair trade pricing, 95
Farm producer cooperatives, 404
Fast-paced markets, 47
FDA. *See* Food and Drug
    Administration
Federal Aviation Administration
    (FAA), 457, 458
Federal government
    product failures, 222
    as source of competitive
        information, 185
Federal Trade Commission Act (1914),
    93–94
Federal Trade Commission (FTC), 91,
    93, 94, 105, 107
*Federal Trade Commission (FTC) v.
    Motion Picture Advertising
    Service Co.,* 93
Feedback, 8
Field market development (FMD)
    personnel, 202
Financial publics, 40–41
Financing, 387
FirstGov, 87, 185
Fit in business strategy, 113
Fixed cost of sales, 365
Flagship product, 214–215
Flexibility and business strategy, 137
FMD personnel. *See* Field market
    development (FMD) personnel
Food and Drug Administration
    (FDA), 94
Forecasting markets, 144, 169–178
    data chart for marketing operations
        forecast (MOF), 177
    forecast types and techniques,
        172–173
    information from field marketing
        operation, 174–178, 174n.10
    marketing operation forecasts
        (MOFs), 144, 157, 172, 173
    Moore's Law, 170
    predictive models, 173
    "rules" of forecasts, 170
Foreign Corrupt Practices Act of 1977
    (FCPA), 465
Form in economic utility, 377

Formal research, 146
Forward-looking incremental costs,
    303–304
Four Ps, 5–9, 374, 377
Free market versus regulation,
    90–91, 106
Free riders, 97
FTC. *See* Federal Trade Commission
Fulfillment firms, 442
Functional spin-off, 381–382

G

Gasoline price increases of 2000, 42
Globalization, 157
GNP. *See* Gross national product
Go/no-go decisions in market
    research, 150, 152–154
Goals and objectives in business
    strategy, 131–132
Goals of the organization, 79, 112, 113
Good forecasts versus useful
    forecasts, 172
Gorilla, 555
Government agencies, 62
Government purchasing, 69
Government units (customers), 36–37
Gross national product (GNP), 36
Growth-share matrix in business
    strategy, 117–120, 142
Guerrilla marketing, 428

H

Hackers, 373
Hard power bases, 400–401, 400n.7
Heterogeneous needs, 196
Hidden costs, 18
Hierarchy of business strategy, 115, 116
High-cost business model, 16
Homogeneous needs, 196
Horizontal competitors, 402
Horizontal management, 79
Horizontal sprawl, 403
Hostile takeover attempts, 477
House accounts, 401
Hubs, 408
Human factors in business decisions,
    80–81
Hypercompetition, 23–24, 295,
    328–330

I

Ignorance of the law, 108
Images, 82–83

Incentives for participation in market
    research, 156n.3, 160
Incremental innovations, 267
Incremental sustaining
    innovations, 272
Incrementalism, logical, 130
Independent agencies, 91
Independent press, 41
Individual ethical behavior, 470–473
Individual ethical standards versus
    performance standards of the
    organization, 466–470
Individual influences on buying, 79
Individual needs in the buying decision
    process, 77
Industrial distributors
    (wholesalers), 35
Industrial end users, 382–384
Industrial standards, 280
Industrial suppliers, 384–385
Inelasticity of demand, 13
Informal research, 146
Information search in consumer buying
    process, 61
Information technology (IT) industry,
    24, 145
    rapid changes in, 156
Information technology (IT)
    systems, 25
Initial public offerings (IPOs), 23–24
Initiating price changes, 321–322
Innovation, 53, 256–277
    competing through innovation,
        265–277
        disruptive technologies, 270–272
        managing innovation, 266–269
        practical aspects of, 273–277
        sustaining innovation, 272–273
    definition, 260
    entrepreneurial marketing, 260–265
        changing the rules, 263
        practical aspects, 263–265
Intangible services, 3
Integrative bargaining, 327
Intellectual property, 104–106, 105n.12
    antitrust implications of, 106
Intensity of distribution, 391–392
Intensity of territory design, 361
Intercorporate stockholding, 93, 96–97
Interlocking directorates, 93, 97
Internal attractiveness in targeting,
    205–206
Internal brands, 68
Internal publics, 42
International marketing efforts and
    pricing, 316
International markets, 16–17

International Rubber Organization (INRO), 12
International Standards Organization (ISO), 17
International trade organizations as source of competitive information, 185
Internet, 24
  and business strategy, 114, 136–137
  and channels, 404–411
  e-commerce, 89, 97
  on-line catalogs, 57
  and pricing, 329–330
  and relationships, 59–60
  as source of competitive information, 167–168, 182–183
  and trademark law, 105n.11
  See also Web
Internet service providers (ISPs), 89, 90
Interpersonal and individual influences on buying, 79
Intranet portals, 3, 34
Inventory management, 388
Inventory services, 7
IPOs. *See* Initial public offerings
ISO. *See* International Standards Organization
IT industry. *See* Information technology (IT) industry

J

Japanese airlines, 318, 333
Jargon, 421
JIT. *See* Just-in-time delivery
Just-in-time delivery (JIT), 319, 377, 383, 398, 403

K

Keiretsu systems, 403–404
Kraft General Foods, Inc. v. State of New York, 98

L

Laggards in technology adoption life cycle (TALC), 212
LANs. *See* Local area networks
Lead users, 272
Learning curve effect, 314–315
Leave-behind materials, 437
Legal environment, 88–109
  antitrust implications of intellectual property, 106

business legislation issues, 96–102
  intercorporate stockholding, 96–97
  interlocking directorates, 97
  legally defined markets, 97, 98
  price discrimination, 99–101
  price maintenance, 97
  price-fixing conspiracy, 102, 103
  quantity discounts, 102
  refusal to deal, 98
  resale restrictions, 98–99
business regulation in a free market, 90–91
  company protection, 90
  consumer protection, 91
  social/environmental protection, 91
enforcement responsibilities, 91
intellectual property, 104–106
legislation affecting marketing, 92–96
  Celler-Kefauver Act (1950), 95
  Clayton Act (1914), 92–93, 94, 95
  Consumer Goods Pricing Act (1975), 95
  Federal Trade Commission Act (1914), 93–94
  Miller-Tydings Act, 95, 97
  Robinson-Patman Act (1936), 94–95, 101, 102
  securities laws, 96
  Sherman Antitrust Act (1890), 92, 93
  Uniform Commercial Code (UCC), 96
  Wheeler-Lea Act (1938), 93
political framework of enforcement, 106
size of companies, 103, 104
substantiality tests, 102–104
Legally defined markets, 97, 98
Leverage, 326
Leveraged demand, 10–13
  See also Bullwhip effect
Licenses, 106
Life cycle, 34
Linkages, 15
List price, 6
Local area networks (LANs), 147, 194
Locational convenience, 7
Logical incrementalism, 130
Logistical linkages, 15
Logistics of business, 71, 72, 387
  See also Channel relationships
Logistics management, 387–391
  See also Channel relationships

Long-term contracts, 81
Loyalty in the buying decision process, 64

M

Macroeconomy, 43
Macroenvironment, 42–47
  competitive, 45–47
  demographic, 42–43
  economic, 43
  natural, 43–44
  sociocultural, 43
  technological, 44–45
Mail order, 97
Maintenance, repair, and operations (MRO) market, 57
Make-or-buy decisions, 248–251
Malicious rumors, 477
Management of supply chain, 25–26
Managing distribution channels, 399–404
  See also Channel relationships
Manufactured materials producers, 38
Manufacturers' representatives, 258, 364–368, 365n.23
Manufacturers' suggested retail prices (MSRPs), 6, 97
Market attractiveness-business strength matrix in business strategy, 122–125, 142
Market development gap, 54
Market generalizations, 34–35
Market intelligence, 146
Market ownership, 114, 115, 128
Market preemption, 104
Market research, 144–162, 182, 350
  designing the research approach, 155–157
    time compression, 156–157, 161
    uncertainty, 157
  differences from consumer markets, 154–155
    concentrated markets, 154
    diversity of interests in the buying center, 154–155, 154n.2
    technical expertise, 155
  performing market research, 157–161
    incentives for participation, 156n.3, 160
    interactions of the buying center, 161
    personal interviews, 154, 158–159

research vendors as source of
competitive information,
185, 186
steps in, 148–150, 182
step (1) define the problem and
research objectives, 149
step (2) design the research
method, 149–150
step (3) data collection, 150
step (4) analyzing the data, 150
step (5) presenting
the findings, 150
types of decision support, 150–154
design decisions, 150, 152
go/no-go decisions, 150,
152–154
targeting decisions, 141–152, 150
See also Customer relationship;
Customers; Organizational
customers
Market share, 71
Market structure, 16
Market up, market down, and market
sideways, 282–283
Market-chosen leader, 55
Market-driven economy, 88
Market-driven organization, 20
Marketing
as direct activity, 19–20
guerrilla, 428
philosophies of, 344
and pricing, 308–316
product development process,
242–244
and relationships, 14–17
See also Business marketing
Marketing channels. See Channel
relationships
Marketing communications
(marcom), 419
Marketing concept, 9
and business ethics, 561
Marketing era, 344
Marketing mix issues, 393
Marketing operation forecast (MOF),
144, 157, 172, 173
data chart for, 177
See also Forecasting markets
Marketing planning forecasts, 172
Markets, evolution of, 50–55
Mass marketing, 16
Mass media, 16, 460
Material requirements planning
(MRP), 173, 389
Material resource planning, 7
Matrix analysis illustration in business
strategy, 120–122

Maximum and minimum price, 302
Measurability, 193
Measuring and tracking results in
business strategy, 113, 133, 134
Media
consumer, 433–434
independent, 41
mass, 16, 460
relations with during a crisis,
477–479
Media buy, 425
Medical devices, 444
Megadamage, 477
Mergers, 109
antimerger acts, 95
Microprocessors, 291–292
Miller-Tydings Act, 95, 97
Minimum price, 302, 302n.4
Mission of the organization, 79, 112,
113, 127–128
Missionary sellers, 79
Missionary sellers/field marketers
(MS/FMDs), 351–352
Modified rebuys, 67
Monopolies, 46, 49, 50, 469
Sherman Antitrust Act (1890), 92
Monopsony, 49
Moore's Law in forecasting
markets, 170
Motivator/problem solver,
347–349
MRO market. See Maintenance, repair,
and operations (MRO) market
MRP. See Materials requirements
planning
MSRPs. See Manufacturers' suggested
retail prices
Multidistribution, 392
Multinational companies, 7
Multioffering companies, 126
Multiple transactions, 343
Mutual dependence and customer
loyalty, 81–82

N

NAICS code. See North American
Industry Classification System
(NAICS) code
NASA, 31, 165
National Plastics Exposition, 442
National Transportation Safety Board
(NTSB), 457, 458, 459
Natural environment, 43–44
Natural law, 466
Need innovation and brands, 282
Need recognition, 80

Need recognition in consumer buying
process, 61
Negotiated price reductions, 224
Negotiated pricing, 322–328
Negotiation, 470
Net value of satisfaction, 18
Network alliances, 48
New businesses, 201, 438
and business strategy, 138
and customer relationship, 348
and forecasting, 175, 176–178
New product development (NPD),
235–242, 240
New task becomes rebuy, 77–78
New tasks, 64, 65, 66–67, 69
New technology and brands, 281
New York American Marketing
Association, 189
Next generation needs, 14
Niche, 54, 213
Non-value producing activities, 21
Nonprofit organizations, 37, 61
North American Industry
Classification System (NAICS)
code, 197
Not-for-profit organizations, 37
NPD. See New product development
NTSB. See National Transportation
Safety Board

O

Objectives of the organization,
112, 113
Occupational health diseases, 477
OEM. See Original equipment
manufacturer
Offerings, 3, 6, 22, 24, 26
Oil crisis of 70s, 13–14
Oligopolies, 45, 49, 70, 79, 159
emergence of, 50–51
On-line catalogs, 57
On-line ordering, 25
One-to-one marketing, 370
Ongoing costs, 303
Ongoing revenue, 303
Open bids, 319
Opportunity costs, 241
Opportunity seeking, 261
Order cycle, 11
Order taker, 345–346
Organizational buying, 58–87
the buying center, 62–63
buying decision processes examples,
72–77
new task example, 74–77
straight rebuy example, 72–74

consumer buying versus organizational buying, 60–61, 80
government purchasing, 69
human factors in business decisions, 80–81
implications for business marketing, 79–80
individual needs in the buying decision process, 77
the Internet and relationships, 59–60
interpersonal and individual influences on buying, 79
modified rebuys, 67
mutual dependence and customer loyalty, 81–82
new task becomes rebuy, 77–78
new tasks, 64, 65, 66–67, 69
organizational influences on buying, 78–79
organizational needs in the buying decision process, 77
process flow buying model, 65–72
stage (1) definition, 66–68
stage (2) selection, 68–70
stage (3) solution delivery, 71
stage (4) end game, 71–72
product specification, 67–68, 80
psychology of the process, 82–84
relationships with customers, 85
request for quotation (RFO) and request for proposal (RFP), 68–69
satisficing behavior, 82
stakeholders, 61, 62, 65
stepwise buying model, 63–65
straight rebuys, 67, 69
value image, 82, 83n.4
variability of rational buying decisions, 80–84
Organizational customers, 35–36
accessory equipment suppliers, 38–39
capital goods manufacturers, 38
component parts and manufactured materials products, 38
government units, 36–37
industrial distributors, 35
nonprofit and not-for-profit, 37
original equipment manufacturers (OEMs), 36
raw materials producers, 37–38
users or end users, 36
value-added resellers, 35–36
See also Customer relationship; Customers; Market research

Organizational levels and business ethics, 465
Organizational model between field and field marketing, 352
Organizational structure and crisis management, 475
Original equipment manufacturer (OEM), 32–33, 36, 291, 374, 376
Outsourcing, 14
Ownership, market, 114
Ownership process, 5

P

Palletizing, 377
Partner networks, 24
Partnership structures, 109
Partnerships, 3, 15–16, 31–33, 47
concerns about, 49–50
Patents, 105
Penetration pricing, 313–315
Performance analysis in business strategy, 134
Performance standards of the organization versus individual ethical standards, 466–470
Personal conscious mind, 83n.5
Personal interviews in market research, 154, 158–159
Personal linkages, 15
Personal selling, 8, 15
Personal service, 8
Personality types, 79
Persuader/sustainer, 346–347
Physical distribution concept, 388–390
Pioneer 1 (space craft), 31
Place in economic utility, 377
Place in the four Ps, 7–8, 374, 377
Plagiarism, 106
Planning. *See* Business strategy
Plant closings, 477
Plant defects, 477
Plant sabotage, 477
PLC. *See* Product life cycle
Policy statements, 456
Political parties, 91
Portal, 3
Portals/exchanges, 218
Portfolios of business, 118, 125–126
Positioning. *See* Segmenting, targeting, and positioning
Positioning statement, 211
Positive law, 466
Possession, 7
Possession in economic utility, 377, 378
Post-sale customer service, 352–354

Postpurchase behavior in consumer buying process, 61
Power and conflict in channel relationships, 400–401, 400n.7
Pragmatists, 53–55
Pragmatists in technology adoption life cycle (TALC), 212
Predatory pricing, 100, 100n.10, 101
Predictive models in forecasting markets, 173
Presidential administration, 91
Press
business and trade, 168
independent, 41
Price discrimination, 99–101
Price discrimination regulations, 90, 102
Price elasticity, 13
Price maintenance, 97
Price negotiations, 6–7
Price in organizational buying, 61, 70
Price reductions and cost coverage, 304
Price skimming, 291, 313–315
Price-fixing conspiracy, 102, 103
Pricing, 6–7, 290–335
auctions, 329–330
and the changing business environment, 328–330
competitive pricing, 291–292
contribution analysis, 304–305, 334–335
definitions, 295–297
demand functions and pricing, 305–308
evaluated, 18–19, 24
manufacturers' suggested retail prices (MSRPs), 97
market-driven, 25
in the marketing mix, 232n.5
and marketing strategy, 308–316
discovery mode, 315–316
international marketing efforts, 316
learning curve effect, 314–315
penetration pricing and price skimming, 291, 313–315
in the PLC and TALC process, 310–313
pricing objectives, 309–310
negotiated pricing, 322–328
predatory, 100, 100n.10, 101
pricing tactics, 317–322
bundling, 317
competitive bidding, 319–321
discounts and allowances, 317–318
initiating price changes, 321–322

reflecting customer value, 297–302
relevant costs, 303–305
value-cost model of the customer,
    300–302
Primary channel participants, 374
Primary market research, 148
    See also Market research
Proactivity, 260
Process flow buying model,
    65–72, 279
Product, core, 5–6, 22, 31–32, 38, 65
Product acceptance, 228
Product announcements and business
    ethics, 467–468
Product brochures, 437
Product capability claims and business
    ethics, 468
Product configurators, 447
Product counterfeiting, 477
Product defects and recalls, 477
Product development process,
    220–254
    collaborators, 246–248
    established products, 233–235
    make-or-buy decisions, 248–251
        factors in, 249–251
        supplier role in the decision, 251
    marketing, 242–244
    new product development process,
        235–242
        (1) idea generation, 235
        (2) product screening, 235
        (3) business case analysis, 236
        (4) product/strategy/plan
            development, 236
        (5) test market, 237
        (6) product launch, 237
        (7) hand off to the
            translation/customer education
            team, 237–238
        concurrent development, 241
        customer/market orientation,
            238–239
        early stages weeding, 240
        no shortcuts, 242
        stage gates, 240
        team approach, 239
    product elimination decisions,
        234–235
    product failures, 221–222, 244–246
        missing marketing plan,
            244–245
        needs of the market,
            245–246
        price of the product, 246
        size of market overestimated, 245
    product life cycle (PLC),
        223–225

product life cycle stages, 225–232
    (1) development stage, 225–226
    (2) introduction stage, 226–227
    (3) growth stage, 227–230
    (4) maturity stage, 230–231
    (5) decline stage, 232
Product differentiation, 228
Product failures, 221–222, 244–246,
    373
Product information, 386
Product life cycle (PLC), 51–53,
    118–119, 126, 223–232
    and distribution, 397–398
Product line maintenance, 401
Product line positioning, 231–215
Product specification, 67–68, 80
Product support and delivery, 387
Product/service offerings, 3
Production era and product era, 344
Products, unsafe, 91
Professional associations, 456
Profitability, 61, 71
Promotion, 8–9
Promotional messages and consumer
    marketing, 4
Proportionately equal terms, 95
Proprietary disclosure agreements, 237
Prototypes, 68, 71
Psycho (type of crisis), 477
Psychology of organizational buying,
    82–84
Public interest groups, 41–42
Public interest and public image, 477
Public sector purchasing, 69
Public stakeholders, 427
Publicity announcements, 168
Publics, 40–42
Purchase decision in consumer buying
    process, 61
Pure competition, 46, 50
Pure monopoly, 46

Q

Quality and brands, 285–286
Quality improvement, 113
Quantity discounts, 90, 102
Quick copy shops, 336, 337

R

Radical innovations, 267–268
Radical sustaining innovations, 272
Rational decision process, 79, 80–84
Raw materials, 266
Realized costs, 303

Recognition of brands, 61
Refusal to deal, 98
Regulation versus free market,
    90–91, 106
Regulatory environment, 88
Relational exchange, 343
Relationship marketing, 14–17
    opportunities through, 15–16
Relationship/value creator,
    349–350
Relationships, 4
    in the buying decision process, 64
    differences between consumer and
        business marketing, 8–9
    and the Internet, 59–60
    and transaction, 323
    See also Customer relationship
Relevant costs, 303–305
Request for quotation (RFQ), request
    for bid (RFB), and request for
    proposal (RFP), 68–69,
    286, 433
Resale restrictions, 98–99
Research and development and
    outsourcing, 14
Research methods, 149–150
    See also Market research
Research vendors as source of
    competitive information,
    185, 186
Resource allocation, 115–116, 125
Response rates in market research, 156
Restraints of trade, 90
Resultant costs, 303
Return on investment (ROI), 135, 232
Revenues, 300
Reward systems, 79
RFQ, RFB, and RFP. *See* Request for
    quotation (RFQ), request for
    bid (RFB), and request for
    proposal (RFP)
Risk aversion, 78
Robinson–Patman Act (1936), 94-95,
    101, 102
ROI. *See* Return on investment
Rolling averages, 173
Routinization of the transaction, 73

S

Sales calls, 360
Sales curve, 52, 53
Sales era, 344
Sales force organization, 359
Sales forces as source of competitive
    information, 184
Sales forecasts, 172–173

Sales teams, 426
Salespersons and sellers, 294n.1, 336
Sample size, 149
Satisficing behavior, 82
SBUs. *See* Strategic business units
SCUBA equipment, 444
Sealed bids, 319
SEC. *See* Securities and Exchange
    Commission
Secondary data, 153
    See also Market research
Securities and Exchange Commission
    (SEC), 167
Securities laws, 96
Security breakdowns, 477
Segmenting, targeting, and positioning,
    188–218
   definitions and relationships,
     191–192
   positioning a product line, 213–215
   segmentation, 193–203
    analytical approach, 197–201
    basis for, 193–195
    discovery approach, 201–202, 238
    value chain and offering, 196
    value-based segmentation,
     195–196
   segmentation framework, 191
   targeting, 203–210
    analytical approach, 206–209
    channel attractiveness, 205
    competitive attractiveness, 205
    discovery approach, 209–210
    factors in assessing segment
     attractiveness, 203
    internal attractiveness, 205–206
    market attractiveness, 204–205
   technology adoption life cycle
    (TALC), 212–213
Segments, 20, 22, 31
Selective attention, 423, 424
Selective exposure, 423
Selective retention, 423, 424
Seller roles, 345-352, 345n.12
Sellers and salesperson, 294n.1, 336
Selling structures, 358–359
Server logs, 446
Service, 22
Service and brands, 281–282
Sexual harassment, 477
Sherman Antitrust Act (1890), 92, 93
SIC code. *See* Standard Industrial
    Classification (SIC) code
Situational ethics, 466–467
Size of companies in substantiality
    tests, 103, 104
Small Business Administration, 185

SMSAs. *See* Standard metropolitan
    statistical areas
Social/environmental protection, 91
Societal marketing concept,
    461–463
Societal/partnering/value network
    era, 344
Society of Automotive Engineers
    (SAE), 17
Society of Plastic Engineers (SPE), 17
Sociocultural environment, 43
Soft power bases, 400–401, 400n.7
Software
   auctioning, 25
   developers of, 258
   and the Web, 26
   word-processing, 269
Software company business model, 26
Spam, 450
Specification standards, 280
Sport utility vehicles (SUVs), 12, 13,
    434–435, 438, 444, 469
Stage gates, 240
Stakeholders, 61, 62, 65
   and business ethics, 464
   customer, 79
   public, 427
   values of, 65
Stand-alone transaction, 323
Standard and brands, 280–282
Standard Industrial Classification
    (SIC) code, 185, 197
Standard metropolitan statistical areas
    (SMSAs), 185
Standards-setting organizations, 62
Standardization, 17, 55
Standardized products, 6
Start-ups, 23
State and local governments as source
    of competitive information, 185
Statistical analyses, 154n.1
Stepwise buying model, 63–65
Straight rebuy example, 72–74
Straight rebuys, 67, 69
Straight-commission compensation
    programs, 362
Straight-salary compensation plans, 363
Strategic business units (SBUs),
    116–117, 118, 142
Strategic forecasts, 172
Strategic management process,
    129–135
    See also Business strategy
Strategy. *See* Business strategy
Structure of the organization, 79
Subscription services as source of
    competitive information,
    184–185

Substantiality, 193
Substantiality tests, 102–104
Substitution, 13
Superior value in business strategy, 113
Superordinate goals, 400
Supplier advantage, 319
Suppliers
   role in make-or-buy decisions, 251
   and switching costs, 15
   See also Vendors
Supply chain, 7
   and bullwhip effect, 11–13
   defined, 21
   logistics-oriented, 13
   management of, 25–26
   and the Web, 25–26
Supply chain analysis, 47
Supply and demand curves, 290,
    305–306
Support activities, 19–22, 48–49
Susan B. Anthony dollar, 222
Sustaining innovations, 268, 272–273
SUVs. *See* Sport utility vehicles
Switching costs, 25, 342
   and suppliers, 15
SWOT (strengths, weaknesses,
    opportunities, and threats), 132
Symbols, 82–83
Systems integrators, 258

T

TALC. *See* Technology adoption life
    cycle
Tangible products, 3
Target markets, 106
Targeting decisions in market research,
    141–152, 150
    See also Segmenting, targeting, and
    positioning
Tariffs, 16
Team approach, 239
Team players, 400
Technical bulletins, 437
Technical expertise and market
    research, 155
Technological change in forecasting,
    170–171
Technological environment, 44–45
Technology, 111, 114, 262, 266–267
   disruptive, 270–272
Technology adoption life cycle
    (TALC), 53–55, 212–213, 225
Technology bank, 57
Technophiles, 54, 212, 373
Telecommunications, 111
Teleconferencing, 360

Territory design, 361
Terrorism, 477
Test reports, 437
Theft, 106
Theory versus practice in business
    strategy, 130–131
Time, 7
    costs in, 18
    in economic utility, 377
    in forecasting, 171
Time compression, 26
    and market research, 156–157, 161
    and pricing, 328–330
    and targeting, 209–210
Time pacing, 273
Tire controversy, 12, 469–470, 479
Tobacco companies, 463
Top-down forecast, 360
Tornado, 53–55
Total offering, 6, 2976
Trade barriers, 16
Trade credit, 380
Trade magazines and journals, 433
Trade organizations as source of
    competitive information, 184
Trade secrets, 105
Trade shows as sources of competitive
    information, 168
Trademark law and the Internet,
    105n.11
Transaction costs, 25
Transaction and relationship, 323
Translation, 175, 176, 178, 201,
    348, 438
Translation tools, 178
Transportation, 388
Treble damages, 92
Trends, 2
Trial-and-error process, 54
TWA Flight 800, 457–458
Tying contracts, 93

U

Uncertainty and market research, 157
Uncertainty and targeting, 209–210
Uniform Commercial Code (UCC), 96
Unique or first-time value network,
    226, 227
United States Bureau of the Census,
    185, 198

United States Department
    of Agriculture, 91
United States Department
    of Commerce, 185
United States Department of Health
    and Human Services, 91
United States Department of Justice,
    91, 103, 104, 105n.12, 107
United States Department
    of Labor, 185
User groups as source of competitive
    information, 183
User training, 386
Users, 36

V

Value, 2, 4, 6
    concept of, 17–18
    creating, 22
    customer, 22
    defined, 18
    future, 31
    maximizing, 8
    misunderstanding of, 21–22
    perception of, 31–32
Value chain, 67, 154n.2, 188, 17–22,
    47–48
    adaptation of, 48
    defined, 19
    direct and support activities of,
        19–22
    implications of, 20–21
    misunderstanding of, 21–22
Value image, 82, 83n.4, 460
Value networks, 47–50, 114, 126, 137,
    163, 404
    and business ethics, 473
    channel relationships, 385–387
    multidimensional, 48–49
Value-added resellers (VARs), 35–36,
    74–77, 398
Value-based pricing, 296, 299
Value-based segmentation, 195–196
Value-cost model of the customer,
    300–302
Variability of rational buying
    decisions, 80–84
VARs. See Value-added resellers
Vendors
    changing, 100, 100n.9
    choice of, 68

research vendors as source of
    competitive information,
    185, 186
    screening, 70
    See also Suppliers
Venture capital, 23–24
Vertical integration, 248, 381
Vertical management, 79
Vertical marketing systems (VMSs),
    402, 403
Virtual entities, 3
Visionaries, 53–54
    in technology adoption life cycle
        (TALC), 212
VMSs. See Vertical marketing systems
Volatility, 10–11, 13–14
    and uncertainty and business
        strategy, 137
Volume of business, 104

W

Warehousing, 389
Web, 24
    as conveyor of products and
        services, 26
    and customer service, 25
    and marketing, 25
    personalized sites, 3
    resources, 3
    and supply chain management,
        25–26
    See also Internet
Web site tools, 147–148, 156, 346,
    404–411, 412
Webinars, 448
Wheeler-Lea Act (1938), 93
Wholesalers, 35
Win-lose, 470–473
Win-win, 470–473
Word-of-mouth diffusion, 428
Word-processing software, 269

Z

Zero-sum, 470–473

Name Index

A

Aaker, David A., 284
Ackerman, Elise, 409
Aeppel, Timothy, 279
Armstrong, Gary, 95

B

Balfour, Frederik, 204
Barmash, Isadore, 221
Bartus, Kevin, 241, 246, 269, 274, 275, 276
Berrigan, John, 193
Best, Roger J., 53, 54
Bradford, Kevin D., 339, 345, 349
Bradford, Robert W., 134
Brandenburger, Adam M., 114
Brewer, G., 461
Brofsky, Keith, 110
Brooke, Lindsay, 271, 356
Brown, James R., 373, 382
Brown, Shona, 273
Brunyee, Janinne, 342, 343
Buzzell, Robert D., 285
Buzzotta, V.R., 339
Byrne, John A., 114

C

Carmody, Carol, 459
Christensen, Clayton M., 268, 270, 271, 272
Churchill, Gilbert A., Jr., 338, 361, 363
Cohen, Andy, 337
Cooper, Robert G., 223, 240, 242, 244, 245, 246
Covin, Jeffrey G., 260
Cummings, Betsy, 463

D

Davis, E. J., 173
Davis, Robert, 458
Dempsey, Jack, 168
Dennis, Kathryn, 284
Dickson, Peter Reid, 115, 163, 170, 182, 193, 259, 262
Donahue, Sean, 406
Dornier, Philippe-Pierre, 11
Doyle, Peter, 197, 207
Duncan, J. Peter, 134

E

Edwards, Cliff, 291
Eisenhardt, Kathleen M., 273
El-Ansary, Adel I., 373, 382, 393, 400, 402
Eng, Robert, 423, 426
Ernst, Ricardo, 11
Ewing, Jack, 111

F

Fadem, Terry J., 264
Fattah, Hassan, 15, 258, 417
Feld, Ric, 278
Fender, Michel, 11
Ferrera, Gerald, 105
Feyerick, Deborah, 458
Fiedler, Edgar R., 170
Fink, Steven, 474
Finkbeiner, Carl, 193
Fisher, Rober, 324
Ford, Henry, 248
Ford, Neil M., 338, 361, 363
Ford, William Clay, Jr., 469
Friesen, Peter H., 260
Funkhouser, G. Ray, 82

G

Gale, Bradley T., 285
Galper, Morton, 423, 426
Gersick, Connie J. G., 273
Gerstner, Lou, 145, 146, 162, 179, 214
Giglierano, Joseph J., 262
Ginter, James L., 193
Glazer, Amihai, 306
Govoni, Norman, 423, 426
Grace, Robert, 44
Grey, Kennedy, 162

H

Haddad, Charles, 382
Hamel, Gary, 114, 116, 117, 120, 124, 263
Harbour, Ron, 356
Hirshleifer, Jack, 306
Hoffman, Lou, 452
Holden, Reed K., 303, 323, 324
Holmes, Stanley, 318

J

Jackson, Thomas Penfield, 104
James, Geoffrey, 189
Jennings, Marianne, 91, 92, 93, 105, 466, 467
Jung, Carl, 83

K

Kaestner, Sven, 204
Kang, Cecelia, 410
Kaplan, Abraham, 182
Kaplan, Robert S., 135
Keller, Maryann, 356
Kirkpatrick, George A., 461
Kobe, Gerry, 36, 356
Kotler, Phillip, 9, 18, 95, 223, 235, 244, 360, 435, 462
Kouvelis, Panos, 11
Kulik, Todd, 350, 364
Kyziridis, Panagiotis, 343, 344, 349

L

Lacey, Robert, 221
Lee, Hau L., 11
Lefton, R. E., 339
Levitt, Theodore, 45, 259
Lopez, Jose Ignacio, 356
Loucks, Vernon R., Jr., 465
Lowry, Tom, 312
Lowy, Alex, 408
Lumpkin, James R., 388

M

McCarthy, E. Jerome, 9
McKenna, Regis, 8, 9, 45, 55, 83, 120, 215, 250, 284, 422
McVay, Ryan, 372
Mann, Richard A., 91, 93, 94
Marchetti, Michele, 360

Miller, Danny, 260
Mintzberg, Henry, 130
Mitroff, Ian I., 474, 475, 476, 477
Moore, Geoffrey A., 53, 55, 212, 228
Morris, Gene, 296, 319, 320
Morris, Michael H., 260, 296, 319, 320, 342, 343

N

Nagle, Thomas T., 303, 323, 324
Nalebuff, Barry J., 114
Nir, Moira Marx, 461
Norton, David P., 135

O

O'Brien, Thomas C., 264
O'Connor, Gina Colarelli, 268, 275

P

Padmanabhan, V., 11
Page, Michael, 342, 343
Pasztor, Andy, 459
Pauchant, Thierry C., 474, 475
Paul, Gordon W., 260
Pelton, Lou E., 388
Peppers, Donald, 370
Perreault, William D., Jr., 9
Peters, Thomas J., 262
Porter, Michael E., 17, 18, 163, 194, 411
Prahalad, C. K., 114, 116, 117, 120, 124, 263

Q

Quinn, James Brian, 130

R

Raeburn, Paul, 306
Ramson, Stuart, 420
Rangan, V. Kasturi, 241, 246, 269, 274, 275, 276
Reinhardt, Andy, 204
Rewick, Jennifer, 410
Ritte, R. Richard, 82
Roberts, Barry S., 91, 93, 94
Robinson, Edward, 213
Rogers, Everett M., 53, 212
Rogers, Martha, 370
Rossant, John, 204

S

Sager, Ira, 145
Saren, Michael, 343, 344, 349
Saunders, John, 197, 207
Sawyer, Christopher A., 165
Sharma, Arun, 343, 344, 349
Sheinwald, Richard, 91
Shell, G. Richard, 323, 326, 327
Sherberg, Manuel, 339
Sherlock, Paul, 82, 83, 127, 242, 247, 296, 339, 345, 391, 397
Sheth, Jagdish N., 46
Shirouzu, Norihiko, 479
Siepler, Dieter, 271
Simison, Robert L., 479
Simon, Herbert A., 82
Sisodia, Rajendra, 46
Slevin, Dennis P., 260
Smith, Wendell R., 193
Southwick, Karen, 23
Stern, Louis W., 373, 382, 393, 400, 402
Steuer, R.M., 95, 109
Strutton, David, 388
Sung, Camay, 127

T

Tapscott, Don, 408
Ticoll, David, 408
Treacy, Michael, 18
Tzokas, Nikolaos, 343, 344, 349

U

Ury, William, 324
Utterback, James M., 267

V

Vine, Terry, 58
Vogel, Richard, 416
Von Hippel, Eric, 272
Von Pierer, Heinrich, 111, 140

W

Walker, Orville C., 338, 361, 363
Waterman, Robert H., 262
Waters, James A., 130
Weitz, Barton A., 339, 345, 349
Welch, Jack, 125
Whang, Seungjin, 11
Wiersema, Frederick, 18
Wong, Andy, 188

Y

Yost, Mark, 356

Z

Zaun, Todd, 479
Zumhagen, Conrad, 490

Company & Product Index

A

Accenture, 417–418, 419, 436
Ace, 402
Adobe, 162
Advanced Car Technology Systems, 33
Advanced Micro Devices (AMD), 52, 291, 292, 314, 333
Airborne, 381
Airbus, 204, 318, 319, 333
All Nippon Airways, 318
AltaVista, 254
Amazon.com, 407
America Online, 50, 109
American Express, 145, 387
Amoco, 95
Andersen Consulting, 417–418, 419, 436
Annuncio, 57
Apple Computer, 221, 222, 285, 373, 376, 381, 386, 392
Arthur Andersen, 417
ArvinMeritor, 12

B

Baxter, 403
BellSouth, 453
Black & Decker, 125
Bloomberg LP, 311
Boeing, 204, 318, 319, 333, 457–459
Boston Consulting Group, 117
Boston Scientific Corporation, 94
BP, 95
Bridgestone/Firestone, 469, 479
Business Wire, 455
Business.com, 409

C

Canon, 280
Carbone of American Industries Corporation, 103
Carrier, 59, 63
CBS, 41
Chemdex, 410
Chrysler, 239, 356, 370
Cisco Systems, 111, 239, 247, 248, 312
Coke, 248
Colonial Oil of Atlanta, 406
Commerce One, 213
Community Publishers, Inc., 98
Compaq, 36, 52, 178, 291, 295
CompuServe, 183
Concorde, 221
Cooper Tire, 206
Covisint, 109, 213
Cyrix, 291

D

Daimler-Chrysler, 45, 356, 370
Dana Corporation, 12, 374, 375, 376, 379, 392, 447
Dell Computers, 52, 178, 291, 295
DHL, 281
Digital Equipment Corporation (DEC), 45
Donrey Corporation, 98
DoubleClick, 11
Dow Corning, 148
DuPont, 222
Duracell, 83

E

Eastman Kodak, 248, 280
Eaton Corporation, 12
eCircles, 183
eGroups, 183
eMarketer, 455
EMC, 15, 329
Emery, 281
E.piphany, 57, 355, 371
Eveready, 83
Explorer Pipeline, 407
Exxon, 476

F

FedEx, 281, 381, 382, 414
Fidelity Investments, 41
Firestone, 11–12, 13, 469, 470, 479
Ford Motor Company, 11–12, 13, 42, 45, 220, 221, 248, 376, 379, 469, 470, 479
Forrester Research, 405
Fortune 1000 firms, 189
FreeMarkets Inc., 59, 63, 65, 73
Fujitsu, 189, 190
Fuld and Associates, Inc., 167

G

Gartner Group, 153
General Electric, 45, 111, 119, 120, 122, 125, 126, 148, 249, 403
General Mills, 45
General Motors, 36, 45, 221, 248, 356, 374, 375, 376, 379
Goodyear, 36, 206, 479
Google, 28, 181, 254
GotMarketing, 57
Government Technology Services, 189

H

Hamilton Sundstrand Corporation, 87
Hewlett-Packard, 83, 94, 120, 178, 215, 260, 288
Hitachi, 189, 190
Honda, 45
Honeywell, 457

I

IBM, 15, 26, 45, 52, 145, 146, 148, 152, 154, 162, 168, 169, 179, 194, 214, 218, 221, 239, 260, 268, 269, 291
Independent Grocers Alliance (IGA), 402
InsightExpress, 161, 181, 211
Intel, 36, 52, 128, 291–292, 293, 307, 314
International Data Corporation (IDC), 153, 405
iPrint, 87

J

JAL, 318
Java, 128
Jupiter Networks, 153, 312

K

Kellogg's, 45

Kinko's, 336, 337, 346, 371
Kolbenschmidt Pierburg AG, 270, 271
Kovair, 218
Kraft General Foods, Inc., 98

L

LandO'Lakes, 404
Landor Associates, 418
Lanier, 45
Lear, 12
Lucent, 312
Luminate, 333

M

McDonald's, 44, 423, 461
McKesson, 402
Magna International, Inc., 33
MarketFirst, 57
MasterCard, 387
MCI, 95
Michelin, 206
MicroAge, 189
Microsoft, 3, 50, 104, 128,
    469, 470
Mitsubishi Corporation, 103, 318
Monsanto, 142
Motion Picture Advertising Service
    Co., 93
Mrs. Fields Cookies, 248

N

Nabisco, 98
NBI, 45
NEC, 189, 190
Netscape, 50
New Coke, 222
Nippon Carbon Co., Ltd., 103
Nokia, 111
Novell, 52

O

Ocean Spray, 404
OfficeMax, 87
Olivetti, 268
Oracle, 26, 414
Otis, 59
Owens & Minor, 403

P

Palm Pilot, 39
Panasonic, 106, 188, 190, 191, 192, 194,
    205, 210, 214, 216
Pentium, 51–52
Pinacor, 189
Polaroid, 248
Pro, 402

Q

Quark, 162

R

RCA, 45, 221, 222
Reuters, 312

S

SAP, 213, 414
SEC Corporation, 103
Sensacon Corporation (fictitious
    company), 229–230, 249, 250, 251,
    282, 283, 432, 432n.4, 434–435,
    438, 444, 455
Sentry Hardware, 402
SGL Carbon AG, 103
Showa Denko Carbon, Inc., 103
Siebel Systems, 355, 371
Siemens, 110, 111, 112, 120–121,
    120n.6, 123–124, 126, 140, 142, 447
Silicon Graphics, 94
Sony, 178, 189, 190
Speed to Market, 241
Sun Microsystems, 3, 50, 128, 257,
    258, 259, 261, 275, 288
Sunkist, 404
Sylvania, 45
System Administration, Networking,
    and Security (SANS) Institute, 254

T

Technology Strategic Planning,
    Inc., 165
Thai Airways, 458
ThreeCom, 247, 286

U

Tibco Software, Inc., 2, 3, 19,
    27, 28, 34
Time Warner, 109
Tokai Carbon Co., Ltd., 103
Topica, 183
Toro, 402
Toshiba, 190
Toyota, 45
Tru-Value, 402
TRW, 12, 30, 31–33, 39, 57, 69, 447
TSNN, 443, 451, 455
TungSol, 45
TWA, 457–458

U

UCAR International, 103
United Technologies, 59, 60, 63, 65,
    69, 84, 87
UNIX, 128
UPS, 381, 382, 414
UpShot, 371

V

Ventro, 410, 414
VerticalNet, 218, 283, 414
Video Storyboard Tests, Inc., 83
Visa, 387
Visteon, 12
Volkswagen, 31–32, 356

W

Wang, 268
Windows NT, 129
Worldcom, 95
W.W. Grainger, Inc., 57

X

Xerox, 222, 268, 280, 295, 296

Y

Yahoo!, 2, 3, 4, 19, 27, 28, 34, 95, 183